CSWE's Core Competencies and Practice Behavior Examples in This Text

Competency	Chapter
Professional Identity	
Practice Behavior Examples...	
Serve as representatives of the profession, its mission, and its core values	1, 9
Know the profession's history	1, 3, 9
Commit themselves to the profession's enhancement and to their own professional conduct and growth	9
Advocate for client access to the services of social work	9
Practice personal reflection and self-correction to assure continual professional development	9
Attend to professional roles and boundaries	8–10
Demonstrate professional demeanor in behavior, appearance, and communication	
Engage in career-long learning	
Use supervision and consultation	9
Ethical Practice	
Practice Behavior Examples...	
Obligation to conduct themselves ethically and engage in ethical decision-making	8, 11
Know about the value base of the profession, its ethical standards, and relevant law	1, 9, 11
Recognize and manage personal values in a way that allows professional values to guide practice	
Make ethical decisions by applying standards of the National Association of Social Workers Code of Ethics and, as applicable, of the International Federation of Social Workers/International Association of Schools of Social Work Ethics in Social Work, Statement of Principles	
Tolerate ambiguity in resolving ethical conflicts	8, 9, 11
Apply strategies of ethical reasoning to arrive at principled decisions	8, 9, 11
Critical Thinking	
Practice Behavior Examples...	
Know about the principles of logic, scientific inquiry, and reasoned discernment	4–6, 12
Use critical thinking augmented by creativity and curiosity	
Requires the synthesis and communication of relevant information	4–6, 12
Distinguish, appraise, and integrate multiple sources of knowledge, including research-based knowledge, and practice wisdom	4–5, 9, 12
Analyze models of assessment, prevention, intervention, and evaluation	5, 8, 10, 12
Demonstrate effective oral and written communication in working with individuals, families, groups, organizations, communities, and colleagues	

Adapted with the permission of Council on Social Work Education

CSWE's Core Competencies and Practice Behavior Examples in This Text

Competency	Chapter
Diversity in Practice	
Practice Behavior Examples...	
Understand how diversity characterizes and shapes the human experience and is critical to the formation of identity	4, 6
Understand the dimensions of diversity as the intersectionality of multiple factors including age, class, color, culture, disability, ethnicity, gender, gender identity and expression, immigration status, political ideology, race, religion, sex, and sexual orientation	4, 6
Appreciate that, as a consequence of difference, a person's life experiences may include oppression, poverty, marginalization, and alienation as well as privilege, power, and acclaim	1, 6, 10
Recognize the extent to which a culture's structures and values may oppress, marginalize, alienate, or create or enhance privilege and power	2, 3, 5
Gain sufficient self-awareness to eliminate the influence of personal biases and values in working with diverse groups	
Recognize and communicate their understanding of the importance of difference in shaping life experiences	
View themselves as learners and engage those with whom they work as informants	
Human Rights & Justice	
Practice Behavior Examples...	
Understand that each person, regardless of position in society, has basic human rights, such as freedom, safety, privacy, an adequate standard of living, health care, and education	1–3, 10, 11
Recognize the global interconnections of oppression and are knowledgeable about theories of justice and strategies to promote human and civil rights	5, 11
Incorporates social justice practices in organizations, institutions, and society to ensure that these basic human rights are distributed equitably and without prejudice	1, 3, 9–11
Understand the forms and mechanisms of oppression and discrimination	3, 7, 11
Advocate for human rights and social and economic justice	9, 11
Engage in practices that advance social and economic justice	5, 7, 9–11
Research Based Practice	
Practice Behavior Examples...	
Use practice experience to inform research, employ evidence-based interventions, evaluate their own practice, and use research findings to improve practice, policy, and social service delivery	4–10, 12
Comprehend quantitative and qualitative research and understand scientific and ethical approaches to building knowledge	4, 6, 12
Use practice experience to inform scientific inquiry	5, 8, 9, 12
Use research evidence to inform practice	1, 4–8, 12

Competency	Chapter
Human Behavior	
Practice Behavior Examples...	
Know about human behavior across the life course; the range of social systems in which people live; and the ways social systems promote or deter people in maintaining or achieving health and well-being	1, 2, 4–6, 10
Apply theories and knowledge from the liberal arts to understand biological, social, cultural, psychological, and spiritual development	5
Utilize conceptual frameworks to guide the processes of assessment, intervention, and evaluation	2, 5, 6, 12
Critique and apply knowledge to understand person and environment	1, 2, 4, 5
Policy Practice	
Practice Behavior Examples...	
Understand that policy affects service delivery and they actively engage in policy practice	1–3, 7, 8, 10–12
Know the history and current structures of social policies and services; the role of policy in service delivery; and the role of practice in policy development	3, 6–11
Analyze, formulate, and advocate for policies that advance social well-being	1, 3, 10–12
Collaborate with colleagues and clients for effective policy action	10, 12
Practice Contexts	
Practice Behavior Examples...	
Keep informed, resourceful, and proactive in responding to evolving organizational, community, and societal contexts at all levels of practice	9
Recognize that the context of practice is dynamic, and use knowledge and skill to respond proactively	2, 6, 9
Continuously discover, appraise, and attend to changing locales, populations, scientific and technological developments, and emerging societal trends to provide relevant services	3, 4, 6, 9, 10
Provide leadership in promoting sustainable changes in service delivery and practice to improve the quality of social services	9, 10

CSWE's Core Competencies and Practice Behavior Examples in This Text

Competency	Chapter
Engage, Assess Intervene, Evaluate	
Practice Behavior Examples...	
Identify, analyze, and implement evidence-based interventions designed to achieve client goals	5–9
Use research and technological advances	5, 8, 10, 12
Evaluate program outcomes and practice effectiveness	8, 12
Develop, analyze, advocate, and provide leadership for policies and services	1, 9, 10, 12
Promote social and economic justice	1, 2, 9, 10, 11
A) ENGAGEMENT	
Substantively and effectively prepare for action with individuals, families, groups, organizations, and communities	5, 9
Use empathy and other interpersonal skills	5, 9
Develop a mutually agreed on focus of work and desired outcomes	5, 6, 9
B) ASSESSMENT	4, 7, 12
Collect, organize, and interpret client data	
Assess client strengths and limitations	5, 9, 12
Develop mutually agreed-on intervention goals and objectives	5, 9
Select appropriate intervention strategies	5, 6, 8–10, 12
C) INTERVENTION	
Initiate actions to achieve organizational goals	10, 12
Implement prevention interventions that enhance client capacities	5, 9
Help clients resolve problems	5, 9, 11
Negotiate, mediate, and advocate for clients	11
Facilitate transitions and endings	5, 9
D) EVALUATION	
Critically analyze, monitor, and evaluate interventions	8, 12

SIXTH EDITION

Mental Health and Social Policy

Beyond Managed Care

David Mechanic
Rutgers, The State University of New Jersey

Donna D. McAlpine
University of Minnesota

David A. Rochefort
Northeastern University

PEARSON

Boston   Columbus   Indianapolis   New York   San Francisco   Upper Saddle River
Amsterdam   Cape Town   Dubai   London   Madrid   Milan   Munich   Paris   Montréal   Toronto
Delhi   Mexico City   São Paulo   Sydney   Hong Kong   Seoul   Singapore   Taipei   Tokyo

Editorial Director: Craig Campanella
Editor-in-Chief: Ashley Dodge
Editorial Product Manager: Carly Czech
Editorial Assistant: Nicole Suddeth
Vice-President/Director of Marketing: Brandy Dawson
Executive Marketing Manager: Kelly May
Marketing Coordinator: Courtney Stewart
Senior Media Editor: Paul DeLuca

Project Manager: Pat Brown
Creative Director: Jayne Conte
Cover Art: Fotolia © Lemonade
Cover Designer: Suzanne Behnke
Editorial Production and Composition Service: Anandakrishnan Natarajan, Integra Software Services
Interior Design: Joyce Weston Design
Text and Cover Printer: Courier/Westford

Library of Congress Cataloging-in-Publication Data
Mechanic, David,
    Mental health and social policy: beyond managed care/David Mechanic, Institute for Health, Health Care Policy and Aging Research, Rutgers, The State University of New Jersey, Donna D. McAlpine, Division of Health Policy and Management, University of Minnesota, David A. Rochefort, Department of Political Science, Northeastern University.—Sixth edition.
        pages cm
    Includes bibliographical references and indexes.
    ISBN-13: 978-0-205-88097-3 (alk. paper)
    ISBN-10: 0-205-88097-5 (alk. paper)
    1. Mental health services—United States.   2. Mental health policy—United States.   I. McAlpine, Donna D.   II. Rochefort, David A.   III. Title.
    RA790.6.M37 2014
    362.19689—dc23

                                                                                    2012039047

10 9 8 7 6 5 4 3 2 1

Contents

PART TWO: SCOPE AND CAUSES OF MENTAL HEALTH PROBLEMS

4. Psychiatric Epidemiology: Science, Counting, and Making Sense of the Numbers   70

5. Controlling Mental Illness: Theory, Research, and Methods of Intervention   102

PART THREE: THE TREATMENT SYSTEM

Preface

Mental Health and Social Policy: Beyond Managed Care provides a multidisciplinary review of mental illness and its treatment. It addresses disease patterns, conceptual debates, services, financing, professional resources, legal issues, and historical and contemporary policy directions related to the field. This text should be well suited to the kind of mental health policy survey course that has become a standard part of the curriculum in undergraduate and graduate programs in social work. It is also intended for students and researchers in other fields, such as public health, human services, psychiatric nursing, psychology, sociology, political science, public policy, and public administration, who may be seeking a broad-ranging analysis of mental health policy in American society.

First published by the lead author in 1969, or more than 40 years ago, this book was written in the early era of deinstitutionalization, a decade in which public mental hospitals were rapidly reducing their patient populations; when many new social programs including Medicare and Medicaid were enacted as part of President Johnson's "War on Poverty"; and when the Vietnam War and its effects began to unravel the fabric of American society.

American psychiatry in the 1960s was still dominated and controlled by psycho-analytic and psychodynamic practitioners, largely working in office-based practice and mostly with middle-class patients having mild and moderate conditions. Meanwhile, a large number of people with serious mental illness, most of them poor, were left neglected and untreated. This was an unusual situation compared to other areas of medicine, where the worst sicknesses and disabilities generally attracted the greatest attention and expertise of the medical profession. The book's first edition had as its central theme the need to correct existing priorities by giving more attention and resources to those with the most severe and persistent mental disorders. Each subsequent edition (1980, 1989, 1999, and 2008), which were also the work of the lead author, reinforced this perspective. Fortunately, priorities have shifted over the decades and persons with serious conditions now receive more treatment than before. Yet inequalities by race, ethnicity, social class, and type of psychiatric condition persist.

Policies concerning mental health and mental health services have become increasingly complex. In developing this sixth edition, it seemed best to extend the range of expertise through collaboration. The book's two new coauthors bring not only an expanded range of knowledge and perspectives about the mental health field but also an informed sense of students' experiences with the book. Donna McAlpine is associate professor and director of the program in Public Health Administration and Policy at the University of Minnesota School of Public Health. Donna completed her Ph.D. in sociology at Rutgers in 2001 and collaborated with David Mechanic over several years on about a dozen papers and chapters on mental health services. David A. Rochefort is Arts and Sciences Distinguished Professor of Political Science at Northeastern University. He has published several books on health and social policy and has researched the mental health services field extensively in the United States and Canada. David also completed a postdoctoral fellowship in 1986–87 at Rutgers in the mental health research training program directed by David Mechanic, and the two wrote papers together on mental health and health care reform and comparative health systems. In this way, the preparation of this sixth edition offered a welcome opportunity for the three colleagues who had benefited from and respected each other's work to come together again and focus on revising a well-established text, keeping it current with the distinctive risks and opportunities of this second decade of the twenty-first century.

Acknowledgments

David Mechanic would like to express his sense of great fortune over the past 33 years for having the close friendship and colleagueship of Gerald Grob and Allan Horwitz at Rutgers, both exemplary contributors to the mental health field. Grob is the preeminent medical historian of mental health services in America; Horwitz is a medical sociologist who has contributed to many areas including conceptions of mental illness, mental health epidemiology, and changing patterns of mental health services.

We would also like to thank Joanne Atay and Judy Teich from the Substance Abuse and Mental Health Services Administration (SAMHSA) for making available early results from *Mental Health, United States, 2010*. Over the years, these data have proved invaluable for describing changes in the U.S. mental health system. We also thank Ron Manderscheid, Executive Director of the National Association of County Behavioral Health and Developmental Disability Directors, for helping us obtain needed data. Ron spent many years at the National Institute of Mental Health and SAMHSA and was instrumental in promoting and maintaining many of the data sources used in this book.

We are all deeply indebted to Margaret (Peg) Polansky, who kept us on course, checked facts and references, and assured that we met all necessary publication requirements. Peg is more than a truly outstanding assistant, and we are very grateful to her.

Much of the research we have carried out that is reported in this book has received generous funding over many years from the NIMH and the Robert Wood Johnson Foundation. We are grateful for their support and confidence in our work.

David Mechanic
Rutgers, The State University of New Jersey

Donna D. McAlpine
University of Minnesota

David A. Rochefort
Northeastern University

Mental Health and Mental Illness as Social Issues

Human feelings and behavior are extremely variable. The same people may be happy or sad, energetic or lethargic, anxious or calm depending on their environment and personal lives at the time. Many emotions and reactions fall within the normal range of response to everyday events. To be sad when a loved one dies and to be anxious about an important but difficult examination are normal responses because such feelings fit the situation. Feelings of sadness, depression, or anxiety by themselves do not constitute mental illness. But what does constitute mental illness remains the subject of debate.

In 1973, David Rosenhan published "On Being Sane in Insane Places," an article reporting the results of what would go on to become one of the most famous of all social science studies. Briefly, the research involved sending pseudopatients to mental hospitals to determine what diagnoses and treatments they would receive. The main conclusion was that mental health professionals inaccurately applied diagnoses of major mental illness (usually schizophrenia in remission) while interpreting the subjects' normal behaviors consistent with these diagnoses. In sum, Rosenhan concluded professionals could not reliably distinguish sane from insane. While the validity of this experiment subsequently became the subject of debate (e.g., Spitzer 1976), it succeeded in casting doubt on the very nature of our definitions of mental illness. The article begins with a question we continue to struggle to answer: "If sanity and insanity exist, how shall we know them?"

DEFINING MENTAL ILLNESS

Much has changed in the decades since the Rosenhan study, including our choice of words. When once to talk of sane versus insane may have seemed sensible, now we talk about mental illness, mental health, and degrees of psychiatric disability. But the central question remains equally salient today as it was in 1973. How do we know what mental illness (or health) is? This question challenges us to take an additional step, and ask: If we do not know what mental illness is, how do we develop social policies that are appropriate and effective?

The struggle to find a valid definition of mental illness continues to preoccupy researchers and policymakers. Even the practice of defining mental illnesses as something apart—different—from physical illnesses seems foolish and has had unintended consequences. The brain is a part of the physical body. The feelings that constitute something like depression play out in the body and are experienced physically. Yet a distinction between mind and body underpins insurance models that historically have funded and delivered mental and physical health services separately. Thinking of mental health as something distinct from general physical health has led to feelings of embarrassment or shame when the designation of mental illness is applied. Similarly, we know that to write about mental illness as though it is one condition or disease is a vast oversimplification. Mental illness encompasses much diversity, from relatively minor forms of emotional distress to often debilitating disorders that substantially interfere with the ability to function over long periods of time. Using the term "mental illness" is simply a convenient communication device; it is not an adequate reflection of the heterogeneity of conditions we might think of as coming under the umbrella of the term.

One approach to defining mental illness is to conceive of it as a deviation from normal reactions or feelings given one's life circumstance. The difficulty with such an approach is that what is normal or deviant is socially and culturally defined. Although a person from a cultural background featuring a belief system based on witchcraft might understandably be fearful of being poisoned or harmed by magic, a similar reaction from a person born and raised in Akron, Ohio, would leave us puzzled and concerned. Such an incongruity might indeed suggest mental illness. Persons with countercultural lifestyles appear bizarre to more conventional persons, but their patterns of dress and action are not necessarily discordant with their peers' beliefs and values.

Another major way of identifying deviations from "normal" is through recognition of personal suffering that is not justified by the circumstances of an individual's life. Although it may be normal for an unemployed person who cannot adequately provide for his or her children, or who is deprived and discriminated against, to feel anxious or depressed, we infer that a person showing a similar reaction under favorable life circumstances and in the absence of any objective provocation may be psychiatrically disordered.

Definitions of mental illness also often take into account some determination of how much the symptoms interfere with our functioning in common roles. The dominant paradigm for defining mental illness in the United States, as expressed in the *Diagnostic and Statistical Manual of Mental Disorders*, for example, specifies that a disorder must produce "clinically significant distress or impairment in social, occupational, or other important areas of functioning" (American Psychiatric Association 1994, p. 7). How one should operationalize significant distress or impairment is, however, not clear.

An important concept in the realm of mental health policy is "severe and persistent mental illness" (SPMI), although again there is no universally agreed upon definition. However, the term is usually intended to convey a history of serious acute episodes, psychiatric comorbidities, continuing residual disability, and high levels of medical and psychosocial need. Patients showing such signs typically have serious problems in many facets of daily living, including work, social relations, and family life, which necessitate special programs and resources.

The notion of "severe and persistent" speaks to the trajectory of the condition and not the diagnosis; thus, it is difficult to obtain an accurate count of this population group, although we will later review best estimates. Even though diagnoses such as schizophrenia encompass a large proportion of patients with SPMI, the diagnosis itself is not a true measure of chronicity. The course of disorder and level of function vary a great deal. Typically, for public policy purposes, estimates of this population are based on duration of illness or treatment or disability, the latter measured by inability to work, or pronounced difficulty in carrying out activities of daily living.

Debates about what constitutes mental illness matter. At the most basic level, they identify groups of special interest in society, that is, categories of individuals considered to be deserving of public expenditures, and target populations for public policy initiatives. For example, the first national review of mental health policies in the United States took place in the late 1950s. It contended that national efforts should concentrate on the needs of people with the most severe impairments, people who at the time were likely to be housed in long-term mental hospitals:

> A national mental health program should recognize that major mental illness is the core problem and unfinished business of the mental health movement, and that the intensive treatment of patients with critical and prolonged mental breakdowns should have first call on fully trained members of the mental health professions. (Joint Commission on Mental Illness and Health 1961, p. xiv)

The period following this report was marked by the large-scale movement of people out of mental hospitals into the community as well as major health initiatives, such as Medicaid, that substantially shifted many responsibilities, especially the financing of care for individuals with the most severe mental disorders, to the federal government. Yet the 1960s was also a period when the nation adopted a more comprehensive vision of community mental health care and began to create a service system devoted to a broad range of assistance for all kinds of disorders, from mild and moderate to severe.

Decades later, under the Clinton Administration, the first Surgeon General's Report on Mental Health took a broad stance on the definition of mental illness and the kinds of problems meriting attention on the national agenda:

> The Nation's contemporary mental health enterprise, like the broader field of health, is rooted in a population-based public health model. The public health model is characterized by concern for the health of a population in its entirety... In years past, the mental health field often focused principally on mental illness in order to serve individuals who were most severely affected. Only as the field has matured has it begun to respond to intensifying interest and concerns about disease prevention and health promotion. (U.S. Department of Health and Human Services 1999, pp. 3–4)

Research and policy in this recent period have tended to focus more on common mental disorders such as depression, and less on disorders that are usually more severe but affect fewer people, such as schizophrenia. Although serious debate was lacking about the trade-offs of implementing policy at the population level versus addressing the needs of people with the most severe mental illnesses, most experts now agree on the benefits of strategies such as screening for mental health problems in primary care. With passage of the federal Patient Protection and Affordable Care Act (ACA) of 2010, the affirmation of its constitutional status by the U.S. Supreme Court, and its many provisions improving behavioral health services through health homes, collaborative care, and other approaches, program initiatives focusing on behavioral health within general medicine will increase.

Neither a broad nor a narrow policy approach is inherently right or wrong. Indeed, it is easy to support the notion that everyone experiencing psychological distress or emotional pain is deserving of attention. But public resources are limited. In addition, medical treatment does not come without side-effects. Encouraging increasing numbers of people to be treated for self-limiting periods of emotional distress seemingly is wasteful and sometimes comes with its own risks. Moreover, there are opportunity costs to consider. If we devote our policies primarily to addressing the more common mental health problems such as depression and anxiety, does this divert attention and resources from much less common, but sometimes more debilitating, disorders? Balancing the needs of persons with very different types of mental health problems remains an essential policy dilemma.

Debates about what constitutes mental illness will never be fully resolved. While there have been great steps forward in our understanding of the chemistry and structure of the brain, there is unlikely ever to be a meaningful biological test to identify depression, anxiety, schizophrenia, or the like. Although we continue to struggle with definitions, accepted practice now relies on clinical judgments based on the presence of specific constellations of symptoms judged to be indicative of disorder. Applying these formal clinical criteria to community samples, researchers have concluded that about one-half of the U.S. population will meet the criteria for one or more types of common mental illness sometime in their lifetime. Even if someone goes through life without such a problem, most people are extremely likely to know someone with a mental illness.

The experience of mental illness is most often intensely private and marked by profound suffering for the individual and his or her close family and friends. First-person narratives by those who have lived with and through this situation remind us powerfully of this reality. Novelist William Styron (1992), in his memoir *Darkness Visible*, describes his own clinical depression as "despair beyond despair." Jay Neugeboren (1997), also a writer, provides an unforgettable account of decades of struggle during which he coped with his brother Robert's severe mental illness. While arguing that persons with all forms of mental illness have the potential to live happy, satisfied lives, he also reminds us that "hundreds of thousands of other human beings, like Robert, despite all forms of treatment and medication, continue to live grim lives of madness, misery and despair" (1997, p. 22). Countless other biographies and autobiographies speak to the plight of individuals living with mental illness. However personal and private the predicaments may be, it is also important to recognize that the experience of mental illness can be shaped by decisions in the public arena, including social policies. Part of the responsibility of policymakers is to understand the consequences of mental illness and to configure programs and policies that may alleviate distress and neglect.

THE CONSEQUENCES OF MENTAL ILLNESS

One of the most tragic consequences of mental illness is suicide. In 2010, there were almost 38,000 deaths by suicide in the United States (Murphy, Xu, and Kochanek 2012). This figure likely vastly underestimates true prevalence because it only includes suicides listed as such on death certificates. Over the decade between 2000 and 2010, suicide ranked as either the tenth or eleventh leading cause of death (Heron et al., 2009; Murphy, Xu, and Kochanek 2012).

Risk of suicide varies significantly by age. As shown in Figure 1.1, between 1950 and 1980 suicide rates declined steeply for persons aged 45 and older, while increasing for the youngest age groups. Historically, persons 65 years and older have had the highest rates of suicide. After 2000, however, middle-aged persons took over this position. The reason for

Figure 1.1 • Suicide Rates by Age Group in the United States: 1950–2010

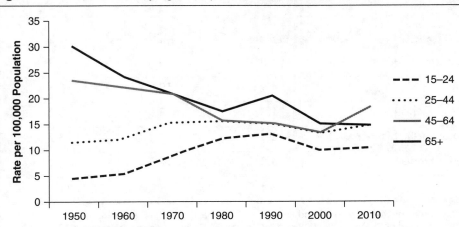

Source: Data from 1950–2000 from National Center for Health Statistics. *Health, United States, 2011: With Special Feature on Socioeconomic Status and Health.* Hyattsville, MD. 2012. Available online: www.cdc.gov/nchs/data/hus/hus11.pdf; Data for 2010 from Murphy, Xu, and Kochanek, 2012; data for age group 65+ not available, estimate based on 2008 data.

this trend is not clear, but it may be due partially to the aging of the baby boom cohort. This cohort of men had increased risk of suicide in adolescence and young adulthood compared to cohorts that came before or after them, and perhaps this risk has persisted into middle age (Phillips et al. 2010). While, in general, older persons have had higher suicide rates than those younger, much of the public's attention is riveted on younger age groups. This is not surprising, given that suicide ranks as the third leading cause of death for persons between 15 and 24 years old, accounting for almost 11 percent of all deaths in this group (Murphy, Xu, and Kochanek 2012).

There are also important race and gender differences in suicide. As shown in Table 1.1, among all racial groups, men have higher rates of completed suicide than women. White and American Indian males have particularly high rates compared to the other racial groups.

It is, of course, difficult to know what proportion of suicides is due to mental illness, although depression and other mental disorders often play a role. Some studies have attempted to make the connection through psychological autopsies that include reviews of administrative data, such as hospital records, and interviews with key informants to try to establish the circumstances of people's lives leading up to death. There is a high level of concordance between estimates of disorder based on personal clinical assessments and reports on comparable measures from a close relative or friend (Schneider et al. 2004). There is also a high level of agreement between diagnosis based on psychological autopsies and those based on information from clinicians who treated the victim (Kelly and Mann 1996). However, it is always difficult to weigh retrospective reports concerning the factors leading up to such a dramatic and shocking event as a suicide given the efforts of informants to attribute meaning to prior events. In a systematic review of studies using psychological autopsy methods, Cavanagh and colleagues (2003) examined the frequency of evidence that suicide victims had previously met the criteria for a *DSM* disorder.

Table 1.1	Age-Adjusted Suicide Rates (per 100,000), 1999–2009		
Race/Ethnicity	Female	Male	Total
Hispanic/Latino	1.8	9.7	5.7
White	4.9	19.8	12.1
African American	1.7	9.5	5.3
Asian or Pacific Islander	3.3	8.4	5.7
American Indian	4.8	17.5	11.1
Total	4.4	18.3	11.0

Source: Centers for Disease Control and Prevention, National Center for Health Statistics. Underlying Cause of Death 1999–2009 on CDC WONDER Online Database, released 2012. Data for year 2009 are compiled from the Multiple Cause of Death File 2009, Series 20 No. 20, 2012, Data for year 2008 are compiled from the Multiple Cause of Death File 2008, Series 20 No. 2N, 2011, data for year 2007 are compiled from Multiple Cause of Death File 2007, Series 20 No. 2M, 2010, data for years 2005–2006 data are compiled from Multiple Cause of Death File 2005–2006, Series 20, No. 2L, 2009, and data for years 1999–2004 are compiled from the Multiple Cause of Death File 1999–2004, Series 20, No. 2J, 2007. Accessed at http://wonder.cdc.gov/ucd-icd10.html

They estimated as many as one-half to three-quarters of all suicides could be avoided if mental illness could be prevented, obviously a utopian possibility. Moreover, they found mental disorder to be a stronger correlate of suicide than other factors such as social isolation, physical health problems, or recent stressful life events.

Many persons who commit suicide have had contact with health services prior to their death. Perhaps as many as three-quarters of suicide victims visited a primary care physician and one-third had contact with a mental health specialist within the year prior to their suicide (Luoma, Martin, and Pearson 2002). More current data concerning contact with health providers by suicide victims in the United States are needed. However, existing research suggests potential opportunities for detection and treatment of mental illness.

A particularly promising point of intervention is hospital emergency rooms (ER), where many persons who attempt to harm themselves first appear. This group is almost six times more likely to commit suicide following hospital discharge than persons in the general population (Olfson, Marcus, and Bridge 2012). A randomized controlled study by the World Health Organization in Brazil, India, Sri Lanka, Iran, and China assessed the effects of an intervention among people who were originally seen in the ER following a suicide attempt. This intervention involving an hour-long information session combined with nine follow-up contacts by phone or in-person over 18 months reduced subsequent deaths by suicide eleven-fold (Fleischmann et al. 2008). A related nonrandomized prospective study in the UK followed for 12 weeks persons who had poisoned themselves. The researchers found that only 10 percent of those receiving psychosocial assessment and support poisoned themselves again while 18 percent who did not receive such an assessment did so (Kapur et al. 2002).

Olfson, Marcus, and Bridge (2012) used national Medicaid claims and other data to assess whether patients who engage in deliberate self-harm received mental health assessment and follow-up outpatient mental health care following an ER admission. Only about half such patients underwent psychological evaluation or had any follow-up within 30 days of discharge. Given the fact that suicide remains a relatively rare event, self-harm ER admissions would appear to be a strategic point for realistic suicide prevention efforts.

That persons with mental illness have greater mortality risk than the general population has been well established. One early study tracked a community sample of persons 40 years of age and older for whom detailed measures of psychiatric disorder were available (Bruce et al. 1994). Nine years after initial assessment of disorder, their survival status was recorded. Overall, depression, alcohol-use disorders, and schizophrenia increased risk for mortality. The leading causes of death for persons with mental illness were circulatory diseases and cancer-related illness, a pattern that largely paralleled the distribution of mortality for the population as a whole.

Another study examined mortality among persons served by public mental health services in eight states from 1997 to 2000 (Colton and Manderscheid 2006). Across all states, the relative risk of death for public mental health clients exceeded that for the general population, adjusted for sex and age. Overall, public mental health clients experienced 13 to 30 years premature loss of life. In general, clients with major mental illness (MMI)—schizophrenia, major depressive disorders, bipolar, delusional and psychotic disorders, and attention deficit/hyperactivity disorders—died at younger ages than clients of public mental health services with non-MMI diagnoses in the same state. For the six states where information was available, the researchers found similar patterns between the general population and persons with mental illness in regard to cause of death, with heart disease, stroke, cancer, diabetes, respiratory illness, and lung diseases topping the list.

Druss and colleagues (2011) studied a nationally representative sample of Americans, some with a diagnosis of mental illness (schizophrenia, affective disorders, substance use, and other mental disorders) and some without, followed for a period of 17 years. Unlike previous studies, these researchers controlled for socioeconomic status (SES), health system factors such as having health insurance, and baseline health status including the presence of comorbid physical conditions, obesity, and self-assessed general health status. Overall, about 27 percent of persons with a mental illness died during the follow-up period, compared to 20 percent of persons with no mental disorder. Death occurred about eight years earlier on average for those with a mental illness. As in previous studies, the causes of death for people with a mental disorder coincided with those for the general population, including cardiovascular disease (34 percent), cancer (21 percent), and pulmonary disease (14 percent). Only about 5 percent of deaths were due to suicide, homicide, or accidents. Controlling for demographics, SES, health system factors, and health status reduced the relationship between mental disorder and risk of death to nonsignificance. In particular, SES and health system factors each accounted for about one-quarter of the excess mortality among persons with mental disorder, highlighting the need to address such risks for this population.

Rates of smoking are much higher among persons with schizophrenia than the general population. The most recent meta-analysis of studies worldwide, which was based on outpatient and inpatient samples, estimated the prevalence of smoking among persons with schizophrenia to be 62 percent (de Leon and Diaz 2005). High rates of smoking have also been observed for persons with many other types of mental illness. In population studies in the United States and Australia, current smoking rates were about twice as high for persons with a mental disorder (anxiety, affective disorders, or substance use) as for others (Lawrence, Mitrou, and Zubrick 2009). Overall, in both studies, about 30 percent of current smokers had a recent mental illness.

Our understanding of why persons with mental illness are more likely to smoke has been hampered by the tobacco industry's involvement in setting the research agenda (Hirshbein 2012). The research that grew out of a collaboration between the tobacco industry and psychiatry proposed that the link between smoking and lung cancer is not as strong for persons with severe mental illnesses as for the general population. Unfortunately, however, mentally ill smokers die of lung and other cancers much like everyone else. This research also suggested that smoking might in a way be beneficial for persons with mental illness by providing a calming effect and acting as a stress modifier. Many mental health consumers and advocacy organizations, while acknowledging the physical consequences of tobacco use, have embraced this more positive view of smoking. The "right to smoke" even became part of the empowerment movement (Hirshbein 2010). Mental health advocacy groups, for example, successfully lobbied for exempting psychiatric hospitals from smoking bans. As a result, until recently there has been little serious attention within public health circles to mental illness and smoking, while clinicians have often regarded smoking as a secondary medical concern in treating persons with mental illness. There is need for better understanding of why persons with mental illness have such strong attachment to tobacco use before we can hope to develop the necessary interventions to reduce smoking (Hirshbein 2010).

Beyond the health hazards associated with smoking, antipsychotic medications contribute to metabolic risk. The side-effects of common atypical antipsychotics, particularly clozapine and olanzapine, include elevated risk of obesity, elevated triglyceride levels, increased fasting glucose levels, high blood pressure, and other components of the metabolic syndrome that increase risk for diabetes and cardiovascular disease (Meyer and Stahl 2009; Newcomer 2007). When patients with serious mental illness receive inadequate medical care, it compounds these problems (Druss et al. 2002; Newcomer and Hennekens 2007).

The disability associated with mental illness exceeds that of many chronic illnesses. Researchers have estimated and compared the disability impacts of common chronic physical conditions (e.g., arthritis, asthma, heart disease, and cancer) with specific mental disorders (depression, anxiety, and impulse control disorders) in four areas of life: home, work, social interaction, and ability to form and maintain close relationships with others (Druss et al. 2009). Overall, having a mental illness is associated with greater impairment than physical disorder in each area of functioning. Depression and bipolar disorder feature the greatest level of impairment, exceeding that of chronic illnesses such as chronic pain syndrome and heart disease. However, disabilities in specific realms of life differ by type of disorder. While the greatest impairments for persons with mental disorder occur in the domains of social functioning and relationships, chronic physical disorders are more likely to interfere with functioning inside the home and work activities.

The aggregate amount of disability associated with mental illness is striking (Merikangas et al. 2007). Disability days are those when one is totally unable to carry out work or other day-to-day activities. On average, common chronic physical conditions account for about 7 annual disability days (arthritis) to 53 days (irritable bowel syndrome), while mental health disorders account for between 14 disability days (specific phobias) and 28 days (major depressive disorders). Taking into consideration prevalence of disorder, mood and anxiety disorders are the second and third most disabling conditions respectively, following musculoskeletal disorders. These results generally confirm an earlier Medical Outcomes Study that found patients with depressive disorders, or even depressive symptoms short of clinical disorder, had comparable or greater disability than patients having eight other chronic conditions such as diabetes, arthritis, ulcers, and spine problems (Wells 1989).

These studies do not include assessments of the disabilities associated with schizophrenia and many other severe disorders, but we know from other research that the latter are even more disabling. Schizophrenia, for example, is perhaps the most disabling of all mental disorders and often associated with problems in living independently, finding work, maintaining social relationships, and managing activities of daily living.

Mental illness and socioeconomic disadvantage also coincide. Even when controlling for other childhood adversities, such as parental neglect or parental mental illness and low socioeconomic status, there is evidence that having an externalizing disorder, such as impulse control or substance use problems, is strongly associated with terminating school early (Breslau et al. 2008). Adults with a mental illness are less likely to be employed (Mechanic, Bilder, and McAlpine 2002). Having a severe mental illness also correlates with lower levels of income when employed (Kessler et al. 2008).

While mental illness proves to be a strong predictor of poor general health, and negative social and economic outcomes, there is much variability depending on type and stage of disorder as well as life circumstances. Behavior disorders in childhood represent one area in which we can readily appreciate the potential gravity of consequences.

CONSEQUENCES OF BEHAVIOR DISORDERS IN CHILDHOOD

Children are one of society's most vulnerable populations but also a group with tremendous future potential regarding all aspects of life. For this reason, it is apt to focus on behavior disorders during childhood as one key indicator of the impact of mental health problems.

According to longitudinal epidemiological studies, antisocial behavior during childhood often results in difficulties later in life (Odgers et al. 2008; Robins 1966, 1979a, 1979b). Resistance to authority during childhood, as reflected in delinquency, drinking, and sexual behavior, is correlated with the development of employment difficulties, problems with the law, alcoholism, drug abuse, and early death in adulthood. Children in this troubled group often begin to stand out early in their school years due to low IQ, poor reading and poor school performance in general, and truancy.

The best research that has followed people throughout their lives comes from the United Kingdom, where four major birth cohort studies (1946, 1958, 1970, and 2000) have been conducted (Richards et al. 2009). The first three of these cohort studies now have data on individuals from childhood into middle and later life. The research team did not directly assess disorders, but instead relied on early reports from teachers or parents concerning poor conduct (such as fighting, lying, and disobedience) and emotional problems (such as fearfulness, worries, and solitariness). Results indicate that behavioral problems in childhood have much stronger repercussions into adulthood than emotional problems. Having a severe, or even mild, conduct disorder in childhood or adolescence goes along with a range of negative outcomes over time, such as lower educational attainment and earnings, greater risk of teenage parenthood, disengagement from economic activity, and problems with the law. Moreover, these risks do not appear to be explained by SES in childhood or psychological variables like early cognitive ability or hyperactivity.

What emerges from many studies is the sad trajectory followed by so many of these children, one in which problems exacerbate with age and have disastrous outcomes for both the affected individuals and society. Although a violent and aggressive childhood does not necessarily ensure such patterns in adulthood, such behavior is unlikely to develop subsequently if it was absent at an earlier age. Social deprivation, low social status, and adverse cultural environments can be overcome. Children living in well-functioning homes under such conditions still do well in adult life. Poor social and economic conditions, however, are conducive to family pathology, child abuse, alienation, and lack of encouragement for achievement, which all increase the probability that children growing up under such conditions will have difficulties. Social deprivation, broken homes, parental deviance, child abuse, and little parental supervision or interest in the child are often interrelated, making it difficult to isolate the central causal factors contributing to the child's maladjustment.

Childhood dysfunction does not thwart all possibility of productivity and fulfillment in adulthood. Children with conduct problems, school difficulties, and poorly developed skills can overcome these issues, but the risk of adult difficulties after such a vexed start in life is considerable. The 40-year follow-up of children from the 1946 British birth cohort found that, while having a conduct disorder during adolescence was associated with lower educational attainment, still 35 percent in this group whose problems were classified as severe managed to achieve educational qualifications (Colman et al. 2009). A major challenge for mental health workers—and for policymakers—is to intervene effectively when children enter into circumstances with poor prognoses so as to maximize their life chances and well-being (Mrazek and Haggerty 1994; O'Connell, Boat, and Warner 2009).

THE IMPORTANCE OF MENTAL HEALTH PROFESSIONS

Mental health care is an intensive form of human service typically delivered on the basis of one-to-one contact between a patient (or consumer) and a specially trained clinical practitioner. For this reason, a critical resource in operation of the mental health system is the supply of mental health professionals within different disciplinary specializations. Changes in the organizational location of professionals, their assigned responsibilities, and the nature of their interaction with each other have often been a focus for mental health program and policy innovations. Just as significant, however, much of the conflict over administrative control and payment practices inside the mental health field has had to do with determining appropriate roles for professional personnel.

According to one classic definition, a profession may be distinguished from other areas of work by its standing in the social structure and the division of labor (Freidson 1988).

A profession possesses control over its work in a specialized domain and is sanctioned by society to exercise this control. Often, though not always, certain attributes go along with this special status, such as superior skill, a theoretical knowledge base, and an ethical code on the part of members of the professional group.

Conceived in this way, no mental health professions existed prior to the founding of mental hospitals. Within the field of medicine, a professional specialty of psychiatry was born out of the asylum system of the 1800s, and its originating concepts and practices were largely a by-product of this setting (Grob 1973). While psychiatrists sought to root their work in science and medical knowledge, they also emerged as a specialty distinctly concerned with questions of institutional management and social control. A key element in this story was formation of the Association of Medical Superintendents of American Institutions for the Insane in 1844 with Dr. Samuel B. Woodward, superintendent of Worcester State Lunatic Hospital in Massachusetts, as its first president. Although the professionalization of psychiatry and mental hospitalization were wedded together as social processes by the early twentieth century, psychiatrists began to forsake public institutions as desirable places for conducting their professional practice, capitalizing on their M.D. status to move to private practice.

As mental hospitals grew rapidly in size, women were recruited to attend female hospital patients. Psychiatric nursing developed out of the need for this group of workers, and many training programs were situated at the asylums (Boling 2003). It was not unusual for psychiatrists and nurses to live nearby the patients on the hospital grounds, so enveloping was the mental institution as a social environment. One leading figure in the development of psychiatric nursing in the United States was Hildegard E. Peplau, who founded the first graduate-level program for clinical nurse specialists in psychiatric nursing at Rutgers University in 1954 (Neeb 2001). As the education of psychiatric nurses became more sophisticated and particular competencies were elaborated, it provided the means for mental health nursing personnel to go beyond the role of handmaiden to psychiatrists and to assume their own significant responsibilities in patient care and administration of services.

The origins of clinical psychology as a profession can be dated a short time after psychiatric nursing, or close to the end of the nineteenth century (Benjamin 2005). These practitioners were university-trained specialists in a new academic field that originally grew out of, and then separated from, philosophy. At first, psychologists were primarily devoted to testing and research, and they were tied to mental hospitals to carry out these activities. Later, when the United States entered World War I, the skills of this group were needed in constructing instruments for selecting recruits into different military occupations and for intellectual assessment of inductees. Psychologists also became involved in diagnosing cases of "shell shock," or what is now called posttraumatic stress disorder. In 1917, the American Association of Clinical Psychologists was established. It would take several more decades, however, and overcoming opposition from psychiatrists, before counseling and psychotherapy were consolidated as main areas of education and practice for psychology and the profession achieved the dominance it enjoys in this sphere today.

By contrast, a community orientation was inherent in the ideology of social work when the specialty of psychiatric social work took shape in the early decades of the twentieth century (Grob 1983; Stuart 1997). In 1907, social work services were added to the neurological clinic at Massachusetts General Hospital. By 1920, Mary C. Jarrett, who earlier had been Chief of Social Service at the Boston Psychopathic Hospital, formed a Psychiatric Social Workers Club that was forerunner to a psychiatric section within the National Association of Social Workers. Social workers became essential personnel in the delivery of aftercare services for discharged psychiatric patients. Soon, their role expanded through participation in a variety of Progressive-era mental health programs, including outpatient mental health services, child guidance clinics, and the promotion of "mental hygiene." Parallel to the rivalry between psychiatrists and psychologists, psychiatric social workers were not always well supported by other practitioners in their quest for professional status and autonomy in the mental health field. Over the decades, however, psychiatric social workers honed a valuable perspective based on clinical expertise combined with sensitivity to the patient's social environment and knowledge of the functioning of community agencies and institutions. This outlook proved indispensable when the community mental health movement arrived (Silverman 1985). Still today, the evolving practice of case management imitates, in some respects, the activities and objectives of the early psychiatric social workers (Stuart 1997).

In mental health care there are other professionals and paraprofessionals—marital therapists, mental health counselors, rehabilitation specialists, and more—as well as subspecialties within categories, such as geriatric and forensic psychiatry and dual-diagnosis practitioners. But the four main groups of psychiatrists, psychiatric nurses, clinical psychologists, and psychiatric social workers define the core mental health professions, and these are the ones we will examine later in this book when reviewing mental health personnel trends and issues.

The state of mental health personnel has been recognized as a serious issue from the time when officials first began formulating mental health policy on the national level. The National Mental Health Act of 1946 included fellowships for individuals and institutional grants for professional training as one of three new areas of federal funding. Nonetheless, by the late 1950s, one systematic review of mental health personnel trends in the United States described a serious mismatch between the public's need for services and the availability of clinical professionals, a situation it characterized as no less than "desperate" and likely to persist for decades to come (Albee and Dickey 1957). Much growth in personnel has occurred since this time, but not so much that concerns about the shortage have abated. In 2009, in order to examine supply issues, researchers grouped mental health professionals into two categories, nonprescribing and prescribing personnel (Thomas et al. 2009). Nationwide, nearly one in five counties had unmet need for nonprescribers, while unmet need for prescribers was nearly universal. The situation is particularly severe for certain specialties. According to one estimate, the number of practicing child psychiatrists satisfies about only one-fifth of national requirements (Huang et al. 2004; Thomas and Holzer 2006). Long waiting lists prevail.

For reasons pragmatic and ideological, the shift to community care in the 1960s inspired development of a team approach among mental health professionals (Burns 2007). The logic was inescapable. If comprehensive mental health care depended on an array of psychological, medical, and social services, attention must be given to organizing and coordinating this multifaceted effort. Community Mental Health Centers pioneered the use of multidisciplinary treatment teams, including, at times, the participation of consumers. Currently, the Assertive Community Treatment program is the most well-known model for providing mental health care in the community by creative utilization of a variety of personnel in management and service delivery roles focused on supporting patients on a long-term basis. Yet teamwork can sometimes produce confusion as well as role strain (Cirpili and Shoemaker 2010; Mancini et al. 2009). As traditional lines of professional functioning become blurred and overlap, new questions of authority, responsibility, and equitable compensation present themselves.

Other forms of professional tension also enliven the contemporary mental health scene. With the spread of managed care, providers have generally not taken kindly to attempts by health insurance gatekeepers to assert themselves as supervisors for clinical decision making. Psychologists continue to battle for prescribing privileges. And some psychiatrists question the progressive narrowing of their role, which has become increasingly devoted to brief medical consultations and less concerned with intimate engagement of patients through in-depth counseling (Harris 2011).

SOCIETAL BURDENS AND POLICY DILEMMAS

The disability, morbidity, and mortality associated with mental illnesses not only have consequences for individuals and their families, they also create a major societal burden. The costs of health care, lost earnings, and disability payments for persons with mental illness exceeded $300 billion in the United States in 2002 (Insel 2008). The World Economic Forum recently estimated the global costs of mental illness (including medical costs and indirect costs such as income loss due to morbidity and mortality) at about $2.5 trillion in 2010, with about 33 percent of this attributable to medical care. Meanwhile, the costs related to lost economic output (which includes lost capital and labor) approximate $16 trillion, a figure higher than similar costs associated with diabetes, cardiovascular disease, respiratory diseases, or cancer (Bloom et al. 2011).

Such calculations are, at best, rough estimates, but they do support the case that mental illnesses produce an immense social burden, one equaling or surpassing most other types of illnesses. Indeed, such estimates are probably conservative because they do not take into account many indirect costs like crime and incarceration, the effects of family disruption on children, special education and social welfare programs, family caregiving for members with mental illness, and homelessness. We do not have good estimates of these amounts, but they are substantial and they represent appropriate subjects of concern within the public policy process.

Sociologist C. Wright Mills (1959) made a classic distinction between personal troubles and public issues. The former has to do with concerns considered to be individual, private, and outside the sphere of government and politics. The latter refers to problems whose breadth and character are such that they impact the functioning of society, they reflect the structure and operation of social institutions, and they cannot be addressed meaningfully without public policy action. Recognition of mental health problems as a public issue goes back to the earliest days of American society when seriously disordered individuals lacking proper supervision were perceived to be a menace to the community and themselves. As we will see, it is a concern still perplexing to American courts in the twenty-first century. Over time, however, a specialized system of organizations, services, and funding gradually sprung up to provide not just custody but also care of those with mental health problems of all types. Today, that effort involves multiple levels of government and a spectrum of professional groups and bureaucratic agencies financed with public dollars. Whether mental illness is a public issue or not has long ago been settled. Yet this does not mean there is agreement on the priority to be given to mental health care versus other social commitments, nor does consensus exist concerning the appropriate content and organization of mental health programs.

Definitions of mental illness shape the scope and purpose of mental health policies. Over the past two decades, the battle over parity insurance coverage for mental health and physical health problems resulted in passage of many pieces of regulatory legislation on the state and federal levels. But the question remains: Which mental illnesses should fall under the umbrella of parity rules and protections? This is a quandary that has stimulated persistent debate among policymakers, and many laws set boundaries by means of definitional approaches such as excluding substance abuse problems or applying the law only to a list of "brain diseases" or "biologically-based disorders." Similarly, when eligibility guidelines for disability programs specify which types of persons and mental health disorders qualify for benefits, it is a means of relegating others to a marginal status for income support initiatives of this kind. The Americans with Disabilities Act (ADA) of 1990 has so far had small effect on persons with mental illness due to narrow court interpretations of the law's applicability. Recent revisions to the ADA taking effect in 2011 could begin to correct this limitation, but it is far too soon to say for sure. One of the most enduring issues within U.S. mental health policy, previously noted, has been the choice between distributing resources across all levels of impairment and targeting assistance according to illness severity (Grob and Goldman 2006). The fact that diagnosis is not a reliable gauge of this latter characteristic only adds confusion to the controversy.

U.S. mental health policy reflects a delicate act of balancing responsibilities among local, state, and federal governments. Prior to the 1950s, states played the lead role, but the impetus shifted to the federal level with such reforms as the Community Mental Health Centers Act and Medicaid and Medicare. Nonetheless, some of the most innovative recent programs, such as assertive case management and the fashioning of community support systems, have emerged at the subnational level. It seems the pendulum of influence and control in mental health policy is always in motion. Over the past few years, economic recession has strained state budgets, diverting resources away from people with mental illnesses. At the same time, the federal Patient Protection and Affordable Care Act (ACA) of 2010 holds promise of greatly augmenting the ability of individuals with mental disorder to access treatment and care. In a mental health policy system like in the United States, however, almost nothing is uniform, and it will be essential to track the way key coverage issues are decided from one part of the country to another. At various places in this book, we will discuss the strengths and weaknesses of general health reform legislation when considered from the vantage point of mental health care issues.

Recent decades have seen the rise of powerful groups vying for decision-making control and resources within the mental health system. Providers, drug manufacturers, insurance companies, and managed care organizations all have a substantial stake in how mental health services are delivered and financed. Sometimes their interests converge with those of consumers, yielding positive results. For example, the profit motive of pharmaceutical companies has been partially responsible for new classes of drugs that have proved effective and lifesaving for many patients. At other times, stakeholder interests may diverge and lead to potentially perverse outcomes, such as when pharmaceutical companies, exploiting their market power, charge so much for their products that some needy consumers are excluded from the benefits.

In general, consumers of mental health services have been a weak political constituency in our society, with sporadic policy influence. This fact is a reflection of the particular forms of disability produced by severe mental illness, inadequate organization and resources, and the difficulties of building a public advocacy movement centering on socially stigmatized conditions. Change is taking place so that an increasing number of mental health advocacy groups have come to the fore. Such interests now have much more say in policy matters than in previous eras, with the greatest gains in recent years being scored by the family movement and by the consumer/survivor movement (Tomes 2006). One drawback, however, is that groups seeking to represent or work on behalf of people with mental illnesses sometimes disagree among themselves. Divisions have been noted not just between families and consumers but within the growing constellation of consumer/survivor groups. Such fracturing disadvantages all parties in a competitive political arena.

Mental health policies have evolved in many ways over time. The first national review of the state of mental health and mental health services in the United States occurred under authority of the Mental Health Study Act of 1955. A Joint Commission on Mental Illness and Health set about the task of describing the existing system as well as formulating recommendations for change. In 1961, the commission issued its report, *Action for Mental Health*, whose preamble acknowledged the gap between rhetoric and reform in past consideration of this issue:

> It would seem futile to content ourselves with restating the problem of the unmet needs of the untreated or poorly treated mentally ill. Such a statement of *what*, as an aftermath of the millions and millions of words which have been written and spoken on the subject in the last fifteen years, would seem useless without at the same time seeking the more important explanation of *why* the words have not moved us. We are prone to boast of progress in mental health, and some has been made, but measured against the over-all dimensions of mental illness, our gains are pitifully small. (Joint Commission on Mental Illness and Health 1961, p. 4)

The report catalyzed important new directions within the mental health system, but not all turned out as planned. Public mental hospitals lost their dominant position in mental health care, but the difficulties of establishing a truly comprehensive and effective array of alternative services were largely unanticipated. The millions of words highlighting unmet needs continued to multiply, often landing on deaf ears.

In 2002, or more than 40 years after the Joint Commission's work made news, President George W. Bush convened the New Freedom Commission on Mental Health. The objective was much the same as with previous such efforts, including President Carter's Commission on Mental Health in the late 1970s and the first Surgeon General's Report on Mental Health in 1999. This was to refocus the national spotlight on the subject of mental health and illness and to compile the best available knowledge on the scope of the problem, its causes, treatments, and recommended services. In its letter to the president introducing the final report, his task force stated:

> Today's mental health care system is a patchwork relic—the result of disjointed reforms and policies. Instead of ready access to quality care, the system presents barriers that all too often add to the burden of mental illnesses for individuals, their families, and our communities.... The time has long passed for yet another piecemeal approach to mental health reform. (New Freedom Commission on Mental Health 2003, p. 1)

The point was not that the period between the first Joint Commission and the New Freedom Commission was one of inaction or constant backsliding. A person with severe mental illness in 2012 is almost certain to have a very different experience, or at least a greater range of options, than one who fell ill in 1961. Much of the information presented in this book will document this reality and the expansion of evidence-based treatments, model programs, and insurance options. Popular television shows feature characters with mental health problems, and celebrities openly discuss their own personal struggles with mental illness in an unprecedented way. All these developments were unimaginable 50 years ago. Yet, as the commission bluntly stated, despite these and other favorable currents, the mental health care system remains deficient and disorganized. Many people with mental illnesses have bleak stories to tell that advertise its failures.

We see the shortcomings of mental health policy in the number of persons with mental illness who are homeless, in the large numbers of people in our jail and prison populations who have mental health problems (mostly untreated), and in the plight of consumers and their families who continue to struggle in navigating a system that seems at best illogical and at worst impossible. The fact is most people who meet the criteria for a mental health problem still do not receive treatment. Quality of care varies widely. Model programs have long waiting lines. Gaps in the system tend to be particularly pronounced within minority racial and ethnic communities, where those diagnostic and treatment services that are available often do poorly in recognizing and responding to cultural diversity.

CONCLUSION

A central question asked throughout this book is why psychiatry and mental health services have not reached a point of greater maturity, confidence, and public support and why mental health care often seems to stand apart from the progress and purposefulness one finds in other major disease sectors. To a great extent, the answer must be sought in our public policy choices, both the approaches we have adopted and those we have rejected or ignored. Debates surrounding mental health care are vital and consequential, not just academic abstractions. Mental illness is real, and so is the suffering of people with mental illnesses and their families and friends. Most persons with a mental illness want what everyone wants—a sense of mattering to others and of being worthwhile, having close relationships, finding something productive to do to occupy one's time and fulfilling one's talents. This book will look at how social policies have made these tasks easier or harder.

References

Albee, George W., and Marguerite Dickey. "Manpower Trends in Three Mental Health Professions." *American Psychologist* 12 (1957): 57–70.

American Psychiatric Association. *Diagnostic and Statistical Manual of Mental Disorders: Fourth Edition (DSM-IV)*. Washington, DC: American Psychiatric Association, 1994.

Benjamin, Ludy T., Jr. "A History of Clinical Psychology as a Profession in America (and a Glimpse at its Future)." *Annual Review of Clinical Psychology* 1 (2005): 1–30.

Bloom, David E., et al. *The Global Economic Burden of Noncommunicable Diseases*. Geneva, Switzerland: World Economic Forum, 2011. Available online: http://www3.weforum.org/docs/WEF_Harvard_HE_GlobalEconomicBurdenNonCommunicableDiseases_2011.pdf.

Boling, Anita. "The Professionalization of Psychiatric Nursing: From Doctors' Handmaidens to Empowered Professional." *Journal of Psychosocial Nursing and Mental Health Services* 41 (2003): 26–40.

Breslau, Joshua, et al. "Mental Disorders and Subsequent Educational Attainment in a US National Sample." *Journal of Psychiatric Research* 42 (2008): 708–716.

Bruce, Martha Livingston, et al. "Psychiatric Status and 9-Year Mortality Data in the New Haven Epidemiologic Catchment Area Study." *American Journal of Psychiatry* 151 (1994): 716–721.

Burns, Tom. "Community Mental Health Teams." *Psychiatry* 6 (2007): 325–328.

Cavanagh, Jonathan T. O., et al. "Psychological Autopsy Studies of Suicide: A Systematic Review." *Psychological Medicine* 33 (2003): 395–405.

Centers for Disease Control and Prevention, National Center for Health Statistics. *About Underlying Cause of Death, 1999–2009*. Atlanta, GA: Centers for Disease Control and Prevention, 2012. Available online: wonder.cdc.gov/ucd-icd10.html.

Cirpili, Avni, and Nancy Christine Shoemaker. "Psychiatric Mental Health Nursing in Community Settings." In *Foundations of Psychiatric Mental Health Nursing: A Clinical Approach*, 6th ed., edited by Elizabeth M. Varcarolis and Margaret Jordan Halter, pp. 87–100. St. Louis, MO: Saunders, 2010.

Colman, Ian, et al. "Outcomes of Conduct Problems in Adolescence: 40 Year Follow-up of National Cohort." *British Medical Journal* 338 (2009): 208–214.

Colton, Craig W., and Ronald W. Manderscheid. "Congruencies in Increased Mortality Rates, Years of Potential Life Lost, and Causes of Death Among Public Mental Health Clients in Eight States." *Preventing Chronic Disease* 3 (2006): 1–14.

de Leon, Jose, and Francisco J. Diaz. "A Meta-Analysis Of Worldwide Studies Demonstrates An Association Between Schizophrenia And Tobacco Smoking Behaviors." *Schizophrenia Research* 76 (2005): 135–157.

Druss, Benjamin G., et al. "Quality of Preventive Medical Care for Patients with Mental Disorders." *Medical Care* 40 (2002): 129–136.

Druss, Benjamin G., et al. "Impairment in Role Functioning in Mental and Chronic Medical Disorders in the United States: Results from the National Comorbidity Survey Replication." *Molecular Psychiatry* 14 (2009): 728–737.

Druss, Benjamin G., et al. "Understanding Excess Mortality in Persons with Mental Illness: 17-year Follow Up of a Nationally Representative US Survey." *Medical Care* 49 (2011): 599–604.

Fleischmann, Alexandra, et al. "Effectiveness of Brief Intervention and Contact for Suicide Attempters: A Randomized Controlled Trial in Five Countries." *Bulletin of the World Health Organization* 86 (2008): 703–709.

Freidson, Eliot. *Profession of Medicine: A Study of the Sociology of Applied Knowledge*. Chicago: University of Chicago Press, 1988.

Grob, Gerald N. *Mental Institutions in America: Social Policy to 1875*. New York: The Free Press, 1973.

Grob, Gerald N. *Mental Illness and American Society, 1875–1940*. Princeton, NJ: Princeton University Press, 1983.

Grob, Gerald N., and Howard H. Goldman. *The Dilemma of Federal Mental Health Policy: Radical Reform or Incremental Change?* New Brunswick, NJ: Rutgers University Press, 2006.

Harris, Gardiner. "Talk Doesn't Pay, So Psychiatry Turns Instead to Drug Therapy." *New York Times*, March 6, 2011, p. A1.

Heron, Melonie, et al. "Deaths: Final Data for 2006." *National Vital Statistics Reports* 57. Hyattsville, MD: National Center for Health Statistics, April 17, 2009. Available online: www.cdc.gov/nchs/data/nvsr/nvsr57/nvsr57_14.pdf.

Hirshbein, Laura. "'We Mentally Ill Smoke A Lot': Identity, Smoking, and Mental Illness in America." *Journal of Social History* 44 (2010): 7–21.

Hirshbein, Laura. "Scientific Research and Corporate Influence: Smoking, Mental Illness, and the Tobacco Industry." *Journal of the History of Medicine and Allied Sciences* 67 (2012): 374–397.

Huang, Larke, et al. "Transforming the Workforce in Children's Mental Health." *Administration and Policy in Mental Health* 32 (2004): 167–187.

Insel, Thomas R. "Assessing the Economic Costs of Serious Mental Illness." *American Journal of Psychiatry* 165 (2008): 663–665.

Joint Commission on Mental Illness and Health. *Action for Mental Health*, Final Report of the Joint Commission on Mental Illness and Health. New York: Basic Books, Science Editions, 1961.

Kapur, Navneet, et al. "Effect of General Hospital Management on Repeat Episodes of Deliberate Self Poisoning: Cohort Study." *British Medical Journal* 325 (2002): 866–867.

Kelly, Thomas M., and J. J. Mann. "Validity of DSM-III-R Diagnosis by Psychological Autopsy: A Comparison with Clinical Ante-Mortem Diagnosis." *Acta Psychiatrica Scandinavica* 94 (1996): 337–343.

Kessler, Ronald C., et al. "Individual and Societal Effects of Mental Disorders on Earnings in the United States: Results from the National Comorbidity Survey Replication." *American Journal of Psychiatry* 165 (2008): 703–711.

Lawrence, David, Francis Mitrou, and Stephen R. Zubrick. "Smoking and Mental Illness: Results from Population Surveys in Australia and the United States." *BMC Public Health* 9 (2009): 285.

Luoma, Jason B., Catherine E. Martin, and Jane L. Pearson. "Contact with Mental Health and Primary Care Providers Before Suicide: A Review of the Evidence." *American Journal of Psychiatry* 159 (2002): 909–916.

Mancini, Anthony D., et al. "Assertive Community Treatment: Facilitators and Barriers to Implementation in Routine Mental Health Settings." *Psychiatric Services* 60 (2009): 189–195.

Mechanic, David, Scott Bilder, and Donna D. McAlpine. "Employing Persons with Serious Mental Illness." *Health Affairs* 21 (2002): 242–253.

Merikangas, Kathleen, et al. "The Impact of Comorbidity of Mental and Physical Conditions on Role Disability in the US Adult Household Population." *Archives of General Psychiatry* 64 (2007): 1180–1188.

Meyer, Jonathan M., and Stephen M. Stahl. "The Metabolic Syndrome and Schizophrenia." *Acta Psychiatrica Scandinavica* 119 (2009): 4–14.

Mills, C. Wright. *The Sociological Imagination*. New York: Oxford University Press, 1959.

Mrazek, Patricia J., and Robert J. Haggerty, eds. *Reducing Risks for Mental Disorders: Frontiers for Preventive Intervention Research*. Washington, DC: National Academy Press, 1994.

Murphy, Sherry L., Jiaquan Xu, and Kenneth D. Kochanek. *Deaths: Preliminary Data for 2010*. National Vital Statistics Reports 60. Hyattsville, MD: National Center for Health Statistics, January 11, 2012. Available online: www.cdc.gov/nchs/data/nvsr/nvsr60/nvsr60_04.pdf.

National Center for Health Statistics. *Health, United States, 2011: With Special Feature on Socioeconomic Status and Health*. Hyattsville, MD, 2012. Available online: www.cdc.gov/nchs/data/hus/hus11.pdf.

Neeb, Kathy. *Fundamentals of Mental Health Nursing*, 2nd ed. Philadelphia: F.A. Davis Company, 2001.

Neugeboren, Jay. *Imagining Robert: My Brother, Madness, and Survival. A Memoir*. New York: William Morrow and Company, Inc., 1997.

Newcomer, John W. "Antipsychotic Medications: Metabolic and Cardiovascular Risk." *Journal of Clinical Psychiatry* 68 (2007): 8–13.

Newcomer, John W., and Charles H. Hennekens. "Severe Mental Illness and Risk of Cardiovascular Disease." *Journal of the American Medical Association* 298 (2007): 1794–1796.

New Freedom Commission on Mental Health. *Achieving the Promise: Transforming Mental Health Care in America: Final Report*. DHHS Publication No. SMA-03-3832. Rockville, MD, 2003.

O'Connell, Mary Ellen, Thomas Boat, and Kenneth E. Warner, Eds. *Preventing Mental, Emotional, and Behavioral Disorders among Young People: Progress and Possibilities*. National Research Council and Institute of Medicine Committee on the Prevention of Mental Disorders and Substance Abuse Among Children, Youth, and Young Adults: Research Advances and Promising Interventions, Board on Children, Youth, and Families, Division of Behavioral and Social Sciences and Education. Washington, DC: The National Academies Press, 2009.

Odgers, Candice L., et al. "Female and Male Antisocial Trajectories: From Childhood Origins to Adult Outcomes." *Development and Psychopathology* 20 (2008): 673–716.

Olfson, Mark, Steven C. Marcus, and Jeffery A. Bridge. "Emergency Treatment of Deliberate Self-harm." *Archives of General Psychiatry* 69 (2012): 80–88.

Phillips, Julie A., et al. "Understanding Recent Changes in Suicide Rates Among the Middle-Aged: Period or Cohort Effects?" *Public Health Reports* 125 (2010): 680–688.

Richards, Marcus, et al. *Childhood Mental Health and Life Chances in Post-War Britain. Insights from Three National Birth Cohort Studies.* Report prepared for Sainsbury Centre for Mental Health and The Smith Institute, 2009. Available online: www.smith-institute.org.uk/file/ChildhoodmentalhealthandlifechancesinpostwarBritain.pdf.

Robins, Lee N. *Deviant Children Grown Up: A Sociological and Psychiatric Study of Sociopathic Personality.* Baltimore, MD: Williams and Wilkins, 1966.

Robins, Lee N. "Longitudinal Methods in the Study of Normal and Pathological Development." In *Psychiatri der Gegenwart*, vol. 1, 2nd ed., edited by Karl Peter Kisker, et al., pp. 627–684. Heidelberg: Springer-Verlag, 1979a.

Robins, Lee N. "Follow-up Studies of Behavior Disorders in Children." In *Psychopathological Disorders of Childhood*, 2nd ed., edited by Herbert C. Quay and John S. Werry. New York: John Wiley and Sons, 1979b.

Rosenhan, David L. "On Being Sane in Insane Places." *Science* 179 (1973): 250–258.

Schneider, Barbara, et al. "Concordance of DSM-IV Axis I and II Diagnoses by Personal and Informant's Interview." *Psychiatry Research* 127 (2004): 121–136.

Silverman, Wade H. "The Evolving Mental Health Professions: Psychiatric Social Work, Clinical Psychology, Psychiatry, and Psychiatric Nursing." *The Journal of Behavioral Health Services and Research* 12 (1985): 28–31.

Spitzer, Robert L. "More on Pseudoscience in Science and the Case for Psychiatric Diagnosis. A Critique of D.L. Rosenhan's 'On Being Sane in Insane Places' and 'The Contextual Nature of Psychiatric Diagnosis.'" *Archives of General Psychiatry* 33 (1976): 459–470.

Stuart, Paul H. "Community Care and the Origins of Psychiatric Social Work." *Social Work in Health Care* 25 (1997): 25–36.

Styron, William. *Darkness Visible: A Memoir of Madness.* New York: First Vintage Books, 1992.

Thomas, Christopher R., and Charles E. Holzer. "The Continuing Shortage of Child and Adolescent Psychiatrists." *Journal of the American Academy of Child and Adolescent Psychiatry* 45 (2006): 1023–1031.

Thomas, Kathleen C., et al. "County-Level Estimates of Mental Health Professional Shortage in the United States." *Psychiatric Services* 60 (2009): 1323–1328.

Tomes, Nancy. "The Patient as a Policy Factor: A Historical Case Study of the Consumer/Survivor Movement in Mental Health." *Health Affairs* 25 (2006): 720–729.

U.S. Department of Health and Human Services. *Mental Health: A Report of the Surgeon General.* Rockville, MD: U.S. Department of Health and Human Services, Substance Abuse and Mental Health Services Administration, Center for Mental Health Services, National Institutes of Health, National Institute of Mental Health, 1999.

Wells, Kenneth B., et al. "The Functioning and Well-Being of Depressed Patients: Results from the Medical Outcomes Study." *Journal of the American Medical Association* 262 (1989): 914–919.

2

What Are Mental Health and Mental Illness?

I f we are to discuss mental health policy, we must be aware of the scope and limits of our topic. If our goal is to develop policies to deal with the prevention and treatment of mental illness and the facilitation of mental health, then we must clearly outline the dimensions of each of these concepts. Are mental health programs to be limited to persons who come under the care of mental health workers or are they to extend to those who see no need for psychiatric services and who have not been defined as individuals in need of attention and care by their communities? Are such programs to be restricted to persons suffering from clear psychiatric syndromes or should they also include those with more ordinary problems, such as nervousness, unhappiness, and social and family conflict? Are deviations such as delinquency and criminal behavior part of the mental health problem or are they more fruitfully dealt with outside the sphere of behavioral health? Are such situations as poverty, discrimination, and unemployment central mental health concerns or do they relate more significantly to other fields of action? Is failure in performance resulting from a low level of education a mental health problem? These are just some of the thorny questions that must be answered to formulate coherent principles of behavioral health care.

Psychiatrists, mental health workers, and the public often disagree about criteria for ascertaining the presence of mental illness. Much of this disagreement stems from a lack of consensus as to how broad or narrow the conception of mental illness should be: some mental health clinicians restrict the definition to a limited set of disorders, while others include a great variety of conditions and situations within the psychiatric sphere.

THE CLASSIFICATION OF MENTAL DISORDER

The classification of mental disorders in the United States has been heavily influenced by the *Diagnostic and Statistical Manual of Mental Disorders* (DSM), first published in 1952 by the American Psychiatric Association (APA). There were previous efforts to develop a classification system, but these were mainly used for collecting statistical data on the prevalence of mental disorder. Incorporating a narrow biological conception of illness, they reflected classes of disorder most often seen among patients in hospital

20

settings. Grob (1991) argues that developments in psychiatry during and after World War II led to a classification system in *DSM-I* largely based on principles of depth psychology and a Freudian psychodynamic approach. Military psychiatrists were exposed to great numbers of soldiers with neuropsychiatric conditions associated with the stress of combat, types of mental illness unlike those seen among hospitalized patients, and they successfully applied interventions for returning individuals quickly to service. As psychiatrists moved out of institutions and into the community after World War II, their involvement with mental health problems expanded far wider in scope than the psychotic conditions seen in institutional settings. Thus, the *DSM-I* emerged from the growing dominance in psychiatry of a psychodynamic approach, but with some additional consideration of biological, social, and environmental conditions (Grob 1991).

DSM-I distinguished between organic and nonorganic mental illnesses and divided psychiatric conditions into three major groups: (1) those conditions caused by or associated with impairment of brain tissue (e.g., disorders caused by infection, intoxication, trauma, and metabolic disturbances); (2) mental deficiency; and (3) disorders without clearly defined clinical cause, those not caused by structural change in the brain, and those attributed to psychogenic causes. The APA further divided the third category into five subcategories:

- psychotic disorders
- psychophysiologic, autonomic, and visceral disorders
- psychoneurotic disorders
- personality disorders
- transient situational personality disorders

The purpose of classifying disorders into subcategories was to depict in descriptive terms the gross reaction patterns recognizable among different kinds of patients. For example, psychoneurotic disorders are characterized by an anxiety reaction, while personality disorders are marked by a behavioral reaction to difficulties in adapting to the problems of life.

The second revision of the *DSM* (*DSM-II*), published in 1968, was designed to bring the manual in line with the eighth revision of the International Classification of Mental Disorders published by the World Health Organization (American Psychiatric Association 1968). The APA believed it important to coordinate the two coding systems and to achieve as much convergence as possible. *DSM-II* expanded the manual's previous diagnostic categories from 3 to 10. Perhaps the most important change was exclusion of the term "reaction" to characterize many disorders, a significant movement away from assumptions about etiology. Otherwise, the *DSM-II* retained the distinction between organic and nonorganic mental disorders, and it continued to describe disorders with brief descriptions. For example, the *DSM-II* categorizes depression according to whether or not the condition has occurred in response to some life event. Involutional melancholia is "characterized by worry, anxiety, agitation and severe insomnia … not due to some life experience" (American Psychiatric Association 1968, p. 36), while depressive neurosis is described as "manifested by an excessive reaction of depression due to an internal conflict or to an identifiable event such as the loss of a love object or cherished possession" (American Psychiatric Association 1968, p. 40).

DSM-I and *DSM-II* were widely criticized for insufficient specificity in their descriptions of disorder. Indeed, the period after the publication of *DSM-II* stands as one of the most divisive periods ever in terms of ideological debates about the classification of mental disorders.

During the 1960s, public interest lawyers, many social scientists, and some psychiatrists championed the liberty interests of patients in the mental health system. As a spokesperson for the extreme libertarian position, Thomas Szasz (1960, 1974), a professor of psychiatry and a psychoanalyst, vigorously maintained that mental illness was a myth and that the standards by which patients become defined as sick were psychosocial, ethical, and legal, but not medical. Although Szasz's use of the myth metaphor did little to stimulate reasonable and rational debate, he presented a point of view that required serious scrutiny.

Szasz argued that the concept of mental illness, strictly speaking, should be associated with biological conditions, such as syphilis of the brain, in which peculiarities in behavior and thought are demonstrably linked with a physiological condition. In contrast, most symptoms designated as mental illness were not the result of brain lesions or biological dysfunctions, but rather deviations in behavior or thinking. Thus, Szasz contended that the metaphor of illness had come to encompass problems having no underlying biological basis, and that judgments of mental illness primarily reflected ethical or psychosocial criteria. He conceded that specific disorders in thinking and behavior could result from brain dysfunctions, but he argued it is better to say that some people labeled as mentally ill suffer from a disease of the brain than to assert that all those called mentally ill are sick in a medical sense. In Szasz's opinion, then, use of the concept of mental illness to characterize both disorders of the brain and deviations in behavior, thinking, and affect due to other causes resulted in confusion, abuses of psychiatry, and the misapplication of medical terminology to deprive patients of their civil liberties through involuntary hospitalization and other forms of coercion.

Issues surrounding the validity of diagnostic categories of mental illness were strenuously debated by advocates of a disease model of schizophrenia versus those characterizing this problem as primarily a deviant response pattern. In the Rosenhan (1973) study, "On Being Sane in Insane Places," which was briefly discussed in Chapter 1, eight "normal" pseudopatients complaining of a bogus symptom presented themselves at 12 hospitals:

> After calling the hospital for an appointment, the pseudopatient arrived at the admissions office complaining that he had been hearing voices. Asked what the voices said, he replied that they were often unclear, but as far as he could tell they said "empty," "hollow," and "thud." The voices were unfamiliar and were of the same sex as the pseudopatient. The choice of these symptoms was occasioned by their apparent similarity to existential symptoms.... Beyond alleging the symptoms and falsifying name, vocation, and employment, no further alterations of person, history, or circumstances were made. The significant events of the pseudopatient's life history were presented as they had actually occurred.... Immediately upon admission to the psychiatric ward, the pseudopatient ceased simulating any symptoms of abnormality. (p. 251)

All pseudopatients were admitted to the psychiatric hospitals. In every case but one, the pseudopatients were discharged with the diagnosis of schizophrenia "in remission." The remaining diagnosis was simply schizophrenia. Length of hospitalization averaged 19 days with a range from 7 to 52 days. Pseudopatients were given a total of 2,100 pills, including antipsychotic agents such as Stelazine, Compazine, and Thorazine. This demonstration captured the powerlessness and depersonalization characteristic of psychiatric hospitalization, as well as the extent to which assumptions about illness influenced interpretations of what patients said and did. Rosenhan (1973) concluded: "[W]e have known for a long time that diagnoses are often not useful or reliable, but we have nevertheless continued to use them. We now know that we cannot distinguish insanity from sanity" (p. 257).

Rosenhan's demonstration drew many critiques. One of the most careful was by Robert Spitzer (1976), a research psychiatrist instrumental in the development of *DSM-III*. Spitzer argued that all Rosenhan had actually demonstrated was that when patients report unusual symptoms frequently associated with a serious psychiatric ailment, they will be suspected of having that ailment and admitted to a hospital. From the perspective of differential diagnosis, the absence of symptoms other than auditory hallucinations excludes most alternative diagnoses. One alternative would be the patient is trying to deceive the physician by malingering—a situation that sometimes occurs—but it is a relatively unlikely alternative because few patients feign schizophrenia, and few benefits can be gained by such deception. Quoting a remark by Seymour Kety (1974), a leader in neuroscience research, Spitzer made the point that if a patient drank a quart of blood and then came to a hospital emergency room vomiting blood, the hospital staff would logically assume the patient had internal bleeding. Kety then asked whether such a demonstration would argue convincingly that medicine does not know how to diagnose peptic ulcers. Furthermore, Spitzer maintained that the discharge diagnosis for all but one of the pseudopatients as schizophrenics in remission is highly atypical, suggesting this group was indeed puzzling to the psychiatrists who evaluated them.

In other words, what Rosenhan showed was nothing more than the duping of hospital staff by individuals reporting a potentially serious symptom not subject to independent validation. In much of medical practice, however, problems are identified by the fact that patients experience pain and discomfort and come seeking help; each patient's history and reports of symptoms are important aspects of an intake assessment. Yet Rosenhan, like many others before him, did raise important issues concerning typical psychiatric practice of this time. His study suggested the bias of physicians toward active treatment in situations of uncertainty, and he showed how readily the decision in favor of psychiatric hospitalization was made, particularly if a patient was receptive to admission. Of course, in today's managed care environment it is far less likely that hospitalization would occur in such circumstances.

Rosenhan's study also illustrated the power of expectancies, an area receiving much more attention recently with the growth of behavioral economics (Kahneman 2011). Rosenhan implemented a small additional study in a hospital whose administrators doubted that such errors as he had documented could occur at their institution. He stated that at some point in the next three months, pseudopatients would seek admission to the hospital's psychiatric unit, and he challenged staff to identify these patients. Yet no pseudopatients were sent. Clinical judgments were obtained on 193 patients, of whom 41 were believed to be pseudopatients by one staff member and 23 were judged as likely pseudopatients by at least one psychiatrist. What we expect very much colors what we see. These expectancies affect professional practice as well as everyday life, not only in psychiatry but in medicine as well (Groopman 2007).

The third major revision to the *DSM* (*DSM-III*) (American Psychiatric Association 1987) took place amidst these sharp ideological debates around the very existence of mental illness. Robert Spitzer, the psychiatrist who criticized Rosenhan's study, headed the Task Force for Nomenclature. This new edition of the *DSM* was a substantial revision that marked a sea change in the nosology of psychiatric disorder. The traditional distinction between organic disorders and functional disorders (those without a demonstrable organic basis or structural abnormality) was discarded as simplistic, while the concept of neurosis was eliminated as too vague. *DSM-III* substantially expanded the universe of disorders to 15 categories, including organic mental disorders such as senile and presenile dementias, substance abuse disorders such as alcohol abuse and dependence, schizophrenic disorders, paranoid disorders, affective disorders such as depression or manic–depressive states, anxiety disorders including phobias and generalized anxiety, and personality disorders. *DSM-III* also set up a multiaxial system with five major levels. Axis I focused on the primary psychiatric diagnosis. Axis II was devoted to recording the presence, where applicable, of personality disorders and mental retardation. Axis III listed general medical conditions, which may be implicated in, or independent of, the psychiatric disorder. Axis IV took account of psychosocial and environmental problems. And Axis V provided for a global assessment of functioning. Although all five axes are important in a well-rounded assessment of patients, in practical terms Axis I, the psychiatric diagnosis, gets most attention.

The most important change in the *DSM-III* was its inclusion of much more specific diagnostic criteria for each disorder. The updated manual outlined particular symptoms for all identified psychiatric disorders—together with frequency or severity thresholds for each—needing to be met in order to reach a diagnosis. *DSM-III* became widely adopted as the official diagnostic system by almost all mental health facilities and by other organizations such as insurance companies and the courts. Efforts to fine-tune *DSM-III*, and correct its errors and inconsistencies, began in 1983. This resulted in the publication of *DSM-III-R* (revised) in 1987.

Work began on *DSM-IV* in 1988, not because a new version was needed but because the World Health Organization was preparing a tenth revision of the *International Classification of Disease*s (ICD) and the APA wanted consistency between the two classification systems. In substance, however, *DSM-IV* (American Psychiatric Association 1994) remains quite close in content and definitions to *DSM-III-R*. While more carefully documented, it contains no substantial innovations. Publication of the *DSM* manual and its various guidebooks and aids is big business. *DSM-III* sold more than one million copies. Some believe the financial returns are no small incentive for frequent revision. In any case, *DSM-IV* is the officially accepted diagnostic manual for mental health services and research in the United States, and it has enormous influence on practice and reimbursement.

Expanding psychiatric diagnoses to 17 categories, the *DSM-IV* continued to refine the symptoms constituting each type of disorder. As an example, consider how a clinician would make a *DSM-IV* diagnosis regarding a major depressive episode. The patient must have had five or more of a list of nine symptoms, present for a two-week period and representing a change from previous functioning. One of these symptoms must be either depressed mood most of the day, nearly every day, or else a marked, diminished interest or pleasure in all, or almost all, activities most of the day, nearly every day. Among the other symptoms are recurrent thoughts of death or suicidal ideation, fatigue or loss of energy, diminished ability to think or concentrate, indecisiveness, insomnia or hypersomnia, feelings of worthlessness or excessive or inappropriate guilt, and so on. To be counted, each of these symptoms should occur almost every day during a two-week period. Moreover, the symptoms should not be due to normal bereavement (of under two months) or the direct physiological effect of a medical condition or a substance, and they should cause clinically significant distress or impairment in social, occupational, or other important areas of functioning. The symptoms should not meet the criteria for a mixed episode of psychiatric illness, which would be classified differently.

CONTESTED CATEGORIES OF DISORDER

Since the third revision, *DSM* has become increasingly central in medical and legal decision making regarding what constitutes a mental disorder. But as it has gained importance, the manual has also become more controversial. The new classification system in *DSM-IV* sought to implement a biomedical perspective quite different from earlier psychodynamic approaches. It distinguished categorically between clinical disorders and nondisorders, moving away from a more continuous view of health and illness. This new system, while pragmatic, is atheoretical and arbitrary in many ways. It also sought to be all-inclusive. With each new version of *DSM* the numbers of diagnoses have expanded, from originally only 106 in *DSM-I*, to 265 in *DSM-III*, to 297 in *DSM-IV* (Mayes and Horwitz 2005).

Since the third revision, *DSM* is often criticized for expanding the types of behaviors properly considered mental illness. The controversy over psychiatric diagnosis is often more political than scientific in character, and compromises are necessary to achieve consensus. One of the bitterest disputes involved classification of neurotic disorders. While psychoanalytic and psychodynamic psychiatrists viewed the concept of neurosis as central to their perspective, more medically oriented psychiatrists saw this designation as vague and unscientific. As Bayer and Spitzer (1985) note in their discussion of the controversy, "the entire process of achieving a settlement seemed more appropriate to the encounter of political rivals than to the orderly pursuit of scientific knowledge" (p. 195). Similarly, a battle erupted over whether *DSM-IV*'s inclusion of premenstrual dysphoric disorder (PDD), a disturbance focusing on behavioral and emotional symptoms related to a woman's menstrual cycle, was a proper exercise in psychiatric labeling (Caplan 1995). By contrast, gay advocacy groups were relieved when the APA removed homosexuality as a disease from its manual in 1973 (Bayer 1981).

Posttraumatic stress disorder (PTSD) offers another example of the kind of political debate that can erupt in response to the expansion of *DSM* (Scott 1990). As mentioned previously, the preparation of *DSM-I* had been partially driven by military psychiatrists in World War II who saw firsthand the psychological consequences of combat. *DSM-I* included "gross stress reaction" as a disorder, characterized as a temporary reaction to extreme stress such as that undergone during combat. This disorder was, however, excluded from the *DSM-II* (Scott 1990). The Vietnam War brought to bear powerful pressures to reconsider mental disorders resulting from wartime service. Scott (1990) describes claims made by antiwar psychiatrists and veterans that the atrocities committed against civilians in Vietnam were understandable as the direct effect of psychological problems brought on by combat. The concept of "post Vietnam syndrome" also emerged to explain the troubles of some veterans in adjusting to civilian life. Antiwar psychiatrists joined with veterans groups to lobby the APA (and the public) for inclusion of "catastrophic stress disorder" in the *DSM-III*; their lobbying was successful and the disorder was named PTSD.

By the time *DSM-IV* came into being, the criteria for PTSD were more encompassing. While originally the disorder was conceived as a reaction to the direct personal experience of extreme stress, *DSM-IV* now included even secondhand exposure, such as witnessing or learning the accounts of others who had faced extreme stresses or traumas, as a possible trigger of PTSD (Summerfield 2001). While serious debate continues about the existence of PTSD as a distinct disorder as well as its expanding boundaries (Spitzer, First, and Wakefield 2007), it now seems firmly ensconced in our diagnostic language.

One advantage of the inclusion of PTSD is that it at least linked the problems of veterans with their military experiences, rather than personal failings. Another was that it gave impetus for the nation's military establishment and the Veterans Administration to develop medical and disability programs specifically focused on addressing the psychological needs of persons who have seen combat. Although there are calls for narrowing the definition of the PTSD disorder in *DSM-5* (Spitzer, First, and Wakefield 2007), any attempt to do so in a substantial way would be greeted with a political firestorm.

To be clear, then, our point is not to raise skepticism about the need for treatment by individuals who are experiencing genuine psychological pain and distress, whatever the label assigned to their disorder, contested or not. Instead, we merely want to highlight the reality that entry of a disorder into *DSM* nomenclature can be driven by political pressure just as much as accumulating scientific evidence. Moreover, the consequences of having a disorder recognized in the *DSM* are important. Hundreds of thousands of veterans from Operations Enduring Freedom and Iraqi Freedom (OEF/OIF) in Afghanistan and Iraq have been diagnosed with PTSD. The long-term costs of providing medical care and disability benefits will be in the billions (Tanielian and Jaycox 2008). Inclusion of PTSD in the *DSM* lends legitimacy to demands for recognition and assistance from this patient group. At the same time, it provides relatively standardized guidance in making clinical diagnoses that are the gateway for important public benefits.

Health insurers, too, depend on *DSM* in decisions concerning eligibility for coverage and documentation of criteria for specific diagnoses. Access to mental health care depends importantly on the willingness of insurance companies to reimburse care and this, in turn, depends on how broad or strict *DSM* criteria are for meeting clinical thresholds. While some clinicians fudge in their use of the manual, insurers are increasingly vigilant that diagnoses and the treatments sought adhere to *DSM* standards.

As we will discuss in Chapter 4, the *DSM* has also been extremely important for research. Criteria based on these definitions of mental illness facilitate defining samples of patients more precisely and clarify the applicability of findings. On the negative side, the codification process can take on a life of its own, such that insurance companies, courts, other social agencies, and researchers may attribute to *DSM* definitions more intrinsic validity than they truly possess.

DEVELOPMENT OF *DSM-5*

In 1999, the APA began its preplanning for the introduction of *DSM-5*, scheduled to be published in May, 2013. Intensive work by various task forces and work groups, involving some 162 psychiatrists and other mental health professionals and more than 300 advisors, began in 2008 and continues as this is being written. A website (www.dsm5.org) was established to publicize many of the relevant materials as deliberations take place. Opportunity exists for professionals and the public to comment on draft proposals, and more than 8,000 have done so.

DSM-5 field trials in academic medical centers and in routine clinical practice settings failed to resolve some contentious issues. For a number of new and established diagnoses, there is a lack of agreement in use by clinicians, which is a problem of low reliability. It is fair to assume that *DSM-5* will be more a fine-tuning of *DSM-IV* than a radical departure. As with earlier efforts, the revision seeks to clarify various criteria and link them as closely as possible with research to achieve the highest utility for clinicians while retaining continuity with earlier editions. Although many of these changes may not seem highly significant, even minor changes can take on momentous importance for those involved in specific clinical areas. It is anticipated that even after the final revision is released, modification will continue to be needed in amended versions such as *DSM-5.1*, *DSM-5.2*, and so on.

Readers can find the latest information on the *DSM-5* website, and it is premature to anticipate fully the 2013 content. Still, it is already possible to describe certain overall changes that are coming. For example, *DSM* chapters will now be organized following a life span approach beginning with neurodevelopmental disorders, which begin very early in life, and progressing with disorder categories likely to arise as one ages. Similarly, within each set of categories, individual disorders will be described following the same life span logic. Greater attention is being given to assessing severity of symptoms and the challenge of co-occurring disorders, as in the case where, for example, one person meets the criteria for both major depression and anxiety disorder.

Potentially one of the most significant and far-reaching discussions about the *DSM* involves the utility of dimensional assessments. Based on the medical model, earlier versions of *DSM* approached diagnosis, first, by assessing whether particular symptoms were present or absent and, second, by setting an arbitrary minimum number of symptoms as marking the threshold for disease. But as is patently obvious, a great deal depends not only on the number of symptoms but also on their severity. While there has been support for appropriate dimensional assessments for some disorders, the reality is that completing this exercise in any comprehensive fashion across most disorders challenges the underlying logic of *DSM*. Thus, it would be greatly disruptive to the goal of maintaining continuity with previous editions of the manual. As noted earlier, *DSM* uses a dichotomous (yes–no) approach in assessing whether patients meet the criteria for a particular diagnosis. A dimensional framework, in contrast, would treat conditions more as continua with quantitative assessment of the extent of symptomatology. Dimensional approaches are unlikely to play a large role in *DSM-5*, although some marginal changes may reflect this way of thinking. The issue remains a controversial one.

One recommended and likely change that has elicited a great deal of commentary and media interest is the establishment of a diagnostic category of autism spectrum disorder that combines autism, Asperger disorder, childhood disintegrative disorder, and developmental disorders not otherwise specified. This new diagnosis would be built around two domains: social and communication deficits, and fixated interests and repetitive behaviors. The task force argued this change would increase diagnostic reliability and validity by reducing present inconsistencies and better reflect scientific evidence about pathology and clinical presentation. The group asserts, further, that previous criteria "were equivalent to trying to 'cleave meatloaf at the joints'" (www.dsm5.org). Among opponents are those members of the Asperger disorder community who worry this proposed diagnosis might prove more stigmatizing than the more neutral designation of Asperger disease. Another concern is that those with limited symptoms might lose access to important services and that a combination of several diagnoses could push individuals with Asperger disorder out of treatment. Changes in the official diagnostic system inevitably have social and political implications, although they cannot always be clearly foreseen.

Much public criticism of *DSM* deals with the expansion of diagnostic entities such as hoarding disorders, avoidant personality disorder, sexual interest/arousal disorder in women, female orgasmic disorder, acute stress disorder, pathological gambling, disruptive mood dysregulation disorder, and the like. The concern is not that these are trivial matters, but that they advance an increasing medicalization of everyday life.

Critics of the proposed revisions of *DSM* abound (Miller 2012). A letter and petition prepared by the humanistic psychology division of the American Psychological Association, which was endorsed by almost 14,000 individuals and some 50 mental health professional and advocacy organizations as of June 2012, provide a thoughtful appraisal (www.ipetitions.com/petition/dsm5). Among concerns cited by this group are lower thresholds for many diagnoses, proposals for new diagnoses lacking scientific merit, and the introduction of certain questionable diagnoses for children and the elderly that are likely to lead to overuse of powerful medications with adverse side-effects. In general, important issues are being raised concerning increased medicalization of the *DSM*, its exaggerated focus on biology, and the de-emphasis of social and cultural factors.

Wakefield (1992), for example, has noted that diagnostic criteria for many conditions in *DSM-IV* contradict *DSM*'s own definition of mental disorder. This latter definition is consistent with Wakefield's notion that a mental disorder is a harmful dysfunction. First, the affects or behaviors must be harmful in some ways, such as being a source of suffering or a disruption to social roles and activities and personal welfare. But to meet the formal definition of disorder, a condition must also be a dysfunction—a product of mental processes inconsistent with how the psyche has been programmed to function by human evolution. Suffering or deviant behaviors alone do not constitute disorder.

How then does one assess how the psyche is meant to function and when there is psychopathology present? Throughout history, laypeople and professionals have used context to make these assessments (Horwitz and Wakefield 2007). In many cases, the inference of psychopathology is relatively easy. When a person for whom life is going well becomes profoundly depressed, or when a person who is hearing voices stabs a perfect stranger, we can reasonably infer that the person's psyche is not working as biologically programmed. But *DSM* stripped evaluations of context from the process of clinical assessment by simply prescribing a diagnosis when various symptomatic criteria are met.

Let's return to the diagnosis of a major depressive episode described above. If individuals meet symptomatic criteria for the periods specified, they receive the diagnosis. The only contextual exception in *DSM* is bereavement of brief duration and moderate severity, because disturbed affect and behavior is a normal response to loss of a loved one and such symptoms might normally persist for some time. Horwitz and Wakefield ask, however, why just this one exception? Is it pathological to have these same types of symptoms after being jilted by a person one loves, or going through an unwanted divorce, or losing one's job and not being able to provide for one's family, or experiencing the ravages of Hurricane Katrina, or suffering the direct effects of 9/11 and loss of friends and relatives? Significant numbers of people meet the definition of major depression following these experiences, but are their responses really a disorder?

Wakefield and colleagues used the National Comorbidity Survey (NCS) to examine, to the extent allowed by the data, whether various outcome measures for uncomplicated depressive symptoms following losses other than bereavement were similar to, or different from, those following bereavement (Wakefield et al. 2007). They consider nine disorder measures including suicide attempts, interference with life, recurrence, and service use. What emerged were very similar profiles of outcomes for those with uncomplicated depression following bereavement versus other losses. The researchers concluded that

uncomplicated depression following other losses, in addition to bereavement, is probably not a disorder. Failure to apply these exclusions exaggerates the prevalence of major
depression in the NCS by about one-quarter.

The *DSM-IV* approach to major depression seems irrational in its neglect of major
stressors and its arbitrary limit of a two-month period for grieving. Psychiatrist/anthropol-
ogist Arthur Kleinman points to the lack of scientific evidence to define a normal period of
grief, as well as the wide range of bereavement behavior cross-culturally (Kleinman 2012).
Many have argued for broadening the grief exclusion to take into account other major
adversities. Yet the proposed *DSM-5* eliminates the exclusion entirely. Instead, it merely
inserts a note to the effect that reaction to significant loss can resemble a depressive disorder, or in other cases it can actually qualify as such a disorder. Clinicians are advised to be
aware of this quandary in making their diagnostic assessments.

It is not surprising that this issue has surfaced as one of the most prickly faced by
DSM-5. Recognizing that the grief exclusion in *DSM-III* and *DSM-IV* would have to be
dealt with one way or another, the Mood Disorder Work Group recommended its elimination. Kenneth Kendler (2010), a member of the work group, has claimed that extending
the principle behind the grief exclusion to other psychological disturbances would require
a major change in diagnostic approach. Adversity plays some part in most major depres-
sions, according to Kendler, and grief is not the same as major depression: most people
who experience bereavement do not develop major depression, and when those in this
group do meet depression criteria, a strategy of "watchful waiting" may be appropriate in
deciding whether treatment is needed.

For Horwitz and Wakefield (2007), by contrast, the test of whether a response is
pathological depends on whether symptoms remit when stressful stimuli are removed
and people's life situations improve. This may not always be testable, but to assume that
pathology exists, regardless of context, is to be highly overinclusive. Although *DSM* does
not require contextual evaluations, many clinicians obviously rely on such data in their
work with patients. Horwitz and Wakefield (2007) direct their critique at the procedure
for making psychiatric diagnoses under *DSM*. They do not speak to the question of who
should receive help when suffering, nor whether a *DSM* disorder should or should not be
a gateway for receiving services.

There is an important distinction between *DSM* and how clinicians practice. While
mental health providers often are required to use *DSM* diagnoses for bureaucratic purposes
and for insurance reimbursement, they do not necessarily accept *DSM* characterizations
of mental disorder. Indeed, clinicians may adopt a variety of "workarounds" that better
fit their practice orientations and their patients' perceived clinical needs. In a fascinating
study, Owen Whooley (2010) interviewed 36 psychiatrists working in a variety of practice
settings in the New York area concerning their views of and implementation of *DSM*. All
felt that insurers and other external actors employed the *DSM* to impose an unrealistic
biomedical model insensitive to the true nature and complexity of mental illness. Thus,
many felt justified in negotiating diagnoses with patients and fudging diagnostic codes on
forms to justify particular treatments or clinical decisions. Even though most psychiatrists
generally supported the biomedical model and saw *DSM* as a constructive effort—or, at
least, a "necessary evil"—they still commonly subverted the manual in practice. However,
about a third of the psychiatrists, those more inclined toward a psychodynamic orientation
and opposed to a strict biomedical model, resorted to workarounds considered "extreme"
by the researcher. Ironically, Whooley found that diagnosis was based less on patients'

symptoms and more on the clinician's beliefs about patient need. As he notes, "Treatment does not follow diagnosis; diagnosis follows treatment. The label is applied after the fact and then quickly discarded to justify a treatment based on the psychiatrist's individual normative assessment of the patient's need. The judgment exercised here is more idiosyncratic and opaque than the standardised assessment championed by the *DSM*" (Whooley 2010, p. 459).

SCHIZOPHRENIA: AN EXAMPLE IN PSYCHIATRIC CONCEPTUALIZATION

Schizophrenic reactions often lead to long-term disability and a continuing need for care. Although comprising a relatively small component of all mental illness, large amounts of public resources are spent on taking care of people with schizophrenia. Thus, schizophrenia constitutes a prototype of the challenge that public policy must intelligently address. Although psychiatrists generally agree that schizophrenic reactions encompass different conditions with surface similarities, little evidence exists that subtypes can be reliably differentiated. Under ordinary conditions of practice, even the gross diagnosis is less than fully reliable. Because schizophrenia is one of the most important psychiatric conditions—and the one perhaps most studied and written about—it is worth illustrating the problems of psychiatric conceptualization using schizophrenia as an example.

Psychiatrists usually diagnose schizophrenia on the basis of bizarre behavior characterized by inappropriate verbalizations and distortions of interpersonal perception as evidenced by the presence of delusions and hallucinations. Persons with schizophrenia often withdraw from interpersonal contacts and can become preoccupied with a strange fantasy life. In its more extreme manifestations, schizophrenia is associated with disregard for conventional expectations and with deterioration of personal habits, including self-care. One early definition (McGhie and Chapman 1961) described schizophrenia as a set of reactions involving disturbances in relating to reality and concept formation, accompanied by intellectual, affective, and behavioral abnormalities varying in kind and degree. The definition identifies early schizophrenia in terms of disturbances in the processes of attention and perception (including changes in sensory quality and in the perception of speech and movement), changes in motility and bodily awareness, and changes in thinking and affective processes. Patients classified as schizophrenic often give the impression that they are retreating from reality and suffering from discontinuous streams of thought. Depending on stage of the condition and level of personal deterioration, schizophrenia may be easy or difficult to identify:

> The diagnosis of schizophrenia is either very easy or very difficult. The typical cases, and there are very many such, can be recognized by the layman and the beginner; but some cases offer such difficulties that the most qualified experts in the field cannot come to any agreement. Such difficulties hardly can be surprising; there is no clear, fundamental definition of schizophrenia. (Redlich and Freedman 1966, pp. 507–508)

DSM-III and *DSM-IV* contributed to clearer diagnostic criteria for schizophrenia and interest in biological models encouraging careful diagnosis. *DSM-IV* notes five characteristic symptoms of schizophrenia: delusions, hallucinations, disorganized speech, gross disorganized or catatonic behavior, and negative symptoms such as affective flattening. A number of approaches have been developed for even more systematic diagnosis. John Wing (2010), for example, developed a technique for interviewing patients—called the *present state examination*—that has been included in a variety of diagnostic studies, particularly in Europe. The procedure involves a set of rules based on clinical experience that guides placement of patients into diagnostic categories. This system has also been computerized—via a program known as CATEGO (Wing, Cooper, and Sartorius 1974)—and possesses high reliability for the classification of schizophrenia in different cultures (Wing et al. 1967; World Health Organization 1973).

Symptoms used in the diagnosis of schizophrenia are divided into various classes. In the case of an acute problem, the central symptoms that account for two-thirds of all clinical diagnoses include beliefs about thought insertion, thought broadcast, and thought withdrawal; auditory hallucinations of a specific type; and delusions of control by people and forces outside the self. Thought insertion, a rare symptom, is the perception that thoughts other than one's own are being placed into the mind. The patient may believe alien thoughts have entered into his or her mind through radar, telepathy, or some other means. Careful questioning is required to establish that the patient is not misstating or exaggerating a commonly occurring experience such as seeming to hear voices in one's mind. Other groups of symptoms may also help to establish a diagnosis of schizophrenia, such as additional types of delusions or hallucinations, or persistent talking to oneself. Still other symptoms are more ambiguous, and it can become difficult to make a clear differential diagnosis between schizophrenia and other clinical conditions. When it comes to more marginal symptoms, agreement among psychiatrists decreases.

The patient with chronic schizophrenia is often highly disabled socially. Two main types of symptoms tend to be present: (1) "a syndrome of 'negative' traits such as emotional apathy, slowness of thought and movement, underactivity, lack of drive, poverty of speech, and social withdrawal"; and (2) "incoherence of speech, unpredictability of associations, long-standing delusions and hallucinations, and accompanying manifestations in behaviour" (Wing 2010, p. 110). The consequences of these types of symptoms and their effects on work, interpersonal relations, and family life present obstacles for community adjustment (Estroff 1981). It is difficult for a patient with schizophrenia to undergo successful rehabilitation, and limiting the chronicity of the condition is itself a challenge. Studies, however, demonstrate that the prognosis for schizophrenia is less discouraging than clinicians have typically believed and that well-conceived and appropriately managed programs of care can significantly limit disabilities associated with the disorder while improving level of function and quality of life (Mechanic 2006). These points are of great importance and require brief attention here.

Clinicians have traditionally expressed pessimism about the inevitable deterioration associated with schizophrenia and the intractability of the disease to intervention. In contrast, long-term studies show extraordinary variability in adaptation and functioning over time, suggesting that patients have much greater potential for recovery than formerly understood (Davidson and McGlashan 1997; Harding, Zubin, and Strauss 1987). In a remarkable clinical investigation carried out over 27 years, Manfred Bleuler (1978) documented the course of disorder among 208 patients in Zurich in various cohorts over two decades. He described the continuing adaptations among these patients, who fluctuated between varying outcomes. One-half to three-quarters of patients with schizophrenia achieved long-term recoveries, and only 10 to 20 percent became severely and chronically ill. This estimate of recovery was conservative, because it included only patients reaching an end state and, as Bleuler noted, the prognosis of all schizophrenia cases combined is better. Moreover, in some patients, even after 40 years of psychosis, marked changes occurred. Long-term studies carried out by Ciompi (1980) in Lausanne, and by Huber, Gross, and Schuttler (1979) in Bonn, confirm Bleuler's conclusion on the variable, often favorable course of schizophrenia.

The earliest study in the United States documenting the variable course of schizophrenia was based on a group of 269 chronic patients from the "back wards" who were discharged from Vermont State Hospital (Harding et al. 1987a, 1987b). The patients were among the most ill in the hospital and had not responded to drug treatment. They were enrolled in a comprehensive rehabilitation program in the hospital and upon release had access to a wide range of services to address health care as well as social needs such as housing and employment. Most were functioning adequately in the community in later life, although 10 years after their release many had made uncertain adjustments and were socially isolated. Approximately 32 years after discharge, between one-half to two-thirds of individuals still alive were significantly improved or recovered, confirming European results.

Using clinical records, the investigators selected and studied the subgroup of 118 patients who had met *DSM-III* criteria for schizophrenia at hospital admission in the mid-1950s (Harding et al 1987b). During follow-up, it was found that most were living in the community and needed little to no help in meeting their basic needs. Two-fifths of patients of working age were employed in the prior year, a majority had few significant symptoms, and about three-quarters were leading "moderate to very full lives."

A comparison study conducted in Maine tracked patients who had been admitted to the state hospital during the same period as the Vermont study (DeSisto et al. 1995). The researchers matched the comparison sample to the Vermont cases on diagnosis, time in the hospital, age, and sex. Unlike the care system in Vermont, Maine's followed a more traditional approach. After-care services were primarily based in community mental health centers, and there was little attention to vocational needs and no early attention to housing needs. Ex-patients from the Vermont system were more likely to be working during the follow-up than their Maine counterparts; they also had fewer symptoms, higher levels of functioning, and better community adaptation. The authors argue that the better-developed rehabilitation system in Vermont accounted for the better outcomes.

While other work following patients for 30 to 40 years found that patients with schizophrenia had a less favorable course than those with affective disorders; a significant number of the former did have "good" outcomes (Tsuang, Woolson, and Fleming 1979). The picture yielded by this body of research departs from conventional clinical pessimism, suggesting that the notion of inevitable deterioration that dominated the psychiatric literature may have been a self-fulfilling prophecy, particularly if it determined assumptions and behavior on the part of some mental health practitioners.

More recent longitudinal studies continue to find much heterogeneity in the long-term course of schizophrenia, with a significant proportion of patients showing long remissions, eventual course improvements, and complete remission later in the illness. A significant negative influence on outcomes is substance abuse among younger clients (Davidson and McGlashan 1997), a form of comorbidity increasingly common in recent years. Poorer outcomes tend to be more characteristic of clients with "negative" clinical symptoms, such as apathy and poor self-maintenance, long recognized as debilitating in social functioning and work. Nevertheless, from a quarter to more than half of all cases seem to resolve with manageable symptoms and some with full remission. Medication adherence is imperative for most clients, but significant numbers of patients lapse (Zygmunt et al. 2002). Early intervention, substance abuse prevention, and medication adherence all seem to contribute to a more favorable course.

How can one reconcile the incongruency between these studies and the pessimism found among some clinicians? Clinicians often remain unaware of the epidemiological picture because they see their patients primarily based on a short-term, cross-sectional perspective (Harding, Zubin, and Strauss 1987). Moreover, many patients who function well may no longer seek or require intensive treatment, giving more visibility to those patients who do not get well and repeatedly return for inpatient care. Difficult and intractable cases thus may come to dominate a clinician's time and perceptions. A longitudinal perspective, in contrast, not only provides a more hopeful picture but also the standpoint necessary for understanding the types of care essential for this needy population. A number of studies, which we will review later, show persuasively that effectively organized community alternatives to hospital care can achieve superior results whether measured by clinical outcomes, psychosocial participation, levels of function, or patient and family satisfaction.

Causes of schizophrenia remain unknown, and disagreement continues about its classification. Etiological theories have ranged from biologically oriented models (Kety 1986) to those that posit the roots of schizophrenia in social interaction and family life (Mischler and Waxler 1966). Is it more accurate to view schizophrenia as a variety of diseases with common manifestations or reaction patterns? In recent years, the dominant view has moved closer to biological and biomedical models, but almost everyone accepts the idea that both biology and environment play some role. As John Strauss (1979) has noted, "No single variable, biological or psychosocial, appears to be necessary or sufficient to make someone schizophrenic" (p. 291). Most researchers now view schizophrenia as a biochemical, genetic, or neurological susceptibility triggered by environmental or interactional events. The factors being investigated are diverse, including genetic propensities, early infection, and nutritional deficiencies, among others.

Many experts have attempted to classify subtypes of schizophrenia based on descriptions of different symptom patterns, but these distinctions have not proved reliable, valid, or useful. Applying tools available from molecular biology and medical imaging to a comparison of brain functioning, researchers have sought a biologically based system of differentiation. Murray and his colleagues (1992) proposed a neurodevelopmental classificatory approach distinguishing between congenital schizophrenia, adult onset schizophrenia, and late onset schizophrenia. They hypothesize that congenital schizophrenia results from aberrant brain development in fetal or neonatal life, or soon thereafter, although the problem may not be immediately recognized. They believe this condition could be a consequence of a genetic defect, resulting in decreased cortical volume and small temporal lobe structures as seen by imaging. Alternatively, similar manifestations may result from a genetic predisposition interacting with some early environmental factor such as maternal influenza, maternal complications, infections, and the like. There is, for example, evidence that famines and starvation increase risk of schizophrenia (Susser, Hoek, and Brown 1998; St. Clair et al. 2005). Persons with this type of schizophrenia have various physical anomalies, deviant child personality and social impairment, negative clinical symptoms of schizophrenia, and cognitive impairment. They come into care early in life, and have relatively poor outcomes. Interestingly, male children predominate.

In contrast, Murray and colleagues (1992) posit that adult onset schizophrenia is much more heterogeneous, likely encompasses several different conditions, and fundamentally differs from the congenital type. These disorders tend to be characterized by "positive" clinical symptoms (such as delusions and hallucinations), more commonly remit and relapse, and appear to be associated with a variety of genes connected with psychotic conditions. Persons developing late onset schizophrenia have good premorbid intellectual and occupational function, are more paranoid than schizotypal, have auditory and visual sensory deficits, and are predominantly women. Researchers believe people have illnesses related to different types of conditions such as paranoid personality, affective illness, and sensory deprivation. Late onset organic changes are proposed as the underlying common pathway in these patients.

IS MENTAL ILLNESS A SOCIAL JUDGMENT OR A DISEASE?

That mental illness is largely a social judgment of deviant and disturbing behavior is a position contested strongly by most psychiatrists, although some ex-patient groups still adhere to these beliefs. The psychiatric disease model contends that mental illness does not simply connote nonconformity but also disturbance of psychological functioning as evidenced by delusions; hallucinations; disorganized thinking; and disturbed emotional states, such as extreme anxiety or depression. (For a classic statement of this view, see Lewis 1953.) Although there are no valid laboratory tests or diagnostic procedures to confirm judgments of psychological dysfunction, the psychiatric establishment believes these psychopathological criteria are as relevant as criteria used in diagnosing physical illness. What leads to such great controversy is the problem that psychiatric assessments of pathology depend almost exclusively on the clinician's judgment, while in physical medicine more objective investigatory procedures are frequently available. In the contemporary context, the debate has focused on the overinclusiveness of *DSM*, not whether schizophrenia and other mainstream diagnoses represent real mental disorders.

Szasz's (1974) notion that mental disease is a myth presents a logical difficulty. The diagnostic approach to identifying disease is a tool for treating and studying persons with particular types of problems. By refining the definition of a disorder, we can then try to ascertain causes and observe what happens to the problem over time, including the way it responds to different types of influences. Most typically, patients come to doctors in distress, when they are suffering and want relief. Differential diagnosis is a technique used by the doctor to identify the specific nature of the problem and what medical knowledge may have to offer. In any given instance, one can ask how useful it is to approach certain types of problems with a disease model as compared with some other approach. To ask whether the disease model is true, however, makes no more sense than asking whether a shovel is true. Both the disease model and shovels are tools—useful for dealing with some problems and not with others. Both can be inappropriate in certain situations and cause more damage than good, as when a shovel is used to try to fix a flat tire or when the disease model is assumed to be relevant for "fixing" a student who has difficulty understanding this book.

Calling a condition a disease is a social judgment based on cultural concepts of what is disturbing. We typically view conditions as diseases if they shorten life, disrupt functioning, or cause pain and distress. But whether we feel pain or not depends not only on our physical being but also on cultural conditioning and social expectations. What may be painful and limiting in one social context may be viewed differently in another. Our goals and definitions of self are culturally shaped. Science and medicine are part of the larger culture and help define the meanings we attribute to various events. Every outcome has causes; the challenge is to identify its determinants correctly. The disease model is one approach for studying causes of the human response patterns that we regard as significant and needing some form of remedy.

Studying a problem also requires us to identify it and differentiate it from other entities. By doing so, we can better locate its determinants, the way it evolves over time, and the possibilities for modification. In the study of disease, efforts are made to identify clusters of symptoms on the assumption they stem from some underlying dysfunction. By accurately describing and studying these symptoms, we are better able to advance our knowledge of them and identify their causes and know how to treat them. Over the years, we have learned a great deal about many diseases—patterns of typical and atypical symptom occurrence, symptom development over time, causes, and effective treatments. In other instances, we have incomplete or very little knowledge. At any given point in time, the physician must work with disease models, some of which are well developed and highly useful while others are incomplete and of more dubious value.

A confirmed disease theory is one that provides all the necessary information concerning the cause of a condition, what is likely to occur if the condition goes untreated, and what regimen is available to correct the condition. Accurate diagnostic assessment thus leads to correct action. It should be obvious why diagnostic reliability is so important; if a patient has pernicious anemia and the diagnosis is tuberculosis, the clinician will be proceeding on incorrect inferences concerning the cause of the problem and appropriate remedies. (For a more complete discussion of this issue, see Mechanic 1978, pp. 95–105.)

Although the debate as to whether a particular problem is a disease or not most commonly occurs in the psychiatric area, no fundamental difference distinguishes between the application of disease models within medicine and psychiatry. Debate rages in psychiatry because the disease theories used by psychiatrists have a lower degree of scientific confirmation than many such theories in general medicine, although both areas have many unconfirmed theories. We are talking about a matter of degree. When a physician assigns the label of pernicious anemia to a patient's medical condition, the doctor's understanding of the illness and its treatment derive directly from the diagnosis. In contrast, if assigning the label of personality disorder to a patient's condition does not affect the choice of therapy or chance of recovery, the advantage of using a disease model can be questioned, especially if it might detract attention from more effective approaches. Psychiatric disease models, however, are not as poor or unspecific as some critics complain. Differentiation of bipolar and other types of depression usually results in specific treatments, and depression is typically treated differently from schizophrenia. In everyday ambulatory medical care, it has been estimated that one-quarter to one-half of all patients do not fit existing models of disease (White 1970), a situation that continues to bedevil and shape primary care practice. Primary care physicians commonly adopt a problem-assessment approach in managing such patients in contrast to imposing disease labels on them.

The defining characteristics of disease models change constantly. What we can or cannot do depends on the state of our knowledge and understanding at the moment. The fact that a confirmed disease theory does not exist for a particular cluster of symptoms, signs, or problems tells us little about the future state of understanding. Knowledge about mental disorders and human behavior is increasing. Although psychiatrists and psychologists adopting a psychodynamic perspective are prone to apply a fairly uniform approach to most conditions they regard as treatable, the more common trend in psychiatry today is to match specific treatments to particular disorders. Even so, there is significant overlap in the treatment techniques recommended for differing conditions, which reflects the ambiguous and uncertain state of the field.

In deciding whether a disease orientation is useful, then, it is necessary to balance gains against disadvantages. Adoption of a disease perspective involves certain risks. Characterizing a particular problem as a mental disease may lead to greater stigmatization than alternative definitions. The implication that the condition lies within the individual rather than the social situation, and that it is not subject to conscious control, may lead to attitudes that are serious deterrents to rehabilitation. The most serious result of using disease models when they yield little information is the possible neglect of alternatives for rehabilitation outside the disease perspective. Gerald Grob (1966), a historian who has studied mental hospital care, has noted the following:

> The continued insistence by psychiatrists that their profession was truly scientific... exerted a profound, though negative, influence over the character of the mental hospital. As we have seen, the assumption that mental disease was somatic in nature invariably led to therapeutic nihilism. Moreover, somaticism often precluded alternative approaches, particularly along psychological and other nonsomatic lines. Lacking any visible means of therapy, psychiatrists tended to engage in a vast holding operation by confining mentally ill patients until that distant day when specific cures for specific disease entities would become available. (Grob 1966, pp. 356–357)

DEVELOPMENTAL MODELS

The major competing view to the disease perspective is one that conceptualizes problems in terms of their psychodynamics or cognitive processes. This is the framework for disorder that informed the original version of *DSM*. Instead of concerning themselves with making a diagnosis of disease, psychodynamic psychiatrists and other mental health professionals, such as psychologists and social workers, may attempt to reconstruct a developmental picture of the patient's personality and life situation. These clinicians believe such an exploration will provide insight into the patient's disturbed state, how problems have developed, and the functions of disturbed behavior in relation to the patient's adaptation to his or her environment. Kolb (1977), in instructing psychiatrists on examination of the patient, made the following observation:

> The purpose of the psychiatric examination is to discover the origin and evolution of such personality disorders as may be interfering with the happiness, satisfactions, efficiency, or social adjustment of the patient. One seeks, therefore, to secure a biographical-historical perspective of the personality, a clear psychological picture of the living person as a specific human being with his individual problems. It will be found that there is a logical continuity in any personality manifestations, whether the manifestations be those that are called normal or those that are called abnormal. The fundamental dynamic laws of behavior and of personality development are the same for both. (Kolb 1977, p. 197)

A basic assumption of the psychodynamic therapist is that disturbed behavior is part of the same continuum as normal behavior and is explained by the same theories that govern our understanding of normal personality development and social functioning. If disturbed behavior is a form of adaptation of the personality in response to particular situations and social stresses, then it is logical to study such behavior from the same perspectives and orientations as those from which we study any other kinds of behavior.

Psychodynamic therapists do not focus on ascertaining whether or not a given patient is mentally ill, for this is not a meaningful perspective within their frame of reference. They assume the existence of mental illness or personality disturbance by the fact that the patient is suffering and has come for help or by the fact that the patient's social behavior is sufficiently inappropriate to lead others to bring him or her to the attention of caregivers. Using a developmental approach, the therapist attempts to ascertain which aspects of the person's past experience have led to those patterns of functioning creating the current difficulty. Strong inferences under this approach are that the source of difficulty resides within the patient's personality and psychosocial development, and that the problem can be alleviated or remedied by changing some aspects of functioning and/or uncovering the roots of his or her emotional imbalance.

Because the psychodynamic perspective does not differentiate mental illness from ordinary mental discomfort or social maladjustment, professionals of this persuasion tend to treat people with a wide variety of problems, including marital dissatisfaction, poor adjustment to school, and feelings of lack of fulfillment. Although such professionals may be attuned, to some extent, to social factors, they basically proceed as if mental health difficulties stem from the personality of the patient rather than the social situation, deprivation and injustice, or other environmental contingencies.

CONCEPTUALIZING MENTAL HEALTH

The *DSM* does not deal with the question of what constitutes "mental health," although in research, policy, and common parlance the term is often presumed to be merely the absence of mental illness as measured by this manual. This is overly simplistic. The WHO (2010) defines mental health much more broadly "as a state of well-being in which an individual realizes his or her own abilities, can cope with the normal stresses of life, can work productively and is able to make a contribution to his or her community." Similarly, the Surgeon General Report on Mental Health insists that mental health is much more than the absence of mental disorders; it is instead "a state of successful performance of mental function, resulting in productive activities, fulfilling relationships with other people, and the ability to adapt to change and to cope with adversity" (U.S. Department of Health and Human Services 1999, p. 4).

Such conceptualizations have rarely been operationalized in practice. A notable exception is the work of Corey Keyes (Keyes 2002, 2007; Keyes, Shmotkin, and Ryff 2002). In a study of adults between the ages of 25 and 74 in the United States, Keyes situated individuals along a continuum of mental health from "languishing" to "flourishing" based on various measures of social, emotional, and psychological well-being. Overall, 18 percent of the sample was characterized as flourishing. More interesting, however, is the finding that about 6 percent of persons who met the criteria for major depression were also categorized as flourishing in terms of mental health, and a further 60 percent were categorized as "moderately mentally healthy." The view that one may have a mental disorder but still achieve mental health is integral to the recovery movement. The goal of recovery focuses less on the absence of disorder as the ultimate goal of treatment, and more on the ability to pursue a life that holds meaning and pleasure combined with a positive sense of self (Slade 2010). The notion that physical health is more than the absence of disorder has been much studied, with a convincing body of evidence that subjective appraisals of health predict outcomes such as functioning and mortality, even when objective measures of health are taken into account (Idler and Benyamini 1997; Idler, Russell, and Davis 2000). We have yet to take equally seriously subjective assessments of mental health and their predictive ability for outcome variations among persons meeting *DSM* diagnostic criteria. And, as yet, there are no signs that this concept of mental health will be integrated into the *DSM-5*.

CULTURE AND THE DEFINITION OF MENTAL DISORDER

The *DSM* originally ignored the role of culture in expressions of distress or interpretation of symptoms, implicitly suggesting that definition of particular disorders and their underlying symptoms were universally applicable. It was not until *DSM-IV* that the APA began to consider cultural factors in defining disorder (American Psychiatric Association 1994). For each disorder, the *DSM-IV* featured a description of cultural features (in addition to gender and age features) that clinicians are advised to take into account when making a diagnosis. For example, criteria for a major depressive episode included the fact that somatic aspects are experienced variably across cultures, and that cultural beliefs such as the feeling one is bewitched should not be viewed as meeting the hallucination criteria for psychotic depression.

In addition, the *DSM-IV* added an appendix section on culture-bound syndromes, described as "locality-specific patterns of aberrant behavior and troubling experience that may or may not be linked to a particular *DSM-IV* diagnostic category" (American Psychiatric Association 1994, p. 844). "Ataque de nervios" is one such disorder. Ataque de nervios is characterized by symptoms of feeling out of control, such as crying, shouting, trembling, fainting, feeling hot, and verbal and physical aggression. The *DSM-IV* describes this syndrome as mainly occurring among Latinos, especially those from the Caribbean. Some critics have argued that placement of culture-bound syndromes in the manual's appendix was too limiting and tended to "exoticize the role of culture" by suggesting it only matters in the diagnoses of individuals from non-White ethnic groups (López and Guarnaccia 2000, p. 576). Indeed, it is not clear why pathological gambling or eating disorders would not also be considered culture-bound syndromes given their dominance in Western cultures (Alarcón et al. 2002).

Finally, the *DSM-IV* presents guidelines for specifying a "cultural formulation" in diagnostic decisions. According to this component, clinicians must note patients' cultural or ethnic group, taking into account cultural idioms for expressing distress as well as cultural factors in experiences and interpretations of stress, social support, and family relationships. The guidelines direct clinicians to weigh how culture plays into their relationship with the patient, for example, how language differences may complicate communication. While inclusion of this cultural formulation has been applauded, and is now integrated into much of psychiatric training, uncertainty remains about how it is being operationalized and whether the result has been improved outcomes for patients (Alarcón et al. 2002; Lewis-Fernandez 2009).

Beyond accepting its relevance for how individuals experience and respond to symptoms, the *DSM-5* will continue to struggle with incorporating culture into a universalist nosology for defining mental disorders (Alarcón et al. 2009). Some see great potential gain if a cultural formulation can be integrated throughout the *DSM*, including increased information regarding practical applications (Lewis-Fernandez 2009).

THE SOCIAL POLICY CONNECTION

It is reasonable to maintain that if people need help, there is a public interest to provide it, whether or not the matter falls within the confines of mental illness. Yet limitations always exist on the resources available. Decisions concerning the way such resources are to be allocated depend, therefore, on our judgments concerning the problems that constitute greater and lesser need.

Because optimal mental health is a utopian ideal, therapeutic practice must confront never-ending layers of personal problems. Since the provision of services itself affects demand, if the field is defined too broadly, infinite amounts of money and time and a large number of personnel could theoretically be absorbed in providing mental health care. Resources, however, are never unlimited. We must weigh investments in mental health care against investments in education, transportation, recreation, housing, and the like; we must base such decisions on some sense of priorities and some notion of the criteria by which priorities will be established.

Priorities always depend on values, and there are two paramount values ordinarily applied in thinking about mental health care. The first is a humanitarian concept of *responding to need* based on the idea that services should be made available to those who require them despite cost or the pressure on resources. The second concept—*producing gain*—is based on the idea that services should be made available when the result achieved is at least equal to the investment or greater than alternative investments. Widespread use of cost–benefit and cost-effectiveness analysis has focused increasing attention on the concept of gain. This objective, however, potentially comes into conflict with humanitarian values at some point and, therefore, public policy usually involves some marriage, however uncomfortable, between producing gain and responding to need.

If mental illnesses differ categorically from ordinary problems in living and are defined not by social standards but by medical diagnosis, public health policy should give highest priority to those patients who are clearly sick in a traditional psychiatric sense. Here we might assume, on the basis of considerable evidence, that many ordinary problems are transitory, while serious psychiatric disease states are more persistent. Thus, public policy must give greatest emphasis to limiting and alleviating the more serious conditions.

In contrast, if psychoses and other serious conditions belong to the same continuum as other disorders, we can treat all such conditions in fundamentally the same way since serious illness and chronic disability may be understood as manifestations of less serious illness that goes untreated and neglected. Early intervention, then, may prevent chronic and severe mental illness. If one accepts these assumptions—and they are assumptions rather than proven facts—it makes sense to devote resources to preventive work and to treating mild and moderate psychological distress.

By drawing these positions too sharply, however, we exaggerate the extent to which two separate camps exist. Most mental health professionals are probably not entirely clear about the assumptions underlying their views of mental illness. They usually hold both a "categorical" and a "continuum" perspective simultaneously, although derivative opinions themselves may be contradictory in a formal sense. Other complications also serve to bring together these two views. Moderate problems (even if they are not regarded as psychiatric illnesses) may become severe problems that incapacitate individuals in carrying out social roles. These serious problems are worthy of help regardless of whether or not they are formally diseases meeting *DSM* criteria.

Coherent public policy depends partially on perspective, but mostly on the resolution of specific empirical questions. Which untreated conditions and problems become chronic, and which ones are transitory? Obviously, no rational person would suggest a large bulk of our medical resources be given to treat the common cold because the condition is self-limiting in any case. In the same way, it is key to identify when psychiatric conditions are analogous to the common cold. We must also be able to specify the effects of varying types of intervention. Which social services and policies limit disability and handicap, and which ones may inadvertently exacerbate such problems? Do preventive psychiatric services increase iatrogenic disturbances or encourage psychological hypochondriasis? Does premature intervention interfere with appropriate development of coping skills? How successful are preventive psychiatric services in insulating persons from future serious morbidity and disability? Although answers to many of these questions are unknown, we must continue to ask the questions in a way amenable to empirical investigation. Although public policymaking often must proceed despite uncertain knowledge, those government agencies financing care need to insist that serious attempts be made to evaluate program effectiveness because of the critical relevance of information of this type.

CONCLUSION

Most typically, psychiatric difficulties are defined in terms of personal distress or the inability to perform social roles. The factors influencing these two aspects of adaptation may vary. Individuals and communities alike have long-range as well as short-range goals, and it may be necessary to incur immediate psychological costs to achieve more important but more distant goals. In addition, successful adaptation as a long-range goal requires learning to cope and to acquire a sense of efficacy, control, and self-esteem. There are both theoretical (Seligman 1975) and empirical reasons (Elder 1974) to believe that exposure to manageable adversity will contribute to coping capacities and well-being in adulthood.

No society in history has devoted itself to eliminating personal discomfort and pain. Usually the aim is to alleviate forms of distress that have no social function. Our most valued social institutions do much to produce psychological stress. We need go no further than the educational system to illustrate this point. Education frequently undermines students' most cherished beliefs. Students in university fail courses and are dismissed. And the educational system is always setting goals that some students cannot meet, potentially resulting in a sense of failure and loss of self-esteem. Implicit in the value structure of universities, however, is the idea that incentives for performance, or the need for acquisition of information and skills, require introducing into students' lives some personal stress and striving and a risk of failure. Most societies operate on the premise that certain kinds of stress can provide meaningful incentives while facilitating the attainment of important instrumental goals. Therefore, although it is often possible to relieve personal distress by reducing obligations and responsibilities, we frequently choose not to do so. In fact, many experts and educators believe that in seeking to reduce stress and bolster young people's self-esteem, American culture has become "soft," or too little demanding of the hard work and mastery needed by someone to compete successfully in an increasingly global economy (Friedman 2006). High expectations, sometimes inducing stress, have a large influence on performance (Bock and Moore 1986).

Thus, a major dilemma for mental health efforts remains the emphasis to be placed on performance in contrast to control of personal distress. Mental health professionals employed by particular social institutions, such as the military, seek to minimize the number of psychiatric casualties while maximizing performance. No doubt, however, performance is achieved at some cost to the psychological comfort of the individuals involved. When a time dimension is factored in, mental health problems become even more complicated to interpret. The value of one alternative in relation to others obviously depends on the long-range goals of individuals and groups, and on the extent to which societal pressures are necessary to achieve goals. If psychological distress is minimized at one stage in a person's life but at some cost to performance and the acquisition of new skills, we may find at a later point that this lack of skills produced even more serious distress. Conversely, if we neglect the issue of personal distress and place value only on the development of performance skills, we may "stress" a person to the extent that he or she is persistently uncomfortable to the point of becoming unable to function at all. The balance between mastery of the environment and individual comfort is paramount, not only for humanitarian reasons but also to facilitate continuing personal growth and adaptation.

References

Alarcón, Renato D., et al. "Beyond the Funhouse Mirrors: Research Agenda on Culture and Psychiatric Diagnosis." In *A Research Agenda for DSM-V*, edited by David J. Kupfer, Michael B. First, and Darrel A. Regier, pp. 219–281. Washington, DC: American Psychiatric Association, 2002.

Alarcón, Renato D., et al. "Issues for *DSM-V*: The Role of Culture in Psychiatric Diagnosis." *Journal of Nervous and Mental Disease* 197 (2009): 559–560.

American Psychiatric Association. *Diagnostic and Statistical Manual of Mental Disorders*. Washington, DC: American Psychiatric Association, 1952.

American Psychiatric Association. *Diagnostic and Statistical Manual of Mental Disorders, Second Edition (DSM-II)*. Washington, DC: American Psychiatric Association, 1968.

American Psychiatric Association. *Diagnostic and Statistical Manual of Mental Disorders, Third Edition, Revised (DSM-III-R)*. Washington, DC: American Psychiatric Association, 1987.

American Psychiatric Association. *Diagnostic and Statistical Manual of Mental Disorders, Fourth Edition (DSM-IV)*. Washington, DC: American Psychiatric Association, 1994.

Bayer, Ronald. *Homosexuality and American Psychiatry: The Politics of Diagnosis*. New York: Basic Books, 1981.

Bayer, Ronald, and Robert L. Spitzer. "Neurosis, Psychodynamics, and *DSM-III*: A History of the Controversy." *Archives of General Psychiatry* 42 (1985): 187–196.

Bleuler, Manfred. *The Schizophrenic Disorders: Long-Term Patient and Family Studies*. New Haven, CT: Yale University Press, 1978.

Bock, R. Darrell, and Elsie G. J. Moore. *Advantage and Disadvantage: A Profile of American Youth*. Hillsdale, NJ: Lawrence Erlbaum Associates, 1986.

Caplan, Paula J. *They Say You're Crazy: How the World's Most Powerful Psychiatrists Decide Who's Normal*. Reading, MA: Perseus Books, 1995.

Ciompi, Luc. "The Natural History of Schizophrenia in the Long Term." *British Journal of Psychiatry* 136 (1980): 413–420.

Davidson, Larry, and Thomas H. McGlashan. "The Varied Outcomes of Schizophrenia." *Canadian Journal of Psychiatry* 42 (1997): 34–43.

DeSisto, Michael J., et al. "The Maine and Vermont Three-Decade Studies of Serious Mental Illness. I. Matched Comparison of Cross-Sectional Outcome." *British Journal of Psychiatry* 167 (1995): 331–338.

Elder, Glen H., Jr. *Children of the Great Depression: Social Change in Life Experience.* Chicago: The University of Chicago Press, 1974.

Estroff, Sue E. *Making It Crazy: An Ethnography of Psychiatric Clients in an American Community.* Berkeley and Los Angeles: University of California Press, 1981.

Friedman, Thomas L. *The World Is Flat: A Brief History of the Twenty-First Century* (expanded and updated). New York: Farrar, Straus and Giroux, 2006.

Grob, Gerald N. *The State and the Mentally Ill: A History of Worcester State Hospital in Massachusetts, 1830–1920.* Chapel Hill: The University of North Carolina Press, 1966.

Grob, Gerald N. "Origins of *DSM-I*: A Study in Appearance and Reality." *American Journal of Psychiatry* 148 (1991): 421–431.

Groopman, Jerome E. *How Doctors Think.* Boston: Houghton Mifflin, 2007.

Harding, Courtenay M., Joseph Zubin, and John S. Strauss. "Chronicity in Schizophrenia: Fact, Partial Fact or Artifact?" *Hospital and Community Psychiatry* 38 (1987): 477–486.

Harding, Courtenay M., et al. "The Vermont Longitudinal Study of Persons with Severe Mental Illness: I. Methodology, Study Sample, and Overall Status 32 Years Later." *American Journal of Psychiatry* 144 (1987a): 718–726.

Harding, Courtenay M., et al. "The Vermont Longitudinal Study of Persons with Severe Mental Illness: II. Long-Term Outcome of Subjects Who Retrospectively Met *DSM-III* Criteria for Schizophrenia." *American Journal of Psychiatry* 144 (1987b): 727–735.

Horwitz, Allan V., and Jerome C. Wakefield. *The Loss of Sadness: How Psychiatry Transformed Normal Sorrow into Depressive Disorder.* New York: Oxford University Press, 2007.

Huber, Gerd, Gisela Gross, and Reinhold Schuttler. *Schizophrenia.* Berlin: Springer, 1979.

Idler, Ellen L., and Yael Benyamini. "Self-Rated Health and Mortality: A Review of Twenty-Seven Community Studies." *Journal of Health and Social Behavior* 38 (1997): 21–37.

Idler, Ellen L., Louise Russell, and Diane Davis. "Survival, Functional Limitations, and Self-Rated Health in the NHANES I Epidemiologic Follow-up Study, 1992. First National Health and Nutrition Examination Survey." *American Journal of Epidemiology* 152 (2000): 874–883.

Kahneman, Daniel. *Thinking, Fast and Slow.* New York: Farrar, Straus and Giroux, 2011.

Kendler, Kenneth S. *Kenneth S. Kendler's Statement Defending the Proposal to Eliminate the Bereavement Exclusion.* Washington, DC: American Psychiatric Association, 2010. Available online: www.dsm5.org/about/Documents/grief%20exclusion_Kendler.pdf.

Kety, Seymour S. "From Rationalization to Reason." *American Journal of Psychiatry* 131 (1974): 957–963.

Kety, Seymour S. "The Interface Between Neuroscience and Psychiatry." In *Psychiatry and Its Related Disciplines,* edited by R. Rosenberg, Fini Schulsinger, and Erling Strömgren, pp. 21–28. Copenhagen: World Psychiatric Association, 1986.

Keyes, Corey L. M. "The Mental Health Continuum: From Languishing to Flourishing in Life." *Journal of Health and Social Behavior* 43 (2002): 207–222.

Keyes, Corey L. M. "Promoting and Protecting Mental Health as Flourishing: A Complementary Strategy for Improving National Mental Health." *American Psychologist* 62 (2007): 95–108.

Keyes, Corey L. M., Dov Shmotkin, and Carol D. Ryff. "Optimizing Well-Being: The Empirical Encounter of Two Traditions." *Journal of Personality and Social Psychology* 82 (2002): 1007–1022.

Kleinman, Arthur. "Culture, Bereavement, and Psychiatry." *The Lancet* 379 (2012): 608–609.

Kolb, Lawrence C. *Modern Clinical Psychiatry,* 9th ed. Philadelphia, PA: W. B. Saunders, 1977.

Lewis, Aubrey. "Health as a Social Concept." *British Journal of Sociology* 4 (1953): 109–124.

Lewis-Fernandez, Roberto. "The Cultural Formulation." *Transcultural Psychiatry* 46 (2009): 379–382.

López, Steven Regeser, and Peter J. Guarnaccia. "Cultural Psychopathology: Uncovering the Social World of Mental Illness." *Annual Review of Psychology* 51 (2000): 571–598.

Mayes, Rick, and Allan V. Horwitz. "*DSM-III* and the Revolution in the Classification of Mental Illness." *Journal of the History of the Behavioral Sciences* 41 (2005): 249–267.

McGhie, Andrew, and James Chapman. "Disorders of Attention and Perception in Early Schizophrenia." *British Journal of Medical Psychology* 34 (1961): 103–116.

Mechanic, David. *Medical Sociology,* 2nd ed. New York: The Free Press, 1978.

Mechanic, David. "Organization of Care and Quality of Life of Persons with Serious and Persistent Mental Illness." In *Quality of Life in Mental Disorders*, 2nd ed., edited by Heinz Katschnig, Hugh Freeman, and Norman Sartorius, pp. 309–319. Chichester/New York: Wiley Interscience, 2006.

Miller, Greg. "Criticism Continues to Dog Psychiatric Manual as Deadline Approaches." *Science* 336 (2012): 1088–1089.

Mishler, Elliot G., and Nancy E. Waxler. "Family Interaction Processes and Schizophrenia: A Review of Current Theories." *International Journal of Psychiatry* 2 (1966): 375–415.

Murray, Robin M., et al. "A Neurodevelopmental Approach to the Classification of Schizophrenia." *Schizophrenia Bulletin* 18 (1992): 319–332.

Redlich, Fredrick C., and Daniel X. Freedman. *The Theory and Practice of Psychiatry.* New York: Basic Books, 1966.

Rosenhan, David L. "On Being Sane in Insane Places." *Science* 179 (1973): 250–258.

Scott, Wilbur J. "PTSD in *DSM-III*: A Case in the Politics of Diagnosis and Disease." *Social Problems* 37 (1990): 294–310.

Seligman, Martin E. P. *Helplessness: On Depression, Development, and Death.* San Francisco: W. H. Freeman, 1975.

Slade, Mike. "Mental Illness and Well-being: The Central Importance of Positive Psychology and Recovery Approaches." *BMC Health Services Research* 10 (2010): 1–14.

Spitzer, Robert L. "More on Pseudoscience in Science and the Case for Psychiatric Diagnosis." *Archives of General Psychiatry* 33 (1976): 459–470.

Spitzer, Robert L., Michael B. First, and Jerome C. Wakefield. "Saving PTSD from Itself in *DSM-V*." *Journal of Anxiety Disorders* 21 (2007): 233–241.

St. Clair, David, et al. "Rates of Adult Schizophrenia Following Prenatal Exposure to the Chinese Famine of 1959–1961." *Journal of the American Medical Association* 294 (2005): 557–562.

Strauss, John S. "The Functional Psychoses." In *Psychiatry in General Medical Practice,* edited by Gene Usdin and Jerry Lewis, pp. 279–302. New York: McGraw-Hill, 1979.

Summerfield, Derek. "The Invention of Post-Traumatic Stress Disorder and the Social Usefulness of a Psychiatric Category." *British Medical Journal* 322 (2001): 95–98.

Susser, Ezra, Hans W. Hoek, and Alan Brown. "Neurodevelopmental Disorders After Prenatal Famine: The Story of the Dutch Famine Study." *American Journal of Epidemiology* 147 (1998): 213–216.

Szasz, Thomas S. "The Myth of Mental Illness." *American Psychologist* 15 (1960): 113–118.

Szasz, Thomas S. *The Myth of Mental Illness: Foundations of a Theory of Personal Conduct,* rev. ed. New York: Harper and Row, 1974.

Tanielian, Terri, and Lisa H. Jaycox, eds. *Invisible Wounds of War. Psychological and Cognitive Injuries, Their Consequences and Services to Assist Recovery.* Santa Monica, CA: Rand Corporation, 2008.

Tsuang, Ming T., Robert F. Woolson, and Jerome A. Fleming. "Long-Term Outcome of Major Psychoses: I. Schizophrenia and Affective Disorders Compared with Psychiatrically Symptom-Free Surgical Conditions." *Archives of General Psychiatry* 36 (1979): 1295–1301.

U.S. Department of Health and Human Services. *Mental Health: A Report of the Surgeon General.* Rockville, MD: U.S. Department of Health and Human Services, Substance Abuse and Mental Health Services Administration, Center for Mental Health Services, National Institutes of Health, National Institute of Mental Health, 1999.

Wakefield, Jerome C. "Disorder as Harmful Dysfunction: A Conceptual Critique of *DSM-III-R*'s Definition of Mental Disorder." *Psychological Review* 99 (1992): 232–247.

Wakefield, Jerome C., et al. "Extending the Bereavement Exclusion for Major Depression to Other Losses: Evidence from the National Comorbidity Survey." *Archives of General Psychiatry* 64 (2007): 433–440.

White, Kerr L. "Evaluation of Medical Education and Health Care." In *Community Medicine: Teaching, Research and Health Care,* edited by Willoughby Lathem and Anne Newbery, pp. 241–270. New York: Appleton-Century-Crofts, 1970.

Whooley, Owen. "Diagnostic Ambivalence: Psychiatric Workarounds and the Diagnostic and Statistical Manual of Mental Disorders." *Sociology of Health and Illness* 32 (2010): 452–469.

Wing, John K. *Reasoning About Madness.* New Brunswick, NJ: Transaction Publications, 2010.

Wing, John K., John E. Cooper, and Norman Sartorius. *Measurement and Classification of Psychiatric Symptoms.* Cambridge: Cambridge University Press, 1974.

Wing, John K., et al. "Reliability of a Procedure for Measuring and Classifying 'Present Psychiatric State.'" *The British Journal of Psychiatry* 113 (1967): 499–515.

World Health Organization. *Report of the International Pilot Study of Schizophrenia,* vol. 1. Geneva: World Health Organization, 1973. Available online: whqlibdoc.who.int/offset/WHO_OFFSET_2_(chp1-chp8).pdf.

World Health Organization. *Mental Health: Strengthening Our Response.* Fact Sheet #220. Geneva: World Health Organization, 2010. Available online: www.who.int/mediacentre/factsheets/fs220/en/index.html.

Zygmunt, Annette, et al. "Interventions to Improve Medication Adherence in Schizophrenia." *American Journal of Psychiatry* 159 (2002): 1653–1664.

3

A Brief History of Mental Health Policy in the United States

In the decades following World War II, a strong coalition emerged emphasizing environmental factors as prominent contributors to mental illness and championing community care as a substitute for the traditional reliance on public mental hospitals. This coalition vastly influenced public policy toward persons with mental illnesses and shaped the federal role in mental health policy (Grob 1987).

Those associated with this movement generally assumed that mental illnesses occurred along a single continuum from mild to severe dysfunction in contrast to a heterogeneous collection of disorders, that early intervention could prevent serious mental disorder, that populations at risk were unchanging, and that use of mental health resources for outpatient psychiatric care was always more cost-effective than hospital care. These were all assumptions in need of testing, but they were mostly accepted on faith. By the 1960s, the rhetoric of community care had developed a momentum of its own, influencing agendas and debates on mental health policy as well as the views of intellectual elites, professionals, and the general public (Grob 1987). In the process, many dedicated reformers lost touch with the varied nature of mental health problems, not to mention the tough realities of designing and implementing programs for those most seriously mentally ill.

Between 1955 and 2002, the number of treatment episodes in mental health specialty organizations increased from 1.7 to 9.5 million (Center for Mental Health Services 2006); the community hospital became an important site for acute inpatient psychiatric care; and the number of mental health professionals of all kinds increased greatly. Despite these changes, there is persistent evidence of neglect of the most seriously ill long-term patients. Indeed, many observers have become pessimistic about the nation's capacity to care appropriately for these individuals in the community. Such negativity results, in part, from the ideological excesses of earlier decades, naive conclusions about the processes of labeling and normalization, and, more recently, the problems of homelessness and criminalization among those with mental illness. For critics it has been easy to focus on the exaggerated claims and obvious failures of community care in denouncing deinstitutionalization as ill founded and misdirected.

Neither exaggerated claims nor sweeping criticisms, however, well serve the needs of those with mental illness, nor do they contribute to a well-informed public. By identifying the dominant misconceptions and defining key issues carefully, we can analyze what has gone wrong, what has worked well, and what should come next in the formulation of mental health policy. But first, planning for the future requires obtaining insights from the past.

A CENTURY OF STATE HOSPITAL CARE

Mental illness is not a new problem. Persons with mental illnesses have always existed in society. Methods of caring for those who are mentally ill have not followed a consistent developmental pattern; rather, they have been characterized by stops and starts, by advances and setbacks. Many of our conceptions of mental illness and many current proposals were not only advocated but also practiced a century ago and more. Milieu therapy, a concept still popular today, existed in the nineteenth century not only in Europe but also in the United States under the rubric of moral treatment (Bockoven 1972). Moral treatment, which originated in the late eighteenth century, was based on the assumption that psychiatric illness could be alleviated if patients were treated in a considerate and friendly fashion, if they had the opportunity to discuss their troubles, if their interests were stimulated, and if they were kept actively involved in some form of communal life, even within the walls of an institution. Close relationships between staff and patients often prevailed, and patients were treated in a personal and sympathetic way.

The idea of moral treatment is attributed to French physician Philippe Pinel, who broke the pattern of harsh custodialism associated with mental institutions by substituting a program based on compassion. Demonstrating that patients with mental illness responded to sympathy and care was not difficult, and Pinel had a profound influence on psychiatrists not only in Europe but also North America. Pinel's program reflected his belief that psychological factors were important causes of emotional disturbance, as were social factors and lack of proper awareness of wholesome ways of living. He believed that treatment of the insane was a form of education and that intelligent understanding of the needs of patients accompanied by a minimum of mechanical restraint would bring good results.

Although moral treatment gradually became established at institutions in different parts of the world, the general sense of social responsibility toward the unfortunate was not very strong in this era. In practice, many patients received no better care than they had previously. During the early 1800s, people with mental illnesses often ended up in jails or local poorhouses, undifferentiated from offenders and the destitute poor. In the United States, it was Dorothea Dix who cast a spotlight on this cruel treatment, and she devoted her life to a far-reaching reform movement to build and expand specialized mental hospital facilities. It is ironic that this effort, inspired by lofty motives, would lead eventually to the development of large custodial institutions. For a while, nonetheless, the mental hospital system marked a real advance from the indiscriminate practices that preceded it. The evidence is that the conditions mental hospitals provided were relatively humane and therapeutic.

Yet history shows that institutions, however idealistic their origins, cannot isolate themselves from prejudices and are not immune to social change. Social conditions accompanying the industrial revolution stimulated an increased tendency to hospitalize those who could not adapt to new demands of the times (Grob 1966). Industrialization during the 1800s changed the nature of work, family life, and community tolerance for bizarre behavior or incapacity. As family structure changed, making it more difficult to contain old and disabled members within the family unit, and as the number of older people increased because of changing mortality patterns, the mental hospital often became a refuge for the elderly. Further, the changing patterns of disease, particularly increasing numbers of patients with paresis and the dementia associated with it, resulted in a growing number of chronic and hopeless patients (Grob 1983).

With limited facilities and resources available, mental hospitals confronted many more patients than they could handle effectively. The burden of their numbers made it more difficult to maintain moral treatment as an active program (Rothman 1971). Thus, hospitals resorted to the regimentation of patients and rigid bureaucratic procedures to facilitate the handling of an overwhelming inpatient census. A large share of state budgets was allocated to mental hospitals throughout this period, and lawmakers kept tight control over funding for staff, programs, and physical improvements (Mechanic and Grob 2011). One humanizing influence near the start of the century was the Mental Hygiene Movement. Begun in 1908 by Clifford Beers, a former patient, this group devoted itself to improving hospital conditions and expanding public concern for those with mental illnesses. Despite these efforts, however, public facilities persisted as large and impersonal institutions characterized by a custodial attitude, meager allowances for active psychiatric treatment, limited professional staff, and dependence on untrained and unskilled personnel. Exceptions existed, and there were variations from one part of the country to another, but the overall picture was undeniably bleak (Grob 1973).

In 1920, 18 percent of all first admissions to mental hospitals in New York State were diagnosed with senility or cerebral arteriosclerosis. By 1940, this patient group accounted for 31 percent of all admissions (Grob 1977). What was true of New York State describes other states as well. In the absence of other social institutions, the mental hospital became a destination for persons unable to cope with society on their own or those without family who could or would take responsibility for their care. Goldhamer and Marshall (1953), in studying the patterns of mental hospitalization in Massachusetts over a 100-year period, could find no evidence that mental illness was increasing, but admissions to mental hospitals for the aged group grew significantly. Brenner (1973), examining the trends in mental hospitalization in relation to changes in the economy over a span of 127 years, found that admissions increased following periods of economic misfortune. During such times, the poor and dependent generally fare the worst, and this helps explain the large inflow to mental hospitals of poor aged persons and immigrants having the least capacity to care for themselves and the weakest community supports. But the extent to which adverse economic circumstances contribute to the prevalence of mental illness or undermine tolerance and supports for those who are mentally ill in the community remains unclear. Whatever the case may be, economic and social instability lead to large number of persons in need of care, and the mental hospital, in the absence of other alternatives, assumed this function in past eras.

The development of a leading mental hospital serves to illustrate these general observations while revealing the social forces and ideologies influencing this sector of care. In a sophisticated historical analysis, Gerald Grob (1966) traced the growth and organization of Worcester State Hospital, which was founded in 1830 as the first state hospital for the mentally ill in Massachusetts. The establishment of a mental hospital in Massachusetts grew out of recognition of the inadequacy of informal methods of caring for the indigent and insane. Prominent among those involved were passionate, enlightened reformers motivated by a strong sense of religious and social responsibility. The new hospital, in its earliest period (1833–1846), practiced moral treatment by offering patients an optimistic and humanitarian climate. Early records of the hospital suggest considerable success at rehabilitation, not because of the efficacy of any particular psychiatric treatment but probably as a result of the hopeful and encouraging climate that supported the patient and inspired a feeling of being helped. Moral treatment, however, did not persist and for most of the rest of the nineteenth century, the hospital became guided by a pessimistic psychiatric ideology that mirrored its custodial nature.

As Grob shows so well, the organization of psychiatric care was responsive to social, economic, and ideological currents in the society at large. Industrial and technological changes in Massachusetts, coupled with increasing urbanization and immigration, brought decreasing tolerance for bizarre and disruptive behavior and less ability to contain persons with deviant behavior within the existing social structure. With the growing number of patients—the mass of them chronically ill and held in low esteem by the community as well as by mental hospital personnel—it was impossible to maintain the administrative and environmental attitudes necessary for moral treatment. Moreover, the onslaught of patients, combined with limited resources, made it necessary to devise efficient custodial procedures. The contempt in which the hospital held its clients, as well as the low social value accorded this group by the society at large, neither stimulated hospital administrators to demand greater resources for patient care nor induced community support.

Other forces, as well, conspired in the hospital's decline. As Grob argues, new psychiatric ideologies and professionalization among psychiatrists did much to retard the care of those who were mentally ill. These ideologies were, in part, the product of psychiatrists' own attitudes and beliefs, molded by their social backgrounds and influenced by a search for status. Grob believes that psychiatrists' insistence on according a scientific status to their profession exerted a negative effect on mental hospitals. An emphasis on somatic factors within the traditional medical model had little to offer in regard to treatment, and it undermined alternative approaches that could have at least communicated to patients a sense of confidence and hope (see, also, Bockoven 1957, 1972). Furthermore, Grob argues that the development of a professional psychiatric subculture erected barriers between psychiatrists and other interested groups in society by excluding the participation of laypersons eager to contribute to improving mental health care. Finally, the trend toward professionalism isolated psychiatry from secular humanitarian ideologies in society, putting in their place a barren, alleged objectivity. Ironically, then, psychiatric professionalization hampered the administration of therapeutic psychiatric care.

THE SHIFT TO COMMUNITY CARE

Psychiatrists became most extensively involved in public policy issues during World War II, initially through their participation in selective service screening. Between January 1942 and June 1945, an estimated 1,875,000 of the 15 million men examined were rejected for service because of psychiatric disabilities. Of the men inducted, a large proportion of those later separated from the armed forces with a disability were discharged specifically for neuropsychiatric reasons (Felix 1967, pp. 28–29). These facts attracted attention while creating great concern about the possible scope of mental health problems in American society. They also stimulated interest in improving basic preventive and treatment services and research in the psychiatric area.

World War II not only alerted the country to mental health needs, it also provided psychiatry with opportunities to develop programs for psychiatrically disabled soldiers. Although the war brought no breakthroughs in psychiatric knowledge, it did provide individual psychiatrists with broad administrative experience and gave considerable stimulus to new treatment techniques for dealing with relatively large groups of patients outside the conventional hospital setting. The practical response of psychiatrists in the military to very difficult psychiatric problems was impressive. Group techniques were used extensively for the first time, and Army psychiatrists experimented with sedation and hypnosis. The problems that occurred under conditions of wartime stress made psychiatrists aware, more than ever before, of the effects of environment on the occurrence of mental illness and the social aspects of psychiatric care.

The publicity given to psychiatric casualties among veterans, combined with large loss of personnel due to psychiatric reasons during induction, galvanized new public policies in relation to mental health. Government officials and informed laypersons alike felt the need to learn more about the causes and prevention of mental illness, to assist the individual states in strengthening their mental health programs, and to build a satisfactory personnel pool in the mental health area. In 1946, Congress passed the National Mental Health Act, creating grant programs for research into the etiology and treatment of neuropsychiatric problems, professional training, and community clinics as pilot and demonstration efforts. The law also established the National Institute of Mental Health (NIMH) to administer this system of grants and to serve as a new focal point within the federal government for addressing mental illness as a major public health concern.

Although significant advances in personnel development and mental health research did take place following adoption of this statute, hospitals gained very little. Direct federal aid to the states for mental health services actually decreased during the Korean War. Although innovations were being developed—notably, psychoactive drugs—most states had neither the facilities and financial resources nor the personnel to implement the new ideas in the mental health field. The Hoover Commission, looking into the issue of government reorganization in the mid-1950s, reported: "Although we believe that the federal government should gradually reduce its grants as the states take up the load for any given health activity, we conclude that the recent reduction in federal support has been too abrupt" (Hoover Commission 1955, p. 72). The commission noted that aid to the states had fallen while research support grew. In the mental health field, this created an imbalance. Individual states were becoming acutely aware of personnel and financial limitations just as a tentative optimistic spirit was emerging because of reports of accelerated release of long-term patients due to intensive personal care and drug therapies.

Concepts of community care were also taking form during this period. Both the work of the Council of State Governments beginning in 1949 and the influential conferences on mental health sponsored by the Milbank Memorial Fund fueled this interest (Grob 1987). In 1954, New York State enacted its Community Mental Health Services Act promoting local mental health boards that could subsidize a range of services, including outpatient care, with state support for up to half of all costs below a specified ceiling. The incentive worked. By 1956, such boards covered 85 percent of the state's population.

Stimulated by these events as well as advocacy from both the American Psychiatric Association and the American Medical Association, Congress passed legislation, the Mental Health Study Act of 1955, establishing a Joint Commission on Mental Illness and Health (Grob 1987). When the act was being considered, government officials no longer believed that large custodial institutions could deal effectively with mental illness. The new emphasis on mental health care in the community was motivated as much by a desire to reduce hospital populations and improve efficiency as by a belief in the therapeutic value of this approach. In its deliberations, Congress gave high priority to considerations of personnel. The feeling was that already existing therapeutic knowledge could not be applied because of shortages of personnel and facilities. Government officials also felt that remedial efforts could be increased substantially via the development of psychoactive drugs, although experience with the latter, while promising, had not yet progressed very far at this time.

The Mental Health Study Act appropriated funds for the Joint Commission to study and make recommendations concerning various aspects of mental health policy. In 1961, the commission published its highly visible report, *Action for Mental Health*, which argued strongly for an increased program of services and more funds for basic, long-term mental health research (Joint Commission on Mental Illness and Health 1961). It recommended that expenditures in the mental health field be doubled in five years and tripled in 10 years. It argued for better recruitment and training programs for mental health workers. It called for expansion of treatment programs for acutely ill patients in all facilities, including general hospitals and mental hospitals. It argued for establishment of mental health clinics, suggesting one for every 50,000 persons in the population. It attacked the large state mental hospitals, proposing their transformation into a regional system of smaller intensive treatment centers with no more than 1,000 beds. And it recommended new programs for the care of chronic patients as well as aftercare and other rehabilitation services. Here was a wide-ranging and ambitious agenda for change that fell on receptive ears in Washington. Many recommendations quickly began to be converted to action because of financial and moral support from the federal government. The most far-reaching initiative was a new community mental health centers program.

It would be wrong, however, to say that many new mental health policies on the federal level flowed directly from the Joint Commission report. *Action for Mental Health* was largely an ideological document, and it was sufficiently ambiguous to allow various interest groups to read into it what they wished. In fact, a vigorous political battle ensued between those psychiatrists with a public health viewpoint, who wished to situate patient care within a context of population-based planning and intervention, and those psychiatrists aligned with the traditional medical model, who sought federal assistance for improving the capacity and quality of mental hospitals. In the end, those favoring a radical break with the past wielded more influence with President John F. Kennedy. The final decision was to establish a nationwide network of comprehensive community mental health centers, not clinics, which would be independent of the old mental hospitals, in other words an alternative for what was viewed as an archaic and obsolete institutional system (Mechanic and Grob 2011). This new approach endorsed the viewpoint that serious mental illness is not inherently different from the larger range of psychological difficulties common in the community.

Timing and circumstance were advantageous for launching this initiative. The U.S. economy was in excellent shape in the early 1960s with abundant funds available for meeting domestic needs. The new president was personally committed to this program in mental health and mental retardation, which did not mobilize any obvious group conflicts or value disputes in contrast to some other contemporary health care proposals. With the public growing more knowledgeable about, and supportive of, helping those with mental illnesses during this period of ascendant political liberalism, a two-tier system giving the rich and poor unequal access to good psychiatric treatment was increasingly unacceptable.

Perhaps most significant, the harmful consequences of custodial hospital environments had been poignantly demonstrated. As previously noted, most state mental hospitals were built in the later part of the nineteenth and early part of the twentieth centuries, influenced by the crusade launched by Dorothea Dix. The setting up of the mental hospitals consti-tuted the first attempt in many areas of the country to make provision for poor people with serious mental illness. But as patients with chronic illness came to comprise an increasing proportion of the institutional caseload, psychiatrists shifted their work to other settings. A feeling of hopelessness set in regarding the possibilities for constructive treatment in the public hospital setting. A series of exposés in the years following World War II, including such works as *The Shame of the States* (Deutsch 1948), broadcast this demoralization to a broad audience.

Administrators themselves were eager to make changes in the operation of state insti-tutions, and the arrival of psychoactive drugs in the mid-1950s rendered this possible. Although drugs were not a cure, they reduced some of the most disturbing symptoms of mental illness; they facilitated control of seriously disordered patients; and they created more opportunities for active treatment by hospital personnel. As established practices came under scrutiny, adjustments took place, including elimination of restraints, reduced security arrangements, and the adoption of early discharge programs. The sense of opti-mism and efficacy among hospital staff was communicated to patients and the community generally, instilling newfound confidence about the ability of patients to cope outside the hospital.

Passage of Medicare, a health insurance program for the elderly, and Medicaid, a program for certain low-income individuals and families, which was later extended to additional groups including persons with disabilities, also occurred in 1965. While neither Medicare nor Medicaid was conceived as part of a mental health policy initiative, both had important effects on the budding community mental health system.

IMPLEMENTING A NATIONAL COMMUNITY MENTAL HEALTH POLICY

The new Community Mental Health Centers (CMHCs) were required to offer five essen-tial services: inpatient care, emergency care, partial hospitalization, outpatient care, and education and consultation. This last item, which aimed at establishing the CMHCs as a source of expertise and education on mental health issues for other community agen-cies, was particularly reflective of the public health orientation of this policy. All centers were mandated to develop a continuum of care by means of linkages among the required services. Other activities, such as preadmission and postdischarge services for hospital-ized patients and specialized diagnostic services, were also suggested (but not required). As time went on, the number of mandated services expanded to 12, including specialized services for children and the elderly, alcohol and drug abuse services, and follow-up care and transitional services for those chronically ill. The initial funding level for the CMHC program was set at $150 million, with a provision for matching dollars to be supplied by the states. Each center approved would become eligible for slightly more than four years of declining grant support—later extended to eight years—after which the sole funding would come from state and local government, and private organizations.

By 1981, a total of 796 CMHCs had been funded, and more than 3.3 million patients per year were receiving services from these agencies (Foley and Sharfstein 1983). They represented an important new source of assistance for mental health problems on the local level, providing access to specialized treatment for many people having few, if any, alternatives. CMHCs played a noteworthy role in helping reorient the U.S. mental health system from its emphasis on 24-hour hospital and residential care to office-based and outpatient treatment. As these developments occurred, the number of people in state and county mental hospitals continued to fall sharply—a decline of approximately 280,000 patients between 1965 and 1975—surpassing the deinstitutionalization goals specified by President John F. Kennedy when first proposing the CMHC Act.

However, only about half of the 1,500–2,000 CMHCs projected as needed by the country came into existence. Although expansion of the CMHC system coincided with a downsizing of public hospitals, it was rare for centers to establish strong operational linkages with state hospitals or to focus on discharged patients as a primary population of concern. In fact, as state facilities depopulated, they experienced a sharp spike in admissions, signaling a "revolving door" problem in which many patients returned for repeated hospitalization episodes after brief periods in the community. Further, states had a financial incentive to move persons from state hospitals to nursing homes given that federal Medicaid funds covered private nursing facilities but not care in mental hospitals. One important study found desinstitutionalization more closely correlated with payments to nursing homes than with the availability of CMHCs (Gronfein 1985). A report by the U.S. Inspector General in the early 1990s concluded that many CMHCs had failed to provide adequate service to patients with serious mental illnesses, such as those discharged from institutions, and it identified this as a significant factor in the growth of the number of homeless people in the nation (Office of the Inspector General 1991).

Dowell and Ciarlo (1989) carried out a comprehensive review of the evaluation literature on CMHCs considering a variety of indicators related to service expansion and accessibility, coordination of resources, decrease of state hospital admissions and residents, prevention of mental disorders, and increased citizen participation in community programs. According to this appraisal, CMHCs deserved credit for expanding mental health services inside their catchment areas, improving availability and accessibility of services for the poor and persons from minority cultural groups, and some exemplary instances of interagency coordination around mental health needs. But CMHCs did not do enough to support patients with chronic illness, their role in deinstitutionalization was inconsistent, and the evidence is unconvincing that they were able to prevent mental disorders. Similarly, even the process goal of involving community residents in the operation of local CMHCs received a low grade.

The Vietnam War, its aftermath, and disillusionment with the "Great Society" of the 1960s resulted in the curtailment of resources for mental health care. Little interested in community mental health centers, the Nixon Administration went so far as to attempt to impound funding for the program. Similarly, mental health research, research training, and professional humanpower programs were phased down, phased out, or allowed to erode with inflation. Still, the situation was far from dismal. Outpatient care and use of psychiatric services were increasing dramatically. With the great shift away from public mental hospitals, more acute psychiatric illness was being treated in general hospitals and private psychiatric facilities. Behavioral techniques had gained growing acceptance, with the treatment of many types of disorders becoming more focused and diversified, on the one hand, and less constricted by psychoanalytic dogmatism, on the other. A vigorous civil liberties movement developed on behalf of patients with mental illness, clarifying and strengthening patients' rights in civil commitment procedures and other areas of care. As people in need came to be recognized and treated more quickly in the community, chances improved for averting secondary disabilities associated with earlier treatment modes. Understanding of new psychoactive drugs, including their sometime adverse effects, also increased. This provided a basis for more sophisticated pharmacological therapy. Private and nonprofit insurance companies ventured into providing inpatient psychiatric benefits, and many expanded outpatient coverage as well. When all is said and done, these were no small achievements.

Meanwhile, the executive branch and Congress became increasingly concerned about alcoholism and drug abuse in the late 1960s and early 1970s. Within the mental health sphere, new political constituencies coalesced to address these problems. What eventually emerged was an umbrella agency known by the acronym ADAMHA (Alcohol, Drug Abuse, and Mental Health Administration), which incorporated the National Institute of Mental Health (NIMH), the National Institute on Alcohol Abuse and Alcoholism (NIAAA), and the National Institute on Drug Abuse (NIDA). These bureaucratic departments acquired responsibility for a variety of service programs, demonstrations, research efforts, and research and professional training, and they were also involved in planning and public education. Ultimately, however, ADAMHA programs came under siege from the Nixon administration, which fought with Congress over dismantling many signature programs of the Kennedy–Johnson era.

It was not mental health legislation, but rather the Social Security Amendments of 1972, which created Supplemental Security Income (SSI), that most positively impacted the lives of persons with mental health problems (Mechanic and Rochefort 1990). These amendments brought previously existing aid programs for the aged, blind, and disabled under stronger federal regulation by requiring states to comply with a standard definition of disability, although states could also provide assistance beyond the federal minimum. Social Security Disability Insurance (SSDI) had existed as a federal benefits program for at least some disabled workers since the late 1950s, but it required that applicants possess a minimum work history to qualify. SSI, in contrast, provided benefits to disabled persons in poverty regardless of their work history, and it extended disability benefits to children. The 1972 amendments defined disability status in this way: "Any person unable to engage in any substantial gainful activity (SGA) by reason of any medically determinable physical or mental impairment expected to result in death or that has lasted or can be expected to last for a continuous period of at least 12 months. For a child under age 18, eligibility is based on disability of severity comparable with that of an adult" (Social Security Administration 2012, p. 19). The level of support was modest. At the time of passage of SSI, the guaranteed income was only $130 a month for qualified individuals (House Ways and Means Committee 1974). In most states, however, SSI recipients also qualified for Medicaid, so that a major effect of the program was to provide medical coverage for substantial numbers of persons with mental illnesses.

MORE ATTEMPTS AT NATIONAL POLICY REFORM

By 1976, when Jimmy Carter became president, activist concerns of the 1960s no longer prevailed, and federal mental health programs had been battered into a vulnerable state. The flaws of deinstitutionalization were undeniable, as was the need for better community services for the most chronically disabled patients. Yet developing accessible and comprehensive community care was expensive, and it seemed doubtful the nation would be enacting a system of universal health insurance any time soon with medical costs steeply on the rise. This reality called attention to the need for garnering funds from various federal, state, and local programs in order to sustain essential networks of community care.

With improved epidemiological data and a renewed concern with primary medical care came the realization that many patients in need of mental health care were not found in psychiatric settings but in general medicine. This fact argued for improving the ability of physicians to recognize and manage psychiatric disorder, for making specialized psychiatric consultations available to the general practitioner, and for establishing sound referral practices. Several experiments or demonstrations in this period suggested that closer integration between general medical and psychiatric services could reduce medical utilization by persons with mental health problems (Cummings and Follette 1968; Follette and Cummings 1967; Patrick, Eagle, and Coleman 1978).

In February of 1977, Carter established a Presidential Commission on Mental Health to review the nation's mental health needs and to make recommendations. This effort, like most such commissions, was highly politicized, but it offered a unique opportunity because Mrs. Rosalynn Carter had a special interest in mental health and she served as honorary chairperson of the commission. The commission made its report in 1978, addressing such issues as the organization of community services, community supports for those most seriously mentally ill, financing, personnel, legal rights, research, prevention, and public understanding. The report argued for greater investment in mental health services, noting that although mental illness ranked as one of the worst problems facing society because of the large number of people affected and the levels of suffering endured, it received only 12 percent of general health expenditures. The commission identified an acute need to invest in community-based services to make them financially, geographically, and socially accessible and to make them flexible so as to serve varying social and racial groups. It also argued strongly for research and training support; for special attention to chronic mental illness; and for meeting the special needs of children, adolescents, and the elderly.

The 1978 commission, compared with its predecessor in the late 1950s, conducted its work in a more difficult and complex social and political climate. Inflation was a prime concern during the Carter years, and health care costs were outpacing prices in the economy as a whole. Government expenditures for this budget area were already high and largely uncontrollable, in part as a result of the structure of the Medicare and Medicaid programs. Policymakers were reluctant to exacerbate this trend by approving new initiatives, while any sharing of limited resources seemed anathema to those benefiting from existing programs.

The Carter commission also had to contend with formidable constituencies anxious to protect their turf. Conflicts among state and local, institutional and community, and advocacy and provider interests were, in large measure, a reflection of the unwieldy and uncoordinated structure brought into being by the national community mental health policy of the 1960s. Difficult deliberations led to a report that was quite general, giving the nod to a broad array of incongruous ideas that mollified most mental health stakeholder groups while failing to face the tough question of financial priorities (Grob 2005). No clear direction emerged, and the attempt to appease competing constituencies may actually have contributed to nasty infighting when time came to turn the commission's recommendations into legislation. As it happened, the lead author of this text (Mechanic) served as the coordinator of the Commission's Task Panel on the Nature and Scope of the Problems. Certainly, the experience was one that underscored the necessity of balancing diverse interests when operating in the political realm, but it seemed unfortunate for this process to occur at the expense of a more direct focus on the needs of those most severely ill. While the latter figured into discussion in an important way, so, too, did vague concepts such as prevention of mental illness.

Drafting the Mental Health Systems Act was long and tortuous, reflecting the conflicting interests involved, competition with other Carter initiatives, and the reality of fiscal constraints. After numerous false starts, a bill was eventually presented to Congress that was then substantially modified in an effort to reach consensus among strongly opposing groups and stakeholders. The entire episode showcased the warring ideologies that animated debate in the mental health sector: comprehensive service approaches versus targeting of categorical groups, local autonomy versus state control in the operation of community mental health centers, active treatment of disturbed persons living in the community versus the right of patients to refuse care, and a dispute over having dollars follow deinstitutionalized patients versus satisfying the concerns of unions like American Federation of State, County and Municipal Employees (AFSCME) that sought to protect hospital employees from job loss (Foley and Sharfstein 1983). And so it went.

President Carter signed The Mental Health Systems Act in October 1980. It was an ambitious but ungainly piece of legislation that extended the CMHC program while addressing its many gaps and shortcomings through a more strongly regulatory approach. The end of the story was anticlimactic and rather sad, given all that had preceded it. The Reagan administration, which took office one month after passage of the act, chose not to implement it, opting instead to incorporate mental health care within the president's "New Federalism" initiative.

The Alcohol, Drug Abuse, and Mental Health block grant bundled together 10 programs previously funded by the federal government on a categorical grant basis, including support for the CMHC program (Rochefort 1997). In general, block grants are a mechanism for providing federal dollars within broadly designated areas of interest while devolving management and priority setting from Washington, D.C., to the states. With respect to CMHCs, then, one important bureaucratic aspect of this change was to establish a new line of accountability dislodging the NIMH from its position of control and installing 50 state mental health authorities in its place. The Reagan administration wanted more than just to decentralize mental health and substance abuse programs, however. It also saw creation of the block grant as an opportunity for budgetary savings. Thus, during its first year of operation in fiscal 1982, the constituent programs in the ADAMH block grant received a cut of approximately 21 percent from what had existed prior to consolidation. By the late 1980s, program funding still stood far below the benchmark figure of the pre-block grant period.

When the CMHCs had been functioning as a categorical grant program managed by the federal government, there were many requirements to be fulfilled in regard to specified services, target populations, interagency coordination, citizen involvement, data collection, and more. The block grant largely relaxed these standards, substituting only a few necessities concerning appropriate use of funds and management by the states. It also set some ground rules for allocations among consolidated programs during the initial few years. A substantial body of research has documented how the switch to block grants impacted CMHC operations and services (Rochefort 1997). Typically, states used their discretion to direct community services to persons with chronic and severe mental illnesses. Other types of activities, including consultation and education, prevention, and alcohol and drug abuse treatment, lost importance. The pattern of services for children and the elderly, two groups prioritized by the federal government in its oversight of the CMHC program during the late 1980s, proved more inconsistent because of varying commitment by individual states.

Putting aside the large funding cuts that were involved, the Reagan administration's decision to give states more authority to manage mental health services within their jurisdictions had some clear merits. Federal actors during the 1960s and 1970s habitually bypassed state authority on the theory that states, long the caretakers of decrepit public institutions, represented an impediment to true mental health reform. Federal bureaucrats interacted directly with local service providers, often ignoring state officials and priorities. This practice had its consequences. Much of the hostility complicating negotiations over the Mental Health Systems Act was, in fact, a reaction to earlier insensitivity by the federal government with respect to state interests. And, in retrospect, it seems fair to conclude that the federal government's approach contributed to the low priority given by CMHCs to serving patients with chronic mental illness.

Yet in ceding control of the CMHC program to the states, block grants fueled another type of problem long upsetting to mental health advocates. This was the wide variation in resources, programs, and interest in mental health care issues from one part of the country to the next. Funding reductions accompanying the block grant also diminished the systemic importance of the CMHC program, previously a cornerstone of the nation's community mental health movement. By this time, for example, Medicaid had become a much more significant revenue source for mental health services in the states. Finding themselves in the midst of an unpredictable new fiscal environment under block grants, many administrators of CMHCs began moving toward a "business model" geared to expanding services for populations able to pay for treatment.

While the Mental Health Systems Act was being developed, the Department of Health and Human Services, at the recommendation of the President's Commission, had been crafting an integrated federal strategy for responding to the multifaceted problems of those with chronic mental illnesses. This was a far-ranging effort that examined the epidemiology of severe mental illness; the range of psychiatric, medical, rehabilitative, housing, and social services available and needed; issues of personnel and recruitment; and financing reforms (U.S. Department of Health and Human Services 1980).

Despite opposition from the Reagan administration, Congress embraced NIMH's plan for a Community Support Program (CSP). The CSP, which was inspired by the innovative Program for Assertive Community Treatment in Dane County, Wisconsin, guided states in fashioning broad systems of care for persons with serious mental illness, using an approach that extended well beyond traditional services to address housing, psychosocial rehabilitation, and other important needs. At the same time, a series of actions on the federal level adjusted such major entitlements as SSDI, SSI, Medicaid, and Medicare to make them more useful for assisting persons with severe mental illness. For example, changes in

Medicaid authorized payment for case management services, allowed reimbursement of mental health clinics, and improved standards for persons with mental illness in nursing homes.

Gradually, in ways often unnoticed and unmeasured, a critical transformation of the mental health system was taking place. The driving forces of change came not so much from mental health policy, but rather other federal programs—income maintenance, housing, medical care, and food stamps. Frank and Glied (2006) characterize this process as the "mainstreaming" of those with mental illness. Medicaid became the most important *de facto* mental health program of them all, subsidizing state investment in a panoply of community-care programs and services. Medicare also broadened coverage for mental illness and defined a new medical management service for medication visits, reducing the usual copayment from 50 to 20 percent. Annual outpatient treatment limits were eliminated, and reimbursement to clinical psychologists and social workers gained approval (Frank and Glied 2006; Grob and Goldman 2006). Between 1987 and 1992, mental health user rates for Medicare beneficiaries increased by 73 percent, while the average number of services per user rose 27 percent. Inflation-adjusted spending per capita on mental health services more than doubled (Rosenbach and Ammering 1997). With the expansion of such government programs and the spread of private mental health insurance coverage, the proportion of mental health care paid for out-of-pocket decreased sharply, from 36 to 13 percent between 1971 and 2001 (Frank and Glied 2006).

Court action also figured into this trend, such as the Supreme Court decision in *Zebley v. Sullivan* that required consideration of global impairment in SSI determinations of eligibility. As we will examine in more detail in Chapter 10, the Social Security Administration retooled the SSI program making it easier for children with serious mental health needs to qualify, and the caseload substantially increased. Fearing the cost of these expansions, Congress tightened up eligibility criteria in 1996, reducing the caseload by approximately 100,000 children. Within a few years, however, the numbers had rebounded.

Similarly, the population of working-age adults receiving SSI due to a mental disability also substantially increased—more than tripling between 1991 and 2010. In 1991, adults with mental disabilities were about 24 percent of all disabled working-age recipients of the program. By 2010, they had increased to 39 percent (Social Security Administration 1992, 2011).

In the 1990s, policymakers chose to revisit the issue of the proper location of the NIMH within the governmental structure. Mental health responsibilities again underwent reorganization. In its earliest years, from 1949 to 1967, the NIMH had been part of the National Institutes of Health (NIH) and was able to thrive due to strong public support for research (Grob 1994). As the NIMH took on a wider range of nonresearch functions during the 1960s, its leadership believed it could better prosper outside the NIH. By 1974, the NIMH had come to be situated within the ADAMHA umbrella department alongside agencies dealing with alcohol and drugs. Many scientists argued, however, that the brain sciences, and the closer relationship between psychiatry and medicine, made bringing mental health research together with other biomedical research a logical step. On the other side, advocates for the services and demonstration components of NIMH argued that separating mental health research from these programmatic activities within the ADAMHA would be damaging in terms of loss of political clout. With support from the National Alliance on Mental Illness, a family-centered advocacy group deeply interested in brain research, the NIMH research program was returned to the NIH in 1992 along with alcohol and drug research, each constituting a new institute. Other mental health programs, including the demonstration authorities, planning and monitoring of state plans, technical assistance, information collection, and clinical training, became organized into a new Center for Mental Health Services within a new umbrella agency, the Substance Abuse and Mental Health Services Administration (SAMHSA).

In a sense, both advocates and opponents of these changes were proved right subsequently. As efforts to reduce the federal deficit forced cutbacks in many government programs, mental health research derived shelter from the prestige and public support of biomedical research and the doubling of the NIH budget in the early 2000s. Yet the services component did sustain an initial round of budget cuts that diminished its capacities, and it has continued to receive less attention and support than the NIH over the years.

A signature accomplishment of the administration of President George Herbert Walker Bush was passage of the Americans with Disabilities Act of 1990 (ADA). Evidence of the social and economic exclusion of persons with disabilities from public life, blatant discrimination against persons with disabilities, and the financial costs of supporting people who could be working if not for this discrimination all provided impetus for the implementation of this act (Burgdorf 1991). It came after a long struggle in the disability rights movement to achieve full equality. Senator Harkin, one of the coauthors of the bill, presented the act on the senate floor as the "20th century emancipation proclamation for people with disabilities" (Harkin 1989).

ADA covered discrimination in employment, public services, public accommodations and services operated by private entities, and telecommunications, among other areas. There was vigorous debate about what would constitute a disability under ADA, with conservative senators Jesse Helms (Republican, North Carolina) and William Armstrong (Republican, Colorado) strongly objecting to many mental health problems being included (Burgdorf 1991). These legislators were successful in obtaining amendments that expressly excluded specific behaviors from coverage including homosexuality and bisexuality; transvestism, transsexualism, gender identity disorder not resulting from physical impairments, and various sexual behavior disorders; compulsive gambling, kleptomania, and pyromania; and substance use disorder resulting from current use of illegal drugs. The list of exclusions is somewhat bizarre, and "it is arguable that the members of Congress relied upon nothing other than their own negative reactions, fears and prejudices in fashioning the list of excluded classes" (Burgdorf 1991, p. 519). Other than these exclusions, the ADA did not specifically enumerate the list of disabilities that could be covered. Instead, a person was defined as protected based on having "a physical or mental impairment that substantially limits one or more of the major activities of such individual; a record of having such an impairment; or being regarded as having such an impairment" (Pub L. No 101-336, 103 Stat. 327, 1990). In the end, the ADA passed with overwhelming bipartisan support and was signed into law by President Bush, who declared it a "historic new civil rights act...the world's first comprehensive declaration of equality for people with disabilities" (cited in Burgdorf 1991, pp. 413–414).

The Clinton administration was sympathetic to mental health concerns. In developing its proposal for national health care reform, the administration gave careful consideration to mental health issues (Rochefort 1997). This was consistent with public opinion at the time, which strongly favored an expansion of insurance for behavioral conditions. When the Health Security Act finally emerged from the president's cloistered task force, it encompassed an array of psychiatric inpatient, outpatient, and intensive nonresidential services together with case management. Advocates were dissatisfied with the utilization limits and cost-sharing provisions associated with some of these services, although in fairness the bill had been modeled on the most comprehensive plans then available on the private market. In this sense, the plan could have been helpful to many, particularly in the context of universal coverage, but Republicans thwarted the administration's health reform aims. This defeat was not a total loss, however, because it served as inspiration for the nation's first federal parity bill on mental health insurance coverage in 1996. Unlike the Health Security Act, the parity effort managed to corral bipartisan support, its leadership in the Senate coming from Democrat Edward Kennedy and Republican Nancy Kassebaum. When the law gained passage with the Clinton administration's blessing, it was reason for celebration within the mental health community, albeit celebration of a muted sort owing to several compromises that weakened the final measure.

Another landmark of the Clinton years came in December of 1999, when Dr. David Satcher issued *Mental Health—A Report of the Surgeon General* (U.S. Department of Health and Human Services 1999), a massive document on the scientific basis, accomplishments, and future needs of the mental health field. The report emphasized the necessity of understanding mental health problems as real health conditions that often greatly disabled people. It also identified a range of effective treatments established through rigorous research inquiry. Bemoaning a gap between what was known and what actually occurred in regard to the practice of mental health care, the report put together a great deal of information in a user-friendly and convincing way, and it garnered considerable media attention, including a front-page story in the *New York Times*. Mental health advocates were heartened that for the first time ever the Surgeon General of the United States had addressed this issue in a major way and with strong endorsement from the White House. Tipper Gore, wife of the vice-president, was herself a vigorous participant in this exercise who spoke publicly about her own serious bout with depression. The mental health community enthusiastically anticipated what a Gore administration might bring (Grob and Goldman 2006), but it was George W. Bush who took the reins of office in January of 2001.

Mental health advocates, who incline toward the Democratic side, did not really expect much from the Bush administration. Yet Bush was not indifferent to persons with mental illness or the larger community of persons with disabilities, and there were powerful advocates on the Republican side who had lived with, and were knowledgeable about, the challenges and tragedies of mental illness within a poorly organized system of care. Notable figures included Senator Pete Domenici and his wife, Nancy, who had a daughter with psychiatric problems. Domenici had long advocated for mental health issues within the legislative arena, and in 2002 the president announced the formation of the New Freedom Commission on Mental Health in Albuquerque, New Mexico, the senator's home state. Bush charged the commission with conducting a comprehensive study of the mental health system for the purpose of recommending improvements, but to do so without exceeding current spending. The president appointed Michael Hogan, a highly respected and astute mental health administrator who was then director of the Ohio Department of Mental Health, as chair.

The group operated on the basis of certain key principles: optimizing personal and social outcomes, defining models for efficient coordination of services and supports, enhancing cost-effectiveness, reducing regulatory barriers, and translating research into practice, all within the context of promoting federalism and public innovation, flexibility, and accountability (Grob and Goldman 2006). Six months into its work, the commission filed an interim report with the president reporting that the "mental health delivery system is fragmented and in disarray" and identifying a range of barriers and gaps in mental health care (New Freedom Commission 2003). The final report defined six goals for a transformed system: integration of care for mental health and health; empowerment of consumers and families; elimination of disparities across different population groups; increased availability of early screening, assessment, and referral; achievement of clinical excellence guided by the latest research; and expanded use of technology to improve access and coordination of care, particularly for underserved populations and residents of remote areas. The commission also endorsed the electronic health record. Many of these goals were laudatory, but the recommendations lacked specificity. Perhaps this fuzzy outcome should have been expected from a process geared to satisfying a myriad of constituencies without any injection of new resources.

The New Freedom Commission quickly dropped below the radar screen, dwarfed by other concerns of the day such as large federal deficits, the Iraq and Afghanistan wars, worries about terrorism, education reform, entitlement spending, and more. Unlike President Carter's Commission on Mental Health, the New Freedom Commission of the Bush administration did not produce a coherent long-term strategy for adapting federal programs with mental health care objectives in mind. Federal agencies were, of course, directed to examine how recommendations of the New Freedom Commission might be implemented through existing programs, and in 2005 several departments responded with an action agenda of this kind (Substance Abuse and Mental Health Services Administration 2005). The plan fell far short of being a clear blueprint, however.

Nonetheless, one useful by-product of the commission was the mobilization of mental health advocacy groups. In 2005, 16 national mental health organizations joined together to organize a Campaign for Mental Health Reform (www.mhreform.org). From this collaboration came a road map for dozens of concrete changes in mental health policy and related areas as member organizations matched up their own priorities with what the New Freedom Commission had put forward (Campaign for Mental Health Reform 2005; Glover et al. 2003).

A pivotal theme on the contemporary mental health scene strongly endorsed by the President's New Freedom Commission is "recovery." This concept means different things to different people (Davidson et al. 2006), although one simple definition is the patient's return to a premorbid state (Jacobson and Curtis 2000). The roots of the recovery movement have sometimes been traced back as far as the early 1800s, but are more typically located in the psychiatric survivors' movement that originated in the 1960s and 1970s as well as psychiatric rehabilitation activities of the past few decades. Recovery is, at heart, an optimistic framing of the aftermath of the experience of mental illness, in terms of reclaiming not only functional capacities in various sectors of living but also a personal sense of independence, empowerment, and social inclusion. According to this perspective, mental health treatment is inadequate if all it means is passive receipt of services chosen and directed by professionals. Rather, consumers need and deserve the right to participate in determining their own path through the mental health system and in building successful lives in the community. While highly idealistic, the recovery movement is also grounded in research over the decades (reviewed in other parts of this book) indicating that many persons who have had even the most serious mental illnesses go on to live satisfying and self-actualized lives, often with the assistance of well-conceived treatment and psychosocial and supportive services (Katschnig, Freeman, and Sartorius 2006).

Under President Barack Obama, the Substance Abuse and Mental Health Services Administration has focused attention on recovery as a philosophical and pragmatic touchstone for mental health reform (www.samhsa.gov/recovery). The agency has consulted broadly with professionals and consumers to formulate a working definition of the concept as "a process of change through which individuals improve their health and wellness, live a self-directed life, and strive to reach their full potential." At the same time, it has begun to identify the implications of a recovery-based model for systemic planning and resource development. Elsewhere, it will be discussed how the administration's general campaign for health reform has also addressed the needs of people with mental illnesses.

DEINSTITUTIONALIZATION: A DEEPER LOOK

"Deinstitutionalization" was at once a rallying cry for those advocating community care and a potent symbol of irresponsibility for critics of the community reintegration movement. Yet both sides used the term imprecisely without clear reference to specific patient populations or relocation sites. This limited its utility for empirical description, while fueling a debate that generated far more heat than light (Bachrach 1976).

No doubt, there has been a remarkable decline in the number of people cared for in public mental hospitals. As shown in Figure 3.1, the resident population declined from over 500,000 in the 1950s to less than 40,000 currently. It is widely assumed that deinstitutionalization began with a vengeance in 1955, the point at which the number of inpatients in public mental hospitals reached its peak. In fact, the timing of deinstitutionalization varied greatly by state. For the nation as a whole, the pace was relatively slow at first, that is, only a 1.5 percent decline per year between 1955 and 1965 (Gronfein 1985). One simplistic explanation, often given, is that the introduction of neuroleptic drugs in the mid-1950s resulted in large-scale deinstitutionalization in the period that followed. Figure 3.1 makes

Figure 3.1 • Year-end Resident Population in State and County Mental Hospitals: 1950–2005

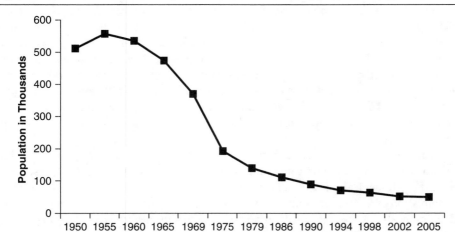

Source: 1950–1965 from Mechanic and Rochefort 1990; 1969–2002 from Center for Mental Health Services 2006; 2005 from Substance Abuse and Mental Health Services Administration 2012.

clear, however, that it wasn't until 1965, and particularly in 1965–1979, that deinstitutionalization accelerated.

The problem in 1955 was that, while new drugs were useful, there were few alternative settings in the community for patients and little financing to support community living. President Johnson's Great Society Program helped create the service infrastructure for placing persons with mental health problems in the community, and SSI cash benefits could help pay for the living costs for patients whether in families, board-and-care facilities, or single-occupancy housing. It became common practice for patients to be transferred from mental hospitals to private nursing homes and for admissions to be diverted from state mental hospitals to general hospitals. In 1983, almost three times as many mental health admissions occurred in general hospitals as state mental hospitals (National Institute of Mental Health 1987). By 1971, the year-end census counted 308,983 residents in public mental hospitals, and the number continued to plummet, reaching 215,573 in 1974 and then 115,000 by the mid-1980s (U.S. President's Commission 1978, vol. II, p. 94).

Federal programs offered an irresistible bargain to state administrators. Medicare covered treatment in general hospitals and private psychiatric hospitals for enrollees. Medicaid paid 50–75 percent of costs for enrollees who entered general hospitals or nursing homes for persons in this program. By directing patients away from public mental hospitals, then, the states could capture huge budgetary savings. Medicaid also provided incentives for private proprietors to vastly expand nursing homes in response to a lucrative business opportunity. In like fashion, these new public funding streams encouraged a boom in private mental hospitals and specialized psychiatric and substance abuse units within general hospitals. Over time, such facilities became the main entry point for acute inpatient behavioral health care. In short, federal health care programs not only financed patient costs, they underwrote the reorganization of the entire mental health infrastructure.

Changing ideologies and cultural values added momentum to these developments. Many young lawyers and activists involved in the civil rights movement of the 1960s extended their efforts to fighting for the civil liberties of persons with mental illness. Substantial abuse plagued the practice of involuntary civil commitment of patients, and this problem supplied a visible target for legal reform (Ennis 1972; Miller 1976). Further, social science researchers and a variety of other critics highlighted the adverse effects of involuntary care and custodial mental institutions (Goffman 1961; Szasz 1963; Wing and Brown 1970). This barrage encouraged a strong antihospital ideology that became widely shared. Finally, the dominance of psychodynamic thinking during this period increased interest in sociocultural and psychosocial factors in mental health care (Caplan 1964; Leighton 1967), and a belief in environmental causation supported the idea that a less coercive and more benign environment could alleviate disturbance in people with mental illnesses.

Yet it is important to appreciate that, even prior to 1955, most inpatients in public mental hospitals eventually returned to the community. In any given year, net discharges and deaths—the typical way of tracking inpatient occupancy—almost equaled the rate of new admissions. In 1950, for example, there were 152,000 admissions, 100,000 discharges, and 41,000 deaths. The longer a patient remained in the hospital, the less likelihood of exit, but a significant proportion of new admissions returned to the community within a few months. Beginning in 1956, net discharges and deaths exceeded new admissions, but only by 7,952 individuals. It was not until 1970 that net discharges (excluding deaths) actually exceeded the number of new admissions during the year (U.S. President's Commission on Mental Health 1978). Moreover, in any given year, the vast majority of patients leaving were those admitted relatively recently.

These simple data indicate that the so-called deinstitutionalized population was somewhat a misnomer insofar as it intermixed a heterogeneous collection of varying patient cohorts (for a discussion of cohorts, see Ryder 1965). Many leaving the hospital in this period would have returned to the community even in the absence of a national community mental health policy. From an analytical standpoint, it would be desirable, yet very difficult, to separate members of this group from those impacted distinctly by reduced lengths of stay and other changes aimed at census reduction.

By 1977, some 668,000 nursing home patients were diagnosed with mental illness or dementia (Goldman, Feder, and Scanlon 1986). This population included those who were transferred from mental hospitals as well as those who entered nursing homes directly from the community. According to Kiesler and Sibulkin (1987), as many as half of the elderly discharged from mental hospitals in the post-1964 years went to nursing homes. As abuses became evident, Congress took action in 1987, mandating preadmission evaluations to ensure that only individuals in need of nursing care were admitted to nursing homes. It also required all facilities to provide active mental health treatment for residents with a primary mental illness. Mechanic and McAlpine (2000), comparing nursing home surveys in 1985 and 1995, found a reduced role for nursing homes particularly for younger patients with mental illness who did not have comorbid physical conditions.

Over time, there was an increasing number of individuals with serious mental illness, mostly comprised of younger people with schizophrenia, raising public fears and concerns in the community. Most of them were not long-stay inpatients, and some have never had a single psychiatric admission. Substance abuse is a common co-occurring disorder for this population. As the organization of mental health services has changed, acute psychoses are treated typically with short inpatient admissions in community general hospitals and in reconstituted public mental hospitals (Mechanic, McAlpine, and Olfson 1998). Only a proportion of these patients would have been long-term residents of mental hospitals in an earlier era, and any description of this group as a problem imposed on the community by the headlong rush into deinstitutionalization is mistaken.

The amount of serious mental illness in the population, with schizophrenia as the prototype, depends on both the rate of incidence and the size of the population at risk. When serious mental illness became more evident in the community in the 1980s, it was not primarily due to sudden deinstitutionalization or even changes in the way psychiatric hospitalization was used, but rather demographic shifts reflecting large subgroups at ages having highest risk of the illness. Morton Kramer (1977) predicted the growth of the numbers of such patients earlier simply by projecting demographic trends.

At the same time, it is true that younger patients with schizophrenia and other seriously disturbed youths have become more aware than ever of their civil liberties and often seem hostile or indifferent to the claims of professional psychiatry. This situation, in some ways, can be seen as the culmination of antiestablishment reform energies that have swept through the mental health sector system over the past 50 years. These younger individuals frequently decline the treatments made available to them, particularly when mental illness is complicated by abuse of drugs and alcohol. At various points in their lives they are hospitalized, jailed, or live on the streets, constituting a significant minority of the homeless population (Lamb 1984; Lamb and Grant 1982). Within this age group are also increasing numbers of minority and disadvantaged youth, for whom the stigma of mental illness combines with the social difficulties associated with color and economic instability.

The ideology of community care originally developed from a realization that long-term hospitalization isolated patients while undermining their motivation and capability to return to the community. The report of the Joint Commission on Mental Illness and Health had attacked large public mental hospitals and advocated their abolition. The commission did support smaller facilities providing intensive care, as well as treatment units in general hospitals and mental health clinics. The objective was for patients to remain close to home and in touch with their family and friends, with a new emphasis on outpatient care and short periods of hospitalization only when truly necessary. Additional alternatives were urged, such as day hospitals, halfway houses, and residential care facilities. Similarly, the perceived importance of patients maintaining their skills and sense of activity led to the added emphasis on vocational services, sheltered workshops, and continuing employment even during a period of hospital stay. Finally, so that patients could remain in their home surroundings whenever possible, there was agreement on the desirability of services that are home based and family inclusive.

Ideologies develop more rapidly than patterns of care. Yet it was not terribly difficult to change institutional policies concerning admission and retention, and as a consequence of population reductions, the public mental hospital was in many instances transformed from a custodial institution into an active treatment unit. It is, of course, difficult to describe conditions across the United States because each state maintains its own mental health system and there is great diversity in the availability of facilities, funding and staffing patterns, and the emphasis put on different aspects of care. Some hospitals are still large and rely on organizational routines that are dehumanizing and that interfere with an individualized approach to the patient. But most hospitals little resemble what they had once been.

When it came to arranging a system of community services that could buttress new hospital policies, however, the obstacles proved considerable. Although the community mental health ideology may be coherent, services provided to patients outside the hospital setting are sporadic and fragmentary. Frequently, the burden that once belonged to the hospital has been shifted, but without the resources needed by families and other social actors to meet crises or deal effectively with the patient and problems of care.

CONCLUSION

There is, of course, no conclusion to history or even sometimes a clear direction. This latter observation is apt in regard to evolution of the mental health system in the United States. Among rival scholarly camps, there is a vigorous debate as to whether pivotal developments such as the establishment of public mental hospitals or the shift to community-based care represent a theme of progressive advancement or regressive social control (Rochefort 1986). In reality, the twists and turns of mental health policymaking defy application of a single overarching model. As we have seen in this chapter, policy directions arise from multiple sources of influence and motivation, and outcomes need not be consistent with the intentions of those who undertake reform. Whatever one's interpretation of the historical record, however, one thing is certain, and that is we all must live with the results of past choices and the pathways they have created (Mechanic and Grob 2006).

Consumers of mental health care have benefited from many systemic changes that occurred over time, including the diversification of service options, improved tolerance and respect for the rights of those impaired by mental disorders, and greater public visibility of the treatments delivered in different settings. The fiscal and regulatory responsibilities of the government with respect to operation of the mental health service system have become enormous and far-reaching, so much so that no one seriously debates any longer whether control should be placed in the hands of state or federal government. Both have acquired fundamental roles that cannot be abdicated if public commitments are to be met and effective planning to take place. However, an unfortunate consequence of elaboration of the nation's mental health system has been to make it increasingly disorganized and unmanageable. A vast array of programs with complicated eligibility criteria has caused much confusion, large variations in care, and difficulty for patients and their advocates who want to access appropriate services. According to one study, there are now more than 40 federal programs relevant to persons with mental illness (Frank and Glied 2006). Meanwhile, ironically, important unmet needs persist (Mechanic and Grob 2006).

As deinstitutionalization progressed, individuals with mental health problems often took up residence in group homes, sheltered care situations, and isolated rooming houses that varied greatly in regard to quality of the environment, supervision, and social contact (Allen 1974; Lamb 1979; Segal and Aviram 1978). Many patients now live in new forms of residential housing and supported housing programs, as well as independent scattered housing. Yet others are simply "dumped" in inadequate community housing in transitional housing areas with little support or assistance, risking victimization by criminal elements. Rapid growth of the homeless population in the 1980s included a substantial proportion of persons with mental disorders, many of them with a history of psychiatric treatment. As this fact came to light, the nation's homelessness problem became a rhetorical bludgeon in the hands of those most critical of the policy of deinstitutionalization (Isaac and Armat 1990; Torrey 1988). Although this connection between homelessness and mental illness was sometimes exaggerated, addressing the relationship between housing and homelessness is now recognized to be an essential component of any comprehensive program serving persons with serious and persistent mental illness.

Historically, there has always been some tension between those who view mental health needs and programs as unique and separate from other public policy concerns and those who believe in the value of mainstreaming so that people with mental illnesses can gain from the reforms and resources of other sectors. The latest issue to crystallize this debate is the struggle for adequate insurance coverage for mental health conditions, which has surfaced in the parity movement and in the drive for national health care reform. It is easy to understand the point of view of those who seek to eliminate longstanding discrimination against mental health conditions within private and public health benefit plans. When coverage is incomplete, it leads to excessive cost and lack of care. But parity is insufficient if it does not also make provision for specialized solutions aligned with the clinical and social support needs of those dealing with mental illness.

Similarly, community mental health care works best at ground level when smoothly coordinated with services from other health and social welfare sectors. This is the lesson of a series of major policy analyses going back to the Carter Presidential Commission on Mental Health and continuing with the recent New Freedom Commission of the Bush administration. Increasingly, it has also become impossible to disentangle mental health and criminal justice systems given the large number of people with mental health problems who become incarcerated, often for minor offenses. Reducing fragmentation, duplication, and gaps in services stands as one of the most commonplace goals of mental health policy reform. There are now many well-documented model programs demonstrating methods of planning, management, organization, and financing effective for this purpose. Yet one of the deepest frustrations experienced by those in need is the partial diffusion of these exemplary initiatives from one section of the country to another, or even from community to community in a single state. When knowledge exists to do better than we have, key questions emerge: How can the use of best practices be expanded within the mental health system? And how can we achieve greater convergence in quality standards regarding service delivery and program administration for all groups and individuals?

The historical data presented in this chapter highlight the critical role of economic factors in mental health system development. Moral treatment in state mental hospitals gave way to a custodial era in no small degree because institutional capacity and conditions deteriorated as state legislatures focused on other funding priorities. By contrast, the shift to community care benefited from the economic upswing of the late 1950s and early 1960s, which supported a more activist federal government interested in social policy matters. Economic trends contribute to both the occurrence of mental health needs and the accessibility of treatments, no matter whether the latter are to be financed out of household or public budgets or the insurance plans paid for by employers and employees (Mechanic and Grob 2011). Availability of funding is a primary determinant in the spread of model programs and their sustainability over time. The economic decline of the current decade takes its place historically as one of the worst in the past half century. The impact of this downturn on mental health care must be examined carefully if its particular challenges are to be understood and responded to meaningfully.

A later chapter will take up these and other contemporary mental health reform issues in greater depth. A strong sense of history is fitting prelude for this discussion. Historical awareness may not identify specific solutions to present problems, but it can remind us where mistakes have occurred, encourage a broader conception of possible future alternatives, and suggest what some of the preconditions for success might entail (Stevens 2006). Historical analysis is a preventive against neglecting those factors and forces that may have faded from memory and hidden from view. The connection with policy formation is thus direct and consequential.

References

Allen, Priscilla. "A Consumer's View of California's Mental Health Care System." *Psychiatric Quarterly* 48 (1974): 1–13.

Bachrach, Leona L. *Deinstitutionalization: An Analytical Review and Sociological Perspective.* Division of Biometry and Epidemiology, Series D, No. 4, DHEW Publication No. (ADM) 76–351. Washington, DC: U.S. Government Printing Office, 1976.

Bockoven, J. Sanbourne. "Some Relationships Between Cultural Attitudes Toward Individuality and Care of the Mentally Ill: An Historical Study." In *The Patient and the Mental Hospital: Contributions of Research in the Science of Social Behavior*, edited by Milton Greenblatt, Daniel J. Levinson, and Richard H. Williams, pp. 517–526. New York: The Free Press, 1957.

Bockoven, J. Sanbourne. *Moral Treatment in Community Mental Health.* New York: Springer-Verlag, 1972.

Brenner, M. Harvey. *Mental Illness and the Economy.* Cambridge, MA: The President and Fellows of Harvard College, 1973.

Burgdorf, Robert L., Jr. "The Americans with Disabilities Act: Analysis and Implications of a Second-Generation Civil Rights Statute." *Harvard Civil Rights-Civil Liberties Law Review* 26 (1991): 413–522.

Campaign for Mental Health Reform. *Emergency Response: A Roadmap for Federal Action on America's Mental Health Crisis*, 2005. Available online: www.mhreform.org/Portals/0/1.3_EmergencyResponseReport.pdf.

Caplan, Gerald. *Principles of Preventive Psychiatry.* New York: Basic Books, 1964.

Center for Mental Health Services. *Mental Health United States, 2004*, edited by Ronald W. Manderscheid and Joyce T. Berry. DHHS Pub No. (SMA)-06-4195. Rockville, MD: Substance Abuse and Mental Health Services Administration, 2006.

Cummings, Nicholas A., and William T. Follette. "Psychiatric Services and Medical Utilization in a Prepaid Health Plan Setting: Part II." *Medical Care* 6 (1968): 31–41.

Davidson, Larry, et al. "The Top Ten Concerns About Recovery Encountered in Mental Health System Transformation." *Psychiatric Services* 57 (2006): 640–645.

Deutsch, Albert. *The Shame of the States.* New York: Harcourt, Brace and Co., 1948.

Dowell, David A., and James A. Ciarlo. "An Evaluative Overview of the Community Mental Health Centers Program." In *Handbook on Mental Health Policy in the United States*, edited by David A. Rochefort, pp. 195–236. Westport, CT: Greenwood Press, 1989.

Ennis, Bruce J. *Prisoners of Psychiatry: Mental Patients, Psychiatrists, and the Law.* New York: Harcourt Brace Jovanovich, 1972.

Felix, Robert H. *Mental Illness: Progress and Prospects.* New York: Columbia University Press, 1967.

Foley, Henry A., and Steven Sharfstein. *Madness and Government: Who Cares for the Mentally Ill?* Washington, DC: American Psychiatric Press, 1983.

Follette, William, and Nicholas A. Cummings. "Psychiatric Services and Medical Utilization in a Prepaid Health Plan Setting." *Medical Care* 5 (1967): 25–35.

Frank, Richard G., and Sherry A. Glied. *Better But Not Well: Mental Health Policy in the United States Since 1950.* Baltimore, MD: Johns Hopkins University Press, 2006.

Glover, Robert W., et al. "New Freedom Commission Report: The Campaign for Mental Health Reform: A New Advocacy Partnership." *Psychiatric Services* 54 (2003): 1475–1479.

Goffman, Erving. *Asylums: Essays on the Social Situation of Mental Patients and Other Inmates.* Garden City, NY: Anchor Books, 1961.

Goldhamer, Herbert, and Andrew W. Marshall. *Psychosis and Civilization: Two Studies in the Frequency of Mental Disease.* Glencoe, IL: The Free Press, 1953.

Goldman, Howard H., Judith Feder, and William Scanlon. "Chronic Mental Patients in Nursing Homes: Re-examining Data from the National Nursing Home Survey." *Hospital and Community Psychiatry* 37 (1986): 269–272.

Grob, Gerald N. *The State and the Mentally Ill: A History of Worcester State Hospital in Massachusetts, 1830–1920.* Chapel Hill: The University of North Carolina Press, 1966.

Grob, Gerald N. *Mental Institutions in America: Social Policy to 1875.* New York: The Free Press, 1973.

Grob, Gerald N. "Rediscovering Asylums: The Unhistorical History of the Mental Hospital." *The Hastings Center Report* 7 (1977): 33–41.

Grob, Gerald N. *Mental Illness and American Society. 1875–1940.* Princeton, NJ: Princeton University Press, 1983.

Grob, Gerald N. "The Forging of Mental Health Policy in America: World War II to New Frontier." *Journal of the History of Medicine and Allied Sciences* 42 (1987): 410–446.

Grob, Gerald N. *The Mad Among Us: A History of the Care of America's Mentally Ill.* New York: Free Press, 1994.

Grob, Gerald N. "Public Policy and Mental Illnesses: Jimmy Carter's Presidential Commission on Mental Health." *Milbank Quarterly* 83 (2005): 425–456.

Grob, Gerald N., and Howard H. Goldman. *The Dilemma of Federal Mental Health Policy: Radical Reform or Incremental Change?* New Brunswick, NJ: Rutgers University Press, 2006.

Gronfein, William. "Incentives and Intentions in Mental Health Policy: A Comparison of the Medicaid and Community Mental Health Programs." *Journal of Health and Social Behavior* 26 (1985): 192–206.

Harkin, Tom. Congressional Record, *135 Cong. Rec.* September 7, 1989: 19801.

Hoover Commission. *Task Force Report on Federal Medical Services*, February 1955.

House Ways and Means Committee. Committee Staff Report on the Disability Insurance Program. *Part III. Background Material A. Legislative History, The Development of the Disability Program Under Old-Age Survivors Insurance, 1935–74.* July 1974. Available online: www.ssa.gov/history/pdf/dibreport.pdf.

Isaac, Rael Jean, and Virginia C. Armat. *Madness in the Streets: How Psychiatry and the Law Abandoned the Mentally Ill.* New York: Free Press, 1990.

Jacobson, Nora, and Laurie Curtis. "Recovery as Policy in Mental Health Services: Strategies Emerging from the States." *Psychiatric Rehabilitation Journal* 23 (2000): 333–341.

Joint Commission on Mental Illness and Health. *Action for Mental Health*, Final Report. New York: Basic Books, Science Editions, 1961.

Katschnig, Heinz, Hugh Freeman, and Norman Sartorius, eds. *Quality of Life in Mental Disorders*, 2nd ed. Chichester/New York: Wiley Interscience, 2006.

Kiesler, Charles A., and Amy E. Sibulkin. *Mental Hospitalization: Myths and Facts About a National Crisis.* Newbury Park, CA: Sage Publications, 1987.

Kramer, Morton. *Psychiatric Services and the Changing Institutional Scene, 1950–1985.* National Institute of Mental Health, Series B, No. 12, (ADM) 77–433. Washington, DC: U.S. Government Printing Office, 1977.

Lamb, Richard H. "The New Asylums in the Community." *Archives of General Psychiatry* 36 (1979): 129–134.

Lamb, Richard H., ed. *The Homeless Mentally Ill, A Task Force Report of the American Psychiatric Association.* Washington, DC: American Psychiatric Association, 1984.

Lamb, Richard H., and Robert W. Grant. "The Mentally Ill in an Urban County Jail." *Archives of General Psychiatry* 39 (1982): 17–22.

Leighton, Alexander H. "Is Social Environment a Cause of Psychiatric Disorder?" In *Psychiatric Research Reports*, edited by Russell Monroe, Gerald Klee, and Eugene Brody, pp. 337–345. Psychiatric Epidemiology and Mental Health Planning. Washington, DC: American Psychiatric Association, 1967.

Mechanic, David, and Gerald N. Grob. "Rhetoric, Realities, and the Plight of the Mentally Ill in America." In *History and Health Policy in the United States: Putting the Past Back In*, edited by Rosemary A. Stevens, Charles E. Rosenberg, and Lawton R. Burns, pp. 229–249. New Brunswick, NJ: Rutgers University Press, 2006.

Mechanic, David, and Gerald N. Grob. "Social Policy and the American Mental Health System of Care." In *Population Mental Health: Evidence, Policy, and Public Health Practice*, edited by Neal Cohen and Sandro Galea, pp. 119–138. New York: Routledge, 2011.

Mechanic, David, and Donna D. McAlpine. "Use of Nursing Homes in the Care of Persons with Severe Mental Illness: 1985 to 1995." *Psychiatric Services* 51 (2000): 354–358.

Mechanic, David, Donna McAlpine, and Mark Olfson. "Changing Patterns of Psychiatric Inpatient Care in the United States, 1988–1994." *Archives of General Psychiatry* 55 (1998): 785–791.

Mechanic, David, and David A. Rochefort. "Deinstitutionalization: An Appraisal of Reform." *Annual Review of Sociology* 16 (1990): 301–327.

Miller, Kent S. *Managing Madness: The Case Against Civil Commitment.* New York: Free Press, 1976.

National Institute of Mental Health. *Mental Health, United States, 1987*, edited by Ronald W. Manderscheid, and Sally A. Barrett, DHHS Publication No. ADM 87-1518. Washington, DC: U.S. Government Printing Office, 1987.

New Freedom Commission on Mental Health. *Achieving the Promise: Transforming Mental Health Care in America: Final Report.* DHHS Publication No. SMA-03-3832. Rockville, MD: U.S. Department of Health and Human Services, 2003.

Office of the Inspector General. *Audit of the Community Mental Health Centers Construction Grant Program—Phase 1.* Washington, DC: U.S. Department of Health and Human Services, 1991. Available online: oig.hhs.gov/oas/reports/region5/59100050.pdf.

Patrick, Donald L., Jeff Eagle, and Jules V. Coleman. "Primary Care Treatment of Emotional Problems in an HMO." *Medical Care* 16 (1978): 47–60.

Rochefort, David A. *American Social Welfare Policy: Dynamics of Formulation and Change*. Boulder, CO: Westview Press, 1986.

Rochefort, David A. *From Poorhouses to Homelessness: Policy Analysis and Mental Health Care*, 2nd ed. Westport, CT: Auburn House, 1997.

Rosenbach, Margo L., and Carol J. Ammering. "Trends in Medicare Part B Mental Health Utilization and Expenditures: 1987–92." *Health Care Financing Review* 18 (1997): 19–42.

Rothman, David J. *The Discovery of the Asylum: Social Order and Disorder in the New Republic*. Boston: Little, Brown, 1971.

Ryder, Norman B. "The Cohort as a Concept in the Study of Social Change." *American Sociological Review* 30 (1965): 843–861.

Segal, Steven P., and Uri Aviram. *The Mentally-Ill in Community-Based Sheltered Care: A Study of Community Care and Social Integration*. New York: Wiley Interscience, 1978.

Social Security Administration. *Annual Statistical Supplement to the Social Security Bulletin, 1991*. Washington, DC: Social Security Administration, June 1992.

Social Security Administration. *SSI Annual Statistical Report, 2010*. SSA Publication No. 13-11827. Washington, DC: Social Security Administration, August 2011.

Social Security Administration. *Annual Statistical Supplement to the Social Security Bulletin, 2011*. SSA Publication No. 13-11700. Washington, DC: Social Security Administration, February 2012.

Stevens, Rosemary A. "Introduction." In *History and Health Policy in the United States: Putting the Past Back In*, edited by Rosemary A. Stevens, Charles E. Rosenberg, and Lawton R. Burns, pp. 1–9. New Brunswick: Rutgers University Press, 2006.

Substance Abuse and Mental Health Services Administration. *Transforming Mental Health Care in America: The Federal Action Agenda: First Steps*. DHHS Publication No. SMA-05-4060. Rockville, MD: Department of Health and Human Services, 2005. Available online: www.samhsa.gov/Federalactionagenda/NFC_TOC.aspx.

Substance Abuse and Mental Health Services Administration. *Mental Health, United States, 2010*. HHS Publication No. (SMA) 12-4681. Rockville, MD: Substance Abuse and Mental Health Services Administration, 2012.

Szasz, Thomas S. *Law, Liberty, and Psychiatry: An Inquiry into the Social Uses of Mental Health Practices*. New York: Macmillan, 1963.

Torrey, E. Fuller. *Nowhere to Go: The Tragic Odyssey of the Homeless Mentally Ill*. New York: Harper & Row, 1988.

U.S. Department of Health and Human Services. *Toward a National Plan for the Chronically Mentally Ill. Report to the Secretary—1980*. DHHS Publication No. ADM 81-1077. Rockville, MD: Department of Health and Human Services, 1980.

U.S. Department of Health and Human Services. *Mental Health: A Report of the Surgeon General*. Rockville, MD: U.S. Department of Health and Human Services, Substance Abuse and Mental Health Services Administration, Center for Mental Health Services, National Institutes of Health, National Institute of Mental Health, 1999.

U.S. President's Commission on Mental Health. *Report of the Task Panel on the Nature and Scope of the Problems*, vol. I, vol. II appendix. Washington, DC: U.S. Government Printing Office, 1978.

Wing, John K., and George W. Brown. *Institutionalism and Schizophrenia: A Comparative Study of Three Mental Hospitals, 1960–1968*. Cambridge: Cambridge University Press, 1970.

Psychiatric Epidemiology

Science, Counting, and Making Sense of the Numbers

Psychiatric epidemiology has to do with determining the number of people affected by mental disorders of various types and identifying possible causes of disorders, an issue addressed in more depth in the next chapter. In this chapter, we focus on how estimates of the population with mental disorders have been developed and the strengths and limitations of such estimates.

Psychiatric epidemiologists face two major challenges in counting the number of people with a specific disorder. The first is to differentiate as carefully as possible new cases from cases that have continued over some period of time. This is the distinction between *incidence* (the number of new cases that occur) and *prevalence* (all cases existing). Each is typically expressed as the number of cases in a period (one month, one year, or lifetime) per person at risk. In order to understand the causes of a disorder, it is essential to differentiate the factors that contribute to the disorder's initial occurrence from those that affect its course—whether it persists, disappears, or fluctuates. For example, the treatment of a streptococcal infection with antibiotics will eliminate the infection, but lack of such treatment, allowing the illness to persist, is not the source of that infection. Although incidence rate will measure new infections that occur during a specified period, the prevalence rate combines these with older infections that continue. Study of prevalence does not allow us to separate clearly the *cause* of a condition from those factors affecting its *course*.

The second challenge, as noted in our discussion of the conceptualization of mental illness in Chapter 2, is to be as precise as possible about the entity being studied. Disorders are extraordinarily varied and complicated, with different causes, natural histories, and biological and social consequences. If the condition being studied is poorly defined and combines different disorders, the knowledge generated will also be confused. Precise definition makes it more likely that we will learn something new and useful in psychiatric epidemiology. Although this field is in part handicapped by inadequacies of our current systems of classification, we should not make matters worse by being careless about case definition.

Psychiatric epidemiology is not just an academic pursuit. Estimates of the number of people with mental illnesses in the population help shape how much public attention is given to a problem, and whether we consider it minor or serious. While it is not always the case that more prevalent diseases, or those that present the greatest social burden in terms of morbidity or mortality, are taken more seriously in the political realm (Armstrong, Carpenter, and Hojnacki 2006), advocacy organizations use large numbers to claim that the problems they are concerned with are important. Similarly, researchers use such information to support requests for more research dollars, while policymakers and program planners factor these estimates into decisions about allocation of resources. Thus, our counts of the number of persons with mental illness matter. Once produced, there is a temptation to view epidemiological data as objective scientific facts, giving them perhaps unwarranted legitimacy. Stakeholders who repeatedly draw on these numbers reify their importance, turning them into symbols of a certain kind. That is not to say researchers produce estimates of the prevalence of any particular disorder for political purposes; most are trying to provide the best information possible to improve our understanding of scope and etiology in order to build knowledge and inform effective policy. But we should be critical consumers of the statistics used to describe any problem.

DEVELOPMENT OF PSYCHIATRIC EPIDEMIOLOGY

Work in the United States to count the number of persons with mental illness has a long history. When the first U.S. census was carried out in 1790, it only collected basic demographic information and included no information on mental illness. However, the 1840 census was more complete and recorded the number of individuals considered "insane or idiotic" (Gorwitz 1974). By 1880, the census employed separate classes of mental illness, and physicians were asked to return forms listing all "idiots and lunatics within the sphere of their personal knowledge" (Gorwitz 1974, p. 181). Results revealed a large increase in the rate of mental illness, from about 50.7 per 100,000 population in 1840 to 183.3 per 100,000 in 1880. The methodology was completely invalid because of its unsystematic approach. However, data from the census were used to support the prejudices against, and oppression of, African Americans that marked this era. The observation that prevalence rates of mental illness were higher among free Blacks than among slaves in the 1840 census bolstered arguments that freedom caused mental illness (Leventman 1968). Writing in the *Journal of the American Medical Association*, one researcher concluded: "Too much liberty and freedom, so far as the laws of health are concerned, is dangerous to the mental and physical integrity of any people" (Powell 1896, p. 1188).

While it would be hard to find a more egregious misuse of population research than occurred in this early period, researchers, advocates, and policymakers continue to draw on epidemiological estimates in making the case for, or against, specific mental health policies. Thus, one must carefully consider both the assumptions underlying the conceptualization of disorder and measurement methodology. All numbers are social constructions, for "Numbers do not exist independently of people; understanding numbers requires knowing who counted what, why they bothered counting and how they went about it" (Best 2005, p. 212).

The field of psychiatric epidemiology has progressed through three generations of research (Dohrenwend and Dohrenwend 1982). Table 4.1 briefly summarizes prevalence estimates using examples of studies conducted during each of these generations.

Table 4.1	Estimates of the Prevalence of Mental Illness from Three Generations of Psychiatric Epidemiology		
Study (Source)	Sample	Case Identification	Prevalence
First Generation			
Insanity and Idiocy in Massachusetts (Jarvis 1855)	Residents of Massachusetts: 1854–1855	Surveys of state hospitals, physicians, clergymen, and others	2,632 "lunatics"; 234/100,000 population
Mental Disorders in Urban Areas (Faris and Dunham 1939)	Chicago: 1922–1934	Census of patients in all private and public psychiatric hospitals	All cases: 110/100,000 population Schizophrenia: 33/100,000 population
Second Generation			
Midtown Manhattan Study (Srole et al. 1962)	Midtown Manhattan residents, 1660 respondents 20–59 Home Interview: 1953–1954	Census of treated cases and self-reports of symptoms; responses assessed by psychiatrists	Treated: 1,290 per 100,000 Community sample: Well: 18.5% Mild symptom: 36.3% Moderate symptoms: 21.8% Marked symptoms: 13.2% Severe symptoms Incapacitated: 10.2%
Stirling County Study (Leighton et al. 1963a, 1963b)	Adult residents of rural county in Nova Scotia: 1,010 respondents; in 1952	Review of institutional records, home interviews, and key informants; Health Opinion Survey; self-reports of symptoms; cases reviewed by psychiatrists	Probability of Disorder: High: 31% Probable: 26% Doubtful: 26% None: 17%
New Hampshire Study (Phillips 1966)	Random sample of 600 adults in New Hampshire	Interviews with respondents: Langner 22-item Mental Health Scale	Psychologically impaired: 28%
Third Generation			
Epidemiologic Catchment Area Studies (Robins and Regier 1991)	20,862 community and institutionalized respondents ages 18+ across five sites (New Haven, Baltimore, St. Louis, Durham, Los Angeles): 1980–1985	Household interview using the Diagnostic Interview Schedule for 14 types of disorder based on *DSM-III*	Lifetime: 32% 12-month: 20%

(Continued)

(*Continued*)

Study (Source)	Sample	Case Identification	Prevalence
National Comorbidity Study (Kessler et al. 1994a)	8,098 community respondents ages 15–54 in 48 contiguous states: 1990–1992	Household interview using Composite International Diagnostic Instrument (CIDI): 14 core diagnostic categories based on *DSM-III-R*	Lifetime: 48.0% 12-month: 29.5%
National Comorbidity Study-Replication	9,282 civilian, noninstitutionalized population ages 18+: 2001–2003	Household interview using WMH-CIDI: 20 approximately types of disorder based on *DSM-IV*	Lifetime: 57.4% 12-month: 32.4%

Note: National Comorbidity Study-Replication 12-month rates are available here: www.hcp.med.harvard.edu/ncs/ftpdir/NCS-R_12-month_Prevalence_Estimates.pdf; Lifetime rates are available here: www.hcp.med.harvard.edu/ncs/ftpdir/NCS-R_Lifetime_Prevalence_Estimates.pdf.

We will not try to cover all studies in each period, but instead concentrate on those demonstrating different methodologies that were particularly influential.

The first generation in psychiatric epidemiology included studies conducted mainly prior to World War II. These were typically based on administrative records or treated cases, sometimes with additional interviews of key informants. An early example is the work of Edward Jarvis (1855) to count the number of "insane and idiotic" in Massachusetts. This study was undertaken in response to the legislature's request for accurate and precise numbers to guide the state's planning efforts, particularly regarding hospital care. Jarvis surveyed every state hospital and physician in the state, as well as others who might have come into contact with the mentally ill, such as clergymen and overseers of the poor. He collected basic demographic information, patients' previous hospital use, and character-istics of different disorders, including prognosis. Names of persons were de-duplicated to arrive at overall estimates of mental illness. It was an impressive research effort. All but four of the commonwealth's 1,319 physicians who were contacted cooperated. One contribution of Jarvis' work was to highlight that a great many (about 50 percent) of those identified as mentally ill were actually living in the community, not institutions (Grob 1994).

A second illustrative example from the period before World War II is Faris and Dunham's (1939) study of the geographic distribution of mental disorders. These research-ers correlated all admissions to private and public hospitals in Chicago with geographic location. (Results were also replicated in Providence, Rhode Island, but here we focus on the Chicago study.) They concluded that "disorganized urban" communities (characterized by a highly mobile population, immigrants from diverse backgrounds, poverty, broken families, and the like) had higher rates of mental disorder than suburban communities. They also suggested that disorganized communities caused severe mental illness such as schizophrenia. The conclusions have proven wrong, but the methodology was common among studies at this time. Despite its flaws, this type of research has been described as an "extraordinary intellectual leap" in psychiatric epidemiology (Horwitz and Grob 2011, p. 638). Prior efforts to count cases of mental illness were primarily driven by the need to understand the institutionalized population for the purposes of planning and policy. Faris and Dunham's research, by contrast, was more concerned with understanding how cases might be distributed in relation to social conditions, a shift in focus that would gain dominance in the second generation of psychiatric epidemiology.

Although a great deal can be learned from the study of treated cases of mental illness, treated cases poorly approximate the sick population in general. Persons with similar conditions may or may not receive treatment. Some will enter the mental health system, while others will come into contact with general practitioners, social workers, or religious counselors. To get a better sense of this group in its entirety, it became necessary to develop new methods sensitive to the true scope of the problem.

The second generation of studies attempted to do so by measuring mental illness in the community. This period of psychiatric epidemiology was heavily influenced by developments during World War II, when the military had a practical need to screen prospective soldiers likely to suffer psychiatric breakdowns. Researchers developed an instrument—the Army Neuro-Psychiatric Screening Adjunct—that could differentiate, to some extent, between mentally ill and healthy populations. Following the war, when epidemiologists turned to the problem of studying psychological disorder in the general population, they used this instrument as a basis for developing measures of impairment.

Some of the earliest efforts during the second generation of epidemiological research to assess the distribution of various types of mental illness involved psychiatrists selecting relatively small communities and systematically interviewing residents and informants to assess the prevalence of varying types of psychiatric conditions. In a classic study in Sweden, Essen-Möeller and colleagues (1956) interviewed all members of a local community to count and describe the types of mental illness that were evident. In 1966, Hagnell carried out a study in the same community following Essen-Möeller's methods (Hagnell 1966). Similar efforts were made elsewhere. For example, psychiatrist Milton Mazer carried out a five-year investigation of predicaments as defined by the investigator rather than specific diagnoses among the population living year round in Martha's Vineyard, Massachusetts, a community of about 4,500 people at the time (Mazer 1974, 1976). While these studies were highly informative and provided much valuable information, they were dependent on the unstandardized psychiatric conceptions of the interviewers and had uncertain reliability and validity. It also was exceedingly expensive for psychiatrists to personally interview large numbers of people in community populations. Efforts soon turned to more standardized and less expensive survey approaches.

Dozens of studies were done in the second generation; we highlight a few that illustrate the dominant method and influenced the field (see Table 4.1). The Stirling County Study was designed to assess the "true prevalence" of psychiatric disorder in a rural community in Nova Scotia, and to investigate the relationship between social environment and mental health (Leighton et al. 1963a, 1963b). Investigators randomly sampled over 1,000 residents of the county, interviewed physicians of the selected respondents, and reviewed hospital administrative records. Psychiatrists scrutinized all information for each respondent to determine probable cases of mental disorder. Overall, the researchers estimated that 57 percent of the adult population had a mental disorder, and only 17 percent were categorized as probably well.

The Midtown Manhattan Study, which began in the early 1950s, included a census of treated cases in public and private hospitals, as well as outpatient clinics and private psychiatrist and psychologist offices (Srole et al. 1962). It also implemented a major methodological innovation—home interviews of a random sample of 1,660 residents that included questions about the occurrence of dozens of symptoms, such as nervousness and feeling weak, as well as questions about functioning. Two psychiatrists reviewed the responses and categorized respondents on a continuum from well to impaired. As in the Stirling County study, only a small percentage (19 percent) of the adult population was categorized as psychiatrically well.

The Midtown Manhattan and Stirling County studies stimulated the development of measures for screening persons in community populations for a variety of symptoms including depression, anxiety, and psychophysiological discomforts. Over time, researchers moved away from having psychiatrists review responses and began to rely solely on self-reports of symptoms, using various cut-points to determine the number of cases of mentally ill persons. In one study that illustrates this approach, Phillips (1966) used the Langner 22-item Mental Health Scale, one of most common measures of the time, to estimate the prevalence of mental illness among adults in New Hampshire (see Table 4.1). The Langner scale was developed based on the Midtown Manhattan research; it differentiated between healthy and treated psychiatric populations and was correlated with such variables as sex, social class, and stressful life events (Dohrenwend and Dohrenwend 1969; Langner and Michael 1963). Examples of the 22 items in the scale are as follows:

- I feel weak all over much of the time.
- I have had periods of days, weeks, or months when I couldn't take care of things because I couldn't "get going."
- Have you ever been bothered by your heart beating hard?
- Are you ever bothered by nervousness?
- You sometimes can't help wondering if anything is worthwhile any more.
- Do you ever have trouble in getting to sleep or staying asleep?

Many items were scored by the frequency with which they occurred (e.g., often, sometimes, or never). On the basis of these data, Phillips (1966) concluded that 28 percent of the nonhospitalized adult population was psychiatrically impaired.

Subsequently, the value of such global measures of psychiatric impairment generated much criticism and debate. At the methodological level, it was argued that these scales suffered from response biases, such as consistent yeasaying/naysaying among certain respondents, distorting effects because of differing perceptions of the social undesirability of items across social groups, and confusion between symptoms related to physical versus psychological illness (Crandell and Dohrenwend 1967; Manis et al. 1963; Phillips and Clancy 1970; Seiler 1973; Tousignant, Denis, and Lachapelle 1974). At the substantive level, concern was raised by the finding that psychiatric outpatients scored higher on such items than more severely disabled inpatients (Dohrenwend 1972), and even well-functioning groups—such as college students—scored extremely high (Mechanic and Greenley 1976). Also, retesting after one year resulted in higher correlation between scores among psychiatric patients than among community samples (Dohrenwend 1972, pp. 485–486). This raised the possibility that among patients the scales measured some stable problem, while among a community sample they reflected only transient stress to a larger extent.

Although many other community studies were carried out using global measures of psychological well-being, prevalence estimates of mental illness varied a great deal—from 1 percent to more than 50 percent—depending on how broad or restrictive the concepts of disorder were. Considering only more thorough studies involving direct interviews with subjects, Dohrenwend and Dohrenwend (1969) noted a tremendous increase in rates for functional psychiatric disorders in studies published after 1950 compared with those before. The only plausible interpretation of these findings was a broadening of definition of psychiatric disorder among researchers. The Dohrenwends (1969, 1974a, 1974b) strove laboriously to synthesize meaningful results from these diverse studies, but it is impossible to reconcile research outcomes based on varying definitions, especially with respect to less disabling nonpsychotic disorders.

Because of their shortcomings the results could not be used for psychiatric diagnostic purposes; however there was evidence that global impairment scales did reliably measure disabling distress, a factor underlying extensive personal suffering as well as the use of many types of medical and psychological assistance (Dohrenwend et al. 1979; Greenley and Mechanic 1976; Wheaton 1978). The scales tapped anxiety, sadness, psychophysiological symptoms, enervation, and a perception of poor health. Rather than a complex of unrelated complaints, a pattern emerged that seemed to reflect a single dimension of psychological malaise (Dohrenwend et al. 1979; Mechanic 1979).

To summarize, studies in this second generation of psychiatric epidemiology made two major contributions. First, they revealed that many more persons in the community had significant levels of psychological distress or emotional problems than was previously thought. More importantly, the research yielded a rich body of findings on the social correlates of psychiatric problems by highlighting that mental illness is not randomly distributed, but instead associated with, and potentially shaped by social context, particularly social class (Horwitz and Grob 2011). And as this reality was established, it galvanized a wave of investigation focusing on how inequality in people's access to power, resources, and status might also help to explain the occurrence of psychiatric problems.

A stumbling block to understanding the range of mental illnesses in the community remained—the lack of valid and reliable measurements for specific types of mental disorder. In the end, it was the introduction of *DSM-III*, and efforts to establish a correspondence between specific clinical diagnoses and research diagnostic criteria, that made possible a third generation of psychiatric epidemiology.

The first important study in this third generation was the Epidemiological Catchment Area (ECA) program (see Table 4.1), designed to gather prevalence rates of specific mental disorders and to examine their relationship to demographic factors, family history, life events, and neurobiological variables. The ultimate purpose was to gain a better understanding of etiology, clinical course, and treatment response in relation to specific disorders (National Institute of Mental Health 1985; Regier et al. 1984; Robins and Regier 1991). The ECA research undertaking was a collaborative epidemiological study of about 20,000 individuals in five sites: New Haven, Connecticut; Baltimore, Maryland; Saint Louis, Missouri; Los Angeles, California; and Durham, North Carolina. Estimates of disorder were weighted to represent the adult population of the United States (Eaton and Kessler 1985).

Here was an important methodological and conceptual shift in psychiatric epidemiology. Instead of symptom scales that measured distress or demoralization, the ECA study drew on a more refined specification of mental illness in line with definitions from *DSM-III* and other diagnostic systems common at the time (Robins and Regier 1991). ECA researchers gathered information about the number of adults living in the community who met clinical criteria for disorder (in other words, who would have been given that diagnosis if they did see a mental health provider). All sites used the Diagnostic Interview

Schedule (DIS), an instrument developed for administration by lay interviewers in 45–75 minutes. Of primary interest were the occurrence of symptoms, their intensity and persistence, and time of first appearance, all information mirroring the checklist of criteria found in *DSM-III* for different disorders. Scoring by computer algorithm defined whether an individual met the criteria for a probable or definite diagnosis for each illness.

ECA results again confirmed the wide scope of mental illness in the general community. Approximately 32 percent of the U.S. population was estimated to meet the criteria for having one disorder in their lifetime, and 20 percent met the criteria for mental illness during the past 12 months (Robins and Regier 1991). The ECA also made clear the wide range of prevalence for specific disorders. The highest 12-month prevalence was found for phobias (8.8 percent), followed by alcohol use/dependence (6.3 percent), with severe disorders such as schizophrenia/schizophreniform disorders being relatively rare (about 1.0 percent).

Following the ECA was the National Comorbidity Survey (NCS), a congressionally mandated study that similarly administered a structured diagnostic interview among a representative sample of the noninstitutionalized civilian population of the United States between ages of 15 and 54 (Kessler et al. 1994a). Unlike the ECA, which was restricted to five population centers, the NCS included respondents from the 48 contiguous U.S. states. The instrument was a modified version of the Composite International Diagnostic Interview (CIDI), itself an adaptation of the DIS from the ECA study. Like the DIS, trained interviewers, not clinicians, administered the CIDI. The format allowed diagnostic estimates consistent with *DSM-III-R* criteria, as well as certain comparisons consistent with *DSM-IV* and the diagnostic criteria for research found in the International Classification of Diseases, Version 10 (ICD-10). Highly sophisticated, the NCS achieved a response rate of 82.6 percent. A supplemental survey followed up aggressively with those who refused to participate in the survey to gauge possible selection bias, and these nonrespondents were found to have higher rates of disorder. As a result, overall rates of disorder were adjusted statistically to take account of this factor.

Like the ECA study, the NCS highlighted the high prevalence of disorder in the community (almost 50 percent met the criteria for at least one lifetime disorder), thereby confirming earlier research (Kessler et al. 1994a). However, valuable new information was collected on patterns of comorbidity. The researchers found that 14 percent of the population met the criteria for three or more disorders over their lifetime, while the majority of those with at least one disorder had three or more. In fact, more than half of all lifetime disorders identified in the study occurred among about one-seventh of the sample having three or more comorbidities. Almost three-fifths of disorders in the prior 12 months also appeared in this same subsample. Thus, the NCS identified a particular segment of the population accounting for most people who have a severe disorder, high levels of impairment, and strong need for mental health services. From a policy standpoint, these individuals with comorbidities constitute the most critical target population in regard to planning public services and supports.

The most recent estimates of disorder come from the National Comorbidity Survey Replication (NCS-R) fielded from 2001 to 2003 (Kessler et al. 1994b; Kessler and Merikangas 1994). This study was designed to provide more up-to-date estimates of the prevalence of disorder while assessing any changes in prevalence, service use, and attitudes toward care since the earlier study. It also encompassed a greater number of disorders than previously. There were certain methodological innovations, but the research continued to employ a diagnostic instrument (the WMH-CIDI) that could be administered by laypersons (Kessler and Ustun 1994).

As shown in Table 4.1, national studies indicate a large increase in mental illness estimates between the time of the ECA and the NCS surveys (e.g., 12-month estimates went from about 20 to 30 percent). Such estimates, however, do not necessarily mean that prevalence actually increased. They reflect differences in methodology, the diagnostic interview used, and the fact that the sample selected for the NCS was younger (15–54) than for the ECA study (18+). Indeed, when Regier and colleagues (1998) re-estimated prevalence using ECA data for the same age group as in the NCS, they found 12-month rates of disorder to be quite similar (24 percent in the ECA, 29 percent in the NCS). When they included further information of past disorders from ECA respondents who were reinterviewed within one year, the rates of lifetime disorder from the two surveys were even closer (47 percent in ECA, 48 percent in NCS). This finding highlights problems of recall as a potential source of bias in estimates of lifetime prevalence. Respondents interviewed at two points in time do not necessarily report the same history of symptoms or service use.

Given that the NCS-R provides the most recent national estimates, we will focus on this survey in examining the prevalence of specific disorders in the United States. One note of caution is in order, however. The NCS-R did not include institutionalized populations (such as people in hospitals, nursing homes, jails, or prisons) or the homeless. To the degree these groups are at increased risk for mental illness, the NCS-R underestimates true population prevalence.

Given the difficulty of obtaining accurate data by asking people to recall the experience of symptoms over long periods of time, we will concentrate mostly on estimates of 12-month disorders. As exhibited in Table 4.2, the most common class of disorder in the NCS-R

Table 4.2 Twelve-Month Prevalence of Specific Disorders in Adult Population (NCS-R)

	12-month		
	Total	Women	Men
Mood Disorder	9.7	11.6	7.7
Major Depression	6.8	8.6	4.9
Bipolar	2.8	2.8	2.9
Anxiety Disorder	19.1	23.4	14.3
Specific Phobia	9.1	12.2	5.8
Social Phobia	7.1	8.0	6.1
Posttraumatic Stress Disorder	3.6	5.2	1.8
Obsessive-Compulsive Disorder	1.2	1.8	0.5
Impulse Control	10.5	9.3	11.7
Conduct Disorder	1.0	0.4	1.7
Attention Deficit/Hyperactivity	4.1	3.9	4.3
Oppositional-Defiant	1.0	1.1	0.9

(Continued)

(Continued)

	12-month		
	Total	Women	Men
Substance Use	13.4	11.6	15.4
Alcohol Abuse/Dependence	3.1	1.8	4.5
Drug Abuse/Dependence	1.4	0.7	2.2
Any Disorder	32.4	34.7	29.9

Source: From www.hcp.med.harvard.edu/ncs/ftpdir/NCS-R_12-month_Prevalence_Estimates.pdf.

Note: Estimates of any mood disorder also include dysthymia; anxiety disorders also include panic, agoraphobia, generalized anxiety, adult separation disorder; any impulse control also includes intermittent explosive; substance use disorders also include nicotine dependence.

was anxiety, with specific phobias (such as fear of animals, flying, or closed spaces) and social phobia the most common types. Substance use disorders were the second most common class if nicotine dependence is included, with alcohol use disorder being more common than drug disorder. Approximately 7 percent of the population reported experiencing an episode of major depression during the preceding 12-month time period.

Consistent with many earlier studies, the NCS-R showed that risk of disorder varies by gender. Women are more likely than men to experience mood and anxiety disorders. In contrast, men are more likely than women to experience impulse control and substance use disorders.

ANALYTICAL QUANDARIES

The third generation of psychiatric epidemiology made a key contribution by document-ing mental illness as a common experience that varies predictably with particular demo-graphic factors. However, the validity of NCS-R results have continued to be the subject of debate (Anthony et al. 1985; McNally 2011; Mechanic 2003; Robins 1985). First, the meth-odological approach relies on individuals' ability to remember symptoms, a questionable assumption. Moreover, the cases of mental illness identified by means of survey interviews are not necessarily those individuals who would be identified as disordered by clinicians. To be sure, clinician judgment is not necessarily reliable or valid; one can question whether such assessments define the "gold standard" of diagnosis. Still, if forced to choose, most people would favor the views of a well-trained clinician over standardized questions easily misunderstood by respondents.

Simply counting the number of people with disorders in the community is also not particularly helpful in policy formulation. Large numbers from the ECA, NCS, and NCS-R projects may alert officials and the public to the potential magnitude of mental health problems, but such estimates combine serious and persistent disorders with others that are transitory or not disabling. There is also good reason to believe that the procedures for approximating *DSM* categories within these surveys are over-inclusive, resulting in many false-positive judgments of illness in the community (Wakefield 1997).

Recognizing these concerns, researchers have tried to produce more refined estimates to take into account the severity of illness. With respect to the NCS-R, when severity is defined by such metrics as whether the respondent had suicide ideation or attempts, reported significant activity limitations or disability days, or presented evidence of nonaffective psychoses, only a minority of cases meeting the criteria for specific types of illness qualify as severe disorders (Kessler et al. 2005a). For example, as shown in Figure 4.1, while about 22 million adults in the United States in 2011 are estimated to have experienced a mood disorder in the past year, as many as 12 million of these are characterized as not serious. Overall, using revised estimates, about 6 percent of the adult population, or about 14 million people in 2011, met the criteria for a serious disorder in a given year.

Results from the NCS-R also point to conceptual problems in trying to classify disorders into distinct types. Kessler and colleagues (2005a) correlated the occurrence of different types of disorders; more than 40 percent of people with one mental disorder during a 12-month period also had a comorbid mental illness. Internalizing disorders such as anxiety and depression tend to co-occur, as do externalizing disorders such as intermittent explosive disorder and substance use problems.

Schizophrenia, one of the most severe and debilitating of all mental illnesses, is a major exclusion from disorders reported by the NCS-R. The ECA study estimated one-year prevalence of schizophrenia to be .06–.07 percent, and the lifetime rate to be about 1.5 percent (Robins and Regier 1991). The NCS estimated the lifetime prevalence of nonaffective psychosis including schizophrenia at about 0.6 percent, with the one-year rate about 0.5 percent (Kessler et al. 1994a). While the NCS-R attempted to screen for cases of nonaffective psychosis, the research group concluded that problems of nonresponse

Figure 4.1 • Estimated Mentally Ill Population Aged 18 and Above by Severity of Illness, 2011

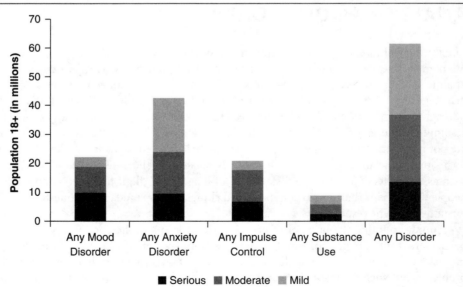

Source: Based on estimates presented in Kessler et al. (2005a) and U.S. Census estimates of the population in 2011 (U.S. Census Bureau 2012), available online: www.census.gov/popest/data/index.html.

for persons with the disorder, coupled with the exclusion of institutional populations, led to invalid estimates (Kessler et al. 2005c).

Psychiatric epidemiologists in at least 46 other countries have gathered data on the occurrence of schizophrenia. Included is a series of international studies, sponsored by the World Health Organization (WHO), which began in 1960 as the International Pilot Study of Schizophrenia (IPSS) (Hopper et al. 2007). Lifetime prevalence estimates derived from this and other work ranged from four to seven cases per 1,000 people (Saha et al. 2005). The most striking finding from worldwide studies was that the prevalence of schizophrenia is higher in developed than developing countries.

The IPSS demonstrated that it was possible to measure schizophrenia across quite diverse cultural settings, and that the course of disorder might depend on the setting. These provocative findings provided impetus for further international studies coordinated by the WHO (Hopper et al. 2007), collectively known as the International Study of Schizophrenia (ISoS). According to this work, the annual incidence of schizophrenia is similar across countries (about 0.1–0.4 cases per 1,000 population), but the prognosis for schizophrenia is worse in developed nations, accounting for the higher prevalence estimates.

CONTINUED USE OF SYMPTOM INDEXES

While diagnostic instruments such as the WMH-CIDI possess the advantage of providing estimates of disorder that reflect the criteria found in *DSM-IV*, they are impractical for public health surveillance for many research purposes. Diagnostic interviews are complicated to administer in community surveys, depend on trained interviewers, are expensive, and require considerable time. The full interview schedule in the NCS-R took about 90 minutes for respondents who had no disorders and an average of 2.5 hours for respondents who did report a disorder (Kessler et al. 1994b). It is not surprising, therefore, that symptom indexes similar to those used in the second generation of psychiatric epidemiology continue to be used frequently. One measure popular since the 1970s is the Center for Epidemiological Studies Depression (CESD) scale (Radloff 1977). The CESD consists of 20 items pertaining to relatively common symptoms of depressed mood—feeling sad, lonely, depressed, completely helpless, or fearful; having crying spells; wondering if anything is worthwhile anymore; not being able to get going; and so on. More recently, there have been shorter versions available (e.g., Andresen et al. 1994). The CESD has high reliability and is successful in screening for a problem of serious depression. However, the measure overlaps greatly with distress in response to life stressors, and large numbers of persons who score high would not be regarded as depressed by clinicians.

Too many of these screening scales now exist to allow a complete review here (see Mitchell and Coyne 2010 for examples of common measures of depression). A few examples should suffice in illustrating their use and limitations within community epidemiological research and clinical settings.

The K6 is a six-item screening scale developed for use in the National Health Interview Survey (NHIS), the largest annual survey of the health of the American population (Kessler et al. 2002, 2003). It was designed to measure nonspecific psychological distress. The six items were chosen from the original 10-item version of the scale (K10) and include common symptoms of depression and anxiety, such as feeling helpless, worthless, and restless or fidgety over the past month (Kessler et al. 2003). The original K6 was validated against a clinical measure, and it adequately discriminated between individuals who met the criteria for a *DSM-IV* depressive or anxiety disorder and who reported problems in functioning versus other respondents. Items were slightly revised in response to the Substance Abuse and Mental Health Services Administration's (SAMHSA) need for state estimates of the number of adults with serious mental illness (SMI), as part of applications for block grant funding to provide community mental health services. K6's appeal was that it could be administered quickly, in less than two minutes, and researchers proposed that a K6 score of 13 or more indicated serious mental illness.

Yet concerns have surfaced regarding K6 as a measurement tool producing too many false positives of SMI. As a result, it was recast, in name only, to serve as a measure of serious psychological distress (SPD). Estimates of serious psychological distress among adults per month have ranged from 2.4 to 3.5 percent between 1997 and 2011. Therefore, about 8.2 million adults experienced SPD in the past month in 2011 (Centers for Disease Control and Prevention 2011).

The acceptance of K6 as a common measure of mental illness is a noteworthy development. Since 1997, the scale has been used as part of the National Health Interview Survey (NHIS). It is included in the mental health and stigma module of the Behavioral Risk Factor Surveillance System (BRFSS), the most important state-based annual survey of health (Croft et al. 2009). Moreover, it is also present in the National Survey of Drug Use and Health (NSDUH), the largest annual survey of the prevalence of substance use (Substance Abuse and Mental Health Services Administration 2010), as well as the Medical Expenditure Panel Survey (MEPS), the most important source of health care cost information in the United States. Now translated into many languages, K6 has played a role in many studies in the United States and internationally (e.g., Browne et al. 2010; Caron and Liu 2010; Castaneda et al. 2010). Nonetheless, very little work has been done validating the scale.

A second common instrument is the Patient Health Questionnaire (PHQ) depression scale (Kroenke, Spitzer, and Williams 2001). This tool was developed with funding from Pfizer, the largest drug manufacturer in the world. The original scale (PHQ-9) had nine items that mirrored the diagnostic criteria for depression from *DSM-IV*, and a cut-point was established to distinguish cases of major depression. Alternatively, the scale can serve as a continuous measure to grade depression severity (Kroenke, Spitzer, and Williams 2001). The PHQ-9 has been used extensively to assess depression in clinical settings and as part of monitoring responses to treatment (Butler et al. 2008). But recently, it has become more common in psychiatric epidemiological work in the community. A version of the PHQ-9 (the PHQ-8) has also been incorporated into the BRFSS (Kroenke et al. 2009); thus, state health departments can choose to estimate the prevalence of depression in the specific populations for which they are responsible. Pressures to reduce the time it takes to detect the presence of depression have led to a two-item version of the scale (PHQ-2) asking only about the frequency of "feeling down, depressed or hopeless" and "having little interest or pleasure in doing things" (Kroenke, Spitzer, and Williams 2003). While follow-up with a full diagnostic interview is recommended in cases of suspected illness, the abbreviated scale is commonly used in screening for probable depression in community and clinical populations.

Short symptoms scales have an obvious appeal. They can readily be incorporated into larger health surveillance efforts to track the prevalence of psychological problems over time and among subgroups of special interest. They can also relatively easily be incorporated into clinical care. In 2002, the United States Preventive Services Task Force (USPSTF) recommended all adults undergo screening for depression as part of receiving primary care (Pignone et al. 2002). Task force members argued that a two-item test like the PHQ-2 performed just as well as much-longer screening tools. In 2008, the American Heart Association recommended screening for depression among cardiac patients (Lichtman et al. 2008). The American Academy of Pediatrics subsequently called for screening mothers for postpartum depression (Earls and The Committee on Psychosocial Aspects of Child and Family Health 2010). And, most broadly, each October there is an annual depression screening day across the United States when the general public is encouraged to undergo screening on an anonymous basis and seek follow-up treatment if probable depression is detected. However, while it may be intuitively appealing to implement programs that identify cases of common mental illnesses, there is as yet no evidence that screening on a large scale in this way results in reductions in symptoms, or increased rates of remission, for persons suffering from depression (McAlpine and Wilson 2004; Mitchell and Coyne 2010; Ziegelstein et al. 2009).

Just as there were concerns about estimates derived from such symptom scales during the second generation of psychiatric epidemiology, so too should there be concerns today about their use. They may overestimate the prevalence of mental health problems while not adequately capturing the most severe cases of disorder. In and of themselves, symptoms do not equate to the need for treatment (Mechanic 2003).

SPECIAL POPULATIONS

Children and Adolescents

Our understanding of the epidemiology of mental health and illness among children and adolescents lags far behind that for adults. When it occurs early in human development, mental illness manifests itself very differently than when it occurs among adults, and the meaningfulness of particular behaviors varies a great deal by age. Unfortunately, because of diagnostic and assessment difficulties, the epidemiology of childhood and adolescent disorders is not well established. The usual difficulties of psychiatric epidemiology reviewed earlier can become compounded for this population group. However, the situation has improved somewhat with the implementation of the National Comorbidity Survey-Adolescent Supplement (NCS-A), and the addition of a mental health diagnostic instrument to the National Health and Nutrition Examination Survey (NHANES).

The NCS-A was a nationally representative sample of adolescents between the ages of 13 and 18 in the 48 contiguous states (Kessler et al. 2012; Merikangas et al. 2010a). It included both a household and a school sample. In addition to parental completion of a questionnaire about each sampled adolescent, the study administered a modified version of the same diagnostic instrument used in the NCS-R study of adults to the adolescent respondents. Adolescent and parental reports were then used in combination to assess whether the criteria for specific disorders were met.

Table 4.3 summarizes the estimates of lifetime prevalence (Merikangas et al. 2010a). As shown, about 50 percent of adolescents met the criteria for lifetime prevalence for at least one disorder, with the most common being anxiety and behavior disorders. Girls were more likely than boys to have an anxiety or a mood disorder, while boys had higher

Table 4.3   Estimates of the Lifetime Prevalence of Specific Disorders in Adolescent Population Age 13–18 (NCS-A)

	Lifetime		
	Total	Females	Males
Mood Disorder	14.3	18.3	10.5
Major Depression or Dysthymia	11.7	15.9	7.7
Bipolar	2.9	3.3	2.6
Anxiety Disorder	31.9	38.0	26.1
Specific Phobia	19.3	22.1	16.7
Social Phobia	9.1	11.2	7.0
Separation Anxiety Disorder	7.6	9.0	6.3
Behavior Disorders	19.6	15.5	23.5
Conduct Disorder	6.8	5.8	7.9
Attention Deficit/Hyperactivity	8.7	4.2	13.0
Oppositional Defiant	12.6	11.3	13.9
Substance Use	11.4	10.2	12.5
Alcohol Abuse/Dependence	6.4	5.8	7.0
Drug Abuse/Dependence	8.9	8.0	9.8
Eating Disorders	2.7	3.8	1.5
Any Disorder	49.5	51.0	48.1

Source: Merikangas et al. (2010a).

Note: Anxiety Disorder also includes agoraphobia, generalized anxiety disorder, panic disorder, and posttraumatic stress disorder.

rates of behavior disorder. Additional research with the NCS-A showed the 12-month prevalence of disorder to be about 40 percent and the one-month prevalence to be about 23 percent (Kessler et al. 2012). Moreover, almost 10 percent of adolescents had three or more disorders in the past year.

Analysis of incidence indicates that anxiety disorders begin very early in life, with the risk leveling off at about age 12 (Merikangas et al. 2010a). In contrast, risk for mood or substance use disorder is low until about age 12, after which it increases markedly.

As with the adult estimates reviewed earlier, one must be circumspect in interpreting these numbers. When we narrow the definition to severe disorder, the estimates become more conservative. Merikangas and colleagues (2010a) estimate that about 22 percent of adolescents have experienced a mental disorder associated with severe impairment in their lifetime.

A second national survey (2001–2004 NHANES) used the NIMH Diagnostic Interview Schedule for Children (DISC-V) to estimate the prevalence of disorder among young people ages 8–15 (Merikangas et al. 2010b). Its estimate of 13 percent prevalence during the preceding 12 months was much lower than NCS-A results, as was the 11 percent figure for significant impairment. These different estimates may be due to the different age ranges and disorders surveyed. However, both studies highlighted that many children and adolescents have mental health problems. Restricting estimates from each study to the most severe impairments yields estimates in 2010 of 5.7 million children ages 13–18 and 3.6 million children ages 8–15 with mental disorder.

An important developmental problem whose prevalence generates significant public health consequences is attention deficit hyperactivity disorder (ADHD). Although initially seen as a problem primarily affecting children and beginning early in life, prior to age 7, today the diagnosis is increasingly being applied to older adolescents and adults who display similar behaviors or attention difficulties. In fact, proposed modifications within *DSM-5* would make up to 12 years old the criterion for beginning age of disorder (American Psychiatric Association 2012). According to experts, there are three different subgroups under the overall category of ADHD: those individuals primarily with hyperactive and impulsive symptoms; those primarily with problems of inattention and distraction; and the most common group combining both types of symptoms. Children often have depression and anxiety comorbidities along with ADHD. Diagnosis is typically made by parent and teacher reports, less frequently by standardized measurement of child behavior. Contact within the medical system is often with pediatricians and general physicians, rather than mental health specialists, so reported estimates can vary greatly. One review reported estimated prevalence rates from less than 2 percent to almost 18 percent (Rowland, Lesesne, and Abramowitz 2002). Estimates tend to be higher for schoolchildren facing attention and conformity demands that are greater and more rigid than usual. Citing the unsystematic diagnostic process based on different types of reports, coupled with a rapidly rising number of cases, some observers dispute whether ADHD is a real disorder as opposed to the medicalization of disruptive behaviors (Conrad 2006; Conrad and Potter 2000). In addition, estimates of ADHD vary widely internationally (Polanczyk et al. 2007). There is little question, however, that ADHD, at its core, represents a serious impairment for some subset of children, one that can imperil success in school, job, and other social contexts (Hinshaw and Scheffler forthcoming). The diagnosis is at least twice as common among boys as girls, although some believe the normal rambunctiousness of boys contributes to this excess.

As Table 4.2 shows, the NCS-R estimated a prevalence rate of 4 percent for ADHD among the population 18 years and older during the preceding 12 months. Table 4.3 shows lifetime prevalence of 8.7 percent for adolescents aged 13–18 in the NCS-A. Generally, estimates in the literature, including *DSM-IV* documents, put the prevalence of ADHD among school-age children at 3–5 percent, but there is no strong empirical basis for this judgment (Rowland, Lesesne, and Abramowitz 2002).

Other important pervasive developmental problems exist that are still not captured by national surveys. An examination of the measurement of autism provides an example of not only the difficult methodological and conceptual challenges faced by psychiatric epidemiology in case identification but also the importance of estimates in shaping public attitudes and policy.

"Autism spectrum disorder" (ASD) is a term referring to an array of neurological and developmental problems (typical autism, Asperger syndrome, and pervasive developmental disorders not otherwise classified) often grouped together in common parlance. Typical age of onset is during the first three years of life, and symptoms include engaging in repetitive or circumscribed behaviors combined with difficulty in socializing and communicating (Fombonne 2009). Historically, autism was considered to be a very rare, but debilitating, disorder. In recent decades, however, the image of autism has changed. In a review of international studies, Williams, Higgins, and Brayne (2006) found a pooled prevalence rate of 7.1 per 10,000 children for typical autism and 20.0 per 10,000 children for ASD, but there was large variation in estimates across studies. What has captured the attention of the public, policymakers, and researchers is an apparent recent increase in autism in the United States and many other nations. In 1983, approximately 4.6 per 1,000 American children were diagnosed with autism compared to about 11 per 1,000 in 2007 (Al-Qabandi, Gorter and Rosenbaum 2011). In 2000, the Centers for Disease Control and Prevention (CDC) implemented the Autism and Developmental Disabilities Monitoring (ADDM) Network to estimate prevalence of ASD based on records of providers who treat, educate, or evaluate children with developmental disabilities (Van Naarden Braun et al. 2007). According to CDC's 2009 report, in the 10 study sites that were included during both periods the average prevalence was 9.4 per 1,000 children aged 8, up from 6 per 1,000 found in 2002, a large increase in four years (Rice 2009). These findings added to growing concern about the prevalence of autism.

The CDC has continued development of its monitoring network, reporting in 2012 on the prevalence of ASD in 14 sites across the United States. Researchers observed a prevalence of 11.3 per 1,000 (one case for every 88 children aged 8 years). ASD was almost five times more common among boys than girls. Rates were much higher among black and Hispanic children, and estimates varied almost fivefold across sites, from 4.8 to 21.2 per 1,000. The 14 sites did not represent the entire United States, and rates might be considerably different in areas for which we have no data. Nevertheless, information regarding these very high rates and their distribution reflects a complex process of ASD identification that is interconnected with services availability, help-seeking processes, and changing sensitivity to diagnosis.

The sense of crisis surrounding autism ripened with the publication of a now infamous article in the British medical journal *The Lancet* by Wakefield and others (1998). It claimed evidence of a connection between childhood immunization and autism, a claim that has since been retracted. Yet concern that the preservative thimerosal used in common vaccines might be responsible for the apparent rise in incidence and prevalence caused a furor (Baker 2008). Congressional investigation followed. The American Academy of Pediatrics and the CDC recommended against vaccination of infants for hepatitis B until new vaccines without thimerosal could be developed. Thousands of claims were taken to the National Vaccine Injury Compensation Program by parents who believed vaccination had caused autism and other disorders in their children (Moreland 2008).

The tumult around the connection between immunization and the incidence of autism took place despite repeated evidence that no link existed (Institute of Medicine 2001, 2004). Analysts grew concerned about whether the apparent rise in autism was real or rather an artifact of greater awareness of the disorder. A related possibility was expansion in the types of behaviors considered under the diagnostic umbrella of ASD. Funding for autism research and treatment outpaced other developmental disorders, including some of which are much more common (Liu, King, and Bearman 2010).

A series of studies examining autism in California offered several explanations for rising incidence rates (King and Bearman 2009; King et al. 2009; Liu, King, and Bearman 2010). Investigators documented the substitution of the diagnosis of autism for mental retardation, a factor that could be extrapolated to account for as much as one-quarter of the upward trend in ASD in the general population. In other work, these same researchers focused on a demographic shift toward later childbearing, which represents an important risk factor for the occurrence of autism (King et al. 2009; Liu, Zerubavel, and Bearman 2010). Also, strong evidence indicated that localities that provide good services for children with ASD draw families who are seeking services for children who appear to have developmental problems.

While a number of studies have observed that older parents are more likely to have children with autism, explanations for this age effect have been highly speculative. In 2012, investigators in Iceland sequenced the genomes of 78 Icelandic trios of mother, father, and child, of whom 44 of the children had autism spectrum disorder. Although it is established that autism is highly heritable, the investigators sought mutations in the child that were not present in either parent, thus resulting spontaneously from sperm, egg, or embryo. Their major discovery was that fathers passed on four times as many mutations in their sperm as women in their eggs and accounted for nearly all the variations in new mutations in children. Moreover, there was a powerful relationship between father's age and such mutations (Callaway 2012; Kong et al. 2012). Sperm is continually produced by dividing cells while women are born with a finite collection of egg cells, explaining the greater likelihood of mutations to occur in sperm. The study also included a smaller number of cases of schizophrenic outcomes (21) with comparable findings. The study does not prove the case but provides a strong suggestion that increases in the prevalence of autism may result, in part, from later marriage and childbearing.

On the one hand, even if the increase in incidence rates is driven by diagnostic changes or demographic shifts, one might argue that greater recognition and awareness is a positive development in its own right, particularly if it means enhanced identification of children with problems who might benefit from early intervention. On the other hand, we should be concerned about the possibility of pathologizing an increasing range of behaviors under the umbrella of autism.

Recent research has extended the investigation of early mental disorders to groups as young as preschoolers (Rescorla et al. 2011). Egger and Angold (2006) reviewed data from four studies assessing a range of disorders in children ages 2–5 by applying *DSM-III* or *DSM-IV* criteria in community or primary care samples. An estimated 22–26 percent of these children had at least one disorder. Overall, oppositional defiant disorder had the highest prevalence, although the rates ranged widely (from 4 to almost 17 percent). Only two studies gauged the seriousness of the disorder. When this more restricted definition was applied, it was estimated that between 9 and 12 percent of preschoolers had a serious emotional disorder. The authors concluded that the prevalence of many mental disorders in preschoolers approaches that found among older children.

These studies suffer from many of the same methodological problems reviewed above for the psychiatric epidemiology of adolescence and adulthood. There is also a larger conceptual issue. Behaviors and emotions that characterize many of these disorders (bad behavior, crying fits, etc.) are part of normal development for many children. It is not clear whether the evidence base exists for carrying over to early childhood categories of mental disorder that were originally developed for understanding adulthood, yet this is the trend in psychiatric epidemiologic studies.

The Elderly

Table 4.4 summarizes data from the NCS-R regarding the association between age and disorder. For each class of disorder, 12-month prevalence is lowest among those 60 years and older. Estimates of the occurrence of any past disorder are several times higher among persons aged 18–29 compared to persons 60 years of age and older. The most common specific disorder for older persons is phobias (5.6 percent), while about 3 percent meet the criteria for major depression during the past year.

While not shown in the tables, lifetime prevalence for each class of disorder reaches its peak in the 30–44 age group and is lowest for persons 60 years and older, a seeming paradox given that older people have had more time at risk to experience a mental illness. At first glance, the declining prevalence of the 12-month disorder would indicate that as

Table 4.4 Estimates of the Prevalence of Disorders by Age Group (NCS-R)

	12-month Prevalence			
	18–29	30–44	45–59	60+
Mood Disorder	12.9	11.9	9.4	3.6
Major Depression	8.3	8.4	7.0	2.9
Bipolar	4.7	3.5	2.2	0.7
Anxiety Disorder	22.3	22.7	20.6	9.0
Specific Phobia	10.3	9.7	10.3	5.6
Social Phobia	9.1	8.7	6.8	3.1
Posttraumatic Stress Disorder	4.0	3.5	5.3	1.0
Obsessive-Compulsive Disorder	1.5	1.4	1.1	0.5
Impulse Control	11.9	9.2	—	—
Conduct Disorder	1.4	0.8	—	—
Attention Deficit/Hyperactivity	3.9	4.2	—	—
Oppositional-Defiant	1.2	0.8	—	—
Substance Use	22.0	13.8	11.2	5.9
Alcohol Abuse with/without Dependence	7.1	3.3	1.6	0.3
Drug Abuse with/without Dependence	3.9	1.2	0.4	0.0
Any Disorder	43.8	36.9	31.1	15.5

Source: From www.hcp.med.harvard.edu/ncs/ftpdir/NCS-R_12-month_Prevalence_Estimates.pdf.

Note: Estimates of any mood disorder also include dysthymia; anxiety disorders also include panic, agoraphobia, generalized anxiety, adult separation disorder; any impulse control also includes intermittent explosive; substance use disorders also include nicotine dependence. Specific types of impulse control disorders were not asked for respondents 45 years and older.

one ages, he or she is less likely to experience a mental illness. A declining prevalence in lifetime disorder, despite increased time at risk, might suggest important cohort differences in risk of disorder. That is, persons born more recently are more likely to experience mental illness than those born in earlier periods (Kessler et al. 2005b).

Conceptual and methodological uncertainties, however, make it premature to draw such conclusions (Mechanic and McAlpine 2011). First, it is not clear whether the diagnostic criteria used to define mental illness in community surveys apply equally well across all ages. The *DSM-IV*, on which diagnostic instruments in community samples are based, does not address potential age differences in the expression of various types of illness. Some research suggests that many older persons experience depression in terms of somatic symptoms, such as feelings of pain, that are not included in common measures of this disorder (Drayer et al. 2005). Second, mental illness is associated with mortality (Piatt, Munetz, and Ritter 2010). Simply put, the most severely ill may die before they reach older age, partially accounting for lower prevalence of disorder among the elderly. Third, in the case of lifetime prevalence, estimates require people to recall symptoms experienced in the past—for the elderly that means looking back decades. In a study of the test–retest reliability of reports of depressive symptoms, Thompson and others (2004) found that approximately 40 percent of those who reported a lifetime history of depressed mood in 1981 did not report such a history when reinterviewed in 1994 (Thompson et al. 2004). While NCS-R included methods to improve recall, it is still likely that age differences in reporting errors distort estimates of age differences in the prevalence of disorder.

Neither of the NCS studies assessed cognitive impairment or dementia, although cognitive impairments, Alzheimer's disease, and other dementias substantially increase at older ages. The largest national study of the prevalence of various types of cognitive impairment over later life is the Aging, Demographics, and Memory Study (ADAMS) (Plassman et al. 2007, 2008). Between 2001 and 2003, individuals 71 years and older from the Health and Retirement Survey were sampled and given in-depth personal interviews and clinical assessments. The project employed key informant interviews for any respondents who, due to cognitive impairment, could not provide self-reported data. Overall, the prevalence of any dementia for persons over the age of 70 was about 14 percent, and the prevalence of Alzheimer's was 9.7 percent. More than one-fifth (22.2 percent) of the population also met the criteria for cognitive impairment without dementia.

As shown in Figure 4.2, risk of cognitive disorder and dementias sharply increases with age. Among persons 90 years of age and above, more than one-third had dementia and almost 30 percent had Alzheimer's disease. A further 39 percent showed evidence of significant cognitive impairment without dementia.

Depression is more common among persons with cognitive impairments, thus community studies such as the NCS that exclude cognitively impaired respondents may underestimate the true prevalence of depression in later life (Steffens et al. 2009). Indeed, the ADAMS project found that approximately 11 percent of the population over age 70 met the criteria for depression, and rates were higher for persons 90 years of age and older (12.1 percent) than for those 71–79 years of age (10.4 percent) (Steffens et al. 2009).

Community studies such as the NCS-R also do not include persons living in institutional settings. Approximately 3 percent of the population over age 65, and 25 percent of the population over age 95, live in nursing homes, and they are excluded from these estimates (Werner 2011). It is difficult to know true prevalence of mental illness in nursing homes,

Figure 4.2 • National Prevalence of Cognitive Impairment and Dementia by Age

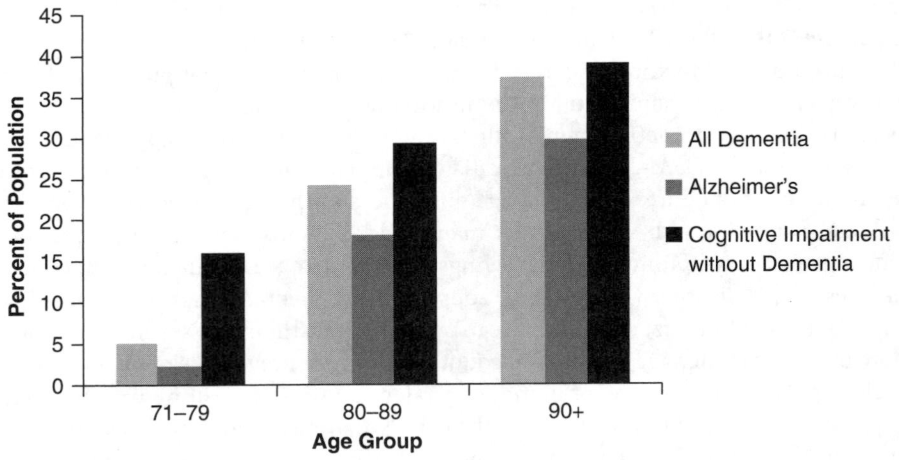

Source: Aging, Demographics and Memory Study, Plassman et al. (2007, 2008).

because researchers typically rely on estimates derived from diagnosed cases. Using this method, Fullerton and others (2009) state that almost one-quarter of persons admitted to a nursing home in 2005 were diagnosed with mental illness—schizophrenia, bipolar disorder, depression, or anxiety disorders—compared to 18 percent admitted with dementia. Further, many nursing home residents have a secondary diagnosis of mental illness, especially depression (Mechanic and McAlpine 2000). People with severe mental illness may be at increased risk for institutionalization in the nursing home setting. In an analysis of Medicaid beneficiaries in New Hampshire, for example, Andrews and colleagues (2009) found that persons with schizophrenia were likely to enter nursing homes at much younger ages (median age 65) than their counterparts without mental illness (median age 80).

Finally, it is important to consider the question of the relationship between age of onset and incidence of disorder. According to Kessler and colleagues (2005b), who analyzed data from NCS-R, the median age of onset for having at least one of the common disorders, such as depression, anxiety, conduct disorder, and substance abuse, was 14 years of age. Risk for anxiety disorder and impulse control disorder occurs earlier in life (median age of onset 11 years) than either mood disorder (30 years) or substance use disorder (20 years). Overall, 95 percent of all cases of any disorder are estimated to have first appeared before the age of 51. While there are methodological issues, the study does confirm many earlier ones that concluded mental disorders often have onset in childhood or young adulthood, and there are few new cases of these types of disorders in late life.

RACE, ETHNICITY, AND CULTURE

In the United States, the typical race and ethnic categories used in research reflect the Office of Management and Budget's classification system: White, Hispanic, Black, Asian, Native Hawaiian or Other Pacific Islander, and American Indian or Alaska

Native (Office of Management and Budget 1997). Most research in the mental health field conceives of race and ethnicity as social, not biological, categories (Williams 1997). Race/ethnic categories reflect shared histories, social conditions, and experiences of oppression or advantage. Of course, culture and race are not synonymous. While researchers often use race or ethnicity as a proxy for cultural differences between groups, culture is much broader. Culture reflects the norms, values, and ways of acting shared by a group that is defined by such characteristics as geography, language, nationality, or race and ethnicity.

In 2001, the U.S. Department of Health and Human Services published *Mental Health: Culture, Race, and Ethnicity* as a supplement to the influential Surgeon General's Report on Mental Health released two years earlier (U.S. Department of Health and Human Services 1999, 2001). The analysis was commissioned, in part, due to the dissatisfaction of stakeholders with the original report's lack of attention to race and culture. Indeed, Nelba Chavez, head of the SAMHSA at the time, refused to sign off on the original Surgeon General's Report on Mental Health because she felt it had given inadequate attention to race, ethnicity, and culture (Chavez 2003). One of the many problems spotlighted by the supplement was the lack of sufficient data at the national level to provide valid estimates of the prevalence of specific disorders among major racial or ethnic groups.

National surveys reviewed in the supplement included the ECA study and the NCS, which had inconsistent findings about race and ethnic variation in mental illness. The ECA research found that Whites and African Americans had similar rates of most disorders, with the exception of depression and phobias (Robins and Regier 1991). African Americans had higher rates of phobias, while Whites had higher rates of depression. More generally, however, the NCS found lower rates of disorder in populations from minority cultural groups compared to Whites. The NCS-R generally replicated these findings that non-Hispanic Blacks and Hispanics have significantly lower risk of disorder than Whites (Breslau et al. 2005).

All these national studies had small samples of persons from minority ethnic groups, and interviews were conducted in English. These factors limited researchers' ability to capture the heterogeneity existing within broad racial categories. African Americans born in the United States are different from Blacks born in Africa, the Caribbean, or South America; Cubans, Mexicans, Puerto Ricans, and those from various South American countries differ as well. Similarly, Asian populations vary enormously in education, cultural background, and life experiences. Few studies have been large enough to capture such subgroup variations, nor are their samples adequate for purposes of multivariate analysis.

To address these problems, two national studies were conducted specifically focused on minority cultural groups, the National Latino and Asian American Study (NLAAS) and the National Survey of American Life (NSAL). Together with the NCS-R, these projects make up the Collaborative Psychiatric Epidemiology Studies (CPES) (Heeringa et al. 2004). The methods of the NLAAS and the NSAL were designed so that comparisons of the prevalence of major disorders could be made with estimates from NCS-R.

The NSAL, fielded between 2001 and 2003, included a random sample of non-Hispanic Whites, African Americans, and Caribbean Blacks (Jackson et al. 2004). Results indicated that rates of lifetime depression were higher among Whites (17.9 percent) than Caribbean Blacks (12.9 percent) and African Americans (10.4 percent), while 12-month and 30-day prevalence were similar among the groups (Williams et al. 2007b). However, depression was more likely to be persistent among African Americans and Caribbean

Blacks than Whites (Williams et al. 2007b). Rates of anxiety disorder for Whites exceeded those for African Americans, with the exception of PTSD (Himle et al. 2009). With regard to subgroup differences, some important patterns emerged from the NSAL. Overall, risk for 12-month disorder was higher for Caribbean Black men than their African American counterparts; however, the opposite pattern held for women. Moreover, the duration of their stay in the United States increased the risk of disorder for Caribbean Blacks, indicating a potential acculturation effect (Williams et al. 2007a).

The NLAAS, fielded between 2002 and 2003 (Alegría et al. 2004; Alegría et al. 2008), was designed to gather information about mental health among the Latino and Asian adult populations. It oversampled Mexicans, Puerto Ricans, and Cubans within the Latino sample, and Chinese, Filipino, and Vietnamese adults within the Asian sample, to capture heterogeneous experiences. Overall, the lifetime prevalence of disorder was lower for Latinos (29.7 percent) than for Whites (43.2 percent), and this difference held for all Latino ethnic subgroups. Latino immigrants generally had lower rates of disorder of any type than their U.S.-born counterparts with the exception of Puerto Ricans, for whom no significant differences appeared. Among the Latino ethnic groups studied, Puerto Ricans experienced the highest rates of disorder. Looking at specific illnesses, the immigrant advantage is apparent for all disorders (mood, anxiety, and substance use) for Mexican Latinos, but only with regard to substance use for Cuban Latinos (Alegría et al. 2008).

Estimates from the Asian subsample of NLAAS indicated lifetime prevalence for disorders of any type of about 17 percent, and a 12-month prevalence of 9 percent, but no significant differences occurred among ethnic subgroups (Takeuchi et al. 2007). The effects of immigration are less clear. Women immigrants were significantly less likely to have any lifetime disorder and were at decreased risk for lifetime mood, anxiety, or substance use disorder compared to their U.S.-born counterparts. In contrast, no immigrant effect appeared for men. Together with the results from NSAL, these findings suggest that assumptions regarding "the healthy immigrant effect" do not hold for all ethnic groups.

The NCS-R does not contain sufficient sample sizes of the American Indian population to provide precise estimates of specific disorders. However, NSDUH, using a different methodology, determined rates for mental illness of any type (excluding substance use disorder) during the past year to be slightly lower for American Indian adults (18.7 percent) than for Whites (20.6 percent) (Substance Abuse and Mental Health Services Administration 2012). However, rates of substance use disorder were much higher in the American Indian population. About 6.2 percent of the adult population met the criteria for drug abuse or dependence, while 14.9 percent met the criteria for alcohol abuse or dependence, compared to 2.6 and 7.3 percent, respectively, in the total adult population. Just as with other broad racial/ethnic groups, there is considerable heterogeneity in the American Indian population not conveyed by these figures.

Many attempts have been made to examine cultural differences in mental illness by examining rates of disorder in various countries. In 1998, the WHO launched the ambitious World Mental Health Survey Initiative (WMH) (Kessler and Ustun 2008; WHO World Mental Health Survey Consortium 2004). About 30 countries (both developed and developing) have participated in the WMH, gathering information related to the prevalence and severity of disorder in the community, as well as etiology and treatment. The NCS-R provides data for the U.S. population, and all national surveys have used the same diagnostic interview (WMH-CIDI). Figure 4.3 presents estimates from selected countries that were included. We should be cautious in interpreting these data, given that the

Figure 4.3 • Twelve-Month Prevalence of Mental Illness in Selected Countries: The WHO World Mental Health Surveys

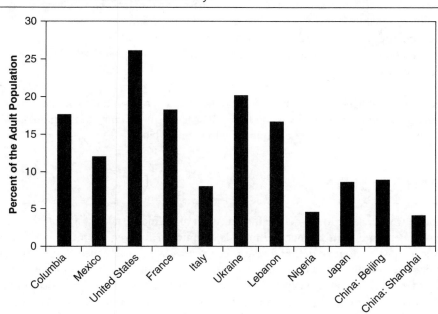

Source: WHO World Mental Health Survey Consortium (2004).
Note: All countries surveyed persons ages 18 and over, except Mexico and Columbia which were restricted to persons ages 18–65 and Japan which surveyed persons 20 years of age and older.

sampling methodology varied substantially across sites, and the U.S. population is probably more familiar with these types of survey questions. These qualms noted, rates of disorder were found to be higher in the United States than any other country presented. Researchers also discovered that anxiety disorders were the most prevalent, and mood disorder the second most prevalent, in almost all the countries included.

An important issue that arises in comparative psychiatric epidemiology is the cultural compatibility of various definitions and measures of mental illness. The use of instruments, such as WMH-CIDI, across different cultures assumes that symptoms representing particular disorders are universal—for example, the symptoms that make up depression in the *DSM-IV* adequately define depression as experienced by populations in North America, Asia, and Africa. Critics of this universalist formulation argue that different racial/ethnic groups vary in the types of symptoms linked to disorder (Alegría and McGuire 2003), and that there are cultural idiosyncrasies in the expression of psychological distress not well captured by standardized instruments. Indeed, we may be committing what Kleinman (1987) calls a categorical fallacy by attempting to apply the concept of mental disorder in a way transcendent of culture. He explains thus:

[I]n many non-Western societies, the phenomenology of depressive disorder is better captured by local syndromes of "soul loss" than by Western existential categories. A psychiatrist from such a society could operationalise the concept and symptoms of soul loss in his society, then organise them into a questionnaire, establish its reliability for use in his society, then translate its items into English, have them back-translated into the original language by another team of bilingual mental health workers, adjust the questionnaire for semantic equivalence, measure its reliability in the hands of native English-speaking clinicians, and apply the questionnaire to a stratified sample of an urban, middle class North American population in an epidemiological survey. He would come up with prevalence data. (Kleinman 1987, p. 452)

Thus, while the WMH studies manage to describe variation across cultures in the experience of symptoms defined as disorder using *DSM-IV* criteria, they do not speak unambiguously to the number of persons in these countries with mental illness.

CONCLUSION

Although we will continue to debate the precision of estimates, taken together the studies reviewed here indicate that mental illness is common. However, from a policy perspective more must be done in defining who needs services. A fourth generation of studies in psychiatric epidemiology is emerging that more seriously takes into account the severity of disorder. As shown previously, the NCS-R does try to estimate severity, although much work remains to be done to demonstrate the relationship between these refined estimates and need for services. Similarly, in 2008 the NSDUH revised its use of the K6 to better capture the severity of disorder and produce state estimates of the SMI population. It now uses modeling based on the presence of a *DSM-IV* disorder, elevated K6 scores, and deficits in functioning to calculate the prevalence of SMI over the past year (Substance Abuse and Mental Health Services Administration 2010).

One suggested strategy for narrowing the definition of disorder is to take into account the clinical significance criteria from the *DSM-IV* when estimating cases (Narrow et al. 2002). For example, if depression is not associated with significant impairment, it should not be considered a case. However, this may not be sufficient. Wakefield, Schmitz, and Baer (2010) analyzed data from the NCS-R to determine whether prevalence rates for major depression would decline if one limited cases to those with significant distress or impairment. However, because over 95 percent of respondents with depression also reported significant distress or impairment, taking into account clinical significance criteria from *DSM-IV* did not substantially change the estimates.

Horwitz and Grob (2011) argue that the central problem of modern psychiatric epidemiology is that it rests on assumptions that the conceptualization and categorization of disorders as presented in the *DSM* since its 3rd edition are meaningful. They maintain that our current approach removes from consideration the social context in which mental health problems arise—someone meeting the criteria for depression following loss of a job, for example, is considered disordered even though this may be a quite normal response to a stressful life event. As long as we rely on this type of methodology, policymakers interested in determining the need for services will be frustrated by the estimates produced by psychiatric epidemiology. High numbers make the case that we should pay attention to mental illness; they are less helpful in targeting services or identifying the social circumstances that put people at risk. This is where analytic epidemiology, discussed extensively in the next chapter, demonstrates its appeal in helping elucidate factors associated with the occurrence and course of mental disorders.

References

Alegría, Margarita and Thomas McGuire. "Rethinking a Universal Framework in the Psychiatric Symptom-Disorder Relationship." *Journal of Health and Social Behavior* 44 (2003): 257–274.

Alegría, Margarita, et al. "Considering Context, Place and Culture: The National Latino and Asian American Study." *International Journal of Methods in Psychiatric Research* 13 (2004): 208–220.

Alegría, Margarita, et al. "Prevalence of Mental Illness in Immigrant and Non-immigrant U.S. Latino Groups." *American Journal of Psychiatry* 165 (2008): 359–369.

Al-Qabandi, Mona, Jan Willem Gorter, and Peter Rosenbaum. "Early Autism Detection: Are We Ready for Routine Screening?" *Pediatrics* 128 (2011): e211–e217.

American Psychiatric Association. *DSM-5 Development: A 06 Attention Deficit/Hyperactivity Disorder.* Washington, DC: American Psychiatric Association, 2012. Available online: www.dsm5.org/Lists/ProposedRevision/DispForm.aspx?ID=383&.

Andresen, Elena M., et al. "Screening for Depression in Well Older Adults: Evaluation of a Short Form of the CES-D." *American Journal of Preventive Medicine* 10 (1994): 77–84.

Andrews, Alice O., et al. "Increased Risk of Nursing Home Admission among Middle Aged and Older Adults with Schizophrenia." *American Journal of Geriatric Psychiatry* 17 (2009): 697–705.

Anthony, James C., et al. "Comparison of the Lay Diagnostic Interview Schedule and a Standardized Psychiatric Diagnosis." *Archives of General Psychiatry* 42 (1985): 667–675.

Armstrong, Elizabeth M., Daniel P. Carpenter, and Marie Hojnacki. "Whose Deaths Matter? Mortality, Advocacy, and Attention to Disease in the Mass Media." *Journal of Health Politics, Policy and Law* 31 (2006): 729–772.

Baker Jeffrey P. "Mercury, Vaccines and Autism: One Controversy, Three Histories." *American Journal of Public Health* 98 (2008): 244–253.

Best, Joel. "Lies, Calculations and Constructions: Beyond How to Lie with Statistics." *Statistical Science* 20 (2005): 210–214.

Breslau, Joshua, et al. "Lifetime Risk and Persistence of Psychiatric Disorders across Ethnic Groups in the United States." *Psychological Medicine* 35 (2005): 317–327.

Browne, Mark A. Oakley, et al. "The Kessler Psychological Distress Scale in Te Rau Hinengaro: The New Zealand Mental Health Survey." *Australian and New Zealand Journal of Psychiatry* 44 (2010): 314–322.

Butler, Mary, et al. *Integration of Mental Health/Substance Abuse and Primary Care.* Evidence Reports/Technology Assessments No. 173. AHRQ Publication No. 09-E003. Rockville, MD: Agency for Healthcare Research and Quality, 2008.

Callaway, Ewen. "Fathers Bequeath More Mutations as They Age." *Nature* 488 (2012): 439.

Caron, Jean, and Aihua Liu. "A Descriptive Study of the Prevalence of Psychological Distress and Mental Disorders in the Canadian Population: Comparison between Low-Income and Non-Low-Income Populations." *Chronic Diseases in Canada* 30 (2010): 84–94.

Castaneda, Anu E., et al. "The Effect of Psychiatric Co-morbidity on Cognitive Functioning in a Population-Based Sample of Depressed Young Adults." *Psychological Medicine* 40 (2010): 29–39.

Centers for Disease Control and Prevention. Figure 13.1: *Percentage of Adults Aged 18 Years and Over Who Experienced Serious Psychological Distress During the Past 30 Days: United States, 1997–June 2011.* Early Release of Selected Estimates Based on Data From the January–June 2011 National Health Interview Survey, 2011. Available online: www.cdc.gov/nchs/data/nhis/earlyrelease/201112_13.pdf.

Chavez, Nelba. "Commentary: The Politics of Science: Culture, Race, Ethnicity, and the Supplement to the Surgeon General's Report on Mental Health." *Culture, Medicine and Psychiatry* 27 (2003): 391–394.

Conrad, Peter. *Identifying Hyperactive Children: The Medicalization of Deviant Behavior*, expanded edition (Ashgate Classics in Sociology). Burlington, VT: Ashgate Publishing Company, 2006.

Conrad, Peter, and Deborah Potter. "From Hyperactive Children to ADHD Adults: Observations on the Expansion of Medical Categories." *Social Problems* 47 (2000): 559–582.

Crandell, Dewitt L., and Bruce P. Dohrenwend. "Some Relations among Psychiatric Symptoms, Organic Illness, and Social Class." *American Journal of Psychiatry* 123 (1967): 1527–1538.

Croft, Janet B., et al. "Public Health Surveillance of Serious Psychological Distress in the United States." *International Journal of Public Health* 54 (2009): S4–S6.

Dohrenwend, Bruce P. "Some Issues in the Definition and Measurement of Psychiatric Disorders in General Populations." In *Proceedings of the 14th National Meeting of the Public Health Conference on Records and Statistics*, pp. 480–489. Washington, DC: National Center for Health Statistics, Health Resources Administration, 1972. Available online: www.cdc.gov/nchs/data/phcrs/phcrs72.pdf.

Dohrenwend, Bruce P., and Barbara Snell Dohrenwend. *Social Status and Psychological Disorder: A Causal Inquiry.* New York: Wiley Interscience, 1969.

Dohrenwend, Bruce P., and Barbara Snell Dohrenwend. "Psychiatric Disorders in Urban Settings." In *American Handbook of Psychiatry*, 2nd ed., vol. 2, edited by Silvano Arieti, pp. 424–447. New York: Basic Books, 1974a.

Dohrenwend, Bruce P., and Barbara Snell Dohrenwend. "Social and Cultural Influences on Psychopathology." *Annual Review of Psychology* 25 (1974b): 417–452.

Dohrenwend, Bruce P., and Barbara Snell Dohrenwend. "Perspectives on the Past and Future of Psychiatric Epidemiology: The 1981 Rema Lapouse Lecture." *American Journal of Public Health* 72 (1982): 1271–1279.

Dohrenwend, Bruce P., et al. "What Psychiatric Screening Scales Measure in the General Population, Part I: Jerome Frank's Concept of Demoralization." Unpublished manuscript, 1979.

Drayer, Rebecca A., et al. "Somatic Symptoms of Depression in Elderly Patients with Medical Comorbidities." *International Journal of Geriatric Psychiatry* 20 (2005): 973–982.

Earls, Marian F., and the Committee on Psychosocial Aspects of Child and Family Health. "Incorporating Recognition and Management of Perinatal and Postpartum Depression into Pediatric Practice." *Pediatrics* 126 (2010): 1032–1039.

Eaton, William W., and Larry G. Kessler. *Epidemiologic Field Methods in Psychiatry: The NIMH Epidemiologic Catchment Area Program.* Orlando, FL: Academic Press, 1985.

Egger, Helen Link, and Adrian Angold. "Common Emotional and Behavioral Disorders in Preschool Children: Presentation, Nosology, and Epidemiology." *Journal of Child Psychology and Psychiatry* 47 (2006): 313–337.

Essen-Möeller, Erik, et al. "Individual Traits and Morbidity in a Swedish Rural Population." *Acta Psychiatrica et Neurologica Scandinavica* 100 (1956): supplement, 1–160.

Faris, Robert E. L., and Henry Warren Dunham. *Mental Disorders in Urban Areas: An Ecological Study of Schizophrenia and Other Psychoses.* Chicago: The University of Chicago Press, 1939.

Fombonne, Eric. "Epidemiology of Pervasive Development Disorders." *Pediatric Research* 65 (2009): 591–598.

Fullerton, Catherine Anne, et al. "Trends in Mental Health Admissions to Nursing Homes: 1999–2005." *Psychiatric Services* 60 (2009): 965–971.

Gorwitz, Kurt. "Census Enumeration of the Mentally Ill and the Mentally Retarded in the Nineteenth Century." *Health Services Reports* 89 (1974): 180–187.

Greenley, James R., and David Mechanic. "Social Selection in Seeking Help for Psychological Problems." *Journal of Health and Social Behavior* 17 (1976): 249–262.

Grob, Gerald N. *The Mad Among Us: A History of the Care of America's Mentally Ill.* New York: Free Press, 1994.

Hagnell, Olle. *A Prospective Study of the Incidence of Mental Disorder.* Stockholm: Svenska Bokförlaget (Norstedt) 1966.

Heeringa, Steven G., et al. "Sample Designs and Sampling Methods for the Collaborative Psychiatric Epidemiology Studies (CPES)." *International Journal of Methods in Psychiatric Research* 13 (2004): 221–240.

Himle, Joseph A., et al. "Anxiety Disorders among African Americans, Blacks of Caribbean Descent and Non-Hispanic Whites in the United States." *Journal of Anxiety Disorders* 23 (2009): 578–590.

Hinshaw, Stephen P., and Richard M. Scheffler. *Myths, Medications, Media, and Money: ADHD's Current Explosion and The Push For Performance.* New York: Oxford University Press, forthcoming.

Hopper, Kim, et al., eds. *Recovery from Schizophrenia: An International Perspective: A Report from the WHO Collaborative Project, The International Study of Schizophrenia.* New York: Oxford University Press, 2007.

Horwitz, Allan V., and Gerald N. Grob. "The Checkered History of American Psychiatric Epidemiology." *The Milbank Quarterly* 89 (2011): 628–657.

Institute of Medicine. *Immunization Safety Review: Thimerosal—Containing Vaccines and Neurodevelopmental Disorders.* Washington, DC: National Academy Press, 2001.

Institute of Medicine. *Immunization Safety Review: Vaccines and Autism.* Washington, DC: National Academy Press, 2004.

Jackson, James. S., et al. "The National Survey of American Life: A Study of Racial, Ethnic and Cultural Influences on Mental Disorders and Mental Health." *International Journal of Methods in Psychiatric Research* 13 (2004): 196–207.

Jarvis, Edward. *Insanity and Idiocy in Massachusetts: Report of the Commission on Lunacy.* Boston: William White, Printer to the State, 1855.

Kessler, Ronald C., and Kathleen R. Merikangas. "The National Comorbidity Survey Replication (NCS-R): Background and Aims." *International Journal of Methods in Psychiatric Research* 13 (1994): 60–68.

Kessler, Ronald C., and T. Bedirhan Ustun. "The World Mental Health (WMH) Survey Initiative Version of the World Health Organization (WHO) Composite International Diagnostic Interview (CIDI)." *International Journal of Methods in Psychiatric Research* 13 (1994): 93–121.

Kessler, Ronald C., and T. Bedirhan Ustun, eds. *The WHO World Mental Health Surveys: Global Perspectives on the Epidemiology of Mental Disorders.* New York: Cambridge University Press, 2008.

Kessler, Ronald C., et al. "Lifetime and 12-Month Prevalence of DSM-III-R Psychiatric Disorders in the United States. Results from the National Comorbidity Survey." *Archives of General Psychiatry* 51 (1994a): 8–19.

Kessler, Ronald C., et al. "The US National Comorbidity Survey Replication (NCS-R): Design and Field Procedures." *International Journal of Methods in Psychiatric Research* 13 (1994b): 69–92.

Kessler, Ronald C., et al. "Short Screening Scales to Monitor Population Prevalences and Trends in Non-Specific Psychological Distress." *Psychological Medicine* 32 (2002): 959–976.

Kessler, Ronald C., et al. "Screening for Serious Mental Illness in the General Population." *Archives of General Psychiatry* 60 (2003): 184–189.

Kessler, Ronald C., et al. "Prevalence, Severity and Comorbidity of 12-Month *DSM-IV* Disorders in the National Comorbidity Survey Replication." *Archives of General Psychiatry* 62 (2005a): 617–627.

Kessler, Ronald C., et al. "Lifetime Prevalence and Age-of-Onset Distributions of *DSM-IV* Disorders in the National Comorbidity Survey Replication." *Archives of General Psychiatry* 62 (2005b): 593–602.

Kessler, Ronald C., et al. "The Prevalence and Correlates of Nonaffective Psychosis in the National Comorbidity Survey Replication (NCS-R)." *Biological Psychiatry* 58 (2005c): 668–676.

Kessler, Ronald C., et al. "Prevalence, Persistence and Sociodemographic Correlates of *DSM-IV* Disorders in the National Comorbidity Survey Replication Adolescent Supplement." *Archives of General Psychiatry* 69 (2012): 372–380.

King, Marissa, and Peter Bearman. "Diagnostic Change and the Increased Prevalence of Autism." *International Journal of Epidemiology* 38 (2009):1224–1234.

King, Marissa D., et al. "Estimated Autism Risk and Older Reproductive Age." *American Journal of Public Health* 99 (2009): 1673–1679.

Kleinman, Arthur. "Anthropology and Psychiatry: The Role of Culture in Cross-Cultural Research on Illness." *British Journal of Psychiatry* 151 (1987): 447–454.

Kong, Augustine, et al. "Rate of *de novo* Mutations and the Importance of Father's Age to Disease Risk." *Nature* 488 (2012): 471-475.

Kroenke, Kurt, Robert L. Spitzer, and Janet B. W. Williams. "The PHQ-9: Validity of a Brief Depression Severity Measure." *Journal of General Internal Medicine* 16 (2001): 606–613.

Kroenke, Kurt, Robert L. Spitzer, and Janet B. W. Williams. "The Patient Health Questionnaire-2: Validity of a Two-Item Depression Screener." *Medical Care* 41 (2003): 1284–1292.

Kroenke, Kurt, et al. "The PHQ-8 as a Measure of Current Depression in the General Population." *Journal of Affective Disorders* 114 (2009): 163–173.

Langner, Thomas S., and Stanley T. Michael. *Life Stress and Mental Health: The Midtown Manhattan Study.* New York: The Free Press of Glencoe, 1963.

Leighton, Dorothea C., et al. *The Character of Danger: Psychiatric Symptoms in Selected Communities.* New York: Basic Books, 1963a.

Leighton, Dorothea C., et al. "Psychiatric Findings of the Stirling County Study." *American Journal of Psychiatry* 119 (1963b): 1021–1026.

Leventman, Seymour. "Race and Mental Illness in Mass Society." *Social Problems* 16 (1968): 73–78.

Lichtman, Judith H., et al. "Depression and Coronary Heart Disease: Recommendations for Screening, Referral, and Treatment: A Science Advisory from the American Heart Association Prevention Committee of the Council on Cardiovascular Nursing, Council on Clinical Cardiology, Council on Epidemiology and Prevention, and Interdisciplinary Council on Quality of Care and Outcomes Research: Endorsed by the American Psychiatric Association." *Circulation* 118 (2008): 1768–1775.

Liu, Kayuet, Marissa King, and Peter S. Bearman. "Social Influence and the Autism Epidemic." *American Journal of Sociology* 115 (2010): 1387–1434.

Liu, Kayuet, Noam Zerubavel, and Peter Bearman. "Social Demographic Change and Autism." *Demography* 47 (2010): 327–343.

Manis, Jerome G., et al. "Validating a Mental Health Scale." *American Sociological Review* 28 (1963): 108–116.

Mazer, Milton. "People in Predicament: A Study in Psychiatric and Psychosocial Epidemiology." *Social Psychiatry and Psychiatric Epidemiology* 9 (1974): 85–90.

Mazer, Milton. *People and Predicaments.* Cambridge: Harvard University Press, 1976.

McAlpine, Donna D., and Amy R. Wilson. "Screening for Depression in Primary Care: What Do We Still Need to Know?" *Depression and Anxiety* 19 (2004): 137–145.

McNally, Richard J. *What Is Mental Illness?* Cambridge, MA: The President and Fellows of Harvard College, 2011.

Mechanic, David. "Development of Psychological Distress Among Young Adults." *Archives of General Psychiatry* 36 (1979): 1233–1239.

Mechanic, David. "Is the Prevalence of Mental Disorders a Good Measure of the Need for Services?" *Health Affairs* 22 (2003): 8–20.

Mechanic, David, and James R. Greenley. "The Prevalence of Psychological Distress and Help-Seeking in a College Student Population." *Social Psychiatry and Psychiatric Epidemiology* 11 (1976): 1–14.

Mechanic, David, and Donna D. McAlpine. "Use of Nursing Homes in the Care of Persons with Severe Mental Illness: 1985–1995." *Psychiatric Services* 51 (2000): 354–358.

Mechanic, David, and Donna D. McAlpine. "Mental Health and Aging: A Life Course Perspective." In *Handbook of Sociology of Aging*, edited by Rick Settersten and Jacqui Angel, pp. 477–493. New York: Springer, 2011.

Merikangas, Kathleen Ries, et al. "Lifetime Prevalence of Mental Disorders in U.S. Adolescents: Results from the National Comorbidity Survey Replication-Adolescent Supplement (NCS-A)." *Journal of the American Academy of Child & Adolescent Psychiatry* 49 (2010a): 980–989.

Merikangas, Kathleen Ries, et al. "Prevalence and Treatment of Mental Disorders among U.S. Children in the 2001–2004 NHANES." *Pediatrics* 125 (2010b): 75–81.

Mitchell, Alex J., and James C. Coyne. *Screening for Depression in Clinical Practice. An Evidence-Based Guide.* New York: Oxford University Press, 2010.

Moreland, Regina. "National Vaccine Injury Compensation Program: The Potential Impact of Cedillo for Vaccine-Related Autism Cases." *The Journal of Legal Medicine* 29 (2008): 363–380.

Narrow, William E., et al. "Revised Prevalence Estimates of Mental Disorders in the United States: Using a Clinical Significance Criterion to Reconcile 2 Surveys' Estimates." *Archives of General Psychiatry* 59 (2002):115–123.

National Institute of Mental Health. *Mental Health, United States, 1985,* edited by Carol A. Taube and Sally A. Barrett. DHHS Publication No. ADM 85-1378. Washington, DC: U.S. Government Printing Office, 1985.

Office of Management and Budget. *Revisions to the Standards for the Classification of Federal Data on Race and Ethnicity.* Federal Register 62 (October 30, 1997): 58782–58790. Available online: gpo.gov/fdsys/pkg/FR-1997-10-30/pdf/97-28653.pdf.

Phillips, Derek L. "The 'True Prevalence' of Mental Illness in a New England State." *Community Mental Health Journal* 2 (1966): 35–40.

Phillips, Derek L., and Kevin J. Clancy. "Response Biases in Field Studies of Mental Illness." *American Sociological Review* 35 (1970): 503–515.

Piatt, Elizabeth E., Mark R. Munetz, and Christian Ritter. "An Examination of Premature Mortality among Decedents with Serious Mental Illness and Those in the General Population." *Psychiatric Services* 61 (2010): 663–668.

Pignone, Mike, et al. *Screening for Depression: Systematic Evidence Review* (Prepared by the Research Triangle Institute—University of North Carolina Evidence-based Practice Center under Contract No. 290-97-0011). AHRQ Publication. No. 02-S002. Rockville, MD: Agency for Healthcare Research and Quality, 2002. Available online: www.ahrq.gov/downloads/pub/prevent/pdfser/depser.pdf.

Plassman, Brenda L., et al. "Prevalence of Dementia in the United States: The Aging, Demographics and Memory Study." *Neuroepidemiology* 29 (2007): 125–132.

Plassman, Brenda L., et al. "Prevalence of Cognitive Impairment Without Dementia in the United States." *Annals of Internal Medicine* 148 (2008): 427–434.

Polanczyk, Guilherme, et al. "The Worldwide Prevalence of ADHD: A Systematic Review and Metaregression Analysis." *American Journal of Psychiatry* 164 (2007): 942–948.

Powell, Theophilus O. "The Increase of Insanity and Tuberculosis in the Southern Negro Since 1860, and Its Alliance and Some of the Supposed Causes." *Journal of the American Medical Association* 27 (1896): 1185–1188.

Radloff, Lenore Sawyer. "The CESD Scale: A Self-Report Depression Scale for Research in the General Population." *Applied Psychological Measurement* 1 (1977): 385–401.

Regier, Darrel A., et al. "The NIMH Epidemiologic Catchment Area Program." *Archives of General Psychiatry* 41 (1984): 934–941.

Regier, Darrel A., et al. "Limitations of Diagnostic Criteria and Assessment Instruments for Mental Disorders: Implications for Research and Policy." *Archives of General Psychiatry* 55 (1998): 109–115.

Rescorla, Leslie A., et al. "International Comparisons of Behavioral and Emotional Problems in Preschool Children: Parents' Reports from 24 Societies." *Journal of Clinical Child and Adolescent Psychology* 40 (2011): 456–467.

Rice, Catherine. "Prevalence of Autism Spectrum Disorders—Autism and Developmental Disabilities Monitoring Network, United States, 2006." *Morbidity and Mortality Weekly Report* 58 (2009): 1–20. Available online: www.cdc.gov/mmwr/preview/mmwrhtml/ss5810a1.htm.

Robins, Lee N. "Epidemiology: Reflections on Testing the Validity of Psychiatric Interviews." *Archives of General Psychiatry* 42 (1985): 918–924.

Robins, Lee N., and Darrel A. Regier, eds. *Psychiatric Disorders in America: The Epidemiological Catchment Area Study.* New York: Free Press, 1991.

Rowland, Andrew S., Catherine A. Lesesne, and Ann J. Abramowitz. "The Epidemiology of Attention-Deficit/Hyperactivity Disorder (ADHD): A Public Health View." *Mental Retardation and Developmental Disabilities Research Reviews* 8 (2002): 162–170.

Saha, Sukanta, et al. "A Systematic Review of the Prevalence of Schizophrenia." *PLoS Medicine* 2 (2005): 413–433.

Seiler, Lauren H. "The 22-Item Scale Used in Field Studies of Mental Illness: A Question of Method, a Question of Substance, and a Question of Theory." *Journal of Health and Social Behavior* 14 (1973): 252–264.

Srole, Leo, et al. *Mental Health in the Metropolis: The Midtown Manhattan Study.* New York: McGraw-Hill, 1962.

Steffens, David C., et al. "Prevalence of Depression among Older Americans: The Aging, Demographics and Memory Study." *International Journal of Psychogeriatrics* 21 (2009): 879–888.

Substance Abuse and Mental Health Services Administration. *Results from the 2009 National Survey on Drug Use and Health: Mental Health Detailed Tables.* NSDUH Series H-39, HHS Publication No. SMA 10-4609. Rockville, MD: Substance Abuse and Mental Health Services Administration, 2010. Available online: samhsa.gov/data/2k10/2k9MHDetailedTables/HTML/TOC.htm.

Substance Abuse and Mental Health Services Administration. *Results from the 2010 National Survey on Drug Use and Health: Mental Health Findings.* NSDUH Series H-42, HHS Publication No. SMA 11-4667. Rockville, MD: Substance Abuse and Mental Health Services Administration, 2012. Available online: www.samhsa.gov/data/nsduh/2k10MH_Findings/2k10MHResults.htm.

Takeuchi, David T., et al. "Immigration-Related Factors and Mental Disorders Among Asian Americans." *American Journal of Public Health* 97 (2007): 84–90.

Thompson, Richard H., et al. "Personal Characteristics Associated with Consistency of Recall of Depressed or Anhedonic Mood in the 13-Year Follow-Up of the Baltimore Epidemiologic Catchment Area Survey." *Acta Psychiatrica Scandinavica* 109 (2004): 345–354.

Tousignant, Michel, Guy Denis, and Rejean Lachapelle. "Some Considerations Concerning the Validity and Use of the Health Opinion Survey." *Journal of Health and Social Behavior* 15 (1974): 241–252.

U.S. Census Bureau. *Population Estimates.* Washington, DC: U.S. Department of Commerce, U.S. Census Bureau, June 2012. Available online: www.census.gov/popest/data/index.html.

U.S. Department of Health and Human Services. *Mental Health: A Report of the Surgeon General.* Rockville, MD: U.S. Department of Health and Human Services, Substance Abuse and Mental Health Services Administration, Center for Mental Health Services, National Institutes of Health, National Institute of Mental Health, 1999.

U.S. Department of Health and Human Services. *Mental Health: Culture, Race and Ethnicity—A Supplement to Mental Health: A Report of the Surgeon General.* Rockville, MD: U.S. Department of Health and Human Services, Substance Abuse and Mental Health Services Administration, Center for Mental Health Services, 2001.

Van Naarden Braun, Kim, et al. "Evaluation of a Methodology for a Collaborative Multiple Source Surveillance Network for Autism Spectrum Disorders—Autism and Developmental Disabilities Monitoring Network, 14 Sites, United States, 2002." *Morbidity and Mortality Weekly Report* 56 (2007): 29–40. Available online: www.cdc.gov/mmwr/preview/mmwrhtml/ss5601a3.htm.

Wakefield, Andrew J., et al. "Ileal-Lymphoid-Nodular Hyperplasia, Non-Specific Colitis and Pervasive Developmental Disorder in Children." *Lancet* 351 (1998): 637–641.

Wakefield, Jerome. "Conceptual Validity of DIS Diagnostic Criteria and ECA Prevalence Estimates." Unpublished paper. Institute for Health, Health Care Policy, and Aging Research, Rutgers University, New Brunswick, NJ, 1997.

Wakefield, Jerome C., Mark F. Schmitz, and Judith C. Baer. "Does the *DSM-IV* Clinical Significance Criterion for Major Depression Reduce False Positives? Evidence from the National Comorbidity Survey Replication." *American Journal of Psychiatry* 167 (2010): 298–304.

Werner, Carrie A. *The Older Population: 2010.* Report C2010BR-09. Washington, DC: U.S. Department of Commerce, Economics and Statistics Administration, U.S. Census Bureau, 2011. Available online: www.census.gov/prod/cen2010/briefs/c2010br-09.pdf.

Wheaton, Blair. "The Sociogenesis of Psychological Disorder: Reexamining the Causal Issues with Longitudinal Data." *American Sociological Review* 43 (1978): 383–403.

Williams, David R. "Race and Health: Basic Questions, Emerging Directions." *Annals of Epidemiology* 7 (1997): 322–333.

Williams, David R., et al. "The Mental Health of Black Caribbean Immigrants: Results from the National Survey of American Life." *American Journal of Public Health* 97 (2007a): 52–59.

Williams, David R., et al. "Prevalence and Distribution of Major Depressive Disorder in African Americans, Caribbean Blacks, and Non-Hispanic Whites: Results from the National Survey of American Life." *Archives of General Psychiatry* 64 (2007b): 305–315.

Williams, Joanna G., Julian P. T. Higgins, and Carol E. G. Brayne. "Systematic Review of Prevalence Studies of Autism Spectrum Disorders." *Archives of Disease in Childhood* 91 (2006): 8–15.

WHO World Mental Health Survey Consortium. "Prevalence, Severity, and Unmet Need for Treatment of Mental Disorders in the World Health Organization World Mental Health Surveys." *Journal of the American Medical Association* 291 (2004): 2581–2590.

Ziegelstein, Roy C., et al. "Routine Screening for Depression in Patients with Coronary Heart Disease: Never Mind." *Journal of the American College of Cardiology* 54 (2009): 886–890.

Controlling Mental Illness

Theory, Research, and Methods of Intervention

Theories of the causation of mental illness have vacillated in their focus on the environment and genetics or biology, reflecting classic debates about the relative importance of "nature versus nurture" for explaining human behavior. Rutter, Moffitt, and Caspi (2006) trace these changing conceptions of causation. During the 1950s and 1960s, they argue that the focus was on the environment, especially the role of early childhood socialization and adversity, in understanding of mental illness. This was followed, in the 1960s through the 1980s, by increased recognition of the role of genetics, a period influenced heavily by studies of twins and adoptees that indicated the importance of heredity. The 1980s through the early 1990s were dominated by genetic determinism. Finally, since the early 1990s we have developed a more complicated appreciation of the development of mental disorder based on the view that there is unlikely to be one cause, that multiple genes and environmental conditions are involved, and that the interaction between genes and environment is essential in explaining variations in risk for disorder.

The current state of knowledge prevents us from coming to any definitive conclusion about the environment–genetics debate. Mental illness is a vague general designation. The relative importance of biological and social influences is likely to depend on the particular condition under consideration. Moreover, it is necessary to separate the effects of environment with respect to the causes of specific psychiatric conditions as opposed to its influence on the development of secondary disabilities (the course of the disorders) (Lemert 1951; Wing 1962) and patterns of illness behavior and responses to care (Mechanic 1978). Most mental health professionals are aware that persons with the same primary condition—such as depression or schizophrenia—may fare better or worse depending on their social and environmental circumstances and the kind of treatment and support they receive. Although in some instances social forces may affect both the occurrence of a condition and subsequent disability, in other instances the environment is most important in determining the extent of the handicap. The challenge is to be as precise as possible about the way environmental factors may affect a condition.

Just as theories and research into the causes of mental disorder have at times highlighted environment or genetics, so too approaches to the control of mental disorder have wavered between biological and psychotherapeutic methods. Our goal here is to present some of the competing positions concerning the etiology and treatment of mental disorders. While our discussion will contrast these views to highlight distinctive aspects, most investigators and mental health professionals adopt an eclectic stance, incorporating elements of each perspective.

GENES, ENVIRONMENT, AND THE BRAIN

Genes play an important causal role for many major mental illnesses. Heritability refers to the amount of variation in particular disorders that is accounted for by genetics (Rutter 2006). Estimates of heritability are based on studies of family concordance in disorders among close versus more distant relatives, studies comparing fraternal versus identical twins, and studies of children raised apart from their biological parents. Table 5.1 summarizes recent estimates of the heritability of major mental illnesses. These are at best rough estimates, but they show that across a number of different types of studies the evidence of a genetic component is strongest for schizophrenia, perhaps because it has been studied more intensively than other disorders. Although these studies are not above criticism (see Rutter 2006 for an extensive review of the strengths and weaknesses of such studies), they do provide a compelling argument for those inclined toward a heredity theory of the etiology of mental disorder. However, looking more closely at the case of schizophrenia provides reason to reject a purely deterministic perspective based on genetics.

Partial evidence for a genetic etiology of schizophrenia comes from studies of the offspring of parents with and without schizophrenia. In a classic study, Heston (1966) compared outcomes of 47 adults born to mothers with schizophrenia with a matched control group born to mothers who were not mentally ill. Those in both the subject and control groups had been separated from their natural mothers beginning in the first few days of life, spending their early years in foster homes. The investigator found the occurrence

Table 5.1 Estimates of the Heritability of Major Mental Illnesses

Type of Mental Illness (Source)	Heritability Estimate (%)
Schizophrenia	80–85
Bipolar Depression	70+
Autism	90
ADHD	39–88
Major Depression	31–75
Substance Use Disorder	25–50

Source: Estimates Derived from Rutter (2006).

of schizophrenia and other pathologies to be higher among the offspring of mothers with schizophrenia than among the matched controls. Because subjects of this study were removed from their mothers shortly after birth, the higher rate of pathology could not have resulted from interaction with a mother who had schizophrenia.

The theory of the genetics of schizophrenia, however, depends mostly upon studies of twins. In a series of influential early studies, Franz Kallmann (1953) found that although schizophrenic concordance varied from 10 to 18 percent among fraternal twins, it was 78–92 percent among identical twins. Subsequent studies of the heredity hypothesis have continued to demonstrate a higher concordance for schizophrenia among identical, as compared with fraternal twins or siblings. In more recent years, however, the level of risk is lower than in prior investigations. In a review of such studies, Tandon, Keshavan, and Nasrallah (2008) determined that the risk of a fraternal twin having schizophrenia if the other twin has the disorder is about 10–15 percent (the same risk associated with having a sibling with schizophrenia), while the risk for a monozygotic twin is between 40 and 50 percent.

Even in instances where both parents have schizophrenia, relative risk of developing the disorder among offspring is between 40 and 60 percent (Tandon, Keshavan, and Nasrallah, 2008). Together, these findings suggest not only that a strong link exists between genetics and schizophrenia but also that there must be environmental factors at play.

But answering the question of which precise environmental factors contribute to a schizophrenic breakdown remains difficult. Evidence shows that psychosis is frequently preceded by a stressful event of some magnitude. Brown and Birley (1968) studied 50 patients suffering from an acute onset or relapse of schizophrenia and 377 healthy people, who comprised the control group. The two groups differed in the proportion experiencing at least one major change in their lives in the three-week period preceding the investigation. Sixty percent of the patient group had such an experience, but only 19 percent of the control group did. Possibly, environmental stress leads to the initiation of treatment rather than the illness itself, and persons similarly ill who do not suffer severe environmental stress are less likely to define themselves as requiring treatment. Because the condition studied, however, was a severe one, this supposition probably would not explain the result obtained. Investigators sorted the social changes experienced by patients into categories of greater or lesser degree of personal control. The relationship between stressful events and illness persisted even when patients could not affect the stressful event, undermining the argument that patients with schizophrenia tend to get themselves into difficulties due to their own symptoms. It is more likely that significant changes in his or her life, especially among those genetically vulnerable, adversely affected a patient's psychological and social functioning. Other studies likewise indicate a relationship between the cumulation of stresses in a person's life and occurrence of psychiatric morbidity, but the causal links are not clearly understood.

The World Health Organization (1973, 1979) conducted an influential international study of schizophrenia that reported little difference in the incidence of schizophrenia from country to country. This finding seems to contradict stress as a key factor triggering the condition because there are certainly large stress differences in regard to lifestyle and social conditions across the countries studied. However, various studies in Europe have identified higher risks of schizophrenia and other psychoses for certain ethnic minorities, particularly members of the African Caribbean population in England. Other research finds a higher incidence of illness in urban environments (Kirkbride et al. 2006). Such discrepancies raise questions about the widely accepted conclusions of the WHO study regarding comparable incidence across nations (McGrath 2007).

Patients with schizophrenia living in family situations featuring high emotional involvement (labeled in the literature as "expressed emotion") characterized by controlling emotional relationships and criticisms are more likely to have a recurrence of symptoms (Brown et al. 1962; Leff and Vaughn 1985; Vaughn and Leff 1976). Those genetically predisposed to schizophrenia may be particularly vulnerable to the intense brain stimulation associated with either stressful life events or intense emotions. Consistent with this conclusion is the fact that social distance from relatives and administration of phenothiazine, a medicine that may block emotional response, seem to prevent a relapse. Study of patients' responses in the home confirms psychophysiological arousal in the presence of "high emotion" relatives (Tarrier et al. 1979). Patients in families with high levels of expressed emotion are also less likely to relapse if they have minimal face-to-face contact with relatives with high levels of expressed emotion (Leff 1978; Vaughn and Leff 1976). Beyond such considerations, persons with schizophrenia may also lack the coping skills necessary for dealing with challenging situations, and the combination of biological vulnerability and personal inadequacy together increases the probability of breakdown. In the end, while there is a growing body of research focusing on both genetic and environmental factors, schizophrenia remains a poorly understood condition. At best, we have some leads and many hypotheses awaiting confirmation; this is still a long way from pinpointing the causes of the illness.

One intriguing finding is that the prognosis of schizophrenia appears to be superior in developing countries (Sartorius et al. 1986). In a two-year follow-up of patients with schizophrenia, the proportion considered recovered varied from 6 percent in Denmark to 58 percent in Nigeria (World Health Organization 1979). More recent research confirms these better outcomes in developing versus developed countries (Menezes, Arenovich, and Zipursky 2006). Reasons for this finding are not well understood. Waxler (1979) maintained it might be due to cultural differences related to the impact of social labeling. That is, in developed nations, serious mental illness is expected to be chronic, characterized by long periods of treatment, involvement with the mental health system, and separation from family. In developing nations, such as Sri Lanka, which Waxler used as a case study, expectations are that the illness will be short-lived allowing the patient to remain integrated with family and social roles. Thus, persons with similar symptoms have different outcomes in line with norms of the society in which they live.

Another alternative is that in rural contexts, persons with schizophrenia can more easily continue to play an economic role and insulate themselves from interpersonal stresses and intense associations. In some cultural contexts, there may be strong mutual expectations within kinship structures that encourage individuals with schizophrenia to maintain their functioning while providing them with community acceptance (Kleinman and Mechanic 1979). Family members may also be less critical of the individual, a factor associated with reduced symptomatology (Leff 1978). While some of the best outcome results have been noted in underdeveloped countries or in rural contexts in developed nations, good outcomes have also been reported from industrialized cities in Europe, suggesting a more complex process than can be explained by gross national or regional comparisons.

The importance of expressed emotion has now been examined across various geographic and cultural groups (Bhugra and McKenzie 2003; Singh, Harley, and Suhail 2011). Findings are somewhat mixed. In India (Wig et al. 1987), a country exhibiting a relatively favorable prognosis for schizophrenia in the WHO studies, hostility of significant others was the primary predictor of relapse. Unlike the West, personal criticism was often not associated with hostility, and criticism by itself was not predictive of relapse. Even more instructive, Indian relatives made fewer critical comments, fewer positive remarks, and demonstrated less overinvolvement with the patient. This was much more the case in rural areas, where the traditional kinship system was stronger than among more expressive city dwellers. However, the relationship between the level of expressed emotion and prognosis has not been consistently found across cultural groups (Bhugra and McKenzie 2003; Singh, Harley, and Suhail 2011). Some have argued that levels of expressed emotion should be judged against normative standards for particular cultures (Bhugra and McKenzie 2003; Singh, Harley, and Suhail 2011). That is, it may not be objective levels of criticism, overinvolvement, and the like that are negative, but whether these reactions are stronger than what is expected in a particular culture.

With respect to affective disorders, both twin and adoption studies support a genetic basis for bipolar (manic-depressive) and unipolar affective illness (Rutter 2006). The degree of causal influence is difficult to estimate because studies vary and no specific process of genetic transmission has been established (Reich et al. 1985). Bipolar disorder appears to differ categorically from unipolar affective illness, with a distinct epidemiology. Siblings and offspring of those with bipolar disorder have an elevated lifetime risk for both bipolar and unipolar disorders, which is higher than in families with unipolar disorders. As shown in Table 5.1, overall bipolar disorder appears to be more closely linked to genetic factors than unipolar depression. However, there are only a few methodologically sound studies of the heritability of the former (Rutter 2006).

Over time, conceptualization and data collection in regard to psychiatric genetics have become more sophisticated. While biologists are using new tools to identify the genes that increase susceptibility to particular mental disorders, researchers in epidemiological genetics are exploring increasingly complex hypotheses about how such susceptibilities may interact with familial and other environmental factors. We know that even very early in life children have temperamental characteristics prone to elicit different environmental reactions that are either damaging or protective in nature (Werner and Smith 1992). We also know that people are not passive actors. Through their temperaments and inclinations—such as impulsivity, warmth, and aggressiveness—they participate in creating the environments around them. Researchers are increasingly exploring the extent to which family environments respond to the unique characteristics of each member or are shared, the extent to which environmental effects may be contemporaneous or long acting, and the extent to which genetic and environmental risk factors vary over time (Kendler 1995). Another line of inquiry seeks to understand whether genes can make individuals more sensitive to the damaging effects of particular environments and how such genes function. Environmental factors are rarely general; they appear to act on people differently depending on susceptibilities (Kendler 1995). Work in genetics is moving toward greater collaboration with the social sciences in an effort to better understand how such complex interactions occur.

In 2003, a paper that appeared in the prestigious journal *Science* aroused much excitement because of its report on the interaction between stressful life events and the serotonin transporter gene (5-HTT) in depression. The paper detailed a longitudinal, prospective study in Dunedin, New Zealand, of a birth cohort of 1,037 children, examining the role of life stress among subjects with one or two copies of the short allele of this gene (Caspi et al. 2003).

One finding that persons with high levels of stress were prone to become clinically depressed has been commonly observed. Capturing attention, however, was the discovery that persons with either one or two copies of the short allele of this serotonin transporter gene proved particularly susceptible to clinical depression under high stress. Regardless of their alleles, study subjects were unlikely to become clinically depressed in the absence of stress, while those with two long alleles had low propensity to clinical depression even under high stress.

Several studies have failed to replicate these G × E (gene–environment) results (Gillespie et al. 2005; Surtees et al. 2006), and others replicate it partially but in idiosyncratic ways (Eley et al. 2004; Grabe et al. 2005; Kendler et al. 2005). These outcomes reflect, in part, differences in sex, age, and other characteristics of the samples studied as well as measurement artifacts. One study, for example, found that social support moderated the risk of depression among maltreated children with the short allele of the serotonin transporter gene (Kaufman et al. 2004). By contrast, Eley and others (2004) reported an extraordinary pattern of interaction wherein female adolescents with two short alleles under low environmental stress comprised a much lower proportion of those with high depressive symptoms as compared with subjects possessing two long alleles. This observation seems to seriously challenge the thrust of the more general G × E hypothesis, but it receives little comment. Brown and Harris (2008) raise a number of methodological and substantive issues about this literature (see, also, Zammit and Owen 2006). They propose that life events as measured by Caspi and colleagues (2003) may mask the more powerful influence of childhood mistreatment and abuse as the key factor interacting with the 5-HTT gene. Further, a range of possible pathways exists through which gene/environment interactions can affect susceptibility to depression. Plainly, there is still a great deal to be learned.

In recent years, a new subfield of biology called epigenetics has gained increasing notice. It seeks to understand how experiences such as sexual abuse, traumatic incidents, and other life events cause changes in the DNA of genes that do not alter the genetic code but affect expression of the gene in ways contributing to psychiatric disorders. In a way yet to be understood, satellite molecules modify the construction of proteins leading to psychological and behavioral changes. These mechanisms close or increase access to genes, altering their manner of expression (Higgins 2008). Intriguing observations have been made from animal studies, and it is hoped that as understanding advances this work will lead to improved treatments.

Exciting developments in genetics and molecular neuroscience, coupled with new imaging and other investigatory tools, inspire hope that we stand at the threshold of significant advances in the understanding and treatment of serious mental illness. But as work progresses, it has become clear that challenges are greater than anticipated, and the complexity of the brain and brain processes poses many scientific barriers to be overcome. Steven Hyman, a neuroscientist and former director of the National Institute of Mental Health, explains the complexity of the issue:

> The brain is the most complex object of investigation in the history of biological science. Its development depends on complex, often non-linear gene-gene and gene-environment interactions, as well as on stochastic processes associated with the interconnection of 100,000 million or more neurons…this complexity, however, has made progress in the neuroscience and genetics of mental illness exceedingly difficult. Each neuron in the brain makes thousands of connections

or synapses with neighbouring and distant neurons; there are probably more than 100 trillion such connections, and across them each neuron may utilize several of more than 100 chemical neurotransmitters. Signals encoded by each neurotransmitter are decoded by the receiving cell, using one or several of the many receptor subtypes that exist for each neurotransmitter...Neurotransmitter receptors initiate complex signalling cascades within nerve cells. These cascades process information, produce immediate outputs, such as a decision to fire, and, at the same time, initiate long-term, activity-dependent changes in the receiving cells which may eventually lead to synaptic plasticity. (Hyman 2000, p. 455)

Genes, in turn, are crucial in the development of brain circuits and their functioning related to all disease processes whether by influencing susceptibility or resistance. Knowledge of causal mechanisms in gene–environment interactions is limited, with very little comprehension of the functional consequences for psychopathology or the influence of genes on one another (Rutter 2002), making applications for practice well in the future (Hyman 2000).

THE PSYCHOSOCIAL DEVELOPMENT PERSPECTIVE

Much research in mental health and illness over the past half century has proceeded according to the premise that early psychosocial environment and family processes are central to personal development as well as distress and disorder over the life course. Earlier years saw a strong focus on psychoanalytic and psychodynamic ideas and processes. Research explored early socialization, the emotional tone of family interaction, and patterns of parental control. Among the factors most commonly studied were punishment methods, parental warmth and criticism, dependency patterns inside the family, and the management of aggression and family role structures. A continuum concept of behavior disorders prevailed that did not carefully differentiate between ordinary distress, unhappiness, and nonconforming behavior, on the one hand, from more serious problems that could appropriately be characterized as disorders, on the other.

Predictors of mental disorder derived from psychoanalytic theory, such as child-rearing practices, modes of family communication, and specific maternal and other parental qualities, have not proved very reliable. In retrospect, blaming parents for the behaviors of children with schizophrenia and autism did a great deal of harm. As interest in social development expanded, and biosocial processes gained broader recognition, the interest in parenting became more specific and concrete, emphasizing attention and neglect; cognitive stimulation; and the acquisition of age-appropriate social skills, including motivation, perseverance, ability to defer gratification, conscientiousness, planning, and related capacities necessary for personal and social adaptation. Further research that examined health and illness in populations clarified how poverty and disadvantage could interfere with the ability of families to provide the nurturance and skills needed by children to make their way in life successfully. There is an unmistakable connection between such factors and later failures, distress, and mild and moderate depression. Just how these factors fit into trajectories of severe mental illness remains uncertain, however.

Careful longitudinal studies have shed some light on this latter question. Aggressiveness, achievement patterns, and initial development of social skills generally become established before adolescence, and childhood problems in these areas frequently persist into adulthood (Robins 1979b). Antisocial behavior in childhood increases vulnerability to a variety of mental disorders, alcoholism, and other problems in adult life. In contrast, children with neurotic problems often do quite well in adulthood, suffering much less illness, disability, and maladjustment than the antisocial child (Robins 1966; Rutter 1972). Children having difficulties with authority figures often end up having drinking, sexual behavior, and legal problems. Seriously disturbed children, such as those with childhood psychoses, commonly have serious and disabling adult disorders. Fortunately, such disorders are infrequent. [For outstanding reviews of the longitudinal studies, see Robins (1979a, 1979b, 1983); Mrazek and Haggerty (1994); and O'Connell, Boat, and Warner (2009).]

Earlier research on child-rearing practices offers limited guidance for preventive work, especially for more severe disorders. Different child-rearing patterns appear to play a small part in producing the profound difficulties we are concerned with here. And, indeed, the relevance of child-rearing practices in personality development, in general, has long been refuted (Sewell 1952). Any relatively warm, accepting family climate that nurtures a sense of self-esteem in the child and provides training experiences consistent with social realities will probably produce a "normal" child, assuming the absence of significant biological vulnerabilities. Despite the myth of the fragile child, children are exceedingly flexible, adaptive, and resilient with respect to modifications in their environments. Adversity in childhood that is manageable may well lead to mastery and strength (Elder 1974). The contexts that appear to breed pathology are emotionally bizarre or highly deprived and are those in which a child experiences profound rejection, hostility, and other forms of sexual, physical, and emotional abuse. Inadequate, ineffective, and incongruous models of behavior are notable.

The more we learn about human development, the more we appreciate its causal intricacies. For example, prenatal and early nutrition can influence the emergence of chronic disease in later life (Barker 2004; Barker et al. 2001, 2005). Mental illness has received relatively little attention in contrast to coronary heart disease, diabetes, and other such conditions, but some of this work on other health problems bears on mental illness, and particularly schizophrenia. Children of pregnant mothers exposed to famine conditions, thus resulting in inadequate nutrition both prenatally and after birth, have a higher risk of schizophrenia in later life (Smith and Susser 2002; St. Clair et al. 2005; Susser, Hoek, and Brown 1998).

Family factors commonly associated in the research literature with adult functioning include "family size, broken homes, illegitimacy, adoption or foster placement, socioeconomic status, supervision by parents, attitudes of parents toward the child, parental expectations for the child's achievement, behavior problems in the parents and siblings, and psychiatric disorders in the parents" (Robins 1979b, p. 488). These factors tend to be intercorrelated, reflecting many aspects of family life and position in the society, in addition to genetic transmission. Moreover, the meaning of concepts such as "broken homes" changes over time as social and demographic patterns change. Definitive causal mechanisms are elusive.

Why has such extensive effort to identify precursors yielded so little understanding of the major mental disorders? The problem may be the superabundance of contingencies in the life course, with outcomes depending on complex pathways that are in no sense inevitable. As George Brown (1986) notes, "the study of various life stages in a series of separate studies is of limited use. For many problems it is necessary to follow an individual from childhood through adult life to determine how various experiences interrelate" (p. 191).

An intriguing study by Quinton and Rutter (1984, 1985) centered on girls in local authority care (the British equivalent of a foster institution) and an appropriate comparison group. It found those who received institutional care were more likely to become pregnant early in adult life, to enter unstable cohabiting relationships, to have serious problems in relating to and caring for their children, and to have psychiatric disorders. They were less likely to plan their relationships with men and more likely to cohabit with a person who had significant personal problems and who provided little support. When such women had a supportive spouse, it alleviated many of the parenting difficulties. Sadly, many noxious patterns of child care and ineffective coping seemed to replicate themselves across generations. The children of women who had received institutional care also were more likely to experience such problems as teenage difficulties, leaving home early because of rejection or conflict, and early pregnancy.

More recently, Rutter and colleagues (Kreppner et al. 2007; Rutter, Kreppner, and O'Connor 2001; Rutter, O'Connor, and the ERA Study Team 2004) have examined the effects of being removed from institutional care on later development. They focus on outcomes for children who were adopted from Romanian orphanages in the early 1990s after the downfall of the Ceausescu regime. These children faced extraordinary deprivation in the institutions where they spent their early lives and then were adopted by relatively affluent families in the UK. The researchers compared outcomes at ages 4, 6, and 11–12 with adoptees born in the UK. Overall, there was substantial variation in cognitive and social outcomes, even among children who had lived for more than two years in an extremely deprived environment. For these investigators, the findings pointed to the resilience of children and the positive effects of removal of early adversities on later life. However, outcomes for children who had lived more than six months in the institutions were less positive than for children who had been adopted earlier. At age 11, about 64 percent of those who were reared in the orphanage for less than 6 months exhibited no sign of impairment across seven domains (cognitive impairment, inattention/overactivity, attachment problems, problems with peers, emotional and conduct problems, autistic patterns) compared to 28 percent of those who lived there between 6 and 24 months and 39 percent of those who lived there for more than two years (Kreppner et al. 2007). About 44 percent of children who had lived in the orphanage for six or more months experienced two or more impairments by age six, and these remained relatively stable up to age 11. The authors propose that the effects of extreme early deprivation (particularly that which lasts beyond six months) may be difficult to reverse for many children, even when the subsequent part of their childhood is spent in positive, well-functioning families. Still, the finding that about one-third of these children showed normal functioning at age 11 indicates resilience and variability in outcomes even following the most extreme adversities in early childhood.

Healthy parents who create a warm and constructive environment for their children, make them feel valued, and encourage acquisition of skills can do much to protect against psychological disorder, although biological vulnerabilities and environmental assaults intrude on the best and most loving environments. Recognizing the importance of high-quality parenting, however, does not equate with blaming parents whose children develop disorder.

Many conditions contribute to poor parenting, including premature parental roles and a lack of child care skills. Parents who are themselves mentally ill or who face life stresses with which they cannot cope have more difficulty attending to the needs of their children

(Feldman, Stiffman, and Jung 1987). Exacerbating these problems are poverty, poor housing conditions, inadequate schooling, and discrimination. Poverty increases risk, but most
poor children acquire the necessary psychological and coping skills. The relative role of
biological predisposition and environment depends, of course, on the specific disorder
being considered. Such issues as altering living patterns, improving housing conditions,
eliminating discrimination, and providing good schools are very much intertwined with
larger social welfare debates. Society will not readily alter its priorities and distribution of
resources merely because mental health workers observe that current conditions may lead
to poor mental health. A political battle will need to be fought, one threatening to at least
some privileged stakeholders under the status quo.

    Income and education are key factors contributing to complex biological and social
trajectories. As James Heckman, a Nobel Prize–winning economist who has studied the
role of inequality, has noted, "Investment in early education for disadvantaged children
from birth to age five helps reduce the achievement gap, reduce the need for special education, increase the likelihood of healthier lifestyles, lower the crime rate and reduce overall
social costs" (Heckman 2011, p. 32). There is massive evidence on the damaging effects of
infant and childhood deprivation and neglect, which is often associated with disadvantage
and the effects of poverty on family structure and processes. What remains less clear is the
role of these adversities and developmental factors in the most serious mental disorders
such as schizophrenia, bipolar disorder, autism, and other conditions that have important
biological precursors.

THE SOCIAL STRESS PERSPECTIVE

Stress has been one of the most active areas of research in social psychiatry. Figure 5.1 depicts
a simplified version of what has come to be known as the stress process (Avison et al. 2009;
Pearlin 2003; Pearlin et al. 1981). To put it briefly, exposure to life events, chronic strains, or

---

Figure 5.1 • The Stress Process

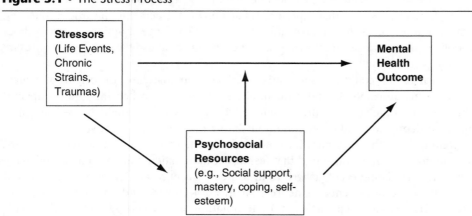

Source: Derived from Pearlin, Leonard, I., et al. "The Stress Process." *Journal of Health and Social
Behavior* 22 (1981): 337–356.

traumas is hypothesized to put one at risk for mental health problems, although most of the research has investigated psychological distress or depressive symptomatology, not disorder *per se*, as outcomes.

Life change events may be hypothesized to play a role in the formation of disease, to trigger a particular disease process to which a given person is constitutionally vulnerable, to stimulate help seeking, or to shape the mode of expression of distress. Brown and Harris (1978), in their classic research, identified life events as a causal influence in depression; however, they argued that not all types of events are important, only certain severe events involving long-term threat:

> The distinctive feature of the great majority of the provoking events is the experience of loss or disappointment, if this is defined broadly to include threat of or actual separation from a key figure, an unpleasant revelation about someone close, a life-threatening illness to a close relative, a major material loss or general disappointment or threat of them, and miscellaneous crises such as being made redundant after a long period of steady employment. In more general terms the loss or disappointment could concern a person or object, a role, or an idea. (Brown and Harris 1978, pp. 274–275)

Subsequent studies of the impact of life change on the development of depressive symptoms and psychological distress have largely confirmed that it is unexpected and negative change that is most important for the development of psychopathology (Pearlin 2003).

One advantage gained by conceptualizing stress as a process is that it highlights the potential long-term trajectories of disadvantage (or the proliferation of secondary stressors and strains) that can emerge after initial exposure to a psychologically damaging event. Brown and colleagues documented a strong relationship between early death of a mother and subsequent depression among women. Harris, Brown, and Bifulco (1987) explicate how and why this event can affect subsequent life transitions. Early maternal loss may be associated with lack of adequate care, which in turn correlates with premarital pregnancy, less effective coping, and early and often unsuitable marriages. Although there is a link between lower social class status and depression, what is most important is the interplay of factors associated with low socioeconomic standing. This perspective on development of the life course assumes that experience at any point is dependent on earlier influences, choices, and resources that, in turn, affect the subsequent range of options. Choices about schooling, job, marriage, childbearing, and their timing establish the conditions for future transitions (Brown 1986).

Brown and his colleagues substantially refined their analysis of the origins of depression by using an elaborate and influential instrument they called the Life Events and Difficulty Schedule (LEDS) (Brown and Harris 1989). Weaving their theoretical thinking about depression and other conditions into a life course perspective, they focus on the contingencies that may push life onto one or another pathway. In research on depression among women, it was found that feelings of humiliation and entrapment following a severely threatening event, as well as measured perceptions of loss or danger, account for most of the occurrence of depression in both clinical and community samples (Brown, Harris, and Hepworth 1995). Humiliation, as defined by the researchers, is associated with events in which a person has been devalued in relation to self or others. Entrapment refers to events lasting at least six months that involve ongoing personal difficulty, marked by indications of persistence or deterioration.

Stress is demonstrably a major factor in depression, anxiety, and psychophysiologi-cal distress, and it can lead to disabling conditions. Increasing attention has been devoted in recent decades to posttraumatic stress disorder (PTSD), defined by the *DSM-IV* as a response to life-threatening events such as combat, natural disasters, serious accidents, personal assaults such as rape and torture, sexual abuse, and other such dire threatening experiences. PTSD can also develop after witnessing, or learning about, such events occur-ring to friends, relatives, or others. The *DSM* attempts to differentiate PTSD from normal responses to extreme stress by duration of symptoms (a month or more), dysfunctions such as flashbacks and nightmares, feelings of detachment and estrangement, recurrent and intrusive recollections, and psychic numbing. Even severe stress, of course, is ubiquitous, and people have stress reactions of many kinds. A majority of the population has experi-enced at least one of the traumas often associated with PTSD. Measures of the incidence and prevalence of PTSD vary a great deal depending on the stringency of criteria applied.

PTSD often occurs in conjunction with psychiatric comorbidity, such as depres-sion, anxiety disorders, and substance abuse. Cases of this type are more severe. PTSD occurs more commonly among certain groups. Almost one-third of soldiers in war zones were said to have experienced PTSD. However, a reanalysis of the 1998 National Veterans Readjustment study, on which these estimates were based, arrived at 19 percent as a more realistic estimate of the number of veterans with war-related PTSD. Nine percent were still suffering with moderate impairments 11–12 years after the war (Dohrenwend et al. 2006).

In recent years there have been numerous studies of American and British troops who were sent to Iraq and Afghanistan, and they provide a picture of less harm. The studies with more careful methodologies that include random sampling among the troops find PTSD rates varying from 2.1 to 13.8 percent (McNally 2012). The most ambitious study, the U.S. Millennium Cohort Study of almost 48,000 service personnel, found that 4.3 percent of forces sent to Afghanistan and 7.6 percent of those who saw combat developed PTSD. The study more intensively followed a subgroup sent to Afghanistan and Iraq who were assessed prior to deployment and then followed by two further assessments at three-year intervals. Among those who were found healthy prior to deployment, 6.6 percent of those with multiple deployments and 4.5 percent with single deployments had PTSD symptoms at later follow-ups (McNally 2012).

The impact of trauma depends on many factors such as the type and intensity of the traumatizing experience, individual temperament, a history of child abuse (especially sexual abuse), attributions people make about the event and their own behavior, and experience in dealing with related events. Men are more likely than women to experi-ence trauma, but women are more than twice as likely to have a lifetime PTSD diagnosis (Kessler et al. 1995). Sexual abuse and harassment appear to play a major role. Rape and sexual abuse account for 100 percent of the excess posttraumatic stress disorder in women as compared with men. Such abuse may play an important role in depressive disorders as well.

Although life events in and of themselves may not create illness, they may induce greater concern with symptoms and result more readily in entrance into treatment. Studies have established a sequence by which stressful events lead to distress, efforts to conceptu-alize and understand one's experience, and decisions on coping and help seeking.

Finally, certain stressful events may influence the way mental illness is expressed. Being fired from one's job will not cause paranoid schizophrenia, but it might provide substance for a patient's existing paranoid ideation. In sum, the pathways and consequences of stress are manifold. Disentangling the link with mental disorder requires isolating the types of stresses involved, the particular disorders referred to, and the distinctive influences that relate the precipitating events to illness process.

While stress is common in people's lives, some manage it much better than others. Attention has thus shifted to intervening variables that either increase vulnerability or contribute to resilience. Such factors include personality, coping strategies, and social support. With respect to the stress process formulated in Figure 5.1, this dynamic is pictured in terms of the potential for resources to buffer or moderate the stress–mental health relationship. According to the stress process model, persons have different vulnerability to life stressors due to differences in access to these resources. Personality traits that seem to amplify the detrimental effects of stress are type A pattern (Friedman and Rosenman 1974), lacking a sense of personal control or efficacy (Rodin 1986), and lack of hardiness (Kobasa 1979). Coping factors include problem-solving approaches, modes of information acquisition, ability to anticipate, and planning (Leventhal 1970); an important contrast is whether persons emphasize problem-oriented or emotion-oriented approaches, with the latter more likely to exaggerate stressful impacts. Social support has been investigated many ways, in terms of both subjective and objective measures of social networks and help that is given and received. The main hypothesis is that the occurrence of negative life events and chronic strain are less damaging on the mental health of persons with high levels of social support.

Vigorous debate surrounds virtually every component of the stress-coping paradigm (measurement of stress, description of social networks, depiction of the coping process). How much emphasis should be placed, respectively, on positive and negative life events, subjective and objective measures, and major life events as compared with daily irritations? Should stressful events be recorded according to respondent report or independent evaluations? What significance does an event's timing have? And how about distinctions between events totally outside an individual's control as compared with those to which the person could have contributed, such as divorce, loss of job, or economic difficulties? These debates have significantly sharpened thinking with respect to assumptions, conceptualization, and methodology in stress research (Brown and Harris 1978; Dohrenwend and Dohrenwend 1981; Lazarus and Folkman 1984).

Although evidence linking social support to health outcomes has been substantial, this area of study is fraught with inconsistencies. The concept of social support may refer to the extent and structure of social networks, the availability of intimate others, the intimacy and frequency of social contacts, voluntary community participation, and similar phenomena. Theories underlying alternative approaches to measurement have not always been clear, and the specific causal mechanisms intervening between support and outcomes are poorly detailed, although specification of alternative statistical models has advanced (Wheaton 1985). Nor has much attention been given to the constraints, responsibilities, and stresses associated with kinship ties and other close interpersonal relations (Thoits 1995).

Decisions about measurement often bear on larger theoretical ideas. Scales that do not differentiate clearly between positive and negative life changes make it impossible to test the assumption that events, independent of positive or negative features, contribute to morbidity. Similarly, the counting or scoring of events, in examining direct relationships between life change and health outcomes, ignores developmental research that suggests growth and competence may be attained through mastering challenging life events (Lazarus and Folkman 1984; Mechanic 1962). When measurement models are not well constructed, they blunt the potential richness of theoretical exploration.

A sense of personal control and the exercise of "mastery" are often considered resources in the stress process and they represent a large and promising research area with practical implications. It is possible to intervene in many social contexts to enhance people's control over their immediate environments (Rodin 1986). This observation is also consistent with developments in clinical psychology and cognitive therapy regarding helplessness and depression. In some contexts studied, such as nursing homes, even small changes in personal control can affect psychological response, health, and even mortality (Rodin and Langer 1977). Questions remain whether these beneficial effects occur only in extreme situations, such as institutional care, or more generally across a range of usual situations. Nor is it evident how enhanced control interacts with personality, attribution styles, cultural values, age, and other variables.

Finally, the stress process model does not fully recognize the potential benefits of successful adaptation to stress on later outcomes. Elder (1974) studied a cohort of children born in 1920–1921 who were part of the Oakland Growth Study and who grew up during the Great Depression. Data were available concerning adult adaptation as reflected in anxiety and tension, psychosomatic illness, behavior disorders, serious somatic illness, and psychotic reactions. Children from the working class faced greater adversities during the Depression and had more problems of adaptation later. More interesting, however, middle-class children who faced deprivation during the Great Depression were more likely to be symptom-free in adult life than those who were sheltered from deprivation. Twenty-six percent of the nondeprived middle class had behavior disorder problems, as compared with 7 percent of the deprived group. Heavy drinking in adulthood was much more common in the nondeprived middle class than in the deprived middle class (43 percent versus 24 percent).

These findings, as well as similar results from other studies, suggest provocative hypotheses. Are persons who are insulated from difficulties that allow for the development of competence and mastery handicapped as a result of a life experience that is too protective? What are the positive social functions of stress, particularly when it is not overwhelming and when persons learn to deal with it effectively? How much stress is necessary in early life as preparation for later adversity? The results of such studies as Elder's are consistent with experimental work in the area of helplessness, suggesting that people's beliefs in their own ability to affect what happens to them are important for well-being (Seligman 1975). Dealing effectively with adversity reinforces a sense of competence and confidence.

Our understanding of the interaction of life events with other factors in the occurrence of psychiatric morbidity, though still in its infancy, provides a rationale for preventive and community mental health efforts. The idea that outcomes depend on the ability of individuals to withstand adverse life events through coping skills and social supports justifies efforts to increase assistance during critical transitions, such as a divorce, while assisting people in actively coping with other enduring problems associated with their life situations. Some self-help groups, such as Parents Without Partners, make assistance available to anyone going through various categories of stressful experience (Weiss 1975). Other groups, such as Alcoholics Anonymous, work with individuals suffering from a specific disorder. Outright prevention of serious mental illness remains uncertain at present, but programs based on a model of teaching coping techniques and expanded social support have succeeded in minimizing secondary disabilities.

INEQUALITY AND RISK OF MENTAL DISORDERS

One of the most persistent findings in the epidemiological literature is the inverse relationship between socioeconomic status (SES) and the prevalence of mental disorder. Socioeconomic status, which is typically operationalized as income, occupation, and education, reflects not only access to material resources but also differences in power, prestige, social and human capital, and the resources that help people to cope with stressful events and strains. Much of the research has focused on the relationship between SES and depression and schizophrenia (Muntaner et al. 2004). Saraceno, Levav, and Kohn (2005) estimated the ratio of current disorder between persons of low versus high SES to be about 3.4 for schizophrenia and 2.4 for depression. Across a number of studies, debate has centered on the relative merits of social causation versus social selection for explaining these relationships.

Social causation explanations, consistent with the stress process paradigm, posit that the adversities and strains associated with low SES status combine with a lack of resources for buffering these strains to produce mental disorder. In contrast, social selection (also called social drift) explanations argue that the impairments associated with having a mental health problem lead one to be selected into a lower SES position. For example, having a mental disorder increases risk of dropping out of school and depresses occupational attainment and income, thereby lowering SES or limiting the rate of advancement characteristic of one's peers.

Bruce Dohrenwend and colleagues (Dohrenwend and Dohrenwend 1969; Dohrenwend et al. 1992) spent several decades exploring the extent to which social selection and social causation explain the relationship between SES and a variety of types of disorder. They developed an unusual strategy to test this idea. The reasoning was that while mental impairments would interfere with social mobility, ethnic discrimination would operate similarly, keeping people from advancing in their socioeconomic status. Thus, ethnic minorities who were not psychiatrically impaired would have difficulty in mobility, while nondisadvantaged groups could move up the social ladder more easily. If schizophrenia was socially caused by the stresses associated with lower SES, ethnic minority groups would be particularly disadvantaged and would be expected to have a higher level of disorder than persons from nondisadvantaged ethnic groups. But if social selection was the predominant influence, healthy ethnic minorities would have difficulty moving upward because of discrimination and blocked opportunities. More of these individuals who remained in the lower social strata would be psychologically healthy than those unlikely to experience discrimination.

Finding an appropriate research setting was a particular challenge for testing this hypothesis. Using Israel's population register, Dohrenwend and his colleagues (1992) identified a birth cohort of 4,914 young Israelis who were born to European and North African families. "Oriental Jews" from North Africa are relatively disadvantaged and experience considerable prejudice and discrimination. Psychiatrists then screened this sample in a standardized way, and those with conditions were given specific diagnoses. These data then allowed examination of comparative illness rates by diagnosis. Rates of schizophrenia were higher for those of European than North African background in low socioeconomic groupings, suggesting support for the social selection hypothesis. In contrast, social causation seemed to be much more influential in the case of depression in women, and substance abuse and antisocial personality in men.

The general conclusion of Dohrenwend and his colleagues—that social selection matters more for explaining the inverse relationship between SES and schizophrenia, while social causation matters more for explaining the relationship of SES with depression—has been generally confirmed over a number of studies using various research designs (Muntaner et al. 2004; Saraceno, Levav, and Kohn 2005). However, the issue is not completely settled. For example, recent large cohort studies have offered the advantage of following groups of people over their lifetimes, allowing an examination of the causal influence of SES in a way previously impossible. Early socioeconomic disadvantage may be a more important cause of serious mental illness such as schizophrenia than was previously thought (Saraceno, Levav, and Kohn 2005).

The ideal design for sorting out the relative influence of social selection versus social causation would, of course, be experimental, but practical considerations make it impossible to experimentally manipulate the SES of individuals. Costello and colleagues (2003), however, were able to make use of a natural experiment to try to assess social causation of common behavioral problems. The Great Smoky Mountains Study is a careful and ambitious longitudinal investigation of childhood mental health based on a random sample of young people ages 9, 11, and 13 in western North Carolina, including an oversample of American Indian children living on a federal reservation in the study area. While the study was being conducted, the reservation began to receive income from a gambling casino, with every person on the reservation receiving a portion of the profits. The effect was essentially to move many American Indian families (by chance) out of poverty, and the researchers were able to examine the impact on levels of psychopathology among children. Prior to opening of the casino, poor American Indian children were more likely to have symptoms of emotional and behavioral problems than nonpoor American Indian children, as would be expected from the extensive literature documenting an inverse relationship between SES and psychopathology. However, the American Indian children who moved out of poverty exhibited a 40 percent decrease in symptoms of behavioral problems in the four years following opening of the casino compared to the four years prior. There was no effect of the added income on levels of psychopathology experienced by American Indian children who were not poor prior to the opening of the casino. After moving out of poverty, children's levels of behavioral symptoms were similar to American Indian children in the sample who were never poor. The researchers also considered whether various stressors may have mediated the relationship between improved SES and behavioral problems. The only significant relationship was with parental supervision, that is, the effect of moving out of poverty on behavioral symptoms appeared to be due to parents being able to better supervise their children. There was no similar effect of moving out of poverty on the experience of children's emotional symptoms (depression and anxiety).

A NOTE ON THE LABELING PERSPECTIVE

One perspective that we have not covered but which was dominant in the 1960s and 1970s was labeling theory. It emerged as part of the ideology inspiring deinstitutionalization and at the same time as debates over the question whether mental illness was a myth (see Chapter 2). Some scholars presented labeling theory as a causal model to explain mental illness while others viewed labeling primarily as a process contributing to chronicity and disabilities beyond those directly resulting from mental disorder. Labeling theory derived from a theoretical approach in sociology that focused less on the origins of deviant behavior and more on those social forces that help structure, organize, and perpetuate deviant identity. Advocates of this perspective argue that deviance is reinforced by social reactions, by the manner in which deviance is labeled, and by the resultant exclusion of, and discrimination against, the deviant. Basic assumptions underlying this approach are that each society produces its own deviants by its definitions and rules and that processes of definition serve to maintain collective boundaries (Erikson 1966; Lemert 1951).

Labeling theory proposes a sequential model in which, over time, a pattern of deviant response has been labeled in a fashion that increases the probability of continued deviance (Becker 1963). As the definition of the deviant response persists, and as normal roles become more elusive for the deviant because of limited opportunities and growing exclusion, there is a tendency for deviant acts to become organized as part of an ongoing social identity. In this way the labeling process itself helps convert transitory, common deviant behavior into a more stable pattern.

Scheff (1984) applied this framework to mental disorder. He maintained that the occurrence of psychological symptoms, or deviant responses, is frequent and usually escapes labeling and definition. When treated within normal and conventional response repertoires, such behavior is likely to be temporary and nonpersistent. However, when the behavior receives explicit identification and labeling, forces that propel the behavior into a social role come into play. Scheff hypothesized that, although deviants do not explicitly learn the role of "a person with mental illness," they are able to assume it readily enough because they have acquired stereotyped imagery of mental illness from early childhood through movies, television, radio, newspapers, and popular magazines. Scheff also believes that deviants labeled as mentally ill may receive a variety of reinforcing advantages, although assumption of this role need not be a conscious process. Later, when such persons attempt to resume normal, or conventional, social roles, their opportunities are restricted, and they may be punished as a result of the stigma associated with past difficulties. This can include problems in obtaining adequate employment and difficulties in relations with others who react harshly or fearfully to someone previously classified as mentally ill. According to Scheff, the transition from mental symptoms as an incidental aspect of social performance to mental illness as a social role is likely to occur under conditions of considerable personal and social stress. In such circumstances, individuals may themselves embrace the societal definition of their status, solidifying their own self-perceptions as deviants.

Although the societal reaction approach is provocative and obviously addresses relevant elements in the trajectory of becoming mentally ill, it is tempting to exaggerate the relative importance of such processes. No one would deny that social labels have powerful effects on individuals, but little evidence supports the inference that labeling processes are major causative influences in producing chronic mental illness. Existing theories are extremely vague in defining the conditions under which labeling will or will not produce deviant behavior. Some patients get well rather quickly and stay well, while others, such as those with schizophrenia, commonly develop chronic disabilities. The theory of labeling does not explain this contrast.

Robins (1975) presented a useful critique assessing labeling theory in relationship to existing knowledge about alcoholism. She noted numerous inconsistencies with regard to important facts. First, predictors of deviance are comparably accurate for both labeled and unlabeled alcoholics if the severity of the problem is taken into account. Second, all common forms of deviant behavior decrease with age, despite the reality that labeling associated with deviance must obviously cumulate over the life span. Third, labeling theory would suggest that persons labeled in a certain way—say, as a prostitute or thief—would increasingly display such behavior. Yet, even when specific types of deviance in younger life are associated with later deviance, often the content of deviant behavior changes. Young girls caught stealing are more likely in later life to attempt suicide, or to be sexually promiscuous or alcoholic, than they are to become adult thieves. Fourth, several studies show that parental deviance is associated with the probability that children will develop schizophrenia or be alcoholics even when the children are separated from their parents and do not know the parents' identification, as in the case of infant adoptees. Moreover, Robins argued, the process of labeling is quite different from theoretical conceptions. The alcoholic, for example, is usually labeled only after many years of excessive drinking, typically by the family not public authorities. Although labels of *alcoholism* are withheld from many heavy drinkers for many years, the behavior is often self-sustaining and may lead to physical dependence. The most popular group approach to containing excessive drinking—membership in Alcoholics Anonymous—actually requires persons to label themselves as alcoholics as part of a strategy for behavior change.

Many people automatically associate the term "mental illness" with psychotic behavior in contrast to the broad variety of emotional problems that occur in populations. For those who do have contact with the mentally ill, perceptions of illness, danger, and degree of stigma grow out of their familiarity (Clausen 1981; Link and Cullen 1986). Individuals test their general impressions against actual experience, often revising their expectations in a favorable direction. While labeling and its consequences may be important, then, the form and content of judgments are highly interdependent with the behavior of those who have mental illness. Some patients may fulfill stereotypes, but most do not, and their families and the community can tell the difference. As Robins' critique suggests, labeling theory is vague in its formulations, in its specification of the ways labeling affects illness, and in the specific types of disorders that may be most affected.

Although labeling theory falls short when it aims to settle etiological questions, the perspective remains valuable for appreciating how the definition of a problem and its management may affect the course or social outcome. In short, the manner in which the community defines and deals with sick and vulnerable people may either encourage or discourage disability, sick role behavior, and dependency. Communicating positive expectations to persons with mental illness cannot help but support improved functioning and adjustment.

PSYCHOTHERAPEUTIC APPROACHES

Views of what causes mental illness influence models of intervention. Psychotherapeutic models for treating mental illness vary in their emphasis on early development, interpersonal communication, family role conflict, behavior modification, and other factors. A variety of counseling approaches, encounter groups, peer and self-help organizations, and recreational sensitivity-group experiences also compete with more formal psychotherapy (Back 1972; Wuthnow 1994). The term *therapy* itself has come to encompass a broad spectrum of ideas, from reasonable approaches that are well grounded in theory and empirical research on the one hand, to various therapy cults on the other. In this arena, it sometimes seems as if anything goes, particularly outside the established professional and medical spheres. Research shows an increase in the number of Americans who received psychotherapy from mental health professionals during the 1990s, with nearly 10 million people in treatment in 1997 (Olfson et al. 2002). More recently, there has been a slight decline in the proportion of the population receiving outpatient psychotherapy, while use of psychotropic medications has increased (Olfson and Marcus 2010).

The relative advantage of psychotherapeutic versus biological approaches depends, of course, on the type of disorder and the invasiveness and safety of the therapies. Although patients with mild and moderate disorders at times benefit from short-term therapy and retain such benefits well into the future, an acute treatment model may not be appropriate for other patients. Many with schizophrenia, for example, require long-term continuing care and quickly relapse when they discontinue medication. An acute care model serves these patients badly, and proper care should be seen as akin to the situation of a diabetic patient who requires insulin and continued monitoring, rather than the situation of a person with an acute infectious disorder who returns to normal after the infection has been treated. The issue of appropriate treatment is crucial for public policy, because application of the wrong model not only contributes to great personal suffering, but also public disillusionment and poor use of resources within the mental health system.

Among the many different psychotherapeutic approaches to psychological disorder, a few have been consistently useful and now enjoy wide acceptance, including learning or behavioral therapy, cognitive therapy, and interpersonal therapy. Following is a brief description of each type of treatment.

Over the years, psychologists have achieved substantial understanding of the learning process. After some faltering early attempts, translating these findings into a therapeutic approach is now a major programmatic investment as well as a focal point for research. One of the first systematic attempts to link learning theory and psychoanalytic practice was presented in *Personality and Psychotherapy*, written by John Dollard and Neal E. Miller in 1950. Bringing together the formulations of Hullian learning theory and psychodynamic insights, these authors tried to specify the conditions under which habits are formed and changed. They reformulated a number of existing concepts—the unconscious, conflict, and repression—into a stimulus–response framework using such terms as *drive*, *cue*, *response*, and *reward*. Thus, repression became understood as the learned avoidance of certain thoughts.

Psychotherapy by Reciprocal Inhibition by Joseph Wolpe (1958) gave considerable impetus to the use of learning theory in psychotherapy. Wolpe maintained that psychotherapeutic effects were due mainly to complete or partial suppression of anxiety responses by means of the simultaneous evocation of other responses physiologically antagonistic to anxiety. He also characterized neurotic behavior as a persistent but learned and unadaptive response acquired in anxiety-generating situations. Such anxiety responses are unadaptive because they continue to manifest themselves in situations lacking objective threat. Given these assumptions, Wolpe and others developed approaches based on desensitization, relaxation, operant conditioning, and other learning techniques now commonly practiced in psychotherapy.

Critics of behavior therapy charged that such procedures altered symptoms without affecting basic causes. They also maintained that, except for specific conditions dominated by a single symptom, such as phobias and sexual impotence, mental conditions comprised complicated syndromes for which it is difficult to discern and develop specific reinforcement schedules or other remedial procedures. For these detractors, one must understand the relevant important cues and stimuli in a patient's illness before proceeding. More frequently than not, they argued, this process requires a long period of therapeutic work.

The contention that behavior therapy merely reduces particular symptoms, or substitutes one symptom for another, has proved to be invalid. Implicit in the claim is the assumption that a more holistic cure is possible, but little evidence supports this conclusion. Changing specific destructive patterns of behavior, such as self-mutilation or fear of leaving one's house, is anything but trivial. The second argument, concerning the difficulty of locating specific cues and the patterns of behavior and thinking with which they are associated, points to a more serious challenge. Over time, however, the techniques of behavior change have been incorporated effectively into a wide variety of other therapeutic approaches concerned with deeper personal investigation.

Many psychotherapeutic approaches are undifferentiated, with little variation from one patient to another regardless of the presenting problem, the patient's familial and social situations, or the need for practical action. Psychodynamic therapists, for example, tend to approach many different types of patients in the same way, taking a global psychological approach to treatment, in contrast to narrowing in on specific difficulties, while defining mutual goals for therapist and patient. A major contribution of the behavioral approach has been its pragmatic emphasis centering on intermediate objectives to be accomplished through modification of complex stimulus–response patterns (Bandura 1969).

Behavior therapy is no panacea, but it has turned out to be a constructive approach for adjusting behaviors that are painful and undermine interpersonal relationships. Even without providing a cure for persons with serious mental disorder, as in the case of schizophrenia, it can facilitate adoption of certain behaviors helpful to the rehabilitation and community adjustment of the patient. Behavior modification may not only be valuable on its own terms but also be a boost to the patient's sense of psychological comfort, self-control, and confidence.

Behavior therapy encompasses a series of techniques including systematic desensitization, flooding, modeling, and stress inoculation (Sutherland 1977). In systematic desensitization, the patient is introduced to a disturbing stimulus in increasing intensity so as to develop tolerance of it. As the patient masters his or her fear in response to one of the graded exposures, rewards, such as encouragement and compliments, may be given. In flooding, the patient is asked to imagine the most frightening examples of feared objects until his or her fear diminishes. This technique may worsen the fear if the patient cannot tolerate imagined scenes, so the method is often combined with tranquilizing drugs to reduce anxiety. In modeling, the patient receives encouragement and rewards for repeating the behavior of the therapist when dealing with some troubling situation. Some mental hospitals create token economies to encourage patients to take increased responsibility and to cooperate in ward endeavors. In stress inoculation, patients learn slow breathing and muscular relaxation (which inhibit anxiety) while being exposed to electric shock. They also learn to reassure themselves and engage in thinking conducive to coping. These learned techniques are then used in real-life situations threatening to the person.

An extension of behavior therapy involves learned self-control, in which the person induces self-selected behaviors without external reinforcement or contingency schedules controlled by outsiders (Halleck 1978). One application is to teach patients how to recognize when they are having symptom exacerbations, how to reduce exposure to events upsetting to them, and how to shape their expressions of emotion in the company of others so as to avoid stigmatization. Improved self-control through self-monitoring and self-evaluation has been useful among patients with psychoses. It has even been suggested it may "be possible to teach schizophrenic patients a behavioral approach for talking themselves out of their symptoms" (Breier and Strauss 1983, p. 1141).

In recent years, there has been a significant resurgence of interest in the role of cognition (Fodor 2006). Cognitive therapy is now perhaps the single most well-established evidence-based therapy, and it dominates the psychotherapy field. Cognitive therapy builds on many successful behavioral techniques, but it concentrates on revising people's self-definitions and attributions. Both cognitive therapy and interpersonal therapy are more purposeful than earlier psychotherapeutic approaches, and empirical support for their usefulness is substantial. Didactic cognitive behavior therapy training is now required in most M.D., clinical psychology Ph.D., Psy.D., and M.S.W. graduate programs (although many schools also continue to teach non-evidence-based approaches such as psychoanalytic/psychodynamic psychotherapy, couples therapy, and group psychotherapy) (Weissman et al. 2006).

Cognitive therapy (CT), often called cognitive behavioral therapy (CBT), is comparable, or even superior, in efficacy to pharmacological interventions for some patients. It is based on three central principles: people can become "aware of the content and processing of their thinking," how people think about themselves and their lives affects their emotional and behavioral responses, and adjustment can be achieved and distress lessened through change of core beliefs and schemas (Beck and Dozois 2011). First introduced by Aaron T. Beck more than 50 years ago, cognitive therapeutic approaches have become refined and popular. CT/CBT regards psychopathology as an exaggerated form of normal adaptive response (Beck 1991), which is in opposition to the medical conception of pathology as discontinuous from normal behavior. Focusing first on unipolar depression, Beck (1991) observed a certain cognitive shift that blocked out positive information while negative information and attributions festered: "...clinically, the patient is more likely to produce exaggerated negative inferences when integrating past events or projecting into the future, when making attributions for which there are no clear-cut criterion[sic] on which to base judgments, or when making vague (but crucial) inferences about his or her character" (p. 372). CT/CBT, in turn, provides a structured process by which the therapist and patient can examine the accuracy and utility of modes of thought through observation, analysis, and experimentation. The goal is to guide the client toward more realistic and adaptive cognitive appraisals while encouraging effective coping skills and problem-solving capacities (Beck and Dozois 2011). How this is done depends on the nature of the psychopathology at hand and context of the problem. According to CT/CBT, common psychotherapeutic elements such as warmth, empathy, and positive regard are necessary but not sufficient for successful personal change. There must be a systematic plan for changing behavior and reinforcing positive responses, and this hinges on new ways of thinking by the patient.

The most rigorously studied psychosocial therapy, CT/CBT has undergone many clinical trials. Generally, the approach works well for patients with unipolar depression, generalized anxiety disorder; panic disorder; phobias; social anxiety; and childhood internalizing problems such as depression, anxiety, and psychosomatic complaints. In these cases, it often works as well or better than medication (Beck and Dozois 2011). Less evidence exists of its value for treating psychotic disorders. However, a recent randomized trial of low-functioning patients with schizophrenia found that when CT was added to standard care, function improved significantly, symptoms such as delusions and disorganization declined, and client motivation increased (Grant et al. 2012). Consensus seems to be emerging that optimal treatment involves combinations of medication and CT/CBT, or comparable therapies such as interpersonal therapy. While Grant and colleagues (2012) argue that such combinations may reduce health costs even for the very expensive population of patients with schizophrenia, combination therapies are uncommon and appear to be the casualty of a desire to contain public expenditures in the short term.

The value of CT/CBT has been observed for PTSD, a disorder that is not easily treated, especially among service personnel who generally are reluctant because of perceived stigma to acknowledge their problems and seek mental health treatment. Moreover, this is not a condition that readily responds simply to drug treatment. The Veterans Administration has developed treatment programs based on interventions that have been found somewhat effective with patients with PTSD in the general population (McNally 2012). These build on the cognitive behavioral therapies (already discussed), structured gradual exposures to revisiting the stressful event with therapist support, and cognitive-processing therapies where patients review the stress event in writing and the therapist and patient work to correct dysfunctional beliefs and attributions about the traumatic occurrence.

Interpersonal therapy (IPT) is an additional type of psychotherapy that has had some success. IPT focuses on interpersonal relations and on conflicts in roles and relationships (Klerman, Weissman, and Rounsaville 1984; Weissman et al. 2006). It is designed to be short term (about 16 weeks) and has been used for a variety of disorders, especially depression. Founders of this approach saw depression as a biological illness that could be helped with antidepressants, but felt that psychotherapeutic treatments would be helpful to deal with the interpersonal conflicts that often accompany depression (Weissman 2006).

The National Institute of Mental Health evaluated the efficacy of IPT compared to CBT and drug treatment (imipramine) in a large clinical trial (Elkin et al. 1989). In the short term, all three approaches performed better than placebo. Imipramine brought improvement more quickly than the psychotherapies, but after three months the drug and therapy groups were comparable. Interpersonal therapy appears to outperform cognitive therapy, particularly for more severely depressed patients.

MEDICATION

For several decades, psychiatry was dependent on a fairly fixed range of drug types and was limited in its understanding of how drugs acted on the brain to modify particular psychiatric conditions. In more recent years, new classes of drugs have been developed and new neuroscience technologies have advanced our understanding of how drugs affect brain receptors. Such methodologies as positron emission tomography (PET) and single-photon emission computed tomography (SPECT) allow for safe examination of brain action as it occurs. Through use of radioligands specific for particular neuroreceptors and the study of brain glucose metabolism, we can now image changes in the brain in response to pharmacological agents (Pickar and Hsiao 1995). Psychopharmacology and its effects on the brain have thus become an expanding and exciting field. Chapter 6 reviews trends in rates of pharmaceutical utilization; here we provide an overview of the different types of medications and their relative effectiveness.

Since introduction of the phenothiazines in the 1950s, antipsychotic drugs have played a major role in reducing the most disturbing psychotic symptoms and helping to manage schizophrenia and other psychotic disorders. Although a number of new antipsychotics have been developed over the decades, no one particular drug has been better than others in antipsychotic effects. Each works better for some patients than others. All the earlier drugs have risks of uncomfortable and often serious side-effects, and none of these drugs is free of dangers. Bothersome side-effects have been a major barrier to maintaining many patients with schizophrenia on neuroleptic drugs, and continuity of medication adherence is a major challenge in psychiatric practice (Zygmunt et al. 2002). The action of antipsychotic drugs is poorly understood, but it is widely believed that psychotic symptoms result from excesses of dopamine or oversensitivity of dopamine receptors in the brain. The antipsychotics seem to interfere with the binding of dopamine to its receptor sites.

The first generation of antipsychotic drugs, mostly antagonists of dopamine D2 receptors, were troubling because of high rates of adverse neurological effects and, in particular, tardive dyskinesia and other extrapyramidal indications. Many patients found these drugs aversive and discontinued treatment. These drugs have largely been replaced by a second generation of antipsychotic drugs. Of the approximately 20 antipsychotic drugs available in the United States by 2006, six were second generation antipsychotics (Tandon and Nasrallah 2006). These new "atypical" drugs have lesser affinity for dopamine D2 receptors and more for other neuroreceptors such as serotonin and norepinephrine (Lieberman et al. 2005). These atypicals constitute about 90 percent of the U.S. antipsychotic market and are believed to be more effective in reducing negative symptoms such as lack of emotion or interest, and to have less onerous side-effects than first-generation antipsychotics. Findings vary among studies and these claims are controversial. One careful meta-analysis of 124 randomized controlled trials and other studies reported that four atypical antipsychotics (clozapine, amisulpride, risperidone, and olanzapine) were more efficacious than earlier drugs (Davis, Chen, and Glick 2003). Six other atypicals were not significantly different in efficacy than first-generation drugs. Clozapine appears to be particularly useful for chronic patients who do not respond to other antipsychotics, but it has potential life-threatening side-effects. This meta-analysis found no major differences in overall efficacy among the other most efficacious antipsychotics.

In 2005, Lieberman and his colleagues (2005) reported on a large, randomized, double-blind, active control clinical trial of 1,493 patients with schizophrenia treated at 47 different U.S. sites. This study compared perphenazine (brand name, Trilafon), a first-line antipsychotic, with four newer atypical medications: olanzapine (brand name, Zyprexa), quetiapine (brand name, Seroquel), risperidone (brand name, Risperdal), and ziprasidone (brand name, Geodon). Although haloperidol (brand name, Haldol) had been the most commonly used older antipsychotic, these investigators selected perphenazine because of its lower potency and more moderate profile of side-effects. The most important finding of this large study, confirming clinical experience more broadly, was that 74 percent of patients discontinued their medication before 18 months, indicating serious problems in the use of all such antipsychotic medications. Olanzapine fared somewhat better than the other drugs, with 64 percent discontinuing the medication, but it was hardly a great success in this regard.

Improvement occurred with all of the drugs. Olanzapine was initially most effective, but its advantage eroded over time. Patients receiving olanzapine, however, gained an average of two pounds a month, and 30 percent gained 7 or more percent of their baseline body weight. Olanzapine had effects consistent with the metabolic syndrome that describes persons at cardiovascular risk. Patients on olanzapine were less likely to be hospitalized for schizophrenia than patients on other medications, but persons in this group were most likely of all patients to discontinue treatment because of intolerable side-effects. Risperidone had the lowest discontinuation rate for this reason (10 percent) but had lower efficacy. There were no significant differences in neurologic side-effects among patients taking the new atypicals but, as clinical experience suggested, more patients discontinued perphenazine, the earlier antipsychotic, due to extrapyramidal effects. The bottom line here is that no obviously superior drug exists, and trade-offs must be considered with respect to patient experience, risks of side-effects, and cost. The glaring fact is that most patients do not adhere to longer-term medication regimens, a significant challenge for improving the outcomes of care (Zygmunt et al. 2002).

An important study in England of patients with schizophrenia reinforces the findings of Lieberman and his colleagues in the United States. Jones and his associates (2006) randomized 227 patients, aged 18–65, in 14 community psychiatric services in the National Health Service (NHS), to receive either a first- or second-generation antipsychotic drug among the medications typically used in clinical practice. Blind assessments were made with a sophisticated quality-of-life measure at 12, 26, and 52 weeks, as well as other measures of symptoms and costs. This study, unlike many of those showing advantages of the second-generation atypical drugs, was carefully executed, had a high 52-week follow-up of 81 percent, had excellent outcome measures, and was financed by the NHS rather than the pharmaceutical industry (Jones et al. 2006; Rosenheck 2006). Contrary to expectations, the study found no advantages of the newer class of drugs in terms of quality of life, symptoms, or associated overall costs of care. The authors concluded that "the hypothesis that SGAs [second generation atypicals] are superior was clearly rejected" (Jones et al. 2006, p. 1085). There was a statistically nonsignificant trend favoring the first-generation antipsychotic drugs. Jeffrey Lieberman, an American authority in research on these drugs, commented on this study and earlier ones, noting that "any reasoned and objective view of the evidence … must lead to the conclusion that with the possible exception of clozapine, the SGAs are not the great breakthrough in therapeutics they were once thought to be; rather, they represent an incremental advance at best" (2006, p. 1071). This remains a charitable perspective. Despite the rhetoric and hype, we unfortunately remain a long way from truly effective drug treatments for persons with schizophrenia.

Accurately understanding side-effects is crucial in decisions about patient management. This task is not uncommonly distorted by aggressive and misleading pharmaceutical marketing efforts, which can be of major consequence. For example, as noted, olanzapine (Zyprexa) possesses some advantages but also presents the risk of weight gain and diabetes, and this has led to much litigation alleging that Lilly, the manufacturer, did not adequately warn of these significant dangers. In 2003, the Food and Drug Administration (FDA) required a change of label that made explicit the diabetes-related risks. Thousands of patient lawsuits were filed against Lilly, and in June 2005 there was a $690 million settlement covering more than 8,000 claims. Documents that became available from other litigation revealed that Lilly had research connecting olanzapine to weight gain and hyperglycemia but the company chose not to reveal it. In fact, executives instructed their sales staff to avoid the issue (Kesselheim and Avorn 2007). In the largest fraud settlement in U.S. pharmaceutical history GlaxoSmithKline agreed to fraud charges, paying $3 billion in penalties. Among their offenses were illegally marketing drugs for unapproved uses—including their high selling antidepressants—and withholding safety data from regulators (Hancock 2012).

The introduction of clozapine (Clozaril) in the United States in the early 1990s was greeted with excitement because this drug almost never causes extrapyramidal motor side-effects and seems to have efficacy in some 30 to 40 percent of patients who have failed to improve with other antipsychotic medications (Pickar and Hsiao 1995). This was the first indication since the introduction of neuroleptics that one drug seemed to be superior to others available. Clozapine, however, has a 0.5 to 2 percent risk of agranulocytosis, a potentially fatal blood-related condition. Its use, thus, requires frequent monitoring of the white blood cell count (Pickar and Hsiao 1995; Yudofsky, Hales, and Ferguson 1991). The drug is recommended only if standard antipsychotic treatment has failed. Other serious side-effects more recently noted include the possibility of myocarditis, a serious heart problem, insulin resistance, and diabetes. Clozapine treatment was initially very expensive and coverage of such treatments put enormous stresses on state mental health budgets that pay for the treatment of most patients with long-term psychoses. Generic clozapine is now available at lower cost, and costs compare reasonably with the newer atypical antipsychotics.

A study in Connecticut found that discharge rates did not differ between those treated with clozapine versus traditional care, but those on clozapine were less likely to be readmitted to inpatient care (Essock et al. 1996). In a cost-effectiveness analysis of patients receiving long-term care in state hospitals in Connecticut that compared clozapine to a range of conventional antipsychotic drugs, clozapine was more effective on most measures than usual care and had advantages in protecting against extrapyramidal side-effects (Essock et al. 2000). Overall, the researchers concluded that clozapine was cost-effective on most measures. As more new second-generation antipsychotic drugs have become available, clinicians have more alternatives. Although there are fewer extrapyramidal symptoms with clozapine, its other serious risks dictate prudent use. Olanzapine appears to have similar advantage in avoiding extrapyramidal symptoms and in overall effectiveness but, as noted earlier, weight gain and diabetes risk are its serious side-effects. Comparative research on the various new antipsychotic drugs is still limited, and most studies do not meet reasonable research standards (Tuunainen and Wahlbeck 2006). Thus, uncertainties remain.

Patients with major depression have a number of major types of drugs as options: heterocyclics (also called tricyclics), monoamine oxidase inhibitors (MAOIs), serotonin-specific drugs, and newer antidepressants that have mixed or compound synaptic effects. None of these drugs has clearly superior effects, and people respond differently. The drugs differ greatly in their side-effects, however, and the ease with which they can be used by distraught patients to commit suicide. According to researchers, depression occurs in the absence of sufficient norepinephrine, epinephrine, or serotonin at the brain's neurotransmitters. These drugs are believed to act partly by blocking the uptake of these chemicals and modifying the mechanisms by which the brain clears them, but modes of action are complex and diverse and not fully understood (Thase and Kupfer 1996). Different drugs act on different biological compounds and through different mechanisms. A common problem in the use of heterocyclic antidepressants like amitriptyline (Elavil), imipramine (Tofranil), or doxepin (Sinequan) is annoying side-effects such as blurry vision, dry mouth, urinary retention, and constipation. There are many other less frequent side-effects, and the drugs also pose risk of unintentional overdose or suicide. MAOIs like phenelzine (Nardil) and tranylcypromine (Parnate) interact with foods to produce potential toxic results due to life-threatening increases in blood pressure. Taking these drugs requires very careful dietary restrictions. Many patients have resisted taking heterocyclics and MAOIs because of annoying and dangerous adverse reactions.

Prozac (generic name, fluoxetine), a serotonin-specific inhibitor, began to dominate the U.S. market in antidepressants in the late 1980s and was an enormous success because of its limited side-effects and comparative safety. Prescriptions increased dramatically and primary care physicians, who were reluctant to prescribe earlier antidepressants, began to prescribe this drug commonly. There were exaggerated claims about the potential of Prozac to modify personality in a positive way, but Prozac was no more effective than most other antidepressants, and significant personality modifications, if they did occur, were rare. Competing selective serotonin reuptake inhibitors (SSRIs) entered the market, and together with sertraline (Zoloft), paraxetine (Paxil), and fluvoxamine (Luvox), world use of antidepressant drugs accelerated, growing at a compound annual rate of 42 percent between 1986 and 1991 (Berger and Fukunishi 1996; DiMasi and Lasagna 1995). Citalopram (Celexa), a more recent market entry, competed successfully for significant market share. By 2006, the antidepressant market was estimated at $15 billion annually, but as these major SSRIs become increasingly available in generic form, price competition is likely to lower this figure over time.

New antidepressants have entered the market in recent years that are different in their structure and neurochemical effects. Among these are the serotonin-norepinephrine reuptake inhibitors (SNRIs), with venlafanine (Effexor) being most commonly used, and other drugs acting on different neurochemicals. With many drugs going to generic form, pharmaceutical companies are looking for new ways of attacking depression and related problems and creating new markets, although no obviously superior drug appears to be on the horizon. Some observers see the next big opportunity, both medically and business-wise, could arise with development of new triple reuptake inhibitors (TRIs) that block the uptake of serotonin, norepinephrine, and dopamine. Increasingly, SSRIs and SNRIs are being approved for other psychiatric diagnoses or are being used off label by clinicians. This trend is occurring without full understanding of complex effects in the brain, which functions in exceptionally multifaceted ways in the brain.

While antidepressants are the most common mode of treatment for persons with depression, in recent years their effectiveness has been seriously questioned. In 2008, Kirsch and colleagues published a highly influential meta-analysis relevant to this question. Unlike much prior research, they included both published clinical trials and unpublished trials that had been approved by the FDA. Overall, there was no evidence that antidepressants were more effective than placebos, except in the case of individuals with the most severe levels of depression. Moreover, even among the latter patients, the clinically significant difference between the subjects who received a placebo and those that received the antidepressant was due to a lower response to the placebo among persons with severe depression, not an increased response to antidepressants (Kirsch 2010; Kirsch et al. 2008). A recent meta-analysis by Fournier and colleagues (2010) confirmed that antidepressants were not effective for persons with mild or moderate impairment, although antidepressants were superior to placebos for persons with the most severe depression. Even if one accepts Fournier and colleagues' more optimistic findings, it still means that antidepressants are not an effective treatment for at least one-half of patients who meet the criteria for clinical depression (Fournier et al. 2010).

Pharmaceuticals are big business. Companies compete in many ways for market share, such as sponsoring professional meetings, special symposia, and lectures; funding medical and postgraduate educational programs; marketing drugs directly to physicians through visits by drug representatives (detailing); advertising in professional medical journals; and engaging in direct-to-consumer advertising (Kassirer 2005). Pharmaceutical companies employ many more personnel for marketing than they do for research and development of new drugs (Angell 2004; Avorn 2004). Although direct-to-consumer advertising is only a small part of total marketing expenditures, it has substantially increased in recent years, and it is a source of great controversy. An estimated $3.8 billion was spent on direct-to-consumer advertising of prescription drugs in 2004 (Bradford et al. 2006). Psychiatric drugs, particularly antidepressants, are among the drugs most widely advertised via television and other popular media. For example, in 2000, Paxil, an SSRI, was the fourth most advertised of all drugs to consumers, only behind Vioxx, Prilosec, and Claritin (General Accounting Office 2002). Brand name drugs that are best-selling are also those most advertised directly to consumers; six of the top ten drugs advertised to consumers in 2000 were among the 20 best-selling drugs. It is difficult to establish causality, but concerns arise. Obviously, the large expenditures on advertising are intended to gain brand identity and increase sales.

Studies find that direct advertising to consumers increases physician visits (Bradford et al. 2006) and often results in patients asking for, sometimes demanding, prescriptions for expensive brand name drugs when comparable less expensive drugs are available and sometimes superior. Most physicians believe that advertising drugs to consumers results in patients seeking unnecessary treatments. Although physicians sometimes use the opportunity to educate patients and suggest alternative treatments, they often accede to patient requests to save time and avoid alienating the patient (Mechanic 2006). In one study, half of the physicians who reported that they prescribed requested drugs believed it was the most effective drug for the patient (Weissman et al. 2004). But physicians often prescribe drugs they believe will have no overall health effect, either good or bad.

The case against advertising directly to consumers is strong. Almost all countries ban such advertising, including the European Union. The reason is that such advertising encourages unnecessary drug use, leads to prescriptions for vastly more expensive drugs, and puts a heavy burden on physicians to spend time trying to help patients understand why the requested prescription is inappropriate. There are also reports of conflicts between patient and doctor that are harmful to the doctor–patient relationship (Abramson 2004). To the extent that physicians accede to patients' requests against their best clinical judgment, it damages medical professionalism.

Proponents of such advertising argue it has informational value by educating the public about available treatments and encouraging medical intervention and treatment. It also may reduce stigma by informing the public about the prevalence of certain clinical conditions. Finally, it might be argued that banning such advertising, as many advocate, is paternalistic and shows little respect for the public's ability to make reasoned judgments. Still, there are numerous instances where advertising has promoted drugs that were not only more expensive than alternatives without definitive clinical advantages but also proved dangerous (Mechanic 2006). Vioxx was the most highly advertised drug directly marketed to consumers in 2000 (General Accounting Office 2002). More than 100 million U.S. prescriptions were written for Vioxx before it was withdrawn from the market because of the risk of heart attacks. Thousands of people died using a drug that was heavily promoted but offered little advantage over safer and much less expensive alternatives.

Psychiatry represents perhaps one area where a reasonable case can be made for direct-to-consumer advertising because many people with serious mental illness who could be helped do not seek and receive available treatments. Some of these people do not want treatment, but others may not understand potentially beneficial therapeutic options or they feel isolated and stigmatized by their conditions. Advertising, however, promotes particular brand medications and often conveys inaccurate or limited conceptions of treatment, failing to note, for example, alternative psychotherapeutic or psychosocial interventions. The FDA now requires such advertisements to report common side-effects, but it does not seriously regulate objectivity. Public detailing to doctors (public information about new medications and treatments by some objective neutral agency) would be far preferable to current promotional efforts by the pharmaceutical industry (Avorn 2004). But given the realities of American culture and the marketplace, this kind of regulatory reform is unlikely to happen (Mechanic 2006).

Indeed, the pharmaceutical industry applies much expertise, resources, and ingenuity in the marketing of their drugs. They encourage new diagnoses that could benefit from their mental health drugs and commonly propose use of these drugs for problems that are not even disorders, such as stresses of everyday life. Increasingly, most research evaluating drugs is financed by the industry itself, and there is much concern about the control exercised over the clinical trials funded by those in the industry together with selective publishing of papers showing positive outcomes. This situation is provoking growing alarm about biases in the scientific literature. Pharmaceutical companies increasingly organize in-house trials of products and then hire information companies to write up the trials and their results for publication (Healy and Cattell 2003). They sometimes recruit well-known physicians and professors to serve as authors for these ghostwritten papers, and it is not clear to what extent the authors see the raw data or assess the integrity of the analyses. Major medical journals have been fighting back against these practices with various initiatives whose success remains unclear. For example, some will not publish results of trials that have not been preregistered; demand considerable declarations of financial and other interests from authors; and require declarations by the authors of their role in the research and writing of the paper, their access to the raw data, and related issues.

An instructive example comes from a study of articles on the SSRI sertraline, marketed in the United States under the brand name Zoloft. The investigators examined articles prepared by ghostwriting companies versus those that were not (Healy and Cattell 2003). Articles prepared by information companies, as well as those sponsored by pharmaceutical companies, were more likely to report positive results than those produced by persons with other sources of funds. The ghostwritten papers had, on average, twice as many authors per paper, some with very high name recognition, and were likely to be published in prestigious, high-profile journals influential among scientists and the media. These companies are quite skillful at what they do; ghostwritten papers on Zoloft were cited almost three times more often than those by other authors. In addition, pharmaceutical companies will distribute many thousands of copies of papers with positive results to those who can potentially prescribe these medications. Obviously, published papers with negative results do not get widely disseminated. Detail personnel also give free samples of drugs to doctors, who often use them to start patients on these medications and later follow up with long-term prescriptions. While efforts are being made to provide more objective information to doctors, it is difficult to compete with the vast sums pharmaceutical companies spend on marketing. In 2002, for example, members of the Pharmaceutical Research and Manufacturers of America reported expenditures of $19.1 billion on marketing, but Marcia Angell (2004), former editor of the prestigious *New England Journal of Medicine*, maintains that $54 billion is a more accurate estimate.

Thus, a great deal can be said about growth of the pharmaceutical industry's dominance over psychiatry and psychiatric knowledge, and its many misrepresentations and marketing abuses (Healy 2012). The federal government has levied large fines for unlawful abuses, and there has been much litigation by states and other parties. However, given the financial stakes involved for the pharmaceutical companies, extending well into billions of dollars, these challenges often seem to be accepted as the cost of doing business. Enormous payments to prominent psychiatrists to promote specific drugs is a conflict of interest, and the publication of drug trials that describe favorable results while negative findings go unreported pollutes the scientific literature. The largest tragedy of these marketing practices is that they confuse treatment, deceive the public and clinicians, and harm patients (Angell 2004; Healy 2012). Advances in drug development are, of course, some of medicine's greatest achievements, but the advent of global pharmaceutical marketing has not been the industry's finest hour.

OTHER SOMATIC TREATMENTS

Prior to the wave of drug treatments that arrived in the mid-1950s, there were few effective therapies for persons with severe mental illness who occupied crowded and understaffed mental hospitals. In the words of one author, it was a time of casting about for "great and desperate cures" (Valenstein 1986). Critics disagree whether these measures were intended more to serve patients' interests or the control aims of institutions and the general society. Plainly, it seems, both motivations were present. Among the panoply of treatments developed were malaria-fever therapy for neurosyphilis, hydrotherapy for psychoses, therapies to induce comas and seizures, and more. For those interested in these interventions and their social contexts, Joel Braslow (1997), a psychiatrist and historian, provides an instructive exploration based on detailed hospital documents and patient records.

During the 1930s and 1940s, António Egas Moniz popularized the approach of cutting connections in the prefrontal cortex of the brain and reported positive results involving more than 100 such operations. For his work, Moniz was awarded the Nobel Prize in 1949. This procedure, referred to as a prefrontal lobotomy, was commonly adopted in the absence of effective alternative interventions for patients with intractable conditions, primarily immobilizing depression. Practitioners in the United States subsequently developed an adaptation in which the operation was simplified and carried out through a patient's eye sockets. This procedure, formally termed "a transorbital frontal lobotomy" but also known informally as an "icepick lobotomy," was easy to do and was taken up by nonsurgeons and even nonphysicians. It was only a matter of time for such a cruel and questionable technique to become discredited, although not before thousands of surgeries had been performed (Mashour, Walker, and Martuza 2005, p. 411). Efficacy was undocumented, and major side-effects often resulted, including unresponsiveness, inappropriate affect, and disinhibition. One patient was Rosemary Kennedy, sister of John F. Kennedy, who suffered permanent incapacitation.

Today, however, surgical procedures have advanced and become more specific for a range of neurological disorders, including epilepsy, Parkinson's disease, and chronic pain. Interventions for psychiatric conditions include anterior cingulotomy, subaudate tractotomy, limbic leukotomy, and anterior capulotomy (for a description of these techniques, see Mashour, Walker, and Martuza 2005). Some neurosurgeons maintain these approaches can be efficacious with carefully selected patients, especially those with severe affective and anxiety disorders. It is very difficult to carry out proper unbiased clinical trials for these techniques, however, because nothing short of sham brain surgery could suffice as a placebo.

Another new approach is to stimulate the vagus nerve in the neck using an attached electrode that is activated by a pulse generator implanted in the chest in the manner of implantable cardiac devices. Neurosurgeons also have hope for new devices that can repetitively stimulate focal brain structures. Similarly, great interest surrounds the use of stem cells and other insertions to repair injured and malfunctioning brains. The prospects for practical treatments arising from these various approaches remain well into the future and are hard to gauge.

Another biologically based treatment that has undergone resurgence in recent decades is electroconvulsive therapy (ECT) (Fink 2009). After first appearing in the 1930s and 1940s, ECT acquired a controversial reputation owing to reports of memory loss and other serious side-effects (Shorter and Healy 2007). The 1975 film *One Flew over the Cuckoo's Nest* dramatically portrayed ECT as a method of institutional coercion. However, improvements in the procedure combined with disappointing outcomes from medication and psychotherapy for many seriously depressed patients have sparked new interest in ECT as a treatment option. An article in the reference work *Massachusetts General Hospital Comprehensive Clinical Psychiatry* presents the following information (Welch 2008). Clinical trials of ECT have reported remission rates from depression of between 70 and 90 percent. The most common indication for treatment is major depression, although ECT is also sometimes used with patients with psychotic illnesses. For most patients, ECT takes place on an outpatient basis, and the procedure is often combined with drug treatment for maximum therapeutic effect. One public figure providing a compelling account of ECT's potential benefits is Kitty Dukakis, wife of former presidential candidate Michael Dukakis. In a book prepared with a former medical reporter from the *Boston Globe*, Dukakis revealed her long-term struggles with depression and substance abuse, the limited effectiveness of a series of medications, and the recovery she was able to achieve through ECT (Dukakis and Tye 2006). The precise mechanism by which ECT affects the brain remains the subject of debate, however. Concerns about side-effects, stigma, and the advisability of attempting drug therapy as an initial course of action are likely to keep ECT as a treatment of last resort for most depressed patients. Currently, it is estimated that approximately 100,000 patients yearly receive ECT (Mental Health America 2012). A more recent medical innovation that appears to change neurochemistry in ways similar to ECT (and antidepressants) is transcranial magnetic stimulation (Mashour et al. 2005).

CONCLUSION

A rich array of theories about mental illness and its origins populate the mental health field. It is certainly possible to emphasize areas of contradiction and discontinuity among different schools of thought. Some of these debates have been carried out with highly charged emotion in the history of mental health policy. However, a more constructive understanding of this situation is also possible. With respect to psychotherapeutic applications, different approaches do not necessarily refute each other but, rather, concern themselves with distinctive points and pathways of intervention. In some instances, important intellectual borrowings have taken place, as in the formulation of early labeling theory based on sociological ideas. In other cases, the simultaneous use of different treatments, such as combined drug and cognitive therapies for depression, is common and recommended. Under circumstances like these, there is a critical role for continued effectiveness research to play in determining optimal clinical practice based on consideration of type of disorder, patient group, and social circumstances.

References

Abramson, John. *Overdosed America: The Broken Promise of American Medicine*. New York: Harper Collins, 2004.

Angell, Marcia. *The Truth About the Drug Companies: How They Deceive Us and What to Do About It*. New York: Random House, 2004.

Avison, William R., et al., Eds. *Advances in the Conceptualization of the Stress Process-Essays in Honor of Leonard I. Pearlin*. New York: Springer, 2009.

Avorn, Jerry. *Powerful Medicines: The Benefits, Risks, and Costs of Prescription Drugs*. New York: Alfred A. Knopf, 2004.

Back, Kurt W. *Beyond Words: The Story of Sensitivity Training and the Encounter Movement*. New York: Russell Sage Foundation, 1972.

Bandura, Albert. *Principles of Behavior Modification*. New York: Holt, Rinehart and Winston, 1969.

Barker, David J. P. "The Developmental Origins of Well-Being." *Philosophical Transactions: Biological Sciences* 359 (2004): 1359–1366.

Barker, David J. P., et al. "Size at Birth and Resilience to Effects of Poor Living Conditions in Adult Life: Longitudinal Study." *British Medical Journal* 323 (2001): 1273–1276.

Barker, David J. P., et al. "Trajectories of Growth Among Children Who Have Coronary Events as Adults." *New England Journal of Medicine* 353 (2005): 1802–1809.

Beck, Aaron T. "Cognitive Therapy: A 30-Year Retrospective." *American Psychologist* 46 (1991): 368–375.

Beck, Aaron T., and David J. A. Dozois. "Cognitive Therapy: Current Status and Future Directions." *Annual Review of Medicine* 62 (2011): 397–409.

Becker, Howard S. *Outsiders: Studies in the Sociology of Deviance*. New York: Free Press, 1963.

Berger, Douglas, and Isao Fukunishi. "Psychiatric Drug Development in Japan." *Science* 273 (1996): 318–319.

Bhugra, Dinesh, and McKenzie, Kwame. "Expressed Emotion Across Cultures." *Advances in Psychiatric Treatment* 9 (2003): 342–348.

Bradford, W. David, et al. "How Direct-to-Consumer Television Advertising for Osteoarthritis Drugs Affects Physicians' Prescribing Behavior." *Health Affairs* 25 (2006): 1371–1377.

Braslow, Joel T. *Mental Ills and Bodily Cures: Psychiatric Treatment in the First Half of the Twentieth Century*. Berkeley, CA: University of California Press, 1997.

Breier, Alan, and John Strauss. "Self-Control in Psychotic Disorders." *Archives of General Psychiatry* 40 (1983): 1141–1145.

Brown, George W. "Mental Illness." In *Applications of Social Science to Clinical Medicine and Health Policy*, edited by Linda H. Aiken and David Mechanic, pp. 175–203. New Brunswick, NJ: Rutgers University Press, 1986.

Brown, George W., and James L. T. Birley. "Crises and Life Changes and the Onset of Schizophrenia." *Journal of Health and Social Behavior* 9 (1968): 203–214.

Brown, George W., and Tirril O. Harris. *Social Origins of Depression: A Study of Psychiatric Disorders in Women*. New York: The Free Press, 1978.

Brown, George W., and Tirril O. Harris, eds. *Life Events and Illness*. New York: Guilford Press, 1989.

Brown, George W., and Tirril O. Harris. "Depression and the Serotonin Transporter 5-HTTLPR Polymorphism: A Review and a Hypothesis Concerning Gene-Environment Interaction." *Journal of Affective Disorders* 111 (2008): 1–12.

Brown, George W., Tirril O. Harris, and Catherine Hepworth. "Loss, Humiliation, and Entrapment Among Women Developing Depression: A Patient and Non-Patient Comparison." *Psychological Medicine* 25 (1995): 7–21.

Brown, George W., et al. "Influence of Family Life on the Course of Schizophrenic Illness." *British Journal of Preventive and Social Medicine* 16 (1962): 55–68.

Caspi, Avshalom, et al. "Influence of Life Stress on Depression: Moderation by a Polymorphism in the 5-HTT Gene." *Science* 301 (2003): 386–389.

Clausen, John A. "Stigma and Mental Disorder: Phenomena and Terminology." *Psychiatry* 44 (1981): 287–296.

Costello, E. Jane, et al. "Relationships Between Poverty and Psychopathology: A Natural Experiment." *Journal of the American Medical Association* 290 (2003): 2023–2029.

Davis, John M., Nancy Chen, and Ira D. Glick. "A Meta-Analysis of the Efficacy of Second-Generation Antipsychotics." *Archives of General Psychiatry* 60 (2003): 553–564.

DiMasi, Joseph A., and Louis Lasagna. "The Economics of Psychotropic Drug Development." In *Psychopharmacology: The Fourth Generation of Progress*, edited by Floyd E. Bloom and David J. Kupfer, pp. 1883–1896. New York: Raven Press, 1995.

Dohrenwend, Bruce P., and Barbara Snell Dohrenwend. *Social Status and Psychological Disorder: A Causal Inquiry*. New York: Wiley Interscience, 1969.

Dohrenwend, Bruce P., et al. "Socioeconomic Status and Psychiatric Disorders: The Causation-Selection Issue." *Science* 255 (1992): 946–952.

Dohrenwend, Bruce P., et al. "The Psychological Risks of Vietnam for U.S. Veterans: A Revisit with New Data and Methods." *Science* 313 (2006): 979–982.

Dohrenwend, Barbara Snell, and Bruce P. Dohrenwend, eds. *Stressful Life Events and Their Contexts*. New York: Prodist, 1981.

Dollard, John, and Neal E. Miller. *Personality and Psychotherapy: An Analysis in Terms of Learning, Thinking, and Culture*. New York: McGraw-Hill, 1950.

Dukakis, Kitty, and Larry Tye. *Shock: The Healing Power of Electroconvulsive Therapy*. New York: Penguin, 2006.

Elder, Glen H., Jr. *Children of the Great Depression: Social Change in Life Experience*. Chicago: The University of Chicago Press, 1974.

Eley, Thalia C., et al. "Gene–Environment Interaction Analysis of Serotonin System Markers with Adolescent Depression." *Molecular Psychiatry* 9 (2004): 908–915.

Elkin, Irene, et al. "National Institute of Mental Health Treatment of Depression Collaborative Research Program: General Effectiveness of Treatments." *Archives of General Psychiatry* 46 (1989): 971–982.

Erikson, Kai T. *Wayward Puritans: A Study in the Sociology of Deviance*. New York: John Wiley and Sons, 1966.

Essock, Susan M., et al. "Clozapine Eligibility Among State Hospital Patients." *Schizophrenia Bulletin* 22 (1996): 15–25.

Essock, Susan M., et al. "Cost-Effectiveness of Clozapine Compared with Conventional Antipsychotic Medication for Patients in State Hospitals." *Archives of General Psychiatry* 57 (2000): 987–994.

Feldman, Ronald, Arlene Rubin Stiffman, and Kenneth G. Jung. *Children at Risk: In the Web of Parental Mental Illness*. New Brunswick, NJ: Rutgers University Press, 1987.

Fink, Max. *Electroconvulsive Therapy: A Guide for Professionals and Their Patients*, 2nd ed. New York: Oxford University Press, 2009.

Fodor, Jerry. "How the Mind Works: What We Still Don't Know." *Daedalus* 135 (2006): 86–94.

Fournier, Jay C. et al. "Antidepressant Drug Effects and Depression Severity: A Patient-Level Meta-Analysis." *Journal of the American Medical Association* 303 (2010): 47–53.

Friedman, Meyer, and Ray H. Rosenman. *Type A Behavior and Your Heart*. New York: Alfred A. Knopf, 1974.

General Accounting Office. *Prescription Drugs: FDA Oversight of Direct-to-Consumer Advertising Has Limitations*. Washington, DC: GAO-03-177, 2002. Available online: www.gao.gov/new.items/d03177.pdf.

Gillespie, Nathan A., et al. "The Relationship Between Stressful Life Events, the Serotonin Transporter (5-HTTLPR) Genotype and Major Depression." *Psychological Medicine* 35 (2005): 101–111.

Grabe, Hans Joergen, et al. "Mental and Physical Distress Is Modulated by a Polymorphism in the 5-HTTransporter Gene Interacting with Social Stressors and Chronic Disease Burden." *Molecular Psychiatry* 10 (2005): 220–224.

Grant, Paul M., et al. "Randomized Trial to Evaluate the Efficacy of Cognitive Therapy for Low-Functioning Patients with Schizophrenia." *Archives of General Psychiatry* 69 (2012): 121–127.

Halleck, Seymour L. *The Treatment of Emotional Disorders.* New York: Aronson, 1978.

Hancock, Jay. "Doc Payments Show Underbelly of Pill Marketing." *Kaiser Health News,* 2012. Available online: capsules.kaiserhealthnews.org/index.php/2012/07/doc-payments-show-underbelly-of-pill-marketing/.

Harris, Tirril O., George Brown, and Antonia Bifulco. "Loss of Parent in Childhood and Adult Psychiatric Disorder: The Role of Social Class Position and Premarital Pregnancy." *Psychological Medicine* 17 (1987): 163–183.

Healy, David. *Pharmageddon.* Berkeley, CA: University of California Press, 2012.

Healy, David, and Dinah Cattell. "Interface Between Authorship, Industry and Science in the Domain of Therapeutics." *British Journal of Psychiatry* 183 (2003): 22–27.

Heckman, James J. "The Economics of Inequality: The Value of Early Childhood Education." *American Educator* 35 (2011): 31–35.

Heston, Leonard L. "Psychiatric Disorders in Foster Home Reared Children of Schizophrenic Mothers." *British Journal of Psychiatry* 112 (1966): 819–825.

Higgins, Edmund S. "The New Genetics of Mental Illness." *Scientific American Mind* 19 (2008): 40–47.

Hyman, Steven E. "The Genetics of Mental Illness: Implications for Practice." *Bulletin of the World Health Organization* 78 (2000): 455–463.

Jones, Peter B., et al. "Randomized Controlled Trial of the Effect on Quality of Life of Second- vs. First-Generation Antipsychotic Drugs in Schizophrenia: Cost Utility of the Latest Antipsychotic Drugs in Schizophrenia Study (CUtLASS 1)." *Archives of General Psychiatry* 63 (2006): 1079–1087.

Kallmann, Franz J. "The Genetic Theory of Schizophrenia." In *Personality in Nature, Society, and Culture,* 2nd ed., edited by Clyde Kluckhohn and Henry A. Murray, pp. 80–99. New York: Alfred A. Knopf, 1953.

Kassirer, Jerome P. *On the Take: How Medicine's Complicity with Big Business Can Endanger Your Health.* New York: Oxford University Press, 2005.

Kaufman, Joan, et al. "Social Supports and Serotonin Transporter Gene Moderate Depression in Maltreated Children." *Proceedings of the National Academy of Sciences of the United States of America* 101 (2004): 17316–17321.

Kendler, Kenneth S. "Genetic Epidemiology in Psychiatry: Taking Both Genes and Environment Seriously." *Archives of General Psychiatry* 52 (1995): 895–899.

Kendler, Kenneth S., et al. "The Interaction of Stressful Life Events and a Serotonin Transporter Polymorphism in the Prediction of Episodes of Major Depression: A Replication." *Archives of General Psychiatry* 62 (2005): 529–535.

Kesselheim, Aaron S., and Jerry Avorn. "The Role of Litigation in Defining Drug Risks." *Journal of the American Medical Association* 297 (2007): 308–311.

Kessler, Ronald C., et al. "Posttraumatic Stress Disorder in the National Comorbidity Survey." *Archives of General Psychiatry* 52 (1995): 1048–1060.

Kirkbride, James B., et al. "Heterogeneity in Incidence Rates of Schizophrenia and Other Psychotic Syndromes." *Archives of General Psychiatry* 63 (2006): 250–258.

Kirsch, Irving. *The Emperor's New Drugs: Exploding the Antidepressant Myth.* New York: Basic Books, 2010.

Kirsch, Irving, et al. "Initial Severity and Antidepressant Benefits: A Meta-Analysis of Data Submitted to the Food and Drug Administration." *PLos Medicine* 5 (2008): 260–268.

Kleinman, Arthur, and David Mechanic. "Some Observations of Mental Illness and Its Treatment in the People's Republic of China." *Journal of Nervous and Mental Disease* 167 (1979): 267–274.

Klerman, Gerald L., Myrna M. Weissman, and Bruce J. Rounsaville. *Interpersonal Psychotherapy of Depression.* New York: Basic Books, 1984.

Kobasa, Suzanne C. "Stressful Life Events, Personality, and Health: An Inquiry into Hardiness." *Journal of Personality and Social Psychology* 37 (1979): 1–11.

Kreppner, Jana M., et al. "Normality and Impairment Following Profound Early Institutional Deprivation: A Longitudinal Follow-up into Early Adolescence." *Developmental Psychology* 43 (2007): 931–946.

Lazarus, Richard S., and Susan Folkman. *Stress, Appraisal and Coping.* New York: Springer, 1984.

Leff, Julian. "Social and Psychological Causes of Acute Attack." In *Schizophrenia: Toward a New Synthesis,* edited by John Wing, pp. 139–165. New York: Grune and Stratton, 1978.

Leff, Julian, and Christine Vaughn. *Expressed Emotion in Families.* New York: Guilford Press, 1985.

Lemert, Edwin M. *Social Pathology: A Systematic Approach to the Theory of Sociopathic Behavior.* New York: McGraw-Hill, 1951.

Leventhal, Howard. "Findings and Theory in the Study of Fear Communications." In *Advances in Experimental Social Psychology,* vol. 5, edited by Leonard Berkowitz, pp. 119–186. New York: Academic Press, 1970.

Lieberman, Jeffrey A. "Comparative Effectiveness of Antipsychotic Drugs: A Commentary on Cost Utility of the Latest Antipsychotic Drugs in Schizophrenia Study (CUtLASS 1) and Clinical Antipsychotic Trials of Intervention Effectiveness (CATIE)." *Archives of General Psychiatry* 63 (2006): 1069–1072.

Lieberman, Jeffrey A., et al. "Effectiveness of Antipsychotic Drugs in Patients with Chronic Schizophrenia." *New England Journal of Medicine* 353 (2005): 1209–1223.

Link, Bruce G., and Francis T. Cullen. "Contact with the Mentally Ill and Perceptions of How Dangerous They Are." *Journal of Health and Social Behavior* 27 (1986): 289–302.

Mashour, George A., Erin E. Walker, Robert L. Martuza. "Psychosurgery: Past, Present, and Future." *Brain Research Reviews* 48 (2005): 409–419.

McGrath, John J. "The Surprisingly Rich Contours of Schizophrenia Epidemiology." *Archives of General Psychiatry* 64 (2007): 14–16.

McNally, Richard J. "Are We Winning the War Against Posttraumatic Stress Disorder?" *Science* 336 (2012): 872–874.

Mechanic, David. *Students Under Stress: A Study in the Social Psychology of Adaptation.* New York: The Free Press, 1962.

Mechanic, David. *Medical Sociology,* 2nd ed. New York: The Free Press, 1978.

Mechanic, David. *The Truth About Health Care: Why Reform Is Not Working in America.* New Brunswick, NJ: Rutgers University Press, 2006.

Menezes, Natasja, Tamara Arenovich, and Robert B. Zipursky. "A Systematic Review of Longitudinal Outcome Studies of First-Episode Psychosis." *Psychological Medicine* 36 (2006): 1349–1362.

Mental Health America. *Electroconvulsive Therapy (ECT).* Alexandria, VA: Mental Health America, 2012. Available online: www.nmha.org/go/information/get-info/treatment/electroconvulsive-therapy-ect.

Mrazek, Patricia J., and Robert J. Haggerty, eds. *Reducing Risks for Mental Disorders: Frontiers for Preventive Intervention Research.* Washington, DC: National Academy Press, 1994.

Muntaner, Carles, et al. "Socioeconomic Position and Major Mental Disorders." *Epidemiologic Reviews* 26 (2004): 53–62.

O'Connell, Mary Ellen, Thomas Boat, and Kenneth E. Warner, eds. *Preventing Mental, Emotional, and Behavioral Disorders Among Young People: Progress and Possibilities.* National Research Council and Institute of Medicine Committee on the Prevention of Mental Disorders and Substance Abuse Among Children, Youth, and Young Adults: Research Advances and Promising Interventions, Board on Children, Youth, and Families, Division of Behavioral and Social Sciences and Education. Washington, DC: The National Academies Press, 2009.

Olfson, Mark, et al. "National Trends in the Use of Outpatient Psychotherapy." *American Journal of Psychiatry* 159 (2002): 1914–1920.

Olfson, Mark, and Steven C. Marcus. "National Trends in Outpatient Psychotherapy." *American Journal of Psychiatry* 167 (2010): 1456–1463.

Pearlin, Leonard I. "Some Conceptual Perspectives on the Origins and Prevention of Social Stress." In *Socioeconomic Conditions, Stress and Mental Disorders: Toward a New Synthesis of Research and Public Policy.* Bethesda, MD: National Institute of Mental Health (NIMH) Office of Prevention and Special Projects, 2003.

Pearlin, Leonard I., et al. "The Stress Process." *Journal of Health and Social Behavior* 22 (1981): 337–356.

Pickar, David, and John K. Hsiao. "Clozapine Treatment of Schizophrenia." *Journal of the American Medical Association* 274 (1995): 981–983.

Quinton, David, and Michael Rutter. "Parents with Children in Care—II. Intergenerational Continuities." *Journal of Child Psychology and Psychiatry* 25 (1984): 231–250.

Quinton, David, and Michael Rutter. "Family Pathology and Child Psychiatric Disorder: A Four-Year Prospective Study." In *Longitudinal Studies in Child Psychology and Psychiatry: Practical Lessons from Research Experience*, edited by Arthur Rory Nicol, pp. 91–134. New York: Wiley, 1985.

Reich, Theodore, et al. "Genetics of the Affective Psychoses." In *Handbook of Psychiatry 3: Psychoses of Uncertain Actiology*, edited by John K. Wing and Lorna Wing, pp. 147–159. New York: Cambridge University Press, 1985.

Robins, Lee N. *Deviant Children Grown Up: A Sociological and Psychiatric Study of Sociopathic Personality.* Baltimore: Williams and Wilkins, 1966.

Robins, Lee N. "Alcoholism and Labelling Theory." In *The Labelling of Deviance: Evaluating a Perspective*, edited by Walter R. Gove, pp. 35–47. New York: Halstead Press, 1975.

Robins, Lee N. "Longitudinal Methods in the Study of Normal and Pathological Development." In *Psychiatri der Gegenwart*, vol. 1, 2nd ed., edited by Karl Peter Kisker, et al., pp. 627–684. Heidelberg: Springer-Verlag, 1979a.

Robins, Lee N. "Follow-up Studies." In *Psychopathological Disorders of Childhood*, 2nd ed., edited by Herbert C. Quay and John S. Werry, pp. 483–513. New York: John Wiley and Sons, 1979b.

Robins, Lee N. "Continuities and Discontinuities in the Psychiatric Disorders of Children." In *Handbook of Health, Health Care, and the Health Professions*, edited by David Mechanic, pp. 195–219. New York: Free Press, 1983.

Rodin, Judith. "Aging and Health: Effects of the Sense of Control." *Science* 233 (1986): 1271–1276.

Rodin, Judith, and Ellen J. Langer. "Long-Term Effects of a Control-Relevant Intervention with the Institutionalized Aged." *Journal of Personality and Social Psychology* 35 (1977): 897–902.

Rosenheck, Robert A. "Outcomes, Costs, and Policy Caution: A Commentary on the Cost Utility of the Latest Antipsychotic Drugs in Schizophrenia Study (CUtLASS 1)." *Archives of General Psychiatry* 63 (2006): 1074–1076.

Rutter, Michael. "Relationships Between Child and Adult Psychiatric Disorders." *Acta Psychiatrica Scandinavia* 48 (1972): 3–21.

Rutter, Michael. "The Interplay of Nature, Nurture, and Developmental Influences: The Challenge Ahead for Mental Health." *Archives of General Psychiatry* 59 (2002): 996–1000.

Rutter, Michael. *Genes and Behavior: Nature Nurture Interplay Explained.* Malden, MA: Blackwell Publishing, 2006.

Rutter, Michael L., Jana M. Kreppner, and Thomas G. O'Connor. "Specificity and Heterogeneity in Children's Responses to Profound Institutional Privation." *British Journal of Psychiatry* 179 (2001): 97–103.

Rutter, Michael, Thomas G. O'Connor, and English and Romanian Adoptees (ERA) Study Team. "Are There Biological Programming Effects for Psychological Development? Findings from a Study of Romanian Adoptees." *Developmental Psychology* 40 (2004): 81–94.

Rutter, Michael, Terrie E. Moffitt, and Avshalom Caspi. "Gene-Environment Interplay and Psychopathology: Multiple Varieties but Real Effects." *Journal of Child Psychology and Psychiatry* 47 (2006): 226–261.

Saraceno, Benedetto, Itzhak Levav, and Robert Kohn. "The Public Mental Health Significance of Research on Socio-Economic Factors in Schizophrenia and Major Depression." *World Psychiatry* 4 (2005): 181–185.

Sartorius, Norman, et al. "Early Manifestations and First-Contact Incidence of Schizophrenia in Different Cultures." *Psychological Medicine* 16 (1986): 909–928.

Scheff, Thomas J. *Being Mentally Ill: A Sociological Theory.* Chicago: Aldine, 1984.

Seligman, Martin E. P. *Helplessness: On Depression, Development, and Death.* San Francisco: W. H. Freeman, 1975.

Sewell, William H. "Infant Training and the Personality of the Child." *American Journal of Sociology* 58 (1952): 150–159.

Shorter, Edward, and David Healy. *Shock Therapy: A History of Electroconvulsive Treatment in Mental Illness.* New Brunswick, NJ: Rutgers University Press, 2007.

Singh, Swaran P., Kath Harley, and Kausar Suhail. "Cultural Specificity of Emotional Overinvolvement: A Systematic Review." *Schizophrenia Bulletin* (2011): doi: 10.1093/schbul/sbr170.

Smith, George Davey, and Ezra Susser. "Zena Stein, Mervyn Susser and Epidemiology: Observation, Causation and Action." *International Journal of Epidemiology* 31 (2002): 34–37.

St. Clair, David, et al. "Rates of Adult Schizophrenia Following Prenatal Exposure to the Chinese Famine of 1959–1961." *Journal of the American Medical Association* 294 (2005): 557–562.

Surtees, Paul G., et al. "Social Adversity, the Serotonin Transporter (5-HTTLPR) Polymorphism and Major Depressive Disorder." *Biological Psychiatry* 59 (2006): 224–229.

Susser, Ezra, Hans W. Hoek, and Alan Brown. "Neurodevelopmental Disorders After Prenatal Famine: The Story of the Dutch Famine Study." *American Journal of Epidemiology* 147 (1998): 213–216.

Sutherland, Norman S. *Breakdown.* New York: Stein and Day, 1977.

Tandon, Rajiv, and Henry A. Nasrallah. "Subjecting Meta-Analyses to Closer Scrutiny: Little Support for Differential Efficacy Among Second-Generation Antipsychotics at Equivalent Doses." *Archives of General Psychiatry* 63 (2006): 935–937.

Tandon, Rajiv, Matcheri S. Keshavan, and Henry A. Nasrallah. "Schizophrenia, 'Just the Facts' What We Know in 2008. 2. Epidemiology and Etiology." *Schizophrenia Research* 102 (2008): 1–18.

Tarrier, Nicholas, et al. "Bodily Reactions to People and Events in Schizophrenics." *Archives of General Psychiatry* 36 (1979): 311–315.

Thase, Michael E., and David J. Kupfer. "Recent Developments in the Pharmacotherapy of Mood Disorders." *Journal of Consulting and Clinical Psychology* 64 (1996): 646–659.

Thoits, Peggy A. "Stress, Coping, and Social Support Processes: Where Are We? What Next?" *Journal of Health and Social Behavior* 35 (1995): 53–79.

Tuunainen, Arja, and Kristian Wahlbeck. *Newer Atypical Antipsychotic Medication Versus Clozapine for Schizophrenia*, 2006. Cochrane Database of Systematic Reviews 2000, Issue 2. Art. No.: CD000966. DOI: 10.1002/14651858.CD000966. Available online: onlinelibrary.wiley.com/doi/10.1002/14651858. CD000966/pdf.

Valenstein, Elliot S. *Great and Desperate Cures: The Rise and Decline of Psychosurgery and Other Radical Treatments for Mental Illness.* New York: Basic Books, 1986.

Vaughn, Christine E., and Julian P. Leff. "The Influence of Family and Social Factors on the Course of Psychiatric Illness: A Comparison of Schizophrenic and Depressed Neurotic Patients." *British Journal of Psychiatry* 129 (1976): 125–137.

Waxler, Nancy E. "Is Outcome for Schizophrenia Better in Non-Industrial Societies? The Case of Sri Lanka." *Journal of Nervous and Mental Disease* 167 (1979): 144–158.

Weiss, Robert S. *Marital Separation.* New York: Basic Books, 1975.

Weissman, Joel S., et al. "Physicians Report on Patient Encounters Involving Direct-to-Consumer Advertising." *Health Affairs Web Exclusive*, April 28, 2004. Available online: content.healthaffairs.org/ content/early/2004/04/28/hlthaff.w4.219.full.pdf+html.

Weissman, Myrna M. "A Brief History of Interpersonal Psychotherapy." *Psychiatric Annals* 36 (2006): 553–557.

Weissman, Myrna M., et al. "National Survey of Psychotherapy Training in Psychiatry, Psychology, and Social Work." *Archives of General Psychiatry* 63 (2006): 925–934.

Welch, Charles A. "Electroconvulsive Therapy." In *Massachusetts General Hospital Comprehensive Clinical Psychiatry*, edited by Theodore A. Stern, Jerrold F. Rosenbaum, Maurizio Fava, Joseph Biderman, and Scott L. Rauch, pp. 635–643. Philadelphia, PA: Mosby, Inc., 2008.

Werner, Emmy E., and Ruth S. Smith. *Overcoming the Odds: High-Risk Children from Birth to Adulthood.* Ithaca, NY: Cornell University Press, 1992.

Wheaton, Blair. "Models for the Stress-Buffering Functions of Coping Resources." *Journal of Health and Social Behavior* 26 (1985): 352–364.

Wig, Narendra N., et al. "Expressed Emotion and Schizophrenia in North India." *British Journal of Psychiatry* 151 (1987): 156–160.

Wing, John K. "Institutionalism in Mental Hospitals." *British Journal of Social and Clinical Psychology* 1 (1962): 38–51.

Wolpe, Joseph. *Psychotherapy by Reciprocal Inhibition.* Stanford, CA: Stanford University Press, 1958.

World Health Organization. *Report of the International Pilot Study of Schizophrenia*, vol. 1. Geneva: World Health Organization, 1973.

World Health Organization. *Schizophrenia: An International Follow-up Study.* Geneva, New York: John Wiley and Sons, 1979.

Wuthnow, Robert. *Sharing the Journey: Support Groups and America's New Quest for Community.* New York: Free Press, 1994.

Yudofsky, Stuart, Robert E. Hales, and Tom Ferguson. *What You Need to Know about Psychiatric Drugs.* New York: Grove Weidenfeld, 1991.

Zammit, Stanley, and Michael J. Owen. "Stressful Life Events, 5-HTT Genotype and Risk of Depression." *British Journal of Psychiatry* 188 (2006): 199–201.

Zygmunt, Annette, et al. "Interventions to Improve Medication Adherence in Schizophrenia." *American Journal of Psychiatry* 159 (2002): 1653–1664.

Illness Behavior and Entrance into Treatment

Among the most difficult issues in the field of mental health are identifying who needs treatment and determining the appropriate types of treatment that will improve outcomes. It is common to hear the discrepancy between the prevalence of disorder and use of services being referred to as "unmet need," or the "treatment gap." This is an oversimplification of a very complex problem. Many persons who meet *DSM* criteria for a disorder do not need or want treatment. The problem may be temporary and self-limiting or the experience of psychological distress may result from a major life change, such as divorce or loss of a job, and will remit when the crisis is over. By contrast, other individuals may be experiencing significant levels of symptoms and disabling psychological distress without actually meeting the official criteria for a *DSM* disorder, and they may benefit from services.

While critical for designing appropriate programs and targeting health care dollars wisely, identifying who needs mental health services can be perplexing. A considerable proportion of the U.S. population has a mental illness as defined by the *DSM*, but such estimates are not very helpful unless we can differentiate the extent to which persons with various conditions suffer distress, are incapacitated, and can successfully be treated. It is misguided to confuse mild and self-limited conditions with those that cause severe discomfort and prevent persons from performing social roles and preferred activities. Although we should help people in distress, in the allocation of scarce treatment resources it is also essential to understand which conditions benefit most from treatment and the relative cost-effectiveness of different treatments. If, in some instances, less expensive drugs and other treatments work as effectively as more expensive ones, it is difficult to justify the latter. At the same time, public policy requires flexibility. Some patients will not be able to tolerate particular therapies, so the optimal choice for them may not be the same as for another patient with similar difficulties. Nonetheless, when the public is subsidizing the cost of services, people cannot simply demand whatever they want.

Except in the case of the clearest psychiatric conditions requiring intervention by authorities, it is very difficult to estimate need for mental health care because need is ordinarily defined less by professional criteria than by the judgments of individuals who decide whether to seek psychiatric care for themselves, or others, and under what circumstances. Because definition and intervention occur within the community, we should understand the social and personal processes through which individuals come to see themselves, or others, as suffering from a psychiatric condition, as well as the way others who have symptoms but do not see themselves as needing care may come to the attention of mental health professionals.

PATTERNS OF SERVICE USE

National data on rates of service use come from the National Comorbidity Survey-Replication (NCS-R), a community study designed to estimate prevalence of disorder in the community and carried out most recently in 2003 (described in more detail in Chapter 4) (Wang et al. 2005a). As shown in Table 6.1, about 20 percent of persons with any recent disorder received care from a mental health professional (defined as psychologists, psychiatrists, social workers, or other counselors). A comparable percentage of persons received care from general medical providers, including family doctors or other physicians and health care professionals. The exclusion of schizophrenia and most other psychoses results in underestimating the work of psychiatrists and social workers. Psychiatrists typically treat the most severely ill patients, and social workers are dominant in many community care programs for persons with severe and persistent disorders. Moreover, it is likely that many respondents cannot differentiate reliably between social workers and counselors. Also, these estimates do not include the large number of people who seek help from alternative sources such as family and friends, spiritual and religious advisors, or self-help groups. Overall, only about 32 percent of persons with a mental disorder in the 12 months prior to the survey received any treatment from a mental health provider or general medical care provider. Results from the NCS-R also suggest that intensity of care is highly skewed (Wang et al. 2005a). For example, about 75 percent of respondents who saw a psychiatrist had fewer than 10 visits in the past year, making up only about 30 percent of the total number of visits. In contrast, 1.6 percent of users made 50 or more visits to a psychiatrist in the previous year, but this represented about 20 percent of all visits. When extremely high utilization occurs within public programs, it raises concern from a cost-effectiveness perspective.

Rates of care vary by type of disorder. Of the classes of disorders included in Table 6.1, persons with mood disorders were most likely to receive treatment while those with impulse control disorders were least likely. About 30 percent of those with substance abuse/dependence disorders received care. Other studies of specific treatment for substance use disorder paint an even dimmer picture. The National Survey on Drug Use and Health, which asks about treatment for alcohol and drug use (not mental health care more generally), found that of the 9.6 percent of the population 12 years of age and older who met criteria for an alcohol or drug use problem in 2010, only 11 percent received specialty services (Substance Abuse and Mental Health Services Administration 2011).

Overall, results from the NCS-R confirm earlier research showing that many persons with mental health problems do not receive any mental health care treatment (Kessler et al. 1994; Leaf et al. 1985; Weissman and Myers 1978). While the NCS-R does not include persons with severe disorders such as schizophrenia, other research confirms suboptimal rates of treatment even among this group. McAlpine and Mechanic (2000) found that only about 43 percent of those with serious mental illness (indicators of schizophrenia, psychosis, or bipolar disorder) used specialty mental health services over the year prior to interview. Similarly, based on the NCS-R, Kessler and others (2005) reported that only

Table
6.1

Twelve-Month Use of Mental Health Services by Persons 18 Years and Older with a Mental Health Disorder

	Psychiatrist	Psychologist	Social Worker	Other Counselor	Any Mental Health Professional	General Medical	Either General or Mental Health Professional
Any Mood Disorder	21.8	12.5	6.1	13.0	33.1	31.8	49.3
Major Depression	19.5	11.3	5.4	12.3	31.5	30.5	48.0
Bipolar	34.2	19.1	9.8	16.7	42.7	37.4	55.1
Any Anxiety Disorder	12.8	6.7	3.7	8.9	20.6	20.4	32.1
PostTraumatic Stress Disorder	22.0	11.7	8.9	13.2	31.5	27.7	43.7
Any Impulse-Control	12.2	7.3	3.9	9.3	20.2	15.9	28.5
Conduct	12.2	7.7	2.5	4.4	14.7	14.6	21.2
Attention Deficit/Hyperactivity	20.2	10.0	5.4	13.2	27.2	23.6	36.9
Any Substance Use	13.9	8.1	5.5	13.3	26.4	14.8	31.0
Alcohol Abuse/Dependence	13.6	8.6	4.5	10.2	24.6	13.0	29.1
Drug Abuse/Dependence	17.4	5.8	9.5	19.1	33.2	19.5	38.4
Any Disorder	11.6	6.8	3.7	8.9	20.4	19.4	31.6

Source: Based on analysis of data from the National Comorbidity Study-Replication, Alegría et al. *Collaborative Psychiatric Epidemiology Surveys (CPES), 2001–2003* (United States), ICPSR20240-v6. Ann Arbor, MI: Inter-university Consortium for Political and Social Research (distributor), 2008a-06-19, doi: 10.3886/ICPSR20240.v6. Available online: www.icpsr.umich.edu/icpsrweb/CPES/index.jsp.

Note: Mood disorders include major depression, dysthymia, and bipolar I and II. Anxiety disorders include panic disorder, specific phobias, social phobias, posttraumatic stress disorder, generalized anxiety disorder, adult separation disorder, and agoraphobia without panic. Impulse control disorders include conduct disorders, attention deficit/hyperactivity, intermittent explosive disorder, and oppositional defiant disorder. Substance use disorders include alcohol and drug abuse and dependence.

Psychiatrists include visits to psychiatrists or a hospital stay for mental health or substance use problem. Other counselor includes counselors or other mental health professionals such as psychotherapists and mental health nurses. General medical includes visits to medical doctors and other health personnel such as nurses.

a minority of persons with serious mental illness (using a broader definition of "serious" than that adopted by McAlpine and Mechanic) received care by a psychiatrist (14.4 percent), other mental health professionals (19.4 percent), or a general medical provider (22.1 percent). Based on a review of available research, Mojtabai and colleagues (2009) suggest that about 40 percent of persons in the community with schizophrenia have had no recent contact with the medical care system, and more than 50 percent have had no recent contact with specialty mental health treatment.

Yet there is some reason for optimism in that mental health care appears to be increasing in frequency (Kessler et al. 2005; Olfson and Marcus 2010). Rates of treatment among persons with a disorder in the past 12 month rose about 62 percent in the decade between the NCS and the NCS-R surveys (Kessler et al. 2005). However, this change was driven largely by higher rates of treatment in the general medical care sector—about 7 percent of persons with a mental disorder received care in this sector in 1990/1992, compared to 17 percent in 2001/2003. Rates of treatment increased regardless of level of severity of the disorder, suggesting that access may not be well aligned with need (Kessler et al. 2005). One would hope that targeted efforts to increase use of mental health services would focus effectively on those having the most serious illnesses. This does not seem to have been the case.

Treatment trends exhibit dramatic changes in the particular sectors that provide care for persons with mental illness. Other parts of this text detail the process of deinstitution-alization that diminished the role of public psychiatric hospitals in the treatment system. Here we focus on changes in inpatient care in general hospitals and outpatient care.

With deinstitutionalization, general hospitals have assumed more responsibility for care of persons with mental illnesses, but utilization trends are far from static. Between 1993 and 2010, the number of discharges from short-stay general hospitals for persons with a mental health diagnosis increased from 1.8 million to 2.1 million (Centers for Disease Control and Prevention 2012a; Graves 1995). Over this same period, however, the average length of stay decreased from 10.3 days to 6.3 days. Taken together, the total days of care in general hospitals have declined, from almost 19 million in 1993 to 13 million in 2010 despite an increase of some 50 million people in the nation's population over this period (see Figure 6.1). Adjusted for changes in the size of the population, this trend represents about a 40 percent decline in days of care for persons with mental disorders.

During the same period, treatment increased in the outpatient sector. Visits to office-based physicians for a mental health problem climbed from 13,039 visits per 100,000 population in 1993 to 18,307 visits in 2009, or a 40 percent increase (Centers for Disease Control and Prevention 2009; Woodwell and Schappert 1995). In 2009, about 39 percent of these visits were to primary care physicians, compared with 55 percent to psychiatrists.

The most dramatic change in care has concerned utilization of psychotropic medi-cations. As shown in Figure 6.2, the number of prescriptions for mental health condi-tions increased 2.5 times from 1996 to 2008 (Substance Abuse and Mental Health Services Administration 2012). Antidepressants are the most commonly used psychotropic medi-cation. While antipsychotics and antimanics/anticonvulsants represent a minority of all prescription fills, they also more than doubled over these 12 years. These estimates count only prescriptions for diagnosed mental illness, but psychotropic drugs are sometimes also prescribed for other conditions.

Increasing use of psychotropic drugs reflects, in part, an expanding range of conditions deemed suitable for treatment with these medications. For example, in 2005 approximately

Figure 6.1 • Days of Care (in millions) in Short-Stay Hospitals and Average Length of Stay (in days) for Patients with a Primary Mental Illness Diagnosis: 1993–2010

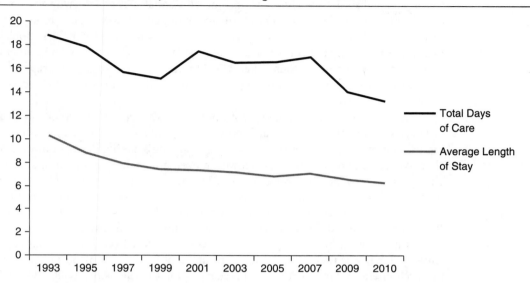

Source: Data from short-stay hospitals come from Centers for Disease Control and Prevention. *National Hospital Discharge Survey.* Atlanta, GA: Centers for Disease Control and Prevention, 2012b. Available online: www.cdc.gov/nchs/nhds.htm.

Note: Mental disorders include first-listed diagnoses of ICD-9 290–319.

Figure 6.2 • Number of Prescription Fills (in millions) for Adults with a Mental Health Condition, 1996–2008

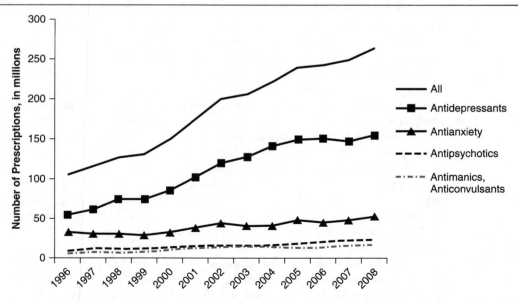

Source: Substance Abuse and Mental Health Services Administration. *Mental Health, United States, 2010.* HHS Publication No. (SMA) 12-4681, Rockville, MD: Substance Abuse and Mental Health Services Administration, 2012, Table 31, p. 139.

14 percent of people receiving antidepressants were being treated for anxiety (Olfson and Marcus 2009). There has been a large marketing campaign to promote antidepressants for social phobia disorder, apparently with some substantial success (Horwitz 2010). Further, certain diagnoses once confined primarily to childhood are now applied more frequently to adults. One key example is ADHD. A recent study by Medco (2011), the nation's largest mail-order pharmacy benefit manager, tracked drug claims by over two million enrollees between 2001 and 2010. It found that ADHD treatment is now growing rapidly among adults, more than doubling in the age group 20–44 during this period (Medco Health Solutions, Inc. 2011).

The upsurge in prescribing psychotropic drugs is also partly the result of population growth as well as the trend toward more prescriptions being written per user, including the common practice of individuals simultaneously taking drugs in more than one class (Mojtabai and Olfson 2010). However, even after taking population and practice changes into account, there remains a substantial increase in psychotropic drugs among persons with mental health conditions. By 2009, just over one in ten adults in the United States had used at least one such medication in the past year for a mental health condition (Substance Abuse and Mental Health Services Administration 2012).

As medication has risen, psychotherapy has declined (Olfson and Marcus 2010). Among all persons treated for a mental health condition, about 11 percent were treated by psychotherapy alone in 2007, a 5 percentage-point decline since 1998. Over the same period, the percentage of treated persons receiving psychotherapy and medication in combination also declined by about 8 percentage points (from 40 to 32 percent). Concomitantly, those treated with only medication climbed from 44 to 57 percent. Of persons receiving psychotherapy in 2007, most saw psychiatrists (52 percent), although psychologists (38 percent) and social workers (14 percent) also played important roles. Some patients may have received psychotherapy by more than one type of professional.

Quality of care is, of course, essential. A persistent problem in health care is that many people do not receive care consistent with evidence-based guidelines, so it is not surprising that the same experience is true for mental health conditions. There are now well-established evidence-based guidelines for the treatment of common mental disorders such as depression (Institute of Medicine 2006; Lehman et al. 2004). Yet a large body of research shows that the quality of care provided to persons with mental illness is not adequate (Bauer 2002; Institute of Medicine 2006; McGlynn et al. 2003; Young et al. 2001). In an analysis of insurance claims for more than 400,000 people between 1991 and 1996, Frank and colleagues (1999) estimated that about 20-26 percent of all spending for treatment of depression went for care not likely to lead to significant improvement. In other words, it is hard not to conclude this was money wasted. More recently, using a crude definition of minimally adequate treatment, Wang and others (2005a) estimated that of all people who received mental health treatment, only about one-third received care consistent with evidence-based guidelines. Unsurprisingly, the proportion of treatment considered minimally adequate was higher in the specialty mental health sector (48 percent) than in the general medical care sector (13 percent).

Similarly, much treatment for schizophrenia is inconsistent with quality guidelines. In the early 1990s, the Agency for Health Care Research and Quality (AHRQ) launched the Schizophrenia Patient Outcome Research Team (PORT) study (Kreyenbuhl et al. 2010). PORT focused on evaluating care given to persons with schizophrenia and making evidence-based recommendations for standards in medication and psychosocial treatment.

These recommendations have been revised a number of times since this research project began. Early work showed that less than one-half of patients had care that met recommendations. Subsequent research using PORT definitions of adequate care continues to show low adherence to guidelines, particularly in providing quality psychosocial treatment (Mojtabai et al. 2009).

ILLNESS BEHAVIOR AND SELECTION INTO CARE

Clearly, need is associated with the probability of receiving care. Persons in the community who meet diagnostic criteria for having a disorder are more likely to receive mental health treatment than persons who do not meet such criteria. Forty percent of those satisfying criteria for a 12-month disorder in the NCS-R received some mental health treatment (using a broader definition of treatment than presented in Table 6.1, including treatment from alternative providers). This group accounted for 69 percent of all visits for mental health treatment and about three-quarters of visits to psychiatrists, other mental health specialists, and general physicians (Druss et al. 2007). Of course, the fact that someone lacks a specific diagnosis does not preclude the possibility of suffering and disability. Druss and colleagues (2007) identified a subgroup having had a disorder at some previous point although not during the most recent 12 months, and a second subgroup with other possible indicators of need such as subthreshold symptoms or a major life event such as divorce. Eighteen percent of the first subgroup used mental health services, as did 13 percent of the second group. Of the 38 percent of the population classified as having no potential need, 4 percent received mental health services, which accounted for 6 percent of visits. This investigation illustrates the meaningful point that a diagnosed condition and need for services are distinct concepts. The fact that this research defined as much as 62 percent of the adult population as needing mental health services underscores the importance, from a public policy viewpoint, of establishing priorities for care.

Taken together, the evidence from large epidemiological studies that some people with no mental disorder seek care while many persons with even the most severe disorders receive little care highlights the reality that factors other than *DSM* criteria influence the help-seeking process and entrance into care. For example, Brown, Craig, and Harris (1985), in analyzing a sample of the population living in Islington, a section of London, England, identified a group of women with levels of depression comparable in severity to depressed patients typically treated by psychiatrists. Those actually referred to psychiatrists did not differ in number of core symptoms of depression compared with those who received care only from general practitioners. However, psychiatric referral tended to occur when the depression was expressed in certain disruptive ways, including threats or plans of suicide, exhibition of socially disruptive behavior such as violent outbursts, and abuse of drugs. This research suggests that referral depends on not only severity of the illness but also the way the illness is expressed in terms of social consequences and high-risk behavior. General practitioners may be more likely to refer patients because they link such indications to more serious illness or feel unable to cope with the behaviors involved.

Many researchers have examined the selective processes by which individuals with various types of symptoms find their way to different types of care (see Mechanic 1982).

Goldberg and Huxley (1980) described the existence of four filters between a community population and potential entry into an inpatient unit. The first filter focuses on who in a population arrives at helpers of first contact. Physicians are a common form of assistance at this stage, but any type of informal or formal care-seeking could be relevant. A second filter concerns whether the source of care (typically a physician) recognizes the patient's psychiatric distress, symptoms, or conditions. A third filter concerns referral to a secondary source of care, such as a mental health specialist. Depending on the symptoms and illness behavior of the patient, the second filter may be bypassed, with patients presenting themselves directly to a mental health specialist. This is a frequent occurrence in the United States. The fourth filter is acceptance for admission into inpatient care of some kind.

This same concept of screening filters can be extended to examine exchanges between acute and chronic beds, hospital beds and nursing home beds, partial-care and total-care beds, and the like, but little analytical power is gained from elaborating the framework past a certain point. The number of filters studied, as well as level of detail in terms of system contacts, depends on the policy issues considered of greatest importance. The basic insight here is that many individual, social, cultural, and economic factors affect the exchange of patients among levels of care and the way individuals negotiate various selective filters (Pescosolido, Gardner, and Lubell 1998). Larger quantitative studies also confirm that referral to psychiatry and admission to a psychiatric hospital are influenced more by risk, such as suicide threats and social disruption, than by severity of symptoms (Mechanic, Angel, and Davies 1991).

All these studies help explain why diagnosis is inadequate, by itself, to explain either need for care or referral processes. Consider, for example, the *DSM-IV* definition of a major depressive disorder. Criteria for diagnosis include five symptoms that must be present during the same two-week period and that represent a change from previous functioning (American Psychiatric Association 1994, p. 327). At least one of these symptoms must be either depressed mood or loss of interest or pleasure, but the other four can be any from a list of seven other possible types of symptoms. This means that, from a diagnostic point of view, the other symptoms assume comparable importance. Symptoms vary, however, from insomnia nearly every day, significant weight loss or gain when not dieting, and fatigue or loss of energy, on the one hand, to a suicide attempt (or specific plan for committing suicide) and observable psychomotor agitation or retardation nearly every day, on the other hand. Clearly, the social risks associated with some of these symptoms are much greater than with others, and doctors and families understandably respond to risk as well as to diagnosis.

Depending on the culture and social group, illness may be readily labeled and self-identified or it may go unrecognized until it rises to a community concern and others demand action. Mechanic (1962, 1978, 1982) employed the term "illness behavior" to refer to variability in how individuals interpret symptoms or feelings, characterize them as illness or not, choose whether or not to seek treatment, and make decisions about types of providers to contact. A wide range of factors affect the recognition of disorder and initiation of care for both physical and psychological complaints:

1. The visibility, recognizability, or perceptual salience of signs and symptoms;
2. The extent to which the person perceives the symptoms as serious
   (i.e., the person's estimate of the present and future probabilities of danger);
3. The extent to which symptoms disrupt family, work, and other social activities;

4. The frequency of the appearance of signs or symptoms, their persistence, or their frequency of recurrence;

5. The tolerance threshold of those who are exposed to and evaluate the signs and symptoms;

6. The information available to, the knowledge of, and the cultural assumptions and understandings of the evaluator;

7. The presence of needs that conflict with the recognition of illness or the assumption of the sick role;

8. The possibility that competing interpretations can be assigned to the symptoms once they are recognized; and

9. The availability of treatment resources, their physical proximity, and the psychological and monetary costs of taking action (including not only physical distance and costs of time, money, and effort but also stigmatization, social distance, and feelings of humiliation resulting from a particular illness definition).

We have no way of predicting the specific response to any condition. Definitions of psychiatric normality by which deviation is judged vary among medical practitioners as well as laypersons. More frequently than not, individuals come to view themselves as ill on the basis of their own standards of functioning as well as knowledge and experience; when marked changes in feelings or behavior emerge, they tend to seek medical confirmation of what is happening. On other occasions, however, individuals may not recognize themselves as sick but come to accept this definition when someone else defines them as ill. Consider that individuals with high blood pressure may be unaware of any problem until receiving a diagnosis as hypertensive. In regard to mental illness, some individuals defined by others as sick vigorously resist this diagnosis. The notion that one is mentally ill involves a considerable change in one's self-identity, and the effects of treatment may be perceived as uncertain or even harmful.

How deviant feelings or behaviors become evident may have varying effects on social life and are associated with varying degrees of stigma. Although some persons with mental illness withdraw from social interaction and cause no disruption in the community, others engage in visible, bizarre behavior that is threatening and frightening to others. An individual whose symptoms are not disruptive is not so readily defined as ill because the public's conceptions of health and mental illness tend to be sharply polarized. Past a certain threshold, when personal behavior seems markedly different from normal, both the mental illness label and stigmatization are likely to go together.

The nine factors that shape illness behavior pertain equally to situations in which individuals define themselves as ill and in which others come to regard someone as "sick." Let us consider how these categories apply to a person suffering from a self-defined depressive condition and someone who abuses alcohol to an extent defined as a problem by the community.

Recognition of a depressive illness may follow a period during which someone experiences feelings of sadness and emptiness more profound than usual, difficulty "getting going," loss of interest in life, and sluggishness. Depression, however, is a fairly common symptom, and the person must recognize this bout of sadness and related disconsolation to be more serious than other passing episodes. This recognition, in turn, depends on the extent to which symptoms disrupt activities, persistence of the depression and associated symptoms, and psychological pain. A self-definition of illness may depend on whether the depressed state is sufficiently severe so that the person cannot get out of bed, get to work, or carry out his or her usual responsibilities and activities and on whether the symptoms are stable or fluctuating. Sometimes, the symptoms may be open to competing interpretations. If there has been some recent adversity, such as death or injury of a loved one or a personal defeat in work or family life, an individual may take his or her feeling state and condition to be a temporary response to a frustrating and unhappy situation. But when symptoms occur independent of adversity or extreme stress, this is when the problem is more likely to be viewed as coming from within the individual.

These categories can be applied equally well to definitions of persons who have alcohol or drug problems. The community is more likely to view individuals as alcoholics when their drinking is visible rather than private, and when their drinking pattern extends beyond that ordinarily thought of as conventional. The definition of, and response of others to, such excessive drinking depends on the extent to which the drinking disrupts work, family, and other community activities and the frequency with which the person becomes drunk. If drinking leads to work absenteeism, conflict within the family, and embarrassing family situations, people are more likely to be defined as having drinking problems than if they drink themselves to sleep at night and do not disrupt family life or fail to meet social obligations. Persons in the community may have more or less tolerance for drinking and drunkenness. They may not take note of a happy inebriate but may react punitively to one involved in fights or driving a motor vehicle. They may react differently to men and women who use substances excessively.

The way people interpret their experiences and the causes of events shape the first stage of illness behavior. Distress may be interpreted in many ways—as a psychological, social, or moral problem, for example. The schemas available in the person's social context may have major effects on the way feelings and experiences are construed (Mechanic 1972). The women's movement provides an interesting example of the emergence, and wide acceptance, of new social explanations for various kinds of women's distress. In earlier decades, housewives feeling a sense of malaise and unfulfillment had difficulty explaining their feelings in terms other than their own inadequacies or failures. They often sought psychotherapy for this problem believing it to be a personal one. The women's movement, however, gave support for explaining such distress less in personal terms and more as a result of inequalities, blocked opportunities, and exploitative role arrangements. Thus, the source of distress became redefined as outside the self, offering different interpretations and opportunities for coping.

Various investigators have studied the conditions under which a particular set of symptoms will be viewed from a psychiatric frame of reference or from another perspective. Charles Kadushin (1958), in interviews with 110 persons using a psychiatric clinic, attempted to ascertain how the decision to undertake psychotherapy had been made. He concluded such a decision involved a five-step process:

1. Individuals must decide that they have a problem and that it is an emotional one.

2. They must decide whether to discuss the problem with relatives and friends.

3. They must decide at some point whether they are adequately dealing with the problem and whether to seek professional help.

4. If they choose to seek professional help, they must choose an appropriate profession from which to seek help.

5. They must select a particular practitioner.

The process of interpreting symptoms as needing treatment is not necessarily linear. Rather, it depends on the interplay between one's own attributions and pressure from social networks. Most persons experiencing a psychological problem consult first with family or friends before deciding they have a difficulty that needs professional care. Or, friends and family may notice the problem, attribute it to mental illness, and encourage the individual to seek help (Horwitz 1977; Pescosolido, Gardner, and Lubell 1998).

Clausen and Yarrow (1955) and their colleagues, in a classic study of mental health definitions, described five scenarios characterizing the process through which wives attempted to cope with their husbands' mental illness and increasingly difficult behavior: (1) the wife's first recognition of a problem depends on the accumulation of behavior that is not readily understandable or acceptable to her; (2) this recognition forces the wife to examine the situation and to adjust her expectations for herself and for her husband to account for his deviant actions; (3) the wife's interpretation of the problem shifts back and forth from seeing the situation as normal on one occasion to abnormal on another; (4) the wife tends to make continuous adaptations to her spouse, waiting for additional cues that either confirm her current definition of the situation or lead to a new one—that is, she mobilizes strong defenses against possible overreaction to her husband's deviant behavior; and (5) finally, the wife reaches the point at which she can no longer sustain a definition of normality and cope with her husband's behavior. Following is an elaboration of this process:

> The most obvious form of defense in the wife's response is the tendency to normalize the husband's neurotic and psychotic symptoms. His behavior is explained, justified, or made acceptable by seeing it also in herself or by assuring herself that the particular behavior occurs again and again among persons who are not ill...when behavior cannot be normalized, it can be made to seem less severe or less important in a total picture than an outsider might see it....By finding some grounds for the behavior or something explainable about it, the wife achieves at least momentary attenuation of the seriousness of it. By balancing acceptable with unacceptable behavior or "strange" with "normal" behavior, some wives can conclude that the husband is not seriously disturbed....Defense sometimes amounts to a thoroughgoing denial. This takes the form of denying that the behavior perceived can be interpreted in an emotional or psychiatric framework. (Yarrow et al. 1955, pp. 22–23)

The strong tendency of individuals, relatives, and the community to normalize difficult patterns of behavior until they can no longer be tolerated has relevance for public policy because it encourages long delays in seeking treatment. The most recent community research from the NCS-R found that relatively few people with various diagnoses sought treatment in the year of onset, varying from about two-fifths for patients with bipolar disorder, dysthymia, or major depressive disorder to less than 10 percent for patients with posttraumatic stress disorder (PTSD) and attention deficit hyperactivity disorder (ADHD). Of those who sought care in later years, the median duration of delay was eight years for major depressive disorder, six years for bipolar disorder, 13 years for ADHD, and 12 years for PTSD (Wang et al. 2005b). Most people with disorders eventually contacted a professional for treatment, but often the delays were very long. This often is true even for individuals with severe disorders. Across studies in the United States, for example, the mean delay between onset of psychosis and first contact with treatment ranged from about 60 to 166 weeks (Marshall et al. 2005).

Failure to recognize mental illness and at times blatant denial of it are not such simple or clear-cut phenomena as they may seem, however. Large costs may be involved in recognizing oneself, one's spouse, or one's child as mentally ill. The act of defining itself often involves major changes in the structure of interaction and responsibilities within the family. Once the definition has been made and action taken, certain consequences are, in many ways, irreversible. The characterizations that members of the family assign to one another have been changed, the stigma of mental illness is difficult to eradicate, and perhaps what is most important of all, mental health assistance may not make any significant difference in restoring "normality" to the situation.

From a policy perspective, there is also the consideration of prudence. Many crises may be transient, with usual patterns of family living prone to restoration without psychiatric intervention. Studies and observations on normalization tend to be extremely biased. They concentrate on situations in which the normalization process has failed and led to further problems. Although adequate data are lacking to make an absolute judgment, situations with dire outcomes like this probably constitute a small percentage of the total population of cases in which disturbing behavior occurs.

Concern about the tendency for long delays in seeking treatment encourages some to argue for expanded public education efforts. Many believe it is necessary to inform the public about recognizing mental illness in its earliest manifestations and to regard timely contact with the treatment system as appropriate. Many efforts have been made to increase public awareness of psychiatric disorder, to increase public understanding about these disorders, and to reduce perceptions of stigma. They vary from programs in which major figures and celebrities talk publicly about their experiences with mental illness to advertising activity such as the NIMH-sponsored Depression Awareness, Recognition, and Treatment campaign and more intensive public mental health "first aid training" programs (Kitchener and Jorm 2002; Mechanic 2007). Highly controversial direct-to-consumer advertising of psychiatric drugs has also played some role in increasing awareness of psychiatric conditions and drugs used for treatment. People are strongly influenced by their immediate social networks, who are more trusted than general media and can have large influence; past research has noted the importance of a social circle of "friends and supporters of psychotherapy" when this exists (Kadushin 1966). All these avenues of communication and persuasion appear to have some impact, but we lack careful conclusive evaluations of their individual effect or how they compare with one another.

As previously noted, illness behaviors are substantially shaped by whether one perceives a need for mental health treatment. About 75 percent of persons with a disorder who used services in the NCS-R indicated they did so because of a felt need for help (Druss et al. 2007). Perceived need is much higher among persons with mood disorders than those with anxiety or substance use disorders, and is higher for disorders associated with more disability or thoughts of suicide (Mojtabai, Olfson, and Mechanic 2002). But among individuals who are experiencing symptoms, variation in perceived need is also associated with attitudes toward mental health care. Those with more positive attitudes toward professional treatment and less sense of stigma are more likely to perceive a need for help (Mojtabai, Olfson, and Mechanic 2002).

We can draw some general conclusions about changing attitudes from a series of studies conducted in the United States from the 1950s to 2006 that examined public views of mental illness, treatment, and stigma (Gurin, Veroff, and Feld 1960; Kulka, Veroff, and Douvan 1979; Pescosolido et al. 2010; Phelan et al. 2000; Swindle et al. 2000; Veroff, Kulka,

and Douvan 1981). First, this research indicates that the public now has a broader awareness of the behaviors and emotions that constitute mental illness than in the 1950s, when
most people described mental illness solely in terms of psychosis or depression and anxiety (Phelan et al. 2000). Second, the public has become more likely to attribute the causes
of disorders such as schizophrenia, depression, and alcohol dependence to biomedical factors, rather than to poor upbringing or moral failings (Pescosolido et al. 2010). Attitudes
toward help-seeking have also become more favorable in recent years; members of the
general public are more likely to endorse getting help both from informal sources, such
as family and friends, and from mental health specialty providers (Pescosolido et al. 2010;
Swindle et al. 2000). However, considerable stigma remains. Between 1950 and 1996, the
percentage of persons in national surveys who described persons with mental illness as
violent or dangerous increased (Phelan et al. 2000).

The last decade has continued to see substantial changes in public conceptions of
mental illness. In 1996 and 2006, the General Social Survey, a large representative survey of
Americans, probed respondents' attitudes toward mental illness using a series of vignettes
describing cases of depression, schizophrenia, and alcohol dependence (Pescosolido
et al. 2010). Among other things, respondents were asked if they believed that individuals with these problems would benefit from treatment. Support for treatment by physicians, psychiatrists, or prescription medicine increased over the decade for all conditions.
(The change in the percentage of respondents who endorsed care by psychiatrists for persons with schizophrenia—from 90 to 92 percent—was not statistically significant, albeit
psychiatric care for schizophrenia has always been very strongly endorsed.) Respondents
were also increasingly likely to support treatment in mental hospitals for persons with
schizophrenia (but not for alcohol dependence or depression).

These changing beliefs notwithstanding, clear signs of stigma were also evident. The
proportion of respondents who preferred to maintain social distance by indicating reluc-
tance about working with persons with a mental illness, having them marry a family member, socializing with them, and so on did not change meaningfully in the decade between
the surveys. Similarly, many respondents continued to believe that persons with mental
illness are violent. For example, 60 percent of respondents thought a person with schizophrenia was very, or somewhat, likely to be violent toward others, 32 percent felt the same
about persons with depression, and 67 percent expressed such feelings about a person with
alcohol dependence. Despite increasingly positive attitudes toward seeking help for mental
disorders, stigma remains and is likely to inhibit the propensity either to admit to a mental
health problem or to enter care. It may also be the case that some members of the public
say they are supportive of treatment and believe it is necessary because of fear of violence
on the part of persons with mental illness.

Illness behavior and attitudes about seeking help are shaped by social circumstances
and access to resources. Overall, taking into account differences in prevalence of disorder,
women are still more likely to seek care for mental health problems than are men (Alegría
et al. 2008b; Kessler et al. 2005; Wang et al. 2005a). This gender difference may reflect
social norms that equate masculinity with self-reliance and stoicism and femininity with
willingness to express emotions (Addis and Mahalik 2003; Courtenay 2000). However,
men are more likely than women to be seen by specialty mental health providers, perhaps
because those who seek care have more severe symptoms.

Socioeconomic status (SES) is also associated with help-seeking behaviors. Of the
traditional measures of SES (occupation, income, and education), education appears to

be most important. One early study found that insured persons with college degrees, as compared with those having a grade school education or less, were six times more likely to seek psychiatric care, and they used office-based psychotherapy visits almost ten times as often as those less well educated (Avnet 1962). These gaps have closed over time as access has increased and as treatment for psychological problems has become more acceptable to the population, but differences remain depending on the type of disorder and treatment. Overall, the NCS-R indicates that education is positively associated with use of specialty mental health treatment (Wang et al. 2005a). However, using the same data, Roy-Byrne and others (2009) did not find substantial differences by level of education in use of services in either the general medical sector or mental health sector for persons with a recent mood or anxiety disorder. In contrast, when looking specifically at psychotherapy, 5.4 percent of persons with 17 or more years of education had an outpatient visit for psychotherapy in 2007, but only 2.6 percent of those with 11 years or less of education had such a visit (Olfson and Marcus 2010).

Health insurance, which is associated with SES, is an important predictor of treatment in the health sector (Wang et al. 2005a). As shown in Figure 6.3, Medicaid enrollees are more likely to receive treatment for mental health problems than people with other types

Figure 6.3 • Percentage of Persons Ages 18 and Older Who Received Mental Health Treatment, 2009

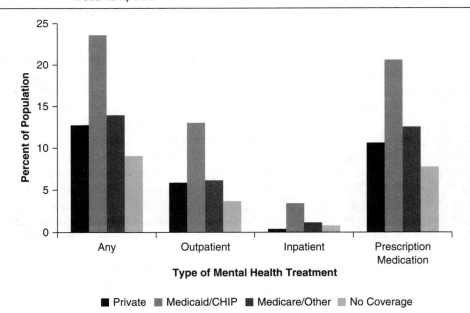

Source: Substance Abuse and Mental Health Services Administration. *Mental Health, United States, 2010.* HHS Publication No. (SMA) 12-4681, Rockville, MD: Substance Abuse and Mental Health Services Administration, 2012, Table 25, p. 129.

Notes: Outpatient includes any mental health treatment at outpatient mental health clinic, office of a private therapist, a doctor's office, a partial day hospital or day treatment program. Inpatient treatment includes an overnight stay at hospital or other facility. CHIP is Children's Health Insurance Program; other insurance includes CHAMPUS, VA, or other types of health insurance.

of coverage, a finding that reflects both need and access to care among this population (Substance Abuse and Mental Health Services Administration 2012). As also shown in Figure 6.3, the uninsured, who frequently are poor or near-poor and also have high mental health need but lack the protections of Medicaid, are less likely to use outpatient, inpatient, or medication treatment than Americans with insurance.

Finally, use of services and the type of service received that also depend on the geographic accessibility of care. Supply of mental health providers in rural areas is about one-half that of urban areas (Ellis et al. 2009). Accessibility in different states also varies enormously; the number of psychiatrists, for example, ranges from a low of about 6.6 per 100,000 in Idaho to 34.6 per 100,000 in Massachusetts (Substance Abuse and Mental Health Services Administration 2012). While we cannot establish a causal relationship, correspondingly about 4 percent of the adult population in Idaho receive specialty mental health outpatient treatment annually, compared to 8 percent in Idaho (Substance Abuse and Mental Health Services Administration 2012).

SPECIAL POPULATIONS

The Elderly

Among individuals with a mental health problem, age is negatively associated with receipt of specialty mental health treatment. This is true despite the fact that older individuals have similar or higher rates of treatment in the primary care sector as younger persons (Klap, Unroe, and Unützer 2003; Wang et al. 2005a). Overall, therefore, the general medical sector plays an even more important role in providing care for older persons with psychiatric problems than it does for younger persons. Unfortunately, the evidence is that much of this care does not meet evidence-based standards for quality (Harman, Edlund, and Fortney 2004; Klap, Unroe, and Unützer 2003; Young et al. 2001).

Low rates of treatment for mental health problems among the elderly may be explained, at least partially, by differences in perceived need for care. Almost all older persons who perceive a need for mental health care do seek treatment (Garrido et al. 2009); however, given existence of a mental health problem, age is associated with lower levels of perceived need (Mackenzie, Pagura, and Sareen 2010). In a national study, Klap, Unroe, and Unützer (2003) found that only 28 percent of persons 65 years of age and older with a mental health problem perceived a need for mental health services, compared to over 40 percent of their younger counterparts.

Treatment choices are also driven partially by constraints of the physician–patient encounter. Primary care physicians spend very little time on each visit and must address multiple concerns. In an in-depth analysis of videotapes from almost 400 office visits, Tai-Seale, McGuire, and Zhang (2007) found that most of the time was spent talking about physical problems, with less than 5 percent of time allocated to concerns about mental health. Small surprise, then, that mental health problems often go undetected by primary care physicians (Mitchell, Vaze, and Rao 2009; Tai-Seale et al. 2005). Some researchers hypothesize that undetected depression may be even more common for older than younger patients (Mitchell, Vaze, and Rao 2010). This could be a consequence of the greater number of competing problems that need to be addressed during the medical visit (Klinkman 1997) or the tendency of older patients to express symptoms of distress somatically (Stewart 2003).

Medicare has also had a 50 percent coinsurance requirement for mental health services, other than for short medication visits, that inhibited utilization. Until mental health parity is fully phased in for Medicare enrollees, the program will continue to pay a smaller proportion of costs for most mental health services than it does for general health services. Indeed, older patients who perceive a need for care commonly cite concerns about cost as a reason for not seeking treatment (Karlin, Duffy, and Gleaves 2008; Mackenzie, Pagura, and Sareen 2010).

Finally, contrary to popular impressions, there is little evidence that older persons have less positive attitudes toward mental health treatment that make them more reluctant to seek care. Using data from the NCS-R, Mackenzie and colleagues (2008) found that older persons overwhelmingly stated they would be comfortable talking to a professional about personal problems, believed in the efficacy of treatment, and would seek help if they thought they had an emotional problem. Similarly, based on analysis of the national Collaborative Psychiatric Epidemiology Surveys (which include the NCS-R), Mackenzie, Pagura, and Sareen (2010) determined that, among older persons who perceived a need for care but did not seek it, stigma was rarely mentioned as a barrier to treatment. Instead, the most commonly cited factor for not entering care was thinking one could handle a problem on one's own (69 percent), followed by not knowing where to go for help (45 percent), concern about how much it would cost (44 percent), and thinking the problem would get better on its own (41 percent).

A persistent concern in psychiatric gerontology is inadequate or inappropriate care for elderly persons with mental illness in nursing homes (Grabowski et al. 2010). Longstanding problems with quality of care, as well as the inappropriate placement of persons with mental illness into nursing homes, spurred passage of reforms as part of the Omnibus Reconciliation Budget Reconciliation Act (OBRA) of 1987. OBRA mandated that nursing homes certified for Medicare and Medicaid must provide prescreening of admissions and annual reviews to identify mental health problems. OBRA also required that residents with mental health problems must receive appropriate care. Still, studies continue to show most nursing home residents with mental health problems do not receive adequate treatment (Grabowski et al. 2010; Shea, Russo, and Smyer 2000).

One highly controversial issue is overuse of psychotropic drugs to sedate nursing home residents and control their behavior. OBRA also prohibited psychotropic medication in the nursing home setting, except when medically necessary, while requiring extensive monitoring and documentation after these medications have been prescribed (Stoudemire and Smith 1996). The Food and Drug Administration, in 2005, issued a black box warning against atypical antipsychotics for patients with dementia or behavioral problems because of increased mortality risk. The agency extended the warning to conventional antipsychotics in 2008. Some research suggests this FDA advisory led to a significant reduction in prescribing of atypical antipsychotics for elderly patients with dementia (Dorsey et al. 2010). A recent study by the Office of the Inspector General that reviewed Medicare claims data and medical charts, however, found levels of prescribing for antipsychotics still strikingly high (U.S. Department of Health and Human Services 2011). About 14 percent of nursing home residents had a Medicare claim for an atypical antipsychotic drug during the first six months of 2007, and almost 90 percent of these claims were associated with a diagnosis of dementia. Moreover, about 50 percent of all claims for atypical antipsychotics did not meet Medicare standards for reimbursement (medically accepted reason documented), and 22 percent of the drugs that had a claim did not comply with standards from the federal

Centers for Medicare & Medicaid Services for nursing home use (either due to evidence of excessive dosing, excess duration, lack of adequate indications for use, lack of adequate monitoring, or drugs that were prescribed in the presence of adverse consequences indicating the dosage should be changed). Critics argue, further, that use of antipsychotics among nursing home residents is the result of aggressive marketing of antipsychotics for off-label uses. Indeed, large pharmaceutical companies have received large fines for this practice (Wilson 2010). For example, in 2009, Eli Lily and company settled for a $1.4 billion fine with the federal government for its off-label promotion of zyprexa, including encouragement of use among elderly patients with dementia. The criminal component of the fine (over $500 million) was the largest to this date in a health care case or in a case against a single corporation in the United States (U.S. Department of Justice 2009).

Children and Adolescents

Children's use of services differs from adults in that children do not typically initiate help-seeking on their own. Instead, it is usually a family member, school authority, or the juvenile justice system that recognizes a problem and directs the child into treatment. The school system is a very common pathway into care (Farmer et al. 2003), with most schools also providing some mental health services of their own (Substance Abuse and Mental Health Services Administration 2012). As shown in Figure 6.4, about three million

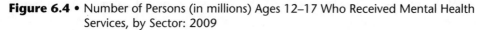

Figure 6.4 • Number of Persons (in millions) Ages 12–17 Who Received Mental Health Services, by Sector: 2009

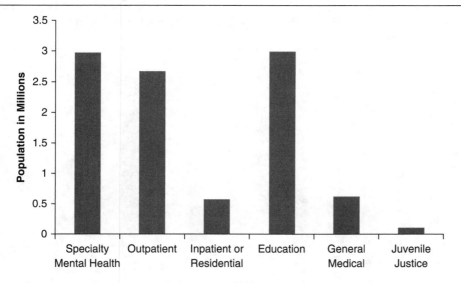

Source: Data for percent of young people who received care in each sector from Substance Abuse and Mental Health Services Administration. *Mental Health, United States, 2010*. HHS Publication No. (SMA) 12-4681, Rockville, MD: Substance Abuse and Mental Health Services Administration, 2012, Exhibit 12, p. 39; Population estimate from U.S. Census Bureau, *The 2011 Statistical Abstract*. Available online: www.census.gov/compendia/statab/2011/2011edition.html.

young people ages 12–17 received mental health services in the educational system in 2009, almost the same number who received specialty mental health care.

Two national surveys allow us to estimate rates of service use for children and adolescents in the community having a range of mental health problems. The National Health and Nutrition Examination Survey (NHANES) defines treatment as seeing "someone at a hospital or clinic or at their office" for symptoms of a disorder (Merikangas et al. 2010b). The NCS-A included a wider range of questions about types of services received for specific disorders, including specialty care, general medical care, care in the human services sector, complementary or alternative medicine, the juvenile justice system, and school services (Merikangas et al. 2010a). The NCS-A also assessed lifetime service use while the NHANES data focused on 12-month use. As shown in Figure 6.5, results from both surveys indicate that most young people with mental health disorders do not receive any treatment (50 percent in the NHANES, and 66 percent in the NCS-A). Children and adolescents with ADHD are most likely to receive treatment, while those with anxiety disorders and substance use problems are least likely (although the latter were only assessed in the NCS-A).

In the NHANES, boys were more likely than girls to receive treatment (Merikangas et al. 2010b). However, data from the NCS-A, which covers older youth, indicate that the impact of gender varies by disorder: boys are more likely to receive care for ADHD, while girls are more likely to receive treatment for anxiety or mood disorders (Merikangas et al. 2010a).

The NCS-A did not contain information on insurance status, and analysis of the NHANES did not discern a relationship between insurance and mental health care. However, other research shows a strong relationship between insurance and use of services. The National Survey of Drug Use and Health, for example, revealed that similar percentages of young people ages 12–17 with a depressive episode received formal care if

Figure 6.5 • Mental Health Service Use by Children and Adolescents with Mental Health Disorders

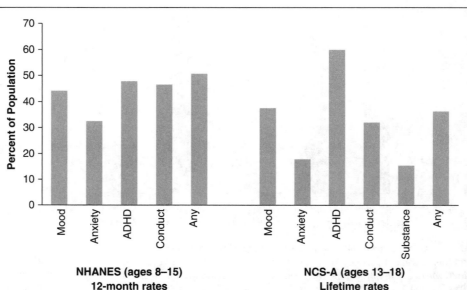

Source: NCS-A: Merikangas et al. (2010a); NHANES: Merikangas et al. (2010b).

they had either private coverage (35 percent) or Medicaid/CHIP coverage (36 percent). But respondents with no health insurance had a lower rate of treatment (26 percent) (Substance Abuse and Mental Health Services Administration 2012).

Parental attitudes can also reasonably be expected to affect use of mental health services by children. Stigma or mistrust of the effectiveness of care may discourage taking a child for treatment. The first national study of the stigma associated with children's mental health care, which was conducted in 2002, yielded mixed results (Pescosolido et al. 2007, 2008). Researchers used vignettes to assess respondents' knowledge of, and attitudes toward, two disorders common in childhood, ADHD and depression. Many adults were able to correctly recognize depression (59 percent) and ADHD (42 percent) based on the symptoms described (Pescosolido et al. 2008). But many others rejected defining these problems as mental illnesses, particularly ADHD. Almost all respondents had positive attitudes toward mental health treatment in that they thought the identified conditions would improve with proper care. However, respondents expressed substantial skepticism about medication. Almost all respondents (86 percent) felt that doctors overmedicate children, while two-thirds thought giving a child psychiatric medication would not help in addressing the "real" problem (Pescosolido et al. 2007).

Given the public's seeming mistrust of psychiatric medication for children, it is somewhat surprising how common drug use has become in the treatment of mental health problems for young people. As new drugs of all kinds have become increasingly available, their use, even with very young children, has skyrocketed. As shown in Figure 6.6, between 1996

Figure 6.6 • Number of Prescription Fills (in millions) for Children Under 18 Years of Age with a Mental Health/Substance Use Condition, 1996–2008

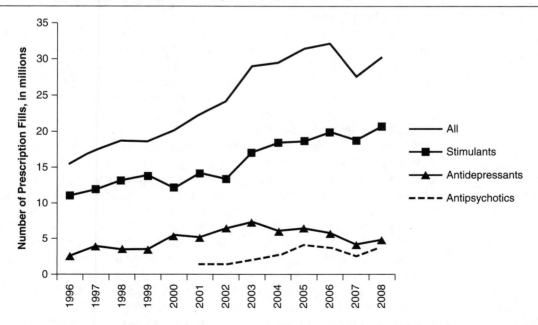

Source: Substance Abuse and Mental Health Services Administration. *Mental Health, United States, 2010*. HHS Publication No. (SMA) 12-4681, Rockville, MD: Substance Abuse and Mental Health Services Administration, 2012, Exhibit 13, p. 41.

Note: Estimates of antipsychotics prior to 2001 are unreliable.

and 2008 the number of prescriptions for mental health and substance use medications for persons less than 18 years old almost doubled, from 15.6 million in 1996 to 30.2 million in 2008 (Substance Abuse and Mental Health Services Administration 2012). In large part, this trend reflects increased diagnosis of ADHD and use of stimulants to treat these children. Early research, still not well understood, indicated that stimulants reduce children's hyperactivity, and Ritalin became the first drug to receive FDA approval for this purpose. Together, these developments set off a cascade in the prescribing of psychotropic drugs for children. In particular, prescriptions increased almost twofold for stimulants between 1996 and 2008 (Substance Abuse and Mental Health Services Administration 2012).

A range of drugs are now available to treat ADHD. Some studies have concluded that stimulants, whose purpose is to reduce distractions and impulsivity, do appear to improve reading and mathematical test scores when administered to elementary school children with a ADHD diagnosis (Scheffler et al. 2009). As such drugs have become more familiar, primary care physicians seem to call upon them readily. Using two major national surveys, Olfson and colleagues (Olfson et al. 2003) estimated that outpatient treatment rates for ADHD increased from 0.9 per 100 children, ages 3–18, in 1987 to 3.4 in 1997. This latter figure corresponds to approximately 2.2 million children. Treatment increases took place almost exclusively in the form of stimulant prescriptions. Meanwhile, the intensity of care actually decreased, despite evidence to support combinational therapies (Jensen et al. 2001).

Overall, about 4.2 percent of children ages 2–17 are now taking medication for ADHD (Substance Abuse and Mental Health Services Administration 2012). Boys (6.1 percent) are more likely to be on such medication than girls (2.2 percent). Children covered by public insurance are more likely to take ADHD medication (6.5 percent) than privately insured children (3.6 percent) or uninsured children (1.5 percent).

While many are concerned about the increasing use of stimulants for children with ADHD, no other approach seems to have strong evidence of success (Rowland, Lesesne, and Abramowitz 2002). One investigation followed 579 children with the combined type of ADHD in the randomized NIMH Collaborative Multisite Multimodal Treatment Study of Children (MTA) over an eight-year period (Molina et al. 2009). Treatments over 14 months included systematic medication management, multicomponent behavior therapy, a combination of these two treatments, and usual community care. In various analyses of outcomes over time, the treatment groups did not differ significantly on ADHD symptoms but those with combined treatment had better short-term outcomes on comorbid symptoms, academics, and peer relations (Hinshaw and Scheffler forthcoming). However, when compared with peers without the diagnosis, the children with ADHD still performed more poorly on 91 percent of test measures. The strongest predictor of outcomes eight years later was the initial severity of symptoms. Initial symptoms, prior conduct, intelligence, and social advantage were all more predictive than any type of intervention during the 14-month treatment period (Molina et al. 2009). If we think of ADHD as a chronic disorder requiring continuing care it should not surprise us that once intensive interventions transition to usual community care, initial gains would no longer prevail eight years later (Hinshaw and Scheffler forthcoming).

Children in the above study were carefully screened prior to participation to ensure they met diagnostic criteria. Many children given the diagnosis of ADHD in usual care situations, however, do not receive particularly thorough assessment. They may have fewer and less severe symptoms and experience different outcomes than study populations, particularly in the contemporary context of an expansion of ADHD labeling. Nevertheless, we have ample evidence that failure to address problems of attention and hyperactivity in our demanding society will be associated with diminished life chances and increased social costs (Hinshaw and Scheffler forthcoming).

For many years, antidepressant drugs were rarely used with children, but this has shifted dramatically. Whether too many or too few children with depression are receiving medications is impossible to judge, but there is reason for concern about a pattern of treatment consisting of rather haphazard prescribing practices coupled with limited clinical attention. As evidence has grown linking Selective Serotonin Reuptake Inhibitors (SSRI) to suicide ideation and attempts, the importance of monitoring also becomes paramount (Olfson, Marcus, and Shaffer 2006). In 2004, the FDA mandated inclusion of a "black box" warning on antidepressants about the risks of suicide among children. This step was prompted by a meta-analysis by Columbia University researchers of dozens of clinical trials highlighting safety issues (Busch and Barry 2009). Prescription fills for antidepressants seem to have peaked around 2003, followed by a downward trend, although between 2007 and 2008 antidepressant prescriptions nudged upward again.

Perhaps of even greater concern is an enormous increase in the number of young children on antipsychotic drugs. Prescription fills soared by almost 90 percent between 1996 and 2008 for children under the age of 18. Antipsychotics for very young children are also becoming more common. In a study of privately insured children between ages two and five, such use doubled between 1999 and 2007 (Olfson et al. 2010). Beyond the fact that we know little about the long-term effects of these drugs on brain development, it is disconcerting that fewer than half of all medicated children received a mental health assessment, saw a psychiatrist, or had a psychotherapy visit. A related study in seven states between 1996 and 2006 found that youth ages 6–17 on Medicaid were three to four times more likely to receive antipsychotic medications than privately insured youth of comparable age, a divergent trend that has been accelerating (Crystal et al. 2009). These two populations are quite different and the discrepancy may be justified, but further inquiry is indicated.

To summarize, by 2008 about 1 in 20 young people had taken a psychotropic drug in the past year for a mental health condition. Moreover, there are now almost as many children and adolescents using antipsychotics as there are using antidepressants.

RACE AND ETHNICITY

As previously noted, studies show that people from minority racial and ethnic groups in the United States have similar or lower rates of *DSM* disorders than Whites. Here we focus on important disparities in the types of treatment and quality of care received by different groups.

Most research has focused on African Americans and Hispanics, finding that these groups are less likely to receive any kind of treatment than Whites (Alegría et al. 2008b; Cook, McGuire, and Miranda 2007; Mills 2012; Wang et al. 2005a; Wells et al. 2001); are less likely to receive specialty mental health care; and may be more likely to seek care outside the health sector (Cook, McGuire, and Miranda, 2007; Mills 2012; Snowden and Pingitore 2002; Wang et al. 2005a; Wells et al. 2001). In addition, there are wide variations in the quality of care provided, including striking ethnic and racial disparities in rates of adequate care for depression and anxiety (Young et al. 2001), schizophrenia (Kuno and Rothbard 2002), use of psychotropic medication (Han and Liu 2005), and detection of mental health problems in primary care (Borowsky et al. 2000).

It is complicated to sort out the effect of race and ethnicity on access to appropriate mental health care as distinct from the role of socioeconomic status and insurance. African

Americans and Hispanics have lower levels of education and income and are more likely to be uninsured than Whites. All these disadvantages contribute to lack of access to mental health care. However, some studies conclude that, even controlling for differences in level of disability, comorbid conditions, and socioeconomic circumstances, disparities in access persist. Examining care for depression, for example, Asians, Hispanics, and African Americans have less access to care and receive lower quality of care than Whites, even after taking disability and SES into account (Alegría et al. 2008b). Cook, McGuire, and Miranda (2007) found that disparities in use of mental health services between Whites and African Americans and Hispanics increased between 2000–2001 and 2003–2004 when controlling for demographics and health status.

There is little evidence, as some suggest (Corrigan 2004), that people from minority racial and ethnic cultural groups hold more negative attitudes toward mental health services. Instead, data from the NCS indicate that African Americans are more likely than Whites to say, first, that they would definitely go for professional help if they had an emotional problem and, second, that they would not be embarrassed if family or friends found out they went for help (Diala and colleagues 2001). Using more recent NCS-R data, Shim and others (2009) confirm that African Americans and Hispanics are less likely to stigmatize mental health treatment than Whites. While bivariate results suggest African Americans are slightly less likely than Whites to feel comfortable talking to a mental health professional, and Hispanics are slightly less likely than Whites to seek professional help for an emotional problem, these differences are accounted for statistically by differences in socioeconomic factors such as education, employment, and income.

While general attitudes about treatment effectiveness may not explain race and ethnic variation in services utilization, different patterns of care may partially reflect treatment preferences. In a study of patients with depressive symptoms, Cooper and colleagues (2003) determined that African Americans and Hispanics were more likely than Whites to believe antidepressants were not an acceptable treatment. While African Americans and Whites did not differ on views of counseling, Hispanics were more likely to consider this form of treatment unacceptable. There is also evidence that Hispanics and Blacks are more likely than Whites to seek care from a spiritual or religious advisor when emotional or mental health problems arise (Mills 2012).

The possible role of physician bias in explaining racial and ethnic variations in mental health care has been understudied, but preliminary investigation from other areas of medical care presents some intriguing hypotheses. Reviewing quality of care and provider practices across a number of different types of medical conditions, van Ryn (2002) argued that providers often bring implicit stereotypes connected to race and ethnicity to the patient encounter. These stereotypes shape treatment expectations, beliefs about whether the patient will follow care instructions, interpretation of symptoms, and diagnostic and treatment decisions. For example, in a study of patients who had received angiograms, van Ryn and Burke (2000) found that physicians assessed African American patients much more negatively than White patients, that is, they felt that African American patients were more likely to use substances, to be nonadherent with physician instructions, to have less social support, and to be less intelligent than White patients, even after controlling for education. Physicians were also less likely to say they saw their African American patients as the type of people they could be friends with, compared with White patients. In general, physicians also held more negative views of patients from lower socioeconomic backgrounds compared to more advantaged patients, independent of race. Such beliefs may play out in the provider–patient relationship. Johnson and colleagues (2004) reviewed audiotapes from about 450 physician–patient visits with 61 different physicians in primary care settings. Overall, visits by African Americans were less patient-centered than visits by White patients; in these instances, physicians were more likely to dominate the conversation and tended to focus exclusively on biomedical, rather than relevant social-emotional, topics during these encounters.

Provider bias has been explored as a potential explanation for the overrepresentation of African Americans in psychiatric inpatient care (McGuire and Miranda 2008; Neighbors et al. 2003; Snowden, Hastings, and Alvidrez 2009; Williams and Harris-Reid 1999). It may be that African Americans have higher rates of schizophrenia, as suggested by some studies, although evidence is too weak to draw any definitive conclusion (McGuire and Miranda 2008). More compelling are data that Blacks are more likely to be given a diagnosis of schizophrenia, while Whites are more likely to receive a mood disorder diagnosis (Neighbors et al. 2003). Clinicians attribute symptoms differently based on the patient's race, with some studies showing, for example, that "negative symptoms" such as blunted affect more often prompt a diagnosis of schizophrenia for African American than for White patients (Trierweiler et al. 2000).

Many studies over the years have found that, while Whites are more likely to seek care voluntarily, Blacks are more prone to be brought into care involuntarily through police intervention (Rosenfield 1984). Patients in the latter group are typically less cooperative, and sometimes more hostile, and they tend to be seen by clinicians as more disordered and dangerous than those seeking care voluntarily. In a study of patients examined in an emergency room, controlling for clinical condition and social class, non-White males were more likely to be involuntarily hospitalized than White males (Rosenfield 1984). However, according to more recent research concerning patients seen in a psychiatric emergency room, Blacks were less likely to be involuntarily hospitalized than Whites when taking into account severity of symptoms and potential dangerousness to self and others (Lincoln 2006). Thus, it is unclear whether historical findings of higher rates of involuntary hospitalization of Blacks still hold true or what the exact reasons for any racial discrepancy might be.

PRIMARY MEDICAL CARE AND THE PROMISE OF INTEGRATION

About 50 percent of all visits to office-based physicians in a given year are made to primary care providers (general and family medicine, internal medicine, or pediatrics) and, as we have seen, much mental health treatment takes place in the primary care sector (Centers for Disease Control and Prevention 2009). Some patients coming to doctors either report or show evidence of serious psychosocial and emotional difficulties, while others may present psychosocial issues through somatic or nonspecific complaints. Although primary care is a natural starting point for improving treatment for psychiatric problems, historically this setting has featured a number of barriers to providing quality mental health care. Primary care physicians (PCPs) are often ambivalent or uncertain about treatment and referral for mental health problems, and they are commonly insecure about making mental health diagnoses and ordering psychotropic medication. They must also determine how to cope with the somatization of psychological distress, part of which reflects the unacceptability of mental health diagnoses to many patients. Studies comparing independent standardized psychiatric assessment of primary care patients with actual diagnosis and management of these patients reveal that primary care physicians often do not recognize psychiatric symptoms, and even less frequently make a mental health diagnosis or prescribe appropriate psychotropic medication for patients with mental health problems (Mitchell, Vaze, and Rao 2009; Wells et al. 1996). Accuracy of diagnosis appears to depend on the way doctors interview patients, their personality, and academic ability. By contrast, accuracy of diagnosis is unrelated to doctors' self-assessment of psychological skills or experience (Goldberg and Huxley 1980).

Of patients seen by primary care physicians, relatively few ever receive referral for specialized care. Even when PCPs believe referral is necessary, as many as two-thirds report they are unable to get quality outpatient mental health care for their patients (Cunningham 2009). Financial barriers interfere with providing quality care in the primary care setting (Kathol et al. 2010). Many insurers carve out mental health services from general medicine, resulting in separate budgets and panels of providers responsible for care in each sector. Moreover, consultations between general and specialty providers are not generally reimbursed, nor are the costs of non-health professionals, such as care managers, to coordinate care between medical specialties.

To overcome these barriers, various models for integrating mental health specialty services into primary care have been developed. Greatest attention has been given to treatment of depression, because the problem is common and it substantially impairs function. While integrated models differ in scope and specific characteristics, all link primary care physicians to mental health specialists to provide varying degrees of collaborative care to patients. One well-known model is the Improving Mood-Promoting Access to Collaborative Treatment Program (IMPACT), which was originally designed to improve depression care for elderly patients in primary care settings (Unützer et al. 2002). IMPACT requires depression screening and diagnostic testing, a care manager to coordinate collaboration and communication between PCP and specialist, and use of a stepped-care approach that consists of close patient monitoring to ensure proper intensity of services and treatment adjustments as necessary, including extensive contacts by the care manager to provide education and to track adherence and symptomatology (for more details of the model see http://impact-uw.org). IMPACT and other models of integrated care have undergone multiple clinical trials. Results suggest they do reduce depressive symptoms and lead to higher levels of remission than usual care (Butler et al. 2008; Gilbody, Bower, and Whitty 2006; Williams et al. 2007). Just which features of this multifaceted approach are necessary to achieve positive outcomes, however, remains unclear.

A central issue in implementing integrated care is whether such models can be sustained outside the research context given current reimbursement limitations. Beginning in 2008, Minnesota implemented a statewide effort to integrate depression care into primary care clinics. By 2012, more than 80 clinics were participating and more than 8,000 patients had been enrolled (Institute for Clinical Systems Improvement 2012). Minnesota overcame the typical reimbursement barriers to integrated care by negotiating with all health plans to provide compensation for a designated bundle of services—such as screening, use of a care manager, and collaboration between PCPs and mental health specialists—that constituted core elements of an integrated approach. While no formal evaluation has yet been published, early results indicate a greater percentage of patients in those clinics that adopted the integrated model achieved remission of depression compared to patients in clinics without the integrated model (Institute for Clinical Systems Improvement 2012). It is unlikely that many states will be able to follow Minnesota's example, however, given that it required all health plans in the state to sign on to new compensation models. Integrated care continues to hold promise, and the concept is likely to be advanced in pragmatic ways through the medical and health homes and accountable care organizations that are central features of national health reform legislation (discussed in more depth later in this book).

CONCLUSION

Any attempt to define precisely the gap between need for treatment for mental health problems and use of services is futile. Estimates of need rest on varying assumptions about how to define mental disorders, while utilization figures depend on which sources of help are included. However, the fact that most people who have mental health problems, even the most severe, do not receive treatment—and if they do, the treatment does not meet accepted standards of quality—should be of great concern. Moreover, persistent disparities by race and ethnicity mean that many people, simply based on cultural background, receive even poorer access and care than the norm. These are public policy issues plain and simple. As we will see in later chapters, interventions that are properly targeted and implemented can go far in improving access to care while enhancing quality for those with the most disabling of mental health conditions.

References

Addis, Michael E., and James R. Mahalik. "Men, Masculinity and the Contexts of Help Seeking." *American Psychologist* 58 (2003): 5–14.

Alegría, Margarita, et al. *Collaborative Psychiatric Epidemiology Surveys (CPES), 2001–2003* [United States]. ICPSR20240-v6. Ann Arbor, MI: Inter-university Consortium for Political and Social Research [distributor], June 19, 2008a. doi:10.3886/ICPSR20240.v6. Available online: www.icpsr.umich.edu/icpsrweb/CPES/index.jsp.

Alegría, Margarita, et al. "Disparity in Depression Treatment Among Racial and Ethnic Minority Populations in the United States." *Psychiatric Services* 59 (2008b): 1264–1272.

American Psychiatric Association. *Diagnostic and Statistical Manual of Mental Disorders: Fourth Edition (DSM-IV).* Washington, DC: American Psychiatric Association, 1994.

Avnet, Helen Hershfield. *Psychiatric Insurance: Financing Short-Term Ambulatory Treatment.* New York: Group Health Insurance, 1962.

Bauer, Mark S. "A Review of Quantitative Studies of Adherence to Mental Health Clinical Practice Guidelines." *Harvard Review of Psychiatry* 10 (2002): 138–153.

Borowsky, Steven J., et al. "Who Is at Risk of Nondetection of Mental Health Problems in Primary Care?" *Journal of General Internal Medicine* 15 (2000): 381–388.

Brown, George W., Thomas K. J. Craig, and Tirril O. Harris. "Depression: Distress or Disease? Some Epidemiological Considerations." *British Journal of Psychiatry* 147 (1985): 612–622.

Busch, Susan H., and Colleen L. Barry. "Pediatric Antidepressant Use After the Black-Box Warning." *Health Affairs* 28 (2009): 724–733.

Butler, Mary, et al. *Integration of Mental Health/Substance Abuse and Primary Care.* Evidence Reports/Technology Assessments No. 173. AHRQ Publication No. 09-E003. Rockville, MD: Agency for Healthcare Research and Quality, 2008.

Centers for Disease Control and Prevention. *National Ambulatory Medical Care Survey: 2009 Summary Tables*. Atlanta, GA: National Center for Health Statistics, 2009. Available online: www.cdc.gov/nchs/data/ahcd/namcs_summary/2009_namcs_web_tables.pdf.

Centers for Disease Control and Prevention. *National Hospital Discharge Survey: Data Highlights—Selected Tables (2010)*. Atlanta, GA: Centers for Disease Control and Prevention, 2012a. Available online: www.cdc.gov/nchs/nhds/nhds_tables.htm#number.

Centers for Disease Control and Prevention. *National Hospital Discharge Survey*. Atlanta, GA: Centers for Disease Control and Prevention, 2012b. Available online: www.cdc.gov/nchs/nhds.htm.

Clausen, John A., and Marian R. Yarrow, eds. "The Impact of Mental Illness on the Family." *Journal of Social Issues* 11 (1955): entire issue.

Cook, Benjamin L., Thomas McGuire, and Jeanne Miranda. "Measuring Trends in Mental Health Care Disparities, 2000–2004." *Psychiatric Services* 58 (2007): 1533–1540.

Cooper, Lisa A., et al. "The Acceptability of Treatment for Depression Among African-American, Hispanic, and White Primary Care Patients." *Medical Care* 41 (2003): 479–489.

Corrigan, Patrick. "How Stigma Interferes with Mental Health Care." *American Psychologist* 59 (2004): 614–625.

Courtenay, Will H. "Constructions of Masculinity and Their Influence on Men's Well-Being: A Theory of Gender and Health." *Social Science and Medicine* 50 (2000): 1385–1401.

Crystal, Stephen, et al. "Broadened Use of Atypical Antipsychotics: Safety, Effectiveness, and Policy Challenges." *Health Affairs* 28 (2009): w770–w781.

Cunningham, Peter J. "Beyond Parity: Primary Care Physicians' Perspectives on Access to Mental Health Care." *Health Affairs* 28 (2009): w490–w501.

Diala, Chamberlain C., et al. "Racial/Ethnic Differences in Attitudes Toward Seeking Professional Mental Health Services." *American Journal of Public Health* 91 (2001): 805–807.

Dorsey, E. Ray, et al. "Impact of FDA Black Box Advisory on Antipsychotic Medication Use." *Archives of Internal Medicine* 170 (2010): 96–103.

Druss, Benjamin G., et al. "Understanding Mental Health Treatment in Persons Without Mental Diagnoses: Results from the National Comorbidity Survey Replication." *Archives of General Psychiatry* 64 (2007): 1196–1203.

Ellis, Alan R., et al. "County-Level Estimates of Mental Health Professional Supply in the United States." *Psychiatric Services* 60 (2009): 1315–1322.

Farmer, Elizabeth M. Z., et al. "Pathways Into and Through Mental Health Services for Children and Adolescents." *Psychiatric Services* 54 (2003): 60–66.

Frank, Richard G., et al. "The Value of Mental Health Care at the System Level: The Case of Treating Depression." *Health Affairs* 18 (1999): 71–88.

Garrido, Melissa M., et al. "Perceived Need for Mental Health Care Among Community-Dwelling Older Adults." *Journal of Gerontology: Psychological Sciences* 64B (2009): 704–712.

Gilbody, Simon, Peter Bower, and Paula Whitty. "Costs and Consequences of Enhanced Primary Care for Depression: Systematic Review of Randomised Economic Evaluations." *The British Journal of Psychiatry* 189 (2006): 297–308.

Goldberg, David, and Peter Huxley. *Mental Illness in the Community: The Pathway to Psychiatric Care*. New York: Tavistock Publications, 1980.

Grabowski, David C., et al. "Quality of Mental Health Care for Nursing Home Residents: A Literature Review." *Medical Care Research and Review* 67 (2010): 627–656.

Graves, Edmund J. *1993 Summary: National Hospital Discharge Survey. Advance Data from Vital and Health Statistics*. No. 264. Hyattsville, MD: National Center for Health Statistics, 1995. Available online: www.cdc.gov/nchs/data/ad/ad264.pdf.

Gurin, Gerald, Joseph Veroff, and Sheila D. Feld. *Americans View Their Mental Health*. New York: Basic Books, 1960.

Han, Euna, and Gordon G. Liu. "Racial Disparities in Prescription Drug Use for Mental Illness Among Population in US." *The Journal of Mental Health Policy and Economics* 8 (2005): 131–143.

Harman, Jeffrey S., Mark J. Edlund, and John C. Fortney. "Disparities in the Adequacy of Depression Treatment in the United States." *Psychiatric Services* 55 (2004): 1379–1385.

Hinshaw, Stephen P., and Richard M. Scheffler. *Myths, Medications, Media, and Money: ADHD's Current Explosion and the Push for Performance.* New York: Oxford University Press, forthcoming.

Horwitz, Allan V. "The Pathways into Psychiatric Treatment: Some Differences Between Men and Women." *Journal of Health and Social Behavior* 18 (1977): 169–178.

Horwitz, Allan V. "Pharmaceuticals and the Medicalization of Social Life." In *The Risks of Prescription Drugs*, edited by Donald W. Light, pp. 92–115. New York: Columbia University Press, 2010.

Institute for Clinical Systems Improvement. *The DIAMOND Program: Success in Primary Care Depression Treatment and Extension to Other Health Care Challenges.* Bloomington, MN: Institute for Clinical Systems Improvement, 2012. Available online: www.icsi.org/diamond_white_paper_/diamond_white_paper_28676.html.

Institute of Medicine. *Improving the Quality of Health Care for Mental and Substance-Use Conditions.* Washington, DC: The National Academies Press, 2006.

Jensen, Peter S., et al. "Findings from the NIMH Multimodal Treatment Study of ADHD (MTA): Implications and Applications for Primary Care Providers." *Journal of Developmental and Behavioral Pediatrics* 22 (2001): 60–73.

Johnson, Rachel L., et al. "Patient Race/Ethnicity and Quality of Patient-Physician Communication During Medical Visits." *American Journal of Public Health* 94 (2004): 2084–2090.

Kadushin, Charles. "Individual Decisions to Undertake Psychotherapy." *Administrative Science Quarterly* 3 (1958): 379–411.

Kadushin, Charles. "The Friends and Supporters of Psychotherapy: On Social Circles in Urban Life." *American Sociological Review* 31 (1966): 786–802.

Karlin, Bradley E., Michael Duffy, and David H. Gleaves. "Patterns and Predictors of Mental Health Service Use and Mental Illness Among Older and Younger Adults in the United States." *Psychological Services* 5 (2008): 275–294.

Kathol, Roger G., et al. "Barriers to Physical and Mental Condition Integrated Service Delivery." *Psychosomatic Medicine* 72 (2010): 511–518.

Kessler, Ronald C., et al. "Lifetime and 12-Month Prevalence of DSM-III-R Psychiatric Disorders in the United States: Results from the National Comorbidity Survey." *Archives of General Psychiatry* 51 (1994): 8–19.

Kessler, Ronald C., et al. "Prevalence and Treatment of Mental Disorders, 1990 to 2003." *New England Journal of Medicine* 352 (2005): 2515–2523.

Kitchener, Betty A., and Anthony F. Jorm. "Mental Health First Aid Training for the Public: Evaluation of Effects on Knowledge, Attitudes, and Helping Behavior." *BMC Psychiatry* 2 (2002): 10–15.

Klap, Ruth, Kathleen T. Unroe, and Jürgen Unützer. "Caring for Mental Illness in the United States: A Focus on Older Adults." *American Journal of Geriatric Psychiatry* 11 (2003): 517–524.

Klinkman, Michael S. "Competing Demands in Psychosocial Care: A Model for the Identification and Treatment of Depressive Disorders in Primary Care." *General Hospital Psychiatry* 19 (1997): 98–111.

Kreyenbuhl, Julie, et al. "The Schizophrenia Patient Outcome Research Team (PORT): Updated Treatment Recommendation 2009." *Schizophrenia Bulletin* 36 (2010): 94–103.

Kulka, Richard A., Joseph Veroff, and Elizabeth Douvan. "Social Class and the Use of Professional Help for Personal Problems: 1957 and 1976." *Journal of Health and Social Behavior* 20 (1979): 2–17.

Kuno, Eri, and Aileen B. Rothbard. "Racial Disparities in Antipsychotic Prescription Patterns for Patients with Schizophrenia." *American Journal of Psychiatry* 159 (2002): 567–572.

Leaf, Philip J., et al. "Contact with Health Professionals for the Treatment of Psychiatric and Emotional Problems." *Medical Care* 23 (1985): 1322–1337.

Lehman, Anthony F., et al. *Evidence-Based Mental Health Treatments and Services: Examples to Inform Public Policy.* New York: Milbank Memorial Fund, 2004.

Lincoln, Alisa "Psychiatric Emergency Room Decision-Making, Social Control and the Undeserving Sick." *Sociology of Health and Illness* 28 (2006): 54–75.

Mackenzie, Corey S., Jina Pagura, and Jitender Sareen. "Correlates of Perceived Need for and Use of Mental Health Services by Older Adults in the Collaborative Psychiatric Epidemiology Surveys." *American Journal of Geriatric Psychiatry* 18 (2010): 1103–1115.

Mackenzie, Corey S., et al. "Older Adults' Help-Seeking Attitudes and Treatment Beliefs Concerning Mental Health Problems." *American Journal of Geriatric Psychiatry* 16 (2008): 1010–1019.

Marshall, Max, et al. "Association Between Duration of Untreated Psychosis and Outcome in Cohorts of First-Episode Patients." *Archives of General Psychiatry* 62 (2005): 975–983.

McAlpine, Donna, and David Mechanic. "Utilization of Specialty Mental Health Care Among Persons with Severe Mental Illness: The Roles of Demographics, Need, Insurance and Risk." *Health Services Research* 35 (2000): 277–292.

McGlynn, Elizabeth A., et al. "The Quality of Health Care Delivered to Adults in the United States." *New England Journal of Medicine* 348 (2003): 2635–2645.

McGuire, Thomas G., and Jeanne Miranda. "New Evidence Regarding Racial and Ethnic Disparities in Mental Health: Policy Implications." *Health Affairs* 27 (2008): 393–403.

Mechanic, David. "The Concept of Illness Behavior." *Journal of Chronic Diseases* 15 (1962): 189–194.

Mechanic, David. "Social Psychologic Factors Affecting the Presentation of Bodily Complaints." *The New England Journal of Medicine* 286 (1972): 1132–1139.

Mechanic, David. *Medical Sociology*, 2nd ed. New York: The Free Press, 1978.

Mechanic, David, ed. *Symptoms, Illness Behavior, and Help-Seeking*. New Brunswick, NJ: Rutgers University Press, 1982.

Mechanic, David. "Barriers to Help-Seeking, Detection, and Adequate Treatment for Anxiety and Mood Disorders: Implications for Health Care Policy." *Journal of Clinical Psychiatry* 68 (2007): 20–26.

Mechanic, David, Ronald Angel, and Lorraine Davies. "Risk and Selection Processes Between the General and Specialty Mental Health Sectors." *Journal of Health and Social Behavior* 32 (1991): 49–64.

Medco Health Solutions, Inc. *America's State of Mind*, A Report by Medco. Medco Health Solutions, Inc., 2011. Available online: www.cchrint.org/pdfs/Psych-Drug-Us-Epidemic-Medco-rpt-Nov-2011.pdf.

Merikangas, Kathleen Ries, et al. "Lifetime Prevalence of Mental Disorders in U.S. Adolescents: Results from the National Comorbidity Survey Replication-Adolescent Supplement (NCS-A)." *Journal of the American Academy of Child & Adolescent Psychiatry* 49 (2010a): 980–989.

Merikangas, Kathleen Ries, et al. "Prevalence and Treatment of Mental Disorders Among U.S. Children in the 2001–2004 NHANES." *Pediatrics* 125 (2010b): 75–81.

Mills, Meghan L. "Unconventional Mental Health Treatment: Reexamining the Racial-Ethnic Disparity in Treatment-Seeking Behavior." *Psychiatric Services* 63 (2012): 142–146.

Mitchell, Alex J., Amol Vaze, and Sanjay Rao. "Clinical Diagnosis of Depression in Primary Care: A Meta-Analysis." *Lancet* 374 (2009): 609–619.

Mitchell, Alex J., Amol Vaze, and Sanjay Rao. "Do Primary Care Physicians Have Particular Difficulty Identifying Late-Life Depression? A Meta-Analysis Stratified by Age." *Psychotherapy and Psychosomatics* 79 (2010): 285–294.

Mojtabai, Ramin, and Mark Olfson. "National Trends in Psychotropic Medication Polypharmacy in Office-Based Psychiatry." *Archives of General Psychiatry* 67 (2010): 26–36.

Mojtabai, Ramin, Mark Olfson, and David Mechanic. "Perceived Need and Help-Seeking in Adults with Mood, Anxiety, or Substance Use Disorders." *Archives of General Psychiatry* 59 (2002): 77–84.

Mojtabai, Ramin, et al. "Unmet Need for Mental Health Care in Schizophrenia: An Overview of Literature and New Data from a First-Admission Study." *Schizophrenia Bulletin* 35 (2009): 679–695.

Molina, Brooke S. G., et al. "The MTA at 8 Years: Prospective Follow-up of Children Treated for Combined-Type ADHD in a Multisite Study." *Journal of the American Academy of Child and Adolescent Psychiatry* 48 (2009): 484–500.

Neighbors, Harold W., et al. "Racial Differences in DSM Diagnosis Using a Semi-Structured Instrument: The Importance of Clinical Judgment in the Diagnosis of African Americans." *Journal of Health and Social Behavior* 44 (2003): 237–256.

Olfson, Mark, and Steven C. Marcus. "National Patterns in Antidepressant Medication Treatment." *Archives of General Psychiatry* 66 (2009): 848–856.

Olfson, Mark, and Steven C. Marcus. "National Trends in Outpatient Psychotherapy." *American Journal of Psychiatry* 167 (2010): 1456–1463.

Olfson, Mark, Steven C. Marcus, and David Shaffer. "Antidepressant Drug Therapy and Suicide in Severely Depressed Children and Adults: A Case-Control Study." *Archives of General Psychiatry* 63 (2006): 865–872.

Olfson, Mark, et al. "National Trends in the Treatment of Attention Deficit Hyperactivity Disorder." *American Journal of Psychiatry* 160 (2003): 1071–1077.

Olfson, Mark, et al. "Trends in Antipsychotic Drug Use by Very Young, Privately Insured Children." *Journal of the American Academy of Child & Adolescent Psychiatry* 49 (2010): 13–23.

Pescosolido, Bernice A., Carol Brooks Gardner, and Keri M. Lubell. "How People Get Into Mental Health Services: Stories of Choice, Coercion, and 'Muddling Through' from 'First-Timers.' " *Social Science and Medicine* 46 (1998): 275–286.

Pescosolido, Bernice A., et al. "Stigmatizing Attitudes and Beliefs About Treatment and Psychiatric Medications for Children with Mental Illness." *Psychiatric Services* 58 (2007): 613–618.

Pescosolido, Bernice A., et al. "Public Knowledge and Assessment of Child Mental Health Problems: Findings from the National Stigma Study-Children." *Journal of the American Academy of Child and Adolescent Psychiatry* 47 (2008): 339–349.

Pescosolido, Bernice A., et al. " 'A Disease Like Any Other?' A Decade of Change in Public Reactions to Schizophrenia, Depression and Alcohol Dependence." *American Journal of Psychiatry* 167 (2010): 1321–1330.

Phelan, Jo C., et al. "Public Conceptions of Mental Illness in 1950 and 1996: What Is Mental Illness and Is It to Be Feared?" *Journal of Health and Social Behavior* 41 (2000): 188–207.

Rosenfield, Sarah. "Race Differences in Involuntary Hospitalization: Psychiatric vs. Labeling Perspectives." *Journal of Health and Social Behavior* 25 (1984): 14–23.

Rowland, Andrew S., Catherine A. Lesesne, and Ann J. Abramowitz. "The Epidemiology of Attention-Deficit/Hyperactivity Disorder (ADHD): A Public Health View." *Mental Retardation and Developmental Disabilities Research Reviews* 8 (2002): 162–170.

Roy-Byrne, Peter P., et al. "Low Socioeconomic Status and Mental Health Care Use Among Respondents with Anxiety and Depression in the NCS-R." *Psychiatric Services* 60 (2009): 1190–1197.

Scheffler, Richard M., et al. "Positive Association Between Attention-Deficit/Hyperactivity Disorder Medication Use and Academic Achievement During Elementary School." *Pediatrics* 123 (2009): 1273–1289.

Shea, Dennis G., Patricia A. Russo, and Michael A. Smyer. "Use of Mental Health Services by Persons with a Mental Illness in Nursing Facilities: Initial Impacts of OBRA87." *Journal of Aging and Health* 12 (2000): 560–578.

Shim, Ruth S., et al. "Race-Ethnicity as a Predictor of Attitudes Toward Mental Health Treatment Seeking." *Psychiatric Services* 60 (2009): 1336–1341.

Snowden, Lonnie R., and David Pingitore. "Frequency and Scope of Mental Health Service Delivery to African Americans in Primary Care." *Mental Health Services Research* 4 (2002): 123–130.

Snowden, Lonnie R., Julia F. Hastings, and Jennifer Alvidrez. "Overrepresentation of Black Americans in Psychiatric Inpatient Care." *Psychiatric Services* 60 (2009): 779–785.

Stewart, Donna E. "Physical Symptoms of Depression: Unmet Needs in Special Populations." *Journal of Clinical Psychiatry* 64, supplement 7 (2003): 12–16.

Stoudemire, Alan, and David A. Smith. "OBRA Regulations and the Use of Psychotropic Drugs in Long-Term Care Facilities. Impact and Implications for Geropsychiatric Care." *General Hospital Psychiatry* 18 (1996): 77–94.

Substance Abuse and Mental Health Services Administration. *Results from the 2010 National Survey on Drug Use and Health: Summary of National Findings.* NSDUH Series H-41. HHS Publication No. (SMA) 11-4658. Rockville, MD: Substance Abuse and Mental Health Services Administration, 2011. Available online: oas.samhsa.gov/NSDUH/2k10NSDUH/2k10Results.pdf.

Substance Abuse and Mental Health Services Administration. *Mental Health, United States, 2010.* HHS Publication No. (SMA) 12-4681. Rockville, MD: Substance Abuse and Mental Health Administration, 2012.

Swindle, Ralph Jr., et al. "Responses to Nervous Breakdowns in America Over a 40-year Period." *American Psychologist* 55 (2000): 740–749.

Tai-Seale, Ming, Thomas G. McGuire, and Weimin Zhang. "Time Allocation in Primary Care Office Visits." *Health Services Research* 42 (2007): 1871–1894.

Tai-Seale, Ming, et al. "Understanding Primary Care Physicians' Propensity to Assess Elderly Patients for Depression Using Interaction and Survey Data." *Medical Care* 43 (2005): 1217–1224.

Trierweiler, Steven J., et al. "Clinician Attributions Associated with the Diagnosis of Schizophrenia in African American and Non-African American Patients." *Journal of Consulting and Clinical Psychology* 68 (2000): 171–175.

U.S. Census Bureau. *The 2011 Statistical Abstract.* Washington, DC: U.S. Department of Commerce, U.S. Census Bureau, 2011. Available online: www.census.gov/compendia/statab/2011/2011edition.html.

U.S. Department of Health and Human Services, Office of the Inspector General. *Medicare Atypical Antipsychotic Drug Claims for Elderly Nursing Home Residents.* OEI-07-08-00150. Department of Health and Human Services, 2011. Available online: oig.hhs.gov/oei/reports/oei-07-08-00150.pdf.

U.S. Department of Justice. "Eli Lilly and Company Agrees to Pay $1.415 Billion to Resolve Allegations of Off-label Promotion of Zyprexa." Washington, DC: U.S. Department of Justice, 2009. Available online: www.justice.gov/opa/pr/2009/January/09-civ-038.html.

Unützer, Jürgen, et al. "Collaborative Care Management of Late-Life Depression in the Primary Care Setting. A Randomized Controlled Trial." Journal of the American Medical Association 288 (2002): 2836–2845.

van Ryn, Michelle. "Research on the Provider Contribution to Race/Ethnicity Disparities in Medical Care." *Medical Care* 40 (2002): I140–I151.

van Ryn, Michelle, and Jane Burke. "The Effect of Patient Race and Socio-Economic Status on Physicians' Perceptions of Patients." *Social Science and Medicine* 50 (2000): 813–828.

Veroff, Joseph, Richard A. Kulka, and Elizabeth Douvan. *Mental Health in America: Patterns of Help-Seeking from 1957 to 1976.* New York: Basic Books, 1981.

Wang, Philip S., et al. "Twelve-Month Use of Mental Health Services in the United States: Results from the National Comorbidity Study Replication." *Archives of General Psychiatry* 62 (2005a): 629–640.

Wang, Philip S., et al. "Failure and Delay in Initial Treatment Contact After First Onset of Mental Disorders in the National Comorbidity Survey Replication." *Archives of General Psychiatry* 62 (2005b): 603–613.

Weissman, Myrna M., and Jerome K. Myers. "Affective Disorders in a U.S. Urban Community: The Use of Research Diagnostic Criteria in an Epidemiological Survey." *Archives of General Psychiatry* 35 (1978): 1304–1311.

Wells, Kenneth B., et al. *Caring for Depression.* Cambridge, MA: Harvard University Press, 1996.

Wells, Kenneth, et al. "Ethnic Disparities in Unmet Need for Alcoholism, Drug Abuse, and Mental Health Care." *American Journal of Psychiatry* 158 (2001): 2027–2032.

Williams, David R., and Michelle Harris-Reid. "Race and Mental Health: Emerging Patterns and Promising Approaches." In *A Handbook for the Study of Mental Health: Social Contexts, Theories and Systems,* edited by Allan V. Horwitz and Teresa L. Scheid, pp. 295–314. Cambridge: Cambridge University Press, 1999.

Williams, John W., et al. "Systematic Review of Multifaceted Interventions to Improve Depression Care." *General Hospital Psychiatry* 29 (2007): 91–116.

Wilson, Duff. "Side Effects May Include Lawsuits." *The New York Times*, October 2, 2010. Available online: www.nytimes.com/2010/10/03/business/03psych.html?pagewanted=all.

Woodwell, David A. and Susan M. Schappert. *National Ambulatory Medical Care Survey: 1993 Summary*. Advance Data from Vital and Health Statistics, No. 270. Hyattsville, MD: National Center for Health Statistics, 1995. Available online: www.cdc.gov/nchs/data/ad/ad270.pdf.

Yarrow, Marian Radke, et al. "The Psychological Meaning of Mental Illness in the Family." *Journal of Social Issues* 11 (1955): 12–24.

Young, Alexander S., et al. "The Quality of Care for Depressive and Anxiety Disorders in the United States." *Archives of General Psychiatry* 58 (2001): 55–61.

7

The Financing and Delivery of Mental Health Services

The availability and use of mental health services depend on financing. For the first half of the twentieth century, mental health services were sharply bifurcated. The poor received little mental health care, but if sufficiently disordered or disturbing, they were maintained in public institutions with minimal active treatment. The rich bought services from private practitioners on a fee-for-service basis; if in need of hospitalization, they would receive care, at least initially, in private mental hospitals. The cost of such care was prohibitive, and even affluent patients with chronic mental illness were frequently transferred to public institutions if they did not respond to treatment after some initial period. This pattern of allocation of services began to shift significantly in the 1960s with the development of community mental health centers, the extension of psychiatric outpatient facilities in hospitals, and the improvement of psychiatric benefits under private health insurance programs (Follmann 1970). With passage of the Medicare Act in 1965, the aged received some modest psychiatric benefits, although on a more limited basis than other types of medical services covered by the program. Similarly, Medicaid provided significant funds to pay for mental health services for the poor. As a public assistance entitlement, however, the program reflects traditional federal–state welfare relationships, including uneven implementation from one place to another (Stevens and Stevens 1974). As a result of various developments in both public and private programs, use of mental health services has increased tremendously, but not in a particularly well-balanced way.

MENTAL HEALTH EXPENDITURES AND COVERAGE

In 2005, the United States spent about $1.9 trillion on health care services, of which $135 billion was for mental health and substance abuse (MHSA) services. Mental health care accounts for about 84 percent of all MHSA spending (Substance Abuse and Mental Health Services Administration 2010a). Despite a large increase in use of services in recent years, growing acceptability of treatment among the public, and efforts to establish MHSA services as a mainstream priority, this sector has not kept pace with growth in other areas of medicine. Between 1986 and 2005, MHSA expenditures actually fell from 9.3 to 7.3 percent of overall health care spending. This is not surprising given the growth in sophisticated expensive technologies within other areas of medicine and the strength of their commercial and professional advocates.

The pattern of expenditures has also changed dramatically in recent decades (Mark et al. 2011). As shown in Figure 7.1, treatment has moved away from institutional care to outpatient care. The area of greatest growth is drug costs. By 2005, the cost of retail prescription drugs constituted about one-fifth of MHSA expenditures (25 percent of MH and 1 percent of SA), increasing by almost 13 times since 1986.

As shown in Table 7.1, public resources account for much more of mental health costs than overall health costs (58 percent versus 46 percent in 2005). Approximately 28 percent of mental health expenditures were from Medicaid as compared with 17 percent of all health expenditures. Although states contributed 30 percent of mental health expenditures, their role as direct providers of service has contracted substantially. Increasingly, state mental health authorities are using their funds to fulfill the required Medicaid match of state to federal dollars. Further, much service provision under state programs takes place through contracts with large managed behavioral health care organizations (Frank and Glied 2006).

In the early twenty-first century, 80 percent of persons with mental illness had some form of public or private health insurance. This level of coverage reflected the expansion of benefits for mental health care within private insurance, as well as the spread of Medicaid and Medicare. However, people with mental health problems are more likely to be uninsured than others in the general population (Garfield et al. 2011; McAlpine and Mechanic 2000).

Figure 7.1 • Spending (in millions) on Mental Health and Substance Abuse Services by Provider and Service: 1986–2005

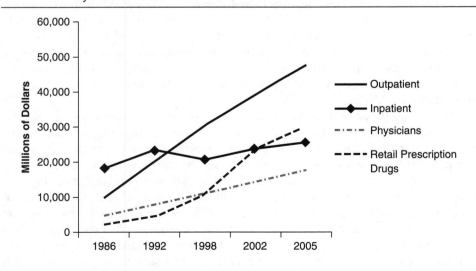

Source: Substance Abuse and Mental Health Services Administration. *National Expenditures for Mental Health Services and Substance Abuse Treatment, 1986–2005*. DHHS Publication No. (SMA) 10-4612, Rockville, MD: Substance Abuse and Mental Health Services Administration, 2010a. Table A.4, p. 48.

	Table 7.1	Percentage of Expenditures by Public and Private Payers for Mental Health and All Health, 2005	

	Mental Health	All Health
Public—Total	58.2	45.6
Medicare	7.7	18.3
Medicaid	27.6	16.8
Other Federal	5.0	4.5
Other State and Local	18.0	5.9
All Federal	28.4	32.5
All State	29.8	13.1
Private—Total	41.8	54.4
Out-of-Pocket	12.2	13.3
Private Insurance	27.0	37.3
Other Private	2.6	3.8

Source: Substance Abuse and Mental Health Services Administration. *Mental Health, United States, 2010*. HHS Publication No. (SMA) 12-4681, Rockville, MD: Substance Abuse and Mental Health Services Administration, 2012, Adapted from Table 75, p. 202.

In addition, coverage of mental health problems has traditionally been limited so that even those with insurance benefits have faced financial access barriers. Nevertheless, among users of mental health services there has been a decline in out-of-pocket spending as a proportion of total mental health service costs, from nearly 36 percent in 1971 to 12 percent in 2005 (Frank and Glied 2006; Substance Abuse and Mental Health Services Administration 2010a). Actual out-of-pocket dollar costs, however, are rising as people use more outpatient care and medications. Deductibles, copayments, and other cost sharing are common in the behavioral health area and have been sizeable, especially when a hospital stay was involved.

Private and public insurers have used a variety of means for restricting coverage for mental health problems over the years. For example, historically in the case of hospital care, most plans restricted care to 30–60 days per year for mental illness, compared with 120 days or unrestricted periods for other illnesses. Plans also typically set lower dollar maximums per year and per lifetime on mental health benefits, such as a $50,000 lifetime cap, and allowed fewer outpatient visits than for other illnesses. Moreover, mental health outpatient insurance usually involved a 50 percent coinsurance rate compared with 20 percent for other medical conditions. Outpatient mental health expenses often could not be used to meet the employee's maximum out-of-pocket expense limit, and the employee had to continue to pay the large coinsurance rate no matter how large the expenditures. Many plans simply excluded specific conditions from coverage, such as eating disorders and substance abuse problems. Discrimination of this type emerged as a major issue for mental health consumers and advocates, giving birth to the fight for mental health insurance parity.

THE PARITY STRUGGLE AND ITS ACCOMPLISHMENTS

The goals of mental health parity legislation are straightforward: to eliminate the discriminatory treatment of mental health conditions within private and public health insurance. The first federal mental health parity statute was passed in 1996 following collapse of the Clinton administration's attempt at national health care reform (Rochefort 1997). Although the law marked an important advance in the parity struggle, it was lacking in many ways. Even though it prohibited differences between coverage of physical and mental illnesses in regard to lifetime and annual dollar benefits, the measure neither prevented employers from dropping mental health coverage nor did it disallow benefit limitations in terms of number of days or visits, copayment rates, and definitions of medical necessity. Also, the law did not apply to small businesses with 50 or fewer employees, thus exempting about 15–20 percent of the workforce from its protections. Frustrated with this timid approach, many states followed up with stricter parity laws of their own. As many as 33 states, including the District of Columbia, had adopted some form of parity legislation by 2001 (Morton and Aleman 2005) and by 2011, all but one state had either parity legislation or a mandate that covered mental health services (National Conference of State Legislatures 2011). The fact that benefit plans of self-insured employers are not subject to state regulation, however, makes state action an inherently poor solution for this issue.

Passage of legislation does not guarantee quick or faithful implementation. In 2000, the General Accounting Office (now renamed the General Accountability Office) surveyed employers in the District of Columbia and 26 states that did not have stricter parity laws than the federal government (General Accounting Office 2000). It found less than full compliance with federal provisions. Eighty-six percent of the employers had standardized annual and lifetime dollar limits for mental health care and medical and surgical services. However, 87 percent of this group had at least one other insurance feature more restrictive for mental health than for other medical or surgical services. Additional information on implementation of the 1996 law comes from analyses by the Department of Labor Statistics (Morton and Aleman 2005). As prescribed by the legislation, there was widespread removal of coverage restrictions related to spending limits. Workers in private industry with inpatient dollar limits fell from 41 percent in 1997 to 7 percent in 2002. Comparable outpatient limits fell from 55 to 7 percent. However, contrary to what advocates had hoped for, restrictions on inpatient days and outpatient visits increased. Seventy-seven percent of workers in 2002 had limits on inpatient care compared with 61 percent in 1997, and limits on outpatient visits increased from 53 percent of covered workers to 75 percent in 2002. In 2008, more than 60 percent of workers were limited to 30 days or less of outpatient care and 30 days or less of inpatient care (Substance Abuse and Mental Health Services Administration 2012).

Federal parity legislation did not address benefits for substance abuse and thus had even less effect in this area, although nearly all workers with health insurance had some alcohol and drug abuse benefits. By 2002, the large majority was eligible for in-hospital detoxification, and four-fifths for inpatient rehabilitation. About nine in ten workers had outpatient alcohol rehabilitation coverage (Morton and Aleman 2005). Nonetheless, utilization restrictions on substance treatment were rampant. In all, only 8 percent of workers with alcohol treatment benefits had inpatient and outpatient rehabilitation coverage equivalent to that for general medical care, and the same was true in regard to drug abuse treatment.

In 1999, President Clinton directed the Office of Personnel Management, which administers the Federal Employees Health Benefits Program, to provide parity mental health and substance abuse benefits in approximately 200 participating health plans covering more than eight million people. This directive applied, as well, to specialty-managed behavioral health providers associated with those plans (Grob and Goldman 2006). The president asked for a study to evaluate the impact of his directive so as to guide future mental health insurance policy. This research was extensive and found only very modest changes in access to care, utilization, costs, or quality as a result of parity requirements (U.S. Department of Health and Human Services 2004). One important positive change was that users of mental health services did have significantly fewer out-of-pocket costs after parity.

In the past, indemnity insurers have defined as legitimate whatever services the designated experts (usually psychiatrists) decided to deliver. Increasingly, however, managed care entities are applying principles of "medical necessity" in narrowing the conditions approved for care as well as types of intervention and length of treatment. Diagnoses not included in the *DSM* are unlikely to be covered, although this guidebook is sufficiently broad to allow most patients to receive a diagnosis. Beyond this, the screening criteria used by managed care reviewers tend to be more or less exacting according to the intensity and cost of services involved. Sustained treatment usually requires a significant diagnosis, such as schizophrenia or major depression, while insurers show little inclination to pay for much care that is associated with common problems in living. Moreover, the objective of managed care is to avoid inpatient admissions where possible, to reduce inpatient lengths of stay, and to truncate long courses of treatment. Long-term psychotherapy has been largely replaced by brief psychotherapy, medications are substituting for psychotherapy, and community treatments are prevailing over inpatient care.

The Mental Health Parity and Addiction Equity (MHPAEA) Act of 2008 represents the most ambitious effort by the federal government to eliminate insurance disparities between mental health and general medical care. The law, which went into effect in 2010, improved upon prior federal legislation by encompassing substance abuse as well as mental illness. While it does not apply to small businesses and stops short of requiring that insurers provide behavioral health coverage, these are limitations that will be corrected over time by implementation of the Affordable Care Act. Also, while Medicare and Medicaid are not legally defined as forms of insurance within the ambit of the 2008 statute, Medicaid managed care is subject to its provisions and parity protections are being phased in separately for Medicare, but on a different schedule.

A significant complication of parity pertains to the so-called "non-quantitative aspects" of coverage that relate to mental health managed care. The quantitative aspects of insurance, such as deductibles, copayments, number of visits, days of coverage, and lifetime limits, are easily measured. But defining comparability of treatment and medical necessity has proven to be much more elusive, often involving different standards and concerns for behavioral health care than for other medical services. A primary political argument for the financial viability of parity was that a carefully managed benefit would not likely result in significant cost increases. When insurers previously had attempted to apply tough managed care controls in the area of medical/surgical services, a public backlash forced them to pull back (Mechanic 2004). But behavioral health care remains subject to close monitoring by means of utilization review within conventional insurance and by the in-house and contracted oversight functions of managed care plans. Interim final regulations for defining comparable non-quantitative aspects of coverage under MHPAEA have yet to be released, and developing criteria that are meaningful and enforceable is challenging. Mental health treatment plans, particularly for individuals with serious and persistent disorders, can involve idiosyncratic trade-offs between levels and types of care, as well as forms of recovery planning that are unique to this sector of medicine. It remains to be seen whether federal policymakers can strike an effective balance between standardized protections and flexibility. However they approach this task, any new federal regulation on such issues is likely to be vigorously litigated given the diverse employer, provider, and consumer interests at stake.

PAYMENT CHANGES AND PROFESSIONAL AND CLINICAL RESPONSES

Not just physicians, but also psychologists, social workers, and other non-MD clinicians face uncertainties as health insurance changes, cost concerns deepen, and insurers and payers seek new ways of reimbursing professional work. Payers are currently encouraging providers to join together in new organizational entities such as Accountable Care Organizations (ACO), Medical Homes (MH), and Health Homes (HH). The objective is improving the efficiency and quality of care, and reimbursements will be designed accordingly. These new organizations will be reimbursed so as to encourage greater quality of care. This development corresponds with a shift in reimbursement arrangements to adjusted capitation, bundled payments, episode payment, and related approaches. The new model of care rests on the experience of tightly organized multispecialty group practices such as Kaiser-Permanente, Mayo Clinic, Geisinger Clinic, and a number of others that have demonstrated the capacity to provide continuous, coordinated, and high-quality care, typically at less cost than prevails elsewhere in the health system. Developing comprehensively integrated models, as well as the kind of professional culture needed for these organizations to function well, promises to be a long and arduous process (Mechanic 2010). Many providers resist the required accommodations. While matching the performance of mature health system models may be a distant target, it should be possible nonetheless to begin nudging the system in the desired direction.

The logic behind moving toward "episode" and "bundled" payments is to induce greater responsibility and accountability in line with the overarching principle of integration. Clinicians may take their responsibilities seriously when treating patients, but the sense of active involvement diminishes once a patient leaves for another setting of care. Thus, even though patients in a hospital are likely to receive excellent care, there is an important missing piece when no one follows up after discharge. As a result, a large number of patients are readmitted within 30 days of discharge from hospital, which is a very expensive pattern to sustain. Episode payment seeks to link clinical responsibility and financing by focusing payment on a single provider, or provider organization, for an entire episode of care that begins when the patient enters the service system—this point may be defined in different ways but typically refers to a hospital admission—and ends at some pre-established point, such as 30–180 days after discharge. Such a payment methodology is calculated to ensure that patients are appropriately followed after discharge, that crises are averted, that patients are assisted with treatment adherence, and that related challenges are planned for and dealt with as necessary. Bundling is a similar concept in which various services logically interrelated but involving different professionals are covered by a single payment to induce continuity of care and seamless coordination among needed services. Many implementation problems remain to be worked out, such as establishing the distribution of payment when various participants are located outside of large integrated medical groups and insurance plans (Mechanic R. 2011; Mechanic and Tompkins 2012). Fortunately, however, some of these capitation-type arrangements are already familiar within the mental health sector due to extensive experience with behavioral managed care organizations and their "carve-out" contracts with private insurers and state authorities.

Parity legislation and other systemic changes currently underway, including those relating to the passage of national health care reform, are certain to alter how treatment plans are managed. In the past, insurers could simply control mental health expenditures by limiting the number of reimbursable providers, relying on high cost sharing, and adopting inflexible utilization and reimbursement ceilings. However, with the present push toward evidence-based practice and quality measurement that is tied to economic incentives, insurers must take on the messy business of assessing which types of mental health problems should be treated and how. This brings medical necessity and appropriate treatment to the forefront, and both are slippery concepts given large gaps in our knowledge base as well as great heterogeneity among patients of different racial and ethnic backgrounds, gender, age, and socioeconomic status.

We can learn from an earlier period, the 1980s, during which payment innovations also provoked waves of turbulence in the organization and delivery of health care. In 1983, concerned about the growing costs of hospital care, Congress passed legislation implementing a prospective payment system (PPS) for acute care hospitals, a payment approach later adapted for use by other federal programs and many private payers. This system provided a predetermined fixed amount to pay for inpatient services for patients whose conditions were categorized according to 468 diagnostic-related groups, or DRGs. However, most private psychiatric hospitals and specialized psychiatric units in general hospitals were exempted from this system because of wide dispersion in costs among patients with comparable diagnoses and because of the difficulty of making reliable predictions regarding inpatient costs for specific diagnostic groups. These exempted providers continued to receive payment based on actual reasonable costs together with a regulated increase tied to historical baseline data for costs per diagnosis.

The relatively favorable reimbursements still flowing to inpatient psychiatry as compared with the general hospital sector spurred the growth of private psychiatric hospitals while providing opportunities for general hospitals to capitalize on unused capacity by developing specialized psychiatric units (Walkup 1997). A favorable profit center, inpatient psychiatry mushroomed. Between 1980 and 1992, the number of private psychiatric hospitals in the United States increased from 184 to 475, and the number of specialized psychiatric units in general hospitals increased from 923 to 1,616 (Center for Mental Health Services 1996).

Other forces converged to help bring about this rapid expansion of the general hospital inpatient sector. The public increasingly had insurance that paid for a number of hospital days for psychiatric illness but provided much less coverage for outpatient service. This created an incentive for inpatient care. As states closed or reduced the size of their public mental hospitals, they also looked to general hospitals as their first line of care in the treatment of acute psychiatric illness. At the same time, states had a powerful fiscal incentive to shift inpatient care to general hospitals because when they did so, the federal government shared the cost for patients in the Medicaid program.

Individual entrepreneurs and hospital chains also recognized the profit potential of inpatient psychiatry and moved aggressively into markets and market niches where bed shortages existed. Private psychiatric hospitals frequently promoted the inpatient care of children and adolescents, an area where treatment standards were particularly uncertain. Private psychiatric hospitals greatly expanded, from 2.7 percent of all psychiatric inpatient beds in 1970 to 16.1 percent in 1992; the number of such hospitals increased from 150 to 475; and admissions grew from approximately 92,000 in 1969 to almost 470,000 in 1992 (Center for Mental Health Services 1996). Full-time-equivalent (FTE) staff in these hospitals increased from 21,504 in 1972 to more than 77,000 in 1992, and patient care FTEs increased more than fivefold. Between 1970 and 1992, inpatient psychiatry in proprietary general hospitals was another growth sector, serving primarily insured persons with less severe problems than those in public and nonprofit general hospitals and disproportionately serving children (Olfson and Mechanic 1996).

Eventually, the conditions that supported this boom in inpatient psychiatry evaporated. Of critical importance was the advent of managed care, which sharply reduced inpatient stays. In the late 1980s, average length of stay for patients with a primary psychiatric diagnosis varied from 10 to 13 days depending on hospital type (Mechanic, McAlpine, and Olfson 1998). By 2000, length of stay varied from 6.7 to 7.7 days (Mechanic and Bilder 2004). Although some patients in general hospitals with primary psychiatric disorders were still being cared for in beds in general medical and surgical units, by the 1990s most such admissions were to specialized units. Between 1986 and 2004, the number of private psychiatric hospitals decreased from 314 to 264, and the number of specialized psychiatric units in general hospitals shrank from 1,287 to 1,230 (Substance Abuse and Mental Health Services Administration 2012). Interestingly, the decline in the number of units and beds in these units in the 1990s did not translate directly into fewer admissions because reduced lengths of stay yielded substantial unused capacity. Admissions to specialized psychiatric units climbed from about 849,000 in 1986 to 1,533,000 in 2004. During this period, admissions to private psychiatric hospitals fluctuated but also increased from 235,000 to 599,000 (Substance Abuse and Mental Health Services Administration 2010b).

After an initial moratorium, psychiatric DRGs also were implemented. The formula for determining prospective payments is complex, with technical details that go beyond our needs in this book. In brief, after an initial severity-DRG classification has been made for a patient, there are adjustments factoring in inpatient operating and capital-related costs, geographic variations in wage levels, patient characteristics such as age, specified comorbidities, and length of stay, and facility characteristics such as whether a hospital is located in a rural area and conducts medical education. Starting in 2005, the PPS system was phased in over three years so that by January of 2008, 100 percent of payments for inpatient treatment of mental health conditions was based on the rates determined under prospective payment (Centers for Medicare & Medicaid Services 2011). Implementation of psychiatric DRGs took place in conjunction with a requirement for budget neutrality. This meant highly efficient inpatient units emerged as winners while less efficient units were losers. Some institutional providers did not survive the conversion from cost-based reimbursement. Simply stated, inpatient psychiatry was no longer the profitable cost center it once was.

The net result of these changes is that while inpatient care is increasingly a smaller part of total costs for MHSA services, the mix of settings has changed. Beginning in 1998 mental health expenditures for care in general hospitals exceeded that of psychiatric hospitals. By 2005, mental health care in general hospitals comprised 56 percent of inpatient mental health expenditures, and 68 percent of this sum went for care in specialized psychiatric units while 32 percent went for care in medical and surgical units. Specialty hospitals, in contrast, accounted for 44 percent of inpatient expenditures (Substance Abuse and Mental Health Services Administration 2012).

UTILIZATION OF SERVICES AND FINANCING PATTERNS

The extension of psychiatric services through expanded insurance benefits has had important implications for the distribution of care. It followed, and may have reinforced, an existing trend toward providing services to groups in the population less in need than some others. The most comprehensive insurance coverage is frequently available to the most advantaged segments of the employed population. Even among those with comparable insurance coverage, persons with higher incomes, education, and greater sophistication use the most services (Leaf et al. 1985), despite the inverse relationship between socioeconomic status and mental health impairment (Dohrenwend and Dohrenwend 1974; Dohrenwend and Dohrenwend 1969; Kessler 1982; Kessler et al. 1994).

Mental health coverage through Medicare and Medicaid has substantially improved access to mental health care, and the latter program provides states with opportunities for more comprehensive coverage. In effect, Medicaid has become the safety net for many persons with serious and persistent mental illness, offering a broad range of services, including case management and psychosocial rehabilitation, in many states. For this reason, Medicaid has been increasing its share of total mental health spending, which rose from 17 percent in 1986 to 28 percent in 2005 (Mark et al. 2011). One consequence is that the poorest of the poor, i.e., those who are most likely to have Medicaid coverage, are almost as likely to have a mental health visit as those with high incomes. Meanwhile, the near-poor have had the lowest rate of such visits among income groups (Olfson and Pincus 1996). The reason is this subgroup is the least likely to be protected by either private or government insurance. Implementation of health reform including the availability of Medicaid to new clients at 133 percent or less of the federal poverty level (up to $30,657 for a family of four in 2012) should help close these disparities and make Medicaid even more important in our mental health services system, although coverage extension is only a state option under the Supreme Court's ACA decision.

THE ECONOMICS OF MENTAL HEALTH CARE

Researchers have learned a great deal about the economics of mental health care; the effects of financial incentives on consumers, professionals, and institutions; and the cost-effectiveness of alternative ways of organizing services. Although our knowledge of the effects of insurance and copayment on the demand for mental health services has advanced, too little attention has been given to the economics of the public mental health sector or to the dynamics of financing care for the most seriously mentally ill.

Not only have cost-sharing features and service limits been more characteristic of mental health care than other medical services, they also have inhibited outpatient services even more in this area than others (Frank and McGuire 1986). One study of psychotherapy conducted among more than 4,000 patients found the use of this service to be quite sensitive to amount of coverage. While not designed to examine the decision whether or not to seek treatment in the first place, the research documented a relationship between adequacy of insurance benefits and volume of care received, particularly among persons with lower incomes (McGuire 1981).

The best source of data on the effects of cost sharing is the Rand Health Insurance Experiment (HIE). This unique study, carried out between 1974 and 1982, randomized 6,970 respondents into insurance plans with varying coinsurance requirements and, in one setting, a health maintenance organization (HMO), Group Health Cooperative of Puget Sound in Seattle. In some cases, there were no coinsurance requirements (labeled the "free care" group), while in other cases families had to pay 25, 50, or 95 percent of their bills up to a $1,000 per-year maximum. There were other coverage variations as well (Newhouse 1974; Newhouse and the Insurance Experiment Group 1993), but for our purposes what is most important is the different obligations imposed on subscribers to absorb the costs of care. Most insurance programs in the United States have some cost sharing, and in recent years such requirements have increased substantially within employment-based coverage. Deductibles and coinsurance also play an important role in Medicare, although the Rand group did not include this program in their study.

The Rand experiment found that use of physicians responded significantly to insurance coverage. Persons in the "free" plan (no coinsurance or deductibles) generated expenditures of about 50 percent more for ambulatory care than those with 95 percent coinsurance (Newhouse et al. 1981). Mean number of physician visits varied from 5.5 to 3.5 across these contrasting groups, and a similar cost-sharing effect was found in all demographic and socioeconomic subgroups studied.

In early publications, the Rand researchers reported that cost sharing affected use of mental health services in a way comparable to other medical services (Wells et al. 1982), but these results stimulated considerable controversy. It was suggested the Rand researchers had underestimated the mental health coinsurance effects due to a special design feature of the experiment, the maximum dollar expenditure (MDE) level for a family (Ellis and McGuire 1984, 1986). Once a family reached the MDE in a particular year, services at that point became free for the remainder of the period. The probability that families in programs with different coinsurance requirements would reach the MDE at varying rates distorted estimates of the impact of cost sharing on mental health expenditures, according to critics.

Responding to these objections, the Rand team extended analysis of their data and concluded that outpatient mental health use is indeed more responsive to price than other types of medical care (Keeler, Manning, and Wells 1988). There was a fourfold variation between extreme coinsurance groups, with those facing 50 percent coinsurance and no limits on cost sharing generating only two-fifths as much spending for mental health care as those with "free care" due to reduced utilization. Coinsurance primarily affected the number of episodes of treatment, but once a person entered care, the duration and intensity varied less. Because relatively few patients seek specialized mental health care whatever their insurance levels, the per-person cost in the study for such services was relatively low. Other factors found to affect use, in addition to mental health status and insurance, included educational level and age (better-educated persons and young adults used more). There were also variations by site, with Seattle and Massachusetts exhibiting more use than Dayton and South Carolina. This site effect was probably because of differences in the availability of mental health providers in the respective locales as well as varying cultural dispositions toward mental health services.

With the growth of mental health managed care, much economic analysis is now directed to studying the supply side of service provision, which can be even more important in limiting utilization than demand factors. Supply-side management first began in prepayment plans.

PSYCHIATRIC CARE UNDER PREPAYMENT PLANS

The pattern of insurance benefits under fee-for-service plans evolved in a way designed to accommodate the existing psychiatric marketplace, which was largely organized around office-based psychotherapy. Stringent controls were seen as necessary by the industry because of concern that psychotherapists, particularly those with a psychoanalytic orientation, might carry out long courses of treatment involving great expense and uncertain efficacy. Another issue was the effect of open-ended coverage of psychotherapy in subsidizing the most affluent and educated groups in the population, who are disproportionately attracted to such services.

An alternative model in many HMOs was to maintain greater control over the referral process and assessment of the need for services. Such programs also provided outpatient benefits without the usual cost-sharing deterrents. Experience in a variety of plans found that outpatient utilization could be maintained at reasonable levels if the primary physician played a gatekeeper role (Cummings and Follette 1968; Follette and Cummings 1967; Fullerton, Lohrenz, and Nyca 1976; Goldberg, Krantz, and Locke 1970). The number of psychiatrists and other mental health clinicians available in the plan and queuing for service set a natural ceiling on how many services could be consumed and with what intensity. When mental health personnel are themselves employees of the plan, when they are conscious of the cost implications of utilization, and when they have no economic incentive to prolong counseling or psychotherapy, treatment tends to be less intensive and to be provided for shorter periods of time. Also, it is likely that such plans select psychiatric personnel who are more attuned to pragmatic approaches to psychiatric care and to short-term treatment.

From an organizational view, prepaid plans offer another advantage in facilitating the use of nonmedical personnel in providing mental health services. Such programs commonly employ psychologists, nurses, and social workers while providing services less expensively than programs that depend primarily on psychiatrists. In contrast, most traditional insurance policies until recently have reimbursed only medical personnel and psychologists in the fee-for-service sector, creating an unnecessary dependence on the most expensive types of personnel when other mental health workers can perform many of the same treatment functions. When health plans receive a fixed amount per enrollee per year, known as capitation, it may facilitate flexibility in the kinds of services or providers made available, and it can lead to a closer alliance between general medical care and more specialized mental health services.

Prepaid group practices or other HMOs often do not provide their own mental health services. Many plans contract with managed behavioral health care companies that specialize in organizing and providing mental health services for employers, health insurance programs, and HMOs. The mental health component of the subscriber's plan thus becomes "carved out" and treated separately from other medical services. A behavioral health company accepts responsibility for managing all mental health services on a contractual basis or, in a pattern that is increasingly common, it may agree to assume financial risk for this one component of medical care on the basis of a "capitated" payment scheme for a defined patient group. This specialty industry has grown very rapidly and now arranges for and manages mental health services for much of the population. Carve-outs are discussed in more detail in Chapter 8.

This is not the place for a detailed review of the large and important literature assessing the development and evolving role of HMOs in the U.S. health system (Mechanic 1986; Miller and Luft 1994; Zelman 1996). Because the way health services are organized importantly affects access, costs, service mix, and health outcomes, however, a brief review of studies of the performance of prepaid practice is appropriate.

A large early literature found that prepaid group practice limited hospital admissions by as much as 40 percent and yielded an overall cost savings of 20–30 percent (Luft 1981; Mechanic 1979, 1986). These differences were found to persist even when controls for population characteristics, out-of-plan use, and other factors were considered. Yet researchers could not exclude the possibility of a significant selection effect, in which enrollees with better health status chose prepaid practice plans for their medical care needs. However, in the Rand HIE families were randomized into a prepaid group practice in Seattle (Group Health Cooperative of Puget Sound). This provided a valuable opportunity to examine the impact of this type of organization independent of possible selection bias (Newhouse and the Insurance Experiment Group 1993).

Group Health was found to have 40 percent fewer admissions than the "free-care" experimental group, although both populations faced no financial barriers to care. Overall, expenditures for those in Group Health were 28 percent below those in the "free-care" experimental group (Manning et al. 1984). A subsequent analysis of health status suggested that poor, sick patients randomized into prepaid practice did slightly less well on outcome measures than those assigned to the fee-for-service "free-care" experimental group (Ware et al. 1986). These data were suggestive rather than conclusive, but they did support other studies that indicated less educated patients may have difficulties negotiating the bureaucratic barriers typical of prepaid practice organizations (Mechanic 1979). It is possible to deal with this issue through well-designed outreach efforts that target enrollees at high risk, although not all prepaid plans include such efforts.

Organization and financing affect mix of mental health services as well. The Rand researchers carried out analyses of the use of mental health care under the fee-for-service conditions as compared with prepaid practice. More enrollees of prepaid practice actually used mental health care than those in the "free-care" fee-for-service condition, but the services were provided much less intensively. Those in prepaid practice were more likely to receive mental health treatment from a general medical provider, and overall mental health expenditures were only one-third of the free-care condition ($25 per year per enrollee versus $70). Further, when prepaid enrollees saw a mental health provider, they had only one-third the number of mental health visits compared to the "free-care" group in fee-for-service. Group Health relied more on social workers than psychiatrists or psychologists and less on individual therapy in contrast to group or family therapies (Manning and Wells 1986; Manning, Wells, and Benjamin 1986). These results paralleled those that have been found in nonexperimental studies.

The Rand experiment also found that when patients received mental health care from general physicians in contrast to the specialty mental health sector, the intensity and cost of services were less. Yet whether patients sought care from general physicians or specialists was unrelated to mental health status at enrollment or to the level of insurance coverage. Those who visited general physicians for a mental health problem accounted for only 5 percent of total outpatient mental health expenditures because of the low intensity of mental health care provided by general physicians (Wells et al. 1987).

Because approximately half of all mental health care occurs in the practice of general medicine, understanding service and spending patterns in conjunction with the quality of care within this sector is important. Most studies find that patients in the mental health specialty sector are more impaired on average than those cared for by general physicians, but there is a large degree of overlap between the sectors. The restricted character of the HIE sample exaggerated the extent of overlap because the population studied underrepresents the most seriously mentally ill, who would be more likely to get care from specialists. The findings alert us to the importance of carefully distinguishing between mental health visits, on the one hand, and the content, appropriateness, and quality of care, on the other. Mental health researchers conveniently differentiate between services provided by general physicians and those provided within the specialty mental health sector. The most seriously mentally ill have complex relationships with various parts of the medical, mental health, and social services systems, and we need an in-depth understanding of the interaction across sectors and how this influences the longitudinal care of patients.

The observation by Rand researchers that there was little difference in the severity of problems between those seeking mental health care from the general medical and specialty mental health sectors reinforces the importance of questions of resource allocation and clinical responsibility. There is, for example, much concern about the failure of general physicians to recognize depression and manage it appropriately as well as their inappropriate use of psychoactive medications (Kirsch 2010; Mechanic 1990; Wells et al. 1996). From a quality point of view, different types of mental health visits are not necessarily equivalent. The cost-effectiveness of one pattern of care versus another requires careful and continuing investigation if we are to make sound policy choices.

Although, in theory, the prepaid model offers the most rational and efficient way to handle mental health problems of the most common type—and evidence supports that promised efficiencies are, in fact, realized—relatively little is known about how well these plans do in terms of outcomes for those with serious mental illness. Thus, although the feasibility of this model has been demonstrated from an economic perspective, it is critical that we gain a better understanding of the referral decisions made by primary care physicians, the pattern of who obtains and who fails to get treatment, and the quality of mental health care provided. The prepaid organization has an intuitive logic to it. This must be supplemented by careful empirical research of the way the system really works for different kinds of patients.

THE STRUCTURE OF INSURANCE
AND NEEDED MENTAL HEALTH BENEFITS

Developing an appropriate structure for mental health benefits is difficult because the needs of persons with mental illness are broad and diverse, requiring decisions about the relationship between acute and long-term care; between medical, behavioral, and social services; and between services provided by physicians and a range of other professionals including psychologists, social workers, psychiatric nurses, and rehabilitation specialists. In this sense, the focus of parity legislation in creating an insurance system that does not discriminate against mental health conditions addresses only part of the coverage problem. Simply providing the same benefits to all insurance subscribers does not recognize the fact that those with serious and persistent mental illness depend on an array of social and rehabilitative services outside the bounds of standard health insurance (Mechanic and McAlpine 1999).

Coverage for mental health comes from a patchwork of private health insurance, Medicaid, Medicare, other public mental health programs, the expenditures of state mental health authorities for institutions and other services, and patients' out-of-pocket payments. Historically, mental health services for persons with serious conditions were a state responsibility, and states and localities made large investments in their mental hospital systems. Over the past half century, however, resident patients in public mental hospitals have declined by more than 90 percent, reaching 33,365 in 2008. Although existing mental hospitals now serve only a small minority of seriously ill patients, and there is broad agreement on the principle that money should follow patients into the community, these institutions retain what many believe to be disproportionate funding. Established state investment in institutions is highly resistant to change. Communities, institutions, and unions representing hospital workers all resist reallocation from inpatient to community care. Moving state funding from institutions is a slow and often politically difficult process, but change is occurring as states redirect their mental health dollars for the purpose of matching resources gained from the federal Medicaid program. In 2008, about 26 percent of state mental health expenditures controlled by state mental health agencies (SMHA) were for state psychiatric hospitals, and 72 percent went to community programming. However, the allocation of spending significantly varies across states, with the proportion of dollars going to inpatient care highest in South Dakota (63 percent) and lowest in Arizona (7 percent) (Substance Abuse and Mental Health Services Administration 2012).

The Medicaid program provides a cornerstone of protection for persons with serious and persistent mental illness and is a core component of the mental health services system for the disabled and many other people in poverty. Medicaid was enacted as a federal–state categorical program to provide medical assistance to low-income families with dependent children and low-income aged, blind, or disabled persons. It came into existence in 1965 and has been modified and expanded many times since, most recently by the Deficit Reduction Act of 2005 and the newly legislated Affordable Care Act (ACA) of 2010. Depending on each state's economic position, the federal government matches state expenditures under the program from 50 to 74 percent in 2012. To receive the funds, states must include certain eligible groups and services, but others are optional. Within certain broad requirements, states can establish criteria for eligibility; determine and administer reimbursement; and define the amount, duration, and scope of covered services. In addition, the federal government may waive some requirements so that states can modify their programs to develop innovative forms of delivery. It is common for state managed care programs to function under the federal waiver authority.

Under Medicaid, states have had considerable discretion in extending eligibility and choosing which of the many optional services to cover. This has been one of the historical weaknesses of the program, resulting in large disparities in coverage among the states. The ACA sought to correct this situation, to some extent, by requiring Medicaid coverage of all citizens at 133 percent or less of the federal poverty level. If applied uniformly, this provision would add some 17 million people to the Medicaid program. After an initial three-year period (2014–2016), in which the federal government would fund 100 percent of the cost of this expansion, states would incrementally assume responsibility for a small proportion of the total, reaching 10 percent by 2020. Thereafter, funding would take place according to a 90/10 federal/state match.

In addition, the ACA gave the federal government authority to withdraw all Medicaid funding from states unwilling to implement this expanded coverage requirement. The Supreme Court, however, found such a threat to be unconstitutionally coercive. As a result of this ruling, states that refuse to participate will now lose the large financial incentives made available for coverage increases, but federal funds already part of their Medicaid programs would not be threatened. As we write this summary, it is soon after the Supreme Court decision. Posturing and inflammatory rhetoric pervade the political atmosphere, with many conservatives hoping to delay and limit implementation of the ACA. Short of a major legislative reversal, however, the ACA will be implemented and the new financial incentives it contains are so generous that it is likely most states, even those with very conservative governors who continue to oppose the ACA, would find it in their interest to participate in Medicaid expansion. A few very poor states, those that are ideologically opposed to the ACA and worried about future financial responsibilities, may not. Here, then, would be another illustration of the limitations of a program like Medicaid, in which federal/state partnership produces benefit disparities and significantly different policy outcomes depending on where one happens to live.

In 2010, Medicaid spending totaled $400.7 billion. ACA provisions are expected to underwrite an increase of another 20 percent or more (Iglehart 2012). Expenditures, however, are distributed very unevenly across various eligible groups. In 2008, for example, children accounted for $2,571 in program spending per capita, while the corresponding figure was $17,332 for persons with disabilities and $16,984 for the elderly, mostly for long-term care (Iglehart 2012; Kaiser Commission 2010, 2011a). Among the 9.2 million persons who are eligible for both Medicaid and Medicare (the so-called "dual eligible" population), most have very low incomes and more severe disabilities than the Medicare and Medicaid populations overall. They have also been the most expensive subgroup covered, accounting for about one-sixth of the enrollment for each of these programs but 27 percent of Medicare expenditures and 39 percent of Medicaid expenditures in 2007 (Medicare-Medicaid Coordination Office 2011). Two-fifths of this dual-eligible population has severe psychiatric disabilities making it a key area for mental health policy.

Mandatory coverage under Medicaid includes the basic hospital and outpatient services traditionally covered under private health insurance. Optional benefits, which sometimes qualify for even more generous federal matching support than other Medicaid services, allow states to develop more comprehensive systems for persons with serious mental illness by incorporating clinical services, occupational therapy, prescribed drugs, psychologist services, diagnostic services, screening services, rehabilitative services, inpatient psychiatric services for persons under age 21 in public hospitals, case management, and transportation services, among others. Such vital benefits as prescription drugs and many community mental health services have been optional for states, as is coverage for certain subgroups of enrollees. According to one analysis, although 29 percent of enrollees nationwide fell into the optional category, fully three-fifths of all expenditures were for optional services (Kaiser Commission 2005). In short, by combining federal and state dollars, skillful and enterprising state administrators have employed Medicaid to build responsive frameworks of mental health care unparalleled under the confines of private health insurance (Mechanic and Surles 1992). In 2010, persons with a primary diagnosis of mental illness represented about a quarter of all adults under age 65 receiving SSI on the basis of blindness or disability, tripling since the early 1990s (Social Security Administration 2011). This growth is a result of aggressive efforts by social workers and other mental health professionals to get clients in the community enrolled in this program not only because of the cash benefits provided but also because of Medicaid coverage.

Despite Medicaid's tremendous contributions, it has been a flawed program from the standpoint of mental health care. Because Medicaid defines inpatient care as a basic benefit, this has helped perpetuate a bias toward inpatient care. Thus, a disproportionate amount of Medicaid expenditures has gone to institutional psychiatric services in general hospitals, private psychiatric hospitals, and other settings. This reality, in turn, limits the use of Medicaid in fashioning community mental health systems backed by appropriate clinical and social service supports. However, spending on Medicaid home- and community-based services has been growing and reached almost $53 billion in 2009, constituting 43 percent of Medicaid long-term care services, or three times more than in 1990 (Kaiser Commission 2011b). The effort by many states to use federal waivers to shift coverage for persons with mental illness into managed care programs has been one strategy to contain inpatient care expenditures.

While some states such as Massachusetts, New York, New Jersey, New Hampshire, California, and Connecticut have capitalized on Medicaid opportunities, other states, particularly in the south and southwest, have not chosen to do as much. In 2009, spending for long-term home- and community-based care services varied greatly by state, from 13 percent in Mississippi to 73 percent in New Mexico (Kaiser Commission 2011b). Even in cases where the federal government pays most of the cost, poor low-tax states have been reluctant to increase their investment in mental health care. In managing the rising costs of Medicaid, states face a trade-off between whom they make eligible for services and how much they spend per recipient. They also face a trade-off between eligibility and benefits, on the one hand, and reimbursement rates to providers, on the other. States aiming at broader coverage of the population often attempt to gain savings through tighter reimbursements, but low payments under this program discourage participation of many physicians and other providers.

Some states resent congressional mandates in a program like Medicaid, insisting they could use the resources better if given more flexibility to design programs as they like. Federal officials, in contrast, believe it important that states meet certain minimum standards and priorities in the use of federal funds. They also argue that the waiver program provides ample opportunity for innovation in state systems, and in recent years the federal government has made it easier to obtain waivers. While it is plausible that some states left on their own to use federal Medicaid funds could become more innovative and effective, the danger is that other states would simply draw back from health care commitments in the face of competing budgetary needs and ideological opposition to "welfare" spending of any sort. Such a response would only worsen disparities in program integrity across the nation. A nationally supervised program maintains a minimum decent standard of care, no matter whether states' own commitment to those with disabilities, poor children and adults, and the elderly is limited. Perhaps a good analogy here is the issue of civil rights where, in the absence of federal standards and oversight, even larger disparities among states would have persisted.

IMPACT OF THE AFFORDABLE CARE ACT

In 2010, the Patient Protection and Affordable Care Act (ACA) became law after a prolonged political battle (Starr 2011). The ACA is the most far-reaching piece of social welfare legislation since Social Security in the 1930s, affecting almost every aspect of health care operations in the United States. Moreover, for the first time, behavioral health, including problems of mental health and substance abuse, has been given centrality in discussions of health reform.

Implementation of this complex legislation involves a timetable spanning several years and has been made even more difficult by continuing partisan attack. The Supreme Court has now resolved legal challenges regarding both the law's "individual mandate" for purchase of insurance coverage and its expansion of the Medicaid program. Meanwhile, the first phases of implementation are proceeding with several popular provisions already in force, such as prohibition of the insurance industry practice of excluding persons with pre-existing conditions (initially children), allowing young people up to age 26 to remain on their parents' insurance policies, and reducing the "donut hole" gap in Medicare's prescription drug program. Many states are busy designing their new insurance exchanges under this law, while demonstration efforts of all kinds are being planned. Officials in other states are moving more slowly.

Many ACA provisions promise to impact access and quality of care for persons with mental illness and substance abuse disorders. Here we can only review some of the most far-reaching changes related to organization and financing. Chris Koyanagi (2010), policy director of the Bazelon Center for Mental Health Law, has prepared a critical analysis of the ACA from a mental health policy perspective that provides an excellent resource for students in need of greater detail.

Under the ACA, private insurance plans that participate in state insurance exchanges are required to provide coverage of MHSA services that meet specified standards and are consistent with federal parity legislation. An extension of Medicaid to persons up to 133 percent of the federal poverty level in states that accept the expansion will cover many currently uninsured persons with mental illness and substance abuse disorders. Other low and moderate income earners up to 400 percent of the federal poverty level will become eligible for federal subsidies through the exchanges. Medicaid eligibility is also being expanded for single adults who previously did not meet disability or care-taking requirements. The Supreme Court decision allowing states to opt out of Medicaid eligibility expansions creates uncertainty concerning the exact impact of this coverage opportunity.

Because of its broad orientation to recovery, Medicaid's enlarged role raises the possibility of the most important innovations in service planning and delivery for mental health care to come out of ACA. For those with more than one chronic condition, a new "health home" concept provides a model for care management and coordination across a variety of providers and agencies together with technology-assisted individual and family support. As an incentive for developing such programs, the federal government will pay 90 percent of all costs for the first two years. Missouri emerged as the first state to amend its Medicaid State Plan to pursue the health home strategy, including both health homes focused on management of chronic conditions in primary care and community mental health care. Building on psychiatric rehabilitation programs, tools from health information technology, nurse liaisons and other special collaborations to integrate services, and wellness and prevention initiatives, Missouri authorities are embracing this opportunity to make wise use of resources and substantially improve care. A number of other states, including New York and Rhode Island, are headed in a similar direction. Health homes are, in fact, a specialized form of "medical home." The latter targets resources more broadly to persons with chronic illnesses, such as those with mental disorders, who would be in need of seamless integration between primary care and more specialized health needs. In either case, the hope is that by changing payment incentives, professionals and program managers will be motivated to provide services that are holistic and well integrated.

As noted earlier, a common way of rationing behavioral health services in private plans has been through inadequate networks of providers and personnel. The ACA requires health plans to maintain networks of services sufficient to meet enrollee need. This is an especially important consideration for the Medicaid program, which pays providers less than other insurance programs. Particularly in the case of MHSA disorders, patients often cannot get access to the specialized services they need. One uncertainty about new coverage mandates concerns the extent to which officials will monitor insurer and provider behavior and enforce all legislative requirements. Initially, enforcement is likely to be more symbolic than real, but careful attention to these operational issues over time could pay dividends in safeguarding consumer interests.

The ACA extends insurance coverage, supports a more holistic approach to patient care, encourages services integration and collaborative care, increases the involvement of patients in their own care, and promotes quality while eliminating duplication and waste. It offers the best opportunity to reform mental health and substance abuse care in many decades. Far reaching and comprehensive, the law explicitly directs attention to persons with serious mental illness and substance abuse disorders, including those with significant comorbidities and continuing care needs. Building on employer-based insurance, the private marketplace, and existing entitlement programs—in contrast to a public takeover as sometimes alleged by opponents—the ACA provides a policy framework for states and provider organizations to refigure their service delivery systems with an eye toward advancing practice approaches, testing new service solutions, and developing and using health personnel in collaborative teams.

The ACA contains a range of economic incentives to induce desired systemic behaviors:

- generous federal contributions for coverage of new Medicaid enrollees (100 percent for the first three years);
- enhanced matching funds for new organizations that meet specified federal standards, such as in the case of new Medicaid "health homes";
- arrangements that allow such entities as Accountable Care Organizations to share with the federal government the financial savings achieved through reducing duplication, avoiding incidents such as unnecessary inpatient readmissions, and providing more efficient care; and
- new forms of capitation including "bundling" and "episode payment."

These reimbursement approaches all qualify as experiments of a sort that are undergoing testing to evaluate whether they can produce theorized outcomes that center on more advantageous patterns of care and support for those most seriously mentally ill.

To this point, the didactic value of the ACA has been enormous, embodying as it does much of the best thinking by experts and practitioners regarding the dysfunctional aspects of current methods of organization and financing health care together with some feasible solutions. By putting new ideas about improving behavioral health care into practice, it will be possible to learn still more from the resulting successes and failures.

CONCLUSION

Health care economist Alex Tabarrok tells the story of how the British government resorted to a new economic approach when grappling with a particularly frustrating problem in the 1700s. Although the government was paying sea captains to transport felons to Australia, large numbers of passengers failed to survive the voyages. Only by shifting the basis of payment, from the number of passengers who boarded in England to the number of (live) passengers who disembarked in Australia, was it possible to achieve better outcomes (Kestenbaum 2010).

This historical tale makes a simple but effective point about the power of incentives in public policy and the need to align rewards so as to encourage desired behaviors. Over the past several decades, a revolution has occurred in thinking about the relationship between the availability and types of payments for health care, on the one hand, and the utilization and impact of these services, on the other. Important changes have resulted affecting the specialty mental health sector, among other areas of health care, including development of a variety of new forms of prospective, capitated, bundled, and other payment practices. With passage of the Affordable Care Act, the creative experimentation will continue as new groups in the population also gain access to behavioral health services and supports.

References

Center for Mental Health Services. *Mental Health United States, 1996*, edited by Ronald W. Manderscheid and Mary Anne Sonnenschein. DHHS Publication No. (SMA) 96–3098. Washington, DC: Government Printing Office, 1996.

Centers for Medicare & Medicaid Services. "Inpatient Psychiatric Facility Prospective Payment System, Payment System Fact Sheet Series." *Medicare Learning Network*, ICN 006839, June 2011. Available online: www.cms.gov/MLNProducts/downloads/InpatientPsychFac.pdf.

Cummings, Nicholas A., and William T. Follette. "Psychiatric Services and Medical Utilization in a Prepaid Health Plan Setting: Part II." *Medical Care* 6 (1968): 31–41.

Dohrenwend, Barbara Snell, and Bruce P. Dohrenwend, eds. *Stressful Life Events: Their Nature and Effects.* New York: Wiley Interscience, 1974.

Dohrenwend, Bruce P., and Barbara Snell Dohrenwend. *Social Status and Psychological Disorder: A Causal Inquiry.* New York: Wiley Interscience, 1969.

Ellis, Randall P., and Thomas G. McGuire. "Cost-Sharing and the Demand for Ambulatory Mental Health Services." *American Psychologist* 39 (1984): 1195–1197.

Ellis, Randall P., and Thomas G. McGuire. "Cost-Sharing and Patterns of Mental Health Care Utilization." *The Journal of Human Resources* 21 (1986): 359–379.

Follette, William, and Nicholas A. Cummings. "Psychiatric Services and Medical Utilization in a Prepaid Health Plan Setting." *Medical Care* 5 (1967): 25–35.

Follmann, Joseph F., Jr. *Insurance Coverage for Mental Illness.* New York: American Management Associations, 1970.

Frank, Richard G., and Sherry A. Glied. *Better But Not Well: Mental Health Policy in the United States Since 1950.* Baltimore, MD: Johns Hopkins University Press, 2006.

Frank, Richard G., and Thomas G. McGuire. "A Review of Studies of the Impact of Insurance on the Demand and Utilization of Specialty Mental Health Services." *Health Services Research* 21 (1986): 241–265.

Fullerton, Donald T., Francis N. Lohrenz, and Gregory R. Nyca. "Utilization of Prepaid Services by Patients with Psychiatric Diagnoses." *American Journal of Psychiatry* 133 (1976): 1057–1060.

Garfield, Rachel L., et al. "The Impact of National Health Reform on Adults with Severe Mental Disorders." *American Journal of Psychiatry* 168 (2011): 486–494.

General Accounting Office. *Mental Health Parity Act: Despite New Federal Standards, Mental Health Benefits Remain Limited.* Washington, DC: General Accounting Office, GAO/HEHS-00-95, 2000. Available online: www.gao.gov/archive/2000/he00095.pdf.

Goldberg, Irving D., Goldie Krantz, and Ben Z. Locke. "Effect of a Short-Term Outpatient Psychiatric Therapy Benefit on the Utilization of Medical Services in a Prepaid Group Practice Medical Program." *Medical Care* 8 (1970): 419–428.

Grob, Gerald N., and Howard H. Goldman. *The Dilemma of Federal Mental Health Policy: Radical Reform or Incremental Change?* New Brunswick, NJ: Rutgers University Press, 2006.

Iglehart, John K. "Expanding Eligibility, Cutting Costs—A Medicaid Update." *New England Journal of Medicine* 366 (2012): 105–107.

Kaiser Commission on Medicaid and the Uninsured. *Medicaid: An Overview of Spending on "Mandatory" vs. "Optional" Populations and Services.* Issue Paper. Washington, DC: Kaiser Commission on Medicaid and the Uninsured, 2005. Available online: www.kff.org/medicaid/upload/Medicaid-An-Overview-of-Spending-on.pdf.

Kaiser Commission on Medicaid and the Uninsured. *The Medicaid Program at a Glance.* Washington, DC: Kaiser Commission on Medicaid and the Uninsured, 2010. Available online: www.kff.org/medicaid/upload/7235-04.pdf.

Kaiser Commission on Medicaid and the Uninsured. *Medicaid Matters: Understanding Medicaid's Role in Our Health Care System.* Washington, DC: Kaiser Commission on Medicaid and the Uninsured, 2011a. Available online: www.kff.org/medicaid/upload/8165.pdf.

Kaiser Commission on Medicaid and the Uninsured. *Medicaid and Long-Term Care Services and Supports.* Washington, DC: Kaiser Commission on Medicaid and the Uninsured, 2011b. Available online: www.kff.org/medicaid/upload/2186-08.pdf.

Keeler, Emmet B., Willard G. Manning, and Kenneth B. Wells. "The Demand for Episodes of Mental Health Services." *Journal of Health Economics* 7 (1988): 369–392.

Kessler, Ronald C. "A Disaggregation of the Relationship Between Socioeconomic Status and Psychological Distress." *American Sociological Review* 47 (1982): 752–764.

Kessler, Ronald C., et al. "Lifetime and 12-Month Prevalence of DSM-III-R Psychiatric Disorders in the United States: Results from the National Comorbidity Survey." *Archives of General Psychiatry* 51 (1994): 8–19.

Kestenbaum, David. "Pop Quiz: How Do You Stop Sea Captains from Killing Their Passengers?" *NPR Planet Money*, September 10, 2010. Available online: www.npr.org/blogs/money/2010/09/09/129757852/pop-quiz-how-do-you-stop-sea-captains-from-killing-their-passengers.

Kirsch, Irving. *The Emperor's New Drugs: Exploding the Antidepressant Myth*. New York: Basic Books, 2010.

Koyanagi, Chris. *How Will Health Reform Help People with Mental Illness?* Washington, DC: Bazelon Center for Mental Health Law, 2010. Available online: www.bazelon.org/LinkClick.aspx?fileticket=HJ7Q6AM8AHM%3D&tabid=221.

Leaf, Philip J., et al. "Contact with Health Professionals for the Treatment of Psychiatric and Emotional Problems." *Medical Care* 23 (1985): 1322–1337.

Luft, Harold S. *Health Maintenance Organizations: Dimensions of Performance*. New York: Wiley Interscience, 1981.

Manning, Willard G., and Kenneth B. Wells. "Preliminary Results of a Controlled Trial of the Effect of a Prepaid Group Practice on the Outpatient Use of Mental Health Services." *Journal of Human Resources* 21 (1986): 293–320.

Manning, Willard G., Kenneth B. Wells, and Bernadette Benjamin. *Use of Outpatient Mental Health Care: Trial of a Prepaid Group Practice Versus Fee-for-Service* (R-3277-NIMH). Santa Monica, CA: Rand Corporation, 1986. Available online: www.rand.org/pubs/reports/R3277.html.

Manning, Willard G., et al. "A Controlled Trial of the Effect of a Prepaid Group Practice on Use of Services." *New England Journal of Medicine* 310 (1984): 1505–1510.

Mark, Tami L., et al. "Changes in US Spending on Mental Health and Substance Abuse Treatment, 1986–2005, and Implications for Policy." *Health Affairs* 30 (2011): 284–292.

McAlpine, Donna D., and David Mechanic. "Utilization of Specialty Mental Health Care Among Persons with Severe Mental Illness: The Roles of Demographics, Need, Insurance and Risk." *Health Services Research* 35, Part II (2000): 277–292.

McGuire, Thomas. *Financing Psychotherapy: Costs, Effects, and Public Policy*. Cambridge, MA: Ballinger, 1981.

Mechanic, David. *Future Issues in Health Care: Social Policy and the Rationing of Medical Services*. New York: The Free Press, 1979.

Mechanic, David. *From Advocacy to Allocation: The Evolving American Health Care System*. New York: The Free Press, 1986.

Mechanic, David. "Treating Mental Illness: Generalist vs. Specialist." *Health Affairs* 9 (1990): 61–75.

Mechanic, David. "The Rise and Fall of Managed Care." *Journal of Health and Social Behavior* 45 (2004): 76–86.

Mechanic, David. "Replicating High-Quality Medical Care Organizations." *Journal of the American Medical Association* 303 (2010): 555–556.

Mechanic, David, and Scott Bilder. "Treatment of People with Mental Illness: A Decade-Long Perspective." *Health Affairs* 23 (2004): 84–95.

Mechanic, David, and Donna D. McAlpine. "Mission Unfulfilled: Potholes on the Road to Mental Health Parity." *Health Affairs* 18 (1999): 7–21.

Mechanic, David, and Richard Surles. "Challenges in State Mental Health Policy and Administration." *Health Affairs* 11 (1992): 34–50.

Mechanic, David, Donna McAlpine, and Mark Olfson. "Changing Patterns of Psychiatric Inpatient Care in the United States, 1988–1994." *Archives of General Psychiatry* 55 (1998): 785–791.

Mechanic, Robert E. "Opportunities and Challenges for Episode-Based Payment." *New England Journal of Medicine* 365 (2011): 777–779.

Mechanic, Robert E. and Christopher Tompkins. "Lessons Learned Preparing for Medicare Bundled Payments." *New England Journal of Medicine* 367 (2012): 1873–1875.

Medicare-Medicaid Coordination Office. *People Enrolled in Medicare and Medicaid, Fact Sheet*. Centers for Medicare and Medicaid Services, 2011. Available online: www.ropesgray.com/files/upload/20120206_HRRC_3.pdf.

Miller, Robert H., and Harold S. Luft. "Managed Care Plan Performance Since 1980: A Literature Analysis." *Journal of the American Medical Association* 271 (1994): 1512–1519.

Morton, John D., and Patricia Aleman. "Trends in Employer-Provided Mental Health and Substance Abuse Benefits." *Monthly Labor Review* 128 (2005): 25–35.

National Conference of State Legislatures. *State Laws Mandating or Regulating Mental Health Benefits.* Washington, DC: National Conference of State Legislatures, 2011. Available online: www.ncsl.org/issues-research/health/mental-health-benefits-state-laws-mandating-or-re.aspx.

Newhouse, Joseph P. "A Design for a Health Insurance Experiment." *Inquiry* 11 (1974): 5–27.

Newhouse, Joseph P., et al. "Some Interim Results from a Controlled Trial of Cost Sharing in Health Insurance." *New England Journal of Medicine* 305 (1981): 1501–1507.

Newhouse, Joseph P., and the Insurance Experiment Group. *Free for All?: Lessons from the RAND Health Insurance Experiment.* Cambridge, MA: Harvard University Press, 1993.

Olfson, Mark, and David Mechanic. "Mental Disorders in Public, Private Nonprofit, and Proprietary General Hospitals." *American Journal of Psychiatry* 153 (1996): 1613–1619.

Olfson, Mark, and Harold A. Pincus. "Outpatient Mental Health Care in Nonhospital Settings: Distribution of Patients Across Provider Groups." *American Journal of Psychiatry* 153 (1996): 1353–1356.

Rochefort, David A. *From Poorhouses to Homelessness: Policy Analysis and Mental Health Care*, 2nd ed. Westport, CT: Auburn House, 1997.

Social Security Administration. *SSI Annual Statistical Report, 2010.* SSA Publication No. 13-11827. Washington, DC: Social Security Administration, August 2011. Available online: www.ssa.gov/policy/docs/statcomps/ssi_asr/2010/ssi_asr10.pdf.

Starr, Paul. *Remedy and Reaction: The Peculiar American Struggle Over Health Care Reform.* New Haven: Yale University Press, 2011.

Stevens, Robert, and Rosemary Stevens. *Welfare Medicine in America: A Case Study of Medicaid.* New York: The Free Press, 1974.

Substance Abuse and Mental Health Services Administration. *National Expenditures for Mental Health Services and Substance Abuse Treatment, 1986–2005. DHHS Publication No. (SMA) 10-4612.* Rockville, MD: Center for Mental Health Services and Center for Substance Abuse Treatment, Substance Abuse and Mental Health Services Administration, 2010a.

Substance Abuse and Mental Health Services Administration. *Mental Health, United States, 2008.* HHS Publication No. (SMA) 10-4590. Rockville, MD: Center for Mental Health Services, Substance Abuse and Mental Health Services Administration, 2010b.

Substance Abuse and Mental Health Services Administration. *Mental Health, United States, 2010.* HHS Publication No. (SMA) 12-4681. Rockville, MD: Substance Abuse and Mental Health Services Administration, 2012.

U.S. Department of Health and Human Services. *Evaluation of Parity in the Federal Employees Health Benefits (FEHB) Program.* Final Report, December 2004. Available online: aspe.hhs.gov/daltcp/reports/parity.pdf.

Walkup, James. "The Psychiatric Unit Comes to the General Hospital: A History of the Movement." In *Improving Inpatient Psychiatric Treatment in an Era of Managed Care*, edited by David Mechanic, pp. 11–23. New Direction for Mental Health Services, No. 73, San Francisco, CA: Jossey-Bass, 1997.

Ware, John E., Jr., et al. "Comparison of Health Outcomes at a Health Maintenance Organization with Those of Fee-for-Service Care." *Lancet* 327 (1986): 1017–1022.

Wells, Kenneth B., et al. *Cost Sharing and the Demand for Ambulatory Mental Health Services* (R-2960-HHS). Santa Monica, CA: Rand Corporation, 1982. Available online: www.rand.org/content/dam/rand/pubs/reports/2007/R2960.pdf.

Wells, Kenneth B., et al. "Cost-Sharing and the Use of General Medical Physicians for Outpatient Mental Health Care." *Health Services Research* 22 (1987): 1–17.

Wells, Kenneth B., et al. *Caring for Depression.* Cambridge, MA: Harvard University Press, 1996.

Zelman, Walter A. *The Changing Health Care Marketplace: Private Ventures, Public Interests.* San Francisco: Jossey-Bass, 1996.

8

Managed Mental Health Care

"Managed care" refers to a variety of organizational and financial structures, processes, and strategies designed to monitor and influence treatment decisions so as to provide care in the most cost-effective way (Mechanic, Schlesinger, and McAlpine 1995). When used generally, the term is confusing because it covers approaches that vary in their incentives, processes, and effects, and that combine in a multitude of ways. Although there is a great deal of discussion about whether managed care is good or bad for the mental health field, such debate is not informative because the answer depends on the specific arrangements that have been put in place. Many complaints about managed care from psychiatrists and other mental health professionals reflect anxieties about how managed care will affect patient flow, incomes, and clinical discretion. Others grow out of concern that service changes are being motivated more by cost reduction than by a desire to improve services and that there are damaging effects on access to care and quality. There is little trust that managed care approaches benefit patients or their providers.

Yet, in considering the impact of managed mental health care, it is useful to remember the deficiencies of traditional indemnity, fee-for-service plans, in which patients often lacked access to needed services and frequently received inappropriate care. Moreover, many patients were in treatment over long periods of time, both on an inpatient and outpatient basis, without clear treatment plans or focused objectives. Clinicians' preferences commonly trumped objective information. Some patients experienced unnecessary hospitalization, their length of stay determined primarily by the number of days covered by insurance plans. Rarely has there been continuity of care between hospital and outpatient care, particularly for patients with the most severe and persistent illnesses. Instead, many persons with mental illness experienced a "revolving door" in and out of hospital facilities that was perpetuated by barriers to community services. *Fragmentation*, *service gaps*, and *lack of coordination*—these are the watchwords of the American mental health system for many. Proponents of managed care describe it as a tool for addressing such issues. The question is does performance live up to promise?

Managed care has a long history in the United States, dating back to the post–World War II years (Starr 1982). It expanded in the late 1980s, but began to dominate the market in the mid-1990s following the failure of President Clinton's health reform legislation;

by the end of the 1990s almost everyone with employment-based insurance was under some type of managed care (Cooper, Simon, and Vistnes 2006). This seemingly had the effect of reducing costs for several years. However, a severe backlash erupted and generated anger toward, and much bad media for, insurers. The key financial mechanisms—capitating payments to providers and applying utilization review and management—infuriated many doctors who saw their autonomy restricted and incomes threatened. Patients became upset as well when faced with explicit rationing by insurance reviewers, who sometimes overrode the recommendations of personal physicians. Most states adopted new regulation over the managed care industry.

In response to the public backlash and increased regulation, health insurers loosened their restraints, leading many observers to declare the "end" or "death" of managed care (Robinson 2001; Swartz 1999). These pronouncements proved premature. At best, we entered a period that might be termed "managed-care lite" (Mechanic 2004).

Nonetheless, traditional indemnity health insurance is now long gone. Whereas in the late 1980s almost three-quarters of workers covered by insurance were enrolled in fee-for-service plans, now less than 1 percent enjoy such coverage (Claxton et al. 2011). Managed care has also rapidly expanded into the public health care market, covering about one-quarter of Medicare enrollees and nearly three-quarters of Medicaid enrollees (Centers for Medicare & Medicaid Services 2012; Gold et al. 2011). Thus, managed care is not dead—it is not even dying—it is alive and well, albeit different from earlier decades.

In the field of mental health, insurers have shown no inclination to pull back in managing services, a function that is predominantly administered by managed behavioral health care organizations (MBHOs). Total enrollment in such organizations has almost tripled since 1993 (from about 63 million enrollees in 1993 to 171 million in 2011) (Oss, Morgan, and Miller 2011). Tough controls continue unabated, and their role and impact deserve careful analysis.

BASIC MECHANISMS OF MANAGED CARE

Four basic mechanisms underlay the practice of managed care: capitation, strategic use of incentives and risks, gatekeeping, and utilization management. Because these elements combine in varying ways under different organizational structures, it is useful to consider them independently.

Capitation is a form of payment involving a fixed, predetermined payment per person for a specified range of services over a fixed period of time (Mechanic and Aiken 1989). The capitation amount received by a provider organization is the same regardless of how many services an enrollee actually uses or what these cost. Some provision can be made to adjust capitation to take account of differences in enrollees age, sex, illness history, or other characteristics, but the basic idea is that prospective payment should induce providers to consider carefully how they use resources. Too many expensive services can lead to financial losses, while efficient practices receive the reward of higher earnings.

Capitation occurs at varying organizational levels. A private employer, or a governmental program, that purchases insurance for a defined group of enrollees can capitate the insurer or a provider organization for each enrollee. Depending on how it procures and delivers services, the provider organization, in turn, can *subcapitate* specific service providers such as physicians, dentists, or psychologists. Just as the incentive underlying fee-for-service provision is to encourage use of services under uncertainty and to over-utilize services in general, the incentive underlying capitation is to be conservative in ordering the use of services in uncertain situations, to substitute less costly alternatives for more expensive ones, and to underutilize services in general. The extent to which different forms of payment actually lead to over- and underutilization depends on professional socialization, the context of practice, other incentives, and the types of quality assurance processes in place.

Capitation as a method of paying direct providers, such as individual or small groups of physicians, was common in an earlier period but has declined dramatically. For example, between 1996 and 2007 the percentage of office visits to physicians that were paid through capitation declined from about 15 to 7 percent, although the percentage is much higher in some regions of the country than others (Zuvekas and Cohen 2010). Ironically, capitation approaches to managing health care, once viewed with such hostility, are making something of a comeback due to uncontrolled health care costs, as well as the widespread realization that fee-for-service medicine contributes to overtreatment and wasteful use of resources. Capitation or quasi-capitation models, such as bundled payment and episodic care, which were discussed in Chapter 7, are seen as pivotal in achieving better coordination of chronic disease care and integration of services through such means as Accountable Care Organizations, Medical Homes, and Health Homes.

Capitation puts the recipient (insurer or provider) at financial risk for a specified period. If they are inefficient, they may be at risk of financial losses or even going out of business. If they function efficiently, they can increase earnings. Managed care organizations can choose to assume the full risk, share the risk with individual providers who are subcapitated, or, in some circumstances, share risk with the purchaser. Sharing of risk may occur in situations where there is uncertainty about the needs of a patient population and the cost of caring adequately for them. This is often the case in attempting to capitate persons with serious and persistent illness or persons with disabilities. Thus, the purchaser—for example, a state mental health department—may agree to share risk with the contracting organization to help protect against unanticipated costs.

Subcapitation is often combined with other mechanisms to fine-tune provider incentives. The latter may come in the form of *withholds* and *bonuses* (Hillman 1987, 1990). Consider, for example, the situation in which primary care physicians are capitated to provide all necessary primary care services for particular patients. One way such physicians might deal with work demands is by making referrals to specialists if they are free of risk for the cost of such referrals. Thus, a primary care physician might direct a patient with moderate depression to mental health specialty services rather than take responsibility for treating the patient directly. To avoid too many referrals, then, a managed care organization might put these primary care physicians at risk for the cost of referrals above a certain threshold. In many cases, part of the physicians' income will be temporarily withheld, with the balance later paid out dependent on meeting expected targets. Alternatively, doctors who stay within utilization targets may receive bonuses that reflect the extent to which they practice in economical ways. Withholds and bonuses are used more commonly with primary care physicians, less so with mental health specialty providers. The latter most typically work under a negotiated fee-for-service arrangement, in which the contracting managed care organization gets clinicians to accept discounted fees and then manages their decisions through various utilization management techniques.

Gatekeeping is a process that limits direct use of specialists, hospitals, and expensive procedures. In many managed care organizations, enrollees are required to select a primary care physician who manages everyday care and becomes a gatekeeper for access to specialists, hospital care, and certain tests and procedures. Patients seeking specialty care or these other services must first consult their primary care physician and obtain a referral through him or her. The organization usually will not pay for services accessed directly by a patient except in emergencies or if the enrollee belongs to a special point-of-service plan that allows outside services (but with larger out-of-pocket costs). Physicians, as just discussed, have incentives to be judicious in making referrals. Patients typically dislike strict gatekeeping, and in recent years these controls have been relaxed significantly.

Utilization management consists of a number of mechanisms, including precertification, concurrent review, case or disease management for high-cost patients, and second-opinion programs. Precertification requires a therapist to seek permission from a utilization reviewer before admitting a patient to a hospital or initiating specified expensive diagnostic and treatment practices. Typically, the clinician, or sometimes the patient, must call the managed care company, describe the symptoms and diagnosis, and seek permission for the procedure. The utilization reviewer at this initial stage is commonly a nurse, who follows various algorithms to decide whether the requested service is appropriate. Most requests for inpatient care are approved initially, but when disapproved, there is an opportunity for appealing the decision to a physician or psychiatrist, who makes a further determination. Higher levels of appeal are also possible, but these involve considerable time, effort, and hassle. It is not really known how often clinicians advocate for their patients when hospitalization or procedures have been refused or how often clinicians simply adapt their practices to what they know utilization reviewers will accept. Utilization review is not standardized. Each company that provides such services has its own criteria, operating procedures, supervision practices, and appeals processes.

Prior-authorization programs are rapidly expanding into pharmaceutical care because of the ever-escalating costs of prescription drugs. Health plans may have a list of preferred drugs, typically generics or those that are less costly, and physicians must start patients on these drugs before switching, if medically necessary, to the more costly alternative (the nonpreferred drugs). To receive authorization to prescribe the nonpreferred alternative, many plans require that physicians document medical necessity. Prior-authorization policies for prescribing psychotropic drugs have potential benefits. If generics are equally as effective as brand drugs, it makes sense to reduce costs by encouraging the use of generics. However, if generics are not equally effective or are associated with side-effects for a particular patient, and if the prior-authorization process introduces barriers to prescribing or filling prescriptions, such policies have the potential to do harm.

Concurrent review of inpatient care is a strategy that seeks to reduce a patient's length of stay and encourage the clinician to find less expensive alternatives to inpatient care. The reviewer may authorize a few days of inpatient care at a time, requiring the clinician to justify each extension. Concurrent review can also be used to monitor other courses of treatment, such as the length of psychotherapy. In high–cost case management, the case manager from the utilization management company works with the clinician to develop a treatment plan for high-cost patients that utilizes less costly alternative care. In indemnity insurance programs that typically use utilization management, the case manager can authorize payment for services not covered under the patients' insurance benefits. The aim is a flexible, efficient treatment plan for high-cost clients.

Disease management (DM) focuses on patients with particular chronic conditions that incur high medical expenditures. Such programs have expanded rapidly in recent years, enrolling about 74 million people in stand-alone programs in 2011, with DM for mental disorders accounting for 25 percent of this overall figure (Oss, Morgan, and Miller 2011). The appeal of disease management is that it allows the health plan to target high-risk patients—for example, those with a diagnosis of major depression—instead of expending resources on managing the care of all patients. DM programs vary widely in approach and scope. Patient education is included in most models, but many also include increased physician education about evidence-based standards of care (Weingarten et al. 2002). Some are fully integrated models, such as the collaborative care approaches described in Chapter 6, while others rely on contracting out services to a disease management company, whose staff contacts enrollees by telephone to educate them about self-management of particular disorders. DM programs are clearly profitable—revenues in the private sector grew from about $85 million in 1997 to more than $600 million in 2002 (Foote 2003). A few companies dominate the market, and one company, Healthways, manages about 52 percent of enrollees (Oss, Morgan, and Miller 2011).

Utilization review and management can occur in any type of insurance program. Private utilization management companies sell utilization services to private employers and government programs. They may do so on a risk basis, where they are financially liable for high levels of utilization, or on an administrative basis, where they provide utilization management services for a fee. Increasingly, however, it is common for managed care companies to contract to manage mental health services on a risk basis, utilizing a variety of strategies to contain cost (Frank, McGuire, and Newhouse 1995). Mental health services are carved out from the entire array of health benefits, and the managed care company assumes responsibility and risk for managing mental health benefits for the defined population covered by the contract.

TYPES OF MANAGED CARE ORGANIZATIONS

Managed care companies offer many combinations of services from a diverse menu of products, including benefit design, employee assistance programs, networks of preferred providers, health maintenance organizations, and utilization management. They also develop incentive schemes, profile the behavior of physicians and other providers, and put in place quality assurance systems. Because they work with employers and governments having varied needs and wishes, managed care companies customize their products and these may vary a great deal from one context to another. As the saying in the industry goes, "When you have seen one managed care plan, you have seen one managed care plan." The variability and changing character of these practices present an enormous headache for mental health services researchers studying the industry and its practices.

There are three basic types of health maintenance organizations (HMOs), with variations of each type. But even these distinctions become blurred as HMOs compete for market share, mixing a wide range of strategies (Zelman 1996). The traditional and most-studied HMO type is the *group model,* in which an insurance plan contracts with one or more large multispecialty groups on a capitated basis to provide services exclusively to its insured population. The professional group is responsible for its internal organization and processes and for distributing income among members, but the insurance plan may provide for hospitals or other needed physical facilities. These facilities may be directly owned by the plan, be available through contracts, or both. *Staff model* HMOs are similar to group models in many ways, but physicians are typically salaried and not personally at risk, although there may be financial incentives for the purpose of shaping practice behavior. The insurance organization and provider groups, however, are capitated and are at risk. Physicians tend to dislike staff models, which make physicians employees, and they commonly convert to group models over time. The best-known and largest group model HMO is Kaiser-Permanente with approximately nine million enrollees. A well-known staff model HMO is the Group Health Cooperative of Puget Sound, which was the HMO included in the famous Rand Health Insurance Experiment (Newhouse and the Insurance Experiment Group 1993).

The dominant form of HMO is the *network/independent practice association (IPA) model*, a type dominated by for-profit organizations. According to this model, an insurance organization builds a network of individual physicians or single-specialty physician groups to serve their subscribers. The insurance plan is capitated and often pays its physician groups capitated fees, while individual physicians are likely to participate on the basis of a negotiated fee schedule. The network of providers is not exclusive; doctors and other providers may participate with several such HMO organizations while also serving fee-for-service patients. The strength of such HMOs is their simplicity to develop, the extensiveness of their networks, and their capacity to offer plan members a wide selection of doctors. However, network/IPA physicians who practice in their own offices or in small groups with a diverse population of insured patients are less likely to establish the special programs, preventive care services, or professional teams commonly seen in large group and staff model HMOs. The latter more easily utilize nonphysician personnel, offer health education and chronic disease management programs, and develop sophisticated ways of monitoring their patient populations. By contrast, they are probably less adaptive and accommodating than small practices once bureaucratization sets in. The flexibility and choice offered by network/IPA HMOs, however, help explain why they grew so much faster than group model HMOs (Freeborn and Pope 1994). Perhaps due to the managed care backlash, enrollment in traditional HMOs has declined from a peak of about 31 percent of covered workers in 1996 to only 17 percent in 2011 (Claxton et al. 2011). Increasingly, their place in the health care market has been taken over by preferred provider organizations (PPOs).

The PPO is not technically a form of managed care because providers are paid through fee-for-service, but enrollees in PPOs typically are subject to many of the management strategies reviewed above. The PPO is an insurance plan that contracts with providers to serve enrollees at a discounted price. Enrollees who use preferred providers have less cost sharing, while those who use outside providers must pay a larger part of costs incurred. PPOs have rapidly expanded in popularity to become the most common type of health plan, covering almost 55 percent of workers with insurance (Claxton et al. 2011).

Various forms of HMOs offer point-of-service options that allow enrollees to see any physician they wish and to be partially reimbursed for this expense. Such plans provide enrollees with the security of knowing they can go outside the plan, albeit with a financial penalty. Point-of-service options increase the competitiveness of HMOs, whose attractiveness to enrollees may otherwise be limited because of restricted physician choice.

Managed care organizations are difficult to study. They combine features in many different ways, and even organizations of the same type may vary significantly on key dimensions (Mechanic 1996). Some early major HMOs were developed by physicians and sponsored by employers, unions, and consumer groups who believed that capitated care was the most appropriate way to organize services for various community populations (Starr 1982). Most early large prepaid practices were organized on a nonprofit basis, but more recent entries are large, profit-oriented firms that are publicly held and pay dividends to stockholders. There is disagreement about whether the profit/nonprofit distinction is important, but it is clear that health insurance plans exhibit significantly different operating philosophies. Plans also vary in regard to how they recruit, select, and supervise physicians and other personnel; their management and quality assurance systems; and the quality of the professionals and facilities in their networks. Plans may or may not own and operate their own hospitals and other facilities; may provide care with varying assortments of doctors, nurses, social workers, and other health workers; may provide a range of financial incentives and evaluation procedures for their professionals; and may differ in the resources devoted to particular functions. From a consumer viewpoint, they provide more or less flexibility in ease of access to care, degrees of choice for specialty referral, different types of special disease management and health education programs, and varying access to patient representatives and grievance processes. In short, the devil is often in the details, and this fact has to be acknowledged to fully understand how particular organizations function.

MANAGED CARE FOR PERSONS WITH MENTAL ILLNESS

It is inevitable that all health plans will include enrollees who need care for mental health problems. Most plans, prior to recent parity requirements, offered a limited number of hospital days and outpatient visits for mental health problems, typically covering 30 visits annually for outpatient visits and 30 days of inpatient care (Substance Abuse and Mental Health Services Administration 2012). By contrast, other plans have developed flexible benefit packages covering persons with severe illness for more services without significant copayment, while other members who are less ill and impaired but want some of these same services must pay more of the cost (Sabin 1995). Under parity requirements, all health plans that provide benefits for behavioral health and medical and surgical care now have to do so comparably and in line with the specifications of federal law.

Managed care plans may possess more or less capacity to provide care for persons with mental disorders. Most deal routinely with common psychiatric problems that are seen in primary care, like depression, with some implementing disease management programs to improve quality of care and coordination of services. Such programs have been credited with a variety of advantages relative to usual care, such as higher patient satisfaction and treatment adherence, greater use of evidence-based guidelines by physicians, improvements in the quality of care, and reductions in symptoms of depression (Badamgarav et al. 2003; Gensichen et al. 2006; Neumeyer-Gromen et al. 2004; Williams et al. 2007). While they increase costs, these programs may be cost-effective in the long run (Neumeyer-Gromen et al. 2004). However, it is difficult to draw meaningful conclusions from this large body of research about what really works in disease management because the components of programs included in these reviews range so widely. Some researchers have suggested that disease management approaches that adopt multiple interventions to substantially restructure how care is developed, such as the integrated models described in Chapter 6, work best (Coleman et al. 2009). Yet even the latter vary immensely in the types of services offered and how they are delivered, making it impossible to come to any certain conclusions about the important essential features of disease management programs.

Few plans have the needed staff expertise to provide appropriate management for persons with severe and chronic disorders such as schizophrenia requiring a great deal more than routine care. These individuals may have insurance through their employers or they are covered as dependents on spousal or parental insurance policies. However, many with the most serious and persistent mental illnesses have no insurance or have completely exhausted their benefits. Depending on circumstances and eligibility, some will be insured through the Medicaid and Medicare programs. Both private insurers and government programs commonly contract with managed care companies to provide services for persons with behavioral disorders.

Managed care organizations handle serious mental illness in many different ways. Some large HMOs have well-developed specialty services and manage most mental illness within the organization, perhaps occasionally using outside providers on a contractual or fee-for-service basis. An alternative approach is for a health plan to *carve-out* the mental health portion of its activity and contract with a managed behavioral health organization (MBHO) to manage services for persons with serious mental illness. Such contracts often include capitated payments assigning financial risk to the MBHO (Frank, McGuire, and Newhouse 1995). The MBHO has developed, or will develop, a network of professionals to provide needed services. How the company fashions this network and arranges financial incentives, reimbursement, utilization control, and quality review will vary (Gold et al. 1995). Companies might, or might not, use subcapitation, negotiated fee schedules, or a combination of reimbursement mechanisms.

Carve-outs offer one distinct advantage to employers who purchase insurance for their employees and for health plans in designing their covered benefits. With regard to mental health care, a relatively small proportion of very sick and needy patients accounts for a large proportion of all expenditures. Further, persons with mental illness have not only more behavioral health costs but also more general medical costs. Competing health plans try to avoid enrolling patients in this category because they are not profitable and often occasion serious financial losses. Health plans that offer better mental health benefits tend to attract more persons with mental illness (a process called adverse selection). As the premiums for such plans become more expensive, it drives away healthy enrollees. Thus, health plans do not seek to be quality mental health providers because it might encourage selective enrollment of high-cost patients. By carving out the mental health services component from the larger insurance program, purchasers and health plans avoid adverse risk selection (Frank and Glied 2006). Carve-outs have an additional advantage because the networks of specialty providers include individuals who are expert in mental health treatments, who are experienced in dealing with serious mental illness, and who probably have heightened understanding and empathy regarding these patients.

One difficulty caused by carve-outs is establishing appropriate boundaries between medical care and mental health care when responsibility is divided between two separate organizations. Persons with serious mental illness often receive poor general medical care; dividing responsibilities makes it more difficult to integrate the two types of care successfully. Moreover, achieving reductions in medical utilization by providing good mental health care may be more difficult when these functions are not well integrated with effective communication among participating providers. Also, a carve-out arrangement, depending on who is responsible for certain costs, such as pharmaceuticals, can lead to efforts to shift costs to another program.

Many persons with serious and persistent mental illness are covered by Medicaid. Since the late 1990s, the states have moved aggressively to enroll Medicaid recipients in managed care (Essock and Goldman 1995), an accelerating trend driven largely by officials' desire to curb rising costs. In 1991, only 2.7 million Medicaid enrollees were in some form of managed care; by 2004, the number reached 27 million, an increase of 900 percent (National Conference of State Legislatures 2011). In 2010, 72 percent of Medicaid beneficiaries were enrolled in some form of managed care plan (Centers for Medicare & Medicaid Services 2012). Initially, disabled populations were excluded from these arrangements because of the treatment complexities involved, but now it is common for states to include this group as well. There are a number of alternative ways for doing this.

One approach is to mainstream the mentally ill population into existing HMOs. Doing so allows integration of general medical care and mental health care, but most HMOs lack the capacity to provide or arrange for comprehensive mental health services. A demonstration program in Minnesota that mainstreamed the mentally ill into existing HMOs had to discontinue this approach when the largest provider refused to continue in the program because of adverse selection (Christianson et al. 1992). A second alternative is for states to contract with comprehensive mental health providers, such as community mental health centers, to take responsibility on a capitated basis for Medicaid recipients with mental illness. A third alternative is for states to contract with one or more MBHO on a capitated basis to develop and manage a network of mental health providers for Medicaid enrollees. The MBHO assumes the risk or shares risk with the state and then manages all aspects of service provision.

One type of integrated mental health HMO that some advocate as a useful approach enlists mental health organizations like comprehensive community mental health centers as the primary provider while providing capitation payments that encompass the entire range of services needed by highly impaired patients (Mechanic and Aiken 1989). Thus, the mental health HMO is capitated not only to provide mental health services but also to take responsibility for arranging needed medical services, housing, supported employment, rehabilitation, and other important resources. As the primary agent responsible for medical as well as mental health care, the mental health specialty organization can accomplish its responsibilities either directly or by agreement with other service providers. The logic is that mental health challenges are primary for patients with serious and persistent mental illness; therefore the appropriate manager for integrating all needed care is a mental health specialist.

The most ambitious demonstration of this idea took place in Rochester, New York, where a nonprofit, voluntary corporation, called Integrated Mental Health, was established to administer a capitation program for persons with serious mental illness (Babigian and Marshall 1989). The program focused on patients treated recently as inpatients in a state psychiatric facility, although this capitation demonstration also had a program for persons who had received treatment on an outpatient basis. The most disabled group, called "continuous patients," included those who had spent at least 270 days in a state hospital in the past two years. Integrated Mental Health had its main contract with the State of New York, but then subcontracted, in turn, with various mental health centers on a capitated basis to take integrated responsibility for care of enrollees. For example, the capitation for continuous patients included all inpatient and outpatient medical, dental, and psychiatric care; medications; and other costs necessary for community living, including housing when required. Two other groups of capitated enrollees were "intermittents" and "outpatients," but the range of responsibility for these groups was more limited.

Developing such complex arrangements involves considerable managerial effort in regard to organizing, financing, and coordinating services. Because the patients being capitated are all very high users of services, risks of high costs cannot be spread over large numbers of patients, many of whom have less need for services. Determining the appropriate capitation payment and methods for handling risk of unexpectedly high expenditures pose difficult problems. The essential challenge in capitating care for the seriously mentally ill and persons with other disabilities is predicting future utilization patterns with reasonable accuracy. Risk adjustment methods in psychiatry are underdeveloped and tend not to adjust correctly for variations in cost among patients. Thus, a mental health provider who is at financial risk and who gets too many very-high-cost patients may suffer large losses. Because many mental health provider organizations are small and cannot take advantage of risk distribution over large numbers of patients, they are vulnerable. Again, mental health organizations recognized as doing an excellent job with the most severely disabled may also attract patients with the greatest needs who are most expensive to treat. They face a penalty for their excellence. A variety of mechanisms exist for managing risk in capitated systems, but working out the specifics can amount to a kind of intricate guesswork. As states develop new health homes, discussed in Chapter 10, there will be further opportunities to learn how to address these issues (Mechanic 2012).

It should be noted here that the motivation for using capitation for persons with serious mental illness may differ from its use in the general medical sector. In the latter, it is assumed patient utilization and costs will vary a good deal, but in any given year most patients will incur low costs. This means the costs for expensive cases are spread across a large population. Capitation, in this context, is primarily a way of inducing clinicians to be more prudent in their decision making and to think carefully about how they allocate resources. In contrast, many more persons with disabilities will be high-cost cases. Important functions of capitation in this context are to integrate funding and clinical responsibility, to coordinate services, to allow flexible trade-offs in decision making between alternative services (rather than limit specific reimbursable benefits, as in indemnity insurance), and to hold mental health providers accountable for each specific patient associated with a capitated payment. All this represents a departure from traditional mental health approaches, in which providers receive budgets to provide services to particular catchment areas but without accountability for the care of any specific individual. Although cost containment is a perennial issue, early efforts in mental health capitation seemed equally concerned with improving the organization of services as with reducing cost. Currently, however, the emphasis in the Medicaid program seems to be tilting more toward cost-containment objectives. As states face more fiscal pressures in their Medicaid programs, they are increasingly requiring managed care for populations with disabilities, such as persons with mental illness, who were previously exempt from managed care coverage (Gifford et al. 2011).

OPPORTUNITIES AND SPECIAL PROBLEMS IN MANAGED MENTAL HEALTH CARE

We have already discussed the lack of clear, agreed-upon standards in mental health practice, the large variability in professional behavior, and the chaotic nature of what often goes on. Mental health practice, and private psychiatry in particular, has been fiercely individualistic and characterized by insistent demands from therapists for autonomy. Medical practice exhibits great variability, but the boundaries of acceptable mental health practice are particularly expansive. Managed care provides an organized framework for better educating both clinicians and patients about evidence-based standards for appropriate treatment and management (Drake, Bond, and Essock 2009; Lehman et al. 2004). Making mental health practitioners more conscious and thoughtful about their decisions, applying quality assurance processes, and establishing guidelines for treating different conditions based on the work being done by professional groups represent pivotal ingredients of this process. The issue is not to impose standards in a rigid way, but rather to induce clinicians to examine current assumptions and practices and to promote a more evidence-based orientation.

Another area in which mental illness differs from most other medical conditions is the extent to which disorders, and particularly psychotic illnesses, are stigmatized. High levels of stigma make it more difficult for persons with mental health problems to navigate large bureaucratically organized systems, to receive appropriate priority relative to other patients, and to advocate effectively for their interests. Stigma is one reason why those with serious mental illness might not fare well when mainstreamed into general HMOs, whose clinicians face heavy work pressures and may not be particularly knowledgeable about the special challenges of mental health care. Indeed, health professionals having little experience with patients who are mentally ill might share some of the same stereotypes as the general public and act on the basis of these misconceptions. Stigma motivates patients, in turn, to establish long-term relationships with trusted clinicians who are especially respectful of confidentiality. Yet the environment of managed care can be antithetical to such aims. Contractual relationships change frequently, and provider networks are disrupted. Confidential patient information may be sought for managerial purposes by the organization. The goals of efficiency and quality may be in tension within the treatment model, with little room for individualistic approaches to care.

Serious mental illness also involves social costs to a greater degree than most other illnesses. Medical studies typically ignore these types of costs. Deinstitutionalization, however, redirected many responsibilities of the mental health system onto families, neighbors, landlords, the police, those involved with the jail system, and others. In short, new public policies that implement the ideology of community care have found great favor with persons with mental illness and their advocates, but they created new burdens in the community. And, so, it needs to be understood in this contemporary setting that any decisions about when to authorize mental health treatment, in what settings, and for how long carry implications for a constellation of actors and interests beyond the patient and the managed care organization.

MANAGED CARE PERFORMANCE

The complexity of organizational strategies, the many ways of combining them, and the different populations studied make it difficult to reach generalizable conclusions about managed care performance. Research is helpful in identifying particularly useful or damaging activities, and when findings are reasonably consistent across settings and populations, we can have more confidence in them. Most studies simply compare some form of managed care organization with some form of traditional care, measuring outcomes such as utilization, costs, rehospitalizations, and functional status. Often, this research treats managed care structures and strategies as a "black box," without gauging the quality and experience of clinicians, operational procedures, financial incentives, risk arrangements, network size and complexity, and so on. These variations, however, have crucial importance and deserve thorough examination. At the outset, researchers were drawn by the novelty of managed behavioral health care, but as it became widely accepted, many investigators have seemed to lose interest and move on to other areas.

Currently, we know a great deal more about prepaid group practices than any other HMO model because it has been a focus of study for many years. Some of this research was discussed in Chapter 7. Repeated findings that organizations of this type could provide services comparable to traditional fee-for-service practice at significantly less cost made them very attractive to policymakers (Luft 1981; Miller and Luft 1994, 1997). Reductions in hospital use and the rate of surgical interventions were a big part of how this was done. In the mental health area, HMOs produced economies by reducing inpatient care and the number of mental health visits. They also substituted less expensive interventions for more expensive patterns of care, employing less expensive therapists in place of psychiatrists and psychologists as well as providing services in group versus individual settings (Wells, Manning, and Benjamin 1986, 1987). The impact of managed care strategies on utilization and cost was confirmed by the Rand Health Insurance Experiment (HIE) discussed in Chapter 7.

No one any longer seriously debates the fact that managed care practices can reduce costs, but there continues to be concern that HMOs seek out and attract healthier enrollees, particularly among the elderly population. This is an issue because a small proportion of sick patients account for the preponderance of costs, and an organization successful at getting a disproportionate number of healthy enrollees can make very large profits. Selecting good risks and avoiding bad ones is, in many ways, an easier task for a managed care organization than competing on the basis of cost, access, and quality of care.

HMOs of both the prepaid practice and network/IPA variety reduce mental health costs for the general population (Miller and Luft 1994). In the Rand HIE, which measured mental health outcomes, patients did as well in the HMO as in fee-for-service practice, but this study covered few persons with serious mental illness and only a limited range of outcomes was measured (Wells, Manning, and Valdez 1990). The results suggest, however, that HMOs are capable of providing appropriate mental health care to the general population. What is less clear is whether these organizations have the capacity or willingness to effectively treat persons with more serious and persistent illness. Some important findings relevant to this question come from the Medical Outcomes Study (MOS), which examined how practice type affected treatment and outcomes for depressive illness. For the most part, this study found relatively few differences (Rogers et al. 1993). Patients in fee-for-service versus HMOs who were treated by all types of mental health therapists (other than psychiatrists) had comparable outcomes. Psychiatrists, however, typically treated more patients who were very ill, and here the investigators found that those treated in HMOs were less likely to have continuity of medication and more likely to have poorer functional outcomes over time than those treated by psychiatrists in fee-for-service settings. This effect was only statistically significant among psychiatrists in IPAs and was inconsistent across sites, again suggesting the importance of getting beyond the "black box" and understanding better the internal variations within HMOs. But this study also provides an important cautionary note about possible harmful effects of managed care that may be difficult to discern when it affects only some patients, treated in only some settings, by particular types of clinicians.

Patients who are most severely and persistently ill are more typically in Medicaid and other government programs, but studies of managed care experiences with this population are too limited to draw any clear conclusions. Evaluation data have been gathered for alternative managed care arrangements (Mechanic and McAlpine 1999), including mainstreaming (Christianson et al. 1992), capitation contracting with community mental health centers (Bloom et al. 2002; Christianson et al. 1995; Cuffel et al. 2002; Manning et al. 1999), capitation with behavioral health companies to develop and manage mental health networks (Busch, Frank, and Lehman 2004; Callahan et al. 1995; Dickey et al. 2003; Leff et al. 2005; Merrick et al. 2010; Ray, Daugherty, and Meador 2003), and specialized mental health HMOs (Babigian et al. 1992). All these approaches successfully reduce costs for the purchaser but not necessarily for patients, their families, or others in the community. Estimates of such cost savings vary a great deal depending on setting and patient subgroup, but a range of 15 to 45 percent seems to apply (Frank and Glied 2006; Mechanic and McAlpine 1999; Zuvekas et al. 2002). In capitation studies in both New York State (Monroe County) and Utah, savings were achieved by a reduction in the number of hospital days either through shorter lengths of stay or the prevention of hospital admissions. In the Utah study, it was not clear whether significant financial savings were captured in regard to patients with schizophrenia over a three-and-a half-year period (Manning et al. 1999). Although budgeted community programs in assertive community treatment technically are not managed care programs, many studies of these quasi-capitation approaches find large reductions in number of inpatient days (Olfson 1990).

In 1992, Massachusetts was first in the nation to implement managed mental health care on a statewide basis for enrollees in its Medicaid program (Rochefort 1999). This MassHealth initiative gave participants the option either to join one of a group of HMOs or to sign up for a Primary Care Clinician Plan, in which mental health and substance abuse services were carved out for management by a for-profit specialty organization. State officials articulated several objectives for their new program, including improved treatment decisions, promotion of community care, and reduced use of hospitalization. Not least, they also hoped to stem rising Medicaid costs in the behavioral health area, which had climbed from $70.1 million to $184.5 million between fiscal years 1989 and 1992.

The Massachusetts program proved exceedingly difficult to assess. The U.S. Health Care Financing Administration, which issued a federal waiver for the Massachusetts plan, required an evaluation after one year (Callahan et al. 1995) and there were a number of other studies by researchers in local universities (e.g., Dickey et al. 1995; Frank et al. 1996; Geller et al. 1998; Hudson, Dorwart, and Wieman 1998; Sabin and Daniels 1999).

What emerged was a diverse set of analyses that focused on different program elements, population groups, and time periods. None included randomization or a control group. Performance measurements often lacked rigor, including data from surveys of provider perceptions. To add to the confusion, in 1995 the state revamped its program by means of an agreement under which the mental health department would begin to purchase all its acute care inpatient and emergency services through the state Medicaid agency, and the carve-out program was switched to a new organizational entity.

One of the authors of this text reviewed developments during the first seven years of the Massachusetts managed mental health care program by drawing on published research, unpublished reports, interviews, and newspaper articles (Rochefort 1999). There were a few noteworthy conclusions. First, the program launched a tumultuous period marked by ongoing adjustments and readjustments in the administration, service arrangements, and organizational framework for behavioral health care for Medicaid recipients in the Commonwealth. Second, despite the abundance of evaluation attempts, program outcomes remained ambiguous. There were cost savings and various new patterns of service delivery, particularly under the carve-out, including a decline in inpatient care (although not, according to some studies, for children) and an increase in outpatient care. But there were no definitive findings on the crucial question of quality impacts, such as could be gained only from detailed information for individual enrollees regarding the content of services delivered and clinical outcomes measured against an objective standard of care. Third, both federal and state officials, as well as advocacy groups, concluded there was insufficient monitoring of the MassHealth program, leading the state Medicaid agency and Massachusetts legislature to judge it necessary to increase their level of oversight.

In general, assessment of quality of care and outcomes under mental health managed care has been limited. Despite the significant reduction of hospital use in capitation studies, there is little evidence overall of lower quality of care or poorer outcomes. Existing data, however, also suggest three important cautions. First, while overall performance in managed care and traditional service settings may be comparable, patients who are most vulnerable are prone to do less well under managed care when a fixed amount of resources is being allocated among many patients. This allocation process, which can be called a "democratization of care," is not in the best interests of persons with severe and persistent mental illness (Mechanic and McAlpine 1999). In these situations, patients with schizophrenia and a history of high utilization seem to get fewer services under capitation and do less well (Manning et al. 1999). This pattern reinforces the need for carefully monitoring the experiences of vulnerable subgroups. Second, adverse effects sometimes observed under capitation seem to increase over time, and this fact should alert us to the need for long-term studies (Lurie et al. 1992; Manning et al. 1999; Rogers et al. 1993; Ware et al. 1996). Patients with such conditions as schizophrenia have a fluctuating course of illness. Patterns of change can only be observed effectively over longer periods, but most managed care studies provide data for only six months or a year. Third, although data are more limited for substance abuse than for mental illness, studies of managed care regarding the former present a more negative picture (Mechanic, Schlesinger, and McAlpine 1995). Hospital treatment of substance abuse was reduced under managed care, but without accompanying increases in outpatient services (Ellis 1992). Another research finding was that managed care organizations sometimes substituted detoxification for treatment for persons with substance use problems (Thompson et al. 1992), although this choice is inconsistent with good treatment standards (Gerstein and Harwood 1990).

Much depends on how a managed care program for serious mental illness is planned and monitored. For example, one of the most careful long-term studies in the state of Colorado compared three models: traditional fee-for-service financing of a community mental health center, capitated care provided by a nonprofit community mental health center, and capitated services provided by a for-profit managed behavioral health care company. Follow-up study of various groups of patients with severe mental illness found substantial per person cost savings (two-thirds in the case of the MBHO company and 20 percent in the case of the capitated mental health center) compared to fee-for-service arrangements over a two-year period. The researchers found few clinical performance differences between the models studied, but when there were differences they generally favored the capitated programs (Bloom et al. 2002; Cuffel et al. 2002). The program has now been studied for five years. Although data are more limited for the later years, the investigators tell us at the time of this writing that the results have held up. One goal of better-integrated care is to avoid emergency room visits and unnecessary hospitalization by providing appropriate care in the community. Catalano and colleagues (2005), using the Colorado data, evaluated the impact of managed care on hospital emergency room visits. Both types of capitation arrangements were associated with a reduction in these visits compared to fee-for-service arrangements. Grieve and colleagues (2008) carried out a cost-effectiveness analysis for the various Colorado reimbursement models using three years of data. They examined the differences in quality-adjusted life years relative to costs and found that the capitated for-profit model was significantly more cost-effective in terms of measured outcomes than either the fee-for-service model or the nonprofit community mental health center model.

The Colorado experience suggests the possibility of certain quality advantages for capitated managed care. However, Busch and colleagues (2004) studied a state Medicaid program that obtained federal waiver authority to implement a private for-profit managed care program in one state region, a situation constituting a kind of quasi-experimental research design when comparing the results in this region to elsewhere in the state. Focusing on how the capitated model affected quality of care for patients with schizophrenia, investigators found substantial reductions in individual and group therapy and psychosocial rehabilitation services in the capitated model. By contrast, the managed care organization was not responsible for the cost of medications, and in this area the likelihood of treatment was not impacted, even with respect to the most expensive medications.

Transitions from one form of care to another are particularly important, requiring careful implementation to avoid disruptions and harm. One study, for example, analyzed continuity of antipsychotic medications in TennCare, Tennessee's Medicaid program, when it converted to a fully capitated behavioral health carve-out (Ray, Daugherty, and Meador 2003). According to researchers, adherence to antipsychotic therapy dropped 18 percent following the transition. Translated into days, 60 days of therapy were lost during the year following the change, a serious gap in treating psychotic illness. Moreover, the effects were largest among those most seriously ill (Mechanic 2003).

Despite the ubiquity of utilization review, we still lack firm knowledge about its effects. It is clear, however, that utilization review successfully reduces costs for the purchaser (employer) by a significant amount (Hodgkin 1992). Although there are few formal studies, data from individual businesses tell a similar story. These employers are not a random sample, but rather those who were motivated to engage utilization review companies due to high mental health care costs. The data indicate that it is possible to achieve significant savings in two ways (Mechanic, Schlesinger, and McAlpine 1995). First, the fact of review itself serves as a deterrent because it makes clinicians more careful about their resource use decisions. Further, as clinicians learn how utilization reviewers define treatment norms, they may accommodate their practice to these expectations to avoid the wasted time, hassle, and frustration involved in appeal and advocacy efforts. Such accommodation may or may not be desirable from a clinical standpoint, but it is the likely reality. Second, savings also occur as a result of decisions made by utilization reviewers to not authorize certain services or to authorize them for shorter periods.

One innovative study in a New York City fee-for-service health insurance plan subjected half the enrollees to sham utilization review where all requested care was automatically approved, while the other half received the usual form of utilization management (Rosenberg et al. 1995). Because all providers believed they were under utilization management, this study does not allow assessment of the magnitude of the psychological deterrent effect. It does, however, highlight actual impacts of the utilization review process. There was a modest but statistically significant reduction in procedures in doctors' offices and in outpatient departments in the non-sham review group compared to the sham group. These were true reductions and not simply delays in treatment until the subsequent year. However, no significant differences occurred in hospital admissions in general or for psychiatric or substance abuse treatment, and there were no differences in length of stay. Reductions from utilization review in this study seem very modest. This may be due to the particular insurance program studied or to the fact that the nature of this research excluded gauging the deterrent effect.

Utilization management and changing provider attitudes have resulted in reductions of inpatient length of stay for all illnesses, but the impact has been most dramatic in the case of mental illness (Mechanic and McAlpine 1999; Wickizer and Lessler 1998). Some believe this management control has gone too far and makes it difficult for patients to get needed care (Appelbaum 2003). If the process of utilization management is to work rationally, one might reasonably expect fewer reductions in care for those most ill, as well as an increase in substituted outpatient services when inpatient care is reduced. In some settings this appears to be the pattern. Goldman, McCulloch, and Sturm (1998), in studying a large West Coast employer, reported a 24 percent reduction in inpatient admissions and a 43 percent reduction in length of stay, but also substantial increases in outpatient treatment and modest increases in residential and day treatment. In too many other instances, however, researchers have found either no increase in alternative treatment or even reductions when utilization management produces cuts in inpatient care (see Mechanic and McAlpine 1999). Even more troubling is the fact that service reductions often do not appear to differentiate between those more and less seriously ill (Wickizer and Lessler 1998), and reductions are sometimes largest among those who are very sick (Chang et al. 1998; Huskamp 1998; Ray, Daugherty, and Meador 2003). Some studies show distinct negative outcomes associated with these practices (Popkin et al. 1998; Ray, Daugherty, and Meador 2003; Wickizer and Lessler 1998).

Utilization management through prior authorization for some types of pharmaceutical treatments is common, but there is little research documenting the effects. At least 46 percent of states have prior-authorization programs for drug benefits (Smith et al. 2011) and while there is insufficient research to draw definitive conclusions, early results are troubling. In 2003, Maine implemented prior authorization for antipsychotics in its Medicaid program (Soumerai et al. 2008). The policy required stepped care for new users of atypical antipsychotics: first the patient had to be tried on a course of the preferred drug (starting with risperidone, followed by one other preferred drug) at full therapeutic dosage for at least two weeks before, if necessary, switching to the nonpreferred drugs (olanzapine and aripiprazole). Alternatively, a physician could obtain authorization to use the nonpreferred drug by documenting that it was medically necessary or that treatment failed on the initial course of medications. Soumerai and colleagues (2008) evaluated the policy by comparing patterns in prescribing of new atypical drugs for patients with schizophrenia in Maine's Medicaid program and for patients in New Hampshire's program, which had no such policy. The prior-authorization policy was successful in reducing use of nonpreferred atypicals. However, the program also increased the risk of treatment gaps in medication therapy, a potentially serious consequence. This study did not examine outcomes such as hospitalization and emergency room use, both relevant indicators of program impact for this patient group.

Researchers have also examined the effect of the Maine preauthorization policy for antipsychotic and anticonvulsant medications on treatment for bipolar disorder (Lu et al. 2010, 2011; Zhang et al. 2009). Similar to the results for schizophrenia, they found that prescribing for nonpreferred drugs decreased after the policy went into effect. However, they also found that the policy decreased rates of initiation of treatment and led to more patients with bipolar disorder discontinuing therapy (Lu et al. 2010; Zhang et al. 2009). They also compared visits for psychiatric care, hospitalizations, and emergency room use for cohorts initiating medication for bipolar disorder prior to, and following, the policy implementation (Lu et al. 2011). Results were analyzed separately for persons with bipolar disorder who were seen at a community health center versus those who were not, under the assumption that patients who use community mental health centers are among the sickest of people with bipolar disorder. Rates of discontinuing medication were higher for both groups in the postimplementation period. However, the sicker patients who discontinued use of medications had fewer visits for outpatient psychiatric care after implementation of the policy, suggesting that they may have become less engaged in other forms of treatment. In contrast, persons who had not attended a community health center but discontinued their medication had greater emergency room use. The authors suggest that this may have been because this group lacked the resources of the community mental health center to monitor symptoms and avoid emergency room care. There was no change in hospitalizations.

Closer examination of the effects of prior authorization for antidepressant use in Michigan's Medicaid program sheds more light on the relationship between such policies and outcomes. Michigan's Medicaid program introduced prior-authorization requirements for nonpreferred antidepressants in 2002. Like the Maine example, the program was stopped due to patient complaints. In their evaluation of the program, Adams and colleagues (2009) found that, similar to the experience in Maine, it reduced prescribing for the nonpreferred drugs. Moreover, there was also a reduction in the number of patients who started on antidepressants. However, the policy was not associated with negative outcomes such as increased hospitalizations and emergency room use in the year following initiation of therapy.

In contrast, Mark and colleagues (2010) found that a prior-authorization policy for antidepressants in private plans had less positive outcomes. They examined treatment patterns for enrollees in plans that required stepped care and prior authorization to use nonpreferred drugs versus patterns for enrollees covered by plans with no such strictures.

The prior-authorization plans required patients to use the preferred drug at treatment initiation or have their physician submit a request for authorization to prescribe the non-preferred drug. Enrollees in the prior-authorization plans had fewer days when antidepressants were supplied, and costs were lower than those for enrollees in comparison plans. In addition, prescriptions for the preferred drugs increased. However, emergency room care, hospital admissions, and outpatient visits were also higher in the prior-authorization plans. While there was a small decline in pharmaceutical spending, it was outpaced by large increases in spending on other medical services.

Management of prescription drugs is still an emerging field that is unlikely to retreat as medication costs make up an increasingly large share of the health care budget, especially for mental health problems. Research results to date should cause some concern insofar as there is evidence of patients discontinuing medications early or physicians prescribing clinically inappropriate drugs. Clearly, it makes sense for health plans to limit overutilization of psychotropic medications and the prescribing of more expensive drugs in place of equally effective but less expensive drugs. However, we need to be cautious in implementing preauthorization policies that might have unintended consequences. The response of patients to medications can be very individualized. Clinicians need to be able to act quickly when medications preferred by a health plan prove ineffective or induce unexpected side-effects.

Overall, the quality of utilization review is only as good as the quality of the criteria used and the experience and judgment of reviewers. Companies that offer these services have different operating procedures, as well as reviewers who may vary in training and experience. Companies also supervise reviewers in different ways. Some depend on carefully worked-out algorithms; others depend to a greater extent on the professional judgments of staff. Some companies make appeals and advocacy on behalf of patients more feasible than others, and the programs may also vary in time, hassle, and paperwork required for approval of treatment decisions. At times, clinicians may develop relationships with reviewers and the two groups will learn to work together cooperatively. When reviewers trust a clinician, they may be less intrusive and more willing to accept clinical judgments, concentrating scrutiny instead on clinicians regarded as less trustworthy. Large utilization review companies often situate reviewers and case managers at major hospitals and medical centers where they can work directly with those involved in patient care decisions.

The National Alliance on Mental Illness (NAMI) began issuing report cards on managed care organizations during the late 1990s (Hall et al. 1997). In the first round of evaluation, NAMI rated various behavioral health companies for performance with respect to the following components: treatment guidelines and practice protocols, inpatient treatment, intensive case management, medication access, response to suicide attempts, involvement of consumer and family members, outcome measures and management, rehabilitation, and housing. The advocacy group concluded that the industry "fails on the basic elements of care that people with serious brain disorders need to survive" (Hall et al. 1997). The latest report card can be found on the Internet at www.nami.org (Aron et al. 2009).

Two systematic reviews of published literature have compiled trends and outcomes in managed behavioral health care from its first appearance in 1990 to the early years of the twenty-first century. The first review examines publicly funded programs, primarily Medicaid waiver programs (Coleman et al. 2005). Findings clearly document cost savings across different program models and settings, although initial efficiency results have not been easy to sustain over time and there are signs of trade-offs, such as reduced access to services; cost-shifting to other public agencies; consumer complaints; and negative impacts for patient groups with extreme or special needs, including those severely ill, patients with dual diagnoses, and children and adolescents. The authors emphasize the critical role of planning and contract formulation in assuring that private contractors will meet public goals, including provision of a defined array of services.

The second review, prepared for the Substance Abuse and Mental Health Services Administration by The Lewin Group, addressed 11 research questions identified by a panel of mental health experts (Mauery et al. 2006). Following is a brief summary of results:

- Application of the techniques of managed care to mental health services delivery is a proven means of saving money.
- Managed mental health care seems to improve access to treatment in general, but there is evidence of restricted access to higher intensity services such as hospitalization.
- There is widespread concern that managed care benefit designs or utilization management harm persons with severe mental illnesses, but empirical data on this issue are inconclusive.
- There are different pluses and minuses for arrangements that "carve in" mental health services as part of an integrated HMO model versus those that "carve out" these services for specialty management through contracting. Purchasers have preferred carve-outs, in part due to greater cost control, but there are concerns with regard to lack of coordination between physical health care and mental health care, access to more intensive inpatient and residential services, and creation of confusion about accessing the service system.
- It is unclear how contractual provisions can be used effectively to achieve coordination of primary care and mental health services under managed care.
- Preventive mental health services can be prioritized in managed mental health care systems, but it requires careful needs assessment, contractual specifications that focus on preventive care, provision of relevant information to enrollees, and monitoring.
- It is unclear how evidence-based standards can be expanded as a guide for practice under managed mental health care.
- It is unclear how principles of consumer-directed care can be expanded under managed mental health care. Medicaid programs have done the most to date by including consumers in the process of program planning, design, and implementation.
- Research data are limited regarding the techniques and circumstances for most effective use of financial risk sharing with providers in managed mental health care.
- Braided funding streams that coordinate, but do not simply pool, resources from multiple sources in regard to service delivery represent the best way to reduce fragmentation of services while maintaining an ability to track the contributions and activities of different participating agencies.

Given the numerous areas in which the literature fails to answer key questions, it is not surprising that the authors call for additional research, especially rigorous quantitative studies adopting longitudinal designs.

THE REGULATORY DEBATE
IN MANAGED CARE

As managed mental health care has been extended to cover more of the U.S. population, it has changed in many ways. The picture remains in flux; however, many key issues are clear.

Managed care, whether in the form of capitation or utilization review, requires a very different way of practicing than is typical in fee-for-service systems. Most clinicians have received training to do whatever they believe would be useful for patients. Regardless of the costs, and however little the actual benefit, the assumption has been that expenditures would be covered. Managed care profoundly adjusts this calculus by requiring provider organizations, as well as individual clinicians, to think much more carefully about how services are organized and selected. It encourages more dependence on research evidence, including the cost-effectiveness of alternative treatment strategies. Clinicians, in the future, will have to rely more on evidence-based practice standards as a guide to treatment while growing accustomed to having their decisions reviewed by others. This will necessitate adaptations in medical and professional education because clinicians-in-training must learn to function within this new practice environment. Further, the issues and quandaries associated with managed care promise to influence the priorities of health care research, including the search for possible methods of prevention, treatment, and management of the most common diseases and disabilities that generate high medical costs.

In the future, individuals will have more information to guide health insurance choices, some of it bewildering. There is great need for meaningful report cards that provide the public with comparable information on the performance of health plans, including such data as patients' perceptions of access, satisfaction with care, and preventive care screening rates. The NAMI report card noted above represents a useful early effort of this type, although much more can, and should, be done. Unfortunately, consumers tend to be primarily interested in the performance of particular clinicians, failing to appreciate the import of information dealing with health plan performance in the aggregate. In addition, report cards thus far have provided little information on specialized services such as ease of referral to mental health specialty providers; the availability of day treatment, residential care, and other supervised arrangements; assistance with housing and supported employment; and the quality and range of mental health staff and programs. Hopefully, the value and reliability of such information will improve in future years.

There is a significant role for public agencies and mental health advocacy groups to play in monitoring managed care, particularly with respect to enrollees having the most severe and persistent illnesses. In situations where public programs purchase services for enrollees, the accountability of provider organizations becomes paramount, no matter whether contractees are for-profit behavioral health companies or nonprofit community mental health centers. Specifications must clearly define the range of expected services—assertive community treatment, assistance with problems of everyday living such as housing and obtaining entitlements, psychosocial rehabilitation, and more—as well as address access to care and quality. Responsibility for providing timely data on such items as expenditures, access to treatment, and service referrals must be clear. All this implies that the contracting and purchase of services at the state level cannot be a closed bureaucratic process. Making known the needs of their constituencies is one step by which mental health advocates can influence the provision of services in constructive ways. In addition, there are real risks surrounding managed care contracting in such areas as deceptive marketing and use of tactics to discourage enrollment of high-risk individuals. These dangers challenge officials and advocates to be *watchdogs*, calling to public attention significant deficiencies in care and providing ways of improving services.

States have followed different approaches in regulating managed mental health care (Rochefort 1996). Some have attempted to protect patients with mental illness by means of broad regulatory provisions applicable to all members of managed care plans. Some have delineated mental health care as one of a number of performance concerns to be addressed by managed care organizations. And some have given specific legislative attention to devising detailed safeguards and remedies for the special risks faced by mental health consumers and providers under managed care. Thus, the regulatory spectrum encompasses actions of varying focus and impact with respect to consumers having mental health and substance abuse problems. In its way, the question of which regulatory method is preferable—grouping persons with mental illness together with other patient populations or giving particular consideration to their distinctive needs and preferences—revisits the dilemma over "exceptionalism" that arises in many public policy debates concerning mental health care.

The technical problems yet to be resolved are many, but the clear solutions available are few. Risk selection occurs even within subcategories of disabled persons, potentially putting the highest quality and most conscientious provider agencies and clinicians in financial jeopardy. To the extent that managed care organizations can play the game of risk selection successfully, they have a disincentive to offer a level of comprehensiveness and quality of care appropriate for needy and expensive clients. We need much better ways of adjusting capitation to take account of complexity of need, and in the absence of such adjustments we require good models for making financial risk manageable. Alternative approaches include stop-loss protection to hold the provider harmless for costs beyond a certain level, and blended systems that combine capitation with fee-for-service as a way of moderating risk. Some state agencies use a gradual process of shifting risk to provider organizations over a period of several years as both the state and the provider gain more experience in the contracting process.

As managed behavioral health care continues to dominate private and public health insurance and as profit becomes a more central motivation in health affairs, maintaining the public's trust is a challenge. Many states continue to work on developing new approaches for regulating managed care. Advocates of competition resist regulation reflexively, believing that in the long run the market will drive out substandard programs. But the complexity of the medical care market, the difficulties of ascertaining quality of care, the inadequacies of information, and the opportunities for abuse lead many people to believe that states should provide strong regulatory guidance (Rodwin 1993, 2011). To the extent that sound processes of nongovernmental accreditation exist, as in the HMO sector where the National Committee for Quality Assurance (NCQA) applies its own sophisticated standards, it makes sense for regulatory enforcement to be calibrated in tandem with the scope of private oversight. Still, when it comes to such specialized issues as mental health, not even a group like NCQA has made much progress in developing relevant and detailed performance criteria (Druss and Rosenheck 1997).

Actors in the managed care sector resist attempts to put any greater regulatory demands on them than on fee-for-service practitioners. The argument is made, not without a certain amount of cogency, that fee-for-service medicine involves its own abuses, such as the provision of unnecessary treatment. The fact of the matter is, however, that the public remains more concerned about the problem of undertreatment than overutilization. There is much greater suspicion toward the distant management of large insurance organizations than small fee-for-service practices with which patients have personal relationships.

What, then, is the appropriate range of regulatory control over HMOs, utilization management firms, behavioral health companies, and the like? No one really questions regulations requiring health insurance programs to have sufficient financial reserves to meet their obligations to enrollees, nor are there major objections to efforts to control mis-leading marketing, lack of access to care, or refusals to meet contractual obligations. There is more disagreement as to the extent of requirements governing information disclosure; data collection and public reporting on access, patient satisfaction, and other performance measures; grievance and complaint processes; and the types of financial incentives used by plans with physicians and other providers, such as withholds and bonuses. Some states are going even further by seeking to protect clinicians from reprisals when they appeal review decisions or criticize managed care arrangements. Micromanagement by state leg-islatures and bureaucrats is not desirable, but some of these measures reflect deep public and professional dissatisfaction, the occurrence of past abuses, and a basic breakdown in trust with respect to the ends and means of managed care (Mechanic 1997, 2004).

CONCLUSION

U.S. health care is an enormous industry with expenditures approaching $3 trillion a year. Its particular structures, and its irrationalities as well as its strengths, reflect our economic and social philosophies, not to mention interest group politics (Mechanic 2006). The health care system is constantly evolving. Thus, the managed care practices we see today may simply be one stage in the movement toward new strategies for wise and efficient use of resources.

The practice of managed mental health care is even less experienced and more uncer-tain than other areas. Reliable performance data are scant. To be sure, it is essential to be vigilant about underservice and other potential abuses. But it is also important to view managed care as an opportunity to define mental health needs more sharply, to develop broader and better integrated systems of mental health management, to define treat-ment norms in line with empirical evidence, and to develop performance indicators for tracking the provision of services. Managed care opens the door for training and using different types of mental health personnel, directing them to tasks badly neglected within a fragmented mental health sector. Managed care is here to stay for the foreseeable future. Simply railing against it has little point. The challenge is to evaluate and shape its constitu-ent components so that the best possible outcomes for persons with mental illness and other disabilities may be achieved.

References

Adams, Alyce S., et al. "Prior Authorization for Antidepressants in Medicaid: Effects Among Disabled Dual Enrollees." *Archives of Internal Medicine* 169 (2009): 750–756.

Appelbaum, Paul S. "The 'Quiet' Crisis in Mental Health Services." *Health Affairs* 22 (2003): 110–116.

Aron, Laudan et al. *Grading the States 2009: A Report on America's Health Care System for Adults with Serious Mental Illness*. Arlington, VA: National Alliance on Mental Illness, 2009. Available online: www.nami.org/gtsTemplate09.cfm?Section=Grading_the_States_2009.

Babigian, Haroutun M., and Phyllis Marshall. "Rochester: A Comprehensive Capitation Experiment." In *Paying for Services: Promises and Pitfalls of Capitation*, edited by David Mechanic and Linda Aiken, pp. 43–54. New Directions for Mental Health Services Number 43. San Francisco: Jossey-Bass, 1989.

Babigian, Haroutun M., et al. "A Mental Health Capitation Experiment: Evaluating the Monroe-Livingston Experience." In *Economics and Mental Health*, edited by Richard Frank and Willard Manning, pp. 307–331. Baltimore: Johns Hopkins University Press, 1992.

Badamgarav, Enkhe, et al. "Effectiveness of Disease Management Programs in Depression: A Systematic Review." *American Journal of Psychiatry* 160 (2003): 2080–2090.

Bloom, Joan R., et al. "Mental Health Costs and Access Under Alternative Capitation Systems in Colorado." *Health Services Research* 37 (2002): 315–340.

Busch, Alisa B., Richard G. Frank, and Anthony F. Lehman. "The Effect of a Managed Behavioral Health Carve-Out on Quality of Care for Medicaid Patients Diagnosed as Having Schizophrenia." *Archives of General Psychiatry* 61 (2004): 442–448.

Callahan, James J., et al. "Mental Health/Substance Abuse Treatment in Managed Care: The Massachusetts Medicaid Experience." *Health Affairs* 14 (1995): 173–184.

Catalano, Ralph A., et al. "The Impact of Capitated Financing on Psychiatric Emergency Services." *Psychiatric Services* 56 (2005): 685–690.

Centers for Medicare & Medicaid Services. *National Summary of Medicaid Managed Care Programs and Enrollment as of July 1, 2010*. Baltimore, MD: Centers for Medicare & Medicaid Services, 2012. Available online: www.cms.gov/Research-Statistics-Data-and-Systems/Computer-Data-and-Systems/MedicaidDataSourcesGenInfo/Downloads/2010Trends.pdf.

Chang, Cyril F., et al. "Tennessee's Failed Managed Care Program for Mental Health and Substance Abuse Services." *Journal of the American Medical Association* 279 (1998): 864–869.

Christianson, Jon B., et al. "Use of Community-Based Mental Health Programs by HMOs: Evidence from a Medicaid Demonstration." *American Journal of Public Health* 82 (1992): 790–796.

Christianson, Jon B., et al. "Utah's Prepaid Mental Health Plan: The First Year." *Health Affairs* 14 (1995): 160–172.

Claxton, Gary, et al. *Employer Health Benefits. 2011 Annual Survey*. Menlo Park, CA: Henry J. Kaiser Family Foundation and Chicago, IL: Health Research & Educational Trust, 2011. Available online: ehbs.kff.org/pdf/2011/8225.pdf.

Coleman, Mardi, et al. "Overview of Publicly Funded Managed Behavioral Health Care." *Administration and Policy in Mental Health and Mental Health Services Research* 32 (2005): 321–340.

Coleman, Katie, et al. "Untangling Practice Redesign from Disease Management: How Do We Best Care for the Chronically Ill?" *Annual Review of Public Health* 30 (2009): 385–408.

Cooper, Philip F., Kosali I. Simon, and Jessica Vistnes. "A Closer Look at the Managed Care Backlash." *Medical Care* 44 (2006): I4–I11.

Cuffel, Brian J., et al. "Two-Year Outcomes of Fee-for-Service and Capitated Medicaid Programs for People with Severe Mental Illness." *Health Services Research* 37 (2002): 341–359.

Dickey, Barbara, et al. "Massachusetts Medicaid Managed Health Care Reform: Treatment for the Psychiatrically Disabled." *Advances in Health Economics and Health Services Research* 15 (1995): 99–116.

Dickey, Barbara, et al. "Guideline Recommendations for Treatment of Schizophrenia: The Impact of Managed Care." *Archives of General Psychiatry* 60 (2003): 340–348.

Drake, Robert E., Gary R. Bond, and Susan M. Essock. "Implementing Evidence-Based Practices for People with Schizophrenia." *Schizophrenia Bulletin* 35 (2009): 704–713.

Druss, Benjamin, and Robert Rosenheck. "Evaluation of the HEDIS Measure of Behavioral Health Care Quality." *Psychiatric Services* 48 (1997): 71–75.

Ellis, Randall P. "Employers Tackle Treatment Costs." *Substance Abuse Issues* 3 (1992): 1–3.

Essock, Susan M., and Howard H. Goldman. "States' Embrace of Managed Mental Health Care." *Health Affairs* 14 (1995): 34–44.

Foote, Sandra M. "Population-Based Disease Management Under Fee-for-Service Medicare." *Health Affairs*, Web Exclusive (2003): doi 10.1377/hlthaff.w3.342. Available online: www.aei.org/files/2004/03/22/20040319_Footearticle.pdf.

Frank, Richard G., and Sherry A. Glied. *Better But Not Well: Mental Health Policy in the United States Since 1950.* Baltimore, MD: Johns Hopkins University Press, 2006.

Frank, Richard G., Thomas G. McGuire, and Joseph P. Newhouse. "Risk Contracts in Managed Mental Health Care." *Health Affairs* 14 (1995): 50–64.

Frank, Richard G., et al. "Developments in Medicaid Managed Behavioral Health Care." In *Mental Health, United States, 1996,* edited by Ronald W. Manderscheid and Mary Anne Sonnenschein, pp. 138–153. DHHS Publication No. (SMA) 96-3098. Washington, DC: Government Printing Office, 1996.

Freeborn, Donald K., and Clyde R. Pope. *Promise and Performance in Managed Care: The Prepaid Group Practice Model.* Baltimore: Johns Hopkins University Press, 1994.

Geller, Jeffrey L., et al. "The Effects of Public Managed Care on Patterns of Intensive Use of Inpatient Psychiatric Services." *Psychiatric Services* 49 (1998): 327–332.

Gensichen, Jochen, et al. "Case Management to Improve Major Depression in Primary Health Care: A Systematic Review." *Psychological Medicine* 36 (2006): 7–14.

Gerstein, Dean R., and Henrick J. Harwood, eds. *Treating Drug Problems, Volume 1.* Washington, DC: National Academy Press, 1990.

Gifford, Kathleen, et al. *A Profile of Medicaid Managed Care Programs in 2010: Findings from a 50-State Survey.* Washington, DC: Henry J. Kaiser Family Foundation, 2011. Available online: www.kff.org/medicaid/upload/8220.pdf.

Gold, Marsha R., et al. "A National Survey of the Arrangements Managed-Care Plans Make with Physicians." *New England Journal of Medicine* 333 (1995): 1678–1683.

Gold, Marsha R., et al. *Medicare Advantage Enrollment Market Update.* Menlo Park, CA: Henry J. Kaiser Family Foundation, 2011. Available online: www.kff.org/medicare/upload/8228.pdf.

Goldman, William, Joyce McCulloch, and Roland Sturm. "Costs and Use of Mental Health Services Before and After Managed Care." *Health Affairs* 17 (1998): 40–52.

Grieve, Richard, et al. "Evaluating Health Care Programs by Combining Cost with Quality of Life Measures: A Case Study Comparing Capitation and Fee for Service." *Health Services Research* 43 (2008): 1204–1222.

Hall, Laura L., et al. *Stand and Deliver: Action Call to a Failing Industry.* Arlington, VA: National Alliance for Mental Illness, 1997.

Hillman, Alan L. "Financial Incentives for Physicians in HMOs: Is There a Conflict of Interest?" *New England Journal of Medicine* 317 (1987): 1743–1748.

Hillman, Alan L. "Health Maintenance Organizations, Financial Incentives, and Physicians' Judgments." *Annals of Internal Medicine* 112 (1990): 891–893.

Hodgkin, Dominic. "The Impact of Private Utilization Management on Psychiatric Care: A Review of the Literature." *Journal of Mental Health Administration* 19 (1992): 143–157.

Hudson, Christopher G., Robert A. Dorwart, and Dow A. Wieman. *The Impact of a Medicaid Behavioral Carve-Out Program on Patterns of Acute Psychiatric Hospitalization: The Massachusetts Experience, FY1996-FY1997.* Salem, MA: Salem State College, 1998.

Huskamp, Haiden A. "How a Managed Behavioral Health Care Carve-Out Plan Affected Spending for Episodes of Treatment." *Psychiatric Services* 49 (1998): 1559–1562.

Leff, H. Stephen, et al. "Assessment of Medicaid Managed Behavioral Health Care for Persons with Serious Mental Illness." *Psychiatric Services* 56 (2005): 1245–1253.

Lehman, Anthony F. et al. *Evidence-Based Mental Health Treatments and Services: Examples to Inform Public Policy.* New York: Milbank Memorial Fund, 2004.

Lu, Christine Y., et al. "Unintended Impacts of a Medicaid Prior Authorization Policy on Access to Medications for Bipolar Illness." *Medical Care* 48 (2010): 4–9.

Lu, Christine Y., et al. "Association Between Prior Authorization for Medications and Health Service Use by Medicaid Patients with Bipolar Disorder." *Psychiatric Services* 62 (2011): 186–193.

Luft, Harold S. *Health Maintenance Organizations: Dimensions of Performance.* New York: Wiley Interscience, 1981.

Lurie, Nicole, et al. "Does Capitation Affect the Health of the Chronically Mentally Ill?: Results from a Randomized Trial." *Journal of the American Medical Association* 267 (1992): 3300–3304.

Manning, Willard G., et al. "Outcomes for Medicaid Beneficiaries with Schizophrenia Under a Prepaid Mental Health Carve-Out." *Journal of Behavioral Health Services Research* 26 (1999): 442–450.

Mark, Tami L., et al. "The Effects of Antidepressant Step Therapy Protocols on Pharmaceutical and Medical Utilization and Expenditures." *American Journal of Psychiatry* 167 (2010): 1202–1209.

Mauery, D. Richard, et al. *Managed Mental Health Care: Findings from the Literature, 1990–2005.* DHHS Pub. No. SMA-06-4178. Rockville, MD: Center for Mental Health Services, Substance Abuse and Mental Health Services Administration, 2006. Available online: store.samhsa.gov/shin/content//SMA06-4178/SMA06-4178.pdf.

Mechanic, David. "Can Research on Managed Care Inform Practice and Policy Decisions?" In *Controversies in Managed Mental Health Care*, edited by Arnold Lazarus, pp. 197–211. Washington, DC: American Psychiatric Press, 1996.

Mechanic, David. "Managed Care as a Target of Distrust." *Journal of the American Medical Association* 277 (1997): 1810–1811.

Mechanic, David. "Managing Behavioral Health in Medicaid." *New England Journal of Medicine* 348 (2003): 1914–1916.

Mechanic, David. "The Rise and Fall of Managed Care." *Journal of Health and Social Behavior* 45 (2004): 76–86.

Mechanic, David. *The Truth About Health Care: Why Reform Is Not Working in America.* New Brunswick, NJ: Rutgers University Press, 2006.

Mechanic, David. "Seizing Opportunities Under the Affordable Care Act for Transforming the Mental and Behavioral Health System." *Health Affairs* 31 (2012): 376–382.

Mechanic, David, and Linda H. Aiken, eds. *Paying for Services: Promises and Pitfalls of Capitation.* New Directions for Mental Health Services, Monograph Series 43. San Francisco: Jossey-Bass, 1989.

Mechanic, David, and Donna D. McAlpine. "Mission Unfulfilled: Potholes on the Road to Mental Health Parity." *Health Affairs* 18 (1999): 7–21.

Mechanic, David, Mark Schlesinger, and Donna McAlpine. "Management of Mental Health and Substance Abuse Services: State of the Art and Early Results." *Milbank Quarterly* 73 (1995): 19–55.

Merrick, Elizabeth L., et al. "Patterns of Service Use in Two Types of Managed Behavioral Health Care Plans." *Psychiatric Services* 61 (2010): 86–89.

Miller, Robert H., and Harold S. Luft. "Managed Care Plan Performance Since 1980: A Literature Analysis." *Journal of the American Medical Association* 271 (1994): 1512–1519.

Miller, Robert H., and Harold S. Luft. "Does Managed Care Lead to Better or Worse Quality of Care?" *Health Affairs* 16 (1997): 7–25.

National Conference of State Legislatures. *Managed Care and the States.* Washington, DC, 2011. Available online: www.ncsl.org/issues-research/health/managed-care-and-the-states.aspx.

Neumeyer-Gromen, Angela, et al. "Disease Management Programs for Depression: A Systematic Review and Meta-Analysis of Randomized Controlled Trials." *Medical Care* 42 (2004): 1211–1221.

Newhouse, Joseph P., and the Insurance Experiment Group. *Free for All?: Lessons from the RAND Health Insurance Experiment.* Cambridge, MA: Harvard University Press, 1993.

Olfson, Mark. "Assertive Community Treatment: An Evaluation of the Experimental Evidence." *Hospital and Community Psychiatry* 41 (1990): 634–641.

Oss, Monica E., Laura Morgan, and Casey Miller. *U.S. Behavioral Health Management Market Directory 2011–2012: Analysis of U.S. Managed Behavioral Health, Employee Assistance and Disease Management Markets.* Gettysburg, PA: Open Minds, 2011.

Popkin, Mike, et al. "Changes in the Process of Care for Medicaid Patients with Schizophrenia in Utah's Prepaid Mental Health Plan." *Psychiatric Services* 49 (1998): 518–523.

Ray, Wayne A., James R. Daugherty, and Keith G. Meador. "Effect of a Mental Health 'Carve Out' Program on the Continuity of Antipsychotic Therapy." *New England Journal of Medicine* 348 (2003): 1885–1894.

Robinson, James C. "The End of Managed Care." *Journal of the American Medical Association* 285 (2001): 2622–2628.

Rochefort, David A. *Regulating Managed Mental Health Care: A Policy Analysis.* Prepared for the Center for Mental Health Services, Substance Abuse and Mental Health Services Administration, Cambridge, MA: The Evaluation Center @ HSRI, 1996.

Rochefort, David A. *Mental Health Care in Massachusetts.* Issue Brief No. 6, Waltham, MA: The Massachusetts Health Policy Forum, 1999.

Rodwin, Marc. *Medicine, Money, and Morals: Physicians' Conflicts of Interest.* New York: Oxford University Press, 1993.

Rodwin, Marc. *Conflicts of Interest and the Future of Medicine.* New York: Oxford University Press, 2011.

Rogers, William H., et al. "Outcomes for Adult Outpatients with Depression Under Prepaid or Fee-for-Service Financing." *Archives of General Psychiatry* 50 (1993): 517–525.

Rosenberg, Stephen N., et al. "Effect of Utilization Review in a Fee-for-Service Health Insurance Plan." *New England Journal of Medicine* 333 (1995): 1326–1330.

Sabin, James E. "Organized Psychiatry and Managed Care: Quality Improvement or Holy War?" *Health Affairs* 14 (1995): 32–33.

Sabin, James A., and Norman Daniels. "Public-Sector Managed Behavioral Health Care: II. Contracting for Medicaid Services—the Massachusetts Experience." *Psychiatric Services* 50 (1999): 39–41.

Smith, Vernon K., et al. *Moving Ahead Amid Fiscal Challenges: A Look at Medicaid Spending, Coverage and Policy Trends. Results from a 50-State Medicaid Budget Survey for State Fiscal Years 2011 and 2012.* Washington, DC: Henry J. Kaiser Family Foundation, 2011. Available online: www.kff.org/medicaid/upload/8248.pdf.

Soumerai, Stephen, et al. "Use of Atypical Antipsychotic Drugs for Schizophrenia in Maine Medicaid Following a Policy Change." *Health Affairs* 27 (2008): w185–w195.

Starr, Paul. *The Social Transformation of American Medicine.* New York: Basic Books, 1982.

Substance Abuse and Mental Health Services Administration. *Mental Health, United States, 2010.* HHS Publication No. (SMA) 12-4681. Rockville, MD: Substance Abuse and Mental Health Services Administration, 2012.

Swartz, Katherine. "The Death of Managed Care as We Know It." *Journal of Health Politics, Policy and Law* 24 (1999): 1201–1205.

Thompson, James W., et al. "Initial Level of Care and Clinical Status in a Managed Mental Health Program." *Hospital and Community Psychiatry* 43 (1992): 599–603.

Ware, John E., et al. "Differences in 4-Year Health Outcomes for Elderly and Poor, Chronically Ill Patients Treated in HMO and Fee-for-Service Systems: Results from the Medical Outcomes Study." *Journal of the American Medical Association* 276 (1996): 1039–1047.

Weingarten, Scott R., et al. "Interventions Used in Disease Management Programmes for Patients with Chronic Illness—Which Ones Work? Meta-Analysis of Published Reports." *British Medical Journal* 325 (2002): 925–928.

Wells, Kenneth B., Willard G. Manning, Jr., and Bernadette Benjamin. "Use of Outpatient Mental Health Services in HMO and Fee-for-Service Plans: Results from a Randomized Controlled Trial." *Health Services Research* 21 (1986): 453–474.

Wells, Kenneth B., Willard G. Manning, Jr., and Bernadette Benjamin. "Comparison of Use of Outpatient Mental Health Services in an HMO and Fee-for-Service Plans." *Medical Care* 25 (1987): 894–903.

Wells, Kenneth B., Willard G. Manning, Jr., and R. Burciaga Valdez. "The Effects of a Prepaid Group Practice on Mental Health Outcomes." *Health Services Research* 25 (1990): 615–625.

Wickizer, Thomas M., and Daniel Lessler. "Effects of Utilization Management on Patterns of Hospital Care Among Privately Insured Adult Patients." *Medical Care* 36 (1998): 1545–1554.

Williams, John W., et al. "Systematic Review of Multifaceted Interventions to Improve Depression Care." *General Hospital Psychiatry* 29 (2007): 91–116.

Zelman, Walter A. *The Changing Health Care Marketplace: Private Ventures, Public Interests.* San Francisco: Jossey-Bass, 1996.

Zhang, Yuting, et al. "Effects of Prior Authorization on Medication Discontinuation Among Medicaid Beneficiaries with Bipolar Disorder." *Psychiatric Services* 60 (2009): 520–527.

Zuvekas, Samuel H., et al. "The Impacts of Mental Health Parity and Managed Care in One Large Employer Group." *Health Affairs* 21 (2002): 148–159.

Zuvekas, Samuel H., and Joel W. Cohen. "Paying Physicians by Capitation: Is the Past Now Prologue?" *Health Affairs* 29 (2010): 1661–1666.

9

Mental Health Professions and Practice

All debates in the field of mental health—over such issues as how we conceptualize mental health or mental illness, the appropriate definitions of need for services, the treatment gaps, the relative value of different financing arrangements, the policies that harm or help, and the like—become real during the encounter between the practitioner and the individual with a mental health problem. People come into care seeking a professional whom they can trust, who will act in their best interest, and who will provide the best care possible. Sadly, however, the stories of people with mental illness and their families are often pervaded by frustration over their haphazard journeys from clinician to clinician, and from one treatment to the next, in the search for something that will relieve their suffering and promote stability.

Most mental health professionals are drawn to the field by altruistic motives and the desire to help. Nonetheless, how one practices is shaped not just by individual motivations and good intentions but also by the particular historical time and social context. Most practitioners today find themselves trying to deliver care in a climate of competing interests and ideologies that, though often unacknowledged, affects their ability to form therapeutic relationships with clients. While much has been made of the importance of having an adequate supply of mental health professionals (which is no doubt important), it is equally imperative to consider whether we are supporting a mental health system that makes possible trusting relationships between people with mental illnesses and the practitioners who have responsibility for their care.

Given the importance of the mental health professions, it is surprising so little good research is available to help us understand the full scope of how care is delivered. This chapter makes use of the best available evidence (although lacking in many areas) to describe the changing roles of mental health professionals. We then look at sociocultural influences on practice patterns and the difficult choices that must be made regarding the allocation of treatment resources.

MENTAL HEALTH PROFESSIONS AND THEIR WORK PATTERNS

As noted in Chapter 1, the four main professions that deliver mental health specialty services are psychiatry, clinical psychology, social work, and nursing. Other groups are also involved in service provision, but they are often less central than the four major mental health professions and they will not be found in every service program. These include case managers, family and marriage therapists, recreational therapists, counselors, specially trained clergy, job coaches and occupational therapists, rehabilitation therapists, and mental health aides. Definitions of these roles tend to be *ad hoc*, varying a great deal from one place to another. Some functions, such as case management, can apply either to master's level or even Ph.D. professionals who perform a complex set of therapeutic, linkage, and administrative responsibilities, or to others with less than a college education and no specialized training. Thus, knowing only the title tells you relatively little about the capacities and responsibilities of a professional or quasi-professional staff member.

It is quite difficult to track the changing work patterns of mental health personnel because many data sources are incomplete and commonly based on inconsistent criteria for inclusion in the enumerated group. Large national data sources, such as the federal expenditure surveys and ambulatory care utilization surveys, are fairly representative but do not include all items of interest, or they exclude nonphysicians. Other studies, based on samples of volunteers who agree to report on their professional practices, are much smaller and typically involve significant sample selection bias. In general, although we have much information on psychiatrists, there is only very incomplete information on many other mental health clinicians, who have become increasingly important for the delivery of care.

Even knowing the size of the workforce is difficult, with each source of potential data having weaknesses (Ellis et al. 2009). Membership lists in national professional organizations miss the many practitioners who are in practice but do not join such organizations. Counts of individuals who are licensed to practice may double count those licensed in more than one jurisdiction, while different jurisdictions may have varying standards for licensing. Neither membership nor licensing takes into account whether or not someone is actively practicing. The Bureau of Labor Statistics collects data on the number of persons employed in different occupations, but it fails to record educational level or licensing status. Another way of estimating the number of mental health personnel is to examine full-time equivalent (FTE) staff in mental health organizations by using data that were collected for many years by the federal government's Center for Mental Health Services (Duffy et al. 2006). Yet this source excludes private practitioners and those practicing in nonspecialty organizations, thereby significantly underestimating the role of psychologists and psychiatrists in office-based practice. Moreover, the most recent data available are from 2000. While we draw on each of these sources to describe changing patterns of work, the numbers of mental health professionals presented in Table 9.1, which reflect the most recent data available, are still rough estimates, at best, of total workforce.

A psychiatrist is a medical doctor who usually has completed four years of a psychiatric residency consisting of intensive training in dealing with clinical psychiatric problems. Even in the case of counting psychiatrists, numbers can be a bit dicey. Any doctor, whether having specialized training in psychiatry or not, can declare himself or herself a specialist in psychiatry, although most doing this work do get board certification that

Table 9.1	**Number of Clinically Trained Mental Health Professionals by Discipline**		
		N	Percent
Psychiatry (2010)		43,732	6.3
Psychology (2010)		93,498	13.5
Social Work (2008)		244,900	35.3
Nursing (2008)		133,791	19.3
Counseling (2008)		128,886	18.6
Marriage and Family Therapy (2006)		48,666	7.0
Total		**693,473**	

Source: Estimates for psychiatrists come from the American Medical Association Physician Masterfiles and exclude inactive physicians (American Medical Association 2012). Estimates for psychologists include APA members in 2010 who indicate that they are not retired (American Psychological Association, Center for Workforce Studies 2011). Estimates for social workers come from the Association of Social Work Boards estimates of the number of licensed social workers with MSW degrees (Substance Abuse and Mental Health Services Administration 2012, Table 109). Estimates for nurses are based on the number who indicated "Psychiatric or mental health substance abuse and counseling" as their speciality area at primary nursing position (U.S. Department of Health and Human Services 2010). Estimates for marriage and family therapists and counseling are from *Mental Health, United States, 2010* (Substance Abuse and Mental Health Services Administration 2012, Table 109, p. 286).

requires residency training and examination. As per data from the American Medical Association (2012), 43,732 psychiatrists were active in patient care in the United States in 2011. Adjusting for size of the country's population, the relative supply of psychiatrists has not changed since 2000. As in the past, psychiatrists continue to be concentrated in large urban states, largely in the Northeast and California, the number varying from about 15 to 35 per 100,000 population. The District of Columbia also has a startlingly high rate at 59 psychiatrists per 100,000. In contrast, psychiatrists are few in number in the Southern states, where rates vary from 7 to 11 per 100,000 persons (Substance Abuse and Mental Health Services Administration 2012).

There are fewer psychiatrists than other mental health professionals, but psychiatrists have a disproportionate role in caring for the sickest patients. Compared with other practitioners, they see relatively more patients with schizophrenia, bipolar disorder, major depression, and substance abuse, and fewer patients with anxiety, less serious depression, and other complaints (Duffy et al. 2006).

Many psychiatrists practice in multiple settings. Over time, however, psychiatrists have become increasingly likely to play administrative roles and less likely to be active in direct patient care (Duffy et al. 2006). Psychiatrists are now also less involved than previously in hospitals and more involved in other organized mental health settings. In general, psychiatrists have begun to gravitate toward work in clinics and individual and group practice.

The content of psychiatrists' work continues to change. According to data from the National Ambulatory Care Surveys, which include visits to office-based physicians, the proportion of all visits to a psychiatrist where a psychotropic drug was prescribed increased from about 73 percent in 1996–1997 to 86 percent in 2005–2006 (Mojtabai and Olfson 2010). At the same time, psychotherapy is less common. Between 1996 and 2005, the percentage of office visits to psychiatrists where psychotherapy was provided declined from 44 to 29 percent (Mojtabai and Olfson 2008). The percentage of psychiatric practices that do not offer psychotherapy also increased from 25 to 29 percent over the study period. Time spent with each patient in office-based practice fell from about 39 minutes in 1999 to 33 minutes in 2006, a reflection of high workloads, less favorable remuneration arrangements, and changing practice orientations (Cherry, Burt, and Woodwell 2001; Cherry et al. 2008).

That psychiatrists can sometimes find themselves playing roles of extraordinary breadth is undoubtedly true. For an intriguing example, one need go no further than the work of a Harvard psychiatrist employed during the 1980s as consultant for the New England Patriots football team. Among his tasks were teaching techniques "to program the mind to achieve peak athletic performance" and "meeting with team members before a game to help prepare them psychologically for a competition" (Nicholi 1987). Other functions included using individual therapy, helping prevent drug use, helping resolve conflicts among team members, and improving relations between coach and players. Curiously, the prestigious *New England Journal of Medicine*, which rations its space in the most parsimonious way, judged this story of psychiatric consultation in football to merit more than five pages of discussion, while articles on the problem of chronic mental illness are a rarity in the publication.

Psychiatrists continue to have the greatest professional influence within the mental health sector, despite their small numbers, because of the prestige of their training and the advantage they have in being recognized by all payers as reimbursable providers. They also have a level of authority regarding care provided in medical settings that is unmatched by other mental health professionals.

A clinical psychologist is not a medical doctor but rather someone who has had several years of graduate work in psychology and a clinical internship. Most clinical psychologists hold a Ph.D. degree; there is also a professional psychology degree (Psy.D.) that is more treatment oriented and provides less training in research. Graduate programs in clinical psychology are a blend of instruction in theory, practice, and conducting research. Although psychiatrists are likely to have a broader understanding of medical issues and in-depth experience with different types of clinical psychiatric problems during their residency training, a clinical psychologist is likely to be better versed in psychological theory and research, to have a clearer understanding of the scientific bases of assessment and treatment, and to have a more critical awareness of the mental health research literature. Clinical psychologists are less likely than either psychiatrists or social workers to treat persons with the most severe and persistent mental disorders. All states license the practice of psychology and most require, in addition to the doctoral degree, two years of supervised clinical training and the passing of a state-administered examination (Dial et al. 1992).

Doctoral-level psychologists largely function as independent professionals, typically in office-based practice, but there are many more individuals holding master's degrees in psychology who work in closely supervised roles within mental health service agencies.

Our estimate of the supply of psychologists in 2010 (93,498), like others (Substance Abuse and Mental Health Services Administration 2012), is based on membership in the American Psychological Association (APA) (American Psychological Association 2011). However, only about 62 percent of these members identify their primary employment as being in the health/mental health fields; thus, a more conservative estimate of the supply of mental health psychologists in 2010 is about 58,000. But again this is very rough, as the figure omits psychologists who are licensed but not members of APA.

In 2008, the APA Center for Workforce Studies conducted a study of members identified as providing health/mental health services, including a supplemental sample of psychologists who were licensed but not members, in order to better understand the work patterns of psychologists providing services in the health field (Michalski and Kohout 2011; Michalski, Mulvey, and Kohout 2010). About 46 percent of the respondents were primarily employed in private practice with only 12 percent employed in hospitals. A subset of the total sample was selected to gather more detailed information about financing of care. Just over one-third in this group indicated they had contracts with behavioral health carve-outs. Overall, approximately 43 percent of psychologists' clients were covered by private insurance, with 21 percent self-pay and only 10 percent Medicaid. Indeed, the vast majority of respondents (about 70 percent) said they did not participate in Medicaid, the program that enrolls many of the nation's most severely mentally ill. The most common reasons for nonparticipation centered on unsatisfactory levels of reimbursement and delays in getting paid.

Another source of information on the changing practice of psychology is a series of surveys conducted periodically between 1960 and 2010 with samples of the membership of the clinical Psychology section of APA (Norcross and Karpiak 2012). Results show a dramatic change in the theoretical orientation of psychologists. While 35 percent of respondents identified psychodynamics as their primary approach to therapy in 1960, only 18 percent did so in 2010. Cognitive approaches to therapy are much more popular currently and have been endorsed as the primary therapeutic method by 31 percent of respondents in 2010, in contrast to about 2 percent of respondents in 1973. However, the percentage of psychologists who said they spend most of their time providing psychotherapy declined from 87 percent in 1986 (the first year this question was asked) to 76 percent in 2010. Simultaneously, there has also been a large decline in the employment of psychologists in hospital settings; respondents who reported they were primarily employed in psychiatric or general hospitals fell from approximately 30 percent in 1960 to 6 percent in 2010.

During the past few decades, clinical psychologists have begun advocating for legal privileges to prescribe a limited range of psychiatric drugs. This proposal has sparked debate among different mental health stakeholders, with strong resistance by professional psychiatry organizations. Another opponent is the National Alliance on Mental Illness, whose concerns include patient health and safety as well as the issue of proper medical supervision. So far, legislation has only been successful in New Mexico and Louisiana, which both require psychologists to complete additional training in psychopharmacology as part of the criteria for certification (Fox et al. 2009). A number of other proposals are pending around the country, and it is difficult to say how the situation will play out. However, due to the shortage of psychiatrists and an ongoing search for efficiencies under managed care, it is likely psychologists will attract at least some allies in their effort to expand existing professional authority.

Social workers make up the largest proportion of the mental health work force reviewed here, but accurate estimates of their numbers are even more difficult to find than for other groups. The master's in social work (M.S.W.) is considered the terminal professional practice degree. A greater number of students receive the bachelor's in social work and have limited clinical experience. The Ph.D. in social work is a research degree. While most who receive this degree also have an M.S.W., some do not. Most states license or certify social workers, although requirements vary. Additional postgraduate qualifications can also be attained by social workers, the most important being admission to the Academy of Certified Social Workers. These qualifications may be necessary for reimbursement of services under some insurance programs.

As with other professional groups, workforce size depends on definitions of who should be counted. The U.S. Bureau of Labor Statistics (BLS) estimated there were about 590,000 social workers in 2011, of whom 115,000 were classified as mental health and/or substance abuse social workers (U.S. Department of Labor, Bureau of Labor Statistics 2012). However, the BLS does not categorize job descriptions by level of education, so it is impossible to know how many of these social workers were master's level or how many were licensed.

The estimate of 244,900 social workers presented in Table 9.1, which comes from the Center for Behavioral Health Statistics and Quality, includes only licensed social workers with an M.S.W. degree (Substance Abuse and Mental Health Services Administration 2012). A survey of social workers in 2004, however, indicated that only 40 percent of licensed social workers identified mental health (37 percent) or addictions (3 percent) as their primary practice specialty (Whitaker et al. 2006).

Looking more carefully at this latter subgroup of "behavioral health care social workers" provides a better sense of practice patterns than examining the entire population of social workers. Behavioral health care workers are most likely to work in either private practice (37 percent) or behavioral health clinics/outpatient facilities (21 percent), with only 8 percent working in psychiatric hospitals. Almost all respondents to the 2004 survey said they spent at least part of their time in direct client care, most seeing clients they identified as having a mental illness (60 percent), depressive disorder (56 percent), psychosocial stressors (87 percent), or some combination of these problems. The most common source of health insurance for clients of these specialty social workers was private coverage (42 percent) followed by Medicaid (33 percent).

Graduate programs in social work have traditionally emphasized psychosocial causes of mental health problems, social casework, and community organization. In recent years, such training has become more diversified, giving attention to coping theory and crisis intervention, cognitive behavorial therapy, family therapy and behavior modification, the development of community care programs, and the administration of social programs.

Historically, psychiatric social workers have not wielded great clout as a member of the mental health professional quartet. Most have worked on a salaried basis in clinics and social agencies, although many are also individual therapists who contract with managed behavioral health organizations. Independent reimbursement is increasingly possible, although clinicians usually require a MSW, 3,000 or more hours of post-masters supervised clinical experience, state licensure or certification, and malpractice insurance coverage. Reimbursement is also provided by Medicaid and Medicare. Reimbursement processes, however, can be onerous for social workers in individual or small practices. Because social work services are less expensive than those provided by psychiatrists and psychologists, managed care organizations have increased use of the former and this has strengthened the position of social work over time, although not necessarily in financial terms.

The final specialty mental health profession considered here is nursing. Nursing plays a major role in mental health services, but there is large variability in personnel ranging from nurses' aides and licensed practical nurses to registered nurses, psychiatric nurses, nurse practitioners, psychiatric nurse specialists, and nurses with Ph.D.s and postgraduate training. In 2008, about 6 percent of the registered nurse workforce (or 134,000 nurses) comprised specialty mental health providers (U.S. Department of Health and Human Services 2010). Nurses in this group have different types of training, from two-year community college associate degrees to the increasingly more common four-year bachelor of nursing degree.

The nursing profession has never wielded influence commensurate with its numbers and central role in inpatient care. Nurses traditionally have been subservient to doctors in all specialties, but nursing has fought vigorously in the last several decades to define sources of independent authority. They have achieved this by requiring increased credentials, by developing new independent roles as nurse practitioners and nurse specialists, and by creating an independent academic structure within universities to train nurse Ph.D.s. The profession has also lobbied successfully for an independent nursing institute at the National Institutes of Health that supports nursing research while elevating the standing of nursing as a profession with its own evidence-based knowledge base.

A graduate degree in psychiatric nursing provides not only more training but also relatively more authority in the mental health system, including the right to prescribe in most jurisdictions. Advanced practice psychiatric nurses (APPN) include nurses with graduate training as clinical nurse specialists (CNS) who specialize in either adult or child and adolescent psychiatry, and nurse practitioners (NP) with additional specialization in psychiatric care. Current reforms for the licensing of APPNs include ending separate credentialing of CNS personnel in psychiatric care, although retaining the credentialing for NPs (Jones and Minarik 2012). In 2008, an estimated 22,471 nurses possessed graduate degrees in psychiatric nursing, with about one-half of them certified.

A national survey of APPNs conducted in 2008 allows us to draw tentative conclusions about practice patterns. Still, the response rate was very low so it is not clear how well the results represent all providers of this type (Drew and Delaney 2009). There has been some movement of APPNs out of hospital care. In 2008, only 20 percent reported working in hospitals, compared to about 29 percent in 1994 (Drew and Delaney 2009). About 30 percent of APPNs were self-employed, with 18 percent working in community mental health agencies. As with psychologists and social workers, the most common psychotherapeutic approach used by practitioners belonging to this group was cognitive/cognitive behavioral therapy. APPNs also appear to be treating the seriously mentally ill, with 11 percent of those who specialize in adult psychiatry naming schizophrenia as the most common diagnosis of their clients.

Curiously, while psychiatric nursing was more central in an earlier period, and also the field from which many national nursing leaders originated, it has not become a dominant profession in the delivery of mental health services (Mechanic and Reinhard 2002). One possible reason is that historically most psychiatric nurses in mental health practiced in institutional settings where medical dominance had strongly established itself. Also, mental health nursing must compete in practice and in politics not only with medicine but also with psychology and social work. Managed care, however, strengthens nursing roles in mental health relative to psychiatry and psychology because nurse services cost less and nurse roles are highly adaptable, ranging from psychotherapy and medication management to unit organization, group therapy, and utilization review.

As already noted, there is longstanding geographic imbalance in the distribution of mental health providers, particularly psychiatrists. In general, mental health services remain concentrated in highly populated urban areas, especially in the Northeast and California, and this pattern holds regardless of type of provider.

TRUST AND THE MENTAL HEALTH PROFESSIONS

Mental health practice is more sensitive to issues of trust than many other aspects of health care because mental illness tends to involve the entire personality and identity of an individual and there are serious threats of stigmatization and discrimination. Moreover, psychotherapy delves into intimate private material in what one thoughtful psychiatrist has referred to as the *confessional model* of psychiatry (Sabin 1997). Thus, patients and their families are rightly concerned that caregivers act on their behalf and as their agents, that they advocate for their needs, and that they rigorously protect confidential information. A study of trust among patients with serious illness, for example, found that patients with mental illness were much more concerned about confidentiality than patients with breast cancer (Mechanic and Meyer 2000). In mental health practice, interpersonal processes are pivotal for relieving distress and achieving personal change, whether in psychotherapy or in rehabilitation. For this reason, the quality and continuity of relationships between patients and practitioners take on even greater importance than in other types of care.

To say that one trusts a mental health professional is to say we anticipate that they will perform their responsibilities competently, that they will act in our interest, and that they will be able to exercise appropriate control over the course of our treatment (Mechanic 1996; Mechanic and Schlesinger 1996). Historically, mental health practice has often deviated from such trust conditions because professionals functioned within organizations that served the community and social control needs as much as the requirements of individual patients. Much care was provided on an involuntary basis. By contrast, in contemporary situations, involuntary care is less common. Yet other challenges to trust have emerged, deriving from the changing organization of care and the practice of utilization management by behavioral health care companies and their reviewers. It is now common for third parties to become involved in the details of a patient's problems and treatment, and for sensitive information to be shared among therapeutic, managerial, and administrative personnel. Beyond the good or bad influences that managed care might have, to the extent that managed care practices jeopardize trust in the system and individual professionals, they reduce the likelihood that patients will seek mental health care, talk about sensitive personal information, and adhere to therapeutic advice or otherwise cooperate in treatment. Achieving and maintaining trust is a major component of effective mental health practice, but it is challenged in the contemporary mental health care environment.

All mental health professionals are affected in their activities and judgments by sociocultural context; by their social and personal biographies; by the perspectives, theories, and scientific conceptions of their respective disciplines and professions; and by the economic and organizational constraints of their practice settings. Mental health practice involves varied, sometimes competing, roles. A social worker who provides therapy may assume different perspectives and responsibilities than a social worker who serves as a utilization reviewer responsible for cost containment. Although mental health workers sometimes select themselves into certain specialized roles and forgo others, many end up playing multiple professional roles with no clear demarcation among them. Deinstitutionalization notwithstanding, professional practice in mental health care retains important social control functions. In general, mental health professionals are inherently political actors to the extent that their practice involves working with individuals in regard to questions of conformity, relationship to authority, and achievement of human potential in a given social context.

Most of the research to which we refer in the following discussion focuses on doctors and psychiatrists; there is much less systematic evidence regarding other mental health professionals. However, most observations apply equally well to mental health care by different categories of practitioners. Indeed, as psychiatrists are increasingly confining their efforts to medication and treatment supervision, more interpersonal therapies and rehabilitation efforts are now being performed by social workers, nurses, psychologists, and other mental health workers.

Freidson (1970), in an influential analysis, noted the basic distinction between practitioners and scientists. The goal of the physician is treatment rather than acquisition of knowledge. The physician believes in his or her treatment recommendations, and this can be beneficial in its own right for both doctor and patient. If therapists truly believe in what they are doing, and communicate their confidence and hope to patients, this becomes a powerful ingredient in care giving. Alternatively, skeptical detachment, so necessary in science, may discourage the patient and undercut the suggestive power of the therapeutic relationship when it becomes too much a part of the practice role. While the scientist seeks to develop or test a coherent theory, the clinician is a pragmatist, depending heavily on subjective experience, and trial and error, in situations of uncertainty. While the scientist seeks to determine regularity of behavior in relation to abstract principles, the clinician is more subjective and suspicious of the abstract. Indeed, the responsibilities of clinical work make it difficult to suspend action, to remain detached, and to operate without faith that one is helping patients.

Thus, the demands of science and the responsibilities of clinical work may collide in the practice of evidence-based medicine (EBM). The Evidence-Based Medicine Working Group, a team of scientists from McMaster University, is credited with introducing its namesake term into the American medical literature (Guyatt et al. 1992). This group stressed the need to base decisions less on intuition and clinical experience and more on objective evidence.

In the last few decades, the industry of producing treatment checklists, guidelines, and the like has flourished. Organizations such as the Cochrane Collaboration, the United States Preventive Services Task Force, and many others have grown in influence while generating thousands of reviews of evidence in various areas of medical care. (For an excellent review of the history and politics of EBM, see Timmermans and Berg 2003.) At least in concept, the medical system has embraced EBM in that it is now integral to the curriculum in many medical schools, insurers are much more likely than they once were to make coverage decisions based on standards of evidence, and the approach underpins the current movement toward use of comparative effectiveness research for assessing different treatment options.

The ideology of EBM has migrated to the mental health arena under the language of evidence-based practice (EBP). The American Psychological Association, for example, endorsed EBP as a policy "to promote effective psychological practice and enhance public health by applying empirically supported principles of psychological assessment, case formulation, therapeutic relationship, and intervention" (American Psychological Association 2005, p. 1). EBP has long been influential in the practice of social work in the United Kingdom, but observers of the U.S. system see its growing influence here too (Cournoyer 2005). The George Warren Brown School of Social Work at Washington University became the first program of its type to fully integrate EBP into its curriculum beginning in 2001 (Howard, McMillen, and Pollio 2003). Subsequently, this effort has caught on in other schools as well. Internationally, the Cochrane model for reviewing medical evidence has been replicated by the Campbell Collaboration, which produces systematic reviews for social welfare interventions (Davies and Boruch 2001).

In sum, EBM/EBP has become the dominant paradigm for discourse around the practice of medicine in general, and in mental health care more specifically. But the model is not without critics (Cooper 2003; Gray, Plath, and Webb 2009). Some view these developments as responsible for an overly standardized and positivistic approach to health care that disregards fundamental uncertainties and complexities in the caregiving process while devaluing the patient's individuality. A disconnect also remains between the belief that evidence matters, on the one hand, and the translation of this belief into actual practice, on the other. Simply put, despite the proliferation of EBP, few practitioners actually deliver care consistent with research-based standards. Some attribute this problem to an essential conflict between the demands of science and the essential nature of mental health practice. Donald Peterson, a figure who was immensely influential in the establishment of professional psychology, summed up the problem concisely: "[S]cience and practice are not the same, and no monistic ideology can make them the same" (Peterson 2004, cited in Tanenbaum 2005, p. 167). Clinicians can see the value of EBP, but they simultaneously hang onto beliefs that experiential knowledge, or idiosyncratic cases, should inform the reality of practice. In a study of faculty in M.S.W. programs, over 90 percent of respondents agreed that evidence from experiments would be sufficient to determine whether an intervention was scientifically supported (Rubin and Parrish 2007), a finding that proponents of EBP should consider encouraging. And yet, more than one-half also thought that qualitative research could be sufficient to support an evidence-based intervention, and more than 40 percent viewed case studies as potentially determinative in a treatment situation.

Divergence between the objectives of science and practice suggests alternative ways of proceeding in the two roles. The mental health researcher must be concerned with precise and reliable diagnosis. Only through careful distinctions among varying clinical entities can knowledge of etiology, course, and effective treatment be acquired (Mechanic 1978). Although efforts to identify new conditions, or make fine distinctions among existing problems, may be uncertain and yield no immediate benefits for the patient, the process is crucial for scientific inquiry and understanding. This same diagnostic orientation, however, when used in a clinical context, may be of little use or even prove dysfunctional. The labeling of questionable conditions may induce anxiety in the patient, add to stigmatization, and even divert constructive clinical interventions.

Consider the situation with the *Diagnostic and Statistical Manual of Mental Disorders* (DSM). The *DSM* undoubtedly has contributed to greater precision in identification of psychiatric disorders, just as it has provided a basis for improved communication among researchers. But to achieve reliability—that is, a high level of agreement among different clinicians when using the manual to assess patients—it has eliminated consideration of context. By contrast, clinicians routinely take into account the context in which symptoms occur (Horwitz and Wakefield 2007, 2012). For example, the *DSM* defines clinical depression by the number of symptoms experienced by the patient, their persistence, and the degree to which they interfere with functioning. A clinician, in contrast, will take into account whether the symptoms might be a normal response to a life event such as the loss of a job or the breakup of a relationship. Even if the patient's symptoms meet formal *DSM* criteria, the clinician may find it much more practical to focus on approaches to dealing with the stressors in the patient's life. Depending on circumstances, the clinician may or may not see a need for medication.

Because mental health treatment is concerned with deviant feeling states and behavior, its standards for illness and well-being intersect with societal conceptions of acceptable behavior, personal worth, and morality. Behavior can be viewed from competing vantage points, and thus is amenable to varying professional stances. In the absence of clear evidence on etiology or treatment, personal disturbance is subject to interpretation as biological in nature; a result of developmental failures; a moral crisis; or a consequence of socioeconomic, social, or structural constraints. Remedies, in turn, may focus on biological restoration, moral realignment, social conditioning, or societal change. Although all these possibilities might coexist in the same situation, the emphasis given to one over another by the clinician has both ideological and practical implications. There is no completely neutral stance. Diagnostic and therapeutic judgments have political and social implications (Halleck 1971).

And, so, the question arises, to whom does the therapist owe primary loyalty? To the extent that he or she acts exclusively as the patient's representative and in the patient's best interest (as far as this can be known), the situation is relatively simple. The patient suffers and seeks assistance; the role of the therapist is to do whatever possible to define available options and to proceed in an agreed-upon manner. Whether intervention occurs at the biological, psychological, or social level, the definition of the endeavor must be in line with the patient's interests, needs, and preferences. In real situations, failure to define treatment options is common, and the clinician's own values, ideologies, and practice orientations may intrude. This is so because clinicians may neither be conscious of their own ideologies and orientations nor acknowledge the underlying assumptions and expectations of the systems in which they practice. Or, clinicians may proceed against patient wishes because they assume greater knowledge of the patient's interests. Despite these complexities, the patient-oriented approach is distinctive in that actions taken are for the sake of the individual in treatment and no other.

It is true that the ethical codes of all mental health professions endorse a responsibility to the patient above all else, but this is one of several possible values and norms of practice. Increasingly, clinicians are expected to be resource allocators as well as advocates, balancing the needs of individual patients against the needs of the collectivity, whether the latter refers to a particular health care organization, the community at large, or the polity and society. Individual patient values sometimes contrast with collective norms—this tension expresses itself in one way or another in many therapeutic encounters. The dynamic also can vary across different societies or across time and circumstance within a single society. A comparative example is instructive here. Historically, in the People's Republic of China, psychiatric practice was a public function with primary commitment to the interests of the state, not the individual (Kleinman and Mechanic 1979). Intervention took place openly and in consultation with family members and community leaders. The situation was handled as a public issue, and information concerning the patient's problems and management commonly was shared with officials and work supervisors. Although the basic content of psychiatry was seen as biological, the social consequences of psychiatric advice received recognition. Recently, with the movement of China to a market economy, the mental health care system has been transformed (Kleinman et al. 2011; Park et al. 2005). Most people lack any access to formal mental health services, community systems of care have dissolved, stigma is high, and there are widespread reports of neglect and abuse of persons with severe mental illness (LaFraniere 2010). Against a tumultuous social backdrop, then, traditional methods of response have unraveled, leaving patients in a kind of no-man's-land between collectivism and individualism marked by fractured clinical responsibilities. In short, professional practice cannot be divorced from existing forms of social organization. As the latter changes, shifts in the former become inevitable.

China and the United States are two very different nations, with two very different mental health systems, but the question of whom the clinician represents, as well as the proper scope of confidentiality, are critical issues everywhere in the care of those who are mentally ill. Many families of patients in the United States express bitter dissatisfaction about their dealings with professionals who seem intent on excluding them from the treatment process concerning a severely ill child or spouse (Copeland and Heilemann 2011; Hatfield 1987; Tessler, Killian, and Gubman 1987). Sometimes the only channel of communication is between the therapist and patient, although patients and their families may have close relationships and mutual obligations, maintenance of which is crucial to the therapeutic enterprise. Further, effective care of patients with chronic mental illness often hinges on communication with landlords, police, employers, and others in a way that strains the ethic of confidentiality for patient–therapist relationships as traditionally practiced.

Individual patients may seek out mental health clinicians for personal reasons using their own funds. These are the circumstances under which professionals tend to enjoy their greatest autonomy in acting as agents for their patients. But there are many other organizational contexts likely to encroach on this orientation (Halleck and Miller 1963). The most dramatic examples are found in totalitarian countries, where psychiatrists are state bureaucrats performing explicit social control functions. A predicament different in degree, but perhaps not in kind, occurs when a clinician practices on behalf of a court system, prison, school, or corporate entity. Whenever the organization that employs the therapist has needs or interests that are potentially at odds with those of the patient, the clinician will be caught in a struggle over divided loyalties. These are hazardous conditions for the mental health practitioner, particularly in regard to the possibility that a mantle of professionalism could be used to cloak the competing agendas surrounding delivery of mental health care. Even in a familial context, couples therapy or therapy involving parents and children typically produces a clash of wills and interests, with resulting demands for the therapist to take sides. In such situations, therapists must walk a difficult line focusing all parties' attention on common ground so that the therapeutic encounter can be sustained to a beneficial outcome.

The influence of outside stakeholders in medical treatment sometimes can be so pervasive that it goes almost unnoticed, yet it may present blatant conflicts of interest. A good case example is involvement of the drug industry in the practice of mental health care. For many years, doctors welcomed drug company representatives into their offices. Clinicians saw no problem accepting gifts, dinners, and lavish trips from these salespeople. Some of the most distinguished psychiatrists in the country routinely received large grants from both the federal government and the pharmaceutical industry to investigate the effectiveness of various psychotropic drugs, while at the same time earning hundreds of thousands of dollars from drug companies in speaker fees to promote these same drugs. Only in recent years have such practices come under serious discussion, with media attention spotlighting the most flagrant examples (Harris and Carey 2008). In response, many universities and some states have implemented measures to prohibit some of these practices and to make others at least more transparent.

This is not to say that psychiatrists who enjoy such ties with the drug industry are necessarily corrupt, although many clearly benefit from the professional prestige that comes with winning research dollars not to mention monetary rewards to their own pocketbooks. The point is that questionable influence is often more subtle than one would expect. In his recent memoir, *Unhinged*, Daniel Carlat (2010), a psychiatrist, gives a fascinating account of the processes at work. What makes his story so relevant and engaging is that he writes not as an outsider, slamming "Big-Pharma," but rather as an insider who once viewed the medical benefits of psychotropic drugs in idealistic terms. Carlat details how the small incentives offered by drug companies, such as lunches, and the larger incentives, such as speaker fees, combined to influence his prescribing behavior. Simply put, he argues, "Drug companies treat doctors like royalty because we hold the keys to their kingdom of riches" (Carlat 2010, p. 105). And being treated as royalty, not surprisingly, influences judgment and behavior. Carlat describes how over time his practice was reduced to short, 15-minute meetings with patients to monitor drug response, and if necessary, to provide referral for counseling with another mental health provider.

Carlat cites a 2006 Gallup poll in which only 38 percent of the public believed that psychiatrists have high or very high ethical standards. The same question was repeated in a survey in 2009, and trust in psychiatrists fell to about 33 percent (Jones 2011). While people seem to trust psychiatrists more than HMO managers (8 percent), or Senators (11 percent), psychiatrists fall much below medical doctors in general (65 percent), or nurses (83 percent). (Nursing has always ranked in these polls as the most trusted health occupation). To the degree these generalized feelings of distrust may inhibit care-seeking and following treatment advice, we should be concerned that so many Americans apparently question the honesty and ethics of the most powerful profession in the mental health field.

SOCIAL INFLUENCES ON PSYCHIATRIC JUDGMENT

In most instances in which psychiatric judgments are made, there are no reliable independent tests to confirm or contest them. Judgments of disorder are tied to social contexts, and the clinician's understanding is based not only on clinical training but also normal life experience. Most laypersons can recognize the bizarre symptoms associated with psychosis. It is the borderline areas that are more at issue, and at these borders it becomes difficult to disentangle subculture, illness behavior, and psychopathology.

As the subcultural situation lies further from the psychiatrist's own firsthand experience, likelihood increases that inappropriate contextual norms will be applied. To the extent that the patient comes to the therapist voluntarily and seeks relief from suffering, the lack of precision in making contextual judgments is less of a concern than when the mental health professional acts on behalf of some other interest. Even in the former situation, however, the prestige of the therapist reinforces considerable personal power in the encounter with the patient. This imbalance between professional and patient may predispose in favor of a particular view of the presenting problem.

The absence of procedures or laboratory tests to establish diagnoses independent of the therapist's judgment makes it relatively easy for critics to insist that psychiatrists label patients on the basis of social, ethical, or legal norms, rather than clearly established evidence of psychopathology (Rosenhan 1973; Szasz 1960). Although such criticisms cannot really speak to the scientific validity of the application of a disease model to the patient's suffering or deviant behavior (Mechanic 1978; Spitzer 1976), they do apply to the multifaceted role of practitioner as both clinician and social agent. The mental health professional who mediates conflicts between husband and wife, between parent and child, between employer and employee, and between citizens and official agencies inevitably intermixes social judgments with assessments of psychopathology. When the practitioner acts as a gatekeeper to justify absence from work or school, to obtain special preference for housing or other program benefits, to document eligibility for disability payments, or to excuse deviant behavior, he or she may present judgments that are, in part, as much social and personal as scientific. For insight into this dynamic, it becomes essential to know something about the social orientations and worldviews of psychiatrists and other clinicians who make these judgments.

PERSONAL AND SOCIAL BIOGRAPHIES

Most of the research on how individuals come to mental health occupations centers on psychiatrists. Psychiatrists have gone through a variety of selective screenings involving entry into medical school; psychiatric specialization; and particular types of psychiatric functions, such as individual psychotherapy, psychopharmacology, hospital work, or administration. This selective process is influenced not only by the applicant's academic performance and interests but also by his or her social background, values and ideologies, and individual aspirations.

Studies show that physicians who select psychiatry differ in social and psychological characteristics from candidates who select other medical specialties and even differ among those choosing different mental health subspecialties. Both the nature of specialties and characteristics of student cohorts change over time, affecting the choices made, but it remains informative to note some of the selection processes observed in various research studies. Some medical specialties (such as surgery, radiology, and urology), for example, have been predominantly male, while others (such as pediatrics, anesthesiology, dermatology, psychiatry, and, more recently, primary care) have had higher representations of women (Hoff 2010). Jewish doctors and more liberal candidates were drawn disproportionately to psychiatry and pediatrics. Earlier studies, when psychodynamics were dominant, found that psychiatry attracted individuals who were playful about ideas and liked abstractions, while family doctors were highly gregarious but not conceptual and surgeons were concrete in their thinking and moralistic. Psychiatry candidates tended to score very high on a scale of Machiavellianism, while surgeons were very low (Christie and Geis 1970; Colombotos, Kirchner, and Millman 1975; Mechanic 1983).

Differences in attitudes, orientations, and even social backgrounds distinguished among psychiatrists who chose varying approaches to practice. In their classic book, *Social Class and Mental Illness*, Hollingshead and Redlich (1958) described the dramatically different social biographies of psychiatrists in New Haven who adopted analytic-psychological orientations as compared with those more directive in their approaches and those focused on organic interventions. More recent books on psychiatric residency training (Klitzman 1995; Luhrmann 2001) describe the two separate cultures of psychiatry—the biological and psychodynamic—that attract adherents with different backgrounds and personalities and are often at war with one another.

Past research has shown that despite the fact that many psychiatrists in office-based practice used both drugs and psychotherapy, those psychodynamically oriented were more similar in social characteristics and perspectives to therapists from psychology and social work than to their colleagues in psychiatry who were more medically inclined (Henry, Sims, and Spray 1971, 1973). Individuals who chose to do psychotherapy, regardless of profession, performed similar activities, had comparable work styles, shared many viewpoints, and had strikingly similar social backgrounds.

The implications of similarities in development and perspective among therapists are not obvious but certainly provocative. It seems reasonable to hypothesize that therapists who share particular backgrounds, personalities, and perspectives and who prefer different specialties and subspecialties (Borges and Savickas 2002) may see social and moral issues differently from other social groups. Because therapists' personalities and orientations are important ingredients in psychotherapy, and because psychotherapy is largely an influence process (Frank 1974), the provider–patient encounter inevitably involves transmission of values. In traditional psychoanalytic therapy, clinicians are careful to reveal very little about themselves in order to encourage the patient to transfer to them psychological reactions developed with parents and other personally significant figures. Even if therapists wish to limit direct personal influence, however, they cannot help but communicate something about what they value and stand for. To the extent that this social identity is transparent to the patient, it may actually be less confusing than when obscured by a professional mystique.

The growth of psychodynamic therapy in the United States can be viewed as a social movement. It developed first among urban patients and practitioners who grappled together with questions and choices that often had a significant existential component (Mechanic 1975). Many practitioners were of urban, middle-class, Jewish origins. Treatment of this type initially attracted clients with social inclinations and characteristics similar to those of therapists. Not surprisingly, however, as the movement grew and therapy became more widely accepted in the culture, it became more heterogeneous in geographic distribution and in the characteristics of both therapists and patients. Data collected by Greenley, Kepecs, and Henry (1981) for Chicago illustrate this trend. Comparing surveys of Chicago psychiatrists in 1962 and 1973, those in 1973 reported seeing more women, Blacks, Catholics, and poor persons as patients, and fewer Jewish patients.

The Chicago data, as well as other research, indicate that psychiatric practice has become more varied and complex (Olfson and Pincus 1996; Redlich and Kellert 1978). Psychodynamic therapy is not as doctrinaire as it once was. The emergence and spread of alternative schools of therapy and practitioners is even more important. Such trends, which represent a healthy diversity within psychiatry and other mental health professions, promise to provide greater opportunity for prospective patients as they seek to locate therapists whose orientations they find compatible and productive.

THE SOCIOCULTURAL CONTEXT

The sociocultural context in which young clinicians develop and mature and within which they practice has a dramatic influence on their worldview as well as the scope of their professional activities. Various historical periods and specific cultural contexts provide their own images of the nature of humanity, the boundaries of deviance, and the role of professionals in psychiatric, as well as social, intervention.

In Europe in the late 1800s, psychiatry was closely aligned with general medical practice. This remained true despite the advent of the Freudian school, which occupied a minor role in European psychiatry and whose "talking cure" largely catered to a well-heeled clientele struggling with neurotic difficulties. When psychoanalytic concepts spread to the United States in the early twentieth century, however, they became more popular than in any other country, and psychiatrists viewed the practice of psychodynamic therapies as more prestigious than taking care of patients with severe and persistent mental illness (Hale 1971). In the post–World War II period, as psychodynamic ideas came to dominate residency programs, they strongly shaped the way psychiatrists defined their roles and practiced their craft. Why the United States and not Europe was the more fertile ground for psychoanalytic ideas is amenable to many interpretations; nevertheless, the fact is that it was, and this reality had important implications for views of psychopathology and the selection and treatment of patients.

The 1960s was a period of great change in U.S. society characterized by social activism and an ideology that government could effectively attack social problems. This ideology had a broad sweep that came to encompass social conceptions of causes of and remedies for mental illness. Caught up in the ethos of the time, psychiatrists began making grandiose claims regarding the potentialities of "community psychiatry." Such advocacy was not grounded in effective implementation of programs for the increasing number of patients with chronic mental illness who were being returned to communities, but rather in far-reaching notions of special societal expertise. In the words of one such advocate, "The psychiatrist must truly be a political personage in the best sense of the word. He must play a role in *controlling* the environment which man has created" (Duhl 1963, p. 73).

Central to this new ideology was the notion that psychiatry could engage in primary prevention to limit the occurrence of mental illness. Gerald Caplan, a noted psychiatrist, maintained that such efforts involved identifying harmful influences, encouraging environmental forces that support individuals in resisting these influences, and preventing the population from succumbing to future illness. In short, the program being offered under the guise of psychiatric expertise was largely a form of social and political action.

Caplan wished psychiatrists to become involved in matters such as morality and values on which there were many views and differences of opinion. He even went so far as to speculate that a psychiatrist might "exercise surveillance over key people in the community and...intervene in those cases where he identifies disturbed relationships in order to offer treatment or recommend dismissal" (1964, p. 79). In the end, Caplan rejected this idea not because he felt psychiatrists lacked ability or knowledge, but because he judged it would be a distasteful role for most psychiatrists to play and because of political and social complications.

Some concepts implicit in early preventive psychiatry were unfortunate not only because they were grandiose, naive, and an obvious projection of political values, but also because they diverted attention from simpler, more pragmatic programs based on actual knowledge and expertise. Preventive care during pregnancy and adequate postnatal care constitute important measures against developmental delays, prematurity, brain damage, and a variety of other difficulties. The system of services in the community for patients with chronic mental illness, still deficient in our own contemporary period, was fragmentary at best 40 years ago. By what set of values should we divert attention away from these pressing issues to pursue illusory goals? The greatest weakness of preventive psychiatry in the 1960s was the substitution of vague ideals for tangible action, as well as a failure to specify how psychiatric expertise could be applied to achieve the goals being advocated.

In general, it is essential from an ethical perspective to differentiate the multiple professional roles one occupies as a mental health professional. In the role of researcher, for example, it is fully appropriate to examine the value of various interpersonal interventions in preventing mental illness. Caplan (1964) maintained that crises and transitional periods in the life span, such as entering school, having a child, going to the hospital for surgery, or moving to a new environment, all pose severe stresses that may burden a person's coping capacities and entail high risk of social breakdown. He asserted that such periods stimulated a heightened desire for, and receptivity toward, professional help. Thus, community psychiatrists should seek out situations in which individuals feel vulnerable and provide them with supportive assistance and new coping techniques. According to this theory, social breakdowns could be prevented either by psychiatric intervention or by more active involvement on the part of other professionals, such as doctors, nurses, teachers, and administrators, who naturally come into contact with people during these crises in such settings as surgical wards, divorce courts, and colleges. The basic hypothesis, and one worthy of continuing detailed inquiry, is that it is possible to give people anticipatory guidance and emotional inoculation to improve their capacity for coping with threatening events (Mrazek and Haggerty 1994; O'Connell, Boat, and Warner 2009).

Yet when the role of a mental health professional moves from research investigation to actual practice, the hypothesis of crisis intervention can raise major ethical dilemmas. First, although aspects of the theory of prevention are promising, the theory is based on the conceptualization that environmental stress and lack of personal coping abilities cause major mental illness, an analysis for which evidence is incomplete and inadequate. Second, although such efforts may be inspired by laudable goals, the evaluation literature is rife with examples of experimental interventions in health care and other fields that not only failed to achieve desired objectives but actually made matters worse (Dishion, McCord, and Poulin 1999; McCord 1978; Robins 1979). Third, there is really very little evidence that many types of troubleshooting advocated by preventive psychiatrists, although perhaps valuable in reducing distress, will have significant impact on the occurrence of mental illness. Despite these concerns, mental health professionals might justifiably engage in such programs with interested community groups to the extent that the latter understand the limitations and elect to participate voluntarily. But interventions of this kind need to be viewed in the same way as any other uncertain therapy whose possible positive and adverse effects must be balanced.

Eventually, in the 1970s and 1980s, psychiatry moved closer to mainstream medicine by adopting a more restricted biological focus, although preventive work has remained an important stream of professional activity. In a 1986 survey of psychiatric residents and faculty at the University of California, Los Angeles, more than half believed preventive interventions in psychiatry are almost always appropriate, and almost four-fifths reported that preventive psychiatric interventions are generally worth the amount of time they take. But a degree of skepticism also surfaced. Almost two-fifths believed or thought it possible that, while preventive psychiatry sounds good in concept, there is little evidence in support of its effectiveness (Linn, Yager, and Leake 1988).

Preventive psychiatry now aspires to identify individuals early who might have mental health problems and to get them into treatment, mostly putting aside the kinds of broad efforts at social change that marked the 1960s. Take, for example, this suggestion from the President's New Freedom Commission on Mental Health (2003): "Emerging research indicates that intervening early can interrupt the negative course of *some* mental illnesses and *may*, in *some* cases, lessen long-term disability" [emphasis ours] (p. 57). This seems an extraordinarily equivocal statement for a major policy, and there is not great depth of analysis to support it. In the case of psychotic disorders, where such an argument is commonly advanced, there is at best only very weak support (Norman and Malla 2001). The commission endorsed a program to give all school youngsters a computer-based behavioral health screening questionnaire. It also advocated training teachers and others to recognize behavioral problems in children and to make appropriate referrals for assessment. All these approaches inevitably involve many false positives. The commission failed to consider the consequences of intervening and labeling children so many of whom, in reality, are merely experiencing transitory and self-limiting difficulties. The fact is parents and teachers already can identify many more students in need than available services can handle. It would be unwise to divert resources away from this population by ambitious new screening approaches that are poorly conceived.

Preventive psychiatry seems intuitively enticing, of course. After all, isn't it always better to prevent illness than to treat it after it occurs? Moreover, proponents typically argue that prevention can save large amounts of money, because treating severe illness is much more expensive than initial preventive care. But as we have learned so well in the area of general medical care, this reasonable-sounding argument is simplistic and often incorrect (Russell 1986, 1987). The success of prevention and potential savings depends on the ability to target individuals who will become more seriously ill without treatment, in addition to the cost and effectiveness of the preventive action. But even when we have interventions believed to be efficacious and not too costly, preventive efforts may still be a bad bargain in the absence of precise targeting. The number of people who become seriously mentally ill is a small proportion of the population. In contrast, the number of people who could become potential targets of prevention is very large. Even a relatively inexpensive intervention averaged over large numbers can result in tremendous aggregate costs. But many of these people get better without formal intervention. Data from the National Comorbidity Study-Replication, for example, have been used to make the claim that about 60 percent of the population possess indicators of needing mental health treatment each year (Druss et al. 2007). Assuming this only applies to adults, that still equates to about 141 million people. An individual intervention costing $100, not a particularly expensive one by psychiatric standards, would be an astronomic expenditure.

Earlier it was noted that mental health professionals often function in bureaucratic roles. Preventive psychiatry is particularly on shaky ground in these circumstances because the "clients" may be neither seeking nor desiring the services. Imposition of mental health interventions in schools, divorce courts, welfare agencies, and the like—with legitimacy derived from the coercive authority of the organization—can be a serious intrusion on privacy and the right of persons to refuse treatment. Even if preventive interventions were more certain and more efficacious than they are, involuntary application of services offered under threat of coercion raises serious ethical questions.

Today, the concept of prevention in mental health care remains in flux, a field of uncertain science in which well-formulated programs and services have, nonetheless, produced persuasive benefits for some at-risk groups, particularly children and adolescents (Lorion and Allen 1989). It does not seem too much to say that psychiatry has two faces—a reformist perspective prone, at times, to social and political overreach versus a more conventional medical model oriented to treating individual patients with medications and other therapies whose effectiveness is often exaggerated. Although each side has something to learn from the other, the relationship between the two has been the source of considerable discomfort and misunderstanding within the profession (Luhrmann 2001). At the same time, it provides a revealing portrait of the fitful process by which psychiatry has evolved as a social institution, all the while continuing to debate its mission and capabilities.

CONSTRAINTS OF PRACTICE ORGANIZATION AND SETTINGS

Professional practice is shaped by organizational context and the manner of payment for services. With utilization review and capitated practice becoming dominant forces in the mental health marketplace, supplanting the once-common fee-for-service plans, the influence of the purchaser on professional decisions is now widely recognized. The only providers still able to escape the dominion of managed care are those who rely solely on revenue from patients who pay out-of-pocket.

Changes in the organization of care lead to changes in the type of treatment that is possible. Traditional psychotherapy was organized in time units of 45–50 minutes as often as every day or a couple of times a week, and the course of treatment often extended for long periods of time, sometimes years. Therapists viewed themselves as solely responsible to their patients, not to insurance programs or abstract notions of community need. The form of payment used—fee-for-service per session—created an incentive for the professional to see the patient often and to continue therapy possibly beyond the point of cost-effectiveness, although no simple method exists for measuring and valuing all the benefits of treatment.

In contrast, clinicians working under capitated models of managed care have a dual role of caring for individual patients while shouldering the burden of reasonable allocation of resources among a larger group of actual and potential recipients of services. Health plans must also consider the economic viability of how they distribute care. Managed care principles prohibit providing services simply to everyone who wants, or even who might benefit from, them. Instead, rationing decisions must be made concerning who in the population most needs specialized mental health services and to what extent. When signing on with such organizations, clinicians yield some of their practice autonomy by accepting an important amount of external influence over the scope and character of the services they will provide.

It is typical for mental health professionals to bemoan the inadequacy of mental health financing and rationing, but it is unlikely that sufficient mental health resources could ever be available to serve all those who might need or request treatment. There are no easy ways out of the dilemma posed by the need to ration, and it is clear that however we ration, we must do so in a way trusted by the public and those who use mental health services. Mental health practitioners have an ethical obligation to evaluate their techniques and approaches in relation to benefits and costs. Increasingly, providers in the mental health sector are approaching this problem through use of evidence-based therapies and interventions.

In allocating mental health treatments, two highly controversial issues concern the services that should be covered and the types of clients who should receive service priority. Mental health practitioners have an intellectual investment in psychotherapeutic services, but there is limited evidence that psychotherapies add much value beyond drug treatment for a large number of people with treatable disorders. Certain patients can do as well with psychotherapy as with medications, but such treatment usually takes longer. Some studies suggest that patients with serious disorders do best with a combination of medication and psychotherapy, but this does not amount to justification of public financing for therapies lacking an evidential basis or that are not cost-effective. The growth of managed care puts great pressure on therapists to formulate treatment plans that are focused and time-limited. Nevertheless, tensions continue to swirl around the question of how much psychotherapy to reimburse and for what patients.

A second contentious issue concerns the definition of which patients should have priority for mental health specialty care. Many people defined in epidemiological studies as having a disorder might not need treatment; others who need it might not be aware of their needs or how to get care; and still others do not want it. Public attitudes about treatment vary a great deal. Public policy should focus on those who have the most serious mental disorders and associated disabilities and the least ability to take care of themselves.

Although, in principle, it is relatively easy to agree that services should be distributed in relation to need and that practice should focus on what is cost-effective, the lack of evidence on cost-effectiveness and the ambiguity of the concept of need provide much to disagree about. Moreover, need and cost-effectiveness may be in conflict. For example, some preventive interventions or treatment of people with minor disorders might yield results, while more intensive and expensive interventions among those with the most severe disabilities might improve outcomes only modestly or not at all. But values also play an important part in this calculation because caring for people with serious disorders in a humane way and offering them hope, even when no effective therapy exists, is a recognized and important goal. Allocating limited resources fairly and intelligently is inherently a challenging task, and one bound to occupy the attention of mental health professionals for many years to come.

CONCLUSION

There is much acrimony inside the mental health arena owing to disputes over treatment and funding priorities among advocacy groups. Mental health constituencies have different views depending on the illness populations they represent (more severe versus less severe disorders), age groups (children, adults, and the elderly), and interest in particular types of services (prevention versus treatment, inpatient care versus outpatient treatment, medications versus psychotherapy, mental illness versus substance abuse treatment, treatment versus rehabilitation). Groups representing these various standpoints compete vigorously and sometimes in a destructive way. Lack of trust across constituencies has made it difficult to develop strategies and approaches that maximize the impact of mental health advocacy or that help resolve competing interests and the ideological and value conflicts involved.

However much we might disdain interest-group politics, the reality is that mental health care, like medicine more generally, has become big business. Many groups have a huge financial stake in how things are done (Mechanic 2006). As we have seen, the pharmaceutical industry is a very formidable participant constantly seeking to develop new and larger markets for psychiatric drugs. They do this by helping define new diagnostic entities that can benefit from medication, by direct-to-consumer advertising, by the practice of detailing to physicians, by sponsorship of psychiatric meetings and publications, by funding clientele groups who demand more access to services, and much more. Many other stakeholders are in the fray as well, including hospital entities, private psychiatric facilities, nursing homes, managed behavioral health care organizations, health plans, consumer and family groups, and the list goes on.

In this light, mental health professionals and their associations must also be seen as a key structural interest in the mental health arena, one whose expertise, numbers, access to decision makers, historical oversight of the system, and social standing virtually guarantee them a voice at the table when important policy choices are made. It is not a position to be taken lightly, nor one that permits any evasion of the essential question: How can the vested interests of the group be advanced while upholding an established code based on values of objectivity, service, fairness, cooperation, quality, and compassion?

References

American Medical Association. *Physician Characteristics and Distribution in the United States*. 2012 Edition. Chicago, IL: American Medical Association, 2012.

American Psychological Association. *Policy Statement on Evidence-Based Practice in Psychology*. August 2005. Available online: www.apa.org/practice/resources/evidence/evidence-based-statement.pdf.

American Psychological Association. *2010 APA Member Profiles*. Washington, DC: American Psychological Association, Center for Workforces Studies, 2011. Available online: www.apa.org/workforce/publications/10-member/tables.pdf.

Borges, Nicole J., and Mark L. Savickas. "Personality and Medical Specialty Choice: A Literature Review and Integration." *Journal of Career Assessment* 10 (2002): 362–380.

Caplan, Gerald. *Principles of Preventive Psychiatry*. New York: Basic Books, 1964.

Carlat, Daniel J. *Unhinged: The Trouble with Psychiatry—A Doctor's Revelations About a Profession in Crisis*. New York: Free Press, 2010.

Cherry, Donald K., Catharine W. Burt, and David A. Woodwell. *National Ambulatory Medical Care Survey: 1999 Summary*. Advance Data from Vital and Health Statistics, No. 322. Hyattsville, MD: National Center for Health Statistics, 2001. Available online: www.cdc.gov/nchs/data/ad/ad322.pdf.

Cherry, Donald K., et al. *National Ambulatory Medical Care Survey: 2006 Summary*. Advance Data from Vital and Health Statistics, No. 3. Hyattsville, MD: National Center for Health Statistics, 2008. Available online: www.cdc.gov/nchs/data/nhsr/nhsr003.pdf.

Christie, Richard, and Florence L. Geis. *Studies in Machiavellianism*. New York: Academic Press, 1970.

Colombotos, John, Corinne Kirchner, and Michael Millman. "Physicians View National Health Insurance: A National Study." *Medical Care* 13 (1975): 369–396.

Cooper, Brian. "Evidence-Based Mental Health Policy: A Critical Appraisal." *British Journal of Psychiatry* 183 (2003): 105–113.

Copeland, Darcy A., and MarySue V. Heilemann. " 'Choosing the Best of the Hells': Mothers Face Housing Dilemmas for Their Adult Children with Mental Illness and a History of Violence." *Qualitative Health Research* 21 (2011): 520–533.

Cournoyer, Barry R. "The Future of Evidence-Based Social Work: An Optimistic View?" *Advances in Social Work* 6 (2005): 68–78.

Davies, Philip, and Robert Boruch. "The Campbell Collaboration Does for Public Policy What Cochrane Does for Health." *British Medical Journal* 323 (2001): 294–295.

Dial, Thomas H., et al. "Training of Mental Health Providers." In *Mental Health, United States, 1992*, edited by Ronald W. Manderscheid and Mary Anne Sonnenschein, pp. 142–162. DHHS Publication No. (SMA) 92-1942. Washington, DC: U.S. Government Printing Office, 1992.

Dishion, Thomas J., Joan McCord, and Francois Poulin. "When Interventions Harm: Peer Groups and Problem Behavior." *American Psychologist* 54 (1999): 755–764.

Drew, Barbara L., and Kathleen R. Delaney. "National Survey of Psychiatric Mental Health Advanced Practice Nursing: Development, Process and Findings." *Journal of the American Psychiatric Nurses Association* 15 (2009): 101–110.

Druss, Benjamin G., et al. "Understanding Mental Health Treatment in Persons Without Mental Diagnoses: Results from the National Comorbidity Survey Replication." *Archives of General Psychiatry* 64 (2007): 1196–1203.

Duffy, Farifteh F., et al. "Mental Health Practitioners and Trainees." In Center for Mental Health Services, *Mental Health, United States, 2004*, edited by Ronald W. Manderscheid and Joyce T. Berry, pp. 256–309. DHHS Publication No. (SMA) 06-4195. Rockville, MD: Substance Abuse and Mental Health Services Administration, 2006.

Duhl, Leonard J., ed. "The Changing Face of Mental Health." In *The Urban Condition: People and Policy in the Metropolis*, edited by Leonard J. Duhl, pp. 59–75. New York: Basic Books, 1963.

Ellis, Alan R., et al. "County-Level Estimates of Mental Health Professional Supply in the United States." *Psychiatric Services* 60 (2009): 1315–1322.

Fox, Ronald E., et al. "Prescriptive Authority and Psychology: A Status Report." *American Psychologist* 64 (2009): 257–268.

Frank, Jerome D. *Persuasion and Healing: A Comparative Study of Psychotherapy*, revised edition. New York: Schocken Books, 1974.

Freidson, Eliot. *Professional Dominance: The Social Structure of Medical Care*. New York: Atherton, 1970.

Gray, Mel, Debbie Plath, and Stephen A. Webb. *Evidence-Based Social Work: A Critical Stance*. New York: Routledge, 2009.

Greenley, James R., Joseph G. Kepecs, and William H. Henry. "Trends in Urban American Psychiatry: Practice in Chicago in 1962 and 1973." *Social Psychiatry and Psychiatric Epidemiology* 16 (1981): 123–128.

Guyatt, Gordon, et al. "Evidence Based Medicine: A New Approach to Teaching the Practice of Medicine." *Journal of the American Medical Association* 268 (1992): 2420–2425.

Hale, Nathan G., Jr. *Freud and the Americans: The Beginnings of Psychoanalysis in the United States, 1876–1917*. New York: Oxford University Press, 1971.

Halleck, Seymour L. *The Politics of Therapy*. New York: Science House, 1971.

Halleck, Seymour L., and Milton H. Miller. "The Psychiatric Consultation: Questionable Social Precedents of Some Current Practices." *American Journal of Psychiatry* 120 (1963): 164–169.

Harris, Gardiner, and Benedict Carey. "Researchers Fail to Reveal Full Drug Pay." *The New York Times*, published June 8, 2008. Available online: www.nytimes.com/2008/06/08/us/08conflict.html?pagewanted=all.

Hatfield, Agnes, ed. *Families of the Mentally Ill: Meeting the Challenges*. New Directions for Mental Health Services, No. 34. San Francisco: Jossey-Bass, 1987.

Henry, William E., John H. Sims, and S. Lee Spray. *The Fifth Profession: Becoming a Psychotherapist*. San Francisco: Jossey-Bass, 1971.

Henry, William E., John H. Sims, and S. Lee Spray. *Public and Private Lives of Psychotherapists.* San Francisco: Jossey-Bass, 1973.

Hoff, Timothy. *Practice Under Pressure: Primary Care Physicians and Their Medicine in the Twenty-First Century.* New Brunswick, NJ: Rutgers University Press, 2010.

Hollingshead, August B., and Fredrick C. Redlich. *Social Class and Mental Illness: A Community Study.* New York: John Wiley and Sons, 1958.

Horwitz, Allan V., and Jerome C. Wakefield. *The Loss of Sadness: How Psychiatry Transformed Normal Sorrow into Depressive Disorder.* New York: Oxford University Press, 2007.

Horwitz, Allan V., and Jerome C. Wakefield. *All We Have to Fear: Psychiatry's Transformation of Natural Anxieties into Mental Disorders.* New York: Oxford University Press, 2012.

Howard, Matthew O., Curtis J. McMillen, and David E. Pollio. "Teaching Evidence-Based Practice: Toward a New Paradigm for Social Work Education." *Research on Social Work Practice* 13 (2003): 234–259.

Jones, Jeffrey M. *Record 64% Rate Honesty, Ethics of Members of Congress Low.* Gallup Organization, December 12, 2011. Available online: www.gallup.com/poll/151460/Record-Rate-Honesty-Ethics-Members-Congress-Low.aspx.

Jones, Jeffery S., and Pamela A. Minarik. "The Plight of the Psychiatric Clinical Nurse Specialist: The Dismantling of the Advanced Practice Nursing Archetype." *Clinical Nurse Specialist* 26 (2012): 121–125.

Kleinman, Arthur, and David Mechanic. "Some Observations of Mental Illness and Its Treatment in the People's Republic of China." *Journal of Nervous and Mental Disease* 167 (1979): 267–274.

Kleinman, Arthur, et al. *Deep China: The Moral Life of the Person, What Anthropology and Psychiatry Tell Us About China Today.* Berkeley: University of California Press, 2011.

Klitzman, Robert. *In a House of Dreams and Glass: Becoming a Psychiatrist.* New York: Simon and Schuster, 1995.

LaFraniere, Sharon. "Life in Shadows for Mentally Ill in China." *The New York Times,* November 10, 2010. Available online: www.nytimes.com/2010/11/11/world/asia/11psych.html?pagewanted=all.

Linn, Lawrence S., Joel Yager, and Barbara Leake. "Psychiatrists' Attitudes Toward Preventive Intervention in Routine Clinical Practice." *Hospital and Community Psychiatry* 39 (1988): 637–642.

Lorion, Raymond P., and LaRue Allen. "Preventive Services in Mental Health." In *Handbook on Mental Health Policy in the United States,* edited by David A. Rochefort, pp. 403–432. Westport, CT: Greenwood Press, 1989.

Luhrmann, Tanya M. *Of Two Minds: An Anthropologist Looks at American Psychiatry.* New York: Vintage Books, 2001.

McCord, Joan. "A Thirty-Year Follow-up of Treatment Effects." *American Psychologist* 33 (1978): 284–289.

Mechanic, David. "Sociocultural and Socio-Psychological Factors Affecting Personal Responses to Psychological Disorder." *Journal of Health and Social Behavior* 16 (1975): 393–404.

Mechanic, David. *Medical Sociology,* 2nd ed. New York: Free Press, 1978.

Mechanic, David. "Physicians." In *Handbook of Health, Health Care, and the Health Professions,* edited by David Mechanic, pp. 432–454. New York: Free Press, 1983.

Mechanic, David. "Can Research on Managed Care Inform Practice and Policy Decisions?" In *Controversies in Managed Mental Health Care,* edited by Arnold Lazarus, pp. 197–211. Washington, DC: American Psychiatric Press, 1996.

Mechanic, David. *The Truth About Health Care: Why Reform Is Not Working in America.* New Brunswick, NJ: Rutgers University Press, 2006.

Mechanic, David, and Sharon Meyer. "Concepts of Trust Among Patients with Serious Illness." *Social Science and Medicine* 51 (2000): 657–668.

Mechanic, David, and Susan Reinhard. "Contributions of Nurses to Health Policy: Challenges and Opportunities." *Nursing and Health Policy Review* 1 (2002): 7–15.

Mechanic, David, and Mark Schlesinger. "The Impact of Managed Care on Patients' Trust in Medical Care and Their Physicians." *Journal of the American Medical Association* 275 (1996): 1693–1697.

Michalski, Daniel S., and Jessica L. Kohout. "The State of the Psychology Health Service Provider Workforce." *American Psychologist* 66 (2011): 825–834.

Michalski, Daniel S., Tanya Mulvey, and Jessica Kohout. *2008 APA Survey of Psychology Health Service Providers: Preliminary Results*. American Psychological Association, Center for Workforce Studies. Washington, DC: American Psychological Association, 2010. Available online: www.apa.org/workforce/publications/08-hsp/report.pdf.

Mojtabai, Ramin, and Mark Olfson. "National Trends in Psychotherapy by Office-Based Psychiatrists." *Archives of General Psychiatry* 65 (2008): 962–970.

Mojtabai, Ramin, and Mark Olfson. "National Trends in Psychotropic Medication Polypharmacy in Office-Based Psychiatry." *Archives of General Psychiatry* 67 (2010): 26–36.

Mrazek, Patricia J., and Robert J. Haggerty, eds. *Reducing Risks for Mental Disorders: Frontiers for Preventive Intervention Research*. Washington, DC: National Academy Press, 1994.

New Freedom Commission on Mental Health. *Achieving the Promise: Transforming Mental Health Care in America: Final Report*. DHHS Publication No. SMA-03-3832. Rockville, MD: U.S. Department of Health and Human Services, 2003.

Nicholi, Armand M., Jr. "Psychiatric Consultation in Professional Football." *New England Journal of Medicine* 316 (1987): 1095–1100.

Norcross, John C., and Christie P. Karpiak. "Clinical Psychologists in the 2010s: 50 Years of the APA Division of Clinical Psychology." *Clinical Psychology: Science and Practice* 19 (2012): 1–12.

Norman, Ross M.G., and Ashok K. Malla. "Duration of Untreated Psychoses: A Critical Examination of the Concept and Its Importance." *Psychological Medicine* 31 (2001): 381–400.

O'Connell, Mary Ellen, Thomas Boat, and Kenneth E. Warner, eds. *Preventing Mental, Emotional, and Behavioral Disorders Among Young People: Progress and Possibilities*. National Research Council and Institute of Medicine Committee on the Prevention of Mental Disorders and Substance Abuse Among Children, Youth, and Young Adults: Research Advances and Promising Interventions, Board on Children, Youth, and Families, Division of Behavioral and Social Sciences and Education. Washington, DC: The National Academies Press, 2009.

Olfson, Mark, and Harold A. Pincus. "Outpatient Mental Health Care in Nonhospital Settings: Distribution of Patients Across Provider Groups." *American Journal of Psychiatry* 153 (1996): 1353–1356.

Park, Lawrence, et al. "Mental Health Care in China: Recent Changes and Future Challenges." *Harvard Health Policy Review* 6 (2005): 35–45.

Peterson, Donald R. "Science, Scientism, and Professional Responsibility." *Clinical Psychology: Science and Practice* 11 (2004): 196–210.

Redlich, Fritz, and Stephen R. Kellert. "Trends in American Mental Health." *American Journal of Psychiatry* 135 (1978): 22–28.

Robins, Lee N. "Longitudinal Methods in the Study of Normal and Pathological Development." In *Psychiatri der Gegenwart*, vol. 1, 2nd ed., edited by Karl Peter Kisker, et al., pp. 627–684. Heidelberg: Springer-Verlag, 1979.

Rosenhan, David L. "On Being Sane in Insane Places." *Science* 179 (1973): 250–258.

Rubin, Allen, and Danielle Parrish. "Views of Evidence-Based Practice Among Faculty in Master of Social Work Programs: A National Survey." *Research on Social Work Practice* 17 (2007): 110–122.

Russell, Louise B. *Is Prevention Better Than Cure?* Washington, DC: The Brookings Institution, 1986.

Russell, Louise B. *Evaluating Preventive Care: Report on a Workshop*. Washington, DC: The Brookings Institution, 1987.

Sabin, James E. "What Confidentiality Standards Should We Advocate for in Mental Health Care, and How Should We Do It?" *Psychiatric Services* 48 (1997): 35–36.

Spitzer, Robert L. "More on Pseudoscience in Science and the Case for Psychiatric Diagnosis." *Archives of General Psychiatry* 33 (1976): 459–470.

Substance Abuse and Mental Health Services Administration. *Mental Health, United States, 2010*. HHS Publication No. (SMA) 12-4681. Rockville, MD: Substance Abuse and Mental Health Administration, 2012.

Szasz, Thomas S. "The Myth of Mental Illness." *American Psychologist* 15 (1960): 113–118.

Tanenbaum, Sandra J. "Evidence-Based Practice as Mental Health Policy: Three Controversies and a Caveat." *Health Affairs* 24 (2005): 163–173.

Tessler, Richard, Lewis M. Killian, and Gayle D. Gubman. "Stages in Family Response to Mental Illness: An Ideal Type." *Psychosocial Rehabilitation Journal* 10 (1987): 3–16.

Timmermans, Stefan, and Marc Berg. *The Gold Standard: The Challenge of Evidence-Based Medicine and Standardization in Health Care*. Philadelphia, PA: Temple University Press, 2003.

U.S. Department of Health and Human Services, Health Resources and Services Administration. *The Registered Nurse Population. Findings from the 2008 National Sample Survey of Registered Nurses.* Rockville, MD: U.S. Department of Health and Human Services, 2010. Available online: bhpr.hrsa. gov/healthworkforce/rnsurveys/rnsurveyfinal.pdf.

U.S. Department of Labor, Bureau of Labor Statistics. *Economic News Release, Occupational Employment and Wages, May 2011*. USDL-12-0548. Washington, DC: U.S. Bureau of Labor Statistics, 2012. Available online: www.bls.gov/news.release/ocwage.htm.

Whitaker, Tracy, et al. *Assuring the Sufficiency of a Frontline Workforce: A National Study of Licensed Social Workers, Special Report: Social Work Services in Behavioral Health Care Settings*. Washington, DC: National Association of Social Workers, 2006. Available online: workforce.socialworkers.org/studies/ behavioral/behavioral.pdf.

10

Building an Effective Community Support System

Knowledge, Aspirations, and Social Policy

Building a comprehensive approach to mental illness and its management requires social policies firmly based on clinical expertise, organizational capacity, and knowledge of evidence-based practice. The "rubber hits the road" when individual patients enter particular treatment settings seeking care, but what mental health professionals can do for patients, and even what consumers can do for themselves, depends on social policies over which neither professionals nor consumers have much immediate control. In a very real sense, providing outstanding care and future opportunities for persons with serious mental illness "takes a village," to borrow a phrase. However excellent the clinician—whether social worker, psychologist, nurse, or psychiatrist—what can be accomplished reflects, in part, the instruments made available and allowable through social policy.

The goal of recovery has gained traction among consumers, advocates, professionals, and administrators over recent years but the concept raises concerns. What, for example, can recovery realistically mean for persons with severe and persistent schizophrenia or bipolar disorder, or a child with severe autism? Working with members of the behavioral health community, the Substance Abuse and Mental Health Services Administration (Substance Abuse and Mental Health Services Administration 2011) identified four essential dimensions: overcoming or managing one's disease(s); having a stable and safe place to live; having meaningful daily activities that give life purpose together with the necessary independence, income, and resources that facilitate social participation; and fashioning social networks and relationships that provide support, friendship, love, and hope. This listing, in turn, is seen as corresponding to 10 guiding principles within the process of recovery: that it emerges from hope; encompasses the whole person; is driven by self-determination; has many pathways; is culturally influenced and relevant; is supported by allies and peers; is built through relationships and social networks; is supported by addressing trauma; involves strengths and responsibilities in relation to self, family, and community; and is based on respect.

Recovery pertains to the fundamental vision now underlying mental health care and is, of course, aspirational for individuals and for the system as a whole. The key from our perspective lies less with definitions and abstract recipes and more with the requisites for programmatic performance. In other words, working within the understood limits of biology and environment, what can be done to structure care and support so as to enhance patient functioning and promote the greatest quality of life possible? A great deal of research data has been compiled, and practical experience gained, over the past 50 years that help us to answer this question. That information is the substance of this chapter.

ASSESSING INSTITUTIONAL AND COMMUNITY ENVIRONMENTS

The realization that mental hospitalization could produce profound disabilities in patients above and beyond the conditions with which they were diagnosed was a major stimulus to the community care movement. Different investigators have described these disabilities as institutional neuroses, institutionalism, and so on (Zusman 1966). There are many indexes of this syndrome, but generally it can be recognized by apathy, loss of interest and initiative, lack of reaction to the environment or future possibilities, and deterioration in personal habits. Patients who have been in custodial mental hospitals, or other such institutions, for a long time tend to be apathetic about returning to a normal life and lose interest in self-maintenance. They may lack simple skills, such as using a telephone or being able to get from one place to another on their own. For a long time, observers believed this set of symptoms was entirely the consequence of psychiatric illness. However, the same disabilities caused by mental hospitals in the past are now being caused by restricted lives in some nursing homes, board-and-care facilities, and other residential contexts (Neugeboren 1997, 1999).

Erving Goffman (1961) provided one of the most provocative analyses of institutional influence on patients. In Goffman's terms, the mental hospital was a "total institution" whose key characteristic is "the handling of many human needs by the bureaucratic organization of whole blocks of people" (1961, p. 6). The central feature of total institutions is bringing together individuals to live in one place and under one authority, a situation that organizes the different features of life within an overall plan while breaking down the barriers usually separating different spheres. People are treated not as individuals but as groups, and are required to do the same things together. Activities are tightly scheduled, with the sequence officially imposed from above. The various enforced activities come under a single rational plan designed to fulfill the official aims of the institution.

In depicting the atmosphere of the overcrowded Saint Elizabeth's Hospital in Washington, DC, Goffman described the plight of mental patients in vivid terms. From his perspective, hospitalization in a mental institution led to betrayal of the patients, deprecated their self-image, undermined their sense of autonomy, and invaded their privacy. Hospital life required patients to adapt in a manner detrimental to readjustment to community life, while the "career" of a mental patient did irreparable harm to his or her future reputation. Goffman was highly sensitive to the deprivations of hospital life and, in particular, to the kinds of abuses commonly seen in large mental hospitals.

Goffman's view was one-sided, however, and very much presented from a middle-class perspective. Many deprivations identified by Goffman were not experienced by all, or even most, mental patients. Certain patients found it a relief to be hospitalized. The community situation from which they came was often characterized by extreme difficulty and extraordinary personal distress. Their living conditions were poor, the conflicts in their lives uncontrollable, and their physical and mental states had deteriorated. Such patients frequently were capable of harming themselves or others, or at least damaging their lives severely. Patients in mental hospitals often reported that hospital restrictions did not bother them, that they appreciated the physical care they received, and that the hospital—despite its restrictions—enhanced their freedom rather than restricted it (Linn 1969; Weinstein 1979, 1983).

Although Goffman made us aware of many aspects of total institutions harmful to patients, total institutions can have good or deleterious effects depending on a variety of factors. Total institutions—hospitals, monasteries, residential schools—are organizations for changing people and their identities. If participants share the goals and aspirations of an organization, their experiences in it may be worthwhile and desirable. If participants are involuntarily admitted and reject the identity assigned to them by the institution, residence in such an organization promises to be extremely stressful and could lead to profound disabilities in functioning. In short, patients who feel they should not be in the hospital and who resent the regimen imposed upon them find hospitalization a distressing experience. But there are many cooperative patients, and it is incorrect to assume that the effect of the hospital is uniformly damaging.

Total institutions vary widely in character. They differ in their size; staffing patterns; the organization of life within them; the pathways by which patients arrive; and expenditures of money, time, and effort. Goffman, in building a general model of total institutions, attributed to them all characteristics that may be specific to the particular hospital he studied, such as its size or staffing pattern. There is evidence that small hospitals with high personnel–patient ratios and large budgets perform their tasks better than those with the opposite characteristics (Ullmann 1967).

Thus, the picture of mental hospitalization is mixed. There are a number of circumstances when such facilities have negative effects on patients:

- Patients may have been involuntarily incarcerated in order to protect the community, and once inside the hospital little of a constructive nature may have been done for them.
- The hospital may not have made sufficient effort to maintain the patient's interpersonal associations and skills after removal from the community, which can deteriorate if the patient remains in the hospital for a significant period of time.
- Hospitalization may lead to stigmatization of the patient.
- The hospital may require adaptations for adjustment to the ward, adaptations that are inconsistent with patterns of behavior necessary for effective reintegration into the community.

In some hospitals, for example, patients have been rewarded for remaining unobtrusive and docile or they may have been punished for attempting to exercise too much initiative. Unwillingness to take initiative, however, may handicap patients in a community setting. Not all total institutions respond in this way; the unit staff often views the participation and initiative of patients as signs of improving health. Our attention should focus not on whether a hospital fits the overarching model of a total institution, but rather on specifying those aspects of such institutions that affect organizational performance.

The variables by which hospital performance may be judged are many. Traditionally, the major concern has been whether facilities protect the public and those patients in danger of harming themselves. Early studies of large institutions concentrated on such issues as how mental hospitals with many patients could be managed by small staffs and few professional personnel. Ivan Belknap (1956) devoted considerable attention to the work system of a large hospital and the manner in which aides developed a reward system for the purpose of maintaining a viable patient workforce. Later researchers evaluated the hospital in terms of its effects on patients' work performance, community participation, self-esteem, sense of initiative, responsibility in performing social roles, reduction of symptoms, and understanding of themselves and their illnesses. Studies of smaller, private hospitals gave greater attention to interaction among patients and staff, communication problems, and administrative conflicts and their effects on patients (Caudill 1958; Coser 1979; Stanton and Schwartz 1954; and for a review of this literature, see Perrow 1965).

Many investigators have been impressed with the importance of hospital ward atmosphere on the functioning and attitudes of patients (Kellam, Schmelzer, and Berman 1966; Stanton and Schwartz 1954). A similar concern with the influence of an environment's atmosphere also extends to other organizations, such as schools and universities. The basic idea is that the emotional tone, tension, attitudes, and feelings dominant on a ward affect the interactions among the patients, between patients and staff, and even among staff. These interactions, in turn, influence the patient's motivation, attitudes, and emotional state. For many years, the investigation of these ideas had been largely impressionistic because of the difficulty of measuring different ward environments and correlating these measurements with performance and symptom measures.

Moos (1974, 1997), however, developed a Ward Atmosphere Scale gauging the climate of ward life in terms of patient and staff perceptions of relationships, treatment, and administrative structure or system maintenance dimensions. Relationships included the involvement of patients on the ward, support among patients and staff, and the degree of open expression and spontaneity. Treatment dimensions included autonomy, practical orientation, personal problem orientation, and expression of anger and aggression. Administrative structure variables included order and organization, staff control, and program clarity. Moos used this scale to study many hospital wards in the United States and England, and profiles of ward atmosphere were used to examine treatment outcomes and patient adjustment. Programs that kept patients out in the community the longest had high scores on open expression of feelings in a context emphasizing a practical orientation, order and organization, staff control, and autonomy and independence. In contrast, programs with high dropout rates had little emphasis on involving patients, few social opportunities, and poor planning of activities. Patients in such programs had little interaction and little guidance, while staff were unresponsive to criticisms or patients' suggestions.

Clearly, in acknowledging the detrimental effects of institutions on people, we should not assume that institutional environments have not produced rehabilitative effects as well. While many traditional mental hospitals offered patients impoverished and unstimulating conditions, this does not reflect recent changes in hospital environments and many current efforts to enhance the personal skills and resources of patients. Too frequently, mental health workers have made the naive assumption that community life is always constructive, although particular family and community environments might have the same adverse effects on a patient's functioning and skills as a poor mental hospital. The issue is not so much whether patients are resident in a hospital as it is whether the environment to which they are exposed is a stimulating one for minimizing incapacities resulting from their illnesses and for maximizing potential for living a life of reasonable quality.

Inpatient care, while less important today than in previous decades, continues to be a major component of management of serious mental illness, although lengths of stay are low. Thus, patterns of inpatient care and their links with subsequent aftercare services have acquired great importance since patients are often still severely ill when leaving the hospital. Unfortunately, we know too little about the effects of varying inpatient interventions on how patients fare after discharge.

Mechanic and colleagues studied this issue in hospitals in New York State for a number of years between 1989 and 1997 (Mechanic 1997). Based on the literature (Olfson, Glick, and Mechanic 1993), they identified seven dimensions of care likely to have a positive effect on how well patients with schizophrenia do following hospital care: linkage of inpatient care to external services, medication education, medication management, illness education, family involvement, substance abuse treatment, and psychosocial rehabilitation. The research group surveyed 178 specialized psychiatric units in general hospitals, virtually all such units in the state, and found large variations in the extent to which staff gave attention to each of the seven dimensions. Units devoting efforts to mobilize family attention and resources also tended to give greater attention to linkage, which is crucial to a pattern of continuing care. Patients who had schizophrenia and also used street drugs proved most likely to fail to maintain their medication and to become homeless, indicating this is a population that needs specially targeted efforts for medication adherence and for linkage with aftercare services.

Relatively few studies have examined the community contexts and environments that stimulate patient functioning and sense of hope versus those associated with a morbid response. In an intriguing study referred to earlier, Brown and his colleagues (1962) followed a group of men with schizophrenia after release from the hospital. They assessed the severity of symptoms just before discharge and saw the patients again at home two weeks after discharge. During this home interview, they measured the amount of expressed emotion in the family, i.e., primarily hostility, dominance, and criticism. Patients returning to live with a relative who showed high emotional content of this type deteriorated more frequently than other patients. This finding was replicated in a variety of settings (Brown, Birley, and Wing 1972; Leff and Vaughn 1985; Vaughn and Leff 1976). Earlier in this book, we noted theoretical explanations of the link between stress and schizophrenic breakdown, and it remains possible that persons with schizophrenia cannot tolerate intense emotions. We still know little, however, about the types of environments that promote control over symptoms and social functioning. We do know that patients who have psychiatric impairments require incentives for activity and involvement, reinforcement for initiative and successful performance, and protection against an environment that is too demanding and too stimulating.

A wide range of treatment environments for patients with schizophrenia characterizes the contemporary era of community care. One early study by Segal and Aviram (1978) examined patients and proprietors of sheltered care in California. Sheltered care residents were disproportionately ages 50–65, had low education and low employment, and almost all had either never been married or had experienced broken marriages (95 percent). Nearly all residents were supported by welfare, with three-quarters receiving SSI. Although only moderately symptomatic and not particularly troublesome to the community, this population constituted a highly disabled group that was dependent on the community for its support.

Segal and Aviram examined the correlates of both *internal* and *external integration* among sheltered care residents. The first concept focused on the extent to which the person was involved in the sheltered facility and the extent to which operators assumed responsibility for mediating the person's needs and relationships with the community. The latter concept measured the relationship of the patient to the community in terms of access and participation. In the sample studied, there was much more internal than external integration. By far the most important factor in external integration was neighbor response, and the most important individual factor was availability of spending money.

Deinstitutionalization not only returned many patients to the community, it also involved transfers of patients from public hospitals to other community contexts, including nursing homes and intermediate care facilities. From a public policy perspective, it should be apparent that providing an effective environment for persons with mental illness is not simply a matter of whether they reside in hospitals or other types of institutions but, more importantly, what quality of life is achieved. We know with some certainty that inactivity, lack of participation, and dependence have an erosive effect on social functioning. Lack of involvement and excessive dependence contribute to diminished coping skills, reduction of effort, and a sense of helplessness. The first requirement of any program for the long-term care of patients with mental illness, as the recovery movement emphasizes, is to activate the potential of patients to fulfill their own needs, to assume some responsibility for their lives, and to participate socially in a meaningful way.

Nursing homes are a primary source of care for older persons with mental illness. Nursing homes sometimes provide superb care, but too often the environment is primarily custodial with staff focused on keeping patients as quiet as possible to minimize supervision requirements. Patients in such settings have often been given heavy doses of drugs and kept in restraints for reasons of institutional convenience. Following a study by the Institute of Medicine of the National Academy of Sciences (1986), the U.S. government adopted regulations requiring facilities that receive funds from Medicare and Medicaid meet certain care standards, including the provision of mental health services to patients. Regulations also required that facilities providing nursing, medical, and rehabilitative care to Medicare and Medicaid beneficiaries carry out comprehensive, standardized assessments of each resident's functional capacity to assist staff in care planning and treatment decisions. As a result of these policies, progress has been made in reducing some of the worst practices, such as use of restraints. Nevertheless, continued monitoring and improvement is needed and great variability in quality of care persists (Mechanic 2006).

The conditions in hospitals and other facilities that affect residents' functioning and quality of life also apply to life in the community. Risk of withdrawal, inactivity, apathy, and victimization can be as large or even greater in the community than in residential institutions, despite the fact that the community offers more opportunity for a higher quality of life. One study found that one-quarter of persons with serious mental illness were victims of a major crime in the previous year, 11 times the rate in the overall population (Teplin et al. 2005). Thoughtful residential placements, however, can enhance the lives of even the most impaired patients. Leff, Trieman, and Gooch (1996) followed a cohort of 737 long-stay patients who returned to the community with the closing of two London mental hospitals. Although very little improvement in patients' psychiatric symptoms and social behavior occurred, the community residential settings where these patients were resettled gave them increased freedom, which they valued, and they reported making more friends. Within these staffed housing arrangements, crime was rare, and only seven patients who were lost to follow-up were presumed to have become homeless. One unexpected consequence was a decrease in contact with relatives following discharge.

Appropriate housing is, of course, only one component of successful community living for persons with severe and persistent illnesses and disabilities. Employment is another. Here we examine recent issues and developments in both critical areas.

MENTAL ILLNESS, HOMELESSNESS, AND HOUSING

There have always been homeless people in large urban areas in this country, but not since the years immediately following the Great Depression had homelessness been so visible as it became in the United States starting in the 1980s (Bassuk 1984a, 1984b). Estimates of the number of homeless are subject to distortion for political reasons and have varied widely. In 1984, the U.S. Department of Housing and Urban Development (HUD) estimated the homeless population at 350,000, and most careful studies and analyses concluded this figure was in the right ballpark (Freeman and Hall 1986; Jencks 1994; Rossi et al. 1987; U.S. General Accounting Office 1985). The nation's shelter population increased perhaps fivefold between 1980 and 1990 (Jencks 1994). By 2008, the U.S. government estimated that approximately 1.6 million people used transitional housing or an emergency shelter. On any given night there were about 664,000 homeless people (U.S. Department of Housing and Urban Development 2009). This is a diverse group, however, including both short-term homeless individuals during transitional periods in their lives and long-term shelter residents and homeless persons. People with serious mental illness and those with substance abuse problems are more prevalent in the long-term group.

There are many reasons why defining and counting the homeless is a complex, shifting process (Lee, Tyler, and Wright 2010). People who do not have a home or apartment may end up many places, including shelters, welfare hotels, subways and bus stations, or on the street. They may also double up with relatives, friends, and acquaintances. In general, the public and public officials are more worried about the visible homeless on the streets than those who may be trapped in unsatisfactory living arrangements. Researchers require a specific definition of homelessness to collect relevant data on this social problem. One useful formulation comes from the Congressional McKinney-Vento Homeless Assistance Act, which identifies people as homeless if they: (1) do not have a regular residence; (2) have a residence that is not meant for housing such as a car, abandoned building, or camp ground; (3) live in a shelter designed to provide only temporary housing; or (4) live in a place not meant for human habitation. The act also includes as homeless those persons about to lose their housing who have no permanent housing identified, and children and adolescents who lack permanent housing (U.S. Congress 2009). Various studies indicate that persons who are homeless have many needs, both medical and social in nature (Bassuk 1984a, 1984b; U.S. General Accounting Office 1985).

Disagreement surrounds the question of what causes homelessness. After careful examination of the issue, Jencks (1994) concluded that the main contributors to homelessness among single adults in the early 1980s included increases in long-term joblessness, tightening of involuntary commitment statutes, deinstitutionalization of state hospitals, growth in the use of crack cocaine, and political restrictions on opening flophouses. Among families, the most important factors were single motherhood, loss of purchasing power among mothers, and possibly increased use of crack cocaine. High rates of homelessness continued into the 1990s even after some of these factors abated. This may have resulted, in part, from public policies that encouraged more of the invisible homeless, particularly those living with friends, to make themselves visible and to seek the benefits of available programs.

It is now clear that homelessness stems from many different types of problems; both societal- and individual-level factors contribute. At the macro level, shortage of affordable housing, economic crisis, and demographic patterns such as the increase in single-parent households may all increase risk of homelessness (Jencks 1994; Lee, Tyler, and Wright 2010). These societal factors interact with individual-level vulnerability. For example, persons with mental illness may be more likely to become homeless given an economic crisis.

One painstaking study of homeless people in Chicago found that more than one in three reported themselves in ill health, a rate twice as high as that found in general population surveys (Rossi and Wright 1987). More than one in four reported having a health problem that prevented employment. Mental illness and psychiatric symptoms were major sources of disability. Almost one in four persons homeless in Chicago reported having been in a mental hospital for stays of more than 48 hours, and nearly half exhibited levels of depression suggesting a need for clinical attention. Contacts with the criminal justice system were frequent. In all, a striking 82 percent of those homeless reported ill health, having been in a mental hospital or detoxification unit, having been sentenced by a court, or they received clinically high scores on psychiatric symptom scales administered by the researchers (Rossi et al. 1987).

Studies suggest that for many people homelessness is a temporary situation reflecting changing economic circumstances and housing markets. Although the housed poor share many problems with the homeless population, the homeless poor often have personal and social risk factors—mental illness, substance abuse, disrupted households, the stigma of arrest and imprisonment, weak family and personal networks, and poor coping skills—that heighten their economic vulnerability. A study in Massachusetts, for example, compared mothers on welfare who were never homeless with a comparable sample in shelters (Bassuk et al. 1996). Those in shelters had less income, less education, a history of more residential instability, and smaller support networks. Both groups included a greater proportion of individuals with mental disorders than the general population, but they did not differ from each other in overall prevalence. However, the psychiatric problems of mothers in shelters were more serious, as reflected in higher rates of treatment and prior hospitalization for a mental disorder or substance abuse.

The demographic profile of homelessness changes with time and circumstance, but certain trends are clear. The homeless population is composed disproportionately of non-White young males with limited education. About two-fifths have substance abuse problems, and a third have serious psychiatric problems or a history of mental illness. A substantial minority of young women with children have never been married or they have disrupted marriages. In short, this is a poor population in a precarious social position (Bassuk 1984a, 1984b; Rossi et al. 1987; Wright 1989).

Precise estimates of psychiatric problems among those who are homeless will vary depending on definitional criteria, the samples studied, and particular time frame, but all studies report high rates of psychiatric symptoms and contact with the specialty mental health system compared to the population as a whole. As reported by respondents, the level of prior hospitalization varies from 11 to 33 percent among the homeless, compared to 3–7 percent among general adult community samples (Institute of Medicine 1988). A study of the skid row homeless population in Los Angeles used measures comparable to those in NIMH's Epidemiologic Catchment Area study, research discussed earlier in this book that derived clinical diagnoses from survey responses. It found 60 percent of those homeless met criteria for a mental illness or substance abuse disorder—about three times the rate in the general population. Summarizing more than two dozen studies, Rossi (1989) estimated that 27 percent of the homeless population had a history of at least some time in a mental hospital. A combination of 17 studies placed the average rate of chronic mental illness at 34 percent. These estimates exceed those derived from studies of other poor populations who are also vulnerable to psychiatric problems. In a review of studies of the prevalence of schizophrenia among homeless people in a variety of Western countries, Folsom and Jeste (2002) found an average prevalence rate of 11 percent, with higher rates among women, younger persons, and those who had been chronically homeless. Persons with serious mental illness are also more likely than others to remain chronically homeless (Susser, Struening, and Conover 1989).

By the mid-1980s, mental health administrators began to appreciate more fully the critical nature of housing problems and to make housing development and placement a significant component of mental health services. Suitable housing with appropriate supervision is an essential part of a good mental health service and a prerequisite for further rehabilitation efforts. Both the federal government and state mental health authorities began to increase a range of housing options geared to the clinical needs of persons with mental illness, but the need is tremendous and the supply of appropriate and affordable housing has yet to catch up. Particularly difficult is finding housing arrangements for uncooperative or disruptive individuals who have substance abuse problems and who get into conflicts with landlords, residence counselors, and other tenants. Some of these residents require supervision but rebel against it and have unstable housing histories.

Susser and his colleagues (1997) developed an innovative homelessness prevention program strengthening participants' links to services, family, and friends and providing emotional and practical support during the transition from shelters to community housing. They randomized 96 homeless men with serious mental illness who were entering community housing to a "critical time intervention" versus usual services. Over an 18-month follow-up, the intervention group, on average, was homeless for 30 nights, compared to 91 nights for the usual care group. The positive impact of the intervention was sustained over the 18 months studied, suggesting its value in helping protect against future homelessness.

A number of programs to combat homelessness have been initiated under the McKinney-Vento Homeless Assistance Act. This law required action by three agencies of the NIH concerned with psychiatric problems, including the National Institute of Mental Health, the National Institute on Alcohol Abuse and Alcoholism, and the National Institute on Drug Abuse. In 1993, a program called Access to Community Care and Effective Services and Supports (ACCESS) was initiated at two sites in each of nine states to assess whether additional resources to integrate services would improve the organization and coordination of care for mentally ill homeless people, thus leading to better mental health outcomes (Grob and Goldman 2006). Sites involved in this five-year demonstration deployed a wide range of strategies, among them interagency coalitions, interagency service teams, joint client tracking systems, cross training of service providers, joint funding, and co-location of services (Randolph et al. 1997). Homelessness was, of course, a core concern with much emphasis given to resolving this problem. A follow-up study of 1,340 participants after a year found improved housing results but few improved psychiatric outcomes (Rosenheck et al. 1998, 2001). The lesson seemed to be that, although integrating services is theoretically enticing, implementation can be extraordinarily difficult.

Finding appropriate and affordable housing in large cities is one of the most critical problems faced by people with chronic mental illness. It is unreasonable to anticipate that community care programs can provide adequate mental health services to patients living on the street, in large shelters, or in dangerous and unsuitable housing. Housing has not typically been a formal responsibility of the mental health sector, but the problem can hardly be ignored.

There is scarcity of housing in many localities, with fierce competition among needy groups for available housing units. Other problems include fear and prejudice toward those with mental illness in many neighborhoods, community resistance to group homes and other sheltered housing arrangements, and a profound lack of understanding about mental illness among those typically responsible for housing development and assignment.

The Robert Wood Johnson Foundation Program on Chronic Mental Illness, which focused on nine large cities, made housing one of its central features. The provision of Section 8 housing certificates to mental health authorities in demonstration cities was a tactic that helped some patients return to independent living (Newman et al. 1994).

There are strong ideological disagreements about what constitutes appropriate housing for persons with serious and persistent illness. At one extreme are those who support supervised residential living, and at the other are those who advocate normalization and scattered site independent living. All would agree, however, that patients have varying needs, requiring a spectrum of housing alternatives.

Initially, the consensus among mental health professionals was that clients should be moved along a residential continuum over time, from more to less supervised housing as particular capacities for independent living increase. Such policies proved highly disruptive, however, because they undermined stability in housing arrangements. Frequent moves were themselves stressful. Larger currents within the mental health field also came to affect the policy discussion over housing, particularly a strong consumer empowerment philosophy. This has resulted in turning away from the model of planners who decide what is best for the "patient" and toward an approach that focuses on "clients" who play an active role in decision making. Now it seems the better approach toward community housing is to find a relatively permanent situation, one that meets the preferences of the client while providing a level of supervision matching individual needs (Carling 1993). Most clients want to live in their own residences, but there are circumstances (such as in the case of substance abuse comorbidities) where this may not be an optimal alternative (Schutt and Goldfinger 1996). In any case, the dominant idea is to wrap services around the client in a setting he or she chooses, if this can be achieved. As clients cope more independently, supervision is relaxed.

Like others, people with mental illnesses are clearly more satisfied when housing arrangements follow their preferences, and they tend to do better under these circumstances. Further, clients understandably tend to prefer independent living arrangements, although they may actually benefit from settings with more support, supervision, and opportunities for interaction, such as group homes (Schutt 2011). Unfortunately, research concerning the interplay of mental status, individual choice, and clinical and social outcomes within the housing area is quite limited.

Federal efforts to create new housing have diminished while the emphasis has shifted from public housing to private-sector development. Currently, government programs are devoted chiefly to helping eligible clients pay rent in the marketplace of community housing. Scattered-site independent housing often is not suitable for patients severely mentally ill who require help and supervision. However, many communities resist the establishment of group homes, board-and-care facilities, supervised apartments, and other special projects directed to housing those with mental illness. Gaining community support presents difficult dilemmas. On the one hand, officials can inform a neighborhood of plans to locate a group house in its vicinity and seek to gain cooperation although fore notice provides an opportunity for opponents to mobilize (Hogan 1986a, 1986b). On the other hand, the strategy of quietly establishing a facility without neighborhood awareness can later result in bitter confrontations along with isolation of the facility and its residents. In reality, the establishment of a facility often has so little effect that when neighbors learn of its existence, they make no complaint. Problems arise when patients with bizarre mannerisms wander onto private property or make their presence obvious. For this reason, community resistance is much less likely to develop in urban commercial zones. Such locations may, in fact, be advantageous if they are close to needed services and facilities, but too often these sites represent the path of least resistance for political reasons.

In 1992, the U.S. Department of Housing and Urban Development (HUD) and the Department of Veterans Affairs (VA) initiated a supported housing program (HUD–VASH) that focused on the integration of clinical and housing services. In one randomized experimental study, researchers studied the use of VA clinicians to provide intensive case management while Section 8 housing vouchers were made available to house homeless veterans with psychiatric or substance abuse disorders (Rosenheck et al. 2003). A second group received intensive case management without housing vouchers, and a third group received usual VA care for homeless persons.

Over three years, the researchers found that those in the HUD–VASH group had 25 percent more days of housing than the standard group and 17 percent more days than the treatment-only group. These results were only statistically significant for the first two years, however. The HUD–VASH group had about 36 percent fewer days of homelessness than either the standard group or those who received only case management services. Clients in the HUD–VASH group were more satisfied with their housing and family relationships than those in the other groups, and they had formed larger social networks. But as in earlier studies of service integration, there were no significant differences on clinical and adjustment measures. Case management alone was no better than standard care. The HUD–VASH group had some significantly better housing results, but the program was more costly. Assessments of cost-effectiveness depended on assumptions made about the value of a day housed as compared with being homeless.

It is now more than 30 years since "the new homeless" attracted attention from researchers in sociology and related disciplines (Lee, Tyler, and Wright 2010). Over this period, homelessness has waxed and waned as a public issue, but information about causes, attributes, consequences, and program interventions has accumulated steadily. The latest national data that estimate the homeless at approximately 664,000 people were derived from a one-day snapshot. The count ranges several times higher if one aims to capture the entire population who experiences homelessness over a defined interval of time. Discharge from treatment facilities providing inpatient psychiatric care emerges as one of the primary junctures leading some people onto the path of homelessness. There is general recognition that reducing homelessness depends on closing the "front door" by which people join the homeless population and opening the "back door" by which they can leave. The former means developing measures of prevention to keep people from becoming homeless in the first place; the latter refers to providing services and resources that make it feasible to obtain housing (National Alliance to End Homelessness 2012). In 2010, the Obama administration released a 10-year plan to end homelessness (U.S. Interagency Council on Homelessness 2010). The objective is worthy and ambitious, but one made all the more intimidating when one considers how little progress has been made in reducing the scope of homelessness over past decades.

Homelessness thus remains a troubling issue for social policy. Nowhere is this observation truer than in regard to persons with serious mental health and substance abuse problems. Housing has become an essential ingredient of needs assessment and treatment planning in community programs. This represents an encouraging trend, aside from the unsatisfactory state of the housing market and its limited offering of possibilities. Increasingly, professionals with expertise in housing issues and mental health have learned to work cooperatively with landlords to gain acceptance and support, providing assurances that professional assistance will be available as a resource should crises or special problems occur. A variety of self-help and group-support mechanisms also provide expanded opportunities for consumers to help one another, as in the independent living movement. The American Recovery and Reinvestment Act of 2009 included $1.5 billion for homelessness initiatives around the country. Even so, this is a period of widespread need for safe, affordable housing among many social groups hard hit by the nation's economic downturn. The interface between housing and mental health care is an area undergoing great ferment marked by new concepts as well as learning from practice. As we have seen with regard to other aspects of community mental health care, however, there is often a frustrating gap between good ideas and resources with which to implement them.

INNOVATIONS IN EMPLOYMENT

Traditionally, public mental hospitals relied extensively on the labor of patients, who maintained the grounds, farmed, prepared food, worked in the laundry, and performed many other vital institutional functions. Indeed, hospitals were sometimes reluctant to discharge key workers on whom they had come to depend for important work assignments in underfinanced and understaffed institutions. There is a considerable history of research on industrial rehabilitation of patients, particularly in England (Wing 1967). According to various studies, persons with chronic schizophrenia who wanted to leave the hospital could be trained successfully. Even older patients who were more resistant to rehabilitation benefited somewhat from work rehabilitation programs. Although rehabilitation units could not replicate all the conditions of an industrial setting, including a majority of noninstitutionalized workers and specific training in work habits appropriate to real conditions, hospitals that prepared patients for work tended to have better clinical outcomes than those that did not.

Most people derive their self-esteem and sense of purpose from the social roles they occupy and productive activities such as work, child care, volunteer services, and the like. Work plays a particularly meaningful part in life, and persons with serious mental illness often say they want more help in finding and maintaining employment. Many persons with persistent illness face the problems of simply keeping busy in some meaningful activity, avoiding the boredom and sameness of every day, and gaining a sense of productivity. Mental health programs have often provided sheltered work outside competitive settings, but such work does not necessarily transfer to competitive employment. In addition, the work itself in sheltered programs, typically some form of assembly task, can be below the capacities and education of participants. Vocational rehabilitation is often made available to those recovering from severe mental illness, but many clients have not found such services responsive to their needs or particularly helpful in finding suitable employment (Noble et al. 1997).

Mechanic, Bilder, and McAlpine (2002) analyzed data from four major national surveys that included information about the work experience of people with mental illnesses—the 1990/1992 National Comorbidity Study (NCS); the National Health Interview Survey (NHIS), Mental Health Supplement, 1989; the National Health Interview Survey of Disability 1994/1995 (NHIS-D); and the Health Care for Communities Survey, 1997/1998. While the employment level of the general population ranged from 75 to 83 percent across these sources, the range among persons with a serious mental illness varied from 48 to 73 percent. In the NHIS-D, which provides detailed information concerning disabilities, 76 percent of persons without mental illness were employed, 62 percent full time, while the comparable figures for persons with any mental illness were 48 percent fully employed and 34 percent employed part-time. As one might expect, the extent of ability to work depends on the nature of the illness and disability. Thirty-seven percent of those with serious mental illness were employed, 24 percent full-time. Among those with schizophrenia, perhaps the most severe illness on average, only 23 percent were employed and only 12 percent full-time. However, the fact that members of this group do work suggests that, with proper accommodations and coaching, perhaps many more could find and retain employment. Research showed that some of the jobs held by those with serious mental illness were demanding administrative and professional positions.

The Americans with Disabilities Act (ADA) of 1990, whose passage was noted in Chapter 3 on mental health policy history, initiated a new era in the life of persons with disabilities. The ADA establishes protections in a number of areas, with Title I focusing on employment. The act covered people with a physical or mental impairment that substantially limits one or more major life activities, persons with a record of such impairment, and persons regarded as having such an impairment. In regard to hiring, the ADA prohibits employers from inquiring about impairments, although employers can still explore an applicant's capacity to perform all tasks necessary to the job. ADA also requires employers to provide "reasonable accommodations" to qualified persons with disabilities unless such accommodations impose an "undue hardship."

Studies have found most requested accommodations are not expensive, but the notions of "undue hardship" and what is "reasonable" are difficult to define clearly except on a case-by-case basis (Mechanic 1998). The Job Accommodation Network (JAN) provides examples of the types of accommodations that might be considered for a variety of disabilities. For example, for someone who has difficulty handing stress at work, JAN suggests a reasonable accommodation might be to allow an employee to make phone calls to a counselor or other source of support during working hours (www.jan.wvu.edu/links/adalinks.htm). In 1997, the U.S. Equal Employment Opportunity Commission (EEOC) issued new enforcement guidance for employing people with psychiatric disabilities under the ADA, including illustrative examples of the types of life activities that might be substantially limited by a mental disability such as thinking, concentrating, interacting with others, caring for oneself, doing manual tasks, and sleeping (U.S. Equal Employment Opportunity Commission 1997).

In the two decades since the passage of the ADA, lobbying and litigation seeking to define its extent and limits have been rife. To cite one such example, in 2007 the EEOC settled an agreement with the Starbucks Corporation involving a barista with a variety of impairments including bipolar and attention deficit disorders. Apparently, the woman had been performing satisfactorily with extra training and support, but a new manager at her store stopped these accommodations and her performance declined. He responded by cutting the employee's hours, berating her in public, and eventually firing her. The case was eventually settled with an award of $75,000 to the barista, an additional $10,000 to the Disability Rights Legal Center that represented her, and the purging of negative material in the employee's file put there by the new manager. The EEOC mandated that Starbucks post its EEOC policy and a notice of this settlement in all its stores (U.S. Equal Employment Opportunity Commission 2010).

Most disability-related cases brought before the EECO, however, end up being dismissed as lacking in merit (www.eeoc.gov/eeoc/statistics/enforcement/ada-charges.cfm). Nor are outcomes typically favorable for cases that go to court. For example, in 2010, of the 341 court cases related to employment under the ADA that were resolved, the employee prevailed only 1.8 percent of the time. Employees who brought claims based on psychiatric disabilities fared even worse; of the 78 cases that were brought on the basis of a mental illness/substance abuse disability, none were resolved in favor of the employee (Allbright 2011).

A major concern with implementing the ADA has been that courts have narrowly interpreted disability (Petrila and Brink 2001). In *Sutton v United Airlines*, two sisters who were experienced pilots applied to United Airlines and were told they did not meet the minimum uncorrected vision standards. The Supreme Court found the women were not protected under the ADA because they were not disabled when they took corrective action (wore glasses). This ruling was particularly important for persons with mental illness because it implied that if one could take a medication to help control the symptoms of the illness, one might not be considered disabled. Subsequently, lower courts favored this kind of narrow interpretation, ruling, for example, in Krocka v. City of Chicago that a police officer with depression was not disabled under ADA because he took antidepressants (Petrila and Brink 2001).

The Supreme Court has also adopted a circumscribed view of the types of life activities that should be considered when assessing limitation, an approach arguably more restrictive than was intended by authors of the ADA. Again in Sutton, it found that because the women could still work in other jobs, they were not substantially limited in a major activity and therefore did not qualify as disabled under the ADA. In a subsequent decision (Toyota Motor Manufacturing v. Williams 2002), the Court ruled that "an individual must have an impairment that prevents or severely restricts the individual from doing activities that are of central importance to most people's daily lives. The impairment's impact must also be permanent or long-term." The life activities considered central included things like bathing and brushing one's teeth, making it much more difficult for claimants to meet the definition of being disabled if they could still perform these basic tasks.

Congress passed the ADA Amendments Act of 2008 in order to broaden the definition of disability and make it easier for a person seeking protection to establish a disability under law (Petrila 2009). Perhaps most significant for persons with mental illness was the clarification that an impairment that is episodic or in remission remains a disability if it would substantially limit a major life activity when active (U.S. Equal Employment Opportunity Commission 2011). The act also clarified that major life activities include brain and neurological functions.

It is too soon to know what effect the revised ADA provision will have. Moreover, research findings have been mixed as to the impact of the ADA of 1990 on employment for persons with disability in general, or persons with psychiatric disabilities more specifically. There is a vigorous debate in the literature about whether employment rates for persons with disabilities declined, stayed the same, or got better after the passage of ADA, with opposing findings seemingly due to how disability is measured (Barrow 2008). Although the ADA offers opportunities for persons already employed to seek accommodation and protect their employment, it is less clear that the law facilitates persons with obvious mental illness gaining employment. Discrimination in hiring of persons with mental illness is very difficult to substantiate.

As with housing, there are strong competing ideologies about how to prepare persons with serious mental illness for employment. A traditional view was that clients had to be introduced to employment slowly by prevocational training, practice in sheltered work situations, and graduated introduction into more competitive work situations. More recent studies suggest it is difficult to predict who will do well in competitive work, and that directly mainstreaming patients into the workforce is often more effective than a gradual approach (Bond et al. 1997; Drake and Becker 1996). The Individual Placement and Support (IPS) work model seeks to place the client directly into competitive work situations, providing whatever support is needed. Job coaches commonly assist the client in job counseling, in dealing with whatever work problems occur, and in providing encouragement and support. The basic idea of supported employment is that clients should become regular employees in usual work settings at the prevailing wage rate rather than spending time in some artificial work setting. Bond and his colleagues (1997) identified six elements common to most supported employment programs: the goal of a permanent competitive job, minimal screening for employability, individualized placement, avoidance of prevocational programs, consideration of client preferences, and continuing support as needed with no time limits. Supported employment has been found to be far more successful in resulting in competitive employment than traditional vocational services (Bond et al. 1997; Drake and Becker 1996).

Many jobs available to clients with mental health problems are not particularly desirable, such as janitorial work, food service, dishwashing, and laundering, and some of these jobs can be very stressful. This may help explain the weak link between work experience, on the one hand, and quality of life, improvements in self-esteem, and reduction in symptoms, on the other. However, there is no evidence that competitive work leads to negative outcomes such as increased relapse rates. Client preference in selecting jobs is important, and such preferences are generally realistic. Clients who obtain competitive employment in preferred areas of work are more likely to stay in such jobs and are more satisfied with them. Becker and her colleagues (1996) conducted six-month follow-up interviews of patients in supported employment and found those who were working in preferred areas held their jobs twice as many weeks as those who did not.

Many patients with mental illness are well educated and have good skills but suffer insecurities in the world of work. It can be difficult to return these patients to suitable employment because most programs concentrate on less educated and less skilled work-ers, who are the more typical clients. Expectations are higher in higher-level jobs and employer tolerance is lower because employers recruit from a more stable labor force than prevails in areas demanding few skills. Employer receptivity, however, depends on how difficult it is to recruit persons with the skills being sought. In tight labor markets, when unemployment is high and employers have many choices, employers may be less willing to deal with deficits disregarded under other circumstances. In general, persons with mental illness with higher levels of education are more likely than others with mental illness to be employed (Mechanic, Bilder, and McAlpine 2002).

Progress has been understandably slow because it requires cultural change, but a large number of employers are cooperating in employment programs for people with men-tal illness, and they are discovering this group is often a source of reliable and excellent employees. Some programs contract with employers to provide a certain number of jobs for job-ready clients. Program managers, for their part, make the commitment that clients will arrive at work as expected and perform at a reasonable level. In emergencies, staff members will even step in to fill the contracted jobs to meet the commitment that has been made. But in well-run programs, employers learn that many patients with psychi-atric illness are often more reliable and perform better than recruits from the standard labor pool. Initially, employers are insecure about inviting persons with mental illness to join their organization, which makes it important that appropriate help is readily available when a mental health problem develops at the workplace.

To date, 17 randomized controlled trials have been carried out confirming the effectiveness of the Individual Placement and Support model (Bond, Drake, and Becker 2008; Drake and Becker 2011), which was described above. Few interventions in the mental health field can claim so strong a base of evidence. While most clients in supported employment work part time, about two-thirds of those who achieve competi-tive employment work 20 hours or more per week. Up to now, however, very few clients have been able to access such programs, and funding for IPS has been highly fragmented in contrast to the more generous support received by less effective programs, such as sheltered workshops. In addition to the lack of a secure funding stream (such as broad Medicaid coverage), the IPS model faces barriers that include negative predispositions and biases on the part of many therapists, slow diffusion of new evidence regarding the IPS model, professional resistance to change, persistence of paternalism toward persons with serious mental illness, and the need for new practice structures to incorporate IPS services (Pogoda et al. 2011).

ONGOING REFORM OF MEDICAID

As discussed in Chapter 7 on financing, Medicaid is the single largest and most important program affecting persons with severe and persistent mental illness. Medicaid involves 53 separate programs in various states and U.S. territories, including Puerto Rico, and while there is some uniformity prescribed by federal law, states have considerable latitude to define the scope, amount, and duration of services. Until recently, states controlled their Medicaid expenditures by the way they reimbursed institutions and providers; in many states, payments to professionals were so low that providers refused to treat enrollees in the program. Instead, states used Medicaid as a way to subsidize public providers and to reconfigure their public mental health systems. Using Medicaid as a base, some states have very wisely built a community support system for persons with mental illness that is attentive to a wide range of needs such as housing and rehabilitation.

Despite the abundant observational studies and experience attesting to the value of Medicaid for persons with disabilities and those with low income, some opponents argue that the poor and disabled might obtain care in other ways or that the program is flawed by poor administration and underpayment of clinicians (Baicker and Finkelstein 2011). Demonstrating the positive role and impact of Medicaid requires randomized comparison of eligible enrollees who do and do not receive the benefits of the program. Obviously, this is a difficult research project to conduct, but an important recent study provides just this kind of examination.

Finkelstein and colleagues (2012) traced the experience of two groups of applicants to Medicaid in the state of Oregon: individuals admitted to the program versus those who were denied. No systematic differences distinguished these two groups because enrollees were selected randomly. Oregon had only limited capacity to increase enrollment of low-income adults (an optional population for state coverage), and it used a lottery as the means for accepting 10,000 enrollees from some 90,000 applicants. Over a period of a year, the investigators collected extensive data on new enrollees and controls not selected in the lottery, including administrative information on hospital discharges, credit information, and mortality. They also conducted a survey measuring a wide range of health outcomes, including substantial information relevant to mental health and illness. As we have noted elsewhere, the Medicaid population includes many persons with psychiatric problems. Among those who applied to this lottery, 10 percent had mood disorders, 3 percent had schizophrenia or other psychotic disorders, and 3 percent had alcohol-related disorders. Many others had depressive symptoms.

Investigators have not yet analyzed the full range of clinical outcome indicators, but they have reported preliminary results from utilization trends and the respondent surveys, sources that are particularly relevant for questions of mental health since few laboratory tests or other objective clinical measurements would be available for this sector. Overall, it was found that the experimental group had considerably more access and used more services than the controls, including much greater use of preventive care (Finkelstein et al. 2012). Moreover, the experimental group fared significantly better on all seven survey measures concerning self-reported health. New Medicaid enrollees were 10 percent more likely than the control group to screen negative for depression, and they also reported fewer days in poor mental health during the prior month. Additional data were collected on happiness. Those who gained coverage by Medicaid had a 32 percent increase on this measure relative to controls, an effect approximately equal to the impact of a doubling of income. We look forward to further results from this unique experiment.

Traditional Medicaid is rapidly fading and many new innovations are on the drawing boards. Elsewhere in this book, we have noted the aggressive movement to managed care that has taken place in most states and is accelerating in the face of growing costs. Officials view this strategy as a means both to control expenditures and to integrate different forms of mental health services. Additional changes lie ahead, and in future years Medicaid will have very different financing methods, ways of organizing providers, and standards of care. In the Deficit Reduction Act of 2005, Congress chose to give states greater discretion in managing their Medicaid programs. Such flexibility provides opportunities for innovation, but it also allows regressive and sometimes poorly formulated approaches that can harm persons with mental illness, such as arbitrary limitations on services and prescriptions. Medicaid changes affect not only patients but also mental health delivery systems and those in the mental health professions. The adoption of rigorous measures of effectiveness is key to high-quality care. Such measures should reflect the amount of care given while encompassing patients' functioning and quality of life, family burden, patient and family satisfaction, and the absence of client victimization, arrest, and imprisonment. When there is deterioration in these latter indicators, they are signs of potential problems in community care, including the operation of managed care.

With an anticipated large expansion of Medicaid under the Affordable Care Act in 2014, there will be numerous opportunities to use additional Medicaid innovations to redesign mental health and substance abuse services in ways that greatly improve care (Mechanic 2012). Health Homes, briefly discussed in Chapter 7, offer promising opportunities to provide the kind of holistic and integrated services needed by persons with serious mental illness. The Missouri Department of Mental Health was the first state mental health authority approved for funding under the Health Home provision. It began providing this service in January of 2012. Increasingly voluminous details are becoming available regarding plans for and implementation of Health Homes elsewhere around the nation, and states seem to be taking advantage of the flexibility being given to them in the design of these programs. With Health (and other Medical) Homes a strong incentive exists to use information technology (IT) to track patients, integrate services across multiple providers, close gaps in care, and avoid unnecessary and expensive crises resulting in emergency room use and hospitalization. The goal is to provide comprehensive management of coordinated care and promotion of improved health and health behavior. There is also increased attention on pivotal transitions, such as follow-up from hospitalization and other types of care. As needed, patients and their families receive support services and appropriate referrals. States may select from a variety of designated providers such as community health centers, rural group practices, home health agencies, or a team of health professionals (social workers, nurses, dieticians, or other personnel) that is linked to a designated behavioral health provider. Medicaid clients eligible for coverage by a Health Home include those with two or more chronic conditions, those with one chronic condition but who are at risk for a second, and persons with a serious and persistent mental health condition. We focus on Missouri's approach here to illustrate how the program might work more generally (http://dmh.mo.gov/about/chiefclinicalofficer/healthcarehome.htm).

Missouri chose two approaches to the organization of Health Homes. One is organized through 27 community mental health centers (CMHCs) and their affiliates and is focused on persons with a serious and persistent mental disorder, an addiction disorder, mental health and addiction comorbidities, or an addiction disorder accompanied by another targeted health condition such as diabetes, developmental disabilities, and cardiovascular disease. Physicians lead the CMHC Health Homes with teams including a director, nurse case manager, primary care physician consultant, and administrative staff. At the state's discretion, these teams might also include a psychiatrist, mental health case manager, employment and housing representatives, and the like. Medicaid reimburses the usual services, and the Health Home receives an additional reimbursement for necessary coordination of the treatment plan. In 2012, such payment in Missouri was $78.74 per month for each patient. The Department website provides a hypothetical Health Home patient scenario to illustrate how the program is intended to work (dated July 18, 2011).

Missouri is also implementing primary care Health Homes administered through federally qualified health centers, physician practices, and rural health centers. These homes will be led by physicians and include a primary care physician or nurse practitioner, a behavioral health consultant, a nurse case manager, a licensed nurse or medical assistant, and administrative staff. The target group is clients with diabetes, asthma, cardiovascular disease, and developmental disabilities. Smoking, a major cause of chronic disease and death, is also included as an eligible criterion. These primary care "homes" also receive a coordination payment but at a lower rate than those for Health Homes.

THE ROLE OF DISABILITY PROGRAMS

Moving patients out of long-stay custodial institutions depended on a government safety net that supported the ability of patients to subsist in the community. Especially important were the federal Social Security Disability Insurance (SSDI) Program and the Supplemental Security Income (SSI) Program. The latter is particularly relevant for those with severe and persistent illness and lacking a sufficient work history to qualify for SSDI.

Growth in disability costs over the 1970s led to the 1980 amendments to the Social Security Act, in which Congress required that states review all awards at least every three years. These reviews resulted in loss of benefits by a large number of persons with severe mental illness, among others, and subsequently much litigation in the federal courts. What became apparent was that application of existing disability criteria seriously underestimated the incapacities of many patients with chronic mental illness to work in a sustained way. Between 1981 and 1983, the benefits of a half million people, many of them mentally ill, were terminated. Eventually, some 290,000 of those terminated gained reinstatement under new psychiatric criteria based on an integrated functional assessment (Osterweis, Kleinman, and Mechanic 1987).

Persons with mental illness were targeted for removal from the disability rolls for a variety of reasons. Members of this group are generally much younger than those with more common medical disabilities, such as heart disease, and in targeting the young, policymakers saw opportunities to achieve large financial savings by removing enrollees likely to remain on disability for many years, if not for life. Also, unlike many medical conditions, psychiatric symptoms are not well correlated with functional capacities. Thus, some persons with serious mental illness do well in the workforce. Yet the symptoms of severe psychiatric illness can fluctuate, and persons who seem superficially capable of work when evaluated may decompensate under realistic work demands. In response to much criticism, as well as a study by the General Accounting Office, Congress passed a number of administrative reforms that included new medical impairment standards.

Expeditious attainment of disability benefits is important in order to stabilize the life situations of patients with chronic mental illness and to plan appropriate care. Yet there are barriers, including common delays in awarding benefits and contradictory eligibility criteria in regard to disability benefits and access to rehabilitation services. In some localities, state agencies administering disability determinations locate government workers in mental health service facilities to make the disability filing process more simple and accessible. But if the potential of this system is to be better realized, the disability system must also be linked to stronger incentives for rehabilitation (Mashaw and Reno 1996a).

Many provisions within the Social Security disability system speak to rehabilitation, but they have clashed with the requirement that recipients prove they cannot work because of long-lasting medical impairment. State vocational rehabilitation agencies also have had little financial incentive to serve most clients with mental illness because the Social Security Administration paid for these services only when a recipient returned to work for a continuous period of nine months (Osterweis, Kleinman, and Mechanic 1987, pp. 70–71). This group of recipients also was prone to a high risk of rehabilitation failure. Small surprise, then, that the rehabilitation provisions of the act were rarely used.

In 1986, Congress extended the Vocational Rehabilitation Act. For the first time, supported work activities were permitted under the act, including transitional employment for persons with chronic mental illness. The legislation specifically included CMHCs among agencies encouraged to collaborate with departments of vocational rehabilitation. But vocational rehabilitation among the millions of persons with mental illness was still highly underdeveloped, and consumers with mental illness often reported dissatisfaction with the service.

One of the ironies of the disability program is that while many persons with disabilities yearn to work, the difficulties of becoming a beneficiary, and the disincentives for leaving the rolls, lead relatively few to return to more than minimal employment. Less than 1 percent of enrollees each year leave these programs, and only 2.5 percent of any new enrollment cohort ever leave (Drake et al. 2009; Thornton et al. 2006). Many people throughout the disability community have been highly critical of state vocational rehabilitation agencies, but advocates for those who are mentally ill have been especially outspoken (Noble et al. 1997).

In 1996, the Ways and Means Committee of the U.S. House of Representatives commissioned a committee of the National Academy of Social Insurance to study the issue of disability and re-employment. The committee, which included the senior author of this book, recommended that SSDI and SSI beneficiaries receive a return-to-work ticket (a voucher) that they could bring to any public or private provider who would, in turn, receive ample payment upon assisting an enrollee to return to work and exit from the benefits program (Mashaw and Reno 1996b). The committee saw this effort as enhancing consumer choice and empowerment, encouraging provider competition, and rewarding providers when they reduced program costs. The question remained, however, whether the incentives were strong enough to mobilize rehabilitation providers when there was doubtfulness about bringing a client to work independence.

The initiative was launched with great fanfare as the Ticket to Work and Work Incentives Improvement Act of 1999. The Social Security Administration (SSA) contracted with Mathematica Policy Research to conduct an evaluation, and findings of the research covering the first two years of implementation were not very encouraging. By September 2004, that is, the end of the implementation period, the Social Security Administration had sent out "tickets to work" to more than 11 million beneficiaries in total. Focusing simply on those in Phase 1, the beneficiaries for whom the program had operated longest, only 1.1 percent went on to assign their ticket to a provider (Thornton et al. 2006). Persons with mental illness had a slightly higher rate of 1.5 percent. By 2005, more than 1,300 agencies had registered as employment networks, most had at the time of evaluation not yet accepted any tickets, and it was increasingly difficult to recruit new providers. Ironically, more than 90 percent of all the tickets cashed were by state vocational agencies, presumably the providers for whom consumers had been seeking alternatives. Providers who had initially been enthusiastic were losing interest.

Cook and colleagues (2006) completed a simulation study to assess the distribution of provider payments that would have resulted had persons with psychiatric disabilities made use of their tickets to work. Researchers had earnings data over two years in eight state study sites for 450 persons with psychiatric disabilities who received state-of-the-art employment rehabilitation services. These data then provided a basis for calculating payments under two formulas used by the Ticket to Work Program to reimburse providers. It was determined that clients' earnings rarely reached levels sufficient to generate provider payments under the program. The conclusion was that the program failed to take account realistically of the rehabilitation challenges faced by persons with serious mental illness.

Mathematica Policy Research has continued to monitor SSA efforts to improve this program. SSA made substantial modifications in 2008, seeking to increase provider participation by enhancing financial benefits and reducing administrative burdens. While some positive changes occurred, enrollee and provider participation remained exceedingly poor relative to the number of eligible beneficiaries (Altshuler et al. 2011; Schimmel et al. 2010). Some providers continued to complain about financial and administrative issues, while evidence of reduced dependency on disability support was lacking.

However, a cohort study of beneficiaries who enrolled in the program during a six-month period beginning October 1, 2009, found that 22 percent of these self-selected clients said they were willing to earn enough to allow some reduction in their SSA benefits, and 13 percent indicated a willingness to give up benefits entirely if earnings were sufficient (Livermore, Prenovitz, and Schimmel 2011). About two-thirds of these enrollees were employed to some extent or seeking employment at entry, and 55 percent of those who received services had some earnings over the next 15 months. Sixteen percent ended up absorbing some reduction to their SSA benefits because of earnings (Livermore, Prenovitz, and Schimmel 2011). Of the group of rehabilitation clients studied, 44 percent had a primary diagnosis of mental illness. More than half (54 percent) of these individuals showed some earnings, averaging $5,946, with 8 percent accruing earnings in excess of the allowable "substantial gainful activity" standard. This, in turn, triggered benefit reductions of $1.7 million among the total sample of about 11,000. Unfortunately, beyond such figures, there are no real outcome data, and the small successes noted cannot be attributed to program effectiveness given methodological limitations of the evaluation.

REDESIGNING COMMUNITY CARE PROGRAMS

Over the past 40 years, excellent models of community mental health care have been developed and evaluated for clients with severe mental illness that provide the essential foundations for a true system of community care. These components are consistent with, and could operate effectively within, new Health Homes that are being organized under the ACA. One of the most innovative of such models is a training program for community living created in Madison, Wisconsin, some four decades ago (Stein and Test 1980; Stein, Test, and Marx 1975; Test and Stein 1980). A group of patients seeking admission to a mental hospital was randomly assigned to experimental and control groups. Subsequent analysis found no differences in significant variables between these two groups, indicating that successful randomization had occurred. The control group received hospital treatment linked with community aftercare services. The experimental group was assisted in developing an independent living situation in the community; given social support; and taught simple living skills such as budgeting, job seeking, and use of transportation. Independent researchers evaluated patients in both groups at various intervals. Compared with patients in the control group, patients in the experimental group made a more adequate community adjustment as evidenced by higher earnings from work, involvement in more social activities, more contact with friends, and greater satisfaction with their life situations. Patients in the experimental group had fewer symptoms at follow-up than the controls. This experiment demonstrated that a logically organized and aggressive program of services and supports could effectively treat even patients with severe impairment in the community.

Wisconsin has had a unique mental health system for many years, and Dane County, the area where this program innovation was situated, does not necessarily face the same range of obstacles to care evident in other communities. This program, however, has been adopted in part or in its totality in other areas of the country, as well as in international settings, with reports of equally promising outcomes. The program seems most successful in small and moderately sized communities, while the problems of providing comprehensive care in large urban areas are more challenging. It is in this latter context that the experience of Sydney, Australia, takes on particular interest.

In the period 1979–1981, psychiatrist John Hoult and his colleagues adopted the Wisconsin model in this large urban Australian area, using a randomized controlled experiment. Researchers obtained patient care and cost-effectiveness outcomes similar to Stein and Test's earlier studies (New South Wales Department of Health 1983). Particularly notable, and consistent with the Wisconsin experience, patients and their families preferred the community care option. For example, at 12-month follow-up, almost two-thirds of patients in the experimental group were very satisfied with treatment, in contrast to less than one-third of those in the control group. Similarly, 83 percent of relatives with whom patients in the experimental group lived were very satisfied with treatment, in contrast to 26 percent of relatives for those in the control group (New South Wales Department of Health 1983).

The Wisconsin experiment, however, had not addressed the intensity of staffing essential to carry out the types of aggressive and continuing care necessary within a large urban program. Limited resources, particularly with regard to staffing, upon which the viability of the community care model depends, is a persistent problem in many areas. The Australian replication was sufficiently favorable despite a lower level of staffing than in Dane County. The state of New South Wales subsequently reorganized mental health services throughout the state using the Wisconsin model (Hoult 1987). At the same time, it signaled the importance of questions of scale in such a program and the need to define minimum resource levels.

The Stein and Test approach, generally known as Assertive Community Treatment (ACT), is now widely used all over the world. These are not exact replications, but in each case at least some ACT elements have guided the design of community treatment. The National Alliance on Mental Illness (NAMI) endorses ACT and has done much to disseminate the model. NAMI recognizes the program's high cost, but views it as cost-effective relative to other alternatives (National Alliance on Mental Illness 2005). Overall, studies of ACT-like models report consistent findings of reduced hospitalization and high levels of patient and family satisfaction in comparison with more conventional care (Olfson 1990; Santos et al. 1995). Patient improvement is more variable, and it remains uncertain whether variation springs from different populations of patients, problems with adherence to medication, differences in local ecology, or differences in program implementation. Specific local events and interprofessional politics also influence program implementation and effectiveness.

For example, the ACT program was replicated in a district in South London in England as a randomized trial between 1987 and 1992. In the first phase of this trial, assertive treatment was compared with existing inpatient and outpatient care (Marks et al. 1994). For the initial 20 months, researchers found small improvement in symptoms and social adjustment but relatively high satisfaction among patients and relatives in the ACT-like program when compared to clients receiving conventional care. Inpatient days in the ACT-like group were much reduced and costs were significantly lower than for controls (Knapp et al. 1994). However, media attention given to the murder of a child by a member of the ACT-like group, 14 months after the incident occurred, created political turmoil. This resulted in the transfer of responsibility for decisions about inpatient admissions to a hospital ward team, thereby undermining the program's authority over care and demoralizing staff. In the subsequent period, most gains from the program, with the exception of patient and family satisfaction, were not sustained (Audini et al. 1994).

Perhaps the most extensive analysis of these holistic intensive case management (ICM) approaches comes from the Cochrane Collaboration, an effort by health professionals to distill the best evidence possible from an accumulation of randomized controlled trials relevant to important health care questions. The Cochrane Collaboration has assessed the state of evidence on assertive (intensive) case management at various times and returned to this topic most recently in its report of 2011 that covered research up through early 2009. In this latest review, Dieterich and colleagues (2010) focused on the most relevant 38 studies involving 7,328 clients. Their core analysis looked at the performance of formal ICM programs as well as less formal but holistic ICM programs, in comparison with standard care.

It was found that ICM reduces hospitalization when compared with standard care, although this advantage is declining as psychiatric services, in general, come to depend less on inpatient care. Differences are greatest when the program being studied adheres closely to the formal ACT model, a principle the literature refers to as "fidelity" (Monroe-DeVita, Morse, and Bond 2012). ACT programs are more likely to retain clients in treatment.

Client outcomes, however, are mixed. ACT improves overall social functioning better than standard care, but not necessarily symptoms, mental status, or even quality of life. The ACT approach possesses greatest advantage in managing the population of persons with severe illness who are at high risk of inpatient care.

With the maturation of ACT has come not only widespread acceptance within professional and advocacy communities but also growing acceptance by government funders. In 1999, the federal government approved ACT as an optional state service under the Medicaid program. The objective was plainly to diffuse ACT as a form of evidence-based practice consistent with principles of community support and the recovery paradigm, and the effect of government reimbursement has been to make it possible for many more patients to receive the benefits of this program. At the same time, however, Medicaid's role has served to highlight certain tensions that can develop within the ACT model concerning standardization versus local adaptation, program design versus program implementation, and cost-control versus innovative service expansion. In detailed case studies of ACT adoption in Oklahoma and New York, Johnson (2011) tracked how Medicaid coverage introduced new forms of regulation-driven rigidity while officials concentrated on selected outcome measures having particular political salience, such as reduced hospitalizations and jail diversions. Discrepancies also arose, to some extent, between ACT's strong professional management and the value of consumer empowerment.

Reviewers have found it difficult to gauge the advantages of a formal ACT approach in comparison with similar holistic services provided less formally. Family-oriented reha-bilitation models based on principles similar to ACT, as well as the clinical research on expressed emotions, have also yielded promising results in both England (Leff et al. 1982) and the United States (Falloon, Boyd, and McGill 1984; Falloon et al. 1985). In a controlled social intervention trial in London, patients with schizophrenia having intense contact with relatives demonstrating high expressed emotion were randomly assigned to either routine outpatient care or an intervention program for patients and their families empha-sizing education about schizophrenia and the role of expressed emotion in exacerbating patients' symptoms (Leff et al. 1982). The intervention also included family sessions in the home and in support groups for relatives. All patients were maintained on psychotropic drugs. After nine months, half of the 24 control patients relapsed, but only 9 percent in the experimental group did so. There were no relapses in the 73 percent of the experimental families where the aims of the intervention were achieved.

In the 1990s, the U.S. federal government established Patient Outcome Research Teams (PORTs) to assess the most established evidence-based treatments and the extent of their use. One team was established for schizophrenia, and after extensive study it found that effective practices were poorly implemented, even in the face of compelling evidence. Medication doses were often outside the recommended range. Patients with schizophre-nia usually did not receive anti-Parkinson medication or antidepressants when they had comorbid depression. Most striking was the very few patients who were receiving appro-priate psychosocial services, including family education and support and employment support (Lehman 1999; Lehman and Steinwachs 1998).

An experimental trial was carried out in California in which family members of patients with schizophrenia were taught about their condition and instructed in problem-solving techniques while efforts were also made to reduce family tensions (Falloon, Boyd, and McGill 1984). Follow-up at nine months found that patients in families receiving such interventions had lesser symptoms than those in a control group receiving clinic-based individual supportive care. Only one patient in the intervention group (6 percent) was judged to have experienced a relapse, in contrast to eight (44 percent) in the control group (Falloon et al. 1982). A less systematic and intensive follow-up after two years found that the lower symptom level was maintained over the longer period (Falloon et al. 1985).

Various studies have confirmed that a psychoeducational approach with families of patients with schizophrenia who display high expressed emotion can reduce or delay relapses. Hogarty and his colleagues (1991) randomly assigned patients with schizophrenia who were expected to return to families exhibiting high expressed emotion to four groups, all of which received medication: (1) family psychoeducation/management (FT); (2) social skills training (SST); (3) a combination of FT and SST; and (4) a control group receiving medications and social support. In the first year, the proportion of patients relapsing in the experimental groups was only half that of the control group. No patient with combined treatment relapsed in the first year. By the end of the second year, about a quarter of those in the groups receiving family treatment relapsed, while half of those receiving only skills training relapsed and three-fifths of the control group relapsed. At the end of the second year, skills training did not improve upon the impact of family psychoeducation, which remained effective in preventing or delaying relapse.

In a somewhat different twist on this theme, McFarlane and his colleagues (1995) randomized patients with schizophrenia into either single or multiple family psychoeducational groups at six New York public hospitals and studied relapses over a two-year period. Patients treated in family groups were less likely to relapse (16 percent) than those treated in single family groups (27 percent). Differences were even larger among patients who were at high risk of relapse. Although it is difficult to know for sure, providing services for patients and their families in groups may provide greater social support, enhance social networks, and provide opportunities to learn from the experiences of other families. The group setting may also affect how emotions and tensions are managed. The researchers reported that overinvolved family members seem to adopt more functional behaviors as they develop relationships with members of other families.

The studies described above are just a small sample from a much larger literature that reveals the value of community care and psychoeducational approaches (Dieterich et al. 2010; Dixon et al. 2001; Gudeman and Shore 1984; Kiesler 1982; Kiesler and Sibulkin 1987; McFarlane et al. 1996; Stein and Test 1978). According to a wide variety of experimental studies, then, alternative care is often more effective than hospitalization across a wide range of populations and treatment strategies (Kiesler and Sibulkin 1987).

Developing and reinforcing the living skills of patients is common to many community care and treatment programs. The emphasis on social learning has been carried to the extreme in experimental work by Paul and Lentz (1977), who successfully applied this model to resocialize patients having long histories of chronic mental illness and inappropriate behavior. Using a highly controlled treatment environment in which all staff adopted responses consistent with learning principles, concerted and continued efforts were made to shape patients' behavior so as to condition more normal responses. The approach used instruction, direction, and reinforcement through reward and punishment. The researchers reported dramatic behavioral improvements and demonstrated quite convincingly that even the most regressed patterns of response can be modified.

Elements of this social learning approach operate in almost all community care and social rehabilitation programs. Community programs, however, can never have the degree of control over patients that characterizes a "total institution." Current concepts of appropriate treatment, civil liberties, and respect for patient preferences make it unlikely that an all-encompassing approach such as the one implemented by Paul and Lentz (1977) would be adopted except under very extreme conditions. Similar techniques have been used in some institutions treating children with severe disabilities such as severe autism, but this behavioral approach is very much in dispute and commonly viewed as unethical and abusive.

Long-term therapy for patients with schizophrenia is further complicated by the fact that antipsychotic medications, a critical component of care, often have unpleasant side-effects and long-term adverse biological effects. Although antipsychotic medication is helpful in controlling delusions, hallucinations, severe excitement, or withdrawal and odd behavior, first-generation antipsychotics occasionally cause extrapyramidal motor reactions and, with prolonged use, a neurological syndrome known as tardive dyskinesia (Berger 1978). The extrapyramidal symptoms, which include uncontrollable restlessness, muscle spasms, and other reactions resembling Parkinson's disease, can be controlled by anticholingeric drugs used for treating Parkinson's. Tardive dyskinesia—which consists of involuntary movements of the lips, tongue, face, and other upper extremities—is less reversible, more dangerous, and stigmatizing. It represents a serious risk for patients on some long-term maintenance antipsychotics. The side-effects of medications, discussed in Chapter 5, have complicated the treatment of patients with chronic schizophrenia, particularly in community settings. First, the side-effects lead patients to discontinue medication, often resulting in relapse. Second, problems of patient cooperation as well as the real medical dangers of these drugs require close supervision and monitoring. The latter constitutes more of a strategic conundrum in the community than on a hospital ward for obvious reasons, necessitating an aggressive and sustained administrative effort.

Development of new neuroleptic drugs, and alternative modes of administration, may contribute to addressing three difficult areas in medicating patients: lack of response to treatment, disturbing side-effects, and failure to take medication. As noted earlier in this book, clozapine appears helpful with patients whose conditions are refractory to other neuroleptic drugs and it has fewer extrapyramidal side-effects. Because of clozapine's other life-threatening potential side-effects, however, patients on this drug regimen must have their blood closely monitored.

When the new antipsychotic atypical drugs came on the market, it was with claims of a superior ability to control symptoms of schizophrenia combined with fewer adverse side-effects. Clinicians were enthusiastic, and patients and families also seemed to prefer these drugs. Much of the subsequent research comparing these new drugs has involved small, short-term studies with high rates of attrition and great patient heterogeneity, so it offers limited guidance. However, initial high hopes have not been confirmed (Geddes et al. 2000). Previously, we reviewed the results of one of the most extensive of such studies involving some 1,500 patients over a period of 18 months (Lieberman et al. 2005). This research compared four of the new atypical antipsychotic drugs to one older drug, perphenazine. The most dramatic finding of the entire study was that 74 percent of patients discontinued medication before 18 months, a fact seemingly inconsistent with rhetoric about the tolerability of newer drugs.

Lieberman and his colleagues carefully analyzed drug safety issues over the course of this trial. There were no significant differences among drugs in terms of severe or moderate adverse events, with a range of 64–70 percent. Similarly, there were no significant differences in neurological side-effects, however measured. Yet significant numbers of patients did experience problems. For example, 13–17 percent across groups had scores above the defined severity criterion for neurological problems. How patients subjectively experience symptoms may differ from objective measures; patients often have idiosyncratic responses in relation to personal needs and preferences. Only 10 percent of patients on risperidone in this study stopped taking the drug because of intolerable side-effects, which was the lowest rate of discontinuation. By contrast, 18 percent stopped taking olanzapine, despite the fact that patients on this medication were least likely to be rehospitalized because of exacerbation of symptoms of schizophrenia. But greater weight gain and metabolic effects were significant reasons why many patients disliked olanzapine. A greater number of patients discontinued perphenazine, the traditional antipsychotic, than the newer drugs due to extrapyramidal symptoms. Incontinence was a relatively uncommon but troubling side-effect that varied from 2 to 7 percent among study participants, with the traditional antipsychotic drug performing best. Insomnia, a more commonly reported concern, varied from 16 to 30 percent, with the traditional antipsychotic about average. Achieving adherence to medication treatment in the face of these and other undesirable secondary results remains one of the most essential challenges in the treatment of schizophrenia (Zygmunt et al. 2002).

One way of assisting patients who have difficulty adhering to medication is use of depot preparations of neuroleptic drugs, that is, medication given by intramuscular injection. Depending on the type of injection, medication levels in the blood can be maintained from three days to a month. Thus, depot medications can be particularly useful when discharging patients with a history of poor adherence from inpatient care to the community. However, patients are often poorly informed about medication matters, and they may neglect to have dosages adjusted when an increase in florid symptoms occurs. Psychosocial programs are giving increasing attention to educating patients in this area.

ISSUES CONCERNING CASE MANAGEMENT

Case management is a tool that has been widely embraced in developing systems of care for those most disabled in the community. We have already discussed studies of intensive case management, but the concept has varied meanings in different contexts. One survey of case management within Medicaid concluded: "In concept and in practice, case management appears to be an ill-defined process that lacks substance" (Spitz 1987, p. 69).

Case management has a long tradition in social work, where case workers help to identify and mobilize a variety of community services on behalf of clients. Many case management approaches used in social work for decades—such as street teams, crisis intervention, and brokering community services—have now been adapted for the purposes of mental health care. Case managers play an important role as part of ACT teams, in less intensive programs focused on coordination of services, and within managed care organizations where clinicians need assistance in planning efficient treatment plans. People with severe and persistent illness who are younger, and those homeless and mentally ill, are often suspicious of the mental health system and traditional service approaches. Case managers can provide crucial outreach to these populations while enhancing continuity of care.

Case managers come in many varieties and may have little in common but their name. They range from masters-trained nurses, social workers, and psychologists (even some with doctorates) to staff with no specialized training. Some case managers have responsibilities for clinical care as well as acquiring services for clients, such as housing, disability insurance, psychosocial rehabilitation, family psychoeducation, and the like. Others are simply brokers with the sole responsibility of linking people with services. At times, case managers may control independent resources for use in enhancing already existing services and entitlements, as in the New York State Intensive Case Management Program (Surles et al. 1992). More typically, case managers must depend on exhortation, having little control over resources and little clout with the providers whose services they must enlist. Intensive case management programs might have professional case managers with no more than 10 clients per manager, whereas other programs might have as many as 40 or 50, or even 100 or more, clients per staff member. Some case management programs, such as the New York program, have been freestanding, focusing on particularly high and expensive utilizers of services; others, such as used in ACT programs, are part of systems of integrated care. Some case managers function primarily as patient advocates, whereas others play a dual role working for clients but also managing scarce resources in the face of bureaucratic pressures to stay within budget.

Case management is loosely thought of as a solution to a wide variety of difficult problems. However, case management has often become bureaucratized, narrow, and depersonalized despite expectations that it will transcend bureaucratic barriers, providing a personalized service in an impersonal society (Dill 2001). Case managers often shoulder unrealistic responsibilities given system disorganization and the types of personnel given these tasks. Thinking about case management in the more restricted medical context, the case manager is the primary care physician who serves as the doctor of first contact, provides continuing care and supervision, and makes appropriate referral for specialized medical and other services. The integrity of this role requires clinical judgment of a high level and broad scope, linkage with specialized services, and authority vis à vis other doctors and professionals, not to mention the patient. What is more important, it requires authority under reimbursement programs or other financial arrangements (Lewis, Fein, and Mechanic 1976).

Case management for persons with severe and persistent mental disorders is inherently more complex than even the multifaceted primary care situation. It not only requires appreciation of general medical and psychiatric needs and care, but also sophistication about such varied issues as housing, disability and welfare benefits, psychosocial rehabilitation, sheltered and competitive work programs, and issues relating to the legal and criminal justice systems. The scope of case management functions, the typical caseload, the level of expected training and experience, and the authority of the case manager all vary enormously, both within and among systems of care. Thus, it is essential to look carefully within the "black box" labeled as case management. In one systematic study, 417 persons with chronic mental illness in Texas were randomly assigned to experimental and control groups (Franklin et al. 1987). Each patient had two or more prior admissions to state or county mental hospitals during an approximately two-year period. Although those in the control group could receive any of the usual services other than case management, those in the experimental group were assigned to a case management unit staffed by a supervisor and seven case managers who possessed undergraduate or graduate degrees in the social sciences and an average of about four years experience working with those with mental illness. During the study, the case management unit spent about half its time providing nonclinical services to clients and two-fifths of its time brokering services. After 12 months, it was clear that patients in the case management group received more services, but they were also admitted to mental hospitals more often and incurred higher costs. Thus, concepts of community care that sound appealing in theory often may not achieve their goals in practice. Clearly, there are important differences between case management as practiced in contexts like this Texas study and a program like ACT.

The concept of the case manager has intuitive appeal, but it remains unclear whether it is appropriate to assign such varied and complex functions to individuals in contrast to teams or subsystems of care. First, there must be a clear definition of continuing responsibility for clients; few professionals other than physicians have traditionally played such roles. Second, given the diverse functions involved, specialization is more likely to lead to effective service. Third, case management in support of clients with chronic illness is a longitudinal process, but the "half-life" of case managers is short and attrition is high. Case managers typically do not have the training and experience, leverage, or professional standing to command resources from other organizations or even to be persuasive with them. Thus, case management, to be most effective, must be embedded in an organizational plan that defines who is responsible and accountable for the care of persons with the most severe disabilities, makes provision for the full spectrum of client needs, and exercises control over the multiple streams of resources that flow into the service system.

APPROACHES TO INTEGRATING SERVICES

A central theme of the Affordable Care Act is managing the trajectory of persons with chronic disease by developing Health Homes, Medical Homes, Accountable Care Organizations, and the colocation of health and social services. The objective is to integrate medical and behavioral health services; primary and specialty care; and a wide array of clinical, social, and rehabilitative services while promoting the philosophy and practice of holistic care. The multiplicity of resources under consideration includes case management, social work services, housing, nutrition and medication counseling, and much more. To the extent that new reimbursement approaches and financial incentives prove successful, they will help break down silos that currently isolate treatments for mental illness; substance abuse; and physical comorbidities such as diabetes, cardiovascular disease, and asthma. In this team effort, the need for effective use of organizational design and the latest information technologies and electronic health records is abundantly clear.

Up to now, responsibility for serving those with mental illness has been fragmented among varying levels of government and categorical service agencies. This has resulted in inefficiencies, duplication, poor use of resources, and outright failures to support people in need. Hospital units are sometimes linked poorly, or not at all, with outpatient psychiatric care and psychosocial services. Admission to, and discharge from, inpatient units often occur without relation to an ongoing system of community services or careful long-term planning based on patient needs. Agencies serving people who are homeless, abuse substances, or have developmental disabilities operate within distinct bureaucracies, making it particularly difficult to accommodate those with a spate of problems. Similarly, inpatient care services under Medicaid and local medical assistance programs often function independently of outpatient care and psychosocial rehabilitation organizations in the community, contributing to inadequate care.

What form should new organizational structures take? A precise answer to this question must await more development and testing. Different structures will likely be needed to fit various political, legal, and service delivery environments. This process can be facilitated if major administrative authorities, such as the Centers for Medicare & Medicaid Services and state mental health authorities, act to promote local diversity and program innovation. By contrast, centralization is prone to lead to reduced flexibility, innovation, and public support. Consider, for example, the situation that arose recently in a major city in Texas. Faced with the option of taking over a number of smaller agencies serving individuals with chronic mental illness, the director of a department having community-wide authority and responsibility for this population chose not to consolidate. The rationale was that each of these agencies had an enthusiastic board with members advocating for improved care, and this reality outweighed any advantages associated with direct control.

The relative merits of organizing mental health services through government agencies, special boards designated by statute, managed behavioral health companies, nonprofit voluntary groups, self-directed consumer groups, or some hybrid of these forms remain unclear. It is not obvious to what degree such entities should strive to be direct service providers as well as planning, financing, and administrative bodies, or whether they should simply restrict themselves to limited administrative and regulatory functions while contracting with providers for treatment services. Decisions of this kind cannot be made in the abstract but, rather, must be weighed in relation to the organization and effectiveness of existing services, statutory requirements, and a locality's political culture. In theory, performance contracting and the competition it implies seem advantageous to publicly organized services, but in practice the funders may become dependent on their contractees with few real options for alternative partnerships (Dorwart, Schlesinger, and Pulice 1986).

During the late 1980s, efforts to develop stronger public mental health authorities in a number of cities contributed to thoughtful consideration of the problem of how to reduce services fragmentation (Goldman 2000). The result was improved continuity of care in certain localities, but without evidence of corresponding benefits in regard to patient outcomes. One major change during this period was the extent to which mental health authorities began to view housing as part of their responsibilities. By creating new housing or cooperating with public housing authorities, they worked to expand access to residential opportunities. Although developing stronger public mental health authorities on the local level did not live up to the high expectations with which these agencies were established, the movement was helpful in keeping mental health issues on the agenda during a period when the American public and policymakers demanded tax relief, and programs for the disadvantaged suffered declining interest.

Rather than focus on new mental health authorities, today the public sector increasingly seeks to handle its responsibilities for mental health care by contracting. Contracting is commonly seen as a way of reforming programs that have become overly bureaucratic, self-protective, risk-aversive, and resistant to innovation. One advantage of the private sector is that it is much less vulnerable to the political clout of unions, professional associations, and elected officials, thereby yielding greater flexibility in confronting redundant and unproductive components of the service system. States have had notorious difficulty in closing institutions, replacing civil service employees, and changing work practices inside the bureaucracy.

A very appealing feature of the Affordable Care Act is its establishment of a new Center for Medicare and Medicaid Innovation with the purpose of assessing revised models of patient care, organizational coordination, new payment and delivery approaches, and strategies for enhancing public health. The legislation directs some $10 billion toward this effort through 2019, signaling a seriousness of intent behind this element of national health care reform.

RECOGNIZING THE ROLE OF FAMILIES

For most people with mental illness, families remain the main source of love, assistance, and support, often at great personal cost and burden to family members. In recent years, as most patients with serious mental illness have been treated in community settings, this issue of burden has received more attention, and research on the topic is increasingly sophisticated in theory and measurement (Awad and Voruganti 2008). For example, researchers have differentiated between objective and subjective burdens, examining the impact of such variables as where the patient resides, familial connection to the patient (whether parent or sibling), and the extent to which families receive assistive services.

The problems that arise in caring for a family member with severe mental illness take many forms. One study in Ohio identified the following types of family burden: attention-seeking behaviors (24 percent), night disturbances (18 percent), embarrassing behavior (18 percent), alcohol use (12 percent), suicide (11 percent), drug use (10 percent), and violence (9 percent) (Tessler and Gamache 1994). In a New Jersey study, Reinhard and Horwitz (1995) found that two-fifths to three-quarters of parents caring for a mentally ill adult child were distracted from their own activities, had their household routines upset, experienced family frictions and reduced leisure time, and had financial strain and reduced social contacts. More than a quarter also reported missing work, neglecting other family members, and friction with others. A particularly prominent worry for these parents was what would happen to their child in the future. It is not surprising, then, that many studies report that caretaker burden results in high levels of stress. There is also evidence that living in a household with a seriously mentally ill family member is associated with reduced physical health as well (Gallagher and Mechanic 1996).

The profile and particulars of burden may reflect different situations, but some level of strain is a transcendent reality within nearly all families affected by serious mental illness. Tessler and Gamache (1994) found that parents living with a mentally ill adult child provided more help and took more measures to control the offspring's behavior than when they lived elsewhere. Yet, even when an adult child who has a mental illness resides elsewhere, parental worry and burden are high. The greater the problem of dealing with disruptive behaviors, or the higher the need for practical aid and emotional support, the more toll it takes (Reinhard and Horwitz 1995). Professional assistance can moderate the weight of responsibility to some extent (Reinhard 1994). A significant policy challenge is identifying the most beneficial types of psychoeducational intervention under these circumstances. Increasingly, the research literature documents the importance of family burden not only in relation to mental illness and dementias, such as Alzheimer's disease, but also for other medical conditions. In all cases, consequences for the physical health and longevity of family caretakers can be significant (Christakis and Allison 2006).

Family interventions need not be complex to be useful. In a study of 462 family members of adults with mental illness located in three cities, the family members were randomized either to 8 modules of education and skill-training of 2 hours or to a waiting list for the program (Pickett-Schenk et al. 2006). On average, relatives attended six of the eight classes. Those in the experimental group reported fewer depressive symptoms (measured with the CES-D and Brief Symptom Inventory) while expressing significantly fewer negative views of the ill relative than the control group. Those participating in the program also reported better role functioning and vitality. Outcomes were still sustained six months after the intervention had ended.

One intriguing study revealed a degree of mutuality between family members and patients in the area of caregiver support (Horwitz, Reinhard, and Howell-White 1996). That is, the more assistance a mentally ill family member could give parents and siblings, the more he or she received in return. This suggests simple interventions aimed at helping persons to be less dependent and more proactive in reducing family burden and stress, whether by means of expressing caring and appreciation, helping with chores, or even such simple things as acknowledging birthdays and other special events important within the family.

Families of individuals with severe and persistent mental illness frequently become puzzled and angry about their interactions with the mental health system and mental health professionals. In situations where family members have received little constructive support and must assume most of the burden, it is understandable some would resist deinstitutionalization while calling for additional beds in public mental hospitals (Isaac and Armat 1990). Studies demonstrate, however, that families, including patients, are much more satisfied with community care than hospitalization when the former includes a coherent and well-organized complement of services complete with clear locus of responsibility within the system for individual patients (Leff, Trieman, and Gooch 1996; Marks et al. 1994; New South Wales Department of Health 1983; Stein and Test 1985).

Family concerns are represented by the increasingly influential National Alliance on Mental Illness (NAMI), formally established in 1980. The organization has grown rapidly in membership, visibility, and political presence (Hatfield 1987). NAMI represents families of the severely mentally ill. Members hold differing points of view and support no single political ideology. Most in the organization, however, believe severe mental illness to be substantially biological in nature, and they strongly support expansion of biomedical research. Many individuals have been angry with mental health professionals who seem to blame families for the occurrence or worsening of the condition of mental illness, but this does not imply hostility to mental health treatment. Further, NAMI actively backs the fashioning of more comprehensive systems of community care, and the group seeks to reduce stigmatization of mental illness. Without a group like NAMI, there would be an important gap to fill in political advocacy inside the mental health field.

It is largely due to the efforts of NAMI and other family advocacy organizations that caretaker burden has become a more visible issue within the mental health field. Relevant services are spreading, and this marks a significant advance from earlier periods when families were excluded from the treatment process, given little information, and often were assumed to be "part of the problem" for patients working toward recovery. Even so, many programs and professionals today still provide inadequate family support, information, and instruction, and they often fail to make use of opportunities to mobilize families as part of treatment planning (Walkup 1997). Therapists who promote a strong ideology of patient independence may inadvertently contribute to tensions within a family unit by challenging members to develop new roles and relationships in responding to the occurrence of mental illness.

The Affordable Care Act (ACA) recognizes the important role of family caregiving for persons with chronic disease and disabilities, together with the difficult personal and financial burdens faced by family caregivers. Indeed, the statute explicitly mentions "family caregivers" 11 times and "caregivers" another 46 times (Feinberg and Reamy 2011). Following are some of the pertinent measures included in the ACA:

- Involving family caregivers in shared decision-making and in assessing how caregivers and consumers experience care;
- Involving caregivers as part of the teams in new models of care;
- Providing education and training for caregivers; and
- Relieving caregiver burden by strengthening support services

In the case of Health Homes, previously discussed, providers must offer family support as well as services for authorized representatives of patients, who often will be family caregivers. It will be many years before we can evaluate how all this will play out, but the blueprint of change is encouraging.

MENTAL HEALTH POLICY AND THE CONTEMPORARY ERA

Historians are prone to describe and explain the past in terms of distinctive periods organized around overarching themes. So it is that in the history of mental health care, we often talk about moral treatment and the spread of mental hospitals in the early and mid-1800s, institutional decline during the late 1800s and early 1900s, the community mental health movement and heyday of deinstitutionalization from the late 1950s to 1970s, and a post-deinstitutionalization era in the latter part of the twentieth century concerned chiefly with devising the concept and practice of community support. In this light, where would we situate the mental health system today, just a few years into the twenty-first century? What are the driving issues that give coherence to contemporary debate and demarcate the direction of change? Based on our review, three forces are dominating influences within the current process of mental health policy formulation.

First is the reality of economic recession. In 2007–2009, the nation underwent an economic crisis from which it has yet to recover. The devastation began with the collapse of the subprime mortgage market. Soon, there followed a round of investment company bankruptcies and bank failures that sent the economy into a tailspin. From a high of more than 14,000 in October of 2007, the Dow Jones average plunged to less than 7,000 in early 2009. *An Economic Report of the President* characterizes the current downturn as "the most severe...since the Great Depression," and it is not over yet (White House 2012). After reaching a high of 10 percent unemployment in October 2009, the country's level of joblessness at the time of this writing, in late-2012, still hovers around 8 percent. Not until the third quarter of 2011 did the real gross domestic product of the United States exceed its value before the start of the recession in 2007. The gap between rich and poor has widened.

High unemployment and falling incomes have contributed to historic shortfalls in state revenues (Oliff, Mai, and Palacios 2012). The situation with regard to mental health care in a period like this may be likened to a fiscal vise. On one side, the prevalence of many mental health problems increases with economic ills (Hodgkin and Karpman 2010). On the other, there are declining budgets to fund treatment services. In 2011, NAMI released a report on state spending cuts for mental health services (Honberg et al. 2011). Twenty-eight states plus the District of Columbia cut their mental health budgets between fiscal years 2009 and 2012. In the 10 states exhibiting the most severe retrenchment, these cuts ranged from 10.4 percent in Mississippi to 39.3 percent in South Carolina.

The second major influence shaping mental health policy on the contemporary scene is the movement for health care reform. In a sense, the mental health community led the way toward more general health reform by setting an example with its fight for parity insurance coverage between mental illness and other health conditions. Parity has dealt mostly with a particular form of *underinsurance* in that, while new federal laws ended most types of coverage discrimination against those with mental health problems, they did not require health plans to include mental health benefits. The Affordable Care Act went well beyond this achievement not only by including mental health and substance abuse services as part of the "essential benefits package" to be covered by all insurance policies offered through state health insurance exchanges, it did so while expanding health insurance coverage among tens of millions Americans. Thus, the ACA increased mental health protections by attacking the dual problems of underinsurance and *uninsurance*.

Yet, as our analysis of the ACA makes plain, the law does more than simply address longstanding issues of mental health insurance coverage. It also provides an important opportunity for mental health system reform in numerous areas. New health care delivery and payment mechanisms could go far in improving the scope and quality of behavioral health care services. This is being done via new options within the Medicaid program, as well as financial support for a variety of other initiatives and service demonstrations supportive of the functioning of community care programs (Barry 2011).

The third pivotal influence on mental health care is the paradigm of recovery. In recent years, the recovery movement has advanced swiftly in this country from a rather vague set of strivings articulated by groups marginal to policy development to a specific body of principles given central consideration within discussions of mental health care. Yet much remains to be worked out regarding the link between concept and practice in this transformation. However, philosophy and vision have always mattered in the evolution of mental health care, as much as organizational and financial realities. The idea of recovery is emerging as a powerful touchstone for imagining what the mental health system should, and can, be doing in years ahead.

Each of these three forces of change presents great opportunity in tandem with great risk. Economic crisis has drawn attention to the need for repairing holes in the safety net of mental health programs and services—including a significant new report on economics and mental health by the World Health Organization (2011)—but the longer economic troubles drag on, the more existing protections are likely to become eroded. Health care reform could prove a boon to the mental health system to the extent that stated objectives are achieved, yet this legislative accomplishment has continued to face relentless attacks and distortions. The concept of recovery injects new energy and idealism into the mental health policy process, but it introduces certain tensions between consumer and professional and family perspectives that may be hard to reconcile in service planning. And as the balance between risk and opportunity gets played out within each of these circumstances, the result will define the nature of the contemporary era in mental health care.

In addition to the impact of these high-profile determinants, the mental health system continues to contend with a long-term gap between knowledge and implementation. Community programs for chronic mental illness have not suffered from lack of innovation or evaluation. Rather, the primary difficulty has been the absence of a public policy framework to facilitate the development of appropriate organizational entities; to bring together essential elements of services, funding, and reimbursement; and to balance the trade-offs between investing in traditional medical and hospital services and a broader range of treatment and supports beneficial for patients with long-term rehabilitative needs (Mechanic and Aiken 1987; Stein and Ganser 1983; Talbott 1985). Many components of effective community mental health care are well understood, but the continued compilation of research evidence, on its own, will do little to correct a situation in which model programs are scattered geographically or available with such inadequate capacity that hundreds, sometimes thousands, of patients are lining up on waiting lists hoping for the chance to gain access to state-of-the-art practice.

CONCLUSION

In 2010, Mark Vonnegut, son of the famous novelist Kurt Vonnegut, published a memoir of his life with mental illness. The book, titled *Just Like Someone Without Mental Illness Only More So*, is actually the author's second foray on this subject, the first volume having appeared in 1975, or shortly after Vonnegut underwent his first schizophrenic breakdown (Vonnegut 1975). Now writing after a lengthy career as a successful pediatrician, Vonnegut recounts the ups and downs of his recovery, including periodic relapses that necessitated rehospitalization. Dr. Vonnegut may not be typical of the majority of patients with severe mental illness, but his story is an instructive one for appreciating the truth that, even if lives may be interrupted by mental health problems of the most serious kind, a person's identity and long-term functioning need not be dictated by this illness experience. The challenge of mental health and social policy is to act on this realization by using all the tools and insights yielded by more than 200 years of hard-won experience providing mental health care on the local, state, and national levels.

References

Allbright, Amy L. "2010 Employment Decisions Under the ADA Titles I and V-Survey Update." *Mental and Physical Disability Law Reporter* 35 (2011): 394–398.

Altshuler, Norma, et al. *Provider Experiences Under the Revised Ticket to Work Regulations.* Washington, DC: Mathematica Policy Research, 2011. Available online: www.ssa.gov/disabilityresearch/documents/Provider%20Experience%20Under%20New%20TTW%20Regulations%20September%202011.pdf.

Audini, Bernard, et al. "Home-Based Versus Out-patient/In-patient Care for People with Serious Mental Illness." *British Journal of Psychiatry* 165 (1994): 204–210.

Awad, A. George, and Lakshmi N. P. Voruganti. "The Burden of Schizophrenia on Caregivers." *Pharmoeconomics* 26 (2008): 149–162.

Baicker Katherine, and Amy Finkelstein. "The Effects of Medicaid Coverage—Learning from the Oregon Experiment." *New England Journal of Medicine* 365 (2011): 683–685.

Barrow, Burt S. "The Employment Rate of People with Disabilities." *Monthly Labor Review* 131 (2008): 44–50.

Barry, Colleen L. *Beyond Parity: Mental Health and Substance Use Disorder Care Under Payment and Delivery System Reform in Massachusetts.* Waltham, MA: Massachusetts Health Policy Forum, Brandeis University, 2011. Available online: masshealthpolicyforum.brandeis.edu/forums/Documents/Barry_Forum_10262011_FINAL.pdf.

Bassuk, Ellen, et al. "The Homelessness Problem." *Scientific American* 251 (1984a): 40–45.

Bassuk, Ellen, et al. "Is Homelessness a Mental Health Problem?" *American Journal of Psychiatry* 141 (1984b): 1546–1550.

Bassuk, Ellen L., et al. "The Characteristics and Needs of Sheltered Homeless and Low-Income Housed Mothers." *Journal of the American Medical Association* 276 (1996): 640–646.

Becker, Deborah R., et al. "Job Preferences of Clients with Severe Psychiatric Disorders Participating in Supported Employment Programs." *Psychiatric Services* 47 (1996): 1223–1226.

Belknap, Ivan. *Human Problems of a State Mental Hospital.* New York: McGraw-Hill, 1956.

Berger, Philip A. "Medical Treatment of Mental Illness." *Science* 200 (1978): 974–981.

Bond, Gary R., Robert E. Drake and Deborah R. Becker. "An Update on Randomized Controlled Trials of Evidence-Based Supported Employment." *Psychiatric Rehabilitation Journal* 31 (2008): 280–290.

Bond, Gary R., et al. "An Update on Supported Employment for People with Severe Mental Illness." *Psychiatric Services* 48 (1997): 335–346.

Brown, George W., James L. T. Birley, and John K. Wing. "Influence of Family Life on the Course of Schizophrenic Disorders: A Replication." *British Journal of Psychiatry* 121 (1972): 241–258.

Brown, George W., et al. "Influence of Family Life on the Course of Schizophrenic Illness." *British Journal of Preventive and Social Medicine* 16 (1962): 55–68.

Carling, Paul J. "Housing and Supports for Persons with Mental Illness: Emerging Approaches to Research and Practice." *Hospital and Community Psychiatry* 44 (1993): 439–449.

Caudill, William. *The Psychiatric Hospital as a Small Society.* Cambridge, MA: Harvard University Press, 1958.

Christakis, Nicholas A., and Paul D. Allison. "Mortality After the Hospitalization of a Spouse." *New England Journal of Medicine* 354 (2006): 719–730.

Cook, Judith A., et al. "Estimated Payments to Employment Service Providers for Persons with Mental Illness in the Ticket to Work Program." *Psychiatric Services* 57 (2006): 465–471.

Coser, Rose Laub. *Training in Ambiguity: Learning Through Doing in a Mental Hospital.* New York: The Free Press, 1979.

Dieterich, Marina, et al. "Intensive Case Management for Severe Mental Illness." *Cochrane Database Systematic Review* 6 (2010): CD007906.

Dill, Ann E. P. *Managing to Care: Case Management and Service System Reform.* New York: Aldine de Gruyter, 2001.

Dixon, Lisa, et al. "Evidence-Based Practices for Services to Families of People with Psychiatric Disabilities." *Psychiatric Services* 52 (2001): 903–910.

Dorwart, Robert A., Mark Schlesinger, and Richard T. Pulice. "The Promise and Pitfalls of Purchase-of-Service Contracts." *Hospital and Community Psychiatry* 37 (1986): 875–878.

Drake, Robert E., and Deborah R. Becker. "The Individual Placement and Support Model of Supported Employment." *Psychiatric Services* 47 (1996): 473–475.

Drake, Robert E., and Deborah R. Becker. "Why Not Implement Supported Employment?" *Psychiatric Services* 62 (2011): 1251.

Drake, Robert E., et al. "Social Security and Mental Illness: Reducing Disability with Supported Employment." *Health Affairs* 28 (2009): 761–770.

Falloon, Ian R. H., Jeffrey L. Boyd, and Christine W. McGill. *Family Care of Schizophrenia.* New York: Guilford Press, 1984.

Falloon, Ian R. H., et al. "Family Management in the Prevention of Exacerbations of Schizophrenia: A Controlled Study." *New England Journal of Medicine* 306 (1982): 1437–1440.

Falloon, Ian R. H., et al. "Family Management in the Prevention of Morbidity of Schizophrenia." *Archives of General Psychiatry* 42 (1985): 887–896.

Feinberg, Lynn, and Allison M. Reamy. *Health Reform Law Creates New Opportunities to Better Recognize and Support Family Caregivers.* AARP Policy Institute Fact Sheet. Washington, DC: AARP, 2011. Available online: assets.aarp.org/rgcenter/ppi/ltc/fs239.pdf.

Finkelstein, Amy, et al. "The Oregon Health Insurance Experiment: Evidence from the First Year." *Quarterly Journal of Economics*, Advanced Access published May 3, 2012. Available online: qje.oxfordjournals.org/content/early/2012/05/03/qje.qjs020.full.pdf+html.

Folsom, David P., and Dilip V. Jeste. "Schizophrenia in Homeless Persons: A Systematic Review of the Literature." *Acta Psychiatrica Scandinavica* 105 (2002): 404–413.

Franklin, Jack L., et al. "An Evaluation of Case Management." *American Journal of Public Health* 77 (1987): 674–678.

Freeman, Richard B., and Brian Hall. "Permanent Homelessness in America?" Cambridge, MA: Bureau of Economic Research, Working Paper No. 2013, unpublished, 1986.

Gallagher, Sally, and David Mechanic. "Living with the Mentally Ill: Effects on the Health and Functioning of Other Household Members." *Social Science and Medicine* 42 (1996): 1691–1701.

Geddes, John, et al. "Atypical Antipsychotics in the Treatment of Schizophrenia: Systematic Overview and Meta-Regression Analysis." *British Medical Journal* 321 (2000): 1371–1376.

Goffman, Erving. *Asylums: Essays on the Social Situation of Mental Patients and Other Inmates.* Garden City, NY: Anchor Books, 1961.

Goldman, Howard H. "The Program on Chronic Mental Illness." In *To Improve Health and Health Care 2000: The Robert Wood Johnson Foundation Anthology*, edited by Stephen L. Isaacs and James R. Knickman, pp. 115–133. San Francisco: Jossey Bass, 2000.

Grob, Gerald N., and Howard H. Goldman. *The Dilemma of Federal Mental Health Policy: Radical Reform or Incremental Change?* New Brunswick, NJ: Rutgers University Press, 2006.

Gudeman, John E., and Miles F. Shore. "Beyond Deinstitutionalization: A New Class of Facilities for the Mentally Ill." *New England Journal of Medicine* 311 (1984): 832–836.

Hatfield, Agnes, ed. *Families of the Mentally Ill: Meeting the Challenges.* New Directions for Mental Health Services, No. 34. San Francisco: Jossey-Bass, 1987.

Hodgkin, Dominic, and Hannah E. Karpman. "Economic Crises and Public Spending on Mental Health Care." *International Journal of Mental Health* 39 (2010): 91–106.

Hogan, Richard. "It Can't Happen Here: Community Opposition to Group Homes." *Sociological Focus* 19 (1986a): 361–374.

Hogan, Richard. "Gaining Community Support for Group Homes." *Community Mental Health Journal* 22 (1986b): 117–126.

Hogarty, Gerard E., et al. "Family Psychoeducation, Social Skills Training, and Maintenance Chemotherapy in the Aftercare Treatment of Schizophrenia II. Two-Year Effects of a Controlled Study on Relapse and Adjustment." *Archives of General Psychiatry* 48 (1991): 340–347.

Honberg, Ron, et al. *State Mental Health Cuts: The Continuing Crisis.* Arlington, VA: National Alliance on Mental Illness, 2011. Available online: www.nami.org/Template.cfm?Section=state_budget_cuts_report.

Horwitz, Allan V., Susan Reinhard, and Sandra Howell-White. "Caregiving as Reciprocal Exchange in Families with Seriously Mentally Ill Members." *Journal of Health and Social Behavior* 37 (1996): 149–162.

Hoult, John. "Replicating the Mendota Model in Australia." *Hospital and Community Psychiatry* 38 (1987): 565.

Institute of Medicine. Committee on Nursing Home Regulation. *Improving the Quality of Care in Nursing Homes.* Washington, DC: National Academies Press, 1986.

Institute of Medicine. *Homelessness, Health, and Human Needs.* Washington, DC: National Academy Press, 1988.

Isaac, Rael J., and Virginia C. Armat. *Madness in the Streets: How Psychiatry and the Law Abandoned the Mentally Ill.* New York: Free Press, 1990.

Jencks, Christopher. *The Homeless.* Cambridge, MA: Harvard University Press, 1994.

Johnson, Sandra J. *Assertive Community Treatment: Evidence-Based Practice or Managed Recovery.* New Brunswick, NJ: Transaction Publishers, 2011.

Kellam, Sheppard G., June L. Shmelzer, and Audrey Berman. "Variation in the Atmospheres of Psychiatric Wards." *Archives of General Psychiatry* 14 (1966): 561–570.

Kiesler, Charles A. "Mental Hospitals and Alternative Care." *American Psychologist* 37 (1982): 349–360.

Kiesler, Charles A., and Amy E. Sibulkin. *Mental Hospitalization: Myths and Facts About a National Crisis.* Newbury Park, CA: Sage Publications, 1987.

Knapp, Martin, et al. "Service Use and Costs of Home-Based Versus Hospital-Based Care for People with Serious Mental Illness." *British Journal of Psychiatry* 165 (1994): 195–203.

Lee, Barrett A., Kimberly A. Tyler, and James D. Wright. "The New Homelessness Revisited." *Annual Review of Sociology* 36 (2010): 501–521.

Leff, Julian, and Christine Vaughn. *Expressed Emotion in Families.* New York: Guilford Press, 1985.

Leff, Julian, Noam Trieman, and Christopher Gooch. "Team for the Assessment of Psychiatric Services (TAPS) Project 33: Prospective Follow-up Study of Long-Stay Patients Discharged from Two Psychiatric Hospitals." *American Journal of Psychiatry* 153 (1996): 1318–1324.

Leff, Julian, et al. "A Controlled Trial of Social Intervention in the Families of Schizophrenic Patients." *British Journal of Psychiatry* 141 (1982): 121–134.

Lehman, Anthony F. "Quality of Care in Mental Health: The Case of Schizophrenia." *Health Affairs* 18 (1999): 52–65.

Lehman, Anthony F., and Donald M. Steinwachs. "Patterns of Usual Care for Schizophrenia: Initial Results from the Schizophrenia Patient Outcomes Research Team (PORT) Client Survey." *Schizophrenia Bulletin* 24 (1998): 11–20.

Lewis, Charles E., Rashi Fein, and David Mechanic. *A Right to Health: The Problem of Access to Primary Medical Care.* New York: Wiley Interscience, 1976.

Lieberman, Jeffrey A., et al. "Effectiveness of Antipsychotic Drugs in Patients with Chronic Schizophrenia." *New England Journal of Medicine* 353 (2005): 1209–1223.

Linn, Lawrence S. "Social Characteristics and Patient Expectations Toward Mental Hospitalization." *Archives of General Psychiatry* 20 (1969): 457–469.

Livermore, Gina, Sarah Prenovitz, and Jody Schimmel. *Employment-Related Outcomes of a Recent Cohort of Work Incentives Planning and Assistance (WIPA) Program Enrollees: Final Report.* Washington, DC: Mathematica Policy Research, 2011. Available online: www.ssa.gov/disabilityresearch/documents/WIPA%20Cohort%20September%202011.pdf.

Marks, Isaac M., et al. "Home-Based Versus Hospital-Based Care for People with Serious Mental Illness." *British Journal of Psychiatry* 165 (1994): 179–194.

Mashaw, Jerry L., and Virginia P. Reno, eds. *The Environment of Disability Income Policy: Programs, People, History and Context.* Washington, DC: National Academy of Social Insurance, 1996a.

Mashaw, Jerry L., and Virginia P. Reno, eds. *Balancing Security and Opportunity: The Challenge of Disability Income Policy.* Washington, DC: National Academy of Social Insurance, 1996b.

McFarlane, William R., et al. "Multiple-Family Groups and Psychoeducation in the Treatment of Schizophrenia." *Archives of General Psychiatry* 52 (1995): 679–687.

McFarlane, William R., et al. "A Comparison of Two Levels of Family-Aided Assertive Community Treatment." *Psychiatric Services* 47 (1996): 744–750.

Mechanic, David. "Cultural and Organizational Aspects of Application of the Americans with Disabilities Act to Persons with Psychiatric Disabilities." *Milbank Quarterly* 76 (1998): 5–23.

Mechanic, David. *The Truth About Health Care: Why Reform Is Not Working in America.* New Brunswick, NJ: Rutgers University Press, 2006.

Mechanic, David. "Seizing Opportunities Under the Affordable Care Act for Transforming the Mental and Behavioral Health System." *Health Affairs* 31 (2012): 376–382.

Mechanic, David, ed. *Improving Inpatient Psychiatric Treatment in an Era of Managed Care*. New Directions for Mental Health Services, No. 73. San Francisco, CA: Jossey Bass, 1997.

Mechanic, David, and Linda H. Aiken. "Improving the Care of Patients with Chronic Mental Illness." *New England Journal of Medicine* 317 (1987): 1634–1638.

Mechanic, David, Scott Bilder, and Donna D. McAlpine. "Employing Persons with Serious Mental Illness." *Health Affairs* 21 (2002): 242–253.

Monroe-DeVita, Maria, Gary Morse, and Gary R. Bond. "Program Fidelity and Beyond: Multiple Strategies and Criteria for Ensuring Quality of Assertive Community Treatment." *Psychiatric Services* 63 (2012): 743–750.

Moos, Rudolf H. *Evaluating Treatment Environments: A Social Ecological Approach*. New York: Wiley Interscience, 1974.

Moos, Rudolf H. *Evaluating Treatment Environments: The Quality of Psychiatric and Substance Abuse Programs*, 2nd ed. New Brunswick, NJ: Transaction Publishers, 1997.

National Alliance on Mental Illness. *ACT: Assertive Community Treatment*. Arlington, VA: National Alliance on Mental Illness, 2005. Available online: www.nami.org/Template.cfm?Section=ACT-TA_Center&template=/ContentManagement/ContentDisplay.cfm&ContentID=132547.

National Alliance to End Homelessness. *Ten Year Plan*. Washington, DC: National Alliance to End Homelessness, 2012. Available online: www.endhomelessness.org/section/solutions/ten_year_plan.

Neugeboren, Jay. *Imagining Robert: My Brother, Madness, and Survival: A Memoir*. New York: William Morrow and Company, 1997.

Neugeboren, Jay. *Transforming Madness: New Lives for People Living with Mental Illness*. New York: William Morrow and Company, 1999.

New South Wales Department of Health. *Psychiatric Hospital Versus Community Treatment: A Controlled Study* (HSR 83-046). Sydney, Australia: Department of Health, 1983.

Newman, Sandra J., et al. "The Effects of Independent Living on Persons with Chronic Mental Illness: An Assessment of the Section 8 Certificate Program." *Milbank Quarterly* 72 (1994): 171–198.

Noble, John H., Jr., et al. *A Legacy of Failure: The Inability of the Federal-State Vocational Rehabilitation System to Serve People with Severe Mental Illnesses*. Arlington, VA: National Alliance on Mental Illness, 1997. Available online: www.nami.org/Template.cfm?Section=Issues_Spotlights&Template=/Content/ContentGroups/E-News/20013/January_20012/Vocational_Rehabilitation_Report__A_Legacy_Of_Failure.htm.

Olfson, Mark. "Assertive Community Treatment: An Evaluation of the Experimental Evidence." *Hospital and Community Psychiatry* 41 (1990): 634–641.

Olfson, Mark, Ira D. Glick, and David Mechanic. "Inpatient Treatment of Schizophrenia in General Hospitals." *Hospital and Community Psychiatry* 44 (1993): 40–44.

Oliff, Phil, Chris Mai, and Vincent Palacios. *States Continue to Feel Recession's Impact*. Washington, DC: Center on Budget and Policy Priorities, June 27, 2012. Available online: sparkaction.org/resources/52171.

Osterweis, Marian, Arthur Kleinman, and David Mechanic, eds. *Pain and Disability: Clinical, Behavioral, and Public Policy Perspectives*. Washington, DC: National Academy Press, 1987.

Paul, Gordon L., and Robert J. Lentz. *Psychosocial Treatment of Chronic Mental Patients*. Cambridge, MA: Harvard University Press, 1977.

Perrow, Charles. "Hospitals: Technology, Structure, and Goals." In *Handbook of Organizations*, edited by James G. March, pp. 910–971. Chicago: Rand McNally, 1965.

Petrila, John. "Congress Restores the Americans with Disabilities Act to Its Original Intent." *Psychiatric Services* 60 (2009): 878–879.

Petrila, John, and Thomas Brink. "Mental Illness and Changing Definitions of Disability Under the Americans with Disabilities Act." *Psychiatric Services* 52 (2001): 626–630.

Pickett-Schenk, Susan A., et al. "Psychological Well-Being and Relationship Outcomes in a Randomized Study of Family-Led Education." *Archives of General Psychiatry* 63 (2006): 1043–1050.

Pogoda, Terri K., et al. "Qualitative Analysis of Barriers to Implementation of Supported Employment in the Department of Veterans Affairs." *Psychiatric Services* 62 (2011): 1289–1295.

Randolph, Frances, et al. "Creating Integrated Service Systems for Homeless Persons with Mental Illness: The ACCESS Program. Access to Community Care and Effective Services and Supports." *Psychiatric Services* 48 (1997): 369–373.

Reinhard, Susan C. "Perspectives on the Family's Caregiving Experience in Mental Illness." *Image: Journal of Nursing Scholarship* 26 (1994): 70–74.

Reinhard, Susan, and Allan V. Horwitz. "Caregiver Burden: Differentiating the Content and Consequences of Family Caregiving." *Journal of Marriage and Family* 57 (1995): 741–750.

Rosenheck, Robert, et al. "Service System Integration, Access to Services, and Housing Outcomes in a Program for Homeless Persons with Severe Mental Illness." *American Journal of Public Health* 88 (1998): 1610–1615.

Rosenheck, Robert, et al. "Service Delivery and Community: Social Capital, Service Systems Integration, and Outcomes Among Homeless Persons with Severe Mental Illness." *Health Services Research* 36 (2001): 691–710.

Rosenheck, Robert, et al. "Cost-Effectiveness of Supported Housing for Homeless Persons with Mental Illness." *Archives of General Psychiatry* 60 (2003): 940–951.

Rossi, Peter H. *Down and Out in America: The Origins of Homelessness.* Chicago: University of Chicago Press, 1989.

Rossi, Peter H., and James D. Wright. "The Determinants of Homelessness." *Health Affairs* 6 (1987): 19–32.

Rossi, Peter H., et al. "The Urban Homeless: Estimating Composition and Size." *Science* 235 (1987): 1336–1341.

Santos, Alberto B., et al. "Research on Field-Based Services: Models for Reform in the Delivery of Mental Health Care to Populations with Complex Clinical Problems." *American Journal of Psychiatry* 152 (1995): 1111–1123.

Schimmel, Jody, et al. *Evaluation of the Work Incentives Planning and Assistance (WIPA) Program: Beneficiaries Served, Services Provided, and Program Costs.* Washington, DC: Mathematica Policy Research, 2010. Available online: www.ssa.gov/disabilityresearch/documents/WIPA%20final%20report-full.pdf.

Schutt, Russell K. *Homelessness, Housing, and Mental Illness* (with Stephen M. Goldfinger). Cambridge: President and Fellow of Harvard College, 2011.

Schutt, Russell K., and Stephen M. Goldfinger. "Housing Preferences and Perceptions of Health and Functioning Among Homeless Mentally Ill Persons." *Psychiatric Services* 47 (1996): 381–386.

Segal, Steven P., and Uri Aviram. *The Mentally-Ill in Community-Based Sheltered Care: A Study of Community Care and Social Integration.* New York: Wiley Interscience, 1978.

Spitz, Bruce. "A National Survey of Medicaid Case-Management Programs." *Health Affairs* 6 (1987): 61–70.

Stanton, Alfred H., and Morris S. Schwartz. *The Mental Hospital: A Study of Institutional Participation in Psychiatric Illness and Treatment.* New York: Basic Books, 1954.

Stein, Leonard I., and Leonard J. Ganser. "Wisconsin's System for Funding Mental Health Services." In *New Directions for Mental Health Services: Unified Mental Health System*, edited by John Talbott, pp. 25–32. San Francisco: Jossey-Bass, 1983.

Stein, Leonard I., and Mary Ann Test, eds. *Alternatives to Mental Hospital Treatment.* New York: Plenum Press, 1978.

Stein, Leonard I., and Mary Ann Test. "Alternative to Mental Hospital Treatment I. Conceptual Model, Treatment Program and Clinical Evaluation." *Archives of General Psychiatry* 37 (1980): 392–397.

Stein, Leonard I., and Mary Ann Test, eds. *The Training in Community Living Model: A Decade of Experience.* New Directions for Mental Health Services 26. San Francisco: Jossey-Bass, 1985.

Stein, Leonard I., Mary Ann Test, and Arnold J. Marx. "Alternative to the Hospital: A Controlled Study." *American Journal of Psychiatry* 132 (1975): 517–522.

Substance Abuse and Mental Health Services Administration. *SAMHSA Announces a Working Definition of "Recovery" from Mental Disorders and Substance Abuse Disorders.* SAMHSA News Release. Rockville, MD: Substance Abuse and Mental Health Services Administration, 2011. Available online: www.samhsa.gov/newsroom/advisories/1112223420.aspx.

Surles, Richard C., et al. "Case-Management as a Strategy for Systems Change." *Health Affairs* 11 (1992): 151–163.

Susser, Ezra, Elmer L. Struening, and Sarah Conover. "Psychiatric Problems in Homeless Men." *Archives of General Psychiatry* 46 (1989): 845–850.

Susser, Ezra, et al. "Preventing Recurrent Homelessness Among Mentally Ill Men: A 'Critical Time' Intervention After Discharge from a Shelter." *American Journal of Public Health* 87 (1997): 256–262.

Talbott, John A. "The Fate of the Public Psychiatric System." *Hospital and Community Psychiatry* 36 (1985): 46–50.

Teplin, Linda A., et al. "Crime Victimization in Adults with Severe Mental Illness: Comparison with the National Crime Victimization Survey." *Archives of General Psychiatry* 62 (2005): 911–921.

Tessler, Richard, and Gail Gamache. "Continuity of Care, Residence, and Family Burden in Ohio." *Milbank Quarterly* 72 (1994): 149–169.

Test, Mary Ann, and Leonard I. Stein. "Alternative to Mental Hospital Treatment III. Social Cost." *Archives of General Psychiatry* 37 (1980): 409–412.

Thornton, Craig, et al. *Evaluation of the Ticket to Work Program: Implementation Experience During the Second Two Years of Operations (2003–2004)*. MPR Reference No. 8977. Washington, DC: Mathematica Policy Research, 2006. Available online: www.hireabilitieshawaii.org/Portals/0/Research/TTW-report-2006.pdf.

Toyota Motor Manufacturing v. Williams. *Supreme Court of the United States, Case No. 00-1089*, 2002. Available online: congressionalresearch.com/RS21105/document.php?study=The+Americans+with+Disabilities+Act+Toyota+Motor+Manufacturing+v.+Williams.

Ullmann, Leonard P. *Institution and Outcome: A Comparative Study of Psychiatric Hospitals.* Elmsford, NY: Pergamon Press, 1967.

United States Congress. *McKinney-Vento Homeless Assistance Act of 1987.* Public Law 100-77, July 22, 1987, 101 Stat. 482, 42 U.S.C. § 11301 *et seq.* Available online: uscode.house.gov/download/pls/42C119.txt.

U.S. Department of Housing and Urban Development. *The 2008 Annual Homeless Assessment Report to Congress.* Washington, DC: U.S. Department of Housing and Urban Development, Office of Community Planning and Development, 2009. Available online: www.hudhre.info/documents/4thHomelessAssessmentReport.pdf.

U.S. Equal Employment Opportunity Commission. *EEOC Enforcement Guidance on the Americans with Disabilities Act and Psychiatric Disabilities.* EEOC Notice Number H915.002, March 25, 1997. Available online: www.eeoc.gov/policy/docs/psych.html.

U.S. Equal Employment Opportunity Commission. *The U.S. Equal Employment Opportunity Commission: Twenty Years of ADA Enforcement, Twenty Significant Cases.* Washington, DC: U.S. Equal Employment Opportunity Commission, 2010. Available online: www.eeoc.gov/eeoc/history/45th/ada20/ada_cases.cfm.

U.S. Equal Employment Opportunity Commission. *Notice Concerning the Americans with Disabilities ACT (ADA) Amendments Act of 2008.* Washington, DC: U.S. Equal Employment Opportunity Commission, 2011. Available online: www.eeoc.gov/laws/statutes/adaaa_notice.cfm.

U.S. General Accounting Office. *Homelessness: A Complex Problem and the Federal Response.* GAO/HRD-85-40. Washington, DC: General Accounting Office, 1985. Available online: www.gao.gov/assets/150/142674.pdf.

U.S. Interagency Council on Homelessness. *Opening Doors: Federal Strategic Plan to Prevent and End Homelessness.* Washington, DC: U.S. Interagency Council on Homelessness, 2010. Available online: www.usich.gov/PDF/OpeningDoors_2010_FSPPreventEndHomeless.pdf.

Vaughn, Christine E., and Julian P. Leff. "The Influence of Family and Social Factors on the Course of Psychiatric Illness: A Comparison of Schizophrenic and Depressed Neurotic Patients." *British Journal of Psychiatry* 129 (1976): 125–137.

Vonnegut, Mark. *The Eden Express: A Memoir of Insanity.* New York: Praeger, 1975.

Vonnegut, Mark. *Just Like Someone without Mental Illness Only More So: A Memoir.* New York: Random House, 2010.

Walkup, James. "Family Involvement in General Hospital Inpatient Care." In *Improving Inpatient Psychiatric Treatment in an Era of Managed Care*, New Directions for Mental Health Services Number 73, edited by David Mechanic, pp. 51–64. San Francisco: Jossey-Bass, 1997.

Weinstein, Raymond. "Patient Attitudes Toward Mental Hospitalization: A Review of Quantitative Research." *Journal of Health and Social Behavior* 20 (1979): 237–258.

Weinstein, Raymond. "Labeling Theory and the Attitudes of Mental Patients: A Review." *Journal of Health and Social Behavior* 24 (1983): 70–84.

White House. *Economic Report of the President, 2012.* Washington, DC: U. S. Government Printing Office, February 2012. Available online: www.gpo.gov/fdsys/pkg/ERP-2012/pdf/ERP-2012.pdf.

Wing, John K. "The Modern Management of Schizophrenia." In *New Aspects of the Mental Health Services*, edited by Hugh Freeman and James Farndale, pp. 3–28. Elmsford, NY: Pergamon Press, 1967.

World Health Organization. *Impact of Economic Crises on Mental Health.* Copenhagen, Denmark: World Health Organization, 2011. Available online: www.euro.who.int/__data/assets/pdf_file/0008/134999/e94837.pdf.

Wright, James D. *Address Unknown: The Homeless in America.* New York: Aldine de Gruyter, 1989.

Zusman, Jack. "Some Explanations of the Changing Appearance of Psychotic Patients: Antecedents of the Social Breakdown Syndrome Concept." *Milbank Memorial Fund Quarterly* 44 (1966, Part 2): 363–394.

Zygmunt, Annette, et al. "Interventions to Improve Medication Adherence in Schizophrenia." *American Journal of Psychiatry* 159 (2002): 1653–1664.

Mental Illness,
the Community,
and the Law

Mental disorders can create significant difficulty for the community as well as for families of those who are mentally ill. Persons with severe mental illness often violate norms for acceptable behavior and disrupt normal social activities. They may be frightening and dangerous or so disoriented or neglectful of themselves that their lives are in danger. Suicide is a common threat in the case of patients with serious and disabling mental disorders. How to deal with problems of care and danger among persons who appear to lack control over their own welfare is a long-standing issue (Shah and Sales 1991).

Involuntary care of those with mental illness has been a source of debate and litigation over many years. This will continue. On one side are those who want either to institutionalize persons with serious mental illness for purposes of care, treatment, and social control or to provide coercive supervision in the community. On the other side are patients themselves, or their advocates, insisting that persons with mental illness be left alone to live their lives as they see fit. In an earlier historical period, the cost of treatment was rarely an issue in hospitalization and, indeed, the threshold for the decision to hospitalize someone involuntarily was rather low. Now, in contrast, the costs of hospitalization are viewed with great concern, and neither the state nor those who manage insurance benefits look with favor on discretionary hospital admissions and extended lengths of stay. Thus, it has become far more common to keep even patients with florid psychoses in community settings. When involuntary treatment occurs, it tends to be relatively brief. Attention in recent years has moved away from inpatient to outpatient commitment, which can take various forms. Public authorities and community agents are still motivated to exercise control over dangerous persons, but concepts of danger and the tripwire for involuntary commitment have changed. Although the impetus for these changes may have developed out of civil liberty concerns over the protection of individual rights, current policies are reinforced by a desire to deal with mental illness in the least restrictive setting because it is consistent with a downscaling of certain areas of government. To understand current circumstances, it is important to review the history of involuntary care and its evolution over recent decades.

INVOLUNTARY HOSPITALIZATION

Civil commitment has four goals: (1) protecting society from persons with mental illness who are dangerous; (2) protecting those who are mentally ill from harming themselves; (3) providing mental health care to those who need it but may not appreciate the severity of their disorder; and (4) relieving families and communities from persons who might not be imminently dangerous but who are bizarre and troublesome and disrupt everyday life.

The battles over involuntary hospitalization have been tugs-of-war between those seeking to protect individual liberties and those viewing the state as parent (*parens patriae*) in ensuring that persons with mental illness be coerced if necessary to receive treatment. Legal activism in mental health developed out of the civil rights movement of the 1960s, and mental health law remained in active ferment for the following two decades. Civil libertarians argued that individual freedom was the highest good and must be protected even against those with the most benevolent of motives. Thus, it mattered little whether diagnosis was reliable, treatment effective, or hospitalization decisions sensible. The value of liberty was foremost, not any empirical fact about psychiatry. Others attacked involuntary commitment because of the unreliability of psychiatric diagnosis and predictions of danger, the large inconsistencies between commitment criteria and their implementation, and selective outcomes from one jurisdiction to another (Miller 1976). Many patient rights lawyers believed that individuals who had mental illness and were facing involuntary confinement, depriving them of their liberties, ought to have the same procedural rights as those available to criminal defendants.

Concerns about civil commitment go back more than 100 years. Institutionalization of persons with mental illness was informally administered on the local level until the middle of the nineteenth century, although the State of Virginia enacted a law for involuntary commitment as early as 1806. By mid-century, however, there was much concern about unjustified hospitalization of persons in mental institutions. In 1845, Chief Justice Lemuel Shaw of the Massachusetts Supreme Court established the precedent that individuals could be restrained only if dangerous to themselves or others and only if restraint would be conducive to their restoration. This principle became the foundation for most state statutes. The idea of insanity itself has been primarily a legal concept, with no real meaning in either medicine or psychiatry. Although initially intended to protect the rights of sane individuals, state statutes ultimately became vehicles to deprive patients with psychiatric disorders of their civil liberties when they were little threat to themselves or the community (Ennis 1972). It was the routine abuse of these statutes that attracted the attention and energy of civil liberties lawyers in the 1960s and 1970s.

Relatives and others in the community who demand that individuals with mental illness be hospitalized against their will may be motivated by multiple interests. These include fear and intolerance of disruptive behavior, as well as real concern that someone with disabling mental illness may not understand the need for treatment. The behavior of persons with active psychotic disorders, particularly when combined with substance abuse, can indeed be dangerous and highly unsettling. Although most simply cause discomfort to others by their presence and inappropriate behavior, others may pose serious threats of suicide or violence, engage in destructive behavior, or demonstrate grossly bizarre and disturbing symptoms.

Two landmarks in civil commitment doctrine were the Lanterman–Petris–Short Act passed in California in 1967 and the *Lessard* decision in Wisconsin in 1972. The California Act was purposely designed to discourage commitment and, particularly, long periods of confinement (Segal and Aviram 1978). The law tightened criteria for involuntary commitment while creating financial incentives for local government to provide alternatives to the large California state institutions. It also established a series of graduated categories requiring more evidence of impairment or danger to justify longer periods of involuntary hospitalization. Continuing review of such decisions was also established, making it difficult to follow the past practice of committing patients indefinitely.

In the *Lessard* decision the court found that patients with mental illness facing civil commitment have rights to timely notice of the charges, notice of right to a jury trial, aid of counsel, protection against self-incrimination, and assurance that the evidence on which a claim of dangerousness has been made be established "beyond a reasonable doubt." The California and Wisconsin developments had a pervasive effect on many other jurisdictions, helping to make criteria for civil commitment more specific in terms of a combination of mental illness and either dangerousness or incapacity to care for oneself. In addition, duration of commitment was specified and curtailed, with due process guarantees in criminal cases extended to civil commitment procedures (Lamb and Mills 1986). Although practices varied from one area to another, civil commitments declined. As Stone noted, "Psychiatrists who once committed people because it was the easiest thing to do are increasingly diffident. Courts are apt to be more scrupulous in reaching their decisions; lawyers are more frequently involved in preventing confinement; and hospitals are more fastidious about their own role" (Stone 1975, p. 43).

Many psychiatrists vigorously opposed such changes, arguing they gave inadequate protection to the community and left patients "to die with their rights on" (Treffert 1973, p. 1041). Critics alleged the new procedures were unduly restrictive, denied needed care to many, and increased the number of homeless with mental illness (Isaac and Armat 1990).

Such claims were exaggerated and supported more by occasional anecdotes and emotionalism than by evidence. Still, they raised important issues and highlighted the fact that legal changes may be a poor remedy for certain human and social problems. New statutes reduced the amount and duration of involuntary hospitalization, but many patients did not get community care services and others were simply "reinstitutionalized" in local jails and prisons. New legislation and court decisions did little to advance the painstaking work of developing well-organized systems of community services.

One celebrated case that dramatized the dispute over involuntary commitment concerned a woman named Joyce Brown (also known as Billie Boggs), who was picked up in 1987 under a policy announced by then New York City mayor Ed Koch to remove homeless people with serious mental illness from the street. Ms. Brown lived on the sidewalk in front of a hot air vent in Manhattan. When Ms. Brown was brought to Bellevue hospital, it was alleged she defecated on herself, burned and cut up paper money, ran into traffic, shouted obscenities at passersby, and wore inadequate clothes for winter. City psychiatrists maintained this was a case of schizophrenia, although psychiatrists for the New York Civil Liberties Union who came to Ms. Brown's defense contested this diagnosis. The judge hearing the case concluded:

> Freedom, constitutionally guaranteed, is the right of all, no less of those who are mentally ill (*O'Connor v Donaldson*, 422 U.S. 563 [1975]). Whether Joyce Brown is or is not mentally ill, it is my finding, after careful assessment of all the evidence, that

she is not unable to care for her essential needs. I am aware her mode of existence does not conform to conventional standards, that it is an offense to aesthetic senses. It is my hope that the plight she represents will also offend moral conscience and rouse it to action. There must be some civilized alternatives other than involuntary hospitalization or the street. (Robert D. Lippmann, Matter of Boggs, 136 Misc.2d 1082, Supreme Court, New York County, 1987)

The judge based his decision on the fact that psychiatrists substantially disagreed in their testimony regarding Joyce Brown's condition, that there were plausible explanations for some of her seemingly strange behaviors, that she had already survived a winter on the streets without apparent difficulty, and that in court she appeared to be logical and coherent. Thus, the criteria for involuntary treatment were not met. Subsequently, the City appealed this ruling, and the case made it as far as the New York State Supreme Court, at which time the judge blocked forced medication of the defendant. Shortly after, the City announced it would release Ms. Brown.

Is civil commitment or involuntary treatment ever justified in the absence of imminent physical danger? Improving due process encourages a more responsible stance from both physicians and the courts, but it hardly solves the individual, familial, and community dilemmas presented by the most serious cases of mental illness. The grounds for commitment should properly be narrow, protections for the allegedly mentally ill rigorous, and use of less restrictive alternatives exhaustive. There are, however, persons who, lacking self-awareness, cause great anguish for others and damage to themselves. In situations where they are sufficiently disturbing, such individuals are likely to be detained by police, thus circumventing the intent of mental health professionals and civil libertarians alike. What really is needed is not rigid avoidance of the use of public authority, but rather a more flexible and constructive response devoted to protecting future life chances of the disturbed patient.

Stone (1975) suggested a five-step procedure through which assessments could be made as to the appropriateness of civil commitment: (1) reliable diagnosis of a severe mental illness, (2) assessment as to whether the person's immediate prognosis involves major distress, (3) availability of treatment, (4) the possibility that illness has impaired the person's ability to make a decision as to whether he or she was willing to accept treatment, and (5) assessment as to whether a reasonable person would accept or reject such treatment. Stone argued that involuntary confinement was justified when there was convincing evidence of a serious illness causing suffering for which treatment is available, where the patient's refusal of treatment is irrational, and where a reasonable person in possession of all faculties under the circumstances would accept such treatment. He called this the Thank You Theory, implying that patients looking back on the circumstances would be grateful for state intervention:

> This is the Thank You Theory of Civil Commitment: it asks the psychiatrist to focus his inquiry on illness and treatment, and it asks the law to guarantee that treatment before it intervenes in the name of parens patriae. It is radical in the sense that it insists that society fulfill its promise of benefit when it trenches on human freedom. It is also radical in that it divests civil commitment of a police function; dangerous behavior is returned to the province of criminal law. Only someone who is irrational, treatable, and incidentally dangerous would be confined in the mental health system. (Stone 1975, p. 70)

Although Stone's Thank You Theory is appealing, it depends on trust in the integrity and reliability of psychiatric assessment and treatment, which are areas of continuing controversy. Many people weigh the values involved differently and would not want to trade-off some patients' civil liberties for treatment that psychiatrists contend is valuable. Those who favored civil commitment primarily as a means to get dangerous and troublesome people off the street found Stone's approach unsatisfactory in that it separated the social control function from civil commitment. Stone's approach, however, was valuable because its main intent was to assist patients who could not appreciate their own needs, not to serve the sometimes narrow interests of the community. The Thank You Theory attempted to struggle with central dilemmas underlying commitment rather than simply stake out an ideological position.

In 1983, the American Psychiatric Association suggested a model state law for civil commitment substantially influenced by the Thank You Theory. A central part of the proposal was to extend the *parens patriae* grounds for commitment to cover cases where the person is likely to suffer substantial mental and physical deterioration and lacks the capacity to make an informed decision. Commitment would occur if a person with severe mental illness would be likely to suffer, or continue to suffer, severe and abnormal mental, emotional, or physical distress associated with deterioration of prior ability to function independently. However, while the objective was to bring into treatment many of those with mental illness languishing on the streets, the criteria were sufficiently ambiguous to apply to other populations of patients. In the words of one critic, the proposal was "extremely broad and ultimately incoherent" (Rubenstein 1985). As with so many other attempts, such language as "substantial deterioration" is difficult to operationalize clearly and consistently (for a useful debate on the issues, see Appelbaum 1985).

Commitment statutes matter, and litigation and court decisions are an important part of defining and improving our procedures. Yet many wise and knowledgeable people have labored over the language of civil commitment procedures, and no language, however astutely drafted, can compensate for the deficiencies of a poorly organized mental health system. Almost all existing statutes contain language sufficiently broad to allow judges to commit patients they believe should be coerced into care. Dangerousness is open to varying interpretations, as is the notion of grave disablement, both common features of state laws. The problem lies less in the specification of legal criteria and more in conflicting views of illness among psychiatrists, lawyers, persons with mental illness, and society at large. Moreover, whatever reasonable principles the courts may establish, the inadequacies of both the mental health and criminal justice systems open up a large gap between theory and reality (Warren 1982). As one very experienced forensic psychiatrist noted:

> My experience suggests that no matter how clear or detailed a law is, judges, police, attorneys, and bureaucrats often ignore or have no knowledge of its fine points. These officials, especially judges, who are often not accountable to anyone, routinely do what they think is best for the patient or what they think the law intends without regard to what the law really says. (Zusman 1985, p. 979)

Civil commitment is part of a larger structure of mental health care, and changes in legal procedures, without improvement in related service areas, are likely to have unanticipated consequences. A study of such legal changes following the murder of an elderly couple in Seattle in 1978 by their 23-year-old neighbor illustrates the issue (Pierce, Durham, and Fisher 1986). Like every other state, Washington had tightened its civil commitment procedures following *Lessard* in Wisconsin. But in 1979, the legislature, in response to public pressure, revised its criteria for commitment to expand the definition of grave disability and allow commitment of persons noncompliant with medication regimens and at risk of severe deterioration. The act also added "danger to property" as a criterion. Admissions increased substantially in the locality where the shocking murder had occurred even before the law was changed, indicating the discretion allowed by earlier criteria. In another part of the state less affected by the murder publicity, admissions also dramatically increased, but only following the legal changes. Thus, it seems that strong public opinion and legal changes can have their independent effects on practice. But the effects were not what policymakers intended or anticipated. In both instances, hospital capacity did not increase, and involuntary commitments displaced persons seeking voluntary admission. This is particularly ironic in light of the fact that the murderer who activated public opinion on this issue had earlier in the day of the murder sought to enter a hospital voluntarily but was refused.

In reviewing these struggles over civil commitment, certain conclusions seem inescapable. The legal process reflects society's need to deal with troublesome issues and demands from the community. However abstract legal terms are defined, courts and mental health professionals will respond to strong public opinion and economic and political pressures in resolving concrete instances. Judges may try conscientiously to apply formal definitions and procedural guidelines, but prevailing time constraints can make this process enormously difficult and often impossible. Some judges do not even seriously try, and simply resort to their own common sense perceptions in the decision-making process. Even with the best of intentions, then, there remains a large gap between legal theory and civil commitment realities (Warren 1982).

Commitment of persons who are mentally ill is also part of a larger social process over which the law has little control. To the extent that the legal system limits civil commitment, other mechanisms may be used to deal with troublesome situations. And so, many people with mental illness now find themselves jailed for minor infractions. The key point is that community pressures encouraging commitment of those who are mentally ill do not disappear simply because legal procedures have been tightened. If hospitalization is difficult to achieve, some other alternative will be used, such as jails or homeless shelters, where vulnerable persons face the danger of victimization.

It is not surprising, thus, that over time the allegedly revolutionary changes brought by legal activism to civil commitment and related areas—such as the right to refuse treatment—were reinterpreted in their implementation, and that mental health professionals, judges, and even lawyers representing those who are mentally ill often accepted the redefinition of terms to allow involuntary treatment when truly needed. There are, of course, exceptions, such as the case of Joyce Brown, that reaffirm sharply the nature of the tensions between libertarian and treatment interests. But looking back, as Appelbaum (1994) convincingly observes, neither the hopes of the most ardent libertarians nor the fears of many mental health professionals have been realized in the commitment controversy. In fact, a commonsense approach prevails, whereby decisions are based on specific facts and circumstances that surround particular cases. He also notes the importance of public opinion on how commitment laws are interpreted as a factor influencing the behavior of clinicians, judges, and lawyers. These influences change from time to time depending on events in the community and how they are handled by the media.

PSYCHIATRIC ADVANCE DIRECTIVES

The "Thank You Theory" sought rules for appropriate decision making for civil commitment and involuntary treatment when it was believed patients lacked the capacity to make their own rational decisions. Such an approach, however, remains paternalistic and challenges the patient's autonomy. Alternatively, patient autonomy and empowerment can potentially be protected by psychiatric advance directives (PADs), which are made when patients are competent. These are legal instruments used to specify a patient's treatment preferences and identify surrogates who can make decisions on a patient's behalf under circumstances of incapacitation and a psychiatric crisis. Among the kinds of items that can be addressed are preferred medications, treatments acceptable and unacceptable, how treatment is administered, and even such issues as who can visit during hospitalization. PADs are modeled on living wills, as well as advance directives and health care proxies common in medicine more generally. However, as in the general health area, there are barriers to appropriate implementation (Srebnik and La Fond 1999).

PADs have great potential advantages to the extent they contribute to a therapeutic alliance, or patient-centered care partnership, with clinicians. But PADs do not require clinician participation in their development, and some mental health advocates believe such participation may impede the patient's expression of true preferences. Under federal law, any facility receiving Medicare or Medicaid funding must offer advance directives. States must also make provision for PADs having their own specifications for execution. Yet relatively few psychiatric outpatients have PADs, despite survey reports among both consumers and providers indicating that there is interest in creating them (Henderson et al. 2008).

In a randomized intervention study, Swanson and colleagues (2006a) provided a 120-minute facilitation session for an experimental group of patients with serious mental illness who received instruction on making needed choices combined with assistance if they decided to complete the forms. A control group received an introduction to PADs, written instructions and needed forms, but no direct help. Of the 239 patients in the experimental group, 149 completed PADs while only 8 of the 230 control group patients did so. The investigators found that, at least in the short term, patients completing an advance directive had a significant improvement in their working alliance with clinicians.

We have relatively little rigorous evaluation of the effects of PADs, however. Investigators reviewed the literature in 2009 and found only two relevant randomized controlled trials comparing usual care to advance treatment directives (Campbell and Kisely 2009). Persons with advance directives required significantly less social work time and engaged in fewer violent acts than persons without such directives, but there were no significant differences in hospital admission, number of outpatient attendances, compliance with treatment, self-harm, or arrests (Campbell and Kisely 2009).

The Bazelon Center for Mental Health Law (www.bazelon.org), a nonprofit organization advocating for persons with mental illness through changes in policy and law, provides detailed instruction on completing psychiatric advance directives. Together with Duke University, the center established a National Resource Center (NRC) on Psychiatric Advance Directives that provides a wide range of valuable information and resources (www.nrc-pad.org). The NRC also provides information and instructions and appropriate forms for each of the states.

OUTPATIENT COMMITMENT
AND MENTAL HEALTH COURTS

Outpatient commitment is a legal option for dealing with many of the problems and dilemmas we have reviewed surrounding hospitalization. Efforts by managed care programs to avoid and minimize inpatient care while providing effective mental health care in the community on an economical basis partially drove the increase in outpatient commitment. Once again, however, the everlasting tension between liberty and treatment interests surfaces.

Although most states have outpatient commitment laws, they are much more frequently used in a few states than others (Petrila and Christy 2008). Even within a single state, there can be large regional variations on how the laws are administered and carried out (Robbins et al. 2010). As with much else in this field, context is all-important. How outpatient commitment works depends on knowledge, attitudes, and cooperation of mental health and criminal justice officials; mental health resources available in the community, including personnel, facilities, and funding; and competing needs and demands of other client groups for the same resources. Public opinion is important and can be shaped significantly by how the media deal with dangerous events involving persons with mental illness.

Earlier studies of outpatient commitment noted that clinicians had little knowledge of the criminal justice system and legal procedures. Nor did they show much interest in collaborating with criminal justice professionals. Those working in the criminal justice system similarly had little knowledge or interest in mental health issues. There was much confusion about appropriate use of outpatient commitment and the responsibilities of the mental health system, concerns about coercive treatment, worry about resources, and anxiety about potential liability should a patient under supervision harm others. Acceptance of community responsibility would, in some instances, shift the costs of commitment from state government (which often pays for inpatient care) to the locality that shares in the costs of treatment under outpatient commitment arrangements. Other complicating difficulties included overly stringent commitment criteria, the failure of laws to specify what was to happen if a patient did not cooperate with the treatment team, and general lack of information and uncertainty about the outpatient commitment process (Torrey and Kaplan 1995). The best early research tracked experience in the state of North Carolina, an innovator in outpatient commitment. These studies illustrated both the potential and complexity of implementing this legal mechanism. Success depends on the attitudes and cooperation of mental health professionals, in addition to the quality of mental health and social services in the community. When the mental health system was receptive, this new mechanism worked well (Hiday and Goodman 1982; Hiday and Scheid-Cook 1987).

Outpatient commitment raises the traditional issue of the grounds for depriving individuals of their liberties. Laws around the country vary with respect to whom can be committed and under what circumstances. Many mental health professionals appreciate the value of outpatient commitment as a tool for facilitating work with patients before they reach a disruptive and dangerous stage, and these same professionals may be reluctant to take responsibility once patients reach this point. However, civil libertarians question the appropriateness of using the state's coercive powers when patients' symptoms have not reached the critical point of danger or grave impairment. According to this perspective, outpatient commitment is simply a convenience to force patients to accept treatment. The Bazelon Center has persistently opposed outpatient commitment. A statement on its website asserts:

> There is no evidence that it improves public safety. Moreover, the evidence is strong that building a responsive mental health system with services like mobile crisis teams, assertive community treatment teams (ACT), and supported housing is the best strategy for ensuring that people receive needed treated (sic). When people are dangerous due to mental illnesses, they should be hospitalized. When safety is not an issue, treatment should be voluntary, because this approach holds the best promise for long-term engagement in treatment. Failure to engage people with serious mental illness is a service problem, not a legal problem. Outpatient commitment is not a quick-fix that can overcome the inadequacies of under-resourced or under-performing mental health systems. Coercion, even with judicial sanction, is not a substitute for quality service. (Bazelon Center for Mental Health Law 2011)

Other mental health advocacy groups, such as NAMI (www.nami.org) and the Treatment Advocacy Center (www.treatmentadvocacycenter.org), see the issues and research findings differently. The latter is a nonprofit organization affiliated with Dr. E. Fuller Torrey, a well-known psychiatric researcher and advocate; other well-known psychiatrists; and various former leaders from NAMI. Following is a statement of its view on outpatient treatment:

> Studies and data from states using AOT [Assisted Outpatient Treatment] prove that it is effective in reducing the incidence and duration of hospitalization, homelessness, arrests and incarcerations, victimization, and violent episodes. AOT also increases treatment compliance and promotes long-term voluntary compliance... (Treatment Advocacy Center 2012)

Since practices differ so much from one place to another, and the research literature is far from definitive, it is understandable that groups with different philosophical orientations approach the issue of outpatient commitment so differently. After finding only two relevant randomized controlled studies, a review in 2009 concluded there was little evidence that outpatient commitment was effective in outcomes such as health service use, preventing hospital readmission within a year, arrests, homelessness, social functioning, mental state, quality of life, or care satisfaction. The evaluators reported a significant reduced risk of victimization (Kisely, Campbell, and Preston 2011). Other mostly nonrandomized studies in particular localities came up with more favorable results.

As of 2011, 44 states had some form of statutory involuntary outpatient treatment, but relatively few actively implement such laws in a preventive sense (Appelbaum 2005; Swartz 2010; Torrey and Kaplan 1995). Public focus on commitment waxes and wanes, typically surfacing as an issue following a highly publicized serious crime committed by a person with severe mental illness. For example, when a man with schizophrenia pushed a young woman, Kendra Webdale, in front of a subway train to her death in New York City, it led to passage of Kendra's Law in 1999, providing for court-ordered assisted outpatient treatment. Ironically, as in the Washington State case discussed earlier, the man with schizophrenia had sought psychiatric assistance prior to his attack and had been denied treatment because of lack of resources. However, the incident triggered new outpatient commitment legislation. Kendra's Law remains highly controversial, with the usual lineup of civil liberties advocates on one side and safety- and treatment-oriented advocates on the other. The legislation was renewed for five more years in June 2005. One of the initial advantages of the New York legislation was that resources were made available to try to provide needed community care in a meaningful way. Renewal came up again in 2010 when New York was facing a fiscal crisis and cutting public budgets. The law was extended for another five years but not made permanent (Swartz 2010).

Although studies of Kendra's Law were done, they were largely descriptive and did not establish definitively whether procedures required by such a statute are superior to good voluntary interventions. In a randomized pilot study at Bellevue Hospital in New York City in 1994, research that was carried out prior to Kendra's Law, Steadman and colleagues (2001) compared 78 patients who received court-ordered treatment, which included an enhancement of services, with 64 patients who received only the enhanced services. Clients were followed up at 1, 5, and 11 months following discharge from a psychiatric hospital. Researchers found no significant differences on any of the major outcome measures in the study. However, the study had two significant limitations. Persons with a history of violence were excluded, and the program did not aggressively pursue noncompliant persons.

Prior to renewal, New York State conducted a study of Kendra's Law (New York State Office of Mental Health 2005). The study was not a randomized trial and had no comparison group. Nevertheless, it reported impressive descriptive results. Between August 1999 and January 2005, 10,078 persons had been considered for a court order, 3,766 individuals received services under an AOT order, and an additional 2,863 persons received comparable enhanced services as a result of the referral process for a potential court order. Large improvements occurred among persons under AOT orders regarding access to and use of services, improved self-care and community living, and reduction in life difficulties such as completing tasks, maintaining attention and concentration, and the like. The positive results are reflected in the authors' summary of findings:

> People in the AOT have been able to improve their involvement in the service system as a result of their participation in the program, and by doing so, they have improved their lives. There has been an 89% increase in the use of case management services among AOT recipients, and substantial increases in utilizing both substance abuse and housing support services...Over a three year period prior to their AOT order, almost all (97%) had been hospitalized (with an average of three hospitalizations per recipient), and many experienced homelessness, arrest, and incarceration...rates for hospitalization, homelessness, arrests, and incarcerations have declined significantly. (New York State Office of Mental Health 2005, pp. 21–22)

Other studies of New York's AOT also provide positive results. A study of 3,576 court-ordered individuals between 1999 and 2007, based on Medicaid claims data and state reports, found that psychiatric hospital admission was reduced by a quarter during the first six months of the court order and by one-third during the subsequent six months. Comparison was made with consumers' base rates controlling for a variety of covariates (Swartz et al. 2010), although one drawback of the study was the absence of a control group. Investigators also found improvements in the use of intensive case management services, more drug treatment, and greater involvement with outpatient services. They used the reports of case managers to compare the experience of the AOT group with another seriously mentally ill group receiving assertive case treatment. The conclusion was that positive results from the AOT mechanism have benefits beyond those from assertive case treatment alone, addressing a common criticism that the success of outpatient commitment programs comes primarily from the reallocation of intensive services to this population.

Link, Phelan, and their coinvestigators studied 183 patients split between AOT clients and others recently discharged from a psychiatric hospital and attending the same outpatient facilities in the Bronx and Queens (Link et al. 2011; Phelan et al. 2010). Although not a controlled experiment, the groups were comparable. The clients were followed for a year by means of interviews, complemented by clinical chart review, arrest records, and other information from the New York State Office of Mental Health. Outcome indicators included arrests, arrests for violence, psychotic symptoms, suicide risk, quality of life, and social functioning, among others. The AOT group had much greater odds of arrest and 8.6 higher odds of arrest for violence before entering the program than after. Those clients not in the program had almost twice the odds of arrest as AOT clients during and shortly after AOT clients entered the program (Link et al. 2011). While suicide risk and serious violence were lower and social functioning higher for those in the AOT program than in the comparison group, the groups did not differ in psychotic symptoms or quality of life (Phelan et al. 2010). Generally, these studies suggest the program met its intended objectives of reducing arrests and violence. The New York program, however, was richly resourced. Results cannot be easily extrapolated to other localities.

Ultimately, what most matters in community care has less to do with legal provisions and more to do with investments in the accessibility and quality of services. Unfortunately, one cannot determine whether a court-ordered approach would be necessary if the same level of services were available and accessible in the first place. It is no accident that, repeatedly, horrendous events alarming to the public have occurred after persons with severe disorders or their family members sought and were refused services. Thus, the essential problem concerns the unavailability, lack of capacity, and fragmentation of the services system for those with the most serious and persistent mental illnesses in many, if not most, communities. California passed its own AOT statute, called Laura's Law, following the violent murder of a college student working in a public mental health clinic (Appelbaum 2006). In 2004 California passed Proposition 63 (known as the millionaire's tax), a 1 percent tax on adjusted gross incomes over one million dollars to support county mental health services, and it will be instructive to monitor how the vast funds generated impact the AOT program (Scheffler and Adams 2005). One program funded through this tax—the full-service partnership program—provides flexible funding for comprehensive services to high-risk clients, including assertive case management and housing. A recent analysis found large reductions in use of emergency department visits when compared to those receiving usual care (Brown et al. 2012). While these intensive programs appear effective in assisting high-risk clients, a study in Los Angeles County observed less success in attaining persistent reductions in voluntary emergency visits among the larger population of mentally ill clients (Bruckner et al. 2012). Even as funding from the millionaire's tax went to local mental health authorities, enormous state deficits in California reduced program support from other streams. Long-range follow-ups are required.

For many years, the state of New Jersey has had a problem addressing long-term stays in public mental hospitals, with about one-quarter of patients remaining more than a year after clinicians approve discharge. These patients no longer need institutional care but remain because of barriers to housing and community placement. In 1983, the New Jersey Supreme Court established a legal basis for continued hospitalization of patients who no longer met formal criteria for confinement but were awaiting appropriate community placement opportunities and, especially, suitable housing. Although a persistent problem, the issue receives only intermittent attention, generally in tandem with budgetary concerns. This patient group is heterogeneous, including subgroups rejected from placement in some residential settings because of stigma, lack of perceived capability of facility administrators, and fear of community reaction. Perhaps the most difficult group to place is patients with prior sexual violations who are publicly identified on the Internet under New Jersey's Megan's Law. Other difficult subgroups are those with serious medical comorbidities, those with a comorbid diagnosis of intellectual disability and patients capable of community living but still manifesting significant behavioral problems. Few localities provide the range of housing options needed to accommodate persons with these varying problems.

Mental health courts are recent innovations fashioned after the drug courts that have now been on the scene for almost two decades. Mental health courts were started around 1997 and now number about 250 across the country (Steadman et al. 2011). Mental health courts function idiosyncratically. As Steadman, Davidson, and Brown (2001) observed, almost any effort to give special attention to persons who are mentally ill within the criminal justice system tends to be given this designation. A mental health court "may be a diversion program with all staff and services circulating around a single judge, or . . . it could simply be the court of jurisdiction within a broader jail diversion program" (Steadman, Davidson, and Brown 2001, p. 458). Relevant to our earlier discussion, the question remains as to whether these courts actually increase the availability of services for the people involved or whether they simply move particular subgroups of patients ahead in the line for limited resources. Boothroyd and colleagues (2005) compared services for mentally ill persons processed by the Broward County Mental Health Court with a matched sample from another comparable Florida county that processed offenders through a misdemeanor court. Researchers found the mental health court increased access to mental health treatment but had little control over the patterns and intensity of services (Boothroyd et al. 2005). Neither the type of court nor whether treatment was received was significantly associated with symptom patterns. Once again, these results suggest that the quality and comprehensiveness of the mental health services system is all-important for outcomes. According to investigations of various mental health courts, involving participants from varying sectors—mental health, criminal justice, housing—in the program from the very start is crucial for success (Hiday and Goodman 1982; Hiday and Scheid-Cook 1987; Watson et al. 2001).

Mental health courts are diverse. Various criteria have been suggested for defining such courts: a single court docket for persons with serious mental illness; the use of a team approach in formulating recommended treatment and supervision, with a designated person to link the mental health and criminal justice systems; assurance of treatment availability before the judicial decision is made; voluntary participation accompanied by mandatory treatment with monitoring; and possible criminal sanctions for noncompliance (Epperson et al. 2011; Steadman, Davidson, and Brown 2001). Most studies, despite methodological weaknesses, find lower arrest rates and days of incarceration over a year or two, and beneficial outcomes often extend beyond the period of court supervision (Hiday and Ray 2010; Ridgely et al. 2007; Steadman et al. 2011). In a systematic study, Steadman and colleagues (2011) followed 447 persons adjudicated in four mental health courts in California, Minnesota, and Indiana together with a comparable group of 600 offenders with mental health problems dealt with in the usual way over 18 months. Their findings proved consistent with anecdotal accounts that those processed in mental health courts have fewer arrests and days of incarceration. Clients who had less intensive experience with the criminal justice system, earlier treatment, a bipolar diagnosis in contrast to schizophrenia or depression, and no use of illegal substances had better outcomes. In general, the literature suggests that reduced incarceration balances the costs of increased mental health interventions in the short term and may result in lower systemic costs over time (Ridgely et al. 2007).

CRIMINALIZATION OF PERSONS WITH MENTAL ILLNESS

Prisons and jails have been a growth industry in the United States. Almost 2.3 million persons were incarcerated in 2009, and over 5 million were under probation and parole (Glaze 2010). A great many of these individuals have serious mental health problems. Estimates of mental illness in prisons and jails depend on the criteria used and the care with which diagnostic assessments are made. Careful evaluations at the Cook County jail in Chicago estimated that 6 percent of men and 12 percent of women had a severe mental disorder, such as schizophrenia/schizophreniform disorder, mania, or major depression (National GAINS Center 2004b). The U.S. Department of Justice studied a large sample of inmates in prisons and jails by means of personal interviews, using symptom ratings and other diagnostic assessments, and concluded that one-half of all inmates in prisons or jails had a mental health problem, amounting to almost 1.3 million people in 2005 (James and Glaze 2006). Defining mental health loosely, the study reported the highest rate of mental disorder was found in local jails (64 percent), followed by state correctional facilities (56 percent), and federal prisons (45 percent). Common symptoms were mania, depression, and psychotic symptoms, such as delusions and hallucinations. High proportions of inmates with mental health problems also had substance abuse and dependence problems, varying from approximately three-quarters in jails and state prisons to two-thirds in federal prison. Among *all inmates*, an amazing 42 percent in state prisons and 49 percent in local jails had comorbid mental health and substance dependence or abuse problems.

Although mental illness is a major problem in correctional institutions, it is not easy to assess whether the prevalence is growing or whether persons with mental illness are increasingly being criminalized. Antisocial behavior, and particularly substance dependence and abuse, often leads to arrests and can be characteristic of mental disorders (Hiday 1999). A substantial proportion of the incarcerated with a mental health problem had drug possession and trafficking as their most serious offense. This involved more than half of those in federal prisons, and a fifth to a quarter of those in state prisons and jails. Persons with the most severe mental illness who use substances often become entangled in our "war on drugs" (Institute of Medicine 2006). In any case, the freedom of living in the community, the fragmentation of mental health services systems, the easy availability of drugs on the street in low-income areas, and limited access to inpatient care all make it inevitable that large numbers of persons with mental illness will be arrested. They are more likely to be found in local jails than other institutions because they often commit nuisance offenses leading to arrest. Moreover, police sometimes make "compassionate arrests" to get troubled people off the streets and out of dangerous situations where they could be victimized. Compared to other inmates, persons with mental health problems were more likely to be homeless during the previous year, to have no employment prior to arrest, and to have a history of physical and sexual abuse (James and Glaze 2006).

Many in jails and prisons have received mental health treatment at some time in their lives (35–49 percent). Among this group, in the year prior to arrest 15–23 percent received treatment, and 18–34 percent received treatment after incarceration. A significant minority of these inmates have committed serious and violent crimes, which may or may not be a product of their mental illnesses (James and Glaze 2006). Mental illnesses are common, and it should not be surprising that some persons with mental illness end up in jails and prisons, as do individuals with other types of illnesses. Nevertheless, all illnesses, physical or mental, warrant appropriate treatment. Most mental health services in correctional institutions are inadequate and lacking in availability. For those with serious mental illness who have committed only nuisance crimes, criminalizing their behavior reinforces the already-challenging problem of stigma and complicates relationships with family, caretakers, employers, and the community. Thus, attention is now being given to ways of diverting persons with mental illness from the correctional system.

Effective diversion programs require understanding and cooperation among participants from multiple sectors, including the police, court personnel, and the mental health system. Each group functions in a distinctive bureaucratic system having its own values and perspectives, definition of roles, and rewards. Communication and cooperation commonly break down. When programs depend on the leadership of a particular sheriff, judge, prosecutor, or mental health professional, they may unravel simply because key individuals move on. But well-organized and cooperative diversion programs offer potentially important benefits, as documented by emerging research in this area (National GAINS Center 2004a; Wood et al. 2011).

In 1992, a national study estimated that only 52 jails in the United States had diversion programs for persons with mental illness. By 2003, the Technical Assistance and Policy Analysis Center for Jail Diversion (TAPA), funded by the federal government, listed 294 such programs (National GAINS Center 2004a). The TAPA center distinguishes between prebooking and postbooking diversion programs. Prebooking programs are focused on avoiding arrest or incarceration while postbooking programs are focused on reducing sentences (Reuland and Cheney 2005).

Perhaps the most common type of diversion involves mental health providers, as in mobile crisis teams that work in cooperation with the police to assess suspects at the scene of a disturbance. Another model involves using mental health professionals either employed by the police or working in partnership with them to provide on-site and telephone consultation to police officers. A third model uses police officers specially trained to respond to crises and to work closely with the mental health system (Reuland and Cheney 2005). Informal qualitative assessment finds the most frequent barrier to these programs is the difficulty of maintaining funding, particularly for the mental health services needed. Other common barriers include unsupportive attitudes of police and other staff, staff shortages, and problems in sharing information (Reuland and Cheney 2005). Success requires good cooperation between law enforcement and mental health personnel, which is not easily achieved given the different cultures and orientations of these two sectors.

In 1997, the federal government funded a demonstration at nine sites around the country to develop knowledge about both pre- and postbooking programs (National GAINS Center 2004a). The programs assessed nearly 2,000 persons with mental illness and comorbid substance use disorders, diverting about half of them. Participants in the study were interviewed at baseline, and at 3 and 12 months, on a wide range of issues. Persons who were diverted in the postbooking period seemed to be more impaired than those diverted earlier. The study found that diverted persons spent more time in the community in the year following contact or arrest than those who were not diverted—a nonequivalent control group—and they received much more mental health treatment. There were no significant differences, however, in arrests during the 12-month follow-up period, suggesting that diversion did not result in additional safety issues. The two groups—diverted and not diverted—did not differ in reduction of symptoms, so the services provided may have been less than optimal. Generally, diversion involved higher mental health costs and lower criminal justice costs, resulting in some higher cost overall. The fact that no measurable difference in symptoms was uncovered raises a question as to what was bought with the additional mental health expenditures. In any case, more rigorous investigation is needed if we are to understand better who can benefit most from these programs.

Whether the topic is outpatient commitment or diversion, such programs cannot fulfill their potential in an impoverished and fragmented community care system. Abuses with civil commitment in earlier periods reflected, in part, the lack of decent community alternatives for people who were mentally ill. With changes in mental health policies and more stringent criteria for civil commitment, many patients who would have been hospitalized remain in the community. Most are probably better off, but others continue to suffer seriously from their problems while leading unhappy and painful lives. There is no reason why a wide variety of alternatives cannot be developed for assisting such individuals without unduly disrupting whatever positive ties remain in the community, but the record so far is poor, particularly for patients with severe and persistent mental illness who are prime candidates for civil commitment. Without alternatives, the community will find some way of dealing with persons who are difficult, disturbing, and frightening. Often, the result will not be in the interests of the patient. If civil commitment presents an affront to the concepts of individual freedom and personal integrity, then less restrictive but more effective alternatives must be devised, in addition to improvements in due process.

A NOTE ON DANGEROUSNESS AND THE RELATIONSHIP BETWEEN MENTAL ILLNESS AND VIOLENCE

The potential for danger is an important consideration in regard to mental illness and the criminal justice system, but the concept of dangerousness remains fuzzy, its discussion often influenced more by ideology than evidence, and research on the topic is difficult. Those without mental health training often focus on bizarre and inexplicable behavior that frightens them, but such behavior is not necessarily predictive of violence and harm. Psychiatrists typically evaluate danger by focusing on a patient's past history, explicit threats of violence, and assessments of such psychological attributes as the presence of deep feelings of rage, a sense of helplessness and feeling trapped, the presence of paranoid delusions and hallucinations (especially when these imply violence), and patients' reports that they find it difficult to control their antisocial urges. Psychiatrists also commonly maintain that aggressive tendencies in association with excessive use of alcohol and drugs are very dangerous. Others, meanwhile, have cited the significance of subcultural factors related to the readiness to express aggression (Rappeport 1967). While predictions of danger based on such criteria may often prove wrong, there is now increasing evidence that alcohol and drug abuse and mental illness, particularly active psychotic symptoms, indicate increased risk of violence (Link, Andrews, and Cullen 1992; Marzuk 1996; Monahan 1992; Steadman et al. 1998; Swanson et al. 1990, 2006b).

Danger and violence are culturally specific to a considerable degree. Acts of violence vary manifold among nations. They are also substantially associated with age, sex, education, and socioeconomic circumstances. Such differences commonly outweigh those between persons with and without mental illness. Moreover, dangerousness and violence are often specific to particular social situations and are not simply an attribute of personality. The same person may have varying risks for violence depending on context. Fortunately, violence is a relatively uncommon event even among those with a greater inclination toward such behavior, and efforts at prediction typically result in large numbers of false positives (Stone 1975).

It should be clear from this discussion that the concept of danger refers to an expectation of physical attack on persons and property, not broader concepts of harm to others that might result from distracted driving due to alcohol or texting, or white-collar criminality such as knowingly manufacturing and selling defective and harmful products. While the latter may be destructive, such behaviors are not inconsistent with broader observation of such behaviors in our culture. What particularly frightens the public about violent acts committed by persons with mental illness is their seeming irrationality and unpredictability.

Pescosolido and her colleagues (1999) examined public views of mental illness and the need for coercion into treatment using data from the General Social Survey, which is based on a representative sample of the U.S. population. In the survey, respondents were given descriptions of persons with various mental illness conditions constructed on the basis of criteria in *DSM-IV*. The conditions included schizophrenia, major depression, drug dependence, and alcohol dependence. Also in the group was a troubled person who did not meet clinical criteria for a *DSM* disorder. Respondents were asked various questions about the people in these descriptions.

In general, the public was more concerned about and less sympathetic with individuals described as meeting the criteria for drug abuse. Persons with schizophrenia, drug dependence, and alcohol dependence were seen as less competent to make treatment decisions. However, two-thirds of respondents thought those with major depression were competent to make decisions, and almost everyone ascribed competence to a troubled person. A similar pattern of judgments was made in regard to individuals' ability to manage money. With respect to views of danger to others and self, drug abusers and persons with alcohol dependence were seen as most dangerous, while persons with schizophrenia occupied an intermediate position. More than two-thirds of respondents did not view persons with major depression as dangerous to others, but many more were likely to see these individuals as dangerous to themselves. The public was much more receptive to coercion in dealing with persons with combined drug problems and schizophrenia than with other types of cases, with persons with alcohol problems alone falling in the middle among the five types of cases.

Persons with mental disorders report committing more violent acts than persons without such disorders (for good reviews, see Marzuk 1996; Monahan 1992, 1997); the highest likelihood of committing a violent act is associated with substance abuse disorders and having pronounced psychotic symptoms. Two early studies have been particularly important in helping to illuminate this issue (Link, Andrews, and Cullen 1992; Swanson et al. 1990). The first used data from the Epidemiologic Catchment Area (ECA) study, described in an earlier chapter, and examined the relationship between having a *DSM* disorder and self-reported violent behavior in the previous year (Swanson et al. 1990). These behaviors included actions like hitting or throwing things at your spouse (partner); fights with others that came to swapping blows; use of a weapon like a stick, knife, or gun in a fight; and physical fights while drinking. While only 2 percent of those with no *DSM* disorder reported such behaviors in the past year, 25 percent of those with alcohol abuse or dependence disorders and 35 percent of those with drug abuse or dependence disorders reported such instances of violence in the prior 12 months. Most other major diagnoses fell in the middle range of frequency: schizophrenia (13 percent), major depression (12 percent), mania or bipolar disorder (11 percent), and so forth. Persons with multiple disorders reported higher rates of violent behavior. When a major mental disorder occurred with a substance abuse disorder, the propensity to engage in violent behavior was significantly higher.

These findings need to be seen in perspective. One major limitation of such a study is that it depends on reports from individuals regarding both their symptoms and violent acts. Yet individuals who are more willing to report socially undesirable symptoms are more likely to report socially stigmatized acts. Also, as previously noted, violent acts of this kind occur commonly in certain subgroups of the population. For example, young males (16 percent) and young females (9 percent) in the lowest socioeconomic group have rates of violence comparable to those among most persons with mental illness. Finally, the survey items used to measure violence, while all reflecting undesirable behavior, encompass incidents varying greatly in severity and danger. Perhaps most important is the fact that even among persons with severe mental illness, such as those with schizophrenia, the vast majority (87 percent) do not report any violent behavior. Thus, while some of these individuals may be more dangerous than the public, identifying them reliably is extremely difficult.

Abuse of alcohol and drugs is commonly connected with occurrences of violence, posing more danger than psychotic symptoms. Tiihonen and his colleagues (1997) in Finland studied a 1966 birth cohort of more than 12,000 individuals over 26 years and assessed the relationship between mental disorder and criminal behavior. Data on crimes came from files maintained by the Ministry of Justice and covered offenses by persons between ages 15 and 25. Psychiatric diagnostic data came from hospital records and outpatient registers. As in other studies, substance abuse proved closely linked with criminal behavior. Offenses were highest among males with alcohol-induced psychoses and males with schizophrenia and coexisting alcohol abuse. In the full cohort studied, 128 individuals had at least one registered violent crime, and the vast majority of such violators (117 persons) had no record of mental illness. However, males with mood disorders with psychotic features and persons with schizophrenia had much higher likelihood of violent criminal behavior relative to those without disorders (adjusted odds ratios of 10.4 and 7.2, respectively).

In one of the best studies on this subject thus far, Link, Andrews, and Cullen (1992) compared mental patients and comparable community residents who never received any mental health treatment on several measures of violent and illegal conduct, based on both official records and self-reports. Sophisticated multivariate techniques were applied controlling for sociodemographic factors and differences in social context, as well as social desirability response bias, a problem noted in the previous ECA study. Results showed that patients with a history of mental treatment reported more violent behavior and also had higher arrest rates for violent crimes. The survey component of this study included a measure of psychotic symptoms, including such items as feeling that thoughts not your own were put into your head, that you were possessed by a spirit or devil, and that your mind was dominated by forces beyond your control. Such symptoms are quite rare in community samples. Link and his colleagues were able to demonstrate that these illness indicators accounted for all the differences in violent and illegal behavior between patients and the never-treated community sample that were not already explained by other sociodemographic and contextual effects. They concluded: "...the excess risk of violence posed by mental patients is modest compared to the effects of other factors. Moreover, only patients with current psychotic symptoms have elevated rates of violent behavior and it may be that inappropriate reactions by others to psychotic symptoms are involved in producing the violent/illegal behavior" (Link, Andrews, and Cullen 1992, p. 290).

In an extension of this study, Link and Stueve (1994) attempted to define more precisely the types of symptoms explaining the relationship between mental illness and violence. Three survey items related to psychosis most successfully predicted future violent behavior (During the past year how often have you felt that your mind was dominated by forces outside your control? How often have you felt that thoughts were put into your head that were not your own? How often have you felt that there were people who wished to do you harm?). The authors suggest that these are "threat/control override symptoms" in which irrational thoughts become accepted as real, and internal controls on concern about irrational thoughts are undermined. These same results were subsequently replicated using data from the ECA study (Swanson et al. 1996).

The role of psychotic symptoms in acts of violence continues to remain uncertain, however. A major study supported by the MacArthur Foundation Network on Mental Health and the Law monitored the occurrence of violent incidents among 1,136 patients with mental disorders every 10 weeks for a year following hospital discharge (Steadman et al. 1998). In Pittsburgh, one of the three study sites, comparable data were also gathered from a sample living in the same neighborhoods as the patients. Researchers determined that comorbid substance abuse disorder was a key factor associated with violence. Reported substance abuse, however, was higher among persons with mental illness than among others in their neighborhoods. The research team also found that persons with mental disorders without comorbid substance abuse did not have significantly more violent behaviors than persons in the community sample. Moreover, while increased violence among persons with comorbid disorders was elevated in the periods prior to and after hospital discharge, over time it fell back to levels characteristic of those in the neighborhoods where they lived. Further, almost 90 percent of violent acts by patients were directed at family and friends; in contrast, more than one-fifth of neighborhood violence was directed at strangers. The investigators did not find, as in some other studies, that psychotic illness in the absence of substance abuse was associated with elevated violence. Of course, issues of sample, measurement, and follow-up periods all affect results from such studies. Link and Stueve (1998) interpreted the concentration of violence prior to and following hospitalization in their study as indication that violence was likely greatest when symptoms were most acute. Patients with serious mental illness discharged from inpatient care often still have acute symptoms given the short length of stay.

In a more recent study, Swanson and colleagues (2006b) examined the prevalence of violence over six months for 1,410 patients with schizophrenia. These data point to the reasons why research might yield inconsistent findings relative to the role of acute psychotic symptoms. They found, consistent with Link, Andrews, and Cullen (1992), and Link and Stueve (1994), that psychiatric symptoms such as the idea of persecution—an example of what psychiatrists call "positive symptoms"—increased risk of violence. In contrast, the "negative symptoms" of schizophrenia such as social withdrawal decreased the risk. Persons with negative symptoms often isolate themselves and have less opportunity to act out beyond their immediate social networks. In the aggregate, the effects of negative symptoms might cancel the effects of positive symptoms, but people who primarily have acute positive symptoms are more violent.

An interesting study of the role of mental illness in violent crime was carried out in Sweden (Fazel and Grann 2006). Sweden differs from the United States in many ways, having few crimes involving guns and a lower incidence of violence in general. It does, however, have a system of national registration (with all persons having a unique identification number) that permits a valuable method of research impossible in the United States and many other countries. Focusing on a 13-year period from 1988 to 2000, this study linked data for all persons age 15 and over and discharged from hospitals with a severe mental illness together with a national register of all criminal convictions. Unlike the United States, criminal convictions in Sweden are unaffected by plea bargaining and include persons sentenced by the courts to mental hospitals or those dealt with in other ways. The study used a broad definition of violent crime, including homicide and attempted homicide (which were rare), assaults that were life threatening in character or caused severe bodily harm, common assault, robbery, threatening behavior, harassment, arson, or any sexual crime (Fazel and Grann 2006).

The study found that about one-twentieth of all recorded violent crimes were committed by persons with a severe mental illness. At the same time, the vast majority of crimes that are of most concern to the public—e.g., homicide, arson, sexual offenses—were committed by others. Swedish women with severe mental illness committed only about one-ninth the number of violent crimes committed by men with such disorders. Despite the fact that they made up a very small part of the violent crime problem, persons with severe mental illness were almost four times more likely to commit such crimes than others in the population. Violent crime was more common for persons with schizophrenia than with other psychoses. Unfortunately, this study does not differentiate between patients with mental illness abusing or not abusing substances, nor can it tell us against whom crimes were perpetrated. The causal picture also remains obscure. It is important to emphasize that this study, like many others, finds the associations of mental illness with violence to be no greater than the effects of age, gender, or socioeconomic status.

In a later study, Fazel and colleagues (2010) used population-based registers to study 3,743 individuals with two or more discharge diagnoses of bipolar disorder, 37,429 population controls, and 4,059 siblings of individuals with bipolar disorder in relation to violent crime. Unlike the earlier study, they examined patients with substance abuse comorbidity. While persons with bipolar disorder were more than twice as likely to commit violent crimes as those in the control group, this pattern primarily occurred among patients with substance abuse comorbidity. For those without substance abuse, there was very minimal increased risk.

Research on dangerousness of patients with mental illness, thus, takes us only a small way in understanding how to identify the small minority likely to threaten the public.

Certainly some patients are dangerous, but much work remains in isolating important indicators that could reduce the number of false positives arising from psychiatric assessments. Predictions of dangerousness will always be uncertain because so much depends on situation and context. As Link and his colleagues note, the dangerous behavior of those with mental illness may well be provoked, at least in part, by harsh and rejecting reactions from other members of society. Research on expressed emotion also supports the notion that it is not solely the presence of illness that precipitates violence but also a propensity to respond in extreme ways to antagonistic interactions with family and others. All of this underscores the need to isolate as clearly as possible the conditions, symptoms, stages of illness, and circumstances most likely to trigger violent behavior.

Concomitant with the tightening of commitment laws has been a legal attempt to define danger in more explicit terms. The *Lessard* decision, for example, equated danger with a "recent act, attempt, or threat to do substantial harm." As Brooks (1978) has noted, even this effort to clarify language raises several questions: What type of act? With what recency? What constitutes an attempt or threat? In practice, psychiatrists and judges read into these definitions whatever they wish, often without distinguishing between real menace versus nuisance and imposition. How should judges deal, as Brooks (1978) asks, with a manic person who depletes family members' resources and exposes them to financial hardship? What about a hysterical person who continually calls others on the phone in the middle of the night, night after night? It appears that decisions by judges and psychiatrists are less determined by precise legal definitions and more by the state of community opinion and pressures at the time. When a psychotic man stabbed 11 people, killing two, on the Staten Island ferry in New York City in 1986 one week after being hospitalized at New York Presbyterian Hospital, psychiatrists began to detain more patients, and psychiatric emergency rooms and hospitals filled to capacity. There was no legal change making detention easier, but public opinion changed, encouraging psychiatrists to feel they would be held responsible for releasing dangerous mentally ill persons. This is the same phenomenon illustrated by experience in the state of Washington discussed earlier (Pierce, Durham, and Fisher 1986).

There are areas other than the law where society must assess whether persons are reliable or whether the risk of dangerous behavior exists. The armed forces must have some assurance that the handling of weapons and other dangerous tasks do not fall to unstable persons. Businesses and industrial firms are concerned that those in positions of responsibility are able to perform without endangering others or the company. A pilot with schizophrenia may be too inattentive to fly an airplane safely. While attempts are made to assess potential employees for particular jobs, the adequacy of these screening programs is in doubt from a psychiatric perspective. Concern even extends to the threat that high-level public officials who become psychiatrically disabled may harm the public because of their illness, but as yet no one has proposed an adequate way to balance these risks against the odiousness of excessive surveillance guided by imprecise knowledge of psychiatric illness and its consequences. Fundamental dilemmas promise to remain.

Overall, however, people with mental illnesses commit a very small proportion of violent crimes in the United States, an estimated 3 percent according to Columbia University professor Paul Appelbaum, a leading specialist in this area. Appelbaum observes poignantly, "If 97 percent of violent acts are committed by the non-mentally ill, targeting them [those with mental illness] as a matter of policy is a peculiar thing to do" (quoted in Levin 2007, p. 1).

THE RIGHT TO TREATMENT

Initial calls for a right to treatment were directed at remedying the horrendous conditions common in many public institutions, but public interest lawyers were ambitious to expand the concept. Kenneth Donaldson, a patient in Chattahoochee State Hospital in Florida from 1957 to 1972, had refused medication and electroshock treatment, claiming at times to be a Christian Scientist. Donaldson had been diagnosed a chronic paranoid schizophrenic, and his efforts to gain release as well as his assertion that he would write a book about his confinement were interpreted as part of his paranoia (see his book, Donaldson 1976). Hospital officials did not take seriously either Donaldson's efforts or those of other caretakers in the community striving to gain his release. Instead, they locked him in a ward for the criminally insane, denying ground privileges despite lack of evidence of dangerous behavior. Ultimately, a jury awarded $38,500 in compensatory and punitive damages, deciding against two hospital doctors who had made the decision for involuntary confinement.

The Donaldson case was brought to the U.S. Supreme Court as a right-to-treatment suit but was decided narrowly in 1975, without recognition of the broad right-to-treatment claim. Instead, the Supreme Court ruled the state could not continue to confine a person with mental illness who was not dangerous to himself or others, who was not receiving treatment, and who was capable of surviving safely outside the hospital (Stone 1984).

There were earlier precedents in right-to-treatment decisions (Stone 1975, pp. 83–96), with a major breakthrough came in 1971 in *Wyatt v. Stickney*. The federal district court in Alabama held that involuntarily committed patients "unquestionably have a constitutional right to receive such individual treatment as will give each of them a realistic opportunity to be cured or to improve his or her mental condition" (quoted in Mechanic 1974, p. 233). The court found, further, that the defendant's treatment program was deficient because it failed to provide a humane psychological and physical environment or qualified staff in sufficient number to administer adequate treatment and individualized treatment plans. Thus, "to deprive any citizen of his or her liberty upon the altruistic theory that the confinement is for humane therapeutic reasons and then fail to provide adequate treatment violates the very fundamentals of due process" (quoted in Mechanic 1974, p. 233).

Siding with the litigants, the court established a large number of standards—defined as "medical and constitutional minimums"—mandating changes in staffing, physical resources, and treatment processes. It goes without saying that if implementation of such standards could have alleviated the horrible conditions documented as prevalent in the state mental hospitals, fairness and decency would be served. It is not clear, however, that such standards achieve the best outcomes possible when costs and benefits are considered as part of an overall mental health strategy, including both inpatient and community care of persons with mental illness. Legal advocacy focused on the involuntarily hospitalized patient because the "handle" for litigation was the argument that deprivation of liberty for humane therapeutic reasons without provision of treatment violated due process of law. This was a narrowly circumscribed view, however, that invited displacement of the problem to other parts of the mental health system not so easily addressed by litigation.

The court's mandated hospital standards reinforced a medical model of treatment. This came just as health experts were increasingly becoming aware of the limitations of physician dominance and rigidly enforced professional roles. The standards encouraged allocation of resources to hospital care in contrast to a network of facilities suited to cost-effective treatment and management of mental health problems in the community. Most perversely of all in view of this last point, such standards provided an incentive for indiscriminate dumping of patients in the community.

Definitive data are not available concerning the full consequences of right-to-treatment decisions, even in Alabama where such major court rulings were applied on a large scale. There is evidence, however, that patients were released from Alabama hospitals following these decisions in greater number than would have been expected on the basis of existing trends in adjacent states (Leaf 1978a, 1978b). Right-to-treatment decisions assisted, if they did not affect directly, efforts to increase Alabama's mental health budget and the staffing patterns in psychiatric institutions. It is difficult to come to any conclusion other than that the *Wyatt* decision contributed to a climate that brought greater support and investment for mental health facilities and programs in Alabama. Although only modest knowledge exists about the fate of patients released to either the community or nursing homes, experiences were not always conducive to a high quality of social functioning. Many remained institutionalized for long periods in settings such as nursing homes (Leaf 1978a). For public interest lawyers, it seemed almost inconceivable that patients could be better off in hospitals given the inadequacies of these facilities. However, some patients with chronic mental illness who are of lower economic status and have serious mental disability sometimes find it more comforting to reside in institutions than the community (Ludwig and Farrelly 1966). Once patients are released to the community, they are no longer protected by right-to-treatment decisions and are at the mercy of prevailing conditions and resources, which can be minimal and more inadequate than those available in a hospital program.

The right-to-treatment theory supported by Judge Frank Johnson in Alabama received little support in *Donaldson*. A Supreme Court majority was not ready to support the theory of a constitutional right in this area. Although Chief Justice Burger strongly opposed assertion of a new right, his concurring opinion has not deterred judges in lower courts from proceeding on this basis (Stone 1984, p. 117). Some judges, in response to public interest lawyers' litigation, have even formulated a right to *community* care, though it is not clear to what degree activist courts can direct state governments on how to establish priorities and allocate limited public resources.

At the least, there is an accepted constitutional right to minimal standards for persons who are mentally retarded. In *Youngberg v. Romeo*, the Supreme Court established that institutionalized patients with mental retardation had a right to "conditions of reasonable care and safety, reasonable nonrestrictive confinement conditions, and such training as may be required by these interests" (U.S. Supreme Court 1982). Federal courts have extended this concept of minimum rights to include treatment to prevent clinical deterioration among institutionalized patients, but it is unknown whether these legal theories can be extended successfully to the mental health system (Lamb and Mills 1986).

In many localities, patients with impairments have been dumped in communities without adequate financial, social, or treatment resources. Many live in low cost, temporary hotels in disorganized urban areas, they find themselves in substandard facilities in the community run for profit by operators who provide few treatment resources, or they lack homes altogether. Given the poor conditions to which they are exposed, these patients frequently experience an exacerbation of symptoms and insecurities and, given their limited coping capacities, face overwhelming life problems. In the case of patients with schizophrenia, aggressive care is often required to prevent regression (Davis, Dinitz, and Pasamanick 1972), but under most circumstances, such care is not available and former patients simply become lost in the community.

Establishing a right to treatment cannot be weighed independent of these other trends. Without considering the mental health system as a whole, we may find that by putting pressure on one aspect of the system, we create more intense problems elsewhere. A major limitation of the litigation approach is the difficulty of approaching the system as a whole in contrast to seeking particular constitutional remedies.

Thus, it is difficult to be confident about the benefits gained through right-to-treatment decisions. Fair and effective rehabilitation for patients with mental illness depends on the entire framework of medical and mental health care, not to mention decisions made through the legislative process. Publicity accompanying right-to-treatment litigation helped make inadequate conditions of mental health care more salient to legislators and aroused the sympathies of the public. It also contributed to eliminating some obvious abuses of institutional care. The concept of right to treatment really means adequate or acceptable treatment, and not *all* that science or knowledge allows. To the extent this legal approach has focused attention on the lack of treatment or unacceptable care, it is a justified strategy. Beyond this, it is necessary to examine treatment across all contexts, not only the hospital, so that resources can best benefit all patients, wherever they are.

THE RIGHT TO TREATMENT UNDER THE AMERICANS WITH DISABILITIES ACT AND THE SUPREME COURT DECISION IN *OLMSTEAD v. L.C.*

As previously reviewed, the Americans with Disabilities Act of 1990 was landmark legislation affecting the civil rights of persons with disabilities, including those associated with mental illness. The act also had the promise of increasing community integration of persons with mental disabilities. Title II of the ADA, perhaps even more important for persons with psychiatric disabilities than others, requires that no one with disability "be excluded from participation in or be denied benefits of the services, programs or activities of a public entity or be subject to discrimination by such entity." The ADA regulations implementing the act specify that programs be administered in the most integrated settings appropriate, and that reasonable modifications be made to protect against discrimination unless this would change the nature of a service, program, or activity (Rosenbaum 2000).

In 1999, the U.S. Supreme Court in *Olmstead v. L.C.* (U.S. Supreme Court 1999) ruled that the ADA created the right to receive care in the least restrictive setting if that right could be implemented with "reasonable accommodations." The case involved two women with intellectual disabilities and comorbid mental health problems in a Georgia mental hospital who had been assessed as able to live in the community by health professionals employed by the state. The Court, influenced by evidence of long waiting lists to obtain Medicaid-funded community services in Georgia, concluded that the state's defense of lack of resources to expand community services was inadequate. The Court's decision prompted a range of responses from exuberance to skepticism. Paul Appelbaum (1999) saw the glass as half empty because of the clause that did not require change if the remedy would fundamentally alter state services. Subsequently, he noted the decision "hardly represents recognition of the thoroughgoing right to treatment of the sort that advocates have urged since the 1960s" (Appelbaum 2006, p. 19).

Attorney Sara Rosenbaum, who has had much influence on Medicaid through her analyses and advocacy, saw the decision quite differently. She argued that the standard set by the court had "striking resemblance" to the "deliberate speed" remedy in *Brown v. Board of Education* (Rosenbaum 2000, p. 228). While acknowledging the difficulty of predicting long-term effects, she believes the decision set a legal standard for "measuring the adequacy of publicly funded health program design for persons with disabilities," an accomplishment that no prior effort had achieved (Rosenbaum 2000, p. 231). Rosenbaum also noted that Medicaid provides most financing for community health services for persons with disabilities and "insufficient funds to support current state plan services has never been a legal defense to a claim for benefits" (Rosenbaum 2000, p. 230). To the extent that states are using Medicaid funds to fund community care, such expenditures must be reasonable, and Georgia failed to fund the community service positions approved by the federal agency that administers the program. Rosenbaum sees three subgroups affected by this decision: those who can reasonably be accommodated in the community, those requiring institutional care, and the large group of people who are at risk of institutionalization because of inadequate community care. It is the latter who offer a variety of opportunities legally to challenge states for inadequate provision of community care.

Overall, the effects of *Olmstead* have been mixed. A variety of federal agencies are exploring how they can use existing programs and regulations to reinforce the trend toward long-term community care and comply with the *Olmstead* decision. Almost all states now have commissions and various types of workgroups to develop plans. When *Olmstead* was decided, about 25 percent of Medicaid funding for long-term services and supports went to home and community services; by 2007 this had increased to 41 percent (Carlson and Coffey 2010).

Yet the process of implementing *Olmstead* and moving to community care has been slow (Fox-Grage, Coleman, and Folkemer 2004). We do not know the number of persons who have been able to avoid or abbreviate institutional care as a result of the *Olmstead* decision. Institutional care is still easier to obtain under Medicaid than is home or community care (Carlson and Coffey 2010). According to Bartels (2011), implementation of *Olmstead* has largely ignored the elderly population, although they make up about one-half of all new admissions to nursing homes for persons with severe mental illness (SMI). For the most part, in the years following this decision, the lower courts have rendered narrow interpretations. *Olmstead* did not require a "fundamental alternation" in the services offered by states; thus there was no requirement to create new home and community supports (Rosenbaum and Teitelbaum 2004). Moreover, while the decision argued that states must show a "reasonable pace" in moving appropriate patients to community care, in legal decisions even the existence of a plan to implement *Olmstead* has sometimes been interpreted as evidence of a "reasonable pace" (Petrila and Swanson 2010; Rosenbaum and Teitelbaum 2004).

Despite the slow pace of change, there is reason for optimism. For example, Petrila and Swanson (2010) cite *Disability Advocates v. Paterson* as an example of a recent decision that promises to extend interpretation of the *Olmstead* decision. Disability Advocates, Inc. (DAI), originally brought the suit in 2003 on behalf of more than 4,000 people in New

York State with mental illness living in adult homes. Placement of persons with serious mental illness in adult homes has been a common solution to deinstitutionalization of the mentally ill from large state hospitals. Residents often live in substandard conditions, segregated from the community, and with little independence. The DAI suit was brought on behalf of residents in adult homes with over 120 beds that had high proportions of people with SMI disabilities (25 percent of the population or 25 residents). The New York Court with jurisdiction decided in favor of the plaintiff and found that the state of New York had violated the requirements of Title II of the ADA by concluding that these adult homes were, in some cases, more segregated and restricted than public mental hospitals. Moreover, the Court decided that provision of supported housing would not result in a "fundamental alteration" of state services. In response, the state developed plans for a limited number of spaces in supported housing. This matter is still working its way through the courts, but the Department of Justice (DOJ) has issued a brief in support of the Court's decision (www.ada.gov/briefs/newyork_olmsteadbr.pdf) and called for even more extensive efforts to build supported housing.

Community care innovations included in the Affordable Care Act are consistent with the goals and directions of the disability rights movement as well as full implementation of the ADA. Transformation of state mental health priorities is a daunting task, and many more years must pass before the full impact of the ADA and, even more so, the ACA will be felt. Remember how long *Brown v. Board of Education* took to have its influence, but it clearly was a landmark decision.

THE RIGHT TO TREATMENT FOR CHILDREN UNDER MEDICAID

In 1967, Medicaid coverage for low-income children incorporated Early and Periodic Screening, Diagnosis and Treatment (EPSDT) as a basic benefit (Rosenbaum and Wise 2007). The legislation has subsequently been expanded but essentially requires states to screen Medicaid enrollees under the age of 21 "to ascertain their physical or mental defects" and provide "such health care, treatment, and other measures to correct or ameliorate defects and chronic conditions discovered thereby" (cited in Rosenbaum and Wise 2007, p. 383). The promise of EPSDT is that once a medical need is identified through screening, the state has an obligation under Medicaid to provide medically necessary services that could improve the condition. In practice, screening has varied widely among states and one of the most difficult determinations is medical necessity, which has often been left to the courts (Perkins 2009). An illustrative case decision is *Rosie D., et al. v. Romney* (later *Rosie D. v. Patrick*), which was brought by eight named children (in addition to a class action suit covering about 15,000 children) in Massachusetts. The suit contended that the state had failed to fulfill the provisions required under EPSDT with "reasonable promptness." The Court agreed that Massachusetts failed in fulfilling the EPSDT requirements for screening for children with serious emotional disturbances and in providing medically necessary services such as case management and home-based supports in a "reasonably prompt" time frame. In response, Massachusetts substantially revamped services for children under Medicaid with mental health problems. While it is too early to ascertain whether this has improved outcomes, rates of screening and identification of children with mental health problems have increased markedly (Kuhlthau et al. 2011).

THE RIGHT TO REFUSE TREATMENT

Malpractice standards based on common law encompass the illegality of a physician treating patients without their consent, except under conditions where consent cannot be reasonably expected, as in medical emergencies. This is an important principle, but the courts have traditionally allowed mental hospitals to treat patients with mental illness involuntarily. In pursuing right-to-refuse-treatment litigation in mental hospitals, lawyers have adopted a constitutional rather than a malpractice approach (Stone 1981).

Right-to-refuse-treatment efforts began in the 1970s with measures to protect involuntary patients in quasi-criminal institutions from experimental drug treatment and psychosurgery (Brooks 1979; Stone 1984). Only later were these suits extended to medications, which is where much of the controversy now centers. Two major cases, *Rennie* in New Jersey and *Rogers* in Massachusetts, account for a large part of today's contentious debate over the regulation of psychiatric treatment.

The difficulty in deciding when someone has a right to refuse treatment comes with balancing individual rights against patient need (Stone 1981). An additional problem is achieving an appropriate balance between regulatory efforts, on the one hand, and the use of limited psychiatric resources in an efficient and meaningful way, on the other.

In *Rennie*, the federal district court in New Jersey accepted the view that involuntary medication with neuroleptic drugs represented an invasion of constitutionally protected privacy. Later, the circuit court of appeals changed the constitutional rationale to "protection from harm." In *Rogers*, the Massachusetts federal district court accepted the further theory, based on the First Amendment guaranteeing free speech and thought, that administration of neuroleptic drugs alters the mind and thus interferes with a constitutionally protected right. Many psychiatrists viewed the Massachusetts decision as particularly offensive, nonsensical, and as an affront to the necessary discretion of clinicians (Stone 1981). The circuit court of appeals later rejected the theory of the federal district court.

Even though court decisions have instituted some checkpoints on psychiatric discretion, they do not prevent psychiatrists from administering medications in emergencies (Appelbaum 1994). In a later decision concerning a Wisconsin case (*Stensvad v. Reivitz*), the United States district court upheld a state provision allowing an involuntary patient under criminal commitment to be medicated without consent (Lamb and Mills 1986). Considerable discretion remains, and hospital practice is believed not to have been much affected. To the extent these cases motivate more thoughtful use of medication, better communication with patients, and greater awareness of how particular medications and dosage may be troublesome for the patient, they probably improve patient care and provide for the type of consideration one would expect in any decent medical encounter.

These cases and court judgments reflect the fact that many medications have serious adverse effects and may cause permanent disability, as in the case of tardive dyskinesia with use of neuroleptics. Public mental hospitals neither attract the best clinicians nor represent the ideal context for a sensitive therapeutic relationship. There is no indication that the formal procedures prescribed by the courts are frequently used, leading some psychiatrists to argue this is all a "tempest in a teapot." In contrast, others believe that the assertion of a right to refuse treatment and establishing procedures to review refusals serve as deterrents to arbitrary and insensitive care while promoting a more humane treatment context. Evidence one way or another remains unclear, but the basic point is not. Treatment should always take place so as to give credence to the patient's wishes and reactions. Good care requires not only the right medication but also calibrating the prescription so that it interferes to the smallest possible extent with the sense of well-being. There may be possibilities for selecting among different drugs, varying means of administration, and using alternative schedules. Moderating the arbitrariness of care thus represents a positive move, unless there is contrary evidence indicating that the regulatory process has either resulted in inability to treat patients who need care or diverted significant resources from patient care to support regulatory mechanisms.

The right to refuse treatment remains a highly contentious issue. In making sense of the debate, Appelbaum (1994) distinguished between those who have a quarantine concept of civil commitment versus those who have a treatment orientation. A quarantine concept holds that the state has a responsibility to protect against danger but should intrude as little as possible once that threat has been addressed. Those who support a treatment view see little sense in detaining people in a hospital, then allowing them to refuse the treatment that might bring them to a more normal state. According to Appelbaum, what makes mental illness different from other forms of danger is that we target behavior prospectively because we believe it derives from an illness that can be treated for the dual benefit of the patient and society. His argument is as follows: "Quarantine is not enough to justify confinement indefinitely, even when harm to others alone motivates commitment. Treatment must also be provided. To fail to treat committed persons, when the treatment is essential for them to regain their liberty, undercuts the rationale that legitimates civil commitment" (1994, p. 148).

Appelbaum (1994) accepts research findings showing that most patients eventually agree to medications, that judges and review panels authorize most emergency requests for involuntary medication, and that the right to refuse treatment often leads to a more thoughtful treatment plan. But he also reviews evidence suggesting that inpatient units with fewer patients medicated are more dangerous places for staff and other patients, and that large amounts of resources are devoted to the administrative review process for treatment refusals. Instead, he suggests a quality review process in which treatment plans would be carefully reviewed for their suitability and appropriateness by attending and outside specialists, just as occurs in other areas of medical care. Sensible though they may be, such views are unlikely to persuade those intent on preserving individual liberties and limiting the coercive authority of the state.

To date, the declaration of a right to refuse treatment has no measurable effect on patterns of mental health care. Relatively few patients actually refuse treatment, and protracted litigation has directly influenced only a limited number of cases. But assertion of this right contributes to better communication and negotiation with patients about their treatment regimen and induces psychiatrists in institutions to be more respectful of patients' concerns (Appelbaum 1994; Lamb and Mills 1986). An alleged cost of such regulation is its damaging effect on the morale of psychiatrists, who are said to view such requirements as intrusive and a reason for becoming apathetic about providing proper treatment (Stone 1981).

THE SOCIAL CONTEXT OF LEGAL REFORM IN MENTAL HEALTH

In the last several decades of legal activism, many other aspects of mental illness have also received sustained attention, including issues related to incompetency to stand trial, the insanity defense, and preventive detention of sexual offenders. Each topic is complicated and important, but has less to do with mental health services for the majority of persons with serious mental illness than areas that have already been reviewed here. However, one item deserving explicit notice is the *Tarasoff* decision on the "duty to warn" and its subsequent modifications creating a "duty to protect." The *Tarasoff* decision arose from a case at the University of California in 1969, where Prosenjit Poddar murdered a fellow student, Tatiana Tarasoff. Poddar had previously told his counselor of his plans. While Poddar's therapist had alerted campus police and argued that the student should be committed, his supervisor overturned the recommendation. Tarasoff's parents brought suit against the university alleging that it should have warned the intended victim. The court decided that therapists have a "duty to warn" intended victims. The California Supreme Court reheard the case and modified the duty to warn to a duty to protect concluding:

> When a therapist determines, or pursuant to the standards of his profession, should determine, that his patient presents a serious danger of violence to another, he incurs an obligation to use reasonable care to protect the intended victim against such danger. The discharge of this duty may require the therapist to take one or more of various steps, depending upon the nature of the case. Thus, it may call for him to warn the intended victim or others likely to apprise the victim of the danger, to notify the police or to take whatever other steps are reasonably necessary under the circumstances. (cited in Weinstock et al. 2006, p. 524)

No set of legal decisions has more upset mental health professionals because the outcome of the *Tarasoff* case seemingly posed a threat to confidentiality and therefore could deter patients' openness with their therapists. Psychiatrists alleged that these decisions would destroy the doctor–patient relationship, imagining countless difficulties harmful to patients, mental health professionals, and even future victims under the rule. Despite widespread predictions of catastrophe, however, little harm resulted. Studies showed that therapists were already taking steps prior to *Tarasoff* to warn victims they feared were in danger, that informing patients of these responsibilities had less negative effect than anticipated and sometimes was seen in a positive light, and that the courts themselves were attentive to the needs and concerns of clinicians in interpreting and revising the relevant statutes. As Appelbaum concludes after an extensive review of the relevant literature, "The duty to protect has complicated life for some clinicians, but it may have made life safer for some potential victims; and it has by no means been the disaster some authorities feared" (1994, p. 99).

Subsequent court decisions have also generally been in favor of mental health practitioners. In a review of 70 cases between 1985 and 2006 that involved a mental health professional or institution being sued for breach of the duty to warn or to protect, Soulier, Maislen, and Beck (2010) found only four cases that had been ruled in favor of the plaintiffs under the *Tarasoff* precedent. In many of the cases decided in favor of the defendant, the court's conclusion was that there was no clear evidence the mental health provider knew of a certain danger, the timing between treatment and the violent act was too long to establish a connection, or the victim already knew of the potential danger.

CONCLUSION

A broad view of the complex relations between mental health and the law suggests the importance of context and the extent to which economic and social realities constrain and modify what may first appear as momentous legal changes. Neither legal doctrine nor the courts function in a vacuum. Both are responsive to changing public opinion, economic problems and budgetary limits, and the need to maintain the stability of community life. Legal reform can, of course, be a force for meaningful change and redressing abuses, but courts are mindful of the obligations their decisions put on government and other community institutions. Furthermore, while the law functions on an important symbolic level, it would be a mistake to confuse legal argumentation with what really goes on in the local courts. As we have seen repeatedly, judges often do not follow the letter of the law in dealing with difficult mental health dilemmas. Rather, they adopt commonsense solutions that seem to work in context. As in the general administration of the criminal law, courts do not operate in practice as they do in theory. Under conditions of crowded dockets and informal deal making among psychiatrists, lawyers, and judges, careful legal procedures often go by the wayside.

Civil commitment, the right to treatment, and the right to refuse treatment are but examples of a large number of complex legal issues affecting the fate of persons who are mentally ill. As treatment procedures change, as our concept of rights evolves, and as we become more aware of patient abuses that once were invisible, a history of litigation develops in neglected areas, sometimes resulting in new standards. The questions involved are complex and cannot be penetrated without methodical research and experienced professional judgment. Inevitably, all confront the dilemma of how to balance the welfare of the individual with that of society as a whole.

References

Appelbaum, Paul S. "Special Section on APA's Model Commitment Law." *Hospital and Community Psychiatry* 36 (1985): 966–989.

Appelbaum, Paul S. *Almost a Revolution: Mental Health Law and the Limits of Change.* New York: Oxford University Press, 1994.

Appelbaum, Paul S. "Least Restrictive Alternative Revisited: Olmstead's Uncertain Mandate for Community-Based Care." *Psychiatric Services* 50 (1999): 1271–1272.

Appelbaum, Paul S. "Assessing Kendra's Law: Five Years of Outpatient Commitment to New York." *Psychiatric Services* 56 (2005): 791–792.

Appelbaum, Paul S. "Twenty-Five Years of Law and Psychiatry." *Psychiatric Services* 57 (2006): 18–20.

Bartels, Stephen J. "Commentary: The Forgotten Older Adult with Serious Mental Illness: The Final Challenge in Achieving the Promise of Olmstead?" *Journal of Aging and Social Policy* 23 (2011): 244–257.

Bazelon Center for Mental Health law. *Outpatient and Civil Commitment.* Washington, DC: Bazelon Center for Mental Health Law, 2011. Available online: www.bazelon.org/Where-We-Stand/Self-Determination/Forced-Treatment/Outpatient-and-Civil-Commitment.aspx.

Boothroyd, Roger A., et al. "Clinical Outcomes of Defendants in Mental Health Court." *Psychiatric Services* 56 (2005): 829–834.

Brooks, Alexander D. "Notes on Defining the 'Dangerousness' of the Mentally Ill." In *Dangerous Behavior: A Problem in Law and Mental Health*, edited by Calvin Frederick, pp. 37–60. Rockville, MD: U.S. Dept. of Health, Education, and Welfare, Public Health Service, Alcohol, Drug Abuse, and Mental Health Administration, National Institute of Mental Health, Center for Studies of Crime and Delinquency, 1978.

Brooks, Alexander D. "The Impact of Law on Psychiatric Hospitalization: Onslaught or Imperative Reform." *New Directions for Mental Health Services* 1979 (1979): 13–35.

Brown, Timothy Tyler, et al. "The Impact of California's Full-Service Partnership Program on Mental Health–Related Emergency Department Visits." *Psychiatric Services* 63 (2012): 802–807.

Bruckner, Tim A., et al. "Voluntary Psychiatric Emergencies in Los Angeles County After Funding of California's Mental Health Services Act." *Psychiatric Services* 63 (2012): 808–814.

Campbell, Leslie Anne, and Steve R. Kisely. *Advance Treatment Directives for People with Severe Mental Illness*. Cochrane Database of Systematic Reviews 2009, January 21 (Issue 1): CD005963.

Carlson, Eric, and Gene Coffey. *10-Plus Years After the Olmstead Ruling: Progress, Problems, and Opportunities*. Washington, DC: National Senior Citizens Law Center, 2010. Available online: www.nsclc.org/wp-content/uploads/2011/07/NSCLC-Olmstead-Report.pdf.

Davis, Ann E., Simon Dinitz, and Benjamin Pasamanick. "The Prevention of Hospitalization in Schizophrenia: Five Years After an Experimental Program." *American Journal of Orthopsychiatry* 42 (1972): 375–388.

Donaldson, Kenneth. *Insanity Inside Out*. New York: Crown Publishers, 1976.

Ennis, Bruce J. *Prisoners of Psychiatry: Mental Patients, Psychiatrists, and the Law*. New York: Harcourt Brace Jovanovich, 1972.

Epperson, Matthew, et al. *The Next Generation of Behavioral Health and Criminal Justice Interventions: Improving Outcomes by Improving Interventions*. Center for Behavioral Health Services and Criminal Justice Research, New Brunswick, NJ: Rutgers University, 2011. Available online: nationalreentryresourcecenter.org/documents/0000/1173/9.21.11_The_next_generation_Monograph_Sept_2011.pdf.

Fazel, Seena, and Martin Grann. "The Population Impact of Severe Mental Illness on Violent Crime." *American Journal of Psychiatry* 163 (2006): 1397–1403.

Fazel, Seena, et al. "Bipolar Disorder and Violent Crime: New Evidence from Population-Based Longitudinal Studies and Systematic Review." *Archives of General Psychiatry* 67 (2010): 931–938.

Fox-Grage, Wendy, Barbara Coleman, and Donna Folkemer. *The States' Response to the Olmstead Decision: A 2003 Update*. Forum for State Health Policy Leadership, National Conference of State Legislatures, February 2004. Available online: www.hcbs.org/files/28/1375/Olmstead03_update.pdf.

Glaze, Lauren E. *Correctional Populations in the United States, 2009*. Office of Justice Programs, U.S. Department of Justice, Bureau of Justice Statistics, NCJ 231681. Washington, DC: U.S. Department of Justice, 2010. Available online: bjs.ojp.usdoj.gov/content/pub/pdf/cpus09.pdf.

Henderson, Claire, et al. "A Typology of Advanced Statements in Mental Health Care." *Psychiatric Services* 59 (2008): 63–71.

Hiday, Virginia A. "Mental Illness and the Criminal Justice System." In *A Handbook for the Study of Mental Health: Social Contexts, Theories and Systems*, edited by Allan V. Horwitz and Teresa L. Scheid, pp. 508–525. New York: Cambridge University Press, 1999.

Hiday, Virginia A., and Rodney Goodman. "The Least Restrictive Alternative to Involuntary Hospitalization, Outpatient Commitment: Its Use and Effectiveness." *Journal of Psychiatry and Law* 10 (1982): 81–96.

Hiday, Virginia A., and Bradley Ray. "Arrests Two Years After Exiting a Well-Established Mental Health Court." *Psychiatric Services* 61 (2010): 463–468.

Hiday, Virginia A., and Teresa Scheid-Cook. "The North Carolina Experience with Outpatient Commitment: A Critical Appraisal." *International Journal of Law and Psychiatry* 10 (1987): 215–232.

Institute of Medicine. *Improving the Quality of Health Care for Mental and Substance Use Conditions*. Washington, DC: National Academies Press, 2006.

Isaac, Rael J., and Virginia C. Armat. *Madness in the Streets: How Psychiatry and the Law Abandoned the Mentally Ill.* New York: Free Press, 1990.

James, Doris J., and Lauren E. Glaze. *Mental Health Problems of Prison and Jail Inmates.* Office of Justice Programs, U.S. Department of Justice, Bureau of Justice Statistics Special Report, NCJ213600. Washington, DC: U.S. Department of Justice, 2006. Available online: www.nami.org/Content/ContentGroups/Press_Room1/2006/Press_September_2006/DOJ_report_mental_illness_in_prison.pdf.

Kisely, Steve R., Leslie Anne Campbell, and Neil J. Preston. *Compulsory Community and Involuntary Outpatient Treatment for People with Severe Mental Disorders.* Cochrane Database of Systematic Reviews 2011, February 16 (Issue 2): CD004408.

Kuhlthau, Karen, et al. "Increases in Behavioral Health Screening in Pediatric Care in Massachusetts Medicaid Patients." *Archives of Pediatric and Adolescent Medicine* 165 (2011): 660–664.

Lamb, H. Richard, and Mark J. Mills. "Needed Changes in Law and Procedure for the Chronically Mentally Ill." *Hospital and Community Psychiatry* 37 (1986): 475–480.

Leaf, Philip J. "Legal Intervention into a Mental Health System: The Outcomes of 'Wyatt vs. Stickney.'" Unpublished Ph.D. dissertation, Dept. of Sociology, University of Wisconsin, 1978a.

Leaf, Philip J. "The Medical Marketplace and Public Interest Law: Part II. Alabama After Wyatt: PIL Intervention into a Mental Health Services Delivery System." In *Public Interest Law: An Economic and Institutional Analysis*, edited by Burton A. Weisbrod in collaboration with Joel F. Handler and Neil K. Komesar, pp. 374–394. Berkeley: University of California Press, 1978b.

Levin, Aaron. "Va. Tech Tragedy Spurs Examination of Commitment, Campus MH." *Psychiatric News* 42 (2007): 1–25.

Link, Bruce G., and Ann Stueve. "Psychotic Symptoms and the Violent Illegal Behavior of Mental Patients Compared to Community Controls." In *Violence and Mental Disorder: Developments in Risk Assessment*, edited by John Monahan and Henry Steadman, pp. 137–160. Chicago: University of Chicago Press, 1994.

Link, Bruce G., and Ann Stueve. "New Evidence on the Violence Risk Posed by People with Mental Illness." *Archives of General Psychiatry* 55 (1998): 403–404.

Link, Bruce G., Howard Andrews, and Francis T. Cullen. "The Violent and Illegal Behavior of Mental Patients Reconsidered." *American Sociological Review* 57 (1992): 275–292.

Link, Bruce G. et al. "Arrest Outcomes Associated with Outpatient Commitment in New York State." *Psychiatric Services* 62 (2011): 504–508.

Lippmann, Robert D. *Matter of Boggs*, 136 Misc.2d 1082, Supreme Court, New York County, 1987. Available online: www.leagle.com/xmlResult.aspx?xmldoc=19871218136Misc2d1082_11025.xml&docbase=CSLWAR2-1986-2006.

Ludwig, Arnold M., and Frank Farrelly. "The Code of Chronicity." *Archives of General Psychiatry* 15 (1966): 562–568.

Marzuk, Peter M. "Violence, Crime, and Mental Illness: How Strong a Link?" *Archives of General Psychiatry* 53 (1996): 481–486.

Mechanic, David. *Politics, Medicine, and Social Science.* New York: Wiley Interscience, 1974.

Miller, Kent S. *Managing Madness: The Case Against Civil Commitment.* New York: Free Press, 1976.

Monahan, John. "Mental Disorder and Violent Behavior: Perceptions and Evidence." *American Psychologist* 47 (1992): 511–521.

Monahan, John. "Clinical and Actuarial Predictions of Violence." In *Modern Scientific Evidence: The Law and Science of Expert Testimony*, edited by David L. Faigman, David H. Kaye, Michael J. Saks, and Joseph Sanders, vol. 1, St. Paul, MN: West Publishing, 1997.

National GAINS Center. *What Can We Say About the Effectiveness of Jail Diversion Programs for Persons with Co-occurring Disorders?* Delmar, NY: TAPA Center for Jail Diversion, 2004a. Available online: gainscenter.samhsa.gov/pdfs/jail_diversion/whatcanwesay.pdf.

National GAINS Center. *The Prevalence of Co-occurring Mental Illness and Substance Use Disorders in Jails.* The National GAINS Center for People with Co-occurring Disorders in the Justice System, 2004b. Available online: gains.prainc.com/pdfs/disorders/gainsjailprev.pdf.

New York State Office of Mental Health. *Kendra's Law: Final Report on the Status of Assisted Outpatient Treatment*. Albany, NY, March 2005. Available online: www.omh.ny.gov/omhweb/kendra_web/finalreport/AOTFinal2005.pdf.

Perkins, Jane. *Fact Sheet: Medicaid EPSDT Litigation*. Chapel Hill, NC: National Health Law Program, 2009. Available online: www.acmhai.org/pdf/Jane_Perkins_-_EPSDT_Litigation.pdf.

Pescosolido, Bernice A., et al. "The Public's View of the Competence, Dangerousness, and Need for Legal Coercion of Persons with Mental Health Problems." *American Journal of Public Health* 89 (1999): 1339–1345.

Petrila, John, and Annette Christy. "Florida's Outpatient Commitment Law: A Lesson in Failed Reform?" *Psychiatric Services* 59 (2008): 21–23.

Petrila, John, and Jeffrey Swanson. *Mental Illness, Law, and a Public Health Law Research Agenda*. A Theory, Practice, Evidence Monograph for the Public Health Law Research Program (PHLR), Temple University Beasley School of Law, 2010. Available online: serp.mc.duke.edu/PDF/Petrila%20%20Swanson%20TPE%20paper-%20Final%20Paginated%20(1).pdf.

Phelan, Jo C., et al. "Effectiveness and Outcomes of Assisted Outpatient Treatment in New York State." *Psychiatric Services* 61 (2010): 137–143.

Pierce, Glenn L., Mary Durham, and William H. Fisher. "The Impact of Public Policy and Publicity on Admissions to State Mental Health Hospitals." *Journal of Health Politics, Policy, and Law* 11 (1986): 41–66.

Rappeport, Jonas R., ed. *The Clinical Evaluation of the Dangerousness of the Mentally Ill*. Springfield, IL: Charles C. Thomas, 1967.

Reuland, Melissa, and Jason Cheney. *Enhancing Success of Police-Based Diversion Programs for People with Mental Illness*. Delmar, NY: Gains Technical Assistance and Policy Analysis Center for Jail Diversion, 2005. Available online: www.nami.org/Template.cfm?Section=cit2&template=/ContentManagement/ContentDisplay.cfm&ContentID=65062.

Ridgely, M. Susan, et al. *Justice, Treatment and Cost: An Evaluation of the Fiscal Impact of Allegheny County Mental Health Court*. Santa Monica, CA: Rand Corporation, 2007. Available online: www.rand.org/content/dam/rand/pubs/technical_reports/2007/RAND_TR439.pdf.

Robbins, Pamela Clark, et al. "Assisted Outpatient Treatment in New York: Regional Differences in New York's Assisted Outpatient Treatment Program." *Psychiatric Services* 61 (2010): 970–975.

Rosenbaum, Sara. "The Olmstead Decision: Implications for State Health Policy." *Health Affairs* 19 (2000): 228–232.

Rosenbaum, Sara, and Joel Teitelbaum. *Olmstead at Five: Assessing the Impact*. Washington, DC: Kaiser Commission on Medicaid and the Uninsured, 2004. Available online: www.kff.org/medicaid/upload/olmstead-at-five-assessing-the-impact.pdf.

Rosenbaum, Sara, and Paul H. Wise. "Crossing the Medicaid-Private Insurance Divide: The Case of EPSDT." *Health Affairs* 26 (2007): 382–393.

Rosie, D., et al., Plaintiffs, v. Mitt Romney, et al., Defendants. Civil Action No. 01-30199-MAP. United States District Court for the District of Massachusetts, *410 F. Supp. 2d 18; 2006 U.S. Dist. LEXIS 3026*, January 26, 2006, Decided. Available online: www.law.berkeley.edu/files/RosieD_v_Romney_410_f_supp2d_18.pdf.

Rubenstein, Leonard. "APA's Model Law: Hurting the People It Seeks to Help." *Hospital and Community Psychiatry* 36 (1985): 968–972.

Scheffler, Richard M., and Neal Adams. "Millionaires and Mental Health: Proposition 63 in California." *Health Affairs Web Exclusive*, W5-212–224, 2005. Available online: content.healthaffairs.org/content/early/2005/05/03/hlthaff.w5.212.full.pdf+html.

Segal, Steven P., and Uri Aviram. *The Mentally-Ill in Community-Based Sheltered Care: A Study of Community Care and Social Integration*. New York: Wiley Interscience, 1978.

Shah, Saleem A., and Bruce D. Sales, eds. *Law and Mental Health: Major Developments and Research Needs*. DHHS Publication No. (ADM) 91-1875. Rockville, MD: U.S. Dept. of Health and Human Services, Public Health Service, Alcohol, Drug Abuse, and Mental Health Administration, National Institute of Mental Health, 1991.

Soulier, Matthew F., Andrea Maislen, and James C. Beck. "Status of the Psychiatric Duty to Protect, Circa 2006." *Journal of the American Academy of Psychiatry and Law* 38 (2010): 457–473.

Srebnik, Debra S., and John Q. La Fond. "Advance Directives for Mental Health Treatment." *Psychiatric Services* 50 (1999): 919–925.

Steadman, Henry J., Susan Davidson, and Collie Brown. "Mental Health Courts: Their Promise and Unanswered Questions." *Psychiatric Services* 52 (2001): 457–458.

Steadman, Henry J., et al. "Violence by People Discharged from Acute Psychiatric Inpatient Facilities and by Others in the Same Neighborhoods." *Archives of General Psychiatry* 55 (1998): 393–401.

Steadman, Henry J., et al. "Assessing the New York City Involuntary Outpatient Commitment Pilot Program." *Psychiatric Services* 52 (2001): 330–336.

Steadman, Henry J., et al. "Effect of Mental Health Courts on Arrests and Jail Days: A Multisite Study." *Archives of General Psychiatry* 68 (2011): 167–172.

Stone, Alan A. *Mental Health and the Law: A System in Transition.* DHEW Publication No. (ADM) 75-176. Rockville, MD: National Institute of Mental Health, Center for Studies of Crime and Delinquency, 1975.

Stone, Alan A. "The Right to Refuse Treatment." *Archives of General Psychiatry* 38 (1981): 358–362.

Stone, Alan A. *Law, Psychiatry, and Morality.* Washington, DC: American Psychiatric Press, 1984.

Swanson, Jeffrey W., et al. "Violence and Psychiatric Disorder in the Community: Evidence from the Epidemiologic Catchment Area Surveys." *Hospital and Community Psychiatry* 41 (1990): 761–770.

Swanson, Jeffery W., et al. Unpublished manuscript (reviewed in Monahan, 1997, p. 305), 1996.

Swanson, Jeffrey W., et al. "Facilitated Psychiatric Advance Directives: A Randomized Trial of an Intervention to Foster Advance Treatment Planning Among Persons with Severe Mental Illness." *American Journal of Psychiatry* 163 (2006a): 1943–1951.

Swanson, Jeffrey W., et al. "A National Study of Violent Behavior in Persons with Schizophrenia." *Archives of General Psychiatry* 63 (2006b): 490–499.

Swartz, Marvin S. "Introduction to the Special Section on Assisted Outpatient Treatment in New York State." *Psychiatric Services* 61 (2010): 967–969.

Swartz, Marvin S., et al. "Assessing Outcomes for Consumers in New York's Assisted Outpatient Treatment Program." *Psychiatric Services* 61 (2010): 976–981.

Tiihonen, Jari, et al. "Specific Major Mental Disorders and Criminality: A 26-Year Prospective Study of the 1966 Northern Finland Birth Cohort." *American Journal of Psychiatry* 154 (1997): 840–845.

Torrey, E. Fuller, and Robert J. Kaplan. "A National Survey of the Use of Outpatient Commitment." *Psychiatric Services* 46 (1995): 778–784.

Treatment Advocacy Center. *Assisted Outpatient Treatment Laws.* Arlington, VA: Treatment Advocacy Center, 2012. Available online: treatmentadvocacycenter.org/solution/assisted-outpatient-treatment-laws.

Treffert, Darold A. "Dying with Their Rights On." *American Journal of Psychiatry* 130 (1973): 1041.

U.S. Supreme Court. *Youngberg v. Romeo*, 457 U.S. 307, 1982. Available online: caselaw.lp.findlaw.com/scripts/getcase.pl?court=us&vol=457&invol=307.

U.S. Supreme Court. *Olmstead v. L.C.*, 527 U.S. 581, 1999. Available online: supreme.justia.com/cases/federal/us/527/581/case.html.

Warren, Carol. *The Court of Last Resort: Mental Illness and the Law.* Chicago: University of Chicago Press, 1982.

Watson, Amy, et al. "Mental Health Courts and the Complex Issue of Mentally Ill Offenders." *Psychiatric Services* 52 (2001): 477–481.

Weinstock, Robert, et al. "Back to the Past in California: A Temporary Retreat to a *Tarasoff* Duty to Warn." *Journal of the American Academy of Psychiatry and Law* 34 (2006): 523–528.

Wood, Jennifer, et al. *Police Interventions with Persons Affected by Mental Illnesses: A Critical Review of Global Thinking and Practice.* Center for Behavioral Health Services and Criminal Justice Research, New Brunswick, NJ: Rutgers University, 2011. Available online: www.temple.edu/cj/people/documents/Police_Interventions_Monograph_March_2011.pdf.

Zusman, Jack. "APA's Model Commitment Law and the Need for Better Mental Health Services." *Hospital and Community Psychiatry* 36 (1985): 978–980.

12

Mental Health Policy Analysis

A recent textbook defines policy analysis as the examination of government decisions and actions for the purpose of assessing their impact and gauging their advantages and disadvantages in comparison with possible alternatives (Mintrom 2012, p. 2). The steps involved in carrying out the process of policy analysis can be broken down in different ways and depend, to some extent, on the type of question being asked. Common tasks involve defining a problem, gathering empirical data on actual or estimated policy impacts, and making a judgment about the most desirable solution. The promise of policy analysis, in mental health care as in other fields, is improved allocation of resources by taking into account trustworthy factual information, relevant social values, and strategic insight regarding the possibilities and limitations of public problem solving.

Policy analysis takes place in a variety of contexts, and there are several audiences for which policy analysis results provide a useful resource (Bardach 2009). Perhaps the most conventional setting is inside the government bureaucracy, where professional staff members formulate advice for officials who must develop or respond to new legislative proposals. Government programs typically affect multiple stakeholders. Policy analysis is a basic tool for these individuals and organizations as they seek to advocate for provisions most beneficial to their interests and those of their clientele. Similarly, public and private administrators charged with implementing laws, rules, and services need to discern their responsibilities as well as discretionary options within an operating policy. The scholarly community in a variety of disciplines, including sociology, political science, social work, economics, public health, and law, is another major source of policy analysis research, whether undertaken for the purpose of contributing to public debate, enhancing critical understanding of government, or addressing questions of social and political theory.

An important finding by public policy specialists is the recognition that government is neither a homogeneous nor consistent entity. Rather, there are different components of the political system organized to respond to specific issues, that is, a series of functional "domains" with distinctive groups of participants, styles of interaction, cultural influences, institutional jurisdictions, and historical background (Burstein 1991). The design of solutions, the play of political interests within policy adoption, and the system's capacity for translating new policies into effective programs all require consideration in appreciating how legislative proposals on a particular issue arise.

Yet it is essential to acknowledge that public policy is not merely what governments do by intention, but also the incentives, opportunities, and restraints created by decisions (and nondecisions) across multiple issues and programs even when the cumulative result may be inadvertent. Kiesler and Sibulkin (1987) make this point in their distinction between *de jure* and *de facto* public policy. For example, deinstitutionalization emerged as operational policy for state mental hospitals and other actors in the mental health system during the 1950s, which was years before the federal government adopted community mental health legislation. The reason was that new medications, administrative and program developments within mental health facilities, and financial factors all began to shift the system of care before federal law confirmed this redirection. Similarly, as discussed in an earlier chapter, one cannot make sense of the course of deinstitutionalization (e.g., its timing and geographic patterns) without taking into account the essential impact of income support and public health insurance programs that were devised by policymakers without having the situation of the mentally ill primarily in mind.

Preceding chapters of this book have covered mental health as a social policy area in terms of its central concepts, epidemiological patterns, professional roles, legislative history, service agencies, financing arrangements, and strategies of reform. This material now provides the foundation for identifying key features of mental health as a policy domain. This discussion, in turn, will set the stage for examining five approaches for conducting policy analysis of mental health care issues.

CHARACTERISTICS OF THE MENTAL HEALTH POLICY DOMAIN

To speak of a "mental health policy domain" is to call attention to the distinctive environment—political, legal, economic, and organizational—within which demands for government action related to mental health care take shape and are negotiated and implemented. This environment is a reflection of prominent characteristics of mental illness as a clinical and social problem; it also reflects the way in which citizens and officials have reacted to these features over the long historical span during which the mental health system emerged and developed into present form.

Persistence of Stigma

Even as mental health services have become increasingly available and utilized by a large segment of the population, stigmatization of mental health conditions and the people affected by them continues. Historical examples of hostility toward, and discrimination against, people with mental illnesses abound in the punitive and exclusionary practices that preceded the contemporary era, including such extremes as demonization, physical abuse, and neglect. Today, the organized social response is much more humane, directed by scientific knowledge, and informed by a commitment to disability rights and other legal protections—although it is true that jails still serve as a setting of control to a surprising extent. Nonetheless, negative public perceptions about mental illness are rampant, showing stubborn resistance to change and an ability to coexist with advances in the efficacy of treatments and their integration into mainstream medicine. In their overview of U.S. mental health care since 1950, Frank and Glied (2006) examined the question of stigmatization and key dimensions of popular attitudes as documented in opinion polls and media coverage. As we have discussed, despite a broadening understanding of mental illness and its causes, they found stable percentages of the general public inclined to put social distance between themselves and those with mental health problems and an increased likelihood to view mental illnesses as linked with violent behavior.

Stigmatization of mental illnesses has decided significance in a political system where public opinion and other cultural currents are central ingredients of the policy process. Schneider and Ingram (1997) explain how social constructions of different groups affect the amount of attention they receive as well as the characteristics of policies adopted to deal with their problems. Groups perceived to be suspicious and frightening generally have little political power and rank low in terms of "deservingness." In this light, views of mental illness as a threatening form of social deviance have produced interventions that are restrictive, coercive, and limited. An example is reliance on underfunded and isolating institutions. Contemporary movements for parity, disability rights, and consumer empowerment represent efforts to combat the long-term stigmatization of people with mental illnesses in our society and to redress the substandard conditions and practices that have characterized many previous policies.

Definitional Ambiguity

At this point in the book, it hardly needs stating that much ambiguity clouds interpretation of the problem of mental illness. The line between nonconformity, on the one hand, and pathology, on the other, can be difficult to draw even for professionals with extensive training and experience and recourse to technical diagnostic resources like the *DSM*. Different societies, and different groups within the same society, may have more or less expansive categories for labeling behavior as abnormal and in need of treatment. As previously noted, some social critics warn about the potential misuse of psychiatry as a framework for individualizing problems more properly seen as disorders of the social system. Notable examples can be cited regarding the psychiatric sector's role in helping to suppress dissent and human rights within oppressive regimes abroad (Perlin 2006). A recent study maintains that American psychiatric professionals influenced by the rise of civil rights protest activity in the 1960s and 1970s reacted with a tendency to diagnose African Americans with the label of schizophrenia much more frequently than Whites (Metzl 2009). This research, which examined the records of patients admitted to Ionia State Hospital, a facility serving the African American population of riot-torn urban Detroit, found that clinical perceptions of the disorder came to be affected by cultural frames and anxieties regarding race in that time period. Aside from such large-scale sociopolitical concerns, the fields of psychiatry and psychology have been split by perennial debates over the etiological significance of environmental, biological, and intrapsychic factors.

Social problems whose causality is debatable tend to be disadvantaged in the competition for scarce public resources. Problems defined as having multiple causal agents are more difficult to deal with than problems believed to result from a single or overriding factor. A problem matched with a widely consensual solution has much greater chance of capturing policymakers' interest and support than one characterized by confusion over the best course of action. Each of these generalizations represents distilled wisdom from a large body of empirical research investigating the disposition of social issues within the process of government decision making (Howlett and Ramesh 1995; Kraft and Furlong 2010; Rochefort and Cobb 1994). The fact that mental illness is a problem characterized by complex causal formulation, ongoing disputes among different theoretical schools, and periodic revolutions in the dominant paradigms for research and treatment has complicated its handling as a public policy matter. Often, the result has been inaction, cautious adherence to the status quo, and the sense that more time and study are needed to chart a decisive course of action.

Service Complexity

For most of the 1800s and the first half of the 1900s, the "mental health system" in the United States was synonymous with a network of public and private hospitals. Community-based services, to the extent any nascent interest in this modality existed, were minimally available, lacking in sophistication, and often poorly connected with institutional care (Caplan 1969). This is not to say, however, that hospital facilities did not offer their own impressive array of services. In addition to attention to their psychological problems, residents received medical care, supervised housing, recreational opportunities, and, in certain instances, job training and employment. Once deinstitutionalization and the community mental health movement took root starting in the 1950s and 1960s, it created a need for arranging these and additional supports in a general social setting. Different sections of this book have reviewed the role of income maintenance programs, temporary shelters, affordable housing, case management, substance abuse treatment, rehabilitation, family services, and new legal and criminal justice provisions in dealing with mental health problems. Such a panoply of resources bears witness to the comprehensive vision of contemporary community integration as well as our increasingly intricate awareness of best practices and model programs in targeting the needs of particular patient groups.

As psychiatrist Howard Goldman (2003) has written, one of the most important questions a clinician can ask a patient is this: How do you pay your rent? This practical query has little to do with psychiatry as a medical specialty, yet it is one capable of exposing serious social vulnerabilities whose resolution may be crucial to effective delivery of mental health services. Commenting on the work of President Bush's New Freedom Commission on Mental Health, Goldman highlighted the broad social policy agenda that is necessary to counter a fragmented system of care. In a word, population needs and service requirements are *complex* in a way paralleled by few other program areas. The enduring challenge for policy development in the mental health domain, then, is either to invent or to coordinate resources that can incorporate this complexity while matching it with flexibility and efficiency in responding to the idiosyncratic circumstances of persons with mental health problems, their families, and their home communities.

Federal Structure

Federalism is a defining aspect of American government. Certain policy domains, like defense, are strictly national responsibilities, while others, like motor vehicle registration (state) and basic municipal services (local), fall under the control of other levels. In this era of the advanced social welfare state, however, most social policies possess an inter-governmental character with respect to their financing, administration, and venues of policy development. Mental health care does not stand out because of the fact that policy is established and maintained through the interaction of multiple levels of government. What *is* noteworthy is the extent to which, historically, pivotal issues concerning the organizational forms and philosophy of the mental health system have been approached simultaneously as decisions about federal, state, and local involvement inside this policy area (Rochefort 1999).

Thus, the advent of a formal mental health system in the United States during the late 1700s and early 1800s, in which state and county mental hospitals were established to remove disordered individuals from local poorhouses and jails, was effectively a deci-sion about which level of government would be accepting the mantle of responsibility for mental illness. Local communities still were required to help pay for this new system of care when their residents counted among those hospitalized. With the exception of the founding of a Government Hospital for the Insane in 1852, later known as St. Elizabeth's Hospital in Washington, D.C., the federal government remained disengaged from men-tal health matters throughout the nineteenth century. That situation did not change until the shift to community-based care after World War II, a systemic reorientation that coin-cided with a reshuffling of state/federal roles in setting the country's mental health policy agenda. Then, during the 1960s and following decades, the progressive integration of men-tal health care into general medicine depended on the inflow of a vast amount of federal financial resources by means of the Medicare and Medicaid programs. Recently, it has been interesting to see the movement for adequate insurance for mental illnesses play out as a debate over state versus federal roles in determining minimum standards for coverage pertaining to this service area.

Historian Gerald Grob (1994) underscores the importance of attention to federalism as a structural factor that can mediate and transform mental health policy. His research documents not only the way that changes in intergovernmental relations have been the vehicle of major innovations throughout the history of mental health care but also the programmatic distortion that can result due to strain, competition, and divided and over-lapping authorities under a federal system. Whenever fiscal resources are at stake, it is pre-dictable for government actors to maneuver to align services and the flow of patients most favorably for their respective interests, such as by shifting responsibility for payment to some other level. The point is that analysts must be attuned to structure as well as program substance in understanding mental health policy development and impacts.

Policy Cycles and Issue Triggers

Few public policy issues maintain a high position on the political agenda continuously. More typical is an "issue attention cycle," in which matters recede into the background after brief periods of prominence, with or without government action to address the prob-lems that have come to the fore (Parsons 1995). This episodic pattern of policy change has been described in terms of a "window" that opens only occasionally when there is fortu-itous alignment of forces related to a social problem, its politics, and the consideration of proposed solutions (Kingdon 1984).

Two patterns are clear when we look at the occurrence of such cycles within the mental health policy domain. First, a historical perspective indicates that it often takes tragic incidents shocking to public sensibilities to garner high-level attention for mental health concerns. The killing of two police officers at the U.S. Capitol building in 1998, the death of a young woman in New York City when she was pushed in front of a subway car in 1999, the 2007 Virginia Tech massacre, the shooting of Congresswoman Gabrielle Giffords and 18 others, six fatally, at a political rally in Tucson, Arizona, in 2011 and the killing of 27 people, most school children, in new town, Connecticut in 2012 are just some of the examples one could cite in which violent actions by people struggling with mental illnesses served to galvanize widespread, but temporary, interest in the state of the nation's mental health system. At times, these events have led quickly to adoption of new laws or an injection of funding for mental health services. Yet crisis-driven policymaking of this type is prone to major disadvantages, including spasmodic responses that neglect program areas of greatest documented need, opportunistic exploitation of the policy process by well-positioned stakeholders, and sudden resource expansion that will not sustain building a planned system of care (Bonnie et al. 2009; Hogan and Sederer 2009).

Second, many scholars have also noted the existence of longer-wave cycles in mental health policymaking fueled by the periodic rediscovery of past intellectual concepts and program themes, particularly as the system has vacillated between different forms of institutional and community care (Rochefort 1988). Eventually, the approaches of one era may run their course as the focus of enthusiasm, only to resurface in new garb at a later time. Some of the elements associated with this cyclical motif include ideas about "curability," prevention, the emphasis on somatic versus psychological factors, and the role of social and environmental forces in the origins and treatment of mental disease. Based on a review of literature, Rochefort (1988) identified 14 different factors proposed by researchers as reasons for the occurrence of mental health policy cycles. One overarching theme in this analysis is repeated frustration with the outcomes of mental health policy reforms that have been oversold, underfunded, and diminished by haphazard implementation.

FIVE APPROACHES TO MENTAL HEALTH POLICY ANALYSIS

Policy analysis is a versatile technique whose particular forms are determined, in practice, by available information, intended audience, disciplinary orientation, and constraints of time and resources (Mintrom 2012). A central objective, however, is to demystify the actions of government and to optimize results from the investment of public resources. To illustrate the utility of this research genre within the domain of mental health care, five types of policy analysis studies have been selected for examination. In each case, our discussion highlights the methodology and findings of a published article or report exemplifying the respective approach.

Analyzing the Politics of Policymaking

Mental health policies come into being through a political process. What is the social problem that prompted official concern? In what way did it come to light? How were proposals for remedying the situation formulated? How did the functioning of decision-making institutions influence consideration of this issue? If a tangible outcome resulted—a new law, ruling, regulatory procedure, administrative change, or budgetary shift—which set of interests emerged victorious and why? Were the goals of those responsible for putting this issue on the agenda satisfied or is there likely to be pressure for subsequent action? Analysts who focus on the politics of mental health policy aim to provide coherent accounts of official behavior to answer these questions.

In the September 2010 issue of *Milbank Quarterly*, Colleen L. Barry and her colleagues Haiden A. Huskamp and Howard H. Goldman published a study of the political development of the Paul Wellstone and Pete Domenici Mental Health Parity and Addiction Equity (MHPAEA) Act. As discussed earlier in this book, this measure, which was adopted in 2008, improved behavioral health coverage for millions of people enrolled in employer-sponsored and state and local government insurance plans by strengthening provisions of the 1996 federal parity statute. These authors sought to relate the passage of MHPAEA to the long-term struggle for mental health parity in the United States and to identify those factors enabling a major new statute to make it through Congress after more than a decade of inaction. The study relies on diverse sources of information, including historical documents, government reports, academic scholarship, the Congressional Record, and public correspondence. Most critical is a collection of more than two dozen key informant interviews with members of Congress, their staffs, lobbyists, advocates, and other contacts.

Barry, Huskamp, and Goldman begin by describing how the problem of inadequate insurance coverage was entwined with the very origins of third-party payment for mental health conditions following World War II. In short, private payers resisted taking on the burden of costs in this sector because they did not want to supplant the financing role historically played by state governments. During the 1970s and 1980s, however, as private psychiatric services and community care proliferated, advocates worked for passage of state benefit mandates regarding alcoholism, drug abuse, and mental illness. Although these were worthwhile advances, such laws nonetheless remained inadequate since they existed only in certain states and stopped short of eliminating coverage discrepancies between general medicine and behavioral health care. Advocates decided to pursue a more thorough corrective by shifting their efforts to the federal level and by framing the mental health parity issue as an antidiscrimination measure. This effort resulted in the Mental Health Parity Act of 1996, a law having more symbolic than practical value, however, due to limitations on size of businesses affected (50 or more employees), the persistence of inequities within certain benefit categories, and exclusion of substance abuse services. Significantly, the statute also did not require coverage of mental health care in health plans.

Within the structure of federalism, political actors frustrated by blockages at one level of government will likely regroup for action at another. For the parity battle during the late 1990s and early 2000s, this meant temporarily refocusing on state legislatures sympathetic to the plight of those needing to use mental health services within the confines of private insurance. Ultimately, dozens of states responded to this challenge, a few with comprehensive laws that were virtually a model of reform, but inconsistencies across different parts of the country continued to be a drawback. Most important, the federal law known as ERISA (the Employee Retirement Income Security Act of 1974) prohibited states from regulating self-insuring private businesses, thereby exempting close to half of all employers from state parity requirements. Only by addressing parity as a federal issue could this obstacle be surmounted.

Three factors made it possible for activists to break the impasse over parity legislation within the U.S. Congress, according to Barry, Huskamp, and Goldman's research. First was the compilation of extensive empirical evidence by investigators inside and outside of government documenting the feasibility of controlling costs for an augmented behavioral health benefit under managed care. Second, a small but effective group of legislators championed the cause of parity. Leaders such as Senators Pete Domenici, Paul Wellstone, and Edward Kennedy and Representatives Patrick Kennedy and Jim Ramstad, who all shared the common link of personal or family experience with mental health or substance abuse problems, were key in crafting the legislation and moving it toward passage. Third, a legislative strategy was fashioned to move forward with different parity approaches in the Senate and House, limited in the former and more ambitious in the latter, in recognition of the political complexion of each body, and then to use the process of reconciliation to find common ground yielding the most progressive law possible under the circumstances.

The study by Barry, Huskamp, and Goldman makes comprehensible a landmark mental health policy initiative that was decades in the making. As a work of political policy analysis, it clarifies the genesis of the parity issue, explains its circuitous path across the landscape of opportunities and blind alleys created by federalism, and examines how changing conditions within the institution of Congress facilitated the breakthrough of 2008. The authors bring their analysis to an end by noting several technical concerns surrounding administration of the new law. Further, the federal parity statute still applied only to large businesses, and it did not require employers to offer behavioral health coverage, only to bring benefits for mental health and substance abuse services into line with other forms of medical care when both types of insurance are available. To be sure, these were design flaws unsettling to parity advocates, but the relevant context of mental health policy formulation suddenly shifted as the Obama Administration next acted to make the treatment of mental illness and substance abuse a basic benefit in its sweeping overhaul of the nation's health system.

Implementation Analysis

In contrast with the previous study of policy formulation, our second type of policy analysis deals with implementation. Implementation is the phase of the policy process that follows adoption, and it is concerned with execution of a new law, regulation, program, or set of services. Often, the political battle between those "pro" and "con" continues as a policy goes into effect. In addition, a rash of other challenges related to administrative behavior, organizational capacity and functioning, coordination of resources, quality control, performance of technology, and "gaming" by affected interests can, and do, arise during implementation. Implementation analysis centers on the progress of a policy once put into action in order to identify those operational elements needing adjustment to produce a better outcome.

An apt study for illustrating implementation analysis is "Challenges in Implementing Disaster Mental Health Programs: State Program Directors' Perspectives," published by Carrie L. Elrod, Jessica L. Hamblen, and Fran H. Norris in *Annals of the American Academy of Political and Social Science* in 2006. At the heart of this inquiry is the Crisis Counseling Assistance and Training Program (CCP), a measure adopted as part of federal disaster and emergency assistance legislation in 1974. As described by these authors, the CCP uses outreach, education, and brief counseling to address mental health needs in communities coping with disaster. The program's emphasis is on short-term intervention, with referral to the existing mental health system for longer-term treatment and support. The database for this research consisted of a sample of 36 interviews with CCP directors in 25 states that received program grants between 1996 and 2001. This time period saw numerous natural occurrences—hurricanes, tornadoes, flooding, wildfires—as well as the D.C. sniper shootings in 2003 and a catastrophic nightclub fire in Rhode Island in that same year. To organize the information gained from interviews and related documentary materials, the authors turned to the actual sequence of activities followed by a state that finds itself facing a disaster. Their framework includes six stages: preparing; implementing the program response; providing CCP services to the community; integrating CCP into community and state systems; phasing out the response; and evaluating the response.

A main finding was that a detailed, comprehensive emergency mental health plan was rarely in place before disaster struck, particularly in states where disasters were uncommon. This meant critical ingredients for mounting an efficient and effective response—designation of resources and supplies, establishment of multiagency relationships, and a protocol for crisis decision-making—were underdeveloped or nonexistent when most needed.

It is during the first week of a disaster that state officials must take action in applying for assistance from the federal government to put CCP into motion. However, a common experience in states having lived through this experience was a kind of bureaucratic chaos that impeded submission of the required paperwork with reliable needs assessment data.

Multiple challenges were uncovered in the delivery of CCP services. Outreach to high-risk target populations suffered due to staffing inadequacies, language and literacy barriers, and sometimes resistance from service recipients. There was confusion regarding the definition of "crisis counseling" among program directors, along with uncertainty about criteria for referrals from CCP to the formal mental health system. And, although rapid training of service providers was judged crucial for implementing a high-quality response in the field, little consensus existed in regard to the content, timing, and audience for this component of the program.

CCP directors must avoid a program response that ignores the existing system of care in their locale, otherwise service duplication and gaps are likely to occur. This research found integration to be a complex task dependent on good communication among a wide variety of agencies, departments, and provider groups; the formation of collaborative relationships; and the navigation of a maze of fiscal management difficulties. Many CCP directors admitted to skill and knowledge deficiencies in one or another of these areas. Turf issues exacerbated the situation.

The winding down of CCP activity typically proved a clumsy matter marked by uncertainty over how to choose the end date as well as irregular staff departures. Only about half the CCPs included in this study attempted any kind of systematic evaluation of their activities. Among those conducting an evaluation, the data collected were of questionable quality and relevance.

As this study by Elrod, Hamblen, and Norris makes plain, it can be dismaying to compare a law's aftermath with policymakers' original intentions. In this case, the provision of mental health services as an essential part of our nation's disaster response system proved to be an ideal undermined by ground-level inconsistencies, inefficiencies, and conflicts. Yet the benefits of an implementation policy analysis of this type, which carefully scrutinizes all integral parts of a program, lie in the guidance it provides for correction. Thus, the research report ends with a series of thoughtful recommendations for enhancing CCP. These include expanded federal support for readiness planning, improved training services for state disaster mental health coordinators, a streamlined federal grant application process, new program manuals to support administrative responsibilities, increased attention to fiscal management issues, and a standardized approach for CCP evaluation. Several of these changes were already in process at the time Elrod and colleagues' article was being written.

Policy Analysis by Normative Criteria

Another useful application of policy analysis is comparison of alternative policies or service systems. This type of study begins with specification of normative criteria, or standards, which will serve as benchmarks for gauging performance. The criteria may be general attributes one would apply in any area of public policy—e.g., effectiveness, efficiency, equity, cost control—as well as objectives and values with particular importance for the domain under review (Kraft and Furlong 2010). The appeal of this method of analysis lies in its structure for organizing a tremendous amount of quantitative and qualitative information while maintaining clear focus on the bottom-line questions of policy evaluation and choice. The approach is also flexible in that researchers not only make use of multiple kinds of indicators, they can also weight criteria differently to identify performance priorities when this seems appropriate for the policy situation at hand.

The study we have selected as an example of normative comparative analysis in mental health care is *Grading the States* published by the National Alliance on Mental Illness (Aron et al. 2009). The NAMI project takes the form of a "report card," an increasingly common device in contemporary policy discourse that ranges in sophistication from simple legislative scorecards to multipronged efforts to gauge the performance of complex systems like school departments, hospitals, and state governments (Coe 2003). As one of the nation's leading mental health advocacy groups, NAMI began rating state mental health programs in 1986 as a means of drawing attention to the strengths and weaknesses of the nation's mental health system. Over time this effort has grown considerably in sophistication, at least in part because of methodological criticisms lodged against earlier studies in the series (e.g., Warner 1989).

For the 2009 policy analysis, NAMI's research team defined four broad categories of normative performance:

1. health promotion and measurement,
2. financing and core treatment/recovery services,
3. consumer and family empowerment, and
4. community integration and social inclusion.

Each of these categories, in turn, included from 8 to 34 component measurements related to service availability, patient outcomes, planning activity, and financing. Reflecting NAMI's judgment about their relative importance, the four master categories have different weights when a state's total score is calculated, with category I at 25 percent, category II at 45 percent, category III at 15 percent, and category IV at 15 percent. Data were gathered primarily by a survey of state mental health authorities, but with supplementation by state documents and a Web-based survey regarding the experiences of consumers and family members residing in different states. Every state but South Dakota participated in the study.

Based on this research, NAMI's overall assessment of the status of public mental health care in the United States is extremely negative, judging the system be "in crisis"

Table 12.1 **NAMI Report Card Results**

	United States	Massachusetts	Minnesota	New Jersey
Health Promotion and Measurement	D	B	D	C
Financing and Core Treatment/ Recovery Services	C	B	C	C
Consumer and Family Empowerment	D	C	C	B
Community Integration and Social Inclusion	D	C	D	D
Overall Grade 2009	D	B	C	C
Overall Grade 2006	D	C	C	C

Source: Aron, Laudan, et al. *Grading the States 2009: A Report on America's Health Care System for Adults with Serious Mental Illness.* Arlington, VA: National Alliance on Mental Illness, 2009. Available online: www.nami.org/gtsTemplate09.cfm?Section=Grading_the_States_2009.

and mired in the past. For the nation as a whole, NAMI issued an average final grade of "D," or no better than the previous study results in 2006. "D" was also the most common state grade; no state received an "A"; and six states received "F." The bulk of the *Grading the States* report provides detailed narratives and data points profiling circumstances within individual states, particularly the reasons for any improvement or decline between 2006 and 2009. Table 12.1 summarizes the findings for the United States as a whole and for Massachusetts, Minnesota, and New Jersey, which are the home states of authors of this edition of *Mental Health and Social Policy*.

The NAMI report ends with policy recommendations presenting no real surprises, since the values and priorities of this advocacy group are, by now, well known, and they are the same touchstones that generated the rubric for these state assessments. However, the authors do elaborate by citing some of the service programs, legislative and regulatory initiatives, and administrative practices considered most praiseworthy in selected locations around the country. The five overarching policy recommendations are as follows: (1) increase public funding for mental health care services; (2) improve data collection, outcomes measurement, and accountability; (3) integrate mental and physical health care; (4) promote recovery and respect; and (5) increase services for people with serious mental illnesses who are most at risk.

Would another research group come to the same conclusions as NAMI in assessing the state of mental health care in the United States? Not necessarily. Is there any scientific basis to the numerical formulas developed by NAMI researchers in compiling their grades? Not really. Should NAMI be able to identify areas of improvement in the scope and quality of data collected as its *Grading the States* venture moves forward? Without doubt. Such questions do not discredit this type of normative analysis, however, they only accent its purpose. This is to galvanize ongoing discussion of a policy issue by formulating transparent standards for assessment; gathering timely and original information pertinent to these standards; and packaging the results in a way suitable for understanding by a diverse group of officials, experts, members of the media, and, not least, users of the system.

Policy Analysis by Patient Case Study

Our fourth type of mental health policy analysis is a very common way of pinpointing flaws in service delivery, although it does not follow any standard textbook methodology. Akin to the tradition of "grand rounds" in medicine, the technique of policy analysis by patient case study focuses intensively on the problems presented by a single patient, but with attention to the response of the system of care. Insofar as gaps and shortcomings are evident, they are viewed as potentially "symptomatic" of broader dysfunctions worthy of discussion and repair.

In 1982, journalist Susan Sheehan published a book titled *Is There No Place on Earth for Me?* giving an account, artfully rendered, of the life of a woman with schizophrenia. This work was not targeted at the mental health community but, rather, a general audience, and it won the Pulitzer Prize for general nonfiction. Nonetheless, Sheehan's portrait of "Sylvia Frumkin," a pseudonym, won acclaim from those most familiar with the mental health system, including professionals and consumers and their families, who valued its clinical detail coupled with meticulous observation of organizations, programs, and services within the psychiatric sector. Shortly after the appearance of *Is There No Place on Earth for Me?* a group of mental health experts subjected the book's material to their own analysis as "a case study for policymakers" (Moran, Freedman, and Sharfstein 1984). They concluded that the case offered a dramatic illustration of system fragmentation and the need for a more encompassing set of supports for those living with serious mental illnesses in the community.

The study we have chosen to illustrate policy analysis by patient case study connects itself directly to this approach of Moran and her colleagues, although it was produced more than a decade later and is based on primary information collected by the authors instead of secondary analysis. "'Sylvia Frumkin' Has a Baby: A Case Study for Policymakers" was published by Joanne Nicholson, Jeffrey Geller, and William Fisher in *Psychiatric Services* in 1996. The article concerns a patient named by the authors "Gloria Morrison," whose psychiatric condition and social circumstances resembled Sylvia Frumkin's. Yet Ms. Morrison belongs to a younger cohort of women with serious mental illness who are more likely to bear and raise children in this current post-deinstitutionalization era. The purpose of this study, then, was to address issues similar to those considered by Moran and associates concerning the delivery of services, clinical treatment, and potential role of families in supporting members who develop serious mental disorders.

Case records indicated that Gloria Morrison's initial hospitalization for depression and suicidal ideation had occurred at age 28, or about three years following birth of her first child. Soon after, her marriage broke up and Ms. Morrison entered a period of her life characterized by increasingly severe psychiatric illness and domestic and employment instability. Multiple hospitalizations occurred during the next four years, typically associated with suicide attempts. Charges of child neglect were filed by teachers, neighbors, and family members. Police took Ms. Morrison, at age 33, into custody after finding her sleeping in a car with her child. Ms. Morrison was pregnant, although she denied this fact. According to various clinicians, she exhibited multiple psychiatric conditions, among them schizoaffective disorder, unspecified personality disorder, and bipolar affective disorder. During the next two years, another round of psychiatric hospitalizations took place, one for a full year at a state psychiatric facility. After the second child was born, both children entered the state's foster care system. Although her parents lived nearby, this did not provide a workable long-term placement option. Upon discharge into the community, Ms. Morrison attempted to regain her parental rights, but the court decided against her resuming these responsibilities. At age 37, Ms. Morrison ended her life by suicide.

Within the area of service delivery, the researchers found Gloria Morrison's case to be a very costly one; however, exact figures were difficult to calculate taking into account direct mental health services together with indirect expenses of the social service and legal systems. The case indicated a need for service expansion in a number of categories— foster placement planning and supports, family-oriented residential and supported housing, flexible program funding to serve parents and children as a family unit, and better coordination of case management across different bureaucracies—to lower such costs and to help avert the tragic outcome of this situation. With respect to clinical treatment, the authors criticized the general lack of care for the pregnancy-related needs of women with severe mental illness, which vary during different phases of pregnancy. They also argued for greater involvement of parents who have mental illness in planning alternate care arrangements when necessary for their children, and for incorporating parenting skills training as a component of psychosocial rehabilitation. Finally, on the subject of family support issues, the facts of this case suggested the need for educational and supportive services targeted at grandparents and other relatives who may have resources worth considering in child placement decisions.

Nicholson, Geller, and Fisher concluded their study by admitting they did not know how many other individuals were in situations comparable to the one faced by Ms. Morrison and her children. This woman may have been a "worst-case scenario" or she just may stand for a large number of others suffering like troubles. In circumstances like this where the mental health service system is hampered by unreliable or absent information, the technique of policy analysis by patient case study can make a simple but vital contribution. If nothing else, it puts the system on alert for detecting similar cases while advising on the careful decision-making these will require. It also delineates issues meriting review by those charged with steering the system as a whole by means of data collection, resource management, and policy advocacy and reform.

Formal Policy Evaluation

Our final type of policy analysis combines rigorously defined input and output measures with formal research design in drawing its conclusions about the impact of mental health policy. According to this approach, every public policy is an "experiment" that needs to be tracked over time. No matter how plausible the arguments of supporters, nor how logical an initiative's design, the goal of formal policy evaluation is to assemble scientifically sound evidence that documents not merely the activities occurring under a program or law but also whether desired effects for an intended population have been realized (Dye 2011). Sometimes studies of this type also calculate costs and benefits as a way of gauging an intervention's economic viability.

It would be rare for a single study to redirect public policy, irrespective of the comprehensiveness or sophistication of the methodology involved. When considering expert advice, officials value consensus, and a preponderance of evidence from numerous investigations, to clearly establish the linkage between an intervention's means and ends. For this reason, an influential form of policy analysis emerging in recent years has been the preparation of research reviews by collecting findings from multiple published sources, a synthesis of information distinguished equally by its quality and its relevance concerning a significant policy issue under review. One leading institutional client for this form of analysis is the federal Agency for Healthcare Research and Quality (AHRQ), and the study chosen as our final illustration of this chapter was completed for this government group as part of its "Evidence Report/Technology Assessment" series.

The review titled "Integration of Mental Health/Substance Abuse and Primary Care" was conducted by Mary Butler and colleagues, among them one of the authors of this text, to examine methods and outcomes of integrating mental health care with general medicine (Butler et al. 2008). The chief studies of interest were randomized controlled trials, together with quasi-experimental designs that simulated or somehow attempted to compensate for the absence of a control group. Supplementing this body of research were descriptive data about program components and operations. The bulk of research concerned care of depression, a handful of studies dealt with anxiety disorders, and single studies of miscellaneous mental illness conditions made up the remainder. Primary care was the principal focus of analysis, although the report also touches on specialty outpatient settings. Six main questions guided the selection of research material for the review:

1. What models of mental health and medical integration have been used in the past, and were the outcomes positive?
2. Do the impacts of integrated programs vary for different patient populations defined by diagnostic, demographic, and other factors?
3. What barriers interfere with successful integration?
4. What was the role, if any, of health information technology in successful integration programs?
5. What was the relationship between financial and reimbursement structures and integration success?
6. What program elements have proven key in successful integration efforts within the "real-world" setting of large health systems?

Given these several lines of inquiry, the findings by Butler and colleagues are too complex to relay in full here, yet there are noteworthy "takeaways." Integration of mental health and general medical care was associated with positive outcomes in regard to symptom severity, treatment response, and remission of illness across the majority of reviewed studies. This literature indicates beneficial impacts for patients of different ages and illness type, although more research would be needed to clarify integration's potential role in combating health disparities across a variety of social groups. Barriers to integration are well understood in such areas as financing (e.g., lack of reimbursement for pivotal integration activities and services), organizational behavior (e.g., resistance to changing staff roles), and sustainability (e.g., problems in scaling up model programs for implementation in larger, less controlled clinical settings). While numerous integration programs have made use of health information technology, research is scant to document technology's effectiveness either in facilitating the process of integration or contributing to its results. No particular type of insurance coverage correlates with the success or failure of integration; however, for practice settings dealing with myriad payers and reimbursement policies, this intricacy generally complicates movement toward integrated care.

Some skeptics have raised doubts about the growing role of evidence-based research in guiding mental health practice and policy (Tanenbaum 2005). Debate centers on such issues as the adequacy of experimental methodology in identifying all potentially useful interventions, the difficulties of translating research findings into clinical and organizational reality, and the need for more critical consideration of the way a concept like "effectiveness" becomes operationalized as an outcome variable. To be sure, the review by Butler and her team has limitations that can detract from evidence-based research. Although the project team found strong support for integration as a central theme of service delivery, it could not confirm a specific link between such inputs as program structure, level of integration, and processes of care, on the one hand, and patient outcomes, on the other. This difficulty notwithstanding, policy analysis by research synthesis represents an irreplaceable tool for grounding policy development in empirical social science and health services inquiry. Reports like this one by Butler and others have come to stand as linchpins in the mounting case for integrating mental health and primary care, now bolstered by support for new demonstration programs in the Affordable Care Act as well as an advisory from the World Health Organization (2008).

CONCLUSION

It should be noted that other approaches to policy analysis exist beyond the ones discussed in this chapter (Mintrom 2012). Comparative examination of activities in other countries offers a way to clarify the influence of culture, social structure, and political institutions within a policy domain. Studies can be designed to trace the impact of policies on persons from minority cultural groups, the poor, individuals with disabilities, and other disadvantaged populations. There is much political discourse surrounding the appropriate role of markets versus government in addressing social issues, and policy analysis studies can be used to examine that dilemma. All these techniques offer tools for the mental health policy analyst, although some rely on specialized procedures and bodies of knowledge that will be more meaningful for certain audiences than others. What we have tried to do in this chapter is to cover a handful of policy analysis strategies relevant for any practitioner with basic social science training, studies whose findings can have broad reach among specialists and nonspecialists alike. When informed by firm understanding of the history, concepts, disease patterns, organizational setting, and past policy choices of the mental health sector, this research is indispensable to the prospects for progress and hope among those who depend on this system.

References

Aron, Laudan et al. *Grading the States 2009: A Report on America's Health Care System for Adults with Serious Mental Illness.* Arlington, VA: National Alliance on Mental Illness, 2009. Available online: www.nami.org/gtsTemplate09.cfm?Section=Grading_the_States_2009.

Bardach, Eugene. *A Practical Guide for Policy Analysis: The Eightfold Path to More Effective Problem Solving,* 3rd ed. Washington, DC: CQ Press, 2009.

Barry, Colleen L., Haiden A. Huskamp, and Howard H. Goldman. "A Political History of Federal Mental Health and Addiction Insurance Parity." *Milbank Quarterly* 88 (2010): 404–433.

Bonnie, Richard J., et al. "Mental Health System Transformation After the Virginia Tech Tragedy." *Health Affairs* 28 (2009): 793–804.

Burstein, Paul. "Policy Domains: Organization, Culture, and Policy Outcomes." *Annual Review of Sociology* 17 (1991): 327–350.

Butler, Mary, et al. *Integration of Mental Health/Substance Abuse and Primary Care.* Evidence Reports/ Technology Assessments No. 173. AHRQ Publication No. 09-E003. Rockville, MD: Agency for Healthcare Research and Quality, 2008.

Caplan, Ruth B. *Psychiatry and the Community in Nineteenth-Century America: The Recurring Concern with Environment in the Prevention and Treatment of Mental Disorder.* New York: Basic Books, 1969.

Coe, Charles K. "A Report Card on Report Cards." *Public Performance and Management Review* 27 (2003): 53–76.

Dye, Thomas R. *Understanding Public Policy*, 13th ed. Upper Saddle River, NJ: Pearson, 2011.

Elrod, Carrie, Jessica L. Hamblen, and Fran H. Norris. "Challenges in Implementing Disaster Mental Health Programs: State Program Directors' Perspectives." *Annals of the American Academy of Political and Social Science* 604 (2006): 152–170.

Frank, Richard G., and Sherry A. Glied. *Better But Not Well: Mental Health Policy in the United States Since 1950.* Baltimore: Johns Hopkins University Press, 2006.

Goldman, Howard H. " 'How Do You Pay Your Rent?' Social Policies and the President's Mental Health Commission." *Health Affairs* 22 (2003): 65–72.

Grob, Gerald N. "Government and Mental Health Policy: A Structural Analysis." *Milbank Quarterly* 72 (1994): 471–500.

Hogan, Michael F., and Lloyd I. Sederer. "Mental Health Crises and Public Policy: Opportunities for Change?" *Health Affairs* 28 (2009): 805–808.

Howlett, Michael, and M. Ramesh. *Studying Public Policy: Policy Cycles and Policy Subsystems.* Toronto: Oxford University Press, 1995.

Kiesler, Charles A., and Sibulkin, Amy E. *Mental Hospitalization: Myths and Facts About a National Crisis.* Newbury Park, CA: Sage Publications, 1987.

Kingdon, John W. *Agendas, Alternatives, and Public Policies.* Boston: Little, Brown and Company, 1984.

Kraft, Michael E., and Scott R. Furlong. *Public Policy: Politics, Analysis, and Alternatives*, 3rd ed. Washington, DC: CQ Press, 2010.

Metzl, Jonathan. *The Protest Psychosis: How Schizophrenia Became a Black Disease.* Boston: Beacon Press, 2009.

Mintrom, Michael. *Contemporary Policy Analysis.* New York: Oxford University Press, 2012.

Moran, Ann E., Ruth I. Freedman, and Steven S. Sharfstein. "The Journey of Sylvia Frumkin: A Case Study for Policymakers." *Hospital and Community Psychiatry* 35 (1984): 887–893.

Nicholson, Joanne, Jeffrey L. Geller, and William H. Fisher. " 'Sylvia Frumkin' Has a Baby: A Case Study for Policymakers." *Psychiatric Services* 47 (1996): 497–501.

Parsons, Wayne. *Public Policy: An Introduction to the Theory and Practice of Policy Analysis.* Aldershot, UK: Edward Elgar, 1995.

Perlin, Michael L. "International Human Rights and Comparative Mental Disability Law: The Role of Institutional Psychiatry in the Suppression of Political Dissent." *Israel Law Review* 39 (2006): 69–97.

Rochefort, David A. "Policymaking Cycles in Mental Health: Critical Examination of a Conceptual Model." *Journal of Health Politics, Policy and Law* 13 (1988): 129–152.

Rochefort, David A. "Mental Health Policy Making in the Intergovernmental System." In *A Handbook for the Study of Mental Health: Social Contexts, Theories, and Systems*, edited by Allan V. Horwitz and Teresa L. Scheid, pp. 467–483. New York: Cambridge University Press, 1999.

Rochefort, David A., and Roger W. Cobb, eds. *The Politics of Problem Definition: Shaping the Policy Agenda.* Lawrence, KS: University Press of Kansas, 1994.

Schneider, Anne L., and Helen Ingram. *Policy Design for Democracy.* Lawrence, KS: University Press of Kansas, 1997.

Sheehan, Susan. *Is There No Place on Earth for Me?* Boston: Houghton Mifflin, 1982.

Tanenbaum, Sandra J. "Evidence-Based Practice as Mental Health Policy: Three Controversies and a Caveat." *Health Affairs* 24 (2005): 163–173.

Warner, Richard. "A Review of *Care of the Seriously Mentally Ill: A Rating of State Programs.* Second Edition: 1988, by E. Fuller Torrey, Sidney E. Wolfe, and Laurie M. Flynn." *Psychiatric Bulletin* 13 (1989): 397–398.

World Health Organization and World Organization of Family Doctors. *Integrating Mental Health into Primary Care: A Global Perspective.* Geneva: WHO Press, 2008. Available online: whqlibdoc.who.int/publications/2008/9789241563680_eng.pdf.

Author Index

Subject Index